Law and School Reform

Law and School Reform

Six Strategies for Promoting

Educational Equity

Edited by Jay P. Heubert

Yale University Press

New Haven and London

Set in Adobe Garamond type by The Composing Room of Michigan, Inc. Printed in the United States of America.

Library of Congress Cataloging-in-Publication Data

Law and school reform : six strategies for promoting educational
    equity / edited by Jay P. Heubert.
        p.   cm.
    Includes bibliographical references and index.
    ISBN 0-300-07595-2 (cloth : alk. paper)
    ISBN 0-300-08296-7 (pbk. : alk. paper)
    1. Educational equalization—United States.   2. Educational law
and legislation—United States.   3. Education—United States—
Finance.   4. Minorities—Education—United States.   5. Special
education—United States.   6. Educational change—United States.
I. Heubert, Jay Philip.
LC213.2.L39   1998
379.2'6'0973—dc21   98–25572

A catalogue record for this book is available from the British Library.

The paper in this book meets the guidelines for permanence and durability of the Committee on Production Guidelines for Book Longevity of the Council on Library Resources.

10   9   8   7   6   5   4   3   2

Contents

Foreword *Harold Howe II* vii

Preface xiii

1 Six Law-Driven School Reforms: Developments, Lessons, and Prospects *Jay P. Heubert* 1

2 Conservative Activists and the Rush Toward Resegregation *Gary Orfield* 39

3 The Law's Role in the Distribution of Education: The Promises and Pitfalls of School Finance Litigation *Molly S. McUsic* 88

4 Cultural, Educational, and Legal Perspectives on Immigration: Implications for School Reform *Marcelo Suárez-Orozco, Peter D. Roos, and Carola Suárez-Orozco* 160

5 Special Education: From Legalism to Collaboration *Thomas Hehir and Sue Gamm* 205

6 Service Integration and Beyond: Implications for Lawyers and Their Training *Martin Gerry* 244

7 School Reform and Enforceable Rights to Quality Education *Paul Weckstein* 306

Afterword: Reform Law and Schools *Martha Minow* 390

List of Contributors 394

Index 397

Foreword

Harold Howe II

This book tells the story of the growing involvement of lawyers in America's public schools in the past half century—why they were needed, what they did, and their possible future roles in improving learning, especially for America's least fortunate children. It reaches, also, to the complexity and promise of partnerships between educators and lawyers. If you have ever wanted to understand the critical role that lawyers and the law play in school reform, you hold in your hands the only book I know that explains the subject, and in terms that make sense to educators and other nonlawyers.

Four of this volume's chapters consider the lessons and prospects of key legal strategies that emerged in the wake of the Supreme Court's momentous *Brown* decision in 1954: school desegregation, school finance reform, educational opportunities for immigrant children, and special education.

In these areas, the involvement of lawyers was not caused by an eager and growing profession seeking new business. Indeed, the material rewards were a step backward for most of the attorneys involved. Lawyers migrated to schools in the past fifty years mostly because the barriers to equal educational opportunity had their source in law.

Court decisions such as *Brown v. Board of Education* (1954) foreshadowed a major shift of public opinion on human rights, a shift that emerged from the civil rights movement for blacks and expanded to include Latinos, women, new immigrants, people with disabilities, and other groups. A broad political coalition of Americans from varied religions and walks of life joined with lawyers and educators to make good on unmet promises. The federal government also got involved. The Elementary and Secondary Education Act, launched in 1965, helps fund remedial education programs for disadvantaged children. It has been reenacted and improved over the years despite the efforts of two presidents to get rid of it. Head Start, a program for poor preschool children, has grown into a widely accepted necessity, and when well operated, it is more than worth its cost, even though it still serves only a portion of those eligible. The Bilingual Education Act provides limited funds for programs to serve immigrant children whose first language is not English.

Gains have been made, but there remain huge gaps in the nation's provision of educational and social services for minority children, poor children, and immigrant children. Today, moreover, many past gains are eroding or treading water.

School desegregation opened new doors to minority students in the 1960s and 1970s, but it lost ground in the 1980s and by the 1990s was largely a forgotten cause. President Clinton's December 1997 gathering in Akron, Ohio, to open a national conversation on race in American society completely ignored the subject. The chapter in this book by Gary Orfield explains what we have gained from school desegregation, how much of it is already lost, and our choices for the future.

In terms of school finance reform, changes toward a fairer system have emerged from many state courts and legislatures, and our knowledge about the relationship between learning and financial resources has grown appreciably. Lawyers, educators, and economists have led the march to this understanding; its conversion to action is discussed here, including some promising legal strategies that call for new levels of collaboration between concerned parties. At the same time, school finance reform efforts have often been stymied by strategies that leave poor children in poor schools and provide much better public schools for the well-to-do. In fact, as Molly McUsic points out in chapter 3, some proposed reforms may do more harm than good: popular school choice programs can worsen educational inequalities by leaving the most disadvantaged students behind in deteriorating schools.

The education of immigrant students has become increasingly challenging.

Immigration into the United States grew unexpectedly in the last half of the twentieth century, both in terms of the number of new people and the variety of their origins. These events caught political leaders and school administrators off guard. Some struggled to serve the children with haphazard planning and inadequate funds; others neglected them. In the 1970s, when Texas tried to banish the children of illegal immigrants from its schools, the Supreme Court said that was unconstitutional, but now California is attempting to follow the same path. Political and legal battles about the costs of immigrant social services, including schools, are a growth stock. Efforts to open the minds of students to the full spectrum of the American experience are challenged by English-only movements and others wary of multicultural perspectives. Now and in the future, the complex challenges of educating immigrant children will be an area of common interest to both educators and lawyers, challenges that require much closer levels of collaboration. These issues are well explored in chapter 4.

Perhaps the most far reaching law-based reforms have been those affecting children with disabilities, who constitute about 11 percent of American youngsters. Unlike racial and cultural characteristics, poverty, and immigrant status, physical and mental disabilities reach across the entire economic and social spectrum of our society. Perhaps for this reason, children with disabilities will look back to the twentieth century as a time of great progress in their schooling opportunities. They began the century with almost no legal rights and now are entitled to an appropriate education, usually in regular classrooms rather than in isolation. Their progress stems from legal action, strong federal legislation, and research showing that many children with disabilities are well served in regular schools and classrooms.

What are the prospects for further progress on school desegregation, school finance reform, services for immigrant children, and special education? What place, if any, is there for lawyers in these realms? As Jay Heubert points out in chapter 1, current reform efforts in these areas increasingly focus on issues of teaching and learning, on what goes on *within* schools and classrooms. Examples include reducing segregation, defining what constitutes an "adequate" education, providing native-language instruction, and including children with disabilities in regular classrooms. He and the other authors argue that lawyers and educators must assume new roles and responsibilities in school reform. As Thomas Hehir and Sue Gamm state in their chapter on special education, "Schools, parents, and lawyers must learn to collaborate, not just litigate."

My sense of these new roles for lawyers in school reform raises two reactions:

three cheers for the conceptualization, and a worry over bringing it about successfully. Why the worry? Because lawyers are better known for litigating—compelling people to do things they are not doing or don't want to do—than they are for collaborating. In situations that clearly deny children services or rights that are legally theirs, forcing action by such means is needed, but sometimes it can be self-defeating to try to change the learning process in this way. Using legal leverage to promote better quality teaching and learning in schools creates dilemmas. To some degree, "legislated learning"—a phrase coined by Arthur Wise, a well-known educator and researcher—seems to me to be an oxymoron.

To be successful, in other words, lawyers will have to be effective diplomats and negotiators, and not just legal activists. They will have to learn more than they typically do about the viewpoints of teachers and researchers regarding the major changes in classroom practice implied by educational reforms. Their success in these roles will depend largely on their ability to enlist rather than compel the participation of educators, parents, politicians, and others whose support and insight they need. Such challenges will require new levels of collaboration between lawyers, educators, and others concerned with improving educational opportunities for America's most vulnerable children. This book offers useful illustrations along this line. For example, the chapter on special education makes clear that "inclusion" is more effective when teachers and parents plan for it than when it is imposed from the outside.

The final two chapters of this book turn to more recent reform strategies, both of which illustrate the need for greater collaboration between educators and lawyers. Chapter 6 addresses the attempt to link service integration—the coordination of social services for children—with educational reform. Chapter 7 grows out of new federal and state mandates calling for higher standards of educational quality and performance for all students.

The need to integrate social services for children and youth has been increasingly evident for many years. In neighborhoods, communities, towns, cities, counties, and states, numerous organizations serve children and youth. Schools are the most evident of such agencies, but health care organizations, preschool programs, child-care programs, recreation programs, mental health services, employment training programs, and teen parenting programs, among others, are also part of the mix.

With the exception of public schools, for which all American children are eligible, social services for poor children are a hodgepodge of separate categorical programs with complex eligibility requirements and funding arrangements that prevent many eligible children and families from receiving the help they need. America's tangled and tattered safety net for children deserves a grade of C-.

How can lawyers and their colleagues in schools enter this complex arena? How can they produce a simplified system that serves young people effectively? In chapter 6, Martin Gerry reports on promising recent experiments and argues for an arrangement that replaces the current collection of fragmented categorical programs. He also describes ways in which lawyers can help to broker the collaboration and change that reform will require.

In chapter 7 Paul Weckstein explores standards-based school reform: the enactment at state and federal levels of educational standards that all schools and students should meet. Weckstein sees standards-based reform as a potential means of building school staff capacity to make use of "the best education policies available."

As a school improvement strategy, standards-based reform raises concerns about legislated learning, because it seems to assume that "best" policies can be identified, agreed upon, and then mandated. Many attributes of successful schools cannot be legislated, however, including the motivation of both teachers and students. The author is plainly aware of this concern, and hopes that standards will bring teachers, parents, and other interested parties together to develop plans of action that best address students' learning needs.

This is a book on the ways in which law has been used—and can still be applied—to improve educational opportunity for America's least fortunate children. As our society rapidly grows more diverse, as childhood poverty rates reach historic highs, its themes and insights become increasingly important. As the chapter on service integration suggests, the latest round of school reform efforts will fail unless it addresses the full range of social deprivations that hinder effective learning. It also matters very much whether children languish in racially or ethnically segregated schools or classrooms; whether poor children attend schools that lack the resources to meet even basic educational needs; whether immigrant children are denied an education altogether or receive instruction in a language they do not understand; and whether young people with disabilities have opportunities to enter the mainstream of our schools and our society.

Reflecting on the experience of the twentieth century in advancing these causes, this book clearly envisions and describes a new alliance of lawyers and educators; furthermore, it leaves us with a well-defined challenge for enriching that alliance in the twenty-first century.

Preface

Traditionally, law has played a central role in efforts to secure equal educational opportunity for those who have been denied it. In the process, litigation, legislation, and regulation have helped shape educational policies and the institutions that provide educational services. Over the past decades, countless units of government at all levels have adopted sweeping measures aimed at improving the quality of public education, and these efforts continue.

In 1991 the Andrew W. Mellon Foundation funded a multiyear project to take stock of this experience and to explore the continuing and future roles that law and lawyers could play in promoting school reform and equality of educational opportunity. Initially, Christopher Edley, Jr., of Harvard Law School, and I were the project's co-principal investigators. When Edley took a leave of absence to join the Clinton Administration, Martha Minow, also of Harvard Law School, took his place.

This volume was designed with several objectives in mind. One was to explore comparatively what leading educators and lawyers believed to be the most important law-driven school reforms. A second was to examine these reform efforts from the perspectives of law, education, research, and practice. A third was to study how each reform effort had evolved over time and to consider ways in which lawyers, educators, scholars, and parents could promote future reform most effectively. A fourth was to produce a study accessible not just to legal experts or scholars but to a wide audience of policy makers, educators, parents, and advocates as well.

We have tried in several ways to achieve these objectives. First, a distinguished panel of educators and lawyers helped us identify the most important topics to include and prospective authors for each chapter. The advisory panel members included Patricia Albjerg Graham, president of the Spencer Foundation and Charles Warren Professor of the History of American Education at the Harvard Graduate School of Education; David Hornbeck, Superintendent of the School District of Philadelphia, former chairman of the Council of Chief State School Officers and for sixteen years Maryland's state superintendent of education; Harold Howe II, former U.S. Commissioner of Education, Vice President for Education at the Ford Foundation, and senior lecturer emeritus at the Harvard Graduate School of Education; Paul Weckstein, co-director of the Center for Law and Education in Washington, D.C.; and (until his appointment to the U.S. Court of Appeals for the District of Columbia Circuit) David Tatel, former partner at Hogan & Hartson and former director of the Office for Civil Rights, U.S. Department of Health, Education, and Welfare. We are deeply grateful for their advice.

Second, we selected the contributors not only because they are leading authorities in the fields of education and law but also because they are highly regarded by policy makers, practitioners, and scholars alike.

Third, the authors were commissioned to produce chapters that would address this project's research objectives in their respective areas of expertise. They were asked to explore school reform efforts from interdisciplinary perspectives; to assess the past, present, and future roles of law in advancing and supporting school reform; to identify the ways in which lawyers, educators, researchers, and others could work together most effectively to improve the lives of young people; to include whatever background information a generalist reader might need; and to write in plain English.

Fourth, the manuscript received careful attention from skilled editors, journalists, and subject-matter specialists. During an eight-month period in 1995-96, Joshua Bogin, a seasoned attorney and educator, helped administer the project and worked with the authors and principal investigators to shape early drafts. Carole Ashkinaze made valuable revisions to chapter 2. Joan McCarty

First, co-director of the National Coalition of Advocates for Students, contributed important sections of chapter 4. Edward Miller's skillful revisions, substantive and editorial, improved three chapters significantly. Each chapter also received three rounds of blind peer review from educators, lawyers, and practitioners. And while the reviewers must remain anonymous, I wish to acknowledge their vital contributions.

At Yale University Press, senior editor Gladys Topkis believed in this project from the start and shepherded it with skill and humor through the many stages of the publication process. Noreen O'Connor provided expert copyediting. It has been a pleasure working with both of them.

I wish to thank all of these people. It has also been a rare pleasure, personal and professional, to work with my coauthors: Harold Howe II, Gary Orfield, Molly McUsic, Carola and Marcelo Suárez-Orozco, Peter Roos, Tom Hehir, Sue Gamm, Martin Gerry, Paul Weckstein, and Martha Minow.

I also wish to thank Stephanie Bell-Rose, Program Officer at the Andrew W. Mellon Foundation, whose support made this undertaking possible. Christopher Edley, Jr., initiated this project, invited me to work on it with him, and provided advice and encouragement throughout. Gary Orfield's suggestions on my chapter and the entire project improved both.

I am also grateful to Martha Minow. As co-principal investigator beginning in 1992, she read each draft and helped shape the book in many ways. She was a constant source of insight, perspective, energy, and humor. I also wish to thank my brother and sister, Alan and Terry Heubert. They made it possible for me to complete this project by assuming heavy responsibilities during an extended period of illness in our family, and by providing constant love and support.

Most of all, I am deeply grateful to my wife, Valerie Aubry. An award-winning editor, she read the second and third drafts of the manuscript with care and insight. Her suggestions significantly improved each chapter and the book as a whole. In addition, her love and faith sustained me, and our new son, Loren, during a challenging period in our lives.

Jay P. Heubert

Chapter 1 Six Law-Driven School Reforms: Developments, Lessons, and Prospects

Jay P. Heubert

INTRODUCTION

In its 1954 *Brown* decision, the U.S. Supreme Court recognized that certain educational policies and practices sanctioned by law can "affect [children's] hearts and minds in a way unlikely ever to be undone" (*Brown v. Board of Education of Topeka,* 1954, 494). This holds true not only for minority children but for immigrant children, poor children, and children with disabilities as well. In the words of journalist John Merrow,

> There were no "good old days" in special education. . . . Burned into my memory is the image of one young man, a quadriplegic with cerebral palsy. Abandoned by his parents and labeled "retarded," he languished for years until one day a sympathetic [school] nurse saw in his eyes the glimmer of a fierce intelligence [and taught him to use a letter board with a small light fastened to a hat]. . . . I "interviewed" him. . . . He told me about his mother, asked questions about my family, and asked me if I believed in God. I cried then, tears of joy for his indomitable spirit, but also tears for the loss of thousands and thousands of lives wasted. (Merrow, 1996, 48, 38)

Since 1954, children, parents, and their lawyers have sought legal redress for state-imposed segregation and other law-based educational policies that diminish children's life chances. In important respects, these efforts have succeeded. State-sanctioned apartheid is now illegal in America. Children with disabilities are no longer consigned to oblivion, and immigrant children may no longer be denied a public education. In many states, school funding formulas have become more equitable.

Moreover, research evidence strongly supports the premises of these reforms. The achievement gap between white students and minority students closed dramatically between the early 1960s and the mid-1990s, and there is powerful evidence that children who attend multiracial schools do better, in school and in life. Since the 1970s, levels of educational attainment have increased dramatically for children with disabilities. There is strong evidence that increased funds for education lead to improved student performance when they are properly directed.

And yet the promise of *Brown* remains to be fulfilled. After a long period of diminishing racial segregation, increasing numbers and proportions of black students (66 percent) and Latino students (74.3 percent) now attend segregated schools in which most students are also poor (Orfield and Eaton, 1996), and many minority children are segregated *within* schools, in low-track classes and classes for children with mental disabilities. After some twenty-five years of school finance reform, there remain in most states large funding discrepancies between the richest and poorest school districts (see chapter 3). Voter initiatives and legislative proposals aim to end affirmative action and to deny public education to children of illegal immigrants (see chapter 4). "Welfare reform" measures drastically reduce supports for poor children, immigrant children, and children with disabilities (see chapter 6).

Worse, many influential Americans either do not seem to notice, or erroneously assume that efforts to equalize educational opportunity have failed. For example, many federal courts are hastily withdrawing their support for desegregation plans, producing immediate and significant resegregation (see chapter 2). In eerie parallels to the rollback of civil rights following Reconstruction, the nation seems bent on undoing some of the important progress made during its second, post-*Brown*, reconstruction.

Can the promise of *Brown* be realized? Can lawyers, working collaboratively with educators, researchers, parents, and others, do more to promote equal opportunity in education?

This volume examines six of the most important law-driven school reforms of the past thirty years: desegregation, school finance reform, special education, education of immigrant children, service integration, and enforceable performance mandates. These reforms remain the subject of debate and experimentation even after a decade of renewed political commitment to such other school improvement initiatives as standards-based reform, deregulation, and decentralization. This volume concludes that, setbacks notwithstanding, law-based reform efforts have evolved in promising directions and still hold great potential for improving the educational opportunities of disadvantaged children.

This volume's authors, recognized as experts in their fields by educators, lawyers, and scholars alike, explore their subjects from the multiple perspectives of law, education, and research. They contribute to research and practice in several important respects.

Law-Driven School Reform: The Stakes, the Prospects

This is perhaps the first work to take stock systematically of a key set of law-based school reform efforts, each aimed at increasing educational opportunity in the United States. Some of these reforms, such as school desegregation, have been national issues for decades, while others, such as service integration and enforceable performance mandates, are of more recent vintage. Treating them together in one volume makes possible worthwhile comparisons, contrasts, and insights about efforts to use law and lawyers in the school reform process.

As discussed more fully below, this volume supports important insights into the history, development, and future prospects of law-driven school reform.

First, the chapters that follow show that the objectives of different law-driven reform efforts have evolved along parallel lines over time. The initial objective, to overcome segregation and categorical exclusions, has broadened to include a greater emphasis on serving children more effectively within schools and on helping students meet high standards for academic achievement.

Second, law-driven school reform efforts, while falling short of their full potential, have produced important educational improvements. Children with disabilities and children of undocumented immigrants may no longer be excluded from schools, for example, and recent empirical research suggests that school desegregation may be the factor most closely associated with significant increases in black students' scores on the National Assessment of Educational Progress (NAEP) between 1971 and 1994 (Grissmer et al., 1996). Similarly, as Thomas Hehir and Sue Gamm point out in chapter 5, educational programs for students with disabilities have led to dramatic improvements in scholastic achievement, high-school graduation rates, and post-high-school employment. The federal and state education statutes that Paul Weckstein discusses in chapter 7 promote use of instructional methods that are demonstrably effective.

Third, lawyers and litigation will continue to play a crucial role in efforts to improve educational opportunity in the United States. Current debates over affirmative action, educational services for immigrant children, special education, school finance, school desegregation, "choice" programs, and many other issues amply illustrate this point. In fact, many of the most controversial educational issues of the late 1990s are already in court, and that, for better or worse, is where many of them will be resolved.

Fourth, equal educational opportunity is well served when legislative enactments provide support and substance to judicially defined constitutional rights. Services for children with disabilities, for example, are more secure than those for other groups studied here because extensive federal statutory protections augment favorable court decisions (Kirp, 1977, 137; Thurston, 1980, 315).

Fifth, the nature of litigation is changing, as are education statutes and regulations. Perhaps because judges and policy makers recognize the limitations of imposing remedies that do not take educational considerations adequately into account, there has been a significant convergence of legal standards and educational norms. In federal discrimination law, for example, what is legal increasingly depends upon what is "educationally necessary." This volume contributes to research and practice both by demonstrating the inextricable link between legal questions and crucial questions of learning, teaching, and educational policy; and by exploring what these developments imply for how educators and lawyers do their work (Heubert, 1997b).

Sixth, this volume's contributors see both opportunities and risks in current school-reform trends, many of which focus on deregulation, decentralization, and an increased focus on "outcome measures" of student achievement. The authors consider, for example, how deregulation and decentralization in education, both of which enjoy broad public support, can be reconciled with traditional civil-rights protections, many based in federal law, which themselves reflect fundamental political and educational values (Heubert, 1997a). Similarly, as Paul Weckstein points out in chapter 7, new statutory performance mandates can provide a powerful tool for improving instruction or, in contrast, a basis for penalizing children who do not know what they have not been taught. This study is particularly timely at a point in American history where many believe that government is not the solution and others consider government itself to be the problem.

Seventh, lawyers who seek school reform cannot function solely as litigators. Working with educators, researchers, and parents, they also need to function effectively in the larger political process, as legislators, regulators, mediators, and consensus builders. Particularly in a climate of diminished concern for disadvantaged children, reformers need to think creatively about how to make their proposals more attractive politically. This volume provides numerous illustrations.

Finally, there is consensus among school reform proponents and policy makers that academic success does not depend solely on the services that schools provide. In chapter 6, Martin Gerry offers suggestions for improving and integrating social services for young people that make for effective learning.

In sum, the chapters that follow demonstrate that current and future efforts to improve educational opportunity through law must take into account emerging trends in education, research, politics, and child advocacy, and provide useful examples of how reform proponents can do so effectively.

The Need for Improved Collaboration

This volume breaks new ground in a second key respect: its effort to study how educators, lawyers, judges, policy makers, parents, and scholars, through improved collaboration and an interdisciplinary understanding of school reform, can contribute more effectively to the solution of basic educational problems. Indeed, as the goals of law-driven reform have evolved—from overcoming exclusion and segregation to improving the quality of education within schools and classrooms—partnerships and tensions between lawyers, educators, researchers, and parents have become more central than ever to the shape and direction of schooling.

For those who seek to use the law to improve education, it has always been important to communicate effectively with judges. Conflict over rights is inherent in a constitutional system that authorizes, indeed commands, judges to give certain values and interests priority over the preferences of political majorities. For the past half century, courts have done so, becoming, in the process, a major source of educational policy (Wirt and Kirst, 1982). Courts are likely to retain this role in education, moreover, both because students' rights are continually evolving and because educational attainment is increasingly decisive in promoting social mobility.

Now, however, courts are not only called upon to review policies of exclusion—such as California's Proposition 187, which requires that children of undocumented immigrants be denied admission to the state's public schools

(*New York Times,* 1996)—but to consider such matters as: whether states are spending the money it takes to educate children adequately (see chapter 3); whether instructional programs for immigrant children are educationally sound (see chapter 4); whether a child with serious disabilities can receive an appropriate education in a regular classroom (see chapter 5); and whether practices that tend to segregate minority children *within* schools are educationally justified. As the issues have evolved and the focus has shifted increasingly to the classroom, there has arisen a greater need for educators, lawyers, researchers, and parents to share their knowledge and to present it clearly to judges, other policy makers, and the public.

It is a task for which many educators are poorly prepared, by training and by inclination. Research consistently shows that educators "seem to have little concept of the law as it relates to them and their day to day school activities. In fact, many educators regard legal principles applicable to public school education with apathy or disinterest" (Reglin, 1992, 30). Moreover, many educators are conditioned to see law as an unwelcome intrusion, something to be avoided, rather than as a powerful tool for promoting effective school leadership, developing wise policy, increasing resources, and advancing educational reform (Heubert, 1997b).

Many lawyers who work with educators are similarly underprepared. Despite powerful empirical evidence that specialized legal expertise produces significantly better outcomes for clients (Kritzer, 1995), research shows that most of the lawyers who work with educators are not school-law experts; they devote more than half their work hours to fields other than education, and most have had little formal training in school law (Rehak, 1986; Lupato, 1973; Jones, 1978; Herbert, 1991). Nor do most lawyers recognize their legal limitations: "One of the most striking aspects of [research on the importance of specific legal expertise] was the apparent belief by many attorneys that they could walk into an unfamiliar, highly specialized setting and apply their general knowledge to that setting. . . . The idea that [it might not] had never occurred to some of these lawyers" (Kritzer, 1995, 23).

Where *nonlegal* knowledge is concerned, moreover, most education lawyers are still less well equipped. Few "know the fields of education and educational administration" (Trotter, 1990, 13), and few know how to read and understand educational research (Levin and Hawley, 1975; Schuck, 1989). Instead, most lawyers have been trained to believe that they can find all the information they need in legal texts, "without recourse to the theories, data, insights, or empirical methods of the social sciences, or to personal or political values: without, in other words, an encounter, necessarily messy, with the worlds of fact and feeling" (Posner, 1995, 20).

As a result, many lawyers simply do not appreciate the ways, often subtle, in which a legal dispute can affect central aspects of a school's operation. Lawyers are therefore likely to miss the educational dimensions of a legal dispute, even though they may be as important as its legal aspects. In court, this can be fatal, and unnecessarily so: "The school district lawyers become . . . the single conduit . . . between school systems and the courts. Those lawyers carry the joint burdens of legal and educational arguments. Yet they are trained to carry only one half of that burden. . . . [As a result,] courts can render decisions that are constitutionally sound but educationally disastrous. That consequence is often unnecessary" (Cunningham, 1978, xvi).

These deficiencies have serious consequences for judges, who rely on the parties to present the relevant information and to characterize the evidence responsibly. Orfield (chapter 2) speaks of a court that, "in its rush to judgment . . . rested important parts of its decision to permit the dismantling of desegregated schools on false premises that could not have withstood critical analysis." Orfield sees this as part of a broader and troubling trend.

The consequences are greatest, however, for educators and the children they serve. Poor collaboration between educators, lawyers, researchers, and parents makes it difficult to use the law to advance important educational aims. Poor collaboration also leads to unnecessary lawsuits, which can can cost thousands or even millions of dollars and can reduce significantly the funds that would otherwise be available for other purposes. Court orders and consent decrees, usually entered when school authorities are unwilling or unable to address problems on their own, can hamstring educators for decades, dramatically reducing discretion and flexibility in addressing central questions of education and school leadership, and giving plaintiffs enhanced leverage over school district policy and behavior (Horowitz, 1977; Kirp and Jensen, 1986; Rebell and Block, 1982; Hogan, 1985). Especially in urban areas, many school districts spend significant portions of their time and money attempting to comply with multiple court orders or consent decrees on such issues as special education, bilingual education, and desegregation.

While court orders and consent decrees often ensure that disadvantaged students receive educational services they would not obtain otherwise, these requirements may also hinder experiments and reforms that could be made compatible with the court's aims (Tatel, 1993). Better collaboration between educators and lawyers reduces such conflicts.

Litigation has other costs as well. These include the loss of staff time, which comes at the expense of other work and poses serious problems in periods of administrative retrenchment. Litigation can also drive wedges between educators and the populations they serve, diminishing public support for the schools (Howard, 1994). As Suárez-Orozco, Roos, and Suárez-Orozco (chapter 4) point out, however, such polarization is less likely when educators work with lawyers and parents to shape the remedies that administrators and teachers will have to carry out.

Some lawyers do combine legal expertise with an understanding of education and research. For example, lawyers who *initiate* school reform litigation typically spend years focusing on a single type of school reform, such as school finance reform or the rights of children with disabilities. In the process, they may work closely with educators, parents, and researchers in devising litigation strategies and advising judges and other lawmakers on possible remedies. As a result, they often gain a better grasp of how legal issues, educational matters, and relevant research interrelate than do education lawyers who are generalists. As the following chapters make clear, the experience of those who have been involved in law-based reform efforts, including many of this volume's authors, offers valuable insights for those who wish to improve educator-lawyer collaboration more generally.

A Book for Those Who Contribute to School Reform

There is a third way in which this volume makes a contribution to research and practice in school law: It has been written not solely for legal experts or scholars but for a general audience of educators, advocates, policy makers, parents, and scholars interested in school reform. This approach is based on the belief that the most useful study of school reform is one accessible to all the groups who must work together if school reform efforts are to succeed.

As each of the following chapters focuses on a single type of school reform, the remainder of this chapter compares and contrasts the six studies with respect to each of the cross-cutting themes the authors have addressed and articulates the conclusions that emerge from the volume as a whole.

In the next part of the chapter, I explore from interdisciplinary perspectives the origins, current status, and future prospects of law-driven school reform. To conclude the chapter, I offer insights into the evolving roles of law and lawyers in school reform and consider approaches for promoting school reform through improved collaboration between educators, lawyers, researchers, policy makers, and parents.

INTERDISCIPLINARY PERSPECTIVES ON THE
ORIGINS, CURRENT STATUS, AND FUTURE
PROSPECTS OF LAW-DRIVEN SCHOOL REFORM

Despite obvious differences—with respect to when reforms occurred, what strategies reformers employed, what remedies advocates sought, and how much success these efforts produced—the chapters that follow reveal some important similarities.

One recurring theme is that most law-driven reform efforts were initially intended to overcome problems of segregation, outright denial of a public education, or educational inequalities so severe that some children were in effect excluded from school. This was true for reform efforts on behalf of children of color (chapter 2), poor children (chapter 3), immigrant children (chapter 4), and children with disabilities (chapter 5). In the next section, "The Original Problem: Educational Exclusion," I discuss these developments.

Explicit segregation and outright exclusion from school have become less common, largely owing to court decisions. As a result, legal reform efforts have focused increasingly on how well students are being educated *within* their schools and classrooms. Segregation in the assignment of students to classes *within* schools has become an important issue. Advocates have also focused on the quality of educational services for students with varied needs, and on reducing the fragmentation of services available to such students. The second section below, "Serving Students Well Once They Are in School: Law and Education Converge," discusses these continuing concerns, which rely more heavily on educational considerations and research findings than on pure questions of law.

This volume also attempts to assess the future prospects of legal efforts to improve educational equity. In assessing new challenges and opportunities, the authors consider, among other things, the current political climate, which does not generally support such efforts, and the potential risks and benefits of current school reform efforts, which include deregulation, decentralization, and an increased focus on outcome measures of student achievement. The third section, "New Challenges and Opportunities," explores how law-driven reforms square with these current trends.

The Original Problem: Educational Exclusion

Many law-based school reform efforts began as challenges to rules that served to exclude certain types of children from public education. In some instances states denied education altogether to children with certain disabilities or to children of undocumented immigrants. In some states, laws explicitly excluded black, Latino, Native American, Asian, and/or disabled students from schools that white students attended. Finally, some types of public school students received such poor educational services that they were "functionally excluded" from school.

SCHOOL DESEGREGATION

As Gary Orfield (chapter 2) and Molly McUsic (chapter 3) point out, school desegregation efforts began by challenging the legality of laws under which certain schools were explicitly reserved for white students, teachers, and administrators, and black students and staff were consigned to separate schools that were vastly inferior in terms of funding, facilities, instructional materials, and educational quality. Nor were blacks the only group subject to deliberate, state-imposed racial segregation; it was also the practice in many states and school districts to assign Latinos, Asian Americans and Native Americans to segregated, inferior schools (chapter 4).

The 1954 *Brown* decision invalidated laws and state constitutional provisions that explicitly required the segregation of black students and white students in public schools. It was 1973, however, before the U.S. Supreme Court applied the principles of *Brown* to racial and ethnic groups other than blacks, and the same year in which the Court declared that *any* deliberate governmental segregation by race or ethnicity, whether by explicit policy or not, is unconstitutional (*Keyes v. School District No. 1*, 1973).

For several reasons, moreover, meaningful remedies for illegal racial segregation arrived late if at all. First, the legislative and executive branches of the federal government acted slowly to support judicially mandated school desegregation. Even after enactment of the Civil Rights Act of 1964, the other branches left it to the courts to define what constitutes illegal segregation and to decide on suitable remedies. As discussed more fully below, many such questions remain unanswered more than four decades after *Brown*.

Orfield also points out that strong support for school desegregation, even within the federal judiciary, has been the exception rather than the rule: "The one period of clear and effective judicial leadership came during the five years from 1968 to 1973," after which the federal courts became decidedly less sympathetic to school desegregation efforts.[1] Finally, Orfield explains how the Supreme Court's elevation of local control to a principle of constitutional dimension, coupled with a reluctance to acknowledge the direct relationships between housing segregation and school segregation, seriously restricted school desegregation efforts in metropolitan areas and other places where housing remains deeply segregated by race and social class.

As a result, many public schools in regions other than the South have never been desegregated, and the current trend is toward greater racial isolation of blacks and, even more, Hispanics. No less important, for reasons McUsic discusses in chapter 3, is the fact that over 50 percent of black and Hispanic students attend schools where most students come from families of low socioeconomic status (SES), compared with 6 percent and 14 percent for whites and Asian-Americans, respectively. This is very bad news; since the Coleman Report (Coleman, 1966), we have known that high concentrations of low-SES students are the factor most strongly associated with poor student performance.

SCHOOL FINANCE REFORM

School finance litigation began in the late 1960s. As Molly McUsic (chapter 3) notes, early school finance suits built on *Brown* and other Supreme Court school desegregation rulings in several ways.

First, the very logic of school finance reform is based on what *Brown* says about the importance of public education and the obligation of states to make it available to all on equal terms:

> Today, education is perhaps the most important function of state and local governments. . . . It is the very foundation of good citizenship. . . . In these days, it is doubtful that any child may reasonably be expected to succeed in life if he is denied the opportunity of an education. Such an opportunity, where the state has undertaken to provide it, is a right which must be made available to all on equal terms. (*Brown v. Board of Education of Topeka*, 1954, 494)

Second, the early school finance cases were based, in part, on claims of racial discrimination. Advocates demonstrated that state funding formulas typically produced higher funding levels per pupil in predominantly white school districts than in those where whites were a minority.

Plaintiffs also claimed that certain categories of children, most often low-SES children and minority children, were being excluded from public education. This exclusion was not absolute, of course, any more than black children had been completely excluded from public education before *Brown*. The argument in early school finance cases was that having to attend grossly underfunded, inferior schools constituted a "functional exclusion" from public education.

The first school finance case, *San Antonio Independent School District v. Rodriguez,* reached the U.S. Supreme Court in 1973. It focused on the funding inequities between school districts in the same state, Texas. As McUsic points out, these discrepancies stemmed from the state's decision to fund public education chiefly through local property taxes, which generate very different per-pupil amounts from one school district to another. The district in Texas with the lowest assessed property value per pupil, even taxing itself at a rate of $1.05 per $100 of assessed value, could raise only $26 for the education of each child in 1967–68, while the district with the highest property tax base, taxing itself at the lower rate of $0.88 per $100 of assessed value, supplied $333 per pupil. Moreover, at that time the state funding formula produced greater support for the wealthier district than the poorer one.

In *Rodriguez,* the U.S. Supreme Court, by a vote of 5 to 4, found no violation of the U.S. Constitution. It concluded both (1) that the Texas funding formula discriminated against poor school districts rather than against poor people or persons of color, and (2) that even students in poorly funded school districts were not being denied a public education altogether. As in some pivotal school desegregation cases, the *Rodriguez* Court placed preservation of local control above the need to ensure educational equality among children living in different communities.

After *Rodriguez,* the prospects for school finance reform under federal law dimmed. But advocates were more successful claiming that school-finance arrangements violated *state* constitutional provisions, in part because they, unlike the U.S. Constitution, explicitly require states to provide public education. Many of these decisions rested on the assumption, explicit in *Brown* (1954, 494), that the opportunity to receive a public education, "where the state has undertaken to provide it, is a right which must be made available to all on equal terms."

McUsic points out, however, that decades after *Rodriguez,* there still remain large funding discrepancies between rich districts and poor ones. These discrepancies can be as large as three to one within some states and even, in Texas as of the mid-1990s, nine to one. There also remain serious funding inequalities between schools within districts, and between the public schools of different states. Federal education funds reduce these disparities, though not substantially. Last but not least, funding discrepancies are still correlated with gaps in educational attainment, as measured by dropout rates, SAT scores, and tests of mathematical proficiency.

IMMIGRANT CHILDREN

Historically, children who are legal or illegal immigrants have also been excluded from public schools in several ways. Advocates have used litigation to challenge these forms of exclusion.

First, state laws that segregated schools based on race or national origin consigned many immigrant children to separate, inferior schools. In the years just before and after *Brown* in 1954, some state courts invalidated explicit school segregation based on national origin, but it was not until 1973 that the U.S. Supreme Court invalidated intentional school segregation involving Latinos and students of other national origins.

Second, some states have enacted laws denying children access to public schools based on their parents' immigration status. The advocates who challenged this categorical exclusion relied heavily on the language and logic of *Brown.* Peter Roos, coauthor of this volume's chapter on immigrant students (chapter 4), argued the key case, *Plyler v. Doe,* in the U.S. Supreme Court and prevailed: In 1982, by a 5–4 vote, the Court declared it unconstitutional for any state to deny public schooling to children whose parents are illegal immigrants. The majority opinion rested both on the impropriety of penalizing children for their parents' legal status, a factor beyond the children's control, and on the importance of educating these children, many of whom are likely to remain in the United States and who will become more productive members of society if they are educated.

This issue has once again become controversial. A 1994 voter initiative, commonly known as Proposition 187, amended the California constitution so as to prevent public schools from educating the children of illegal immigrants. Proponents acknowledge that portions of Proposition 187 are inconsistent with *Plyler.* They hope, given changes in the Supreme Court's composition since 1982, that the current justices will overrule that split decision if the opportunity arises.

For now, even as federal legislation patterned on Proposition 187 has been introduced in Congress, lower federal courts have enjoined enforcement of the California initiative. As Suárez-Orozco, Roos, and Suárez-Orozco point out, however, such actions create fear in immigrant communities that deters parents from enrolling their children in school.

Third, there have been successful efforts in Congress and in some states to deny illegal immigrants certain government benefits and services. As Martin Gerry argues, for example, changes in federal welfare law in 1996 impose heavy burdens on poor families and make it harder for poor immigrant children to attend school, even in states where no law expressly prevents them from doing so (chapter 6). Moreover, some of these restrictions apply to immigrant children who reside in the United States legally.

Fourth, for many years immigrant children who had not mastered oral or written English were functionally excluded from school because administrators and teachers did not adapt assessment or instruction to the educational needs of these students who are English language learners. There are still schools in which new immigrant children are tested for special education using English language tests and then inappropriately placed in special education programs where all instruction is conducted in English. These and other issues of teaching and learning are discussed more fully below.

CHILDREN WITH DISABILITIES

As Thomas Hehir and Sue Gamm point out in chapter 5, during the first half of the twentieth century, the eugenics movement sought not only to institutionalize disabled persons but also to sterilize them so they could not pass on to their children what the eugenicists considered inferior genetic stock.

In such a climate, it is not surprising that children with disabilities were regularly excluded by law from public education.[2] Those who were admitted to public school were typically placed in segregated classes where little education took place. Journalist John Merrow, who visited classes for disabled children before the federal law offered protection to disabled persons, describes one such class as "rows and rows of children and adults strapped to their chairs in a dimly lit room, a cacophony of moans and screams [in which] four or five attendants stood watch over . . . about a hundred 'students'" (Merrow, 1996, 48, 38).

In the late 1960s, advocates began a concerted effort to challenge such practices through litigation. Their arguments relied heavily on the logic and language of *Brown,* as did the decisions of federal and state courts that declared unconstitutional the categorical exclusion and segregation of children with disabilities (*Mills v. Board of Education,* 1972; *Pennsylvania Association for Retarded Children v. Pennsylvania,* 1972). These decisions plainly contributed to the enactment of comprehensive federal laws and regulations that now give children with disabilities the legal entitlement to a "free appropriate public education" and protect children and adults with disabilities against discrimination.[3]

As Hehir and Gamm note (chapter 5), the combination of constitutional protection and statutory and regulatory entitlements has been a powerful one. The result is that law-based school reform has benefited disabled children more than any other group of children that has faced exclusion and discrimination in America's public schools.

SUMMARY

As a result of law-based school reform, far fewer students than in the past are excluded from school by force of law:

- State-imposed segregation in education, whether by race or national origin, has been significantly reduced if not eliminated. Black-white discrepancies, in student achievement and in high school graduation rates, are far smaller than in 1954 or even 1984.
- In at least some states, school finance formulas are more equitable today than they were in 1972, when the Supreme Court decided *Rodriguez*.
- The Supreme Court has invalidated laws that deny a public education to immigrant children, whether or not the children reside legally in the United States.
- The U.S. Constitution and federal statutes guarantee a free appropriate public education to every child with a disability, regardless of how severe the disability is or how costly it may be to educate the child appropriately.

These developments represent significant progress. At the same time, efforts to end educational exclusion have not succeeded fully:

- Racial isolation is growing, for blacks and especially for Hispanics. This is especially true in regions outside the South, and in the cities and suburbs that comprise metropolitan areas. Segregation *within* schools is also a serious and continuing problem.
- The gaps between "haves" and "have nots" seem to be increasing, despite strong evidence that such gaps produce highly undesirable educational consequences for the "have nots."
- Powerful forces seek both to overturn *Plyler v. Doe,* which guarantees immigrant children access to public education, and to deny legal and illegal immigrants services that are linked to school attendance, good academic performance, and completion of high school.

In sum, efforts to end educational exclusion have not succeeded fully—and huge inequities remain even where formal exclusion has ended. Some groups have fared better than others, moreover; children with disabilities have made greater educational progress than have children in other groups once excluded or segregated by law. While the reasons for this are complex, one obvious explanation is political: Minority children, poor children, and immigrant children do not enjoy as much political or legal support as do children whose defining characteristic—disability—cuts across all economic classes and racial groups.

Serving Students Well in School:
Law and Education Converge

Some optimistic integrationists thought that ending legally mandated segregation and exclusion would itself produce equality of opportunity. Educational equality depends, however, not only on passing through the schoolhouse gate but also on what occurs afterward, inside schools and classrooms. Unfortunately, in many cases earlier forms of segregation and exclusion were simply replaced by new forms of segregation and unequal educational opportunity *within* schools.

As educational inequality has taken different forms, lawyers and parents have responded, often by initiating new legal challenges. Some of these law-based reform efforts have succeeded. But there have also been significant obstacles.

One obstacle has been political. As discussed more fully below, support for traditional civil-rights enforcement has declined during the past three decades, among the federal judiciary and the public at large, as has concern for the well-being of disadvantaged children. Racial stereotypes also remain; as recently as 1991, polls showed that nearly half of white Americans considered blacks and Latinos to be less intelligent than whites, and 37 percent believed that black children "could not be motivated to learn" (Welner and Oakes, 1996, 451).

A second complication is that what goes on within schools and classrooms involves educational considerations as well as legal ones. Whether a particular educational practice is discriminatory often hinges, at least in part, on what educators and researchers see as its educational consequences. If a practice is educationally necessary, desirable, or even justifiable, judges are less likely to see it as illegal.

This has several implications. First, in situations involving alleged discrimination in education, the key legal standards are increasingly and expressly defined in terms of what is necessary or appropriate educationally. In other words, there has been a convergence of legal standards and educational norms.

Second, this convergence has vastly increased the need for effective inter-disciplinary analysis and collaboration between lawyers, educators, advocates, parents, and researchers. Where disputes hinge on judgments that are at least as much educational as legal, it is difficult—and unwise—for educators and their lawyers to do their jobs without close collaboration.

Third, establishing illegal discrimination will be more difficult when there is disagreement among educators and researchers about the value or necessity of the educational policy or practice in question.

The remainder of this section describes some of the ways in which reformers have attempted to use the law to address in-school problems such as continued segregation, inadequate education, and the fragmentation of educational and other services for children who are in danger of school failure.

TESTING AND CLASSROOM PLACEMENTS

After the courts had declared it illegal to exclude children from schools based on race, national origin, or disability, many schools, school districts, and entire states began to assign students to largely or completely segregated classrooms *within* schools. For minority children these included both low-track classes, in which schools set low academic expectations for students, and classes for children with mild mental disabilities. Educators justified these results on the basis of (1) tests that purported to measure children's knowledge in one or more academic subjects, and (2) a belief in the educational desirability of homogeneous grouping. Meanwhile, disabled children were often placed in segregated settings in which they had little contact with their nondisabled peers.

Desegregation As Gary Orfield has noted, the benefits of school desegregation are not known to penetrate concrete walls. Advocates for black children and Latino children have therefore challenged "ability" grouping plans that produce racial isolation.

They have used three basic arguments. In some cases, the legal claim was that such placements were intentionally discriminatory. With few exceptions, courts have been reluctant to recognize such claims unless attorneys could demonstrate that minority children with high test scores had been placed in lower-track classes than white children with lower scores. A second claim, available only in districts operating under desegregation orders, has challenged in-school segregation on the ground that it preserves the effects of past illegal segregation and is inconsistent with a previously segregated district's obligation to achieve the greatest possible extent of actual desegregation (*McNeal v. Tate County School District,* 1975). These cases have been successful, at least where the minority children in low-track classes had themselves attended illegally segregated schools. Over time, however, there have been fewer children who could satisfy this condition (*Georgia State Conference of Branches of NAACP v. Georgia,* 1985).

In these student-assignment cases, the legal claims that have been most successful are those in which legal standards are based on educational norms.

Under regulations for a federal civil rights statute known as Title VI,[4] for example, school officials must justify as *educationally necessary* the use of any test that produces disproportionate adverse impact by race, color, or national origin. Even if school officials can meet this burden, moreover, plaintiffs can still prevail by showing that there exist *equally practical assignment practices that produce less racial identifiability* in classroom assignments. There are similar obligations where tests used to assess students for special education produce similar results by race or national origin.[5]

In 1985, one appeals court found the educational benefits of homogeneous grouping sufficient to meet this "educational necessity" test (*Georgia State Conference of Branches of NAACP v. Georgia,* 1985), but in the intervening years it has become clear both that there is little scholarly support for "skill grouping" (Mosteller, Light, and Sachs, 1996) and that there are powerful educational justifications for heterogeneous classroom grouping (Welner and Oakes, 1996). Moreover, there is considerable research showing that heterogeneous grouping is a "practical assignment practice" that reduces significantly racial identifiability in classroom assignments (Lynn and Wheelock, 1997).

The consequence of this recent research is a "new susceptibility of school tracking systems to legal challenges" (Welner and Oakes, 1996, 451). This illustrates the growing convergence of legal standards and educational norms and the increased likelihood of legal success when claims are based on strong educational research.

It also demonstrates the importance of effective collaboration between educators, lawyers, researchers, and parents. It is the rare educator who can quote the elements of the legal test that courts apply to ability grouping disputes. At the same time, it is the rare lawyer who knows why it is "educationally necessary" to use a particular student assignment strategy, or whether use of an alternative test, having less disproportionate impact by race or national origin, would be feasible; once the lawyer provides the applicable standard, it takes an educator to determine whether the school's assignment plan meets the educational criteria on which the legal standard is based.

A second consequence, perhaps related to the first, is that many school districts appear to be moving from homogeneous to random (heterogeneous) grouping of students within schools; according to one national study, the proportion of middle schools practicing random grouping rose from 25 percent to nearly 50 percent between 1988 and 1993 (Lynn and Wheelock, 1997).

Hehir and Gamm (chapter 5) confirm that there are similar efforts to reduce overrepresentation of minority children in many programs for children with disabilities. They caution, however, that the greater incidence of poverty among children of color, coupled with the greater incidence of medical and developmental problems among poor children, suggests that overrepresentation of minority children in *some* special education programs may reflect the actual incidence of poverty-related disabilities.

Other cautions are also in order. First, racially heterogeneous grouping is possible only in schools that are themselves multiracial; recent trends cited earlier, however, suggest that segregation of black and especially Latino children is now increasing. Second, integration of children by *socioeconomic* status—the importance of which James Coleman recognized in his landmark report (Coleman, 1966)—is also declining, as the concentrations of poor children increase, particularly in urban schools. This is an issue that recent scholarship (Fuller, Elmore, and Orfield, 1996; Orfield and Eaton, 1996) discusses, and that Molly McUsic explores at some length in chapter 3, on school finance reform.

Children with Disabilities Like minority children and poor children, children with disabilities continue to face isolation within schools. This is true despite court decisions, laws, and regulations stating that such children must be educated with their nondisabled peers "to the maximum extent appropriate."[6]

Since the federal special education statute, now known as the Individuals with Disabilities Education Act (IDEA),[7] went into effect in 1977, views have changed considerably on how much integration of disabled children is, in fact, appropriate. Until 1989, there were relatively few cases in which courts were asked to rule on the appropriateness of placing students with disabilities in regular classes (Hehir and Gamm, chapter 5). Since that time, however, the views of many judges and educators have evolved, largely due to research showing the benefits of instruction in regular classrooms and studies demonstrating how disabled children can be educated in such settings.

There now exists a legal presumption that disabled children, often even those with severe mental disabilities such as autism and Down syndrome, can be educated appropriately in regular classrooms and programs with necessary supplementary aids and services—unless the school can prove otherwise. While "inclusion" is not without its detractors, federal courts increasingly require schools both to restructure regular classrooms to accommodate a wider range of student needs and to justify carefully any placement outside the regular classroom (*Sacramento City U.S.D. v. Holland,* 1994; *Oberti v. Bd. of Ed. of Clementon School Dist.,* 1993; and *Daniel R.R. v. State Bd. of Ed.,* 1989).

Moreover, this trend provides another powerful example of the convergence of law and education: the meaning of a legal standard, calling for inclusion "to the maximum extent appropriate," has evolved dramatically as educational research has altered perceptions of what is, in fact, appropriate. Lawyers who once focused on special education's detailed timelines and procedures must now understand as well the pedagogical issues of where, what, and how a child with disabilities should be taught.

EDUCATIONAL QUALITY

The law-driven reforms discussed in this volume also share a focus on improving the quality of education that students receive. These efforts, like those concerning testing and classroom placements, reflect a growing convergence of legal standards and educational knowledge.

School Desegregation In a 1977 decision known as *Milliken II* (*Milliken v. Bradley,* 1977), the U.S. Supreme Court ruled that remedies for segregated, inferior schooling should include not only desegregation but also programs to address the harmful educational effects of segregation. Since that decision, many school boards, especially in urban areas, have used school desegregation suits to secure substantial state funding with which to improve their educational programs. Unfortunately, the Supreme Court's 1977 decision came too late to benefit most students in the South, where many desegregation cases had already ended. Equally unfortunate, there is evidence (Orfield and Eaton, 1996) that *Milliken II* funds have not been spent on measures that produce the greatest improvements in student learning.

This is not entirely the fault of the districts in question, however. As Orfield explains in chapter 2, two key Supreme Court decisions (*Milliken v. Bradley,* 1974; and *Missouri v. Jenkins,* 1995), place serious limits on the use of remedies that, by reducing high concentrations of poor children in urban schools, are most likely to produce improved student achievement. These cases illustrate how political resistance to reform can lead courts to downplay or ignore critical educational and social science research.

School Finance Reform Proponents of school finance reform have also expanded their objectives and strategies to take educational factors into greater account. Initially concerned with equalizing overall per-pupil expenditures within a state, reformers started asking whether overall equalization is the proper remedy in a variety of circumstances:

• In school districts that serve large numbers of students who are particularly costly to educate, "What should equality mean for those who are different?" (Minow, 1991a, 399).
• In districts that face significantly higher noninstructional costs than others, such as those for school security, heating fuel, and building maintenance.
• In districts that value education more and are willing to tax themselves at higher rates to pay for public education.
• If gross per-pupil equalization leaves districts without the resources they need to educate each student adequately.
• If there is no guarantee that new funds will be applied in the ways most likely to produce improved teaching and learning (Murnane, 1994).
• If a factor other than money itself—dramatic change in school governance, as in Kentucky, or, as McUsic argues in chapter 3, integration of students by socioeconomic class—may be a *sine qua non* of improved student learning.

Thus, far more than in the past, school finance cases turn less on traditional legal questions than on complex questions of education, economics, and politics. Such cases therefore require sophisticated collaboration between educators, lawyers, researchers, parents, and state-level policy makers. In a number of states, collaboration on issues such as these has transformed school finance cases into ambitious statewide school reform efforts (*Rose v. Council for Better Education,* 1986; *Abbott v. Burke,* 1990 and 1994; and *McDuffy v. Secretary of the Executive Office of Education,* 1993).

Immigrant Children Immigrant children are deeply affected by the educational quality issues discussed above, including homogeneous grouping, disproportionate placements into special education classes, and school finance reform;

indeed, the principal Supreme Court decision on school finance reform, *Rodriguez,* involved many school districts that were largely Latino. Federal disability law forbids discrimination in the assessment and placement of children and requires that educational services and communications with parents be in the child's or parents' primary language. Title I, a federal program serving many low-achieving disadvantaged children, now contains provisions to ensure that English language learners (ELLs) eligible for Title I are not denied services (Weckstein, chapter 7).

Advocates for immigrant children have raised other educational concerns. In *Lau v. Nichols* (1974), the U.S. Supreme Court ruled for the first time that public schools could not rely solely on the "sink or swim" method in serving ELLs enrolled in public school. Federal funds under the Bilingual Education Act, as well as post-*Lau* guidelines from the U.S. Office of Education, helped promote use of transitional bilingual education as a means of helping immigrant children keep up in class while learning English. Programs to teach English as a second language have also flourished. *Lau* raises fundamental questions about the legality of efforts, in California and elsewhere, to forbid the use of native-language instruction with ELLs.

The federal statute that has been used most effectively to address the educational needs of immigrant students is the Equal Educational Opportunities Act of 1974 (EEOA),[8] one section of which requires state and local educational agencies to take "appropriate action to overcome language barriers that impede equal participation by its students in its *instructional programs.*"[9]

In defining a legal standard by which to assess compliance with the statute, judges crafted a standard that illustrates well the convergence of legal and educational norms. The legal test asks (1) whether programs for LEP children are *based on a sound educational philosophy,* (2) whether the state and school district are providing *resources sufficient to ensure proper program implementation,* and (3) whether the program *actually enables students to overcome language barriers that impede their educational progress.*[10] Once again, the standard is one that requires collaboration between lawyers and the litigants.

As chapter 4 points out, immigrant children have used the EEOA to address a wide range of educational deficiencies in instructional programs for immigrant children. These include, among others, inadequate criteria for determining students' English abilities; use of aides (rather than bilingual teachers) in serving ELL students; inadequate criteria for assessing teachers' oral and written skills in the ELL students' language; improper teacher recruitment and assignment practices; inadequate curricular materials; insufficient evaluation of student progress in academic subjects and in acquisition of English; insufficient resources to ensure proper program implementation; and inadequate efforts to stem high dropout rates among ELL students.

These legal protections are less impressive in practice, however, as Suárez-Orozco, Roos, and Suárez-Orozco point out (chapter 4). Many eligible students receive no special instruction. Many programs for ELL children fail to meet minimal requirements. ELL students are sometimes tested for special education in English, and assigned to special education classes in which instruction is entirely in English. There are frequent shortages of staff members who can provide counseling services and school-to-work transition programs for ELL children. Children whose first language is neither English nor Spanish are particularly ill-served in many schools, partly due to shortages of trained bilingual staff. Moreover, the current political climate—in which even legal immigrants are losing important government benefits, undocumented immigrants may lose their right to attend school altogether, and native-language instruction is under assault—makes it even harder for immigrant children to succeed in school. It is not surprising that many immigrant groups are among those whose children fare least well in the nation's public schools.

Enforceable Performance Mandates In chapter 7, Paul Weckstein describes how important federal statutes, including Goals 2000, Title I, the IDEA, and the Perkins Vocational Education Act, have been amended to promote promising educational practices and to improve the performance of teachers and students alike.

First, children in Title I programs, students with disabilities, ELL students, and students in vocational programs now have federally protected rights to an education that will teach them what they must know to meet the same high standards as other children.

Second, if such students fall behind in school, they are entitled to an accelerated, enriched curriculum so that they can catch up rather than fall further behind.

Third, schools are subject to periodic evaluations using tests that measure students' basic and higher-order skills. If students are failing to meet those standards, schools must demonstrate that they are adopting new instructional strategies that are likely to succeed, based on educational research.

Fourth, parents have rights of participation at many stages of the planning and implementation process, as well as rights to challenge systemic educational failure through litigation.

These federal statutes, as amended in the 1990s, also illustrate a convergence between law and education. Eligible students have legal rights to the services that will enable them to meet certain educational standards, and parents have a legal right to insist on implementation of instructional strategies that have been shown to be effective. Questions of legal compliance and of legal remedies will thus require interdisciplinary perspectives and collaboration. As Weckstein points out, they will also depend on the capacity to educate and mobilize parents of disadvantaged children, particularly given a tradition of lax federal enforcement of rights under these statutes.

FRAGMENTATION OF SERVICES TO CHILDREN

Another recurring theme among these six law-driven reforms is an emphasis on reducing fragmentation of programs and services for children. Such fragmentation can occur within schools as well as between schools and other agencies that serve children. Addressing such problems requires collaboration between service providers, parents, lawyers, and the policy makers who draft statutes and regulations.

In-School Fragmentation Within many public schools there reside multiple instructional staffs: one each for special education, Title I, bilingual education, vocational education, and "regular" education. The director or coordinator of each typically has little influence over staff in other programs. Too often, these staffs work in relative isolation.

The balkanization of the teaching staff makes it difficult for a school to establish or maintain a clear instructional vision. It also has obvious implications for students whose needs cannot be met by any single program. As chapter 4 points out, there are ELL students who would benefit from special education but who cannot find special education classes in their native languages; they are obliged to choose between the wrong curriculum in the right language and the right curriculum in the wrong language. Title I students who receive instruction outside the regular classroom lose out if their teachers do not work together to ensure that student needs are met. If students with disabilities are to be integrated wherever appropriate in regular classrooms, special education staff and "regular" teachers will need to meet regularly to coordinate (Hehir and Gamm, chapter 5). The school schedule must be designed to permit such collaboration.

In the past, one source of fragmentation has been federal and state regulations. Title I funds, for example, were available only to address problems due to educational disadvantage, while special education funds were available only to address disability-related needs, and Bilingual Education Act grants were to help children overcome language barriers. In practice, of course, children's needs are rarely so easy to categorize. Federal accounting requirements have been another source of fragmentation; Title I's "supplement not supplant" provision, for example, encouraged schools to use pullout programs to show that Title I children were receiving something other children were not.

But educators' attitudes and lack of knowledge have also created obstacles. Though school-level administrators have authority over the school schedule and the entire instructional staff, few use that authority to ensure close coordination between federal programs and "regular education." Perhaps they are too busy. Many principals lack knowledge about how these programs operate and about how they could promote the kinds of collaboration that would improve teaching and learning. Perhaps some would sooner steer clear of programs that involve extensive legal requirements and that raise the prospect of possible litigation. Some principals may empathize with the "regular" kids, who do not benefit from "special" programs or federal grants. For their part, some teachers may fear that greater collaboration will reduce their autonomy and promote turf battles; they may dislike the idea of having to work with teachers in other programs.

In chapter 7, Weckstein discusses ways in which federal statutes have recently been amended to reduce legal obstacles to collaboration within schools. Lawyers and educators can work together to identify and address remaining obstacles so that the in-school fragmentation can be reduced.

Service Integration As Martin Gerry points out in chapter 6, recent years have seen numerous efforts to strengthen collaboration between educators and the people outside schools who provide services to children and families. Educators and scholars have long recognized that improving the academic performance of children depends not only on improving schools but on addressing the larger social forces that affect children's lives and can threaten their well-being (Graham, 1992; Howe, 1993; Fossey, forthcoming).

Gerry analyzes a variety of efforts to integrate education, health services, food and nutrition services, mental health services, child welfare services (such as adoption and foster care), family support services, substance abuse prevention and treatment programs, pregnancy prevention programs, delinquency prevention programs, and school-to-work transition programs for young people. He identifies obstacles to effective collaboration among social service providers, including the same kinds of programmatic fragmentation and complex eligibility requirements that frustrate collaboration between teachers within schools. Indeed, he points out that the purpose of service integration is precisely "to offset some of the worst features of the disjointed array of categorical programs."

Based on the results of various efforts to improve collaboration among existing programs and service providers, Gerry concludes that such approaches are insufficient, and argues for the creation a new network of community-based child-wellness systems. He sees a crucial role for lawyers in bringing this about: to refrain from designing and maintaining categorical program structures, and to "work closely with educators, families, communities and other service professionals to design, implement and support . . . equitable service integration initiatives."

Conclusion The law-driven reforms that this book discusses have evolved: From an initial concern with exclusion, which has still not been addressed completely, and segregation, which remains pervasive despite success in desegregating some school systems, advocates have increasingly focused on addressing such problems as segregation within schools, inadequate education, and the fragmentation of educational and other services for children who are in danger of school failure. The experience with recent reform efforts underscores the need for more effective collaboration between lawyers, educators, researchers, and parents.

New Challenges and Opportunities

What is the current context within which advocates attempt to mount law-driven school reform efforts? It includes both (1) the current political climate, in which many children's rights are being curtailed and the welfare of children is deteriorating; and (2) a round of new school reform efforts that seek to deregulate schools and decentralize school governance in exchange for greater accountability for improving student achievement. Most of the chapters that follow see in these trends both challenges and opportunities for advocates of law-driven school reform.

THE CURRENT POLITICAL CLIMATE

One challenge is a political climate in which there have been many challenges to desegregation, affirmative action, services for immigrants, and programs for disadvantaged people generally. The prevailing wisdom is that discrimination is a thing of the past, and many citizens and policy makers seem unaware of how current trends reflect continuing, unremedied vestiges of segregation and inequality in education, housing, employment, and other domains. In dismantling desegregation plans, courts are sending children back to neighborhoods that themselves reflect long patterns of illegal segregation and are producing single-race schools as surely as in the past (Tatel, 1993; Orfield and Eaton, 1996).

We live in an age in which many children's rights—such as those of immigrant children to attend public school—are in jeopardy, and in which the overall welfare of American children, particularly disadvantaged children, is poor and deteriorating rapidly, with enormous educational consequences. In 1991, the National Committee on Children concluded that in the United States

> children growing up in poverty are frequently undernourished and inadequately clothed, and live in substandard housing. For them, the world is often a dangerous and threatening place to grow up. It is crime-ridden streets . . . or desolate rural areas without adequate roads and running water. It is dilapidated homes with broken windows, poor heating, lead paint, rats and garbage. It is a world in which children grow up ashamed of the way they live, where they learn basic survival skills before they learn to read. They experience the most health problems but live in the least healthful environments and have the least access to medical care. They are at the highest risk of academic failure but have the fewest social supports. (Gerry, chapter 6)

By 1994, a Carnegie Corporation panel reported, 3 million children, nearly one-fourth of all American infants and toddlers, were living in poverty (Chira, 1994), and a year later scientists confirmed that deprivation early in childhood impairs subsequent brain development (Nash, 1997).

These findings were available to the Congress that enacted the 1996 federal "welfare reform," which, according to researchers' predictions (see chapter 6), will throw 1.1 million additional children into poverty: Some "2 million children (23% of the current caseload) will lose AFDC support [and] over 2.2 million children (16% of the current caseload) will lose food stamp eligibility" (Gerry, chapter 6, citing Urban Institute, 1996).

Plainly these trends hinder efforts to use law-based reforms to improve education for disadvantaged students. Some scholars argue that school reformers must pay greater attention to the larger forces that threaten children's well-being (Fossey, forthcoming; Graham, 1992; Howe, 1993).

They are right, of course, but doing so increases the political challenges that law-based school reforms must face. As Martha Minow (1987, 217–218) points out, "it should not be surprising that the more powerfully the legal claims on behalf of children effectively push for change at the deeper, structural level, the more likely are objections, from many quarters, to the use of law to reform society itself." This phenomenon may explain why law-driven school reform efforts have encountered increasing resistance as their objectives have broadened. It also underscores the need for lawyers and educators to help educate the public and mobilize political support for needed reforms.

Each chapter in this volume describes major political obstacles to current law-driven reforms on behalf of disadvantaged students: judicial developments that threaten to undermine not only the integrationist spirit of *Brown* but even the "separate but equal" guarantees of *Plessy v. Ferguson* (1896) (chapter 2); the opposition of wealthier school districts and powerful interest groups to increased funding for poorer districts (chapter 3); hostility toward immigrants, perhaps most evident in efforts to exclude undocumented immigrant children from public education altogether and to deny social benefits to legal immigrants as well (chapter 4); efforts to cut special education funding (chapter 5); reduced funds for social programs for poor children, leaving fewer services to integrate (chapter 6); and proposals to replace new federal education statutes with block grants, which eliminate programs that can be an important source of rights for eligible children (chapter 7).

How to alter these political constraints or work most effectively within them is an important question that each author addresses, in some cases by attempting to frame reform efforts in ways that will attract broader political support. This issue is discussed below, as well as in other chapters.

TRENDS IN SCHOOL REFORM: DEREGULATION, DECENTRALIZATION, AND THE SHIFT FROM INPUTS TO OUTCOMES

There is a second context for current and future efforts to use law to improve the schools: new school reform efforts of the past decade that seek to deregulate schools and decentralize school governance in exchange for greater accountability in improving student achievement. Better measurement of student achievement, coupled with accountability measures, should support the law-driven reform efforts studied here, though reliance on outcome measures for students carries risks as well as opportunities.

The Opportunities Though each chapter focuses on different school reforms, this book's authors see important opportunities in the current effort to place greater emphasis in public education on students' academic performance.

Most important, standards-based reforms show a growing consensus on the need to ensure that each child receives a high-quality education, on the content of a high-quality education, and on what it takes to provide it (Weckstein, chapter 7).

This emphasis is fully consistent with many law-driven reform efforts and the legal rights and protections that such reform efforts have secured. For example, as noted above, many school finance reform cases and court decisions have gone beyond the question of equalizing dollars and instead attempted to define both what constitutes an adequate education and how to ensure that each student in a state receives one.

Moreover, in each state that has defined an adequate education—as have most states, through statutes that spell out in some detail the knowledge and skills that students should possess at different grade levels—the political process has already produced consensus on one of the most challenging and potentially controversial questions associated with school finance litigation.

A similar concern with educational outcomes has long been evident in advocacy on behalf of immigrant students. For example, there has been great concern with high dropout rates among Latino and some Asian immigrants, the college-going rates among immigrants, and the rates at which immigrant students take and pass state competency tests. There has been litigation over homogeneous grouping and disproportionate placement of immigrant children in special education classes, in both cases motivated by a desire to ensure that each child receives the best possible education and acquires the basic and higher-order skills that young people will need in college and the workplace. Even on a politically and educationally charged issue such as native-language instruction, advocates and parents want schools to monitor ELL students' progress in different types of programs.

Earlier versions of the Individuals with Disabilities Education Act were known for focusing almost entirely on compliance with extensive timelines and procedures. The assumption, which many have questioned, has been that good process will lead to good placement decisions for children with disabilities.

This exclusive reliance on inputs is now changing. The 1997 version of the IDEA focuses on outcomes such as promotion rates, graduation rates, and employment rates after graduation. It also requires that students with disabilities be included in state assessment programs, so that parents can evaluate their children's educational attainments in relation to those of nondisabled children (Hehir and Gamm, chapter 5). Where special education differs from other school reforms is that the emphasis on outcomes is in addition to, rather than in place of, compliance with requirements governing timelines, procedures, and other input requirements, such as those governing teacher certification.

The most recent versions of Goals 2000, Title I, the IDEA, and the Perkins Vocational Education Act also place greater emphasis than before on educational outcomes, and they incorporate into federal education law student performance objectives similar to those in American education generally. These changes in federal law are designed to be consistent with similar trends among the states.

The situation is somewhat more complex—and, perhaps, ironic—where desegregation is concerned. The Supreme Court's 1968 decision in *Green v. New Kent County School Board* made *outcomes* the measure of a desegregation plan's adequacy: if the plan actually eliminated the vestiges of state-imposed segregation, it was constitutionally adequate; if not, it was insufficient. The Supreme Court's decision in *Milliken II (Milliken v. Bradley,* 1977) seemed to say that the Constitution requires elimination of the *educational* vestiges of prior, illegal segregation. In short, if educational outcomes are the measure of a desegregation plan's success under *Green* and *Milliken II,* these decisions would be congruent with the approach that recent reforms take, focusing less on inputs and more on student performance.

In 1995, however, the Supreme Court held (5–4) in *Missouri v. Jenkins* that the adequacy of educational remedies should not depend on proof that black students in the district have attained academic parity with their white peers. The meaning of *Jenkins* remains somewhat vague—it did not rule out all crossracial academic comparisons, for example. The trend in desegregation cases, however, as in affirmative action cases, is to diminish the focus on educational results as a measure of whether students have been educated adequately. Ironically, the results-based approach that educators consider most effective in other contexts may be less available in the desegregation context as a means of assessing progress toward educational equality.

In conclusion, the current shift from inputs to student outcomes is in many ways consistent with the remedies that advocates of law-driven school reform have traditionally sought.

The Risks For many disadvantaged children, the increased reliance on outcome measures presents possible risks, especially in a political climate where educational and other programs for such children are being cut.

One risk inherent in standards-based reforms is that standards, rather than stimulating improvement of educational programs and affording each child a real opportunity to learn, "will only validate, rather than help eliminate, vast inequalities in educational outcomes and economic opportunity" (Weckstein, chapter 7). If society defines the knowledge and skills that students need but then denies some students the opportunity to acquire them, imposing penalties on low-scoring test takers reinforces the inequality and provides a basis for further unequal treatment.

Such risks are particularly acute for English language learners, for whom it is often difficult to evaluate fairly the meaning of a test administered in English, and for students with disabilities, whose capacities a test may measure less fairly than the student's success at completing the requirements of his or her individualized educational program (IEP).

Current school reforms involve not only an increased emphasis on student achievement but also an emphasis on deregulation and decentralization.

Here too there are possible conflicts. For example, "School reform initiatives that incorporate choice . . . are likely to face strong opposition from school desegregation advocates and invalidation by courts unless they are controlled to ensure compliance with court-ordered racial guidelines" (Tatel, 1993, 64). As Tatel points out, "One source of the conflict is political. . . . The two movements have different constituencies. . . . A second source is structural. School desegregation orders tend to exert a 'centralizing' force on school systems, while the recent school reform movement has been 'decentralizing'" (65). Similar conflicts arise where charter schools do not respect their obligation to serve children with disabilities. In both cases, the challenge is to reconcile deregulation and decentralization with traditional civil-rights protections (Heubert, 1997a). Working together, educators and lawyers should be able to find ways of reducing potential conflicts without costly, avoidable litigation.

THE EVOLVING ROLES OF LAW AND LAWYERS IN SCHOOL REFORM

The evolution, opportunities, and risks described above have important implications for lawyers, educators, and others who seek to promote school reform through the law.

First, as each of the following chapters suggests, lawyers and litigation will continue to play a prominent role in law-based school reforms, particularly those aimed at attaining equality of educational opportunity.[11] School finance reform is still largely litigation driven, and the thoughtful class-integration remedies that McUsic proposes (chapter 3) have thus far emerged more often through litigation than through the political process. Disputes over the rights of immigrant students also continue to find their way into court, whether the issue is Proposition 187, denial of services to legal immigrants, affirmative action, bilingual education, bilingual special education, teacher testing, or student assessment programs that fail to take language barriers into account adequately.

In special education, legalization and due process have long been a way of life and are likely to remain so, in part because they are linked with improved educational programs for children with disabilities (Hehir and Gamm, chapter 5). Where enforceable performance mandates are concerned, both the threat of litigation and actual lawsuits are likely to play an important role, the former as educators and parents make initial decisions about what educational programs to adopt and the latter where existing programs have failed to produce improved student achievement (Weckstein, chapter 7). School desegregation litigation is also likely to continue despite the unseemly haste with which some judges are seeking to dismantle desegregation plans. This is so whether the issue is the legality of the judicial behavior that Orfield describes in chapter 2, the desirability of seeking unitary status, or the adequacy of educational remedies for past discrimination.

Second, the growing convergence of legal standards and educational norms—which reflects a recognition that legal remedies for educational problems are likeliest to succeed if they take educational considerations properly into account—affects virtually every law-based school reform effort, and will influence the roles that lawyers, educators, researchers, parents, and courts play in the reform process.

Third, though lawyers have always played roles other than those of litigators, their nonlitigation roles will assume increased importance. Some education lawyers may require additional training to operate effectively outside the litigation context.

One such area is the practice of preventive law, something that few law schools teach and about which many lawyers do not know enough (Heubert, 1997b). Lawyers who work for school districts must help educators avoid legal conflicts and promote programs and practices that serve disadvantaged children well. This will involve educating clients, helping to implement legal mandates effectively, anticipating possible conflicts, and reconciling competing interests and educational objectives. Given current trends in school reform, there will be a recurring need to integrate efforts to deregulate schools and decentralize educational decision making with traditional civil rights protections (Heubert, 1997a). Mediation is also important in many situations; in special education disputes, for example, one urban special education director was able to reduce special education litigation in his district by two-thirds—simply by encouraging staff lawyers to work with parents in a more cooperative spirit.[12] Each of the following chapters provides powerful examples of ways in which lawyers can help educators and parents reach consensus and avoid unnecessary litigation.

Another set of nonlitigation roles in which lawyers can be helpful are those of lobbyist, consensus builder, and drafter of statutes, regulations, and policies that make the best use of educational knowledge and social science research. For example, Weckstein (chapter 7) shows how educators, lawyers, advocates, and policy makers used current educational research as they drafted federal vocational-education statutes and argues that collaborating from the start is the best way of avoiding litigation later. This assumes, of course, that lawyers either know what constitutes best educational practice or can make sense of social-science research. And while understanding research is not something that most law schools train their students to do, acquiring such skills is not beyond the capacities of most lawyers; indeed, advocacy lawyers, who frequently work for years on a single set of legal and educational issues, often do master the relevant research. McUsic (chapter 3), Suárez-Orozco, Roos, and Suárez-Orozco (chapter 4), Hehir and Gamm (chapter 5), Gerry (chapter 6), and Weckstein (chapter 7) all offer valuable insights on what lawyers and educators need to understand to function effectively in the lawmaking process.

Even outside the lawmaking process, lawyers can play an important role in bringing together diverse constituencies and in helping them develop and implement programs: "Indeed, lawyering is clearly valuable during the process of reaching compromise on policy goals, solving problems of program organization, and creating mechanisms of accountability and enforcement. A lawyer's instincts and experience on such matters constitute an agenda which complements . . . the agendas of educators at the policy making table" (Edley, 1991, 298). Along these lines, Martin Gerry (chapter 6) writes that "lawyers, because they are neither service professionals nor academic researchers, are best positioned to play the key roles of translator, broker, and problem-solver which lie at the heart of the crafting and successful integration of service integration initiatives." Suárez-Orozco, Roos, and Suárez-Orozco (chapter 4) agree, seeing an important role for lawyers in helping schools establish collaborative relationships with ethnic-constituency-based organizations.

Last but not least, parents, educators, and advocates need to pay closer attention to political issues, particularly in the current climate. As McUsic (chapter 3) notes, "Just as it will be hard to find buyers for a new model car unless it is designed, manufactured, and marketed with an eye on the needs and concerns of consumers, so will it also be hard to gain an order from the courts— or laws from the legislature—that effect real change, unless the remedies are carefully crafted with an eye to political realities, which means that they reflect the fears, concerns, and aspirations of all parties."

School reformers are likelier to achieve their aims when they build coalitions and craft their proposals in ways that maximize their political appeal. For example, parents trying to desegregate urban school districts allied themselves successfully with district officials in seeking state funds under *Milliken II* for programs to address the continuing educational effects of prior segregation; the result has been significant additional support for financially strapped urban schools. McUsic (chapter 3) provides another example: Having won a court order requiring the legislature to modify its school finance formula, the plaintiffs' lawyers immediately hired lobbyists and began a grass roots and public relations campaign to influence the legislators on a remedy.

The Need for Collaboration

Even in litigation there is a growing need for improved collaboration between lawyers, educators, scholars, and parents, particularly where legal standards and educational norms are closely intertwined. McUsic (chapter 3) describes how lawyers must rely on educators and scholars in shaping all aspects of school finance litigation, even the legal theories on which a lawsuit is based. Suárez-Orozco, Roos, and Suárez-Orozco (chapter 4) describe how lawyers worked with educators and researchers to explain complex issues of language acquisition to a judge. Disputes over appropriate placements for students with disabilities likewise call for multidisciplinary expertise.

The same is true for the nonlitigation roles for lawyers described above. Each one requires extensive collaboration between educators, lawyers, parents, policy makers, advocates, and other concerned interest groups. Preventive law is by definition a collaborative process that helps people anticipate and resolve disputes before they blossom into litigation. Collaboration is equally important for lawyers who wish or need to serve as lobbyists, consensus builders, and drafters of rules and agreements that enjoy wide support.

There are significant obstacles to effective collaboration between lawyers and those they serve. Some of these obstacles are due to limited knowledge, others to limiting assumptions that lawyers, educators, researchers, and parents make about themselves and others. Still others stem from structural factors, such as fee arrangements; for example, educators with access to in-house counsel are more likely to speak regularly with their attorneys than are educators whose lawyers charge by the hour (Heubert, 1997b).

These are issues that educators, lawyers, parents, and policy makers will have to address if law-driven school reform efforts are to achieve their objectives, old and new. This volume's authors offer useful information both on the specific reforms they explore and on ways in which those involved in the reform process can work together more effectively to address the needs of disadvantaged children.

NOTES

1. Chapter 2 also summarizes the key Supreme Court school desegregation decisions issued during the 1968–1973 period: *Green v. New Kent County School Board,* 391 U.S. 430 (1968); *Swann v. Charlotte-Mecklenburg Board of Education,* 402 U.S. 1 (1971); *Davis v. Board of School Commissioners,* 402 U.S. 33 (1972); and *Keyes v. School District No. 1,* 413 U.S. 189 (1973).

2. State compulsory education laws frequently exempted disabled children, and many states gave school districts the authority to exclude altogether children with certain kinds of disabilities.

3. These include the Individuals With Disabilities Education Act (IDEA), 20 U.S.C. §1401 et seq., with accompanying regulations found at 34 C.F.R. §§300.1 et seq.; Section 504 of the Rehabilitation Act of 1973, 29 U.S.C. §§794 et seq. and its accompanying regulations, found at 34 C.F.R. §§104 et seq.; and the Americans with Disabilities Act of 1990 (ADA), 42 U.S.C. §§12131 et seq. and its accompanying regulations, found at 28 C.F.R. §§35 et seq.

4. Title VI of the Civil Rights Act of 1964, 42 U.S.C. 2000(d) et seq.

5. Section 504 of the Rehabilitation Act of 1973 (Section 504), 29 U.S.C. §§794 et seq. and its accompanying regulations, found at 34 C.F.R. §§104 et seq.; and Title II of the Americans with Disabilities Act of 1990 (Title II), 42 U.S.C. §§12131 et seq. and its accompanying regulations, found at 28 C.F.R. §§35 et seq.

6. 34 C.F.R. §§300.550(b)(1). "Special classes, separate schooling or other removal of children with disabilities from the regular education environment *should occur only when the nature or severity of the disability is such that education in regular classes with the use of supplementary aids and services cannot be achieved satisfactorily.*" 300 C.F.R. §300.550(b)(2) (emphasis added).

7. 20 U.S.C. §1401 et seq., with accompanying regulations found at 34 C.F.R. §§300.1 et seq.

8. 20 U.S.C. §1701 et seq.

9. 20 U.S.C. §1703(j) (emphasis added).

10. *Castaneda v. Pickard,* 648 F.2d 989 (5th Cir. 1981).

11. This is consistent with an important role that constitutions and judges play in our

governmental scheme: protecting individuals and groups whose interests may not receive adequate weight and attention in the majoritarian political process.

12. Conversation with Thomas Hehir, director, Office of Special Education Programs, U.S. Department of Education, March 1996.

REFERENCES

Abbott v. Burke, 575 A.2d 359 (1990), 643 A.2d 575 (1994).

Brown v. Board of Education of Topeka, 347 U.S. 483 (1954).

Castaneda v. Pickard, 648 F.2d 989 (5th Cir. 1981).

Chira, S. (1994). Study confirms worst fears on U.S. children. *New York Times* (April 12): A1, A11.

Coleman, J. (1966). *Equality of educational opportunity.* Washington, D.C.: U.S. Government Printing Office.

Cunningham, L. L. (1978). Foreword. In *The courts and education: The seventy-seventh yearbook of the National Society for the Study of Education,* part I, ed. C. P. Hooker, xi–xix. Chicago: University of Chicago Press.

Daniel R.R. v. State Bd. of Ed., 874 F.2d 1036 (5th Cir. 1989).

Davis v. Board of School Commissioners, 402 U.S. 33 (1972).

Edley, C. F., Jr. (1991). Lawyers and education reform. *Harvard Journal on Legislation* 28 (Summer): 293–300.

Fossey, R. (forthcoming). Improving our children's future: Looking beyond law-based school reforms.

Fuller, B., R. Elmore, and G. Orfield, eds. (1996). *School choice: The cultural logic of families, the political rationality of institutions.* New York: Teachers College Press.

Georgia State Conference of Branches of NAACP v. Georgia, 775 F.2d 1403 (11th Cir. 1985).

Graham, P. (1992). *S.O.S.: Sustain our schools.* New York: Hill and Wang.

Green v. New Kent County School Board, 391 U.S. 430 (1968).

Grissmer, D., et al. (1996). Explaining trends in NAEP achievement scores. Paper presented at the Emory University conference "Intelligence on the Rise: Secular Changes in IQ and Related Measures," April 12–14, 1996, Atlanta.

Herbert, D. J. (1991). An analysis of the acquisition, utilization, and compensation of legal services in public school districts in the United States. Ed.D. diss., Indiana University.

Heubert, J. (1997a). Schools without rules? Charter schools, federal disability law, and the paradoxes of deregulation. *Harvard Civil Rights–Civil Liberties Law Review* 32 (2): 301–353.

———. (1997b). The more we get together: Improving collaboration between educators and their lawyers. *Harvard Educational Review* 67(3): 531–582.

Hogan, J. C. (1985). *The schools, the courts, and the public interest.* 2d ed. Lexington, Mass.: D.C. Heath and Company, Lexington Books.

Horowitz, D. L. (1977). *The courts and social policy.* Washington, D.C.: Brookings Institution.

Howard, P. K. (1994). *The death of common sense: How law is suffocating America.* New York: Random House.

Howe, H. (1993). *Thinking about our kids.* New York: Free Press.

Jones, J. H. (1978). The role of the school attorney in Mississippi public school districts. *Dissertation Abstracts International* 39:3272A

Keyes v. School District No. 1, 413 U.S. 189; rehearing denied, 414 U.S. 883 (1973).

Kirp, D. L. (1977). Law, politics, and equal educational opportunity: The limits of judicial involvement. *Harvard Educational Review* 47 (May): 117–137.

Kirp, D. L., and D. N. Jensen, eds. (1986). *School days, rule days.* Philadelphia: Falmer Press.

Kritzer, H. M. (1995). "First thing we do, let's replace all the lawyers": A comparison of lawyers and nonlawyers as advocates. Paper presented at meetings of the Law and Society Association, June 1–4, Toronto, Canada.

Lau v. Nichols, 414 U.S. 563 (1974).

Levin, B., and W. D. Hawley. (1975). The courts, social science, and school desegregation. *Law and Contemporary Social Problems,* parts I and II, 39 (1, 2): 1–432.

Lupato, B. F. (1973). A study of the conditions of employment and levels of compensation of public school attorneys in the state of Indiana. Ed.D. diss., Indiana University.

Lynn, L., and A. Wheelock. (1997). Making detracking work. *Harvard Education Letter* 13 (1): 1–4.

McDuffy v. Secretary of the Executive Office of Education, 415 Mass. 545 (1993).

McNeal v. Tate County School District, 508 F.2d 1017 (5th Cir. 1975).

Merrow, J. (1996). What's so special about special education. *Education Week* (May 8): 48, 38.

Milliken v. Bradley, 418 U.S. 717 (1974).

Milliken v. Bradley, 433 U.S. 267 (1977).

Mills v. Board of Education, 348 F. Supp. 866 (D.C. 1972).

Minow, M. (1993). Law and social change. *UMKC Law Review* 62 (1): 171–183.

———. (1991a). School finance: Does money matter? *Harvard Journal on Legislation* 28: 395–400.

———. (1991b). Breaking the law: Lawyers and clients in struggles for social change. *University of Pittsburgh Law Review* 52:723–751.

———. (1987). Are rights right for children? *American Bar Foundation Journal* 1: 203–223.

Missouri v. Jenkins, 115 S. Ct. 2938 (1995).

Mosteller, F., R. Light, and J. Sachs. (1996). Sustained inquiry in education: Lessons from skill grouping and class size. *Harvard Educational Review* 66 (4): 797–843.

Murnane, R. (1994). Will school finance reform improve education for disadvantaged children? *Education Policy* 8 (4): 535–542.

Nash, J. M. (1997). Special report: Fertile minds. *Time* 149 (5): 48–56.

National Society for the Study of Education. (1978). *The courts and education: The seventy-seventh yearbook of the National Society for the Study of Education,* Part I, ed. C. P. Hooker. Chicago: University of Chicago Press.

New York Times, Judge halts California cutoff of prenatal care to illegal aliens. *New York Times* (November 28, 1996): A27.

Oberti v. Bd. of Ed. of Clementon School Dist., 995 F.2d 1204 (3d Cir. 1993).

Orfield, G., and S. Eaton. (1996). *Dismantling desegregation: The quiet reversal of Brown v. Board of Education.* New York: New Press.

Pennsylvania Association for Retarded Children v. Pennsylvania, 343 F. Supp. 279 (E.D. Pa. 1972).

Plessy v. Ferguson, 163 U.S. 537 (1896).

Plyler v. Doe, 457 U.S. 202 (1982).

Posner, R. A. (1995). *Overcoming law.* Cambridge: Harvard University Press.

Rebell, M. and A. Block. (1982). *Educational policy making and the courts: An empirical study of judicial activism.* Chicago: University of Chicago Press.

Reglin, G. L. (1992). Public school educators' knowledge of selected Supreme Court decisions affecting daily public school operations. *Journal of Educational Administration* 30 (2): 26–31.

Rehak, R. W. (1986). Characteristics of school attorneys and satisfactory school district-school attorney relationships. Ed.D. diss., Indiana University.

Rose v. Council for Better Education, 790 S.W.2d 186 (Ky. 1986).

Sacramento City U.S.D. v. Holland, 14 F.3d 1398 (9th Cir. 1994).

San Antonio Independent School District v. Rodriguez, 411 U.S. 1 (1973).

Schuck, P. H. (1989). Why don't law professors do more empirical research? *Journal of Legal Education* 39:323–336.

———. (1993). Public law litigation and social reform. *Yale Law Journal* 102 (May): 1763–1786.

Steinberg, J. (1996). New York City budget analysis shows 43% goes to classrooms. *New York Times* (November 21): p. 1.

Swann v. Charlotte-Mecklenburg Board of Education, 402 U.S. 1 (1971).

Tatel, D. (1993). Desegregation versus school reform: Resolving the conflict. *Stanford Law and Policy Review* (Winter 1992–93): 61–72.

Thurston, P. (1980). Is good law good education? In *Review of Research in Education,* vol. 8. American Educational Research Association.

Trotter, A. (1990). Flagrante dilecto. *American School Board Journal* (December): 12–18.

Tyack, D., T. James, and A. Benavot. (1987). *Law and the shaping of public education, 1785–1954.* Madison: University of Wisconsin Press.

Urban Institute. (1996). *Potential effects of congressional welfare reform legislation on family incomes.* Washington, D.C.: Urban Institute.

Welner, K., and J. Oakes. (1996). (Li)Ability grouping: The new susceptibility of school tracking systems to legal challenges. *Harvard Educational Review* 66 (3): 451–470.

Wirt, F. M., and M. W. Kirst. (1982). *Schools in Conflict.* Berkeley, Calif.: McCutchan Publishing Corporation.

Yudof, M. G. (1980). The future of law-and-education research. *Education Digest* 45 (February): 32–35.

———. (1981). Legalization of dispute resolution, distrust of authority, and organizational theory: Implementing due process for students in the public schools. *Wisconsin Law Review* 1981 (September–October): 891–892.

Zirkel, P. A. (1978). A test on Supreme Court decisions affecting education. *Phi Delta Kappan* 60:521–555.

———. (1980). A quiz on recent court decisions concerning student conduct. *Phi Delta Kappan* 62 (November): 206–208.

———. (1985a). An instrument for a legal review of public school curriculum policies and procedures. *Preventive Law Reporter* (August): 9–16.

———. (1985b). Test your legal savvy. *Instructor* (November–December): 68–69.

Chapter 2 Conservative Activists and the Rush Toward Resegregation

Gary Orfield

In 1994, as the United States celebrated the fortieth anniversary of *Brown v. Board of Education,* the most famous court decision in the twentieth century, the courts were in the process of dismantling desegregated education, and educational leaders in many communities were working to return to segregated neighborhood schools. During decades of struggle for desegregation the lower federal courts had usually moved slowly, often delaying even token desegregation for a decade or more. During the civil rights era, educational leaders in most communities had fought desegregation and tried to shift the entire responsibility to the courts. No major urban school district except Seattle complied with the constitutional requirement for desegregation until it was ordered to do so, even when the law was perfectly clear. When the courts finally ordered compliance, they were often denounced as judicial activists interfering in education.

Once efforts to release school districts from their obligations began in earnest, however, in several important early cases, lower courts and local school officials played a very different role. Some judges speeded things up, interpreting ambiguous marching orders that authorized termination of desegregation plans under certain conditions as clear directives for assertive judicial leadership to end court supervision quickly. Local educators argued that they could offer better education in segregated neighborhood schools. Activist conservative courts often rushed to judgment, sometimes dismantling desegregation plans many times faster than the same courts had desegregated the schools. The active moves for the restoration of segregation received none of the intense political criticism that the much slower moves toward integration had provoked. In fact, they usually received positive treatment in the local press and were ignored by the research community.

The changing role of the courts and education leaders in some communities, from adversaries in a struggle over an expansion of minority rights to collaborators in the termination of judicial protection of those rights, reflects several aspects of relations between law and education seldom discussed in either profession. The first is that both courts and administrators can be strongly affected by large political changes, such as the appointment of judges with different ideologies and the remaking of the language of the policy debate during a long period of conservative domination. The second is that educators tend to respond to conservative signals from the courts and politics on racial issues without serious examination of the educational dimension. Most school superintendents refused to prepare plans for desegregation, forcing the courts to impose their own orders. The superintendents thought that they would risk their jobs if they were identified with desegregation. Many are very willing, however, to design and defend plans for a return to segregation. The third is that when courts make rapid sweeping judgments about the local record of educational equity, they tend to reach dubious conclusions that later cannot be supported. When virtually all the evidence judges hear in a case is constructed by one side to shape the outcome, the problem is particularly acute. The fourth is that when the courts end protection of excluded groups, their withdrawal can signal a resumption of old political patterns of control by the dominant social and economic groups who are uninterested in issues of racial inequality.

Given the high stakes involved in reversing a nearly half-century battle for desegregated schools, it is important that educational leaders and judges devise ways to consider fully the consequences of decisions, obtain the best possible evidence, and recognize conflicting tendencies in a legal process that attempts to realize both the goals of *Brown* and the great desegregation decisions that followed it, as well as the Rehnquist Court's goals of increased local control and judicial restraint. The way educators and lawyers are now working together has often led to decisions that read very selectively from the law and to plans that create highly segregated and unequal schools. As was true a century ago with *Plessy*, the courts may be embracing a "solution" that will create a long-term trend toward greater racial inequality and polarization. A better process with a larger role for lawyers representing minority students and more care by the courts in fully considering the issues could bring substantial improvements. Fortunately, the courts in a few communities are departing from the pattern of rushing toward resegregation and are devising methods to permit a more careful consideration of the alternatives.

WHY DESEGREGATION MAKES A DIFFERENCE FOR EDUCATION

Ever since the Supreme Court concluded in 1954 that separate schools were "inherently unequal" there has been a fierce attack on the courts for imposing "race mixing" or "social planning" instead of letting the educators get on with the business of educating minority youth. In communities facing current legal battles these issues are constantly raised by those urging the courts to end the desegregation orders. In assessing the role of the courts it is important to have an idea of the educational stakes for minority students. Though there is not space to develop the full arguments here I would like to summarize my view of the best evidence on the educational consequences of segregation and desegregation:

1. Segregated schools are unequal, in terms of achievement and competition, graduation rates, teachers teaching in their fields, and many other ways.[1]
2. Racially segregated schools are very likely to be high poverty schools and such schools face many additional social and educational problems. Only one-twentieth of schools that are almost all white have majorities of low-income students, compared to nine-tenths of schools that are more than 90% African American and Latino.[2]
3. On average, black students attending desegregated schools have modestly better test scores.
4. Minority students who go to integrated high schools are more likely to attend and complete college and live outside ghettos and barrios.
5. The educational benefits of desegregation can be strengthened through relatively simple efforts by teachers to engage students in cooperative learning projects including students of different races.
6. Almost all desegregation plans of the past two decades include not only desegregation but also educational reforms, often including choice and the

creation of new curricula. Most choice schools in the United States grew out of desegregation plans and thus any educational gains from them are part of the educational effects of desegregation orders.[3]

In other words, desegregation is an educational treatment. It has important documented educational benefits and it is related to a variety of educational experiments. Contrary to many press reports there is strong support by African Americans for desegregated education and no significant shift toward opposition; support is particularly high among families of students of all races who have actually been desegregated, even if busing was necessary.[4] Segregation is usually highly unequal, to a considerable extent because it concentrates the problems of poor families and communities. The best evidence of the effects of the return to segregation in communities which have dismantled their plans shows the rapid reappearance of extremely unequal schools for many nonwhite students.[5]

THE CHANGING ROLE OF THE COURTS: CYCLES AND IMPACTS

During the desegregation era, courts tended to act very slowly and trials tended to be massive undertakings with weeks or months of hearings, followed by months or years of consideration by a court before it reached a judgment. Even then the judgment was usually for very gradual change and token integration, until the Supreme Court finally created unambiguous standards binding the lower courts and forcing rapid change in the South from 1968 though the early seventies. A decade after the *Brown* decision 98% of Southern black students were still attending 100 percent black schools. The speedup came only after a generation of token changes. The courts provided clear leadership only after Congress acted in 1964 and 1965 to transform civil rights law and the Johnson Administration employed both the threat of cutoff of federal funds and the Justice Department's power to file lawsuits to break the back of resistance in thousands of Southern districts.[6]

The one period of clear and effective judicial leadership came from 1968 to 1973, when the country turned in a much more conservative direction under President Nixon but the Court expanded desegregation law, began major urban desegregation, and ended delays.[7] In the 1950s and early 1960s, of course, the Supreme Court had provided important symbolic leadership in undermining the legitimacy of the Southern apartheid system and stimulating protest, but actual change was very limited. With the exception of a few heroic district judges and the Fifth Circuit Court of Appeals, the courts in the South tended to drag their feet as long as possible and then to order very little change until the Supreme Court eventually issued unambiguous requirements.[8] Thus, the only period in which the courts themselves produced a clearly measurable gain in school segregation was immediately following the most active period of political and social mobilization for civil rights since Reconstruction.

The only period in which the courts provided strong leadership with clear consequences on desegregation without any mobilization in the country was the 1990s. But this time, the activism on the Supreme Court was toward resegregation. Without significant pressure from Congress or the public, thin majorities on the High Court were marshaled to limit civil rights—setting the tone for subsequent lower-court efforts to match or outpace them.

The courts had been a primary target of conservative protests in the 1970s and were ultimately transformed by the most intensely ideological judicial selection process in modern history. The High Court was changed by four appointments by President Nixon; the tradition of unanimity forged in 1954 was soon a thing of the past and a divided court began to limit desegregation in the 1974 Detroit case, *Milliken v. Bradley.*

The period of active insistence on prompt and full desegregation by the Supreme Court has covered less than one-eighth of the forty-year period since *Brown*. Before that time there had been no requirements for prompt and comprehensive remedies. After the 1974 *Milliken* decision, the country was set on a path toward growing racial isolation with only occasional detours such as *Dayton II* and *Columbus II*.

The conservative critique of the civil rights era holds that judges became judicial activists, imposing their social theories on American education, and that school officials lost sight of their educational responsibilities in their futile pursuit of social reform.[9] This assessment is based in part on criticism of the arguments and evidence on which the Supreme Court had relied in *Brown*, as well as on the theory that the Court's role should be a modest one—rarely interfering with the elected branches of government and never trying to supersede them in the operation of government.[10]

The true story is one of judicial reform pursued in an unclear and often ineffective way, and delayed and watered down for many years in the lower courts. The Court had not acted in isolation in *Brown*; both the Truman and Eisenhower Justice Departments had urged a finding that school segregation was unconstitutional. The courts were not displacing local education officials and elected leaders who had been moving to resolve violations. The typical story of educational and political leadership, except in some university towns, was one of decades of denial and resistance until a court or federal agency took the initiative—and then one of minimal compliance.

In this chapter I will argue that today's activist conservative judges and educators are pushing much harder and faster for resegregation than their predecessors ever did for integration, and accepting uncritically the claims of local school officials to justify ending the rights of local minority students. This chapter describes the ways in which this is happening and raises questions about the professionalism and fairness of some of those who've led the way. It will conclude with some suggestions of the ways in which judges, lawyers, and school administrators might approach the coming decisions about segregation in U.S. schools.

The discussion that follows relies on research that shows that the kinds of policies now being abandoned by courts and educators were essential to create significant desegregation, that segregated or resegregated schools in the contemporary United States are unequal in easily measurable ways, and that there has been no clamor to terminate desegregation from Congress or the general public. This is a very large and consequential change in social policy triggered by judicial activism on the right.

Major progress in desegregation of black students occurred in the years of most active enforcement and began to be reversed as the Rehnquist Court took control.[11] Recent studies of districts returning their students to neighborhood schools show intense segregation by race and income and very different levels of educational achievement.[12] Evidence of surveys from the 1970s to the 1990s shows that busing has ceased to be a leading issue, that both white and minority support for integration has increased, and that parents of children bussed for desegregation report a strongly positive experience. Although a substantial white majority continued to oppose busing, the issue had disappeared from the politics of many communities until the Supreme Court reopened it.[13] Congress enacted many anti-busing measures from the late 1960s through the 1970s but has not since.[14] In fact, after the Supreme Court began narrowing the reach of the Voting Rights Act, the 1964 Civil Rights Act, and other civil rights measures, Congress repeatedly passed legislation strengthening those laws in the 1980s.[15]

The conservative reaction, though strongly pushed by several Republican Presidents, had to be carried out through the courts and was part of a much larger set of changes in civil rights policy by the courts. Congress actually strengthened civil rights legislation during the Reagan era, and the Reagan

Administration itself never reversed the presidential executive orders on which affirmative action was based. The judicially initiated changes, however, challenged all group-based civil rights remedies, including voting rights and affirmative action, reflecting the new Supreme Court majority, which was consolidated with the 1991 confirmation of Justice Clarence Thomas.

The new majority was, however, a thin majority, often a single vote. The close division often produced decisions that included both clear signs of reversal and reaffirmations of previous decisions that were not wholly consistent. There was no majority prepared to repudiate directly either *Brown* or any other major desegregation case. Therefore, the way in which the trial courts read the uncertain standards of the Supreme Court was extremely important.

This chapter explores the way in which the judicial reversal is being carried out through the lower courts. Before those issues can be explored, it is first necessary to briefly summarize the major developments in the law of school desegregation.

The Development of the Law and the Changes in Segregation

A small number of legal turning points explain more than forty years of development of desegregation law by the Supreme Court. The Court took relatively few school desegregation cases and typically handed down only two or three major decisions in each decade; these decisions when implemented in the trial courts were of great importance, in beginning desegregation slowly, then accelerating desegregation, and, later, in authorizing a return to segregation under some conditions. The other major force was the role of the federal executive branch. In the Johnson Administration it greatly accelerated desegregation, but in the Nixon, Reagan, and Bush Administrations it worked to appoint more conservative judges, reverse the position of federal civil rights officials, and limit desegregation.

The leading court decisions of the 1950s and early 1960s established the principles that the schools of the South should be desegregated (open to students regardless of race); that the law must be enforced even in the face of intense public resistance; that courts could prevent the closing of public school systems; and that very gradual change was all that was necessary. *Brown v. Board of Education* (1954) began a constitutional revolution when the Supreme Court said that the 1896 *Plessy* decision which made "separate but equal" the lodestone of constitutional law for race relations did not apply to public education; indeed, experience had shown that "separate was inherently unequal" and that imposed segregation did irreparable harm. The Supreme Court, however, put off defining the enforcement process until the following year when it set the vague standard of "with all deliberate speed" but provided no clear delineation of what fully desegregated schools and school districts would look like, leaving that to the judgment of scores of district courts across the South. Change came very slowly and was nearly stopped altogether in 1957 when Governor Orval Faubus blocked the entrance of nine black students to all-white Central High School in Little Rock, Arkansas.[16] In its *Cooper v. Aaron* decision (1958), the Supreme Court insisted that the law be enforced in spite of local resistance.[17] Six years later, responding to the decision of a Virginia county to shut down public education altogether for several years rather than desegregate, the Court sustained court orders reopening public schools.[18] A decade after *Brown,* however, 98 percent of the black students of the South remained in all-black schools and desegregation was slight and gradual.[19]

The breakthrough in desegregation came from Congress and the Johnson Administration. In the 1964 Civil Rights Act, Congress made federal funding dependent on nondiscrimination and authorized the Justice Department to file civil rights cases. The next year Congress passed the largest program of federal aid to education in U.S. history. The Johnson Administration's determination to enforce the law meant that both the sanctions facing districts and the incentives for compliance were increased immensely.[20] The administration, working in close conjunction with the Fifth Circuit Court of Appeals, quickly moved to shorten the time frames and moved from standards about theoretical opportunities for desegregation to standards requiring its actual accomplishment. The burden of change shifted from black families and civil rights groups to the school districts. In 1968, the Supreme Court wrote this understanding into the Constitution in *Green v. New Kent County.*[21] That unanimous decision defined the goal of the desegregation process for the first time. The goal was the abolition of separate white and nonwhite school systems and the creation of a single unitary system in which all the students, faculties, staffs, activities, transportation, and facilities are integrated.

The following year, in response to a Nixon Administration effort to further delay desegregation in Mississippi, a unanimous Court said that henceforth desegregation must be accomplished immediately, that the time for "deliberate speed" had passed.[22] The final question that needed to be answered in order to desegregate the South was whether or not neighborhood school assignments would legitimize segregation in areas with a history of discrimination. In the

1971 *Swann* decision, the Supreme Court said no and authorized busing as a remedy.[23]

This period, from the late 1960s through the early 1970s, was the only time in which there were unambiguous goals and timetables supported by a unified Supreme Court. Those goals applied only to the seventeen states with a history of segregation mandated by state law. Those states had, however, by far the highest percentages of black students and the most intense segregation. By 1970 they would be the most desegregated parts of the United States, a distinction they would hold for two decades.[24]

The early 1970s brought a succession of decisions that elevated desegregation law to its high point, expanding desegregation requirements outside the South and to Latino students. A changing court, however, rejected Court-ordered equalization of funding for schools and, in 1974, put rigid limits on city-suburban desegregation in metropolitan areas. During the last part of the decade there were long court battles about whether or not to cut back on existing desegregation orders.

The Court extended desegregation requirements to individual school districts in the North and to the rapidly growing Latino communities in *Keyes,* a 1973 Denver case. *Keyes* rejected both the argument that segregation was inherently illegal, whatever its origins, and the argument that desegregation should be limited to the South because segregation was not mandated by state law in the North. It was proved to be the result of deliberate acts of segregation by government officials and in that sense was mandated by state authority. In other words, it differed from Southern segregation in that the actions and policies that brought about and perpetuated separate systems of education in the South were explicitly required by state law.

Divided by the time of *Keyes,* the High Court created policies that put a substantial burden of proof on civil rights organizations, requiring large investments and protracted court proceedings, but then imposed district-wide desegregation.[25] Outside the South, however, the minority population was often highly concentrated in the central cities of the largest metropolitan areas, surrounded by rings of independent suburbs where there had been a powerful outmigration of white families since World War II.[26] The root of the segregation was not within but among districts. This dilemma was presented to the Supreme Court in the 1974 Detroit case after the lower federal courts had concluded that the city's children had been illegally segregated but that there was no solution in a system that was already three-fourths black and white enrollment was declining. Detroit, then the nation's fifth largest system, and Chicago, the second largest, together had more than half the black children in the Midwest.[27]

In its 5–4 decision, in *Milliken v. Bradley* (*Milliken I*), the Supreme Court ruled in favor of suburban autonomy, drawing a line of legal protection around the suburbs. The Court held that the Constitution did not require desegregation beyond the city limit unless there was proof that segregation in the city had been caused by intentional acts of segregation by suburban officials, something very difficult to prove in intensely segregated suburbs that had few minority students. The Court excluded the housing issue from its consideration,[28] even though school segregation and city-suburban segregation had plainly been caused by decades of discrimination in federal, state, and local housing policies. Substantial desegregation progress ended with that decision, and the Detroit metropolitan region and the state of Michigan became national leaders in the intensity of their educational segregation.[29]

When the Detroit case went back to the district court for the development of a plan, the judge decided that the only thing that he could do, aside from desegregating a small minority of the students, was to order educational improvements to make up for the admitted harms of segregation. The judge knew that something had to be done but he did not know what to do, so he relied on local educational leaders for recommendations. In essence, he was trying to add resources to make separate schools equal. The state of Michigan fought the issue to the Supreme Court, but the High Court sustained the judge in the 1977 *Milliken II* decision, recognizing that the courts had authority to repair the educational damage of segregation.[30]

Implicitly, these courts rejected the *Brown* decision's conclusion that separate schools were inherently unequal, on the assumption that courts could figure out what the educational damage was and how to cure it since desegregation was impossible under *Milliken I*. However, the *Milliken II* decision said very little about the nature or scope of the remedy that could be approved or how to determine when enough had been done.

The remainder of the 1970s was devoted to a struggle over cutting back on the district-wide desegregation policy from *Keyes*. A minority led by Justice William Rehnquist wanted to limit desegregation to particular schools where a violation could be documented, but it lost and the *Keyes* approach remained in force.[31]

The 1980s were a transitional period. The Court was deeply divided and there was no majority for any substantial changes in school desegregation law until Justice Thurgood Marshall was replaced by Justice Clarence Thomas in 1991. There were, however, decisions limiting civil rights remedies in voting rights, in antidiscrimination requirements for federal programs, and in affirmative action, but most rested on interpretation of statutes rather than the Constitution. Congress limited the reach of those decisions by strengthening the laws.[32] In mid-decade, President Reagan nominated Justice Rehnquist, the Court's most consistent opponent of school desegregation, as Chief Justice in the most closely divided Senate confirmation battle on a chief justice in U.S. history.[33]

The most important change in the law came from a massive and successful effort to create a more conservative judiciary through the power of appointment. The Reagan and Bush administrations adopted a form of White House-controlled ideological screening previously unknown, ending the normal deference to senators of the President's party in the selection of federal district judges; senators were now required to submit several names for rigorous ideological vetting.[34] The White House sought young conservatives likely to serve a long time and to reflect a fundamentally different set of judicial values than their predecessors. Reagan was only the third president in the twentieth century to have an opportunity to appoint half of all federal judges.[35]

The selection process was originally under White House Counselor and future Attorney General Edwin Meese, a fierce opponent of race-conscious remedies for civil rights violations.[36] One of the conservative African Americans appointed by Ronald Reagan to a civil rights enforcement job, Clarence Thomas, would be the ultimate beneficiary of the judicial search process when he became the final appointment and the fifth member of a new Supreme Court majority that reversed school desegregation requirements. Thomas had been a determined critic of the school desegregation decisions of the past two decades, which he described three years before his appointment as "a disastrous series of cases requiring busing and other policies that were irrelevant to parents' concern for a decent education."[37] Thus, he turned his back on three decades of research showing a clear relation between integration and black success in schools and adult achievement.[38] He was confirmed by a narrower margin than any previous justice.

In the mid-1990s more than 60 percent of district court judges, nearly 70 percent of appellate judges,[39] and five of the nine Supreme Court Justices had been appointed by Presidents Reagan and Bush. This campaign to change the courts operated under the banner of "judicial restraint." The Reagan Administration, said Edwin Meese, wanted judges "committed to the philosophy of judicial restraint." It had hoped to depoliticize the courts "to ensure that they played a truly judicial role, rather than usurping the authority of the elected branches of government."[40] Solicitor General Charles Fried outlined the goal: "The tenets of the Reagan Revolution were clear: Courts should be more disciplined, less adventurous and political in interpreting the law, especially the law of the Constitution."[41] The liberals, conservatives claimed, had reached out for power to change society beyond the boundaries of established legal principles. Conservative judges should not.

There was, of course, an inconsistency in the conservative program. The movement wanted judicial restraint, but it also wanted to reverse principles of civil rights law that had been established for decades and implemented in hundreds of cases. Changing the constitutional requirements for school desegregation was a clear and basic goal of the conservative movement and so was judicial restraint. The necessity for race-conscious remedies had been integral to civil rights law since the Voting Rights Act and had been approved many times by the Supreme Court. This was common sense: since the violations were race based, the remedies had to be as well. Conservatives would have to break established precedents to create new principles in the appellate courts, and trial courts would have to step out of the passive role most took in implementing civil rights remedies to turn around existing cases—particularly in circumstances where neither party really wanted to end a plan for integration and/or educational compensation. This chapter examines the ways in which the theory of judicial restraint often gave way to a new and unacknowledged form of judicial activism, and how that played out in individual cases.

The effects of the conservative capture of the courts became apparent in their treatment of affirmative action in 1989, and produced sweeping changes in school desegregation law in three major decisions from 1991 to 1995. The 1991 *Dowell* decision adopted the Reagan Administration's basic argument that desegregation was to be temporary and that local school districts should then gain the authority to reinstitute neighborhood schools, even if they turned out to be segregated.[42] The *Pitts* decision (1992) eased the standards, allowing termination of student desegregation even when other legal requirements for full desegregation had not been met.[43] The *Jenkins* case (1995) held that educational remedies and voluntary desegregation incentives under *Milliken II* should be limited and temporary. It also said that minority student achievement did not have to improve before districts could end their programs for addressing the educational vestiges of segregation, and that courts should not even try to create voluntary attractions for white children from private and suburban schools in overwhelmingly minority school districts.[44] Thus, while the first Detroit case had made mandatory interdistrict remedies virtually unobtainable, *Jenkins* slammed the door on the voluntary possibilities. By 1995, the Court had created a legal context for encouraging resegregation and reducing the separate-but-equal requirements to the provision of brief and unexamined sets of programs included in a court order.

The changes, however, came from a closely divided Court, which left standing previous decisions that set out comprehensive requirements for full desegregation in districts where it was feasible. Thus, the lower courts were encouraged to turn authority back to local officials as soon as possible but were also still under orders to desegregate school districts completely. As there was no Supreme Court majority to repudiate basic school desegregation decisions, the new policies were announced as if they were merely the spelling out of the final stages of desegregation orders, specifically: how courts should retire *after* the constitutional obligations of districts had been fully met. The lower courts had nothing like the clear marching orders of the 1968–1973 period that had led to substantial desegregation in the South. Much depended upon the way that the lower court judges chose to interpret an ambiguous mandate.

In retrospect, it seems clear that the most dramatic impact of the conservative movement that dominated politics during the 1970s and 1980s was on the creation of legal principles through the courts. *Milliken I* left judges trying to maintain desegregation in central cities with shrinking white minorities and few resources. When the Rehnquist Court gave judges discretion to shut down plans, even less conservative judges sometimes moved to end plans that seemed unworkable.

In the broad sweep of desegregation law the focus had moved from vague goals and gradual desegregation to urgent, immediate, and comprehensive desegregation in the South. Then came a limited effort to change Northern segregation, followed by a long deadlock. The Supreme Court decisions of the 1990s clearly encouraged judges to end desegregation plans, but were unspecific, like those of the 1950s, setting no deadlines and offering no clear standards.

District judges had to work with both the existing tough requirements for full desegregation in the decisions of the past generation and the clear signals that there should be a return to local control. It was not at all evident how a lower court should determine the meaning of such vague criteria as "good faith" compliance, "vestiges of discrimination," and "maximum practicable desegregation" or judge the quality of education offered to minority students.

So it was up to the lower court judges, increasingly conservative and skeptical of court-ordered desegregation, to decide whether or not a district had done everything feasible to desegregate and repair the educational harms of segregation. District judges thus had enormous discretion.

A finding of unitary status, which would have wiped out the entire historic debt of a local school district and ending the authority of the court to override local policies with obviously discriminatory consequences, required complex and difficult judgments by courts. The idea of unitary status was that a plan had completely uprooted the segregated "dual school system" and created a single "unitary" system where the effects of the history of segregation had been eliminated. The Supreme Court's decisions of the 1990s sought to restore local control as soon as possible, but also emphasized that this was to follow the trial court's finding of full and good faith compliance with court orders and (as noted above) maximum feasible desegregation. In the 1995 *Jenkins* case, for example, the Court limited *Milliken II* educational remedies to redressing specific historic violations found by the courts but offered no direction on how to assess such violations generations later.[45] And yet, local judges were supposed to comprehensively assess the possibilities of system-wide transformation and to sort out somehow all the strands of causation between the obviously discriminatory past and the present conditions. Continuing a court-ordered program for upgrading low reading sources of minority children, for example, might require proof that there had been intentional discrimination affecting this program in earlier periods and evidence that the present problem was linked to the past discrimination. Proving such linkages for each program would put an overwhelming burden on the plaintiffs as well as create a task of surpassing complexity for the judges.

Courts have responded in a variety of ways to these responsibilities. Some judges have looked at their local school systems and decided that it is premature to consider ending judicial supervision. Others have scheduled full hearings to try to explore the complex issues.

A number of the major decisions, however, showed that other judges were only too willing to exercise their considerable discretion suddenly to reverse remedies. In striking contrast to the very gradual and deliberate pace of desegregation after *Brown*, a number of courts have taken a conservative activist posture: rushing the dismantling of desegregation plans, and assuming with little evidence that these plans had failed and that segregated neighborhood schools would work better. Some of their decisions have ignored or dismissed continuing violations, made sweeping findings about the good faith of the local districts, and cited normal school activities, such as the decision to build a new school, as a justification for ending supervision and allowing resegregation.[46]

The new Supreme Court standards call on judges to balance various considerations, such as local control and educational equity, in resolving a number of questions that defy simple answers. How they strike that balance depends, in part, on the way in which their experience and values lead them to answer such questions as:

- Are there continuing serious racial inequalities in the public life of my city?
- Can the court trust the claims of school administrators and board members now or must there be firm evidence of gains for nonwhite students?
- Can partial fulfillment of a court order be interpreted as full good faith compliance?
- To what extent are the severe persisting inequalities in academic achievement traceable to a history of discrimination and to what extent should they be dismissed as the products of defective values or culture or social and economic status in the minority communities?
- Is the system of spreading residential segregation simply a reflection of private preferences or is it a continuing effect of a history of public discrimination in housing, education, and other domains?

In a larger sense: Do civil rights and compensatory education policies make a difference or are they merely a failed liberal social experiment? If a judge is convinced that they have failed, the balancing process may be very simple.

PERSPECTIVES FROM THE TRIAL COURTS

As there have been only a limited number of cases tried and decided so far, this chapter should not be taken as an analysis of the entire federal judiciary. What emerges, however, is that fateful decisions to end desegregation plans and approve a return to segregated neighborhood schools are often being taken in ways that resemble the kinds of uninformed judicial activism that conservatives had accused the liberal courts of doing a decade earlier. For the first time since the early 1960s we have a court-led effort to restructure race relations in the schools. In contrast to the tepid effort to enforce *Brown*, however, the conservative activism is embraced by many local officials and educators and is actually changing racial patterns significantly as many of the country's largest school systems abandon desegregation. Prof. Garrett Epps noted that "in the area of civil rights, conservative activists on the lower courts now regularly follow their own law, made up of neoconservative aphorisms and snippets from Justice

Antonin Scalia's dissents."[47] These decisions are in striking contrast to those of a few courts that are taking a far more thoughtful approach to these critical decisions.

Judicial Activists and Social Planners

What we are seeing now in some cases is a form of activism that far exceeds that of the Warren Court era. This judicial activism, which overturns settled desegregation plans and policies in communities where desegregation had become noncontroversial, is rapidly turning much of urban American toward resegregation. These changes are not being driven by intense public opinion—the issue does not even appear on the list of leading concerns in national surveys about schools.[48] This is not to suggest that racial issues generally have ceased to concern people, or that renewed opposition to school desegregation might not bubble to the surface if the courts began taking strong, activist positions.

The signs of the new activism are clear. Orders that have the effect of resegregating the schools are often fast and sweeping, issued through proceedings conducted as if there are no important issues to be examined. In a few cases such as Oklahoma City (*Board of Education v. Dowell,* 1991), judges rushed to adopt factual conclusions that would later be proven false. This judicial activism for segregation has been welcomed and treated as noncontroversial by many of the same forces that attacked the courts for their "activism" in initiating desegregation.

Resegregation has been happening with very little attention from legal commentators, on the basis of rushed and superficial proceedings and findings based on "evidence" created by professional witnesses, which is often in sharp conflict with other scholarship that is not presented in court. Some of the same courts that provided all deliberation and no speed in desegregation have been engaged in an unseemly rush to resegregate. Sometimes there is little or no representation of the minority students whose rights are being extinguished.

Consequences of Ideological Change
in Politics

A number of the decisions reflect the judge's skepticism about the concept of desegregation or the possibility of educational improvements for minority students. There is a profound pessimism about the possibility of racial justice, oddly mixed with a thoroughgoing optimism about the degree to which discrimination has ended and the degree to which state and local governments are now free of its taint. The ideology closely parallels that of the Reagan and Bush

Administrations. Judges quietly dismiss the goal of *Brown* as unattainable, without ever saying so, while the entire burden of a history of discrimination is assumed to be easily erased by brief implementation of court-ordered plans, even if they have shown no measurable benefits for the children in groups who were the historic victims.

Liberals are often being hurt now by a view of the courts that they fostered in earlier days. During the period of the Warren Court, many civil rights supporters responded to public attacks on desegregation requirements by stating that the Constitution required them and that what the Court found to be required by law was the morally correct alternative. This argument, equating Supreme Court decisions with morality, led to the widespread celebration of the Court as the institution that guaranteed minority rights, giving the Court a role it had never previously had. The special role of the Court in the 1950s and 1960s, which was often discussed as if protection of minority rights was inherent in the role of a modern independent judiciary, was actually due to the judicial appointments of several presidents and a major change in American politics and public opinion after World War II. Because liberals denied the political role of the more liberal courts and later voted to confirm profoundly conservative judges on the assumption that the judges would not read their views into the Constitution, they were left without a basis on which to challenge reactionary Supreme Court decisions.

During the desegregation era, except for the rapid change in the late 1960s and early 1970s, there were only a handful of new desegregation orders in a given year. By 1995, however, the announcements of resegregation and moves to request resegregation came almost weekly: Denver's court order was dropped. Minneapolis asked for an end to desegregation. Buffalo's court order was terminated. Cleveland's order was ended. Indianapolis filed for the termination of its plan. There was resegregation in Madison, Wisconsin. And massive battles loomed over some of the largest county-wide desegregation plans in Florida, Nevada, and elsewhere.

Although there had been no changes on this scale for a quarter of a century, there has been surprisingly little discussion of them—even those that radically reversed racial policy in some of the nation's largest school systems.

In fact, there appears to have been quiet acceptance of a number of sweeping assumptions about desegregation, education reform, public attitudes, and the conduct of state and local governments. The most radical of these assumptions is that separate but equal is now a viable policy because of the transfer of local school leadership in some cases to predominantly black boards or administrations. And yet in cities such as Atlanta, where black leaders negotiated control over the school system in lieu of busing, we now have more than twenty-five years of evidence that intense segregation and declines in assessment scores and high school graduation for minorities follow hand-in-hand.[49]

Another common assumption is that the passage of civil rights laws and a few years under a court order have ended the continuing effects of generations of official segregation and discrimination. The underlying assumption, for which the courts offer no evidence, is that civil rights laws are much more powerful and fast acting than the policies of official discrimination that lasted many times as long. Had earlier courts followed this reasoning, the intense Southern resistance in Little Rock and elsewhere after the *Brown* decision would have led to a return to apartheid schools instead of to further, stronger decisions that made the South the nation's most integrated region and produced a massive shift in these states toward support of integrated education.[50]

A third assumption is that the discrimination and segregation that do remain are private and cannot be cured because they express "natural" forces that only create greater problems when they are tampered with. Intense white resistance, by this logic, should lead to the abandonment of remedies.

In educational terms, the decisions reflect a change from the assumption that education can remedy historic racial inequalities to the assumption that it is futile to seek an actual remedy as schools have no power to make outcomes more equal. Critics might argue that desegregation, which some disdain as social engineering, has distracted us from improving education. In fact, the most fundamental assumptions about who is responsible for ensuring quality education have changed as well. The widespread assumption among judges that state and local officials should be ordered to make up for the harm of segregation has been replaced with an assumption that state and local officials know what is needed educationally and should be trusted to provide it.

THE RUSH TO RESEGREGATE
IN THE TRIAL COURTS

Some lower court judges are reading the ambiguous words of recent decisions, through the lens of their ideological assumptions, as simple mandates to shut down a case after a superficial hearing. Although the Supreme Court's recent decisions maintain the test for creation of a fully desegregated (unitary) school system from the Court's 1968 *Green* decision, and add to it requirements of local good faith and educational fairness, some courts seem to assume that desegregation is over and the courts should withdraw quickly. The courts appear to be reacting to the tone of the decisions rather than the legal formulations. Just as the *Brown* decision's command of "all deliberate speed" was read by lower courts of its day as if it meant "delay as long as possible before beginning even the slightest token integration," the current decisions are being read not as mandates for judges to end court supervision after carefully evaluating compliance with all requirements but, rather, as mandates to end desegregation as rapidly as possible.

School desegregation cases have long been notorious for their greatly protracted proceedings, and for the vast records which are typically accumulated before a new desegregation plan is implemented. In fact, this was one of the reasons why only a handful of the early urban cases could be litigated by civil rights lawyers in any given year. Judges often delayed for years in reaching decisions after the trials.

Now, suddenly, many of the largest districts are in court and decisions are coming rapidly from many directions. In some courts, judges are taking a kind of leadership unknown in the desegregation phase of the cases—pushing cases into court for changes even when no party has raised the issue of terminating the court order. This extraordinarily unusual initiative could terminate desegregation in a district where school officials were not even asking for that change.

A Sense of Urgency in Tampa

The federal district court in Tampa, Florida, provided an example of the rush to terminate court supervision of desegregation in a November 1995 decision. The local NAACP had sued, claiming that the city board had failed to enforce the consent decree and had illegally allowed an expansion of segregated education. The school board had opposed this claim before a federal magistrate. Neither party, however, had moved for a unitary status declaration or for ending court supervision. When the federal judge supervising the case, Elizabeth Kovachevich, received the report from the magistrate, however, she suddenly transformed the case with an order directing a hearing on unitary status.

Pointing out that the desegregation case had been filed thirty-seven years earlier and that the first busing order was twenty-four years old, Judge Kovachevich noted grimly that without some action, "supervision of this case may well extend into the next millennium. It is this Court's express intention to avoid such a result and it is for that reason that the Court now expands the scope of the inquiry in this case to a determination of unitary status."[51] The judge announced, in other words, before hearing any evidence, that she wanted the matter finished by the next "millennium," which would come in four years. She quoted the Supreme Court language in *Freeman v. Pitts* that "returning schools to the control of local authorities at the earliest practicable date is essential to restore their true accountability in our governmental system."[52] After outlining the issues to be considered in the review, she concluded, "Should there be any remnants of the prior constitutional violation, they must be identified and an immediate solution proffered to remedy the violation."[53] Although plaintiffs were arguing that there were serious new violations, she said in advance that there could be only "remnants," which could be immediately solved.

Judge Kovachevich, in other words, wanted the case finished promptly, wanted to turn back to local control as soon as possible, and wanted to order immediate solutions for remaining problems so that the case could be closed rapidly. As the issue went to court, less than one-fifth of district children in the large county-wide district encompassing the city and the suburbs of Tampa were being bussed for desegregation purposes. The NAACP Legal Defense Fund had gone to court because sixteen of the district's schools were well above the black proportion set out in the court order. Five heavily black schools of concentrated poverty had been designated by state school authorities as "critically low performing" schools. NAACP Legal Defense Fund attorney Warren Dawson pointed to these educational problems and to resegregation the district had allowed elsewhere. Local NAACP President Ann Porter observed, "If there is no court supervision, we're going to slowly go backward." Local reporter Stephen Hegarty wrote that "everyone on either side of the issue agrees that without court supervision, the School Board will be under considerable pressure to reduce or eliminate mandatory busing," thus resegregating its schools.[54]

It had taken thirteen years from the time the court case was originally filed to the time of the first busing order that actually desegregated the district. The system, like all educational systems in Florida, had been segregated by state law from the time that public schools were created until the *Brown* decision was enforced. Even before hearing any evidence on the claim of black parents that the order was being violated, the judge announced her intention to end it as soon as possible in the nation's twelfth largest district.[55]

Judges do, of course, have the authority to apply new constitutional standards to pending matters before their court even if they are not raised by one of the parties. I am not aware, however, of any federal judge ever initiating an action to require *more* desegregation, even when the Supreme Court provided clear desegregation requirements.

"No Basis to Enforce" in Broward

On the other side of Florida in Broward County, the nation's seventh largest school district, which serves Ft. Lauderdale and its suburbs, U.S. District Judge Kenneth Ryskamp ruled in August 1995 that the school district had been needlessly maintaining its busing plan for the previous sixteen years, having fulfilled all constitutional requirements by 1979.[56] This decision affected a vast district which in 1991 enrolled 170,000 students, four times as many as Pittsburgh, St. Louis, or Seattle.[57] Without even conducting a trial, the judge ruled for a group of white parents who were protesting a boundary change intended to aid desegregation. The school board had responded to another suit, filed in 1983 and alleging that its actions were increasing segregation, by signing a consent decree agreeing to maintain desegregated education. A school-board-appointed committee concluded that the district was far from fulfilling all the requirements for unitary status. The court now suddenly said that there was no basis to enforce this decree, though there had been no trial on the allegations of additional violations that led to the 1983 consent agreement. In effect, the court was holding that the consent decree it had accepted years earlier had no legal basis, without permitting any serious exploration of the issues.

School board chair Miriam Oliphant praised the ruling, saying it showed the district had done a "good job." Ali Waldman, co-chair of the school district's Desegregation Task Force, on the other hand, said that "our task force report clearly shows that we are no longer unitary."[58]

The legal issues in Broward County were important ones. The county's school system had been declared unitary many years before the Supreme Court's 1991 *Dowell* decision had established the standards for finding a district unitary or recognized that such a declaration opened the path for resegregation. The issue of whether or not the county was, therefore, unitary under the *Dowell* definition, and questions about the status of a consent decree responding to claims of subsequent violations, were not easy to resolve. The court, however, did not consider these questions or even ensure that the lawyers representing the system's African American children had an opportunity to argue their side of the issue.

What was remarkable in both the Tampa and Broward cases was the fact that the courts were moving very fast, without any pressure from the school systems they claimed to empower, to terminate the courts' role in supervising desegregation. In neither of these cases was any attention given to the civil rights claims that recent school board actions were compounding segregation problems. In spite of the specific requirements in the Supreme Court decisions for demonstrating that a school system was unitary, judges moved to pull out rapidly even when neither party had asked. The school boards are the historical constitutional violators; even when the violators believed that there was still work to do to meet responsibilities, a judge acting on his or her own could rapidly end a desegregation plan. In the case of Broward County, there was no opportunity for the black community to be heard before its rights were suddenly extinguished.

Limiting Evidence and Issues: Oklahoma City

After the first Supreme Court resegregation case, *Dowell,* was decided in 1991, the case was sent back to the federal district court, where the judge was directed to determine whether or not the district was eligible for a release from court supervision. Instead, the district court decided to permit no new evidence and to close the record retroactively to a point several years earlier. The plaintiffs, who had not been aware of the stakes in the earlier hearing, faced a situation in which all current evidence was excluded and there was little opportunity to expand the examination of the past. The result of this procedure was the court's adoption of several kinds of findings that deeper analysis would have proved to be ill founded. The most obvious was a simple error. Judge Luther Bohannon cited, as an important example of the good faith of local authorities, an oversight committee they had set up to see to it that the educational remedies for black children were delivered. He did not know, because he permitted no evidence, that the committee had been dissolved two years earlier. NAACP Legal Defense Fund attorney Janelle Byrd offered five types of new evidence but was refused an opportunity to present it by both the trial court and the court of appeals. After the district disbanded the committee and fired the equity officer after the committee filed a negative report, the NAACP Legal Defense Fund also filed suit on behalf of the officer, a matter still pending in 1996.[59]

Similarly, the judge accepted the district's own account of the remarkable educational success and parental involvement in its resegregated schools without looking carefully at the basis for either claim. Had there been any serious examination, the court might well have discovered that the district was doing two things in its operations that gave a very unrealistic picture of its academic success: First, it was testing a smaller percentage of its students than almost any other similar system; if poorly performing students are not tested, of course, the apparent average achievement goes up. Second, the district was engaged in a grade-retention policy which resulted in large numbers of flunked students being tested at the same level as they had been the year before, rather than with the test normally given to students of their age. This would also raise apparent achievement.[60]

The parental involvement issue was a little more complex. Parental involvement, in terms of PTA membership, did go up in black resegregated schools. It also went up in the white schools, as there was a district-wide campaign for parental involvement. Both trends were cited to show that the neighborhood schools produced more involvement of parents, something that is commonly accepted as important. Thus the judge would seem to have had reasonable grounds for finding some value in the return to neighborhood schools. The court was not aware, however, that parental involvement went up even more in the schools in the upper grades where mandatory busing was retained. Nor did the court know that it later fell in all types of schools as the impact of the special drive wore off.

This court, like many others, treated the district's claims as conclusive and took none of the obvious steps needed to ensure that these relations were not misinterpreted. None of these relations could be adequately explored without comparisons over time and across districts, comparisons that could be greatly aided by knowledge of reports and research. Full exploration of the issues, perhaps with the aid of a court-appointed expert, might well have made an important difference. It turned out that the last chance the lawyers had to provide information on the key issues had passed years earlier during the initial trial where the civil rights side had struggled with very limited resources. In its rush to judgment, however, the Oklahoma City court excluded such information and rested important parts of its decision to permit the dismantling of desegregated schools on false premises that could not have withstood critical analysis.

The basic problem is that it is extremely difficult to persuade higher courts to change findings of fact by trial court judges, and there is often no opportunity to introduce new evidence on these questions once a trial has been closed. If judges in the lower courts and the appellate courts share the same ideological biases, basic findings about constitutional rights can be made on the basis of what turn out to be obviously false claims. On the basis of such claims, often resting on evidence that would be utterly unpersuasive in a first-year college sociology paper, the entire historic debt of a school system to minority children can be canceled, and they can be resegregated with no legal recourse.

THE PRACTICALITY PRINCIPLE

Obviously, a court should not be required to implement a change that is not practically possible. The standard of practicability is set forth inside decisions in which the precondition for unitary status was compliance with the factors set forth in the 1968 *Green* decision and the additional requirements outlined in *Pitts*. *Green*'s central emphasis is upon sweeping changes to eliminate the racial identifiability and the inequality among schools for nonwhite and white children. The basic questions are: What is the proper relationship between assuring full compliance with the *Green* factors and practicality? And what is the standard for judging whether or not something is practical? On the margins, these are not difficult questions. If there has been a very substantial effort, and all but one of the schools are in compliance with the student and faculty desegregation standards, and that school has some problem related to its location, that would be an obvious exception. If, on the other hand, the demographics were feasible for full desegregation and three-quarters of the schools were segregated, there would be an obvious violation. Many other cases are much less clear-cut, however, and require the courts to sort out much more serious conflicts between the values of *Green* and school district claims about what is practical.

The basic problem is that school authorities are always inclined to say that what they are already doing is all that is practical. If courts simply accept such claims, the requirement that there be even temporary compliance with the provisions of the *Green* decision would go by the boards, and the real meaning of the constitutional requirements for desegregation would be merely to do for a while whatever the local officials believed to be practical. Such an interpretation would give local school officials supported by a trial judge the authority to unilaterally limit the reach of the *Green* decision, and the demands of the Constitution would have no meaning apart from the choice of the local judge. Because many years of experience between the *Brown II*[61] enforcement decision in 1955 and the *Green* case convinced the High Court that clear and unambiguous standards were necessary for substantial desegregation, this would be a major change.[62] Very few school boards have ever desegregated voluntarily.

Savannah Rules

The tendency of the courts to accept local views is apparent in many decisions. In his 1994 decision on unitary status in Savannah, Georgia, for example, Judge Avant Edenfield rejected the argument of civil rights lawyers and the Justice Department that the court should not release the district while one-fourth of the schools remained segregated under the court's relatively loose standards (plus or minus 20 percent from the district-wide racial composition). The court concluded that "because of demographics, there is little else, if anything, the District can do to bring them further into compliance, save mandatory busing."[63] The appropriateness of busing when necessary to achieve desegregation, had, of course, been a central conclusion of the Supreme Court's 1991 *Swann* decision, but Judge Edenfield simply ignored the issue and said that the district had done enough without meeting the goals of its desegregation plan and without using a technique approved in hundreds of other cases.

Savannah had adopted a purely voluntary plan with the very active support of the Reagan Administration, which prevailed in the district court. After six years, this court order was terminated. After a minimal two-day hearing, the court adopted page after page of findings based on the testimony of the school board's expert witness. Plaintiff's expert testimony was ignored. The judge ruled that the district "has desegregated its schools to the maximum extent practicable" and, therefore, "federal judicial control is no longer necessary or justified."[64]

The language of the court reflects the political ideology in many contemporary decisions: "The Court is not deaf to the exhortations of those who point to various shortfalls and would have the Court manage the affairs of the School District indefinitely. Unfortunately, perfection, albeit enticing, is frequently unattainable. If the District is not allowed to reap the rewards of its momentous efforts, and is instead admonished to accomplish the near-impossible, the Court then shifts from ensuring racial integration to imposing an exercise in futility."[65]

The full remedy for generations of intentional segregation in Savannah turned out to be a few years of voluntary partial desegregation followed by an abrupt end of judicial supervision. The court undertook no examination of the educational equity, simply relying on the school district's own claims of its success and the testimony of its hired witness.[66]

Viewing Local Educators' Claims Uncritically and Writing Theories of Conservative Experts into the Law

After forty years of struggle to desegregate and produce equal education for the Wilmington, Delaware, region's black students, plaintiffs pointed out that massive inequalities remained and that the systems had failed to fulfill the requirement of the desegregation plan, which included a number of educational dimensions such as those mentioned in the Supreme Court's 1977 *Milliken II* decision. Metropolitan Wilmington had been desegregated under an order combining all city and suburban systems and then breaking the region into four pie-shaped city-suburban districts, each of which was desegregated. The plan, which was possible because of a record of state violations, made Delaware one of the nation's two most desegregated states, with Kentucky.

One part of the Wilmington order provided that "to prevent resegregation under the guise of curriculum or program choices, the Board shall institute an effective and nondiscriminatory counseling and guidance program. This counseling and guidance program must insure that students are counseled on a racially nondiscriminatory basis." There were many other provisions, including "an appropriate human relations program throughout the unitary school system."[67] The court order called for equity in discipline and special educational placement. The plaintiffs pointed to persisting massive racial disparities on all these issues as basic reasons for maintaining court supervision. In the Wilmington trial, and in previous filings, the plaintiffs had shown very large racial inequalities in enrollment in college prep courses, honors courses, and other special programs, and a tendency for students to be enrolled in sets of courses at differing levels by race. The plaintiffs brought in Jeannie Oakes, perhaps the most influential scholar of the tracking issue, to try to explain the consequences of tracking and the forces that kept minority parents from obtaining the best placements for their children.[68]

The court, however, relied on the administrators' listing of their programs that were intended to address the issue and the arguments of David Armor and other defense experts that the difference in course taking, academic achievement, and discipline could be ignored because they simply reflected differences in the social and economic structure of black and white communities. The court decision contains paragraph after paragraph listing these sociological differences and reporting one defense witness's equations showing the statistical relationships between these factors and inequalities in test scores.[69] One defense expert justified the disparities in suspension by pointing to the racial disparities in criminal arrests in the state.[70]

None of these problems was seen by the court as caused by continuing effects from the history of discrimination by schools and other public agencies or as something the court should try to remedy. Ironically, one of the leading social background differences that the court relied on to explain why the schools cannot solve the problems is the fact that black families are "2.54 times as likely as white households to have a reporting householder who lacks a high school degree."[71] This difference, which is a key to a number of other differences the court cites—such as the fact that blacks are six times as likely as white households to have children growing up in poverty—is assumed to be something that simply exists, not the product of unequal education provided in the past to blacks in the greater Wilmington area or to a tradition of unequal treatment in the job markets based in part on the perception that black candidates would often be less educated because of their inferior schools.

If social and economic inequalities in parental education and arrests are legitimate reasons to hold a school district innocent of unequal treatment of a group of students, it will be virtually impossible to enforce any actual gains for a disadvantaged minority since those characteristics are very basic parts of the reality of being disadvantaged in urban society. The conservative side in civil rights cases tends to argue for a limited and formalistic definition of responsibilities, in which a sharp line is drawn between schools and other institutions, interactions are not examined, and other forms of inequality are assumed to be the reflection of nongovernmental forces or "societal" influences that simply happen without any violations. Another key limiting assumption is that implementation of a remedy, by definition, cures the problem and that any remaining inequalities are assumed not to be the responsibility of the court.

In her decision, Judge Sue L. Robinson concluded that the Wilmington district had complied with the specific orders, at least in the sense of taking some actions at some time during the period of court supervision, whether or not they worked, and that it was unreasonable to expect anything like equality in outcomes or even in levels of courses taken because the "school environment cannot be expected to make up for deficiencies in the child's extramural [home and community] environment." She said that these deep remaining differences were not of concern to the court unless the plaintiffs could prove that they "can be attributed to the former *de jure* segregated school system." This, she conceded, would be difficult because there was "no base line from which to compare the plaintiff class's educational progress in the desegregation process."[72] In other words, there was no way to meet the burden of proof, which she shifted to a group of plaintiffs with far fewer resources than the school district in the battle of hired experts.

Judge Robinson dismissed the evidence of classroom segregation and unequal access to the college-preparatory curriculum and unequal special educational placement of blacks as "more a philosophical debate among educators on educational issues that the identification of vestiges of past discrimination in the former *de jure* segregated school system."[73] Although the school district was under an obligation to uproot the dual school system "root and branch" in a way that eliminated the vestiges of segregation, the large-scale operation of segregated classrooms was not seen as something that they could be held accountable for or as an impediment to realizing the goals of desegregation.

The Wilmington decision approved ending the desegregation order after a few months of legal battle, in contrast to the three decades of legal struggle which had been required to obtain it. Judge Sue L. Robinson conducted a hurried hearing ending on January 6, 1995.[74] The State Board of Education and the four districts created out of the previous thirteen districts in the metropolitan area wanted to end the order and spent a great deal of money producing data for the court. The civil rights side had limited resources to try the case and was not allowed to bring rebuttal witnesses to challenge the evidence created for the school officials.[75] In her decision, Judge Robinson relied heavily on the data produced by the state consultants and ruled that the school systems had complied with the desegregation requirements of the original order, including requirements for retraining faculty and staff, cultural pluralism, non-discriminatory counseling and course assignment, and faculty desegregation.

The decision reflected a recent pattern, conceding that there were major problems remaining but finding that they were either simply reflections of other social problems, or that schools should not be expected to do anything about them. The neoconservative argument about the intractability of social problems became a justification for assuming that none of the racial inequalities in the schools could be remedied by stronger or longer court supervision. Remedying the "harms of segregation," neoconservatives claim, does mean changing racial inequalities in education, and it is unreasonable to look at what happened to the minority children. In effect, the court was concluding that access to better schools had no effect; that the destiny of minority students was determined by their being born into less well-placed families, and, implicitly, that *Brown* was a wasted effort because it could not be expected to make any difference. The decision was on one side of a very intense division in the academic world, in which the weight of the research came to very different conclusions—that better education can be expected to make a difference.

In her decision, Judge Robinson noted that large differences remained between blacks and whites in dropouts, achievement, suspensions, access to college prep courses, and other aspects of schooling. She accepted the testimony of the school agencies' witnesses, however, that these differences did not arise from discrimination but from deep social and economic differences between white and black families that the schools could not be expected to overcome.

Her decision relies primarily on three witnesses for the school districts who supported the dismantling of desegregation plans. The witnesses who appeared for the civil rights groups were given no significant attention in the decision except when they agreed with the state government position.[76] Witnesses prepared to rebut the testimony by the school district witnesses were not permitted to testify.[77] The Wilmington case was complicated by division among attorneys representing the plaintiffs and a lack of resources to vigorously defend the court order. The Court of Appeals upheld the Wilmington decision.

PRETTY GOOD IS CLOSE ENOUGH

Among the many complexities of the 1990s resegregation decisions is the simultaneous presence of language saying that a number of constitutional standards and relevant court orders must be met for court monitoring to end, and language giving federal judges discretion to determine what is practicable. Under these decisions the trial judges could surely order completion of the specific requirements of the court orders as a minimal threshold for initiating a unitary status finding. After all, their courts had devised these local requirements, which have been either not appealed or sustained on appeal. A number of judges are holding, however, that large-scale failure to comply with their own courts' orders can be excused because the districts have done what is practical. Often these findings are made with no specific evidence to justify them. Sometimes they are accompanied by discussions of other positive things that the school district is doing—such as building or repairing schools.

This pattern was apparent, for example, in 1994 and 1995 unitary status decisions in Buffalo and Dallas. The 1995 Buffalo decision terminated an order providing magnet schools and extensive voluntary desegregation in a school district whose school board argued that there had not yet been full compliance with the court order and that the city would not provide the money to maintain what the school authorities believed to be central parts of the remedy if the court ended jurisdiction. In his decision, Judge John Curtin, who had supported desegregation in the past, now supported the city government's effort to end the desegregation, although more than one-third of the schools were out of compliance with court-ordered desegregation standards. He also did so even though the board maintained that another stage of educational efforts was necessary to meet the requirements of the plan and the city was actually cutting back funding to the schools in ways that threatened key components of the plan. Latino and handicapped students affected by the decree maintained that the board had not fulfilled its obligations to them.

Judge Curtin concluded that the basic problem was that the city was pressed for funds and that it was not fair to require more. In other words, the court did not enforce the primacy of constitutional requirements. He concluded that although the school district itself said it could and should do more to realize the goals of the desegregation plan, what it and the city had done was all that was practical. He praised the city for coming up with some supplemental and school capital funds for the next four years, though there were no assurances after that. Although he conceded that there were a number of unfinished dimensions, Curtin did not take advantage of the *Pitts* directive to declare the district only partially unitary in such circumstances.

The Supreme Court had decided the 1992 *Pitts* case in an effort to solve one major part of this dilemma. It permitted courts to declare unitary status with regard to one or more parts of the *Green* requirements while maintaining judicial supervision over others until compliance was assured. This decision was clearly meant to cover cases where there was clear compliance with part but not all of the requirements, permitting the court to shed responsibility by stages. This decision opened a path for a court to sort out the situation issue by issue.

Some courts, however, have tended to simply say that everything has been done to the greatest practical extent, and to end all supervision even when some clear unitary status requirements have not been met. In these recent decisions, the implication has been that the *Pitts* decision can be treated not as a requirement to judge each component carefully but as a general encouragement to get rid of supervision. Judge Curtin conceded that there were "numerous concerns" about some of the unmet commitments but that, "in the overall picture, they do not prevent the court from reaching a finding of unitary status in this case." Continually citing Supreme Court language about practicality and the need for local control, the court ended the desegregation order.

The judge's acceptance of a one-time, four-year commitment of funds, mostly for school construction needs was, ironically, going full cycle. A very common strategy in the South after the *Brown* decision was to pump money into construction in the black schools to try to persuade citizens and black organizations to accept the segregated system.[78] The judge terminating the Dallas case was similarly impressed by a school district promise to build a "super magnet" school in his decision ending the order.

The Buffalo Board of Education faced very serious fiscal problems and severe white flight after the end of the desegregation order and was struggling to maintain its magnet schools, which had been the centerpiece of the plan and a very strong positive asset for the district and the city. Less than a year after the court bowed out and left the issues to local politics, however, one local white family sued to end the desegregation standards in the magnet schools since their daughter had not been admitted to a school she preferred, though her scores were higher than several black children who were admitted.[79] The attorney representing the family argued that the school board had to adopt a race-neutral policy regardless of what happened to access for minority students.[80] Even before this lawsuit, the district's fiscal troubles, intensified by the unitary status decision, had resulted in the elimination of many of the special features of the magnet programs that had enabled Buffalo to maintain considerable desegregation without coercion over a long period of years and during a serious downturn in the city's economy.[81] There had been a sharp decline of applications for the magnet schools, a fall of one-third in four years. The white applications had dropped by half. The declines were accelerating.[82]

There are practical limitations to the ability of school districts to comply with court orders. The problem in this approach, however, is extremely severe. Because the Supreme Court now suggests that compliance with whatever happened to have been placed in a district court order in the past fulfills all constitutional obligations, and because minority students' rights disappear as soon as a court makes a finding of adequate compliance with prior court orders, every district has a massive incentive to argue that whatever it has not done is not practical.

By way of comparison, imagine the chaos that would be introduced into our tax system if everyone were authorized to decide how much of their bill it was practical for them to pay, and the courts deferred to such judgments. From the standpoint of the plaintiffs, this new trend suggests that while it becomes almost impossible to expand requirements in court orders, they can be shrunk unilaterally without due process or even an explanation. In the worst cases, this means that there is no law, in the sense of a seriously enforced requirement, and that the plaintiffs who win a school desegregation case win nothing that a judge cannot change whenever he or she wants to terminate the entire order by ruling that what has already been done is all that is practical.

LIP SERVICE FOR LOCAL CONTROL: FLORIDA AND MISSOURI

Judges often write of the urgent need to return the schools to democratically elected local control in their decisions withdrawing court supervision. This is an important element in the Supreme Court decisions from the time of *Milli-*

ken I to *Missouri v. Jenkins.* In a number of cases, however, the courts have terminated plans that the locally elected officials believe to be essential to educating minority children. For example, the Buffalo case was terminated at the behest of the city government, which wanted to cut funding obligations, over the objection of the school board, which argued that the educational goals had not been met. School boards were not seeking to end desegregation in either Tampa-Hillsborough, Broward County, or Charlotte, North Carolina, where courts suddenly raised the issue. In the Supreme Court decision in Kansas City, there were many words of praise for local control but the decision was actually a victory for a state government, which was fighting to reduce expenditures over the objection of a local school board that believed it essential to maintain the magnet school plan. The Kansas City schools were "freed" from funds needed to maintain their educational improvements and choice process. Such deference by the courts to "local control" is deeply misleading, both in its treatment of history and in its lack of respect for local control when it is the desire of local officials to maintain a court-ordered desegregation plan.

Some unitary status decisions actually limit local control, prohibiting local authorities from taking voluntary action on behalf of desegregation. In the decision terminating the Denver decree, for example, the court upheld a state law banning busing. The law was unconstitutional in Denver when it con-flicted with a federal court order, but after the court ended the constitutional obligation, the state had authority to prohibit the city from maintaining deseg-regation, even if local officials wished to.[83] In Boston, the school board was forced to end policies maintaining 35 percent of the seats in the elite Boston Latin High School for blacks and Latinos in an 80 percent black and Latino district. These were policies that the board was maintaining voluntarily and believed to be necessary in a city with a large majority of nonwhite students and with few public high schools providing good college preparation.[84] Thus, under the theory of local control, a school district can be stripped of its authority to maintain its commitments and may lose the right to even take voluntary local action to accomplish the original purpose of the school deseg-regation cases.

Assumptions About Housing and Demographics: Missouri

During the 1970s, the courts typically chose to focus on the desegregation mandate, ignoring the possibility of declines in white enrollment. By the 1980s and 1990s, however, it was clear that courts skeptical about desegregation, including the Supreme Court in *Missouri v. Jenkins,* tended to accept both the theory of white flight from school desegregation and the theory of white flight from integrated neighborhoods as justifying a policy of return to local control and neighborhood schools—even if they led to resegregation. In other words, though white resistance had been forcefully rejected as an adequate constitutional justification for retention of segregation in the South, it was increasingly accepted as a justification for resegregation of the educational systems of the cities. Conclusions about the way in which housing changes make further desegregation unfeasible abound in the district court decisions, often on the basis of little evidence.

JUDICIAL SHELL GAMES: ENDING REMEDIES UNLESS THE COURTS HAD MADE FINDINGS THAT WERE NOT REQUIRED WHEN THE PLAN WAS ORDERED

The Supreme Court, in its resegregation decisions, requires much stronger and more specific judicial findings to justify continuing either desegregation or court-ordered educational prograr..s than to justify ending them. During the 1970s the Supreme Court, in the *Keyes* case, created a presumption that city-wide total desegregation would be presumed to be needed if significant violations were shown in part of a city. During the period when a school district was under judicial supervision, the courts generally held that actions that increased segregation were discriminatory and could be prohibited. Although there was language in the decisions indicating that the judicial interventions were not to be permanent, the decisions required a fundamental remaking of local conditions before returning authority to the local agencies which had been the historic violators of minority rights.

The *Milliken II* decision, allowing remedial education programs paid for by the state government as part of a desegregation remedy, recognized a broad equitable power in the trial courts to address these issues. Its goal was to "restore the victims of discriminatory conduct to the position they would have occupied in the absence of such conduct."[85] In other words, courts were given broad powers and real gains were expected.

The Supreme Court's 1995 decision in *Missouri v. Jenkins,* however, retroactively changed the requirements to justify continuing a civil rights remedy, shifting the burden of proof to plaintiffs, limiting the authority of federal judges, and overruling the Kansas City trial judge's effort to focus attention on actual academic gains for black students.

If the courts were to read the *Jenkins* decision as concluding that nothing could be done to equalize education for minority students, then, of course, the *Milliken II* remedies could be terminated even if the inequalities growing out of the period of segregation and discrimination remained untouched or grew. This would reduce *Milliken II* from a command to repair the damage from illegal segregation to a formalistic requirement to transfer a fixed sum of dollars from the state government to the school district for a limited number of years, after which the minority students' rights would be ended whether or not the programs had produced any actual benefits.

On the other hand, if the decision is read as a command to identify the harms and then produces a remedy that resolves them, the role of the courts in considering termination of a plan would be fundamentally different. Both possibilities find support in various parts of the decisions.

Without acknowledging it, the Court, in *Jenkins,* reversed the conclusions it had reached between 1971 and 1979 and required much more detailed findings to justify continuation of a remedy. This meant that minority children will face resegregation and the loss of educational programs designed to remedy deseg-regation unless the courts made (or make) findings that were unnecessary under the previous constitutional standards and which, therefore, were rarely in-cluded in court opinions. The Supreme Court did not remand the case to see if the trial judge could make such findings: it simply overruled large parts of the plan. Under *Jenkins,* a court could cancel an educationally necessary remedy because there was not a specific kind of conclusion in the decision years earlier about the violation it was to correct. It is as if a company had made a contract to buy property in dollars and then was told later that it would lose the property unless payment had been made in German marks several years earlier. Minority students could lose their rights to certain programs because a judge had not known what kind of findings would be required by the Supreme Court a generation later.

Facing this retroactive change, courts have two basic options. One is simply to see whether earlier decisions contained the findings needed to sustain the current remedies. Since they rarely did, the logical consequence of this ap-proach would be to eliminate the remedy. This is a neat, simple, and rapid procedure, and it is being used. The basic problem is that it is fundamentally unjust, since it involves eliminating rights without examining whether or not the local facts would have permitted, and would still permit, making the findings. It is important for lawyers representing minority plaintiffs to re-examine the record for the kind of specific testimony and other evidence that might sustain arguments for particular remedies and to be prepared to re-open examination of past violations to obtain such evidence if it is not in the record.

LATINOS AS THE UNACKNOWLEDGED VICTIMS
OF THE NEW LEGAL PRINCIPLES

If the law continues to develop along its current course, one of the issues that will be hardest to understand will be how the rights of the largest minority group of students were eliminated with virtually no discussion. Latino students will surpass black students around the turn of the century and account for about one-fourth of the entire school-age population by 2050.[86] By 1991 they were already the largest minority group in fifteen states. They are also the most segregated group of American students by both race and poverty and have by far the lowest high school graduation rates.[87] There is a very strong link between segregation and inferior educational opportunity for Latino students.[88]

The Supreme Court recognized the rights of Latinos to desegregation remedies in the 1973 *Keyes* case, but very few cases were ever brought to desegregate Latinos. Since the time of *Keyes* the Justice Department has never actively pursued integration for Latinos. Unfortunately, Latino rights were not recognized by the courts until after the conservative movement had captured the executive branch. When the Carter Administration began to resume enforcement, Congress limited its powers in the Eagleton-Biden Amendment, which limited assignment of students to schools outside their neighborhoods.

The growth and concentration of Latino populations and the lack of desegregation enforcement has produced a steady rise in segregation of Latinos since the 1960s, radically reducing their contact with non-Hispanic white students. In fact, the only state to show a clear contrary trend was Colorado as a result of the *Keyes* case in Denver. In Denver, however, resegregation was approved in 1995.[89]

The majority of Latinos live in California and Texas, each of which has many small, segregated school districts in the metropolitan areas in which most Latino students are concentrated. Thus, Latinos were deeply affected by the 1974 *Milliken I* decision against metropolitan desegregation.

Los Angeles, which partially desegregated under a state order in 1978, was the first major city in the United States to resegregate, after California voters adopted a constitutional change limiting desegregation rights under state law in 1981.[90] The Reagan Administration dropped the Carter Administration's case for the desegregation of metropolitan Houston in 1981. Dallas, Austin, and Fort Worth were among the first cities in which resegregation was approved by courts.

If minority children's rights to desegregation and to special programs that deal with the educational results of segregation are extinguished before Latino children receive either, the nation's largest minority community will never receive any benefits from the constitutional struggle over two generations.

Many Latinos have very severe educational problems; they are doing far worse than blacks, for example, in high school and college completion, and rank far below whites and Asians on all measures of school achievement. They attend schools that have the highest level of concentrated poverty of any ethnic group.

This economically marginal and socially threatened population has brought hard-working but poorly educated families into big cities, where they must either make a connection leading to education and jobs or risk sinking into the urban slum syndrome of isolation, inequality, hopelessness, crime, and separation from the rest of the society in succeeding generations. Although Latino leaders have been deeply divided on the issue, surveys show a strong Latino preference for integrated schools.[91]

In schools where a remedy was devised for black children but there has subsequently been a large growth of Latino children without any attention to their needs or rights under a desegregation plan, the court should not terminate Latinos' rights without any representation or investigation of violations. In many school districts with relatively small Latino populations, for example, the Latinos were simply combined with the whites in drawing up the desegregation plan or were not targeted for desegregation relief. If such a district subsequently became 10 or 20 percent Latino and the Latino students were in separate and unequal schools, there is an obvious question about whether or not the courts have protected their rights as required by Supreme Court's 1973 decision in the *Keyes* case. In San Francisco, for example, the school desegregation case was filed by the NAACP when black students were the largest single group of students in the schools. By the early 1990s, however, there were more Chinese and Latino students than African Americans. The Court's monitoring process disclosed that Latino students confronted many problems identical to those experienced by African American students, and the consent decree was modified to reflect that reality in 1993.[92] Many school districts have experienced such transitions within the past two decades, but the courts have taken no notice of the changes.

The first resegregation decision of the Supreme Court resulted in this very problem. In Oklahoma City, as resegregation was settling in, no one noticed the significant growth of Latino students, and the Court did not address their situation. The Court has announced that all historic violations by the city school district ended—*before* even the slightest effort had been made to deal with the rights of Latinos.

APPEALS COURTS' INCONSISTENCIES: DEFERRING TO TRIAL JUDGES WHO LIMIT REMEDIES BUT OVERRULING THOSE FINDING THEM NECESSARY

One mechanism which may well change the outcomes of cases while appearing to be a technical matter of court management is the degree of discretion accorded to trial courts relative to higher courts. For fifteen years after *Brown v. Board of Education* there was an initial grant of vast discretion to trial courts under the 1955 decision *Brown II*. When it became apparent that district judges would do very little, the Supreme Court tightened its standards and gave increasingly unambiguous and insistent directions in the 1968 to 1971 period. The requirements for far-reaching district-wide desegregation lasted with few changes from the late 1960s through the 1980s. Meanwhile, conservative presidential administrations were remaking the courts through the appointment process.

The Supreme Court's resegregation decisions of the 1990s went back to a situation like that in the mid-1950s, with courts receiving complicated and seemingly inconsistent policies. The idea was that trial judges would find ways to apply the new requirements to local circumstances.

Not all district courts approached the issues from the same perspectives, however, and consistent treatment by courts of appeals should have supported the judgment of those who heard the evidence in the trials. In fact, however, the decisions by the courts of appeals were inconsistent. For example, the court hearing the appeal from the Wilmington case affirmed the end of the desegregation order, asserting that it had neither the right nor the authority to second-guess the trial judge unless there was a clear abuse of discretion. In the Rockford, Illinois, case, *People Who Care v. Rockford Board of Education,* however, the trial court found extensive local violations, appointed an expert to advise the court, and ordered sweeping reforms, including a change in the district's tracking system. This case went to an appeals panel headed by one of the nation's most prominent conservative judges, Richard Posner. This court sweepingly overturned orders of the trial judge in a 1997 decision, often with brief and even sarcastic comments. In other words, the discretion accorded to a trial judge sometimes appeared to depend more on the outcome of the decision than on a principle of respect for the conclusions of the "finder of fact."

The Wilmington court praised the lower court's termination of the court order as a move to make it possible for local educators "to resume their full role in the larger social and political effort to make our nation worthy of the best ideas of its members."[93] The court noted "the extended social and economic burdens that continued supervision would impose on generations of innocent school children and their families," clearly reflecting a belief that desegregation was a cost for whites and that white rights were now most seriously at risk.[94]

The court held that it had a limited role in reviewing the factual findings, citing many cases suggesting that it could overturn only "clearly erroneous" conclusions. Quoting an earlier opinion, the appeals court said it should overturn a trial judge only when its finding "either (1) is completely devoid of minimum evidentiary support displaying some hue of credibility, or (2) bears no rational relationship to the supportive evidentiary data."[95] Confronting evidence, for example, that black students with the same test scores as white students were likely to be placed in lower levels of courses, the court noted that the findings were "potentially troubling" but said that "our task here is not to engage in such broad speculation, nor to choose among possible inferences" but rather to defer to the trial judge.[96]

The court in Rockford made a much more extensive effort to investigate the facts, including appointing an expert directly responsible to the court, and reached a different judgment on the issues of classroom segregation. The trial court ordered the school district to initiate changes in its classroom segregation patterns as an integral part of the desegregation remedy. In this case, however, the court of appeals freely rejected the conclusions of the lower court and imposed its own judgment. In this case there was no deference to the lower court findings. Rather there was an obvious willingness to impose judgments without significant consideration of the evidence.

Judge Posner's decision begins by recognizing the broad power of district courts in finding facts and developing remedies and then proceeds to overturn many parts of the remedy, often with condescending asides suggesting that the lower court and others supporting the remedy don't really know what schooling is about and are really engaged in discrimination against whites and education policies the appeals court panel prefers.

The opinion says that education remedies make the court "a super school board."[97] Desegregation remedies are defined as creating white victims, and the faculty desegregation and affirmative action provisions would mean "these white teachers are to be made victims of court-decreed racial discrimination."[98] Raising the percentage of black teachers, the court concludes without citing any evidence, would bring "a reduction in quality" since hiring would not be "on the basis purely of merit."[99] Here the court assumes that the previous pattern was fair and that black teachers are inferior.

In discussing the order for desegregation of classes, the court concludes first that "lawyers and judges are not competent to resolve the controversy" over tracking and then rapidly announces its analysis. It would "say to parents of the brighter kids that their children don't really belong in the public school system." The court dismisses a well-researched student note on the issue in the *Harvard Law Review* by attacking the author, "who at the time of writing the note was neither a public school student nor, it is a safe guess, a parent."[100]

The court goes on to dismiss an order for an educational remedy directed at narrowing the racial achievement gap by concluding that it was an impossible goal. It then rejected the lower court's analysis of the part of the gap that was due to past discrimination, posing a standard of proof for such estimates that could not conceivably be met in any school district, given the limits on historic education data and the complexity of the issues studied. The analysis then turns to an assertion that the gap may not be greater in Rockford than in communities that have "not been found to have discriminated against their black and Hispanic students."[101] Since virtually every city ever sued has been found to have discriminated, the court must be assuming that cities that have not been sued and had court findings, such as Chicago, did not have a history of discrimination.

The decision goes on to overrule findings about the harm of concentrating black students in compensatory education programs. It does not require desegregation of extracurricular activities, rarely dealing with any of the empirical research on these issues or discussing the rationale of the lower court judgment.

The basic reality of these two appeals court decisions is troubling. One gives virtually total deference to the trial judge who wishes to dismantle a desegregation plan after a hurried and limited procedure. The other gives no deference to a trial court that examined the facts much more energetically and brought in impartial expertise. There is no consistent pattern of respect for lower court judgments and some of the results are only understandable as reflections of the values of the judges. This is precisely the kind of goal-oriented use of procedures that conservatives claimed that activist liberal courts used in the 1960s.

COURTS THAT HAVE TAKEN THEIR
RESPONSIBILITIES SERIOUSLY

Not all courts dealing with efforts to terminate all or part of desegregation plans have rushed to judgment or brushed aside important questions of the adequacy of the remedy. Nor have all courts relied on obviously unequal representation of the interests of the plaintiffs and defendants or simply decided to insert their personal views into the decisions. Some have rejected unitary status motions as premature, imposed clearer standards for assessing full compliance, or used their powers to create a more comprehensive and less partisan review of the status of the desegregation plan. In San Francisco and Prince George's County, Maryland, for example, the courts appointed panels of experts nominated by the parties to prepare findings and recommendations for the use of the court and the parties. The court in the Little Rock case appointed experts of diverse perspectives to testify. When the school district responded to the testimony by asking that unitary status proceedings be suspended for a time and that the court's monitors try to help the parties find resolutions to problems with the desegregation plan, the court agreed and stepped aside for a period.

Clearly, there is a need for better mechanisms and procedures to deal with the serious problem of courts being forced to reach irreversible conclusions in cases where only one side has had the resources to produce major social science evidence and all that evidence is bought and paid for and not subject to any evaluation by peers. The appointment of experts responsible to the court can greatly reduce the possibility that the court will rely on a "fact" widely known to be false or unsubstantiated in the research and professional communities. It also permits a continued search for better answers to disputes that may be resolved without court intervention if new proposals can be framed that meet the objectives of both parties in a way likely to enhance the remedy.

The U.S. Court of Appeals for the Eleventh Circuit handed down an opinion in August 1996 outlining a much higher standard for ending desegregation orders than that used in most trial courts. In *Lockett v. Board of Education of Muscogee County,* the court held that the district court had wrongly ignored failures of the school board to meet all requirements of its court order until unitary status was granted. It also held that the school board was under a continuing obligation, based on *Green,* to "take whatever [affirmative] steps might be necessary to convert to a unitary system in which racial discrimination would be eliminated root and branch."[102] The courts could not conclude that resegregation was merely the result of private housing action but had the burden of proof to show that it was not substantially caused by school zoning, transfer policy, and site selection for new schools.[103] This demanding standard requires inquiries far more stringent and probing than those undertaken by most courts terminating desegregation plans.

CONCLUSIONS AND RECOMMENDATIONS

This chapter spells out the changes in the decisions and the way in which they are being applied. It also assesses the empirical and procedural changes and suggests ways in which trial judges and lawyers could follow the Supreme Court's decisions without engaging in legal sleights-of-hand that eliminate the rights of minority children. Legal standards that have been changed retroactively are being used to eliminate desegregation and educational opportunity programs, without determining that the remedies either have accomplished their purpose or need to be extended and improved. At a minimum, plaintiffs deserve a fair chance to meet those standards before a court hands down what is probably an irreversible and severe limitation of the rights of minority children in a community.

Another option is to recognize the need for new hearings on the nature of the historic violations and to make the necessary findings about the grounds for specific remedies now. A fair protection of constitutional rights for minority children in circumstances where courts retroactively change the rules is to reopen the process and consider what findings that evidence justifies. This would be a complex process, involving reexamination of evidence already in the record, and acceptance of new testimony and briefs on the specific issues that earlier courts had not had to consider. The advantage of this procedure is that it would offer due process to minority children before their constitutionally mandated remedies are ended—unilaterally canceled because judges ten years ago did not know what kind of findings the Rehnquist court would later require. If the proceedings are to be more than a charade, they must not impose standards of proof that are impossible to meet.

The many problems documented in this chapter show a tendency, at least in some cases, toward speedy and superficial consideration of the complex and critical decisions involved in choosing between segregated and integrated public education, and in deciding to continue or to terminate remedies for historic violations. Since these decisions will play a vital role in determining the racial future of American communities, a process which reflects the complex cross-cutting legal imperatives and impartially explores the social and educational realities is an urgent necessity.

Equitable Approaches to Termination Decisions

Courts must, of course, apply the law of the land as determined by the Supreme Court. In many respects, however, many lower courts have been reading the Supreme Court decisions selectively, rushing to terminate orders where there are important unresolved issues. It is vital for courts to recognize that the law is in considerable disarray because the Court has left standing basic desegregation decisions including *Green, Swann,* and *Keyes* and that its decisions to restore local control contain contradictory elements. Some reaffirm the goals of fully disestablishing the old dual systems and repairing historic harm, while others reduce desegregation to a temporary mechanical process. In this situation the responsibility of courts is to strike a careful balance, reaching decisions that reflect the diverse elements of current law, that are fair to all parties and that incorporate sound educational policies. Courts should honor the law and improve education results through the following procedures, which civil rights lawyers should urgently request:

(1) Consider fully and fairly claims of new violations or of a failure to provide remedies for previously neglected minority children, such as Latinos. Until a district is declared to be unitary, public decisions that increase segregation are violations of the Constitution and should trigger appropriate remedies. However, many school districts have planned and opened segregated schools while under desegregation orders. This point is often neglected when courts rush to judgment; civil rights groups hesitate to raise new violations for fear that a court may dissolve the entire case. If a group entitled to a remedy has never received one, that should be rectified before closing a case.

(2) If the court did not make the kind of specific findings about the educational harm of segregation that are required by *Missouri v. Jenkins,* it should schedule a hearing and appoint expert witnesses with acknowledged skill in the field to assist in considering this difficult question. It is not enough to rely on witnesses-for-hire who always oppose desegregation and testify that local school officials have done everything necessary. The court should then identify

specific educational measures that will remedy these violations. Failure to do this retroactively eliminates educational remedies for minority children simply because their lawyers and the judge at a previous point in time failed to meet standards that did not then exist.

(3) If there is a court monitoring committee or a court-appointed expert, the judge should request a report on the status of rights and opportunities for minority students under the desegregation remedy, informing the court's judgment with the best available data. The court should not defer judgment on these key questions to expert witnesses whom the defendants have hired to justify termination of court control. The court should take into account the obviously unequal resources available to plaintiffs and defendants to address such questions, and use its authority to ensure that the best possible information is obtained before the rights of minority children are terminated. The court should require that all statistics submitted by the school district show results for each minority group separately.

(4) If there is no monitoring committee or court-appointed expert, the court should direct the preparation of such a report by the school district, with the requirement that it consult an individual with professional expertise in successful desegregation and the education of children from the minority groups involved in the case.

(5) The court should permit ample time for discovery and for argument of the unitary status motions, requiring that all school district data as well as reports be made available to all parties and that requested tabulations of data be prepared.

(6) If a court has no past record of initiating orders to increase desegregation on its own motion, it should not, in the interest of equal justice, initiate termination proceedings on its own motion.

(7) The court should permit intervention of Latino civil rights groups if they wish to participate, allowing them to be heard before their rights are terminated.

(8) Professional educators should recognize the critical importance of termination decisions and the fact that such decisions will not only end their opportunity to obtain *Milliken II* funds from state governments, but may also make it impossible to take even voluntary actions needed to maintain racial equity in the future. When faced with decisions of such importance, school districts should be instructed to consider the issues very carefully. Many educators have no understanding of what they will lose with unitary status. It may be possible, for example, to negotiate solutions to unworkable parts of the court order, thus

obtaining key benefits of unitary status, while avoiding the costs of a divisive legal battle and the risk of ending up without any authority to address key racial problems.[104] School district lawyers should apprise their clients of these risks.

(9) Courts and parties in the case should take seriously the findings of the Supreme Court in a number of major school desegregation cases that school segregation decisions can affect housing segregation, as well as vice versa, and should examine the degree to which segregation and resegregation in the housing market are due, at least in part, to school policies and to deficiencies in school desegregation plans.

There are also specific steps plaintiffs and their attorneys can take to ensure that relevant testimony and information are sought and heard in cases such as these. With limited resources, plaintiffs and their lawyers may not be fully aware of the options and procedures open to them.

Lawyers for plaintiffs need to realize that the context in which courts consider these issues is often characterized by exhaustion, the perception that the Supreme Court has given much clearer direction than it has, and a local political climate that strongly suggests that there are no risks in ending the case. Judges are also often disturbed that the plaintiffs' lawyers have not raised problems with the court order for many years and may be appearing to neglect the case. The first necessity of the lawyers is to raise serious questions about compliance with the specific court order and about general assumptions in the district plan for equity after the return to segregated neighborhood schools. It is important that these issues be raised both in court and in the community, citing specific evidence from other communities and from research. Those claims should be tied directly to requests for specific data and for expert, independent assessment of the data not paid for by the school district or other parties.

If the lawyers lack the resources to defend against a unitary status motion, they should make clear their lack of resources and apply for funding from community groups and local organizations and foundations, explaining the serious and irreversible nature of unitary status decisions and the consequences of such decisions elsewhere. They should also file motions asking the court to direct fact finding on the most important issues and to appoint an expert or committee responsible to the court. The key necessities are to raise the awareness of the issue, clearly present the ambiguities and responsibilities under the current law, and take the initiative in laying out a set of factual questions that are essential prerequisites to making the judgments required by the court.

The goals of better procedures are to permit lawyers, educators, and representatives of the victims of discrimination to avoid a rush toward thoughtless, ideologically and politically driven reimposition of segregation in a way that eliminates the rights and harms the education of minority students. Supreme Court decisions must be obeyed, but by recognizing the complexity of Supreme Court directives and actively using the discretion of the trial court, judges can address community concerns and render wiser and more thoughtful judgments.

NOTES

1. Samuel S. Peng and Susan T. Hill, *Understanding Racial-Ethnic Differences in Secondary School Science and Mathematics Achievement* (Washington, D.C.: U.S. Department of Education, February 1995), 19–21; Phillip Burch, *The Dropout Problem in New Jersey's Big Urban Schools: Educational Inequality and Government Inaction* (Bureau of Government Research, Rutgers University, 1992); Gary Orfield and Lawrence Peskin, "Metropolitan High Schools: Income, Race, and Inequality," in Douglas E. Mitchell & Margaret E. Goertz (eds.), *Education Politics for the New Century* (1991).

2. Gary Orfield, Mark Bachmeier, David James, and Tamela Eitle, "Deepening Segregation in American Public Schools," *Equity and Excellence in Education*, 30, no. 2 (September 1997), 5–24.

3. Rolf K. Blank, Roger E. Levine, and Lauri Steel, "After Fifteen Years: Magnet Schools in Urban Education," in Bruce Fuller and Richard F. Elmore, *Who Chooses? Who Loses? Culture, Institutions, and the Unequal Effects of School Choice* (New York: Teachers College Press, 1996), 154–172.

4. Gary Orfield, "Public Opinion and School Desegregation," *Teachers College Record*, 96, no. 4 (Summer 1995), 654–670.

5. Jennifer Jellison, "Failed Promises of Local Control in Oklahoma City," Working Paper, Harvard Project on School Desegregation, 1996; Gary Orfield and Susan E. Eaton, *Dismantling Desegregation* (New York: New Press, 1996).

6. Gary Orfield, *The Reconstruction of Southern Education: The Schools and the 1964 Civil Rights Act* (New York: John Wiley and Sons, 1969).

7. Effectiveness is used here to indicate a period when the Court, acting without support from the other branches, made a clearly measurable impact on the statistical level of segregation.

8. Don Shoemaker (ed.), *With All Deliberate Speed: Segregation-Desegregation in Southern Schools* (New York: Harper and Brothers, 1957); J. W. Peltason, 58 *Lonely Men: Southern Federal Judges and School Desegregation* (New York: Harcourt, Brace and World, 1961); Leon Friedman (ed.), *Southern Justice* (New York: Pantheon, 1965); Jack Bass, *Unlikely Heroes* (New York: Touchstone Books, 1981).

9. J. Harvie Wilkinson III, *From Brown to Bakke: The Supreme Court and School Integration, 1954–1978* (New York: Oxford University Press, 1979), 32–39.

10. Critiques include: Herbert Wechsler, "Toward Neutral Principles of Constitutional Law," *Harvard Law Review*, 73 (1959), 31–34; Nathan Glazer, *Affirmative Discrimination* (New York: Basic Books, 1975); David L. Kirp, *Just Schools: The Idea of Racial Equality in*

American Education (Berkeley: University of California Press, 1982); Lino Graglia, *Disaster by Decree: The Supreme Court Decisions on Race and the Schools* (Ithaca: Cornell University Press, 1976).

11. Gary Orfield, with Sara Schley, Diane Glass, and Sean Reardon, *The Growth of Segregation in American Schools: Changing Patterns of Separation and Poverty Since 1968* (Alexandria, Va.: National School Boards Association, 1993), especially tables 1–5.

12. Orfield and Eaton, *Dismantling Desegregation*. Gary Orfield, "Public Opinion and School Desegregation."

13. Orfield, "Public Opinion and School Desegregation."

14. Gary Orfield, "Congress, the President and Anti-Busing Legislation, 1966–1974," *Journal of Law and Education* 4 (January 1975): 81–139.

15. Gary Orfield, "Congress and Civil Rights: From Obstacle to Protector," in *African Americans and the Living Constitution*, ed. John Hope Franklin and Genna Rae McNeil (Washington, D.C.: Smithsonian Institution Press, 1995).

16. *Brown v. Board of Education,* 349 U.S. 294 (1955).

17. *Cooper v. Aaron,* 358 U.S. 1 (1958).

18. *Griffin v. County School Board of Prince Edward Co.,* 375 U.S. 391 (1964).

19. Orfield, with Schley, Glass, and Reardon, *Growth of Segregation,* table 5.

20. Orfield, *Reconstruction of Southern Education;* Reed Sarratt, *The Ordeal of Desegregation* (New York: Harper and Row, 1966), 349–360; U.S. Commission on Civil Rights, *Southern School Desegregation, 1966–67* (Washington, D.C.: Government Printing Office, 1967).

21. *Green v. Board of Education of New Kent Co.,* 391 U.S. 430 (1968).

22. *Alexander v. Holmes County,* 365 U.S. 1218 (1969).

23. *Swann v. Charlotte-Mecklenburg Board of Education,* 402 U.S. 1 (1971).

24. Orfield, with Schley, Glass, and Reardon, *Growth of Segregation;* Gary Orfield, "Why It Worked in Dixie: Southern School Desegregation and Its Implications for the North," in Adam Yarmolinsky, Lance Liebman, and Corinne S. Schelling (eds.), *Race and Schooling in the City* (Cambridge: Harvard University Press, 1981), pp. 24–44.

25. *Keyes v. School District No. 1, Denver,* 413 U.S. 189 (1973).

26. *Minority* is used here as shorthand for blacks and Latinos.

27. Computations from U.S. Office for Civil Rights data tapes, 1988–89.

28. *Milliken v. Bradley,* 418 U.S. 717 (1974). The five-vote majority included Nixon's four appointees and one of Eisenhower's; the dissenters were Justices appointed by Johnson, Kennedy, Roosevelt, and Eisenhower.

29. Computations from the Common Core of Education Statistics, 1992–93.

30. *Milliken v. Bradley,* 433 U.S. 267 (1977).

31. *Columbus Board of Education v. Pennick,* 443 U.S. 449 (1979); *Dayton Board of Education v. Brinkman,* 443 U.S. 526 (1979).

32. Orfield, "Public Opinion and School Desegregation."

33. Sue Davis, *Justice Rehnquist and the Constitution* (Princeton: Princeton University Press, 1989), 56–60, 199.

34. Lincoln Caplan, "The Reagan Challenge to the Rule of Law," in Sidney Blumenthal and Thomas Byrne Edsall (eds.), *The Reagan Legacy* (New York: Pantheon Books, 1988), 231;

Edwin Meese III, *With Reagan: The Inside Story* (Washington, D.C.: Regnery Gateway, 1992), 317–318.

35. Kaplan, "Reagan Challenge," 232.

36. Meese ridiculed "various 'affirmative action,' quota, minority-set-aside, and other schemes that had surfaced in the preceding decade. The most combustible example, perhaps, was busing school children for purposes of racial balance." Such policies, he said, had "devastating" social consequences. Meese, *With Reagan,* 314.

37. Clarence Thomas, "Civil Rights as a Principle versus Civil Rights as an Interest," in David Boaz (ed.), *Assessing the Reagan Years* (Washington, D.C.: Cato Institute, 1988), 393.

38. Janet Ward Schofield, "Review of Research on School Desegregation's Impact on Elementary and Secondary School Students," in J. A. Banks and C. A. M. Banks (eds), *Handbook of Research on Multicultural Education* (New York: Macmillan, 1995).

39. Neil A. Lewis, "Selection of Conservative Judges Guards Part of Bush's Legacy," *New York Times,* July 1, 1991, A13; Neil A. Lewis, "Partisan Gridlock Blocks Senate Confirmations of Federal Judges," *New York Times,* November 30, 1995, 16; Amy Waldman, "Taking a Hard Right," *Washington Monthly,* September 1995, 39–43.

40. Meese, *With Reagan,* 318.

41. Charles Fried, *Order and Law: Arguing the Reagan Revolution* (New York: Simon and Schuster, 1991), 17.

42. *Board of Education v. Dowell,* 498 U.S. 237 (1991).

43. *Freeman v. Pitts,* 112 S. Ct. 1430 (1992).

44. *Missouri v. Jenkins,* 115 S. Ct. 2938 (1995)

45. Id.

46. Ironically, many southern districts attempted unsuccessfully in the 1950s to persuade the court that the new brick schoolhouses they suddenly built for black students after the desegregation case was taken by the Supreme Court made desegregation unnecessary.

47. Garrett Epps, "Black Robe Activism," *The Nation,* May 5, 1997, 7.

48. The annual Gallup Poll for the education magazine *Phi Delta Kappan* has not shown busing or desegregation as one of the top concerns of the public about schools for two decades (Orfield, with Schley, Glass, and Reardon, "Public Opinion and School Desegregation").

49. Gary Orfield and Carole Ashkinaze, "The Closing Door: Conservative Policy and Black Opportunity (Chicago: University of Chicago Press, 1991), chapter 5.

50. A 1994 Gallup Poll showed that white southern opposition to integrated schools fell from 81% in 1954 to 15% in 1994 (*U.S.A. Today,* May 12, 1994, 8A).

51. *Mannings v. The School Board of Hillsborough County,* slip opinion, M.D. Fla., Case No. 58-3554-CIV-T-17, November 17, 1985, at 2.

52. Id., at 4.

53. Id., at 6.

54. Stephen Hegarty, "Judge's Move Could Lead to Busing's End," *St. Petersburg Times,* November 21, 1995.

55. The federal magistrate recommended granting unitary status to the school district in August 1997 finding that Hillsborough County was desegregated to the "extent practica-

ble." While not favoring busing, the *St. Petersburg Times* editorialized in February 1998: "Yet it also would be dishonest to label busing a failure and to understate the threat facing the black community. . . . The court order expanded educational, extracurricular and employment opportunities, promoted high-quality 'magnet' academic programs. . . . Without the court order, Hillsborough's desegregation efforts would fall prey to legal Challenged by whites, who, under the claim of reverse discrimination, have laid Waste to similar programs throughout the country. . . . Officials are fooling themselves and the public by insisting that the tools for Voluntary desegregation are already in hand. They are not. While it may not be 1958, the school district has a poor record of keeping in step with the moral cause of history" (*St. Petersburg Times,* Editorial "Desegregation Continued," 1 February 20, 1998).

56. *Washington v. School Board of Broward County,* S.D. Fla., Case No. 92-6177-CIV-Ryskamp.

57. "The 100 Largest Public School Districts," *Education Week,* May 18, 1994.

58. Bruce Taylor Seeman and Lisa Arthur, "New Era for Broward's Students?" *Tampa Herald,* August 19, 1995, 1A, 12A.

59. Interview with Janelle Byrd, NAACP Legal Defense Fund, October 8, 1996.

60. This pattern was disclosed by a reporter participating in an Education Writers of America project and documented in a report by Jennifer Jellison of the Harvard Project on School Desegregation. Jennifer Jellison, *Resegregation and Equity in Oklahoma City,* Working Paper, Harvard Project on School Desegregation, September 1996.

61. The Supreme Court declared the right to desegregation in 1954 but put off a remedy until a year later when it required "all deliberate speed."

62. Gary Orfield, "Why It Worked in Dixie: Southern School Desegregation and Its Implications for the North," in Adam Yarmolinsky, Lance Liebman, and Corinne S. Schelling (eds.), *Race and Schooling in the City* (Cambridge: Harvard University Press, 1981), 24–44.

63. *Stell v. Board of Public Education,* 860 F. Supp. 1563, 1571 (S. D. Ga. 1994).

64. Id., at 1578.

65. Id., at 1584.

66. Id., at 1578, n. 25.

67. 1978 order quoted at *Coalition to Save Our Children v. State Board of Education of the State of Delaware,* 901 F. Supp. 784, at 791.

68. Jeannie Oakes, *Keeping Track: How Schools Structure Inequality* (New Haven: Yale University Press, 1985).

69. *Coalition to Save Our Children,* 818–821.

70. Id., at 817.

71. Id., at 88.

72. Id., at 104.

73. Id.

74. The Wilmington case had made Delaware one of the two most desegregated states in the United States for black students. The other was Kentucky, which had a similar order in its largest metropolitan area (Orfield, *Growth of Segregation*). Obviously, the argument that the area had achieved a rare degree of student desegregation was correct.

75. In the Court of Appeals' 2–1 decision supporting the district court judgment, the dissenter, Judge Sarokin, pointed to the exclusion of rebuttal testimony as one of the serious problems with the trial, noting that the Court of Appeals had sustained the importance of hearing rebuttal testimony in a number of major cases, but the other two judges disagreed. (*Coalition to Save Our Children v. State Board of Education,* CA 3, July 24, 1996, slip opinion, 74–78.)

76. *Coalition to Save Our Children v. State Board of Education of the State of Delaware,* D.C., Del., Civil Action No. 56-1816-1822-SLR, August 14, 1995.

77. The author was one of those witnesses.

78. Richard Kluger, *Simple Justice: The History of Brown v. Board of Education and Black America's Struggle for Equality* (New York: Knopf, 1975).

79. James Heaney, "School Suit Claims Reverse Bias," *Buffalo News,* October 2, 1997, A1, A8.

80. James Heaney, "Quotas at Schools Under Fire," *Buffalo News,* October 4, 1997, A1, A5.

81. James Heaney, "Dollar Delusion: Magnets Get No Extra Funds," *Buffalo News,* June, 1997, A1, A6.

82. James Heaney, "Magnets: Losing Their Attraction," *Buffalo News,* June 6, 1997, A1, A12.

83. *Keyes,* 902 F. Supp. 1274 (D. Colo. 1995).

84. *McLaughlin v. Boston School Committee,* Civil Action No. 95-11803-WAG, Complaint, U.S. District Court, 1995.

85. *Milliken v. Bradley,* 97 S.Ct. 2749 (1977).

86. Census Bureau projections in *Education Week,* March 27, 1996, p. 3.

87. U.S. Census Bureau, Orfield with Schley, Glass, and Reardon, *Growth of Segregation.*

88. Reuben Donato, Martha Menchaca, and Richard R. Valencia, "Segregation, Desegregation, and Integration of Chicano Students: Problems and Prospects," in Richard R. Valencia (ed.), *Chicano School Failure and Success* (London: Falmer Press, 1991*)*, 27–63.

89. 902 *F. Supp.* 1274 (D. Colo. 1995).

90. Gary Orfield, "Lessons of the Los Angeles School Desegregation Case," *Education and Urban Society* (May 1984).

91. Orfield, "Public Opinion and School Desegregation."

92. "Desegregation and Educational Change in San Francisco: Findings and Recommendations on Consent Decree Implementation," Report to Federal District Court, July 1992.

93. *Coalition to Save Our Children v. State Board of Education,* CA 3, 1996, slip opinion, at 6.

94. Ibid., at 14.

95. Ibid., at 11.

96. Ibid., pp. 20–21.

97. Rockford Slip Opinion, April 15, 1997, at 4.

98. Ibid., at 6.

99. Ibid., at 7.

100. Ibid., at 9.

101. Ibid., at 12.

102. *Lockett v. Bd. of Educ. of Muscogee County,* 92 F. 3d 1092 (11th Cir. 1996), 1097.

103. Id.

104. Gary Orfield and David Thronson, "Dismantling Desegregation: Uncertain Gains, Unexpected Costs," *Emory Law Journal,* 42, no. 3 (Summer 1993), 759–790.

Chapter 3 The Law's Role in the Distribution of Education: The Promises and Pitfalls of School Finance Litigation

Molly S. McUsic

Every school child in the country, it seems, has an innate sense of distributive justice. Whether the decision is who gets to keep a new-found tennis ball, who gets the better half of an ice cream sandwich, or who has to be "it" in a game of tag, the kids in the schoolyard are adept in developing just methods for dividing their small society's goods. Perhaps less just than the children's methods for deciding who gets what in the schoolyard are their parents' methods for deciding who gets what schoolyard—and the academic and career opportunities that go along with it.

The distribution of educational resources is remarkably unequal in the United States, skewed across lines of race and class. In Texas, per-pupil expenditures range from $2,112 to $19,333, with an average difference of $2,000.[1] In Vermont, some schools spend 160 percent more than others.[2] On Long Island, per-pupil spending ranges from $7,305 to $17,435.[3] Children schooled in New Jersey, with the second highest per capita income, enjoy the nation's highest per-pupil expenditures. Children schooled in Mississippi, with the lowest per capita income, suffer the lowest per-pupil expenditures.[4]

This inequality of educational resources would not be so noted (or perhaps so notable) if it were not matched with inequality of educational achievement. African Americans' proficiency test scores in reading, writing, mathematics, and science at ages nine, thirteen, and seventeen are all significantly lower than test scores of white students.[5] Black and Hispanic students are far more likely than whites to drop out of high school.[6] Poor children do not read as well as wealthy children.[7]

The legal system that delivers this order of educational inequality is a unique combination of unfunded federal mandates affecting local districts unequally, state legal structures that deliver and fund education on a geographical basis (segregating children largely by race and class), and a subsidized system of private schools that serves fewer than 10 percent of schoolchildren. These three central features of school funding guarantee inequities and inadequacies in the delivery of education to American schoolchildren.

As these educational inequities spring from a legal structure created and preserved by lawyers (and lawmakers), it seems fitting that lawyers should play a role in its remedy—and they have. School finance litigation has been the major legal effort over the past twenty years to force a change in the legal structure of the education delivery system. In fact, litigation must play a central role in any hope for transforming the educational delivery system, as school finance reform favoring poor students does not occur in the usual course of legislative action. The political arena does not prefer the poor school district, and at least in the past twenty years or so has seldom preferred increased educational funding over reduced taxes. In that climate, courts appear to provide the only political leverage available for altering the system.

The earliest school finance cases—an outgrowth of courtroom desegregation efforts—were a species of civil rights litigation, although they did not seek an explicitly racial remedy. These cases, first brought under the federal equal protection clause, were dealt a blow in 1973 when the Supreme Court held that discrepancy in funding from district to district did not violate the federal constitution. Since then attorneys have taken up the issue in state courts, seeking remedies both under their state constitution's equal protection clause and its education clause and, under either clause, making an argument for equality under the law.

Equity claims, however, foundered on theoretical difficulties and practical political problems. What was to be divided equally? If it is funding that must be divided equally, how do plaintiffs dodge the implication that all government funding—for housing or health, for example, must also be divided equally? If it is educational achievement that must be divided equally, then how do plaintiffs prove that more funds will buy more educational achievement? Even where judges accept that funding should be equalized (either for its own sake or for the sake of equalizing achievement), how does one equalize educational funding in the face of unequal educational needs?

In fact, judges often feel unqualified to decide how much money it would take to give children of unequal needs an equal education and so would return the issue to the legislature, where the same political forces that shape the current system dominate in shaping its remedy. And, of course, the prevailing political forces resist any remedy; new funds could come from only three sources—from the state's taxpayers generally, from wealthy districts exclusively, or from elsewhere in the existing state budget—and none has proven an obliging source. Thus, while the equity cases enjoy a number of victories in the courtroom, it has been harder to carry that victory through the legislature to the classroom. Even cases that succeed in court (less than half of all cases filed) often fail to equalize funding or educational opportunity.[8] Moreover, despite litigation in nearly every state over the past two decades, interdistrict disparities in the United States have not diminished.[9]

Despite these generally disappointing results, the number of challenges to school finance systems is growing, and there is hope of more substantial success in the future.[10] While the results of past school finance cases highlight the pitfalls of such litigation, they also hold some promise. Past experience suggests that the paradigms used have sometimes failed to address the underlying legal structure that systematically produces the substantive injustice attacked in the cases. A different approach that addresses that legal structure—where the legal standard is not equity, but adequacy—offers an avenue around some of the political and legal obstacles that have bedeviled earlier efforts.

Ironically, the crucial lesson to be learned from past litigation is that if lawyers hope to alter the legal distribution of education fundamentally, they cannot rely, as they have in the past, primarily on traditional legal concepts and remedies. Instead, they must turn to advances in educational policy made outside the courtroom and shift their litigation to reflect the knowledge acquired by educators over the past few decades. While standards of equity revolve around concepts familiar to lawyers and legal discourse, a case built around a constitutional right to an "adequate" education demands an educator's input. In adequacy cases, lawyers must explicitly rely on what educational experts and the political majority say constitutes an adequate education and— in the remedy phase—what educators say will promote that education.

Adequacy claims owe their growing strength to the trend—begun by state governments in the 1980s—of defining explicit educational standards for public schools, commonly in the form of end-of-year tests given to each grade level. This approach clarifies the legal complaint by relying not on the plaintiff, defendant, or the judge for a definition of "adequate education," but on the policy established by education experts and endorsed by the legislature or the state department of education. As a result, the judge is expected to decide not the state's educational policy, but only whether the state is adhering to that policy. And because the plaintiffs demand an adequate education, rather than just more money, the plaintiff may be freed from establishing the link between money and a better education. This, too, can be left to educational experts and the legislature; the experts decide what changes are required to provide an adequate education, and the legislature is then obliged to appropriate the funds necessary to accomplish it.

The greatest strength of the adequacy claim, however, is its potential in the remedy stage to bypass the usual focus on reallocating money in favor of directly altering the institutional structures of education to improve the school performance of the most disadvantaged. Two models of reform—the class integration model and the whole state reform model—offer the possibility of an enduring remedy to education inadequacy.

The first, class integration, is fashioned from education research that has determined that the quality of education plunges in schools where the percentage of poor students rises above a particular threshold. Poor students perform better when studying among students who are not poor; and students who are not poor do worse studying among those who are. This discovery has led to reform approaches designed to relieve the heavy concentration of poor students in certain schools—in ways that could prove more politically palatable than one might first think. These approaches preserve local financing and local control. They include financial and educational incentives for enticing wealthier students to attend previously high-poverty schools, and enticing wealthier schools to accept students from high-poverty schools. Moreover, they would appear to require a more modest financial remedy than equity claims. All these elements should enhance the appeal of a class integration approach to improving education, particularly when the educational research strongly supports the efficacy of such an approach.

The whole state remedy is appropriate in circumstances where virtually all the state's schools are inadequate and underfunded. Here the remedy requires not just increased funding, but relies on those who have expertise in education to develop and implement the programs that will use that funding to improve education. The remedy is only in part about finance, and in greater part about reforming the educational system to deliver a better product. The adequacy claim, by focusing judicial and legislative attention on the lack of education received by students rather than inequities in funding, is likely to create a more enduring political commitment to large-scale funding than if reform is limited to pouring money into schools perceived as mismanaged and impotent.

Adequacy claims elevate the role of educators in school finance litigation. Educators, to begin with, leave their imprint on the adequacy claim by defining the standards used to measure adequacy. But they must also play a central role in construction of a remedy, establishing for the legislature the link between greater resources and greater achievement, whether the resources are measured in money or middle-class students or effective classroom programs. Neither the judge, nor the public, nor public officials will accept the obligation of a changed system and greater financial investment unless the plan is endorsed by respected educational researchers and practitioners.

This chapter argues implicitly for a greater role for educators in school finance litigation as it describes the legal structure of American education; documents its inequalities; traces the evolution of school finance reform litigation; and reviews three proposed school finance remedies. The chapter contends that of all the possible approaches, adequacy claims based on the state education clause—claims that seek a class integration remedy where weak schools are surrounded by wealthy schools, or a whole state remedy where the state's schools are uniformly weak, and are prepared with intense and ongoing collaboration with professional educators—represent the best combined opportunity for a victory in the courtroom that calls forth a remedy that is both politically and financially feasible, and—most important—has the greatest likelihood of making a durable difference in the quality of education offered to those least served by the current system.

ENSURING INEQUALITY: THE LEGAL STRUCTURE OF AMERICAN EDUCATION

Lawyers must play a pivotal role in addressing the unequal distribution of education if only because it is the law that has created the unequal distribution. Three distinguishing features of the American school finance system ensure inequality: First is the federal unwillingness to equalize resources between states, and instead its tendency to exacerbate resource inequalities through unfunded mandates that, in effect, require school districts to elevate the educational needs of "special" students (who are not evenly distributed among or within the states). Second is local control of schools, which means that the majority of the decisions that affect level of curriculum, hiring, and most important, the funding of schools are made not by the federal or state government, but by over 15,000 school districts with dramatically different levels of local wealth and student needs. Third is the existence of private and parochial schools, which—although they receive various forms of state subsidies—offer an educational option only to children whose families are willing and able to pay the tuition (with exceptions for scholarships). Whatever their merits, an undeniable demerit of these features is a school finance system that guarantees an unequal distribution of education within and among the states. Unfunded federal mandates that affect local districts unevenly, a state legal structure that delivers education on a geographical basis, and an alternative system for the relatively wealthy reflect—rather than remedy—existing societal inequalities, and thus lock in a legal structure for American education that is unequal for all and inadequate for many.

The greatest assault on this legal structure has been led by lawyers who sought the help of the federal courts in ending racial segregation in public schools. Desegregation lawsuits succeeded, in some cases, in redrawing district and school lines, and thus to some extent equalizing resources. But the effort to desegregate schools has largely stalled and in some cases its results been dismantled under unsympathetic judicial decisions, leaving the present-day wave of state-based school finance litigation as the most promising—if not the only—effort afoot to alter the inherent inequality in the legal structure of American education.

A Primer on the Legal Structure
for Delivering Education

There are almost as many variations in legal structure for school systems as there are school districts and more laws that affect schooling than can usefully be described here. But the basic legal structure of the American elementary and secondary school system has been both fairly uniform and basically unchanged since the 1800s, when states enacted compulsory schooling laws and established locally controlled districts providing free public schooling from kindergarten through grade twelve.

FEDERAL LAW

Schools are not financed or managed at the federal level: that is the central fact and feature of education delivery in America. Instead, responsibility for both financing and structuring schools has been left to the states. The federal government since the 1980s has contributed only a small portion of elementary and secondary school funding—barely 6 percent;[11] and for the most part the federal government has not issued guidelines to govern schools in their choice of curriculum, standards, or even in their use of federal funds.

The largest federal spending program, with appropriations of $6.6 billion in 1993, is Title I (also known as Chapter 1).[12] Started in 1965 as Title I of the Elementary and Secondary Education Act, it provided grants for elementary and secondary school programs for children of low-income families, with the aim of making educational spending and attainment more equal throughout the United States.[13] But the same political forces that shape and preserve the current legal regime also shaped Title I, turning it, in effect, into a pork barrel program with funds for every congressional district, and thereby turning federal funds intended to be more or less equalizing across states and districts into payments that were more or less equal across states and districts.[14] As of 1993, approximately 90 percent of the nation's school districts and 71 percent of all public elementary schools received Title I funding.[15] In addition, because of the complex funding formula, many schools with high poverty levels and many low achieving children do not receive any money, while less needy schools do.[16] In 1994 renewed attempts were made to concentrate the funds in the poorest, least successful school districts.[17] But even these efforts, while clearly enhancing educational funding for some poor children and thus reducing the fiscal inequities among states—are too small to have a substantial impact on the structure of education financing.

Without sufficient federal aid to compensate areas with fewer resources, the state-based finance system guarantees different resource levels. The wealthiest districts in Alaska and New York spent more than $25,000 per pupil at the same time the poorest district in Texas spent only about $1,200 per pupil.[18] Mississippi does not have the wealth of Massachusetts, and as long as school funding is state-based, schoolchildren in Mississippi will not have the same access to educational resources as children in Massachusetts.[19] And the disparity in educational resources mirrors a disparity in educational attainment. The percentage of high school dropouts, as well as college graduates, varies state to state by as many as ten percentage points,[20] average scores on the Scholastic Aptitude Test vary between states by over one hundred points, and the average proficiency in math by over twenty percentage points.[21]

The most significant federal law affecting the primary and secondary education system is the Individuals with Disabilities Education Act (IDEA) and related laws establishing the educational rights of handicapped children.[22] The IDEA requires, in part, that schools provide all children with disabilities "a free appropriate education which emphasizes special education and related services designed to meet their unique needs."[23] The extra effort by the school district to ensure this "free appropriate education" can be as cheap as taping classes for an ailing student who is home sick for en extended period or as steep as covering the cost of a private education at a special facility.[24] To ensure enforcement, the Act details extensive due process guidelines, protects parents' rights to participate in the decisions affecting their child's education program, and requires that each year the local school district develop an Individualized Education Plan with educational and behavioral goals tailored to each child.[25] Parents can enforce these requirements through a state administrative process, and—if still unsatisfied—by suing in state or federal court.[26]

Like Title 1, the IDEA is a funding statute, which means, theoretically, that the state is free to ignore the act's guidelines if it is willing to forgo the federal funds. However, much of the act's mandates, including the most important substantive requirement of providing a free appropriate education for all handicapped children, are already enacted in Section 504 of the Rehabilitation Act of 1973 and other federal laws.[27] Because the federal mandates for much of IDEA's provisions already existed, there was nothing to dissuade all fifty states from accepting the funding and the attached strings.[28] The federal funding, however, does not come close to paying for the cost of the federally mandated special education. Under the IDEA, the federal government was supposed to provide 40 percent of the national average per-pupil expenditures in elementary and secondary schools for each student receiving special education services in a state.[29] In practice, the federal payment has never reached even 13 percent (in fiscal year 1980), and in the 1990s has paid between 7 and 8 percent.[30]

Even that limited funding, however, overestimates the percentage of the cost actually paid by the federal government: special education costs more than the average per-pupil expenditures.[31] Average costs in 1989–90 dollars range from $1,000 per pupil for students with speech or language impairments to over $30,000 per pupil who is deaf and blind.[32] Overall, the estimated national average per-pupil expenditure for regular education in 1990–91 was $5,266, while the estimated national average expenditure per special education pupil was $12,112.[33] Extrapolating from these figures, special education programs in the 1990–91 school year served 4.8 million students with disabilities at a price tag of $58 billion—$33 billion above the cost of providing a regular curriculum.[34] Of that $33 billion, the federal government paid less than $2 billion, approximately 6 percent of the additional educational cost, and 3.5 percent of the total educational cost.[35] The remaining $31 billion, or 94 percent of the federally mandated expense, was borne by the states and the local school districts.

This law aggravates an already unequal distribution of education among states. It practically assures that a nonspecial education student in a state with a high population of special education students will have more education funding diverted from his or her instruction than will a nonspecial education student in a state with a low population of special education students. Students in special education programs are more likely to be African American, have a family income of less than $25,000, have a household head that is not a high school graduate, and live in a one-parent household.[36] Such students are not uniformly dispersed throughout the nation, and some states bear a greater financial burden.[37] Moreover, the federal government does not calibrate its aid to the actual type, cost, or duration of special education services provided by the state, so while the federal government bears 6 percent of the overall cost of the mandate, the states who incur higher cost may get lower relative assistance.[38] For example, the 1994 federal allocation per pupil in New York State was only $300, a mere 2 percent of New York's total average in-district per-pupil cost of approximately $14,000.[39]

The final federal legal piece that plays an important role in creating educational funding inequities is the requirement for bilingual education or English as a second language for children who have limited English proficiency (LEP students). Title VI of the Civil Rights Act of 1964 and the Equal Educational Opportunities Act of 1974 are the primary bases for the federal requirement that school districts take appropriate action to overcome language barriers.[40] These laws do not provide the particularized requirements and due process rights of the IDEA, but parents can sue to enforce the requirements.[41] Federal funding for educating LEP students began with the Bilingual Education Act of 1968. However, as with the IDEA, federal funding has not kept pace with the demand. In the past decade, funding for the key federal program directed to LEP students decreased by 40 percent, while the number of eligible students increased by almost 26 percent.[42] In 1990–91, the last year the Department of

Education issued a report to Congress, the federal government, under the Bilingual Education Act, was covering the cost of educating only 251,000 of the more than 2.3 million LEP students.[43] The cost for the remaining children was left to the states and to local districts. This created an unequal burden, as students with limited English proficiency are also not uniformly dispersed throughout the country.[44] Forty-six percent of the students in the Los Angeles school district are nonnative English speakers.[45] In New York City the number is 15 percent. In the Charlotte, North Carolina, school district, only 2 percent of the students have limited English proficiency.[46]

The failure of the federal government to meet its funding commitment has not released the state and local school districts from their legal obligation to provide a free appropriate education to special education students or non-English speaking students.[47] Because there is no equivalent federal right to an appropriate education for nonspecial education students, the IDEA, and to a lesser extent the Bilingual Education Act, are a federally mandated priority for special programs. To comply with the law, a school district must first allocate in its budget the cost of an appropriate education for its special education and bilingual children and then apportion the remainder of the budget to serve the remainder of the students. The predictable result of this law, and the growing number of LEP and special education students, is that a greater share of elementary and secondary school spending over the past twenty years has been allocated to special needs leaving a shrinking share available for nonspecial education.[48] With both special education and English as a second language children concentrated in certain states, nonspecial education students in those states are unequally affected.

STATE LAW

Outside the federal requirements for special education and compensatory aid, the basic legal structure of schooling in the United States—all the decisions as to the selection of teachers, the nature of the curriculum, the length of school year, the money appropriated, and the tax rate levied—is left to the states. States, however, delegate an extraordinary amount of this authority to the 15,000 local school districts.[49] All states but Hawaii divide their territory into geographically based school districts which are entrusted with the power and the responsibility to run the schools.

In almost all states, school districts are required to educate all the students whose parents or guardians live within the geographic boundaries. Usually students are permitted to attend other public districts for the price of tuition. However, admissions decisions are left to the discretion of the district, which is legally obligated first to meet the needs of the students living within its borders. As a result, the number of students permitted to transfer is limited.[50] In addition, the government usually provides free transportation only for students attending their own districts' schools.

A defining feature of these local districts is their power to levy taxes on real estate within their district and use the taxes to fund the schools. Because no state draws its school district boundaries to equalize the value of property in each district, districts are able to raise differing amounts of money for their schools. Property-rich districts can finance abundantly with low property taxes; property-poor districts can provide inadequate finances even with high taxes. For example, in Arizona, the least wealthy district has $749 in taxable property wealth per pupil, while the wealthiest school district has an assessed property value per student of $6.5 million.[51] Assessed valuation per pupil in Nebraska for the ten poorest school districts averaged $46,814 per student, while the ten wealthiest districts assessed tax bases with an average of over $2.7 million per pupil.[52] Most states have no cap on the amount of money that can be raised locally, although some do have caps on the rate of property taxes. While a cap on the rate does limit local spending, it will not equalize it; if all districts tax themselves at the cap, property-rich districts will still produce more revenue (and higher per-pupil expenditures) than property-poor districts.[53]

Providing public education through a geographically based structure also means that the inequities in residential housing are reflected in schools. Most of the neighborhoods in the United States are segregated by class and race. Because financing of schools is based substantially on the value of real estate in the school district, many families have been able to send their children to better schools by buying homes in residential areas with a high ratio of land value to number of school-age children. This high ratio is a cachet for residential communities and is maintained through zoning and covenant restrictions that keep land values high by limiting the supply of new housing, and keep the school-age population low by limiting intensive residential uses of land such as apartments.[54] Poorer families are segregated into neighborhoods with the opposite ratio. The result is highly class-segregated school districts: middle-class students attend school with middle-class students, and poor children attend school with other poor children. Children who attend these high-poverty schools suffer severe educational disadvantages; by every measure of educational achievement and success, they do worse than their counterparts who attend schools with wealthier students.[55]

In an effort to address funding disparities, all state governments make supplemental appropriations to local school districts. In the 1970s, states began to assume a greater and greater share of education funding, peaking at just under 50 percent in school year 1986–87. By school year 1992–93, however, the average state share had dropped to 45.6 percent of school funding, with the local government covering 47.4 percent, and the federal government providing the balance.[56] The amount of state funding is usually inversely proportional to the property wealth of the district.[57] In these cases, the purpose is to supplement the funding of property-poor districts and those with greater student need and move the state's districts toward greater equality. However, in no state does the supplemental funding actually eliminate spending inequalities.[58] In fact, in a few states where funds are allocated without regard to local wealth, the supplemental funding may aggravate inequality. This persistent difference in financing capability leads to wide district-by-district differences in per student spending and to wide differences in student achievement.[59]

STATE AND FEDERAL LAW: SUSTAINING AND SUBSIDIZING
A PRIVATE SCHOOL SYSTEM

The last important piece in the legal structure of education is the explicit inclusion of a parallel private school system. The state compels students to attend school (but does not make them attend *public* school), accredits and approves private schools, and permits private schools to deny admission as they choose (unless that choice is based on an illegal criterion such as race). The government also provides a myriad of subsidies to private schools from funding private school transportation, lending textbooks to private school students, providing remedial programs to parochial students on public school premises, granting tax deductions and credits for private school tuition, and reimbursing private schools for the cost of state-imposed examinations.[60] The state also subsidizes nonprofit private and parochial schools through exemptions from property, sales, payroll, and other taxes. This parallel, state-subsidized system offers a slice of the school-age population (those from families who can afford the taxes to support the public schools as well as the tuition of the private schools) an option for attending a school other than the one they are assigned to by law.[61] If standardized test scores can serve as a measure of student achievement, this alternative private schooling system offers these children of the relatively well-to-do a superior education,[62] and the availability of a superior education to a small sector of society aggravates the educational inequality created by current federal and state public school financing regimes.

The Desegregation Challenge

The biggest legal threat to this structure of public school finance was the flurry of lawsuits in the 1960s and early 1970s seeking a court-ordered end to racially segregated schools. Federal litigation after *Brown v. Board of Education* gradually forced the elimination of the legally segregated school system in the former Confederacy. The remedies ordered by the federal courts were wide reaching, including redrawing district and school borders, restaffing schools, busing students to a school other than their neighborhood school, and stipulating racial quotas for each school's student body.[63] The federal courts also blocked "freedom of choice" programs that would have provided students with state-financed vouchers to attend private (segregated) schools.[64]

In the north and west, although school districts were not explicitly segregated by law, organizing schools by geographic district (in a nation with widespread residential segregation) also led to white and black school districts, particularly when coupled with explicitly segregative steps taken by school officials. In Detroit, for example, the racial divide of a predominantly black city surrounded by white suburbs was exacerbated by a city school board that had created and maintained "optional attendance zones" which allowed white students to avoid identifiably black schools, used busing to transport black children past nearby white schools to more distant black schools, designated attendance zones to minimize interracial conduct, and used school construction decisions to maintain the racial identity of schools.[65] In such cases, where litigants could show that government action played an explicit role in segregating schools, federal courts also ordered desegregation.[66]

Desegregation often had an equalizing effect on the distribution of education. Coupled with desegregation orders almost always came greater financial resources, in effect redistributing resources to the education of racial minority children.[67] Moreover, where litigation actually served to integrate the schools, the results appear to show improvement in educational achievement. Early studies of the effect of integration on academic achievement and later economic success were mixed.[68] But by the 1980s, more than a decade after the wave of desegregation lawsuits had begun, the positive results of integration seemed clearer. Nationwide, achievement scores for African American students had risen overall and relative to whites, and scores had increased more dramatically in the south, where court orders had done most to integrate schools.[69] More specifically, African American students attending desegregated schools improved their academic performance, when measured over the long term.[70]

If court-ordered desegregation had sustained the pace—or even preserved the gains—of the 1960s and early 1970s, the legal landscape of public schools might look completely different. Because African American students are poorer on average than white students, school desegregation would have dismantled the legal structure needed to sustain both the economically isolated as well as the racially isolated district school system. For the most part, however, desegregation stalled in the 1970s in the north and west, and has begun to be dismantled in the 1990s in the south.

In 1974, the Supreme Court in *Milliken v. Bradley* held that desegregation orders had to respect local district lines.[71] That voided a district court order requiring Detroit suburban schools to participate in a plan to integrate Detroit city schools. Allowing judges to order desegregation only within a district and not across districts immediately exempted most suburbs from any court order, and allowed city-dwelling whites to duck integration by moving to the suburbs, where realities of race and economics made it unlikely black families would follow.[72] The combination of the court doctrine in *Milliken* and the scorching political opposition to busing (which prompted jittery state and federal officials to drop the issue) ended virtually all new efforts at desegregation in the nation's northern and western cities, and these areas remained highly segregated.[73]

Although *Milliken* effectively derailed desegregation efforts in the United States, it did have one equalizing effect on the delivery of educational resources. On remand from the Supreme Court, the district court—now unable to order meaningful integration—ordered instead that the defendants, including the state of Michigan, spend money to develop educational programs within the Detroit schools that might aid in overcoming the vestiges of the prior discrimination.[74] This approach, approved by the Supreme Court in *Milliken II,* was followed in other cases where the prohibition against desegregation across school district lines, coupled with a high percentage African American population within a given district, prevented interracial reassignment of students.[75] The most celebrated example is the St. Louis desegregation case, *Jenkins v. Missouri.* There the district court (initially upheld by the Supreme Court) required the expenditure of several hundred million dollars from the state for capital improvements in Kansas City schools in an effort to make those schools comparable to the suburban (white) schools.[76]

Nonetheless, the scope of these remaining federal court desegregation efforts was too limited to alter significantly the prevailing school finance system. After *Milliken* there was no practical remedy for minority students concentrated in school districts with few white students; and that describes the experience of most minority students in the north and west.[77] The legal difficulties in proving intentional discrimination remained an important barrier to any successful desegregation lawsuit, and the removal of integration as a practical remedy in most of the north and west left litigants little to win, even if they won.[78] In the south, subsequent federal court decisions also stalled further desegregation efforts and actually permitted resegregation, as the Supreme Court in the 1990s limited the district court's ability to counter the effects of "white flight" on the integration remedy and offered local districts an easy route out of court supervision and desegregation programs.[79] And in the second *Jenkins v. Missouri* case in the Supreme Court, the Court restricted the compensatory remedies approved in *Milliken II*. It disallowed district court orders intending to woo white suburban schoolchildren into black urban schools, invalidated orders to raise salaries in the segregated district in order to keep and attract skilled personnel, and blocked district court efforts to examine test scores to ensure that the remedy was actually helping black children.[80]

SCHOOL FINANCE LITIGATION

Background

School finance litigation is the offspring of school desegregation lawsuits, born of the effort to make the legal structure for distributing education more hospitable to children of low-income (and overwhelmingly minority) families. As the momentum behind desegregation stalled, school finance litigation became the primary method for seeking equal educational opportunity. This litigation was a species of civil rights litigation which sought equality and integration in all sectors of public life.[81] The two movements were driven by the same theory, the same goals, and the same lawyers. As former Congressman Augustus F. Hawkins explained, "Equity in education is a political and ideological requirement, not an educational one."[82] Educators presented evidence of unequal education and its devastating economic and social impact, and lawyers—working from the ideal of equal treatment central to civil rights litigation—made the logical and legal connection between an unequal education and a constitutional violation.

School finance litigation began in earnest in the late 1960s and early 1970s under both the federal and state constitutions. But litigation under the federal constitution has been dormant since the 1973 Supreme Court case *San Antonio Independent School District v. Rodriguez.*[83] The case, brought on behalf of Texas schoolchildren, contended that the method of funding violated the federal equal protection clause because per-pupil spending was dramatically unequal and based on where the student lived. The plaintiffs won in the district court, but were reversed in the Supreme Court. In a 5–4 decision, the Court held that the Texas system was rationally related to the state's interest in local control of schools, effectively ending federal equal protection claims over financing based on property wealth. Since *Rodriguez,* some commentators have continued to insist that the federal constitution does provide a basis for state school finance reform, but no case has yet succeeded.[84] And with a politically conservative federal judiciary there seems little potential anytime soon for a court-declared federal right to a changed school finance system.

Plaintiffs basing their claims on state constitutions have been more successful. State school finance litigation attacks the statutory financing schemes on the basis of one of two provisions of the state constitution: the equal protection clause or the education clause. The dominant theory under both provisions has been the dominant legal theory in all civil rights litigation over the period: equality under the law.[85] The particular argument in school finance litigation is that the legal financing structure fails to provide an equal education to all the state's students, an obligation of the state under either the equal protection or education clause.

Prior to 1989, virtually every school finance case made its equity claim under the state constitution's equal protection clause.[86] Most state constitutions contain one or more provisions that either parallel the federal equal protection clause or have been interpreted to impose substantially the same limitations. But the doctrinal structure judges built around equal protection analysis made success difficult. Although states are not required to adopt the doctrinal tools of the federal courts in interpreting their equal protection clauses, most do.[87] As a result, state equal protection claims faced the same rigid analysis of federal claims: Inequalities in government treatment based on race or regarding a fundamental right are almost always unconstitutional; other inequalities are constitutional if the government can provide a rational reason. In school financing the rational reason is the legal structure of local financing which places a high value (in theory) on local control.[88]

Two state courts have held that the state's interest in local control is not even rationally related to the school finance scheme.[89] But most state courts have required litigants to show that education is a fundamental right like the right to vote, or that poverty is a suspect classification like race, which would require the state to meet a tougher standard in justifying the inequalities. In cases that succeeded, courts found education to be a fundamental right under the state constitution (in contrast with the federal) at least by partially relying on the inclusion in their state constitution of a right to a free public education.[90]

Most courts, however perhaps fearing the implications of such a finding, remained unpersuaded. Given the wide variety of minutia found in many state constitutions, it seemed that whatever basis justified extending fundamental status to education would justify extending it to an unmanageable number of human needs. Courts were also wary of voiding school finance statutes on the grounds that they discriminate on the basis of wealth, because it could subject any state program that involves a money classification to invalidation.[91] Similarly, if rational review means that courts do not defer to the legislative judgment but begin closely examining the link between the means and ends of all state programs—as they did in finding local financing an irrational means to fund local control of schools—little legislation would be safe from invalidation at the hands of an activist court.[92] Perhaps for these reasons, claims under state equal protection clauses have been less successful recently than those urging equity through the state education clause.[93]

Every state has an education clause in its constitution requiring the legislature to provide citizens with free public schools. Most of these include some language expressing standards for the educational system—the system must be "efficient" or "uniform" or "adequate," for example.[94] It is this language that is used by plaintiffs seeking school finance reform. Although the precise form of the argument may vary depending on the language of the clause, the plaintiffs' basic argument is that the education clause of the state constitution mandates some measure of equality that the state financing laws fail to provide, and perhaps cannot provide so long as they heavily rely on local property wealth.[95] This argument avoids the rigid doctrinal structure of the equal protection clause jurisprudence, and because the federal constitution has no parallel education clause, state courts had neither the obligation nor the prerogative to follow federal interpretation. Moreover, a decision under the education clause can be limited to education, without calling for a reformulation of a broad array of state programs.

The usual remedy sought in both education clause and equal protection claims is substantial equality of educational funding for all schoolchildren. Because school funding is based in part on local property taxes, it is inevitably unequal. If the litigants succeed in establishing that those inequities violate the state constitution, they generally seek a regime that does not depend on local property wealth.

The Pitfalls

School finance equity cases have succeeded by many measures. Plaintiffs have won nearly half of all cases; even the threat of lawsuits has, at times, led to school finance reform;[96] and most data indicate that the school finance regimes adopted under court order have generally led to more equitable funding. What successful school finance suits have failed to do, however, is translate success in the courtroom into success in the classroom. Instead, often after prolonged and bruising legislative battles, a somewhat more equitable funding system is devised, but for a variety of reasons even this system does not result in measurably greater educational achievement for low-income students. Ironically, it appears that the more plaintiffs succeed in weaning the school funding system from its dependence on local property taxes, the less money will be spent overall on education. The difficulties faced by plaintiffs in winning the cases, winning the right remedies, and turning those remedies into higher educational achievement for low-income students all flow from the theoretical and practical complications in the equity paradigm, difficulties that have often bedeviled other civil rights litigation as well.

THE WRONG: THE DIFFICULTIES INHERENT IN THE EQUITY PARADIGM

Although "equality" appears to be the clearest of standards, its precise application has confounded judges, lawyers, and commentators. Equity theories (in school finance and in civil rights cases generally) have traditionally stumbled when it comes to specifying equality of what? Equity may be framed in terms of equality of the education delivered, equality of education received, equality of funding, or equality of other inputs.[97] Each has weaknesses that have undermined plaintiffs' claims for equality and invited courts to leave the school finance decision to the legislature.

In its most straightforward form the equality requirement in school finance cases demanded equal funding: the state could not vary the amount of taxes spent on each child's education. Under this theory (which has powerful implications outside education) all citizens are entitled to the same amount of money spent on any government service. Individual students must be treated uniformly wherever they live and whatever the financial circumstances of their parents. The state itself is not permitted to create inequities. This seemingly simple notion of "one student–one dollar," however, has failed to appease any party to the litigation.

Plaintiffs generally oppose strict financial equality because it fails to consider the different needs of students. Equal funding of unequal needs is not true equality.[98] Districts with a high percentage of poor children, for example, often must spend far more money on special needs such as bilingual or special education than other school districts. The City of New York in 1994, for example, spent nearly twenty-two cents of every public school dollar on special education students.[99] The Greenburgh Central Seven School District in Hartsdale, New York, spends ten cents.[100] Eighty-one percent of the state's pupils with limited English proficiency attend New York City schools.[101] School districts in high poverty areas can suffer higher costs than their suburban neighbors in other areas also. School districts serving large percentages of poor students typically find it more difficult to staff their schools with qualified teachers, and need to provide greater economic incentives than wealthier districts to recruit and retain good teachers.[102] These school districts also need to compensate for the high mobility of students, unqualified and burned-out teachers, students with untreated serious health problems, developmental disabilities, hunger, family disruption, and violence.[103] They often have higher security costs. Their buildings are usually much older than in more recently developed suburban areas, and often in need of continuous expensive repairs; they are often overcrowded.[104] After these and similar costs are subtracted, the amount available to spend on an academic program for an eleventh grader, for example, is far less than what is available in a more affluent district, even if that district started out with the same per-pupil funding. Because of these greater costs, equal educational opportunity according to plaintiffs requires that more money be spent on poor students than on middle-class students.

Defendants, especially suburban school districts, often also agree that equality of per-pupil funding is a poor proxy for equality of education, but they come to that conclusion from the opposite direction. They point out that property-poor districts are often filled with poor children; studies show that poor children do less well academically, regardless of other factors, including money. Thus, defendants argue, poor children would not benefit from, and do not have the same need for, the expensive advanced college prep program needed in suburban high schools. They agree that equality depends on need, but argue that need should be measured not by a standard uniform measure across school districts, but by a demonstrated ability to make profitable use of educational resources.[105]

The problems that arise from defining equality of education as equality of per-pupil funding have encouraged plaintiffs to seek a definition of equality that takes into account the differing educational needs of the students, but that approach itself is greeted by pitfalls. From the earliest litigation, plaintiffs lost cases because courts were reluctant to try to fashion a remedy of meeting student needs. Defining what inputs a student would need in order to achieve an equal level of education struck courts as an issue incapable of being resolved in a principled judicial manner; they often concluded it was a policy question to be resolved in the legislature.[106] Some courts did tackle the issue by adopting the standard of equality of per-pupil expenditures,[107] but other courts were convinced by litigants and commentators that equalizing per-pupil expenditures would be unresponsive to the alleged constitutional wrong, and so instead found no constitutional violation.[108]

But those trying to base equality on some measure of equal education faced a related hurdle as well. Defendants in all finance cases contend that education gained does not correlate with money spent. Students might be promised an equal education under the state constitution, the argument goes, but the state cannot make that happen by providing equal funding. There is no sense pouring good money after bad into poor districts, because there is no evidence that equalizing funding would equalize education.

The argument has proved powerful because it is based on a germ of truth. It is undisputed that factors other than money affect the level of education attained by a student, most notably parents' education level, wealth, and involvement in schools.[109] It is also undisputed that while the amount spent on education over the past twenty years has increased substantially, it has not led to dramatic increases in any measure of educational attainment. Finally, specific input-output studies have often failed to find a correlation between money spent and various measures of academic success such as test scores.[110] The result has been a broad-based coalition (including education reformists sympathetic to the plight of poor districts) united behind the idea that spending more money on poor school districts will not improve education.[111] As a result of the lack of social science consensus, many courts have been predictably reluctant to declare funding inequalities a constitutional violation when they may be doubtful that certain state funding increases will make any difference in education.[112]

Another common measure of inequality—educational inputs—suffers from the same critiques. Plaintiffs frequently document extensive and striking evidence of the inequities in educational resources. Some districts in Arizona, for example, have indoor swimming pools, a domed stadium, specialty science labs, a television studio, 30,000-volume libraries, satellite dishes, and telephones in every classroom, while other districts have school buildings with leaky roofs, safety hazards, overloaded wiring, dirt playgrounds, and no libraries, science labs, computer rooms, art programs, gymnasiums, or auditoriums.[113] But proving inequalities in educational services—while apparently essential to any successful case—has been insufficient evidence for many judges that the education system is unconstitutional. It is not clear that the state system of unequal funding is the cause of the unequal inputs (rather than, say, administrative judgments and skills) or that constitutional equality requires equal class size or teacher salaries or facilities for students of different backgrounds or capabilities or that solving the unequal inputs will equalize the level of educational achievement.

The failure of any of these measures of equality to demonstrate a clear causal connection between government policy that guarantees unequal resources and an educational system that produces unequal results has tempted courts to leave the defining of an equal education system to the policy debates of the legislature.

THE REMEDY: POLITICS MEETS EQUAL EDUCATIONAL FINANCING

Winning in the courtroom is not the same as winning in the classroom. Because it is not the courts but the legislatures that ultimately establish and fund a school financing system, successful school finance litigation under state constitutions is a legislative process as well as a court procedure. State courts have been much less inclined to order radical measures than were federal courts in desegregation cases. State courts, even when holding for the plaintiffs, have been loath to clarify the full content of the rights they recognize, or to prescribe for state legislatures the remedial steps necessary to bring the school funding system into constitutional compliance. The courts' most common course has been to declare the system unconstitutional and send it back to the legislature to create a constitutional system, without the explicit guidance of the court. That put yet another hurdle in the path of the plaintiffs—converting successful litigation into successful legislation.

Equalizing school district expenditures can occur in only two ways. Money can be redistributed from the rich districts to poor districts until they reach the same level of spending, or rich districts may be allowed to retain their property tax money (perhaps with a cap) and general tax revenue (from a tax hike or budget reallocation) is redistributed to poor districts in order to supplement their property revenue. The realpolitik that dominates state legislatures hinders both options.

Voters in well-financed school districts and their legislators strongly oppose any effort at redistribution from their districts. Parents, educators, and public officials clearly believe that reducing the resources to their schools will impair the education of their children. They have an expectation that property taxes are "theirs" to be spent in their local community, not in the rest of the state. As property owners, they know that if the advantage of their school district over their neighbors is diminished, their property values will diminish as well.[114] Moreover, wealthier white voters often do not want their tax money redistributed to families of another race, who may be perceived as unwilling to support their own education.[115] These voters have proved to be a powerful constituency, and no state legislature has yet implemented a plan that fully equalizes spending by redistributing property taxes from rich districts to poor districts.[116]

The more common remedy is to preserve the basic district structure, but add supplemental funding for low-wealth schools to help them come nearer the spending levels of the wealthier districts. This remedy requires redistribution from other uses—either from private spending through higher taxes or from reallocations of the state budget.

State legislatures have concocted a complex array of school finance programs in an effort to get more money to property-poor districts without taking it directly from the property taxes of the rich districts. One method does not eliminate local financing but "power equalizes" it. The goal is to guarantee each district the same amount of money for local taxpayer effort. Local districts retain their power to set budgets and levy taxes, but the state gives an equalizing payment to the poorer districts so that every district in the state could raise the same number of dollars per student at whatever levy rate it sets.[117] Another common method is to have the state set an "equalization base" that is intended to provide a roughly equal per-pupil funding base for each district. If a district cannot fund its equalization base out of local property taxes at a uniform tax rate assumed by the state, then the state will make up the difference in the form of state aid to the district.[118] The per-pupil funding base is usually adjusted for special needs such as special education, transportation, desegregation, or migrant parents. Other states leave local financing alone, but supplement the poor districts with flat grants based on some measure of need.[119] Most states adopt a complicated mixture of these programs.[120]

These legislative responses to legal challenges (or threatened legal challenges) appear almost always to provide greater financial help to property-poor districts, at least for a time.[121] Even modest victories (such as the first round of legislative response in Arizona, which produced an additional $30 million for capital needs in poor districts) bring benefits that would not have been realized without litigation.[122] However, the patchwork of remedies usually brought on by litigation may—both in design and effect—do more to relieve the political pressure for equalization more than it achieves either equal funding or equal educational opportunity.[123]

While "power equalizing" and setting an "equalization base" make it easier for property-poor districts to raise local tax money, they do not equalize spending. Property-poor district residents often cannot or will not vote to increase their taxes.[124] A poor family may find a 1 percent property tax far more onerous than a wealthier family and be unwilling to pay the rate the suburban families will.[125] Moreover, many state equalization plans undercut their own effectiveness in a variety of ways: by permitting finance options outside the plan, creating proxies in their funding formula for student need that have no relationship to actual need, or by not including important expenses such as capital. For one or all of these reasons, equalization plans fail to equalize funding.

In addition, the complexity created by the blend of unequal funding and unequal need results in some remedies that may aggravate at least one measure of inequality. There is not a perfect match between low-income students and low-wealth districts. High-poverty urban districts often have valuable commercial and industrial property. These districts, which may be the least adequately funded districts in the state based on student need, may nonetheless have above-average per-pupil funding, and thus are harmed by efforts to equalize the tax base.[126]

The most important reason these partial measures fail to equalize spending, however, is that they always turn out to cost too much. Giving poverty districts funds "equal" to the wealthiest districts, especially after taking into account the greater need, is extremely expensive. In Massachusetts, for example, a wealthy state without gross disparities in school funding, a study done by the Federal Reserve Bank of Boston indicated that it would take $700 million annually in additional aid to bring the poorest one-half of the communities to the current statewide per-pupil average—a funding supplement that would require an immediate permanent across-the-board tax hike of over 5 percent.[127] And on average, Americans already spend generously on education—more than virtually all other industrialized countries both as a total per pupil and as a percentage of government expenditures.[128] In fact, in many states, poor school districts with highly needy students are funded at levels higher than the state average.[129]

However, even these generous spending levels are insufficient to bring disadvantaged students to an average level of educational attainment. In school district after school district, large funding increases have proved inadequate to overcome the educational disadvantages faced by poor, underachieving students.[130] Connecticut is an example. In the 1991–92 school year, the Hartford school district was first among all districts in the region in overall district expenditures per pupil. However, after subtracting the expenditures for special needs programs, actual per-pupil spending on regular academic programming—instructional services, textbooks, instructional supplies, library books, equipment, and plant operation—was far less in Hartford than the regional or state average; by one measure Hartford was 133rd in the state and last in the region. Despite the millions of dollars in state resources spent on the Hartford schools, students attending them had the lowest test scores and the highest dropout rates in the state.[131]

Seen against this backdrop, it is doubtful that any commitment to a sufficient increase in educational spending for property-poor school districts could be sustained by a legislature that must also address changing economic conditions, new emergencies, and the desires of a public whose attention shifts rapidly from issue to issue.[132] As a result, states often pass ambitious programs to equalize poor district funding and then underfund them, or just resign themselves at the outset to the fact that any politically feasible financing scheme will never fully equalize educational spending.[133]

Although state legislative response to school finance suits almost always involves some shift from local to state financing,[134] occasionally states have sought greater equalization through a more dramatic restructuring, where financing is shifted primarily from local property taxes to statewide taxes. This is done usually through some combination of capping the property tax rate, forcing districts to tax at a uniform rate, capping the amount that can be spent in wealthy school districts, and increasing statewide taxes such as the income tax, sales tax, and lottery. These plans have a more significant effect on distribution; they lead to more equal spending, as proponents would expect, but they also appear to lead to an unintended and undesirable consequence—a distribution of resources away from education to other state needs.

Two populous states, Michigan and California, provide examples of systems not based primarily on property wealth. California has one of the most equally financed school systems. At nearly the same time that the California Supreme Court in *Serrano v. Priest* required the state to reduce wealth-related disparities in per-pupil expenditures, voters passed Proposition 13, which severely capped property taxes.[135] As a result, California transferred most financing to the state level and financed per-pupil expenditures relatively equally.[136] The equalization effort has not been perfect; wealthy districts such as Beverly Hills still receive greater tax revenue and are able to supplement those revenues with monies from tax-exempt foundations set up to aid them, but the spending is far more equitable than it was.[137]

Michigan, formerly one of the more unequally financed states, has now (under the prodding of the anti–property tax movement rather than a school finance lawsuit) adopted a system that transfers most of the cost of schools to the state and is intended to lead to more equity in spending.[138] Here, too, there are exceptions for well-off districts, but the plan promises to result in greater equality in per-pupil expenditures than has previously been the case.[139]

Ironically, both school finance reform efforts, though relatively successful in equalizing funding, run the risk of redistributing resources from education to other budget priorities. California is now becoming the best argument against its own school financing approach—a case study of what happens when control over educational spending is shifted from the local to the state level (and equalized). California, eighth in the nation in per capita government spending, is now forty-sixth in the share of its income it spends on public education. Only seventeen states spend less per pupil on public education, and Mississippi is the only state with lower average reading proficiency scores.[140] While California has unusual demographics, those who fear the same result in other states have some basis for their fears; the limited empirical studies and theories of voter behavior warn of the same result.

Local governments are usually majoritarian governments—they are dominated by the interests of the majority of voters rather than special interest groups.[141] The great postwar suburban school systems were created in part by parents choosing to live in places with good school districts and willingly paying for it. At the same time, many urban areas became dominated by taxpayers who had little interest in public schools. This pattern continued from the 1950s until the 1990s, even as some cities enjoyed a resurgence. The gentrification of cities in the 1980s and 1990s occurred in part because the new urban dwellers had no interest in good public schools, and so had little interest in living in suburbia.[142] The result of all these demographic changes was the decline of the formerly superior urban schools and the rise of the formerly inferior (or nonexistent) suburban school systems.

Given these demographics, the shift from local direct financing to state financing is likely to lead to less money for the suburban districts. With locally

controlled financing, there are a number of factors that encourage high investment. School tax elections are an easy and uncomplicated method for reflecting
preferences. Voters directly choose whether they prefer to give their money to
the schools or keep it for themselves.[143] Families with children in the public
schools have a clear incentive to favor higher taxes. Their children benefit
directly, and their taxes are leveraged by the payment of other taxpayers with no
children. It is a more efficient use of their education resources to pay them in a
higher uniform tax rate than to give directly to the PTA or library or sports
team.

But even taxpayers with no children may have a strong economic reason to
support higher school taxes. While higher property taxes are generally reflected
in a lower market value of a house, good public schools lead to a higher market
value. In areas where good schools are scarce (neighboring districts are perceived as worse and there are few private schools), the property value enhance-
ment from a good public school system can outweigh the drop in value from
higher taxes.[144]

These incentives to invest in public schools are lost when school financing is
moved primarily to the state level. As a first step, the budgetary process becomes
far more complex. In any given year the legislature is choosing budgetary
priorities from within a fixed budget. Assuming a public choice model where
legislators act so as to be reelected and react to the special interests that have the
most clout, the success of education funding depends not on whether a majority of voters would approve it in a direct vote but on how powerful the
education lobby is compared with other interests competing for state dollars,
including advocates for prisons, highways, human services, state salaries, and
tax cuts.[145] It is unlikely that education will always win that battle. Moreover,
because antitax sentiment runs high, legislators are unlikely to vote for a tax
increase to pay for schools even if a majority of voters might have done so in a
direct vote.

The obstacles the state-level budget debate presents for educational funding
are compounded by what would likely be a diminished interest among the
electorate to pay higher taxes for education under this new funding scheme.
Taxpayers lose most of the advantage of higher taxes for education when
education funding is moved to the state level. Higher taxes no longer lead to
higher property values, thus removing any economic interest in higher taxes for
voters with no school-age children. Even for those with school-age children, the
link between higher taxes and education becomes far more attenuated. General
tax increases may produce very little difference in funding at the local school.

For a middle- or upper-class family, the efficiency calculation is now reversed. It is far better to pay money directly to the PTA—or a local foundation set up to benefit the public schools—than to vote for a statewide increase, because wealthier parents will almost certainly pay out more money in taxes than will return to them in appropriations.

This resistance to education taxes will be exacerbated if the public schools are perceived as declining. Although parents will be unable to move to find better public schools unless they are willing to leave the state, the state funding solution does not alter the private school alternative. As the difference in quality between public education and private education increases, more parents will abandon the public school system. Having opted out of the system, these parents are even less likely to support taxes to pay for the education of others.[146]

The very limited empirical data available seems to support these assumptions. Broadly, of the fourteen states where local financing makes up less than 30 percent of the total for elementary and secondary education, all but three (Alaska, Delaware, and Washington) spend less than the national average per pupil.[147] Specific studies of changes in school funding in the aftermath of equalization efforts inspired by school finance litigation are hampered by scarce data, but they too show that on average, states that adopt plans that reduce local funding inequalities tend to see lower than average growth over time in educational spending.[148]

All of which suggests that the California example is not an aberration. A movement away from property taxed local financing should lead to fewer total dollars spent on public schools. The beneficiaries of such a move are the wealthiest families who paid the majority of property taxes and now pay a lesser percentage of the more regressive sales taxes, liquor tax, lottery ticket returns, and relatively flat income tax that partially replace property taxes as the funding source.[149] Even these families with children are likely beneficiaries because they can afford either to send their children to private school or to move to the few remaining unequal districts, the Beverly Hills of the system. The poorest families may also benefit. If they live in property-poor districts, their schools will almost certainly receive more resources absolutely and in comparison with the formerly well-funded suburban schools. The poor families' tax rate is increased—the replacement taxes are more regressive than the property tax—but because they by definition have very little income anyway, it is almost certain that the gain to the schools will be greater than the amount of taxes they pay. Of course, the gain must be seen in light of the far greater needs of the poor, especially in urban school districts—needs that mean the average student will still have far less spent on his or her education than in a district populated by the middle class or wealthy.[150] But on balance, the shift is still likely a positive one for the poorest families, while the negative distributive impact falls on the middle class, who now pay a greater share of the more regressive taxes and attend inferior public schools.

In sum, the results of courtroom efforts to equalize spending and educational opportunity are disheartening. Equity claims are hard to win, and even when won are exceedingly difficult to implement. Past litigation efforts have succeeded in reducing funding disparities and generated more money for poor school districts, but they have not approached equal financing and seem to have had even less impact on the inequalities of educational opportunity. At their boldest, equalization schemes lead to the abandonment of local property wealth as a determinant of funding, but that result redistributes from the middle to the rich and poor, and from education to other state interests.

THE CAPACITY OF SCHOOL FINANCE LITIGATION TO ALTER EDUCATIONAL DISTRIBUTION

Despite these relatively modest results, school finance reform litigation is in the midst of a renaissance. Since 1989, supreme courts in twelve states have ruled on the constitutionality of their education finance systems, and over half of all states are now embroiled in litigation. The rising number of lawsuits may be due less to worsening inequalities than to an approach to school finance litigation that offers the promise of deeper and more enduring results. A confluence of ideas from law and education suggest an avenue for litigation that could transcend some of the conceptual complexities and political limitations of past cases. The greatest hope for improvement lies not in reallocating resources within a highly structured system, but in directly altering the institutional structures in order to improve the school performance of those who are disadvantaged.

The key to this change is the willingness of lawyers to adapt their theories of litigation to evolving theories of education. This approach requires lawyers to frame the lawsuit around education theory, rather than legal theory—on what works, rather than what is "equal."

The Wrong: The Adequacy Paradigm

Although the equity paradigm has dominated school finance litigation in the past, there has been a movement in scholarship—and the beginnings of a shift in the litigation—toward an alternative model, one that focuses not on equality but on the substantive right of every student to an adequate education. Adequacy arguments rely on the same state constitution education clauses as equity arguments. However, rather than focusing on the clauses' implications for equity, adequacy claims measure the level of educational services delivered and contend that those services are insufficient to satisfy the state's minimal constitutional obligations. The right seized upon and highlighted in an adequacy claim is not the right to an equal education, but the right to an adequate education—one that meets a particular standard. While courts in successful school finance cases have simultaneously addressed the inequities in school finance systems, since 1989 all but two have based their decision on an adequacy claim, and in three cases (Massachusetts, New Hampshire, and Idaho), the court has focused exclusively on adequacy arguments.[151]

Adequacy arguments were used in early school finance cases but little emphasis was given them by the plaintiffs, and they generally did not form the basis for court decisions.[152] The idea that adequacy might be an independent right of students was first suggested in the 1970s in Justice Powell's opinion upholding the constitutionality of the Texas schools in *Rodriguez,* where he distinguished the facts of that case from situations where the financing system might "fail to provide each child with an opportunity to acquire the basic minimum skills."[153] The federal claim was never successfully developed, but litigants recognized it as an additional basis for relief under state constitutions.

The early difficulty of adequacy claims lay in defining an adequate education. Courts, believing that defining educational adequacy was not within their sphere of competence, skirted the issue by adopting a definition of adequacy based on standards fixed by the legislature—number of classes for graduation, hours of instruction, courses offered—or by adopting a circular definition: The educational resources provided each school district by the legislature must be adequate.[154] Under these definitions, no student was denied an adequate education. Gradually, however, litigants and courts became more adept at finding measures that could provide a legally enforceable criteria of an adequate education.

A few state courts circumvented the difficulties in finding an objective measure of educational quality by meshing the adequacy and equality claims; they inferred a quality standard by comparing education among districts.[155] An educational system that precluded the students of poorer districts from competing in the same market and society as their peers could not, by definition, be providing an adequate education. Defining an adequate educational standard through comparison remains one of the most frequently used methods.

Some courts have also been willing to plunge into the definitional debate full force by inferring from their education clauses long litanies of skills that comprise an adequate education: "ability to appreciate music, art and literature, and the ability to share all of that with friends;"[156] "sufficient oral and written communication skills to enable students to function in a complex and rapidly changing civilization;"[157] "prepar[ation] for useful and happy occupations, recreation, and citizenship;"[158] "sufficient grounding in the arts to enable each student to appreciate his or her cultural and historical heritage."[159]

But for those who must seek a changed finance system from more prosaic courts, a more promising route is to define adequacy through the academic standards developed in the past decade. As part of growing alarm over the condition of America's schools, both states and the federal government began during the 1980s to define explicit standards for education. Now virtually every state has defined (through an elected branch of government, either the legislature or the state department of education) what standards a student should meet at various grade levels.[160] Some standards are highly elaborate and complete; others are described primarily in terms of passing a particular exam. But in all cases, the standards provide a voter-validated definition of minimum educational standards, which can provide a basis for an effective adequacy claim. With state standards in place, the court can defer to the political majority while still ordering a forceful remedy.[161]

The future promise of using state standards to define a constitutionally adequate education will depend on educators and legislators creating substantial and measurable content-based standards, and much of that work remains to be done.[162] By 1997, only one state court finding for the plaintiffs has been confident enough in state standards to rely exclusively on them for defining the constitutionally mandated adequate education.[163] But the growing political enthusiasm for standards suggests that in the future courts will have meaningful and explicit standards they can draw on. And political pressure should assure a high standard. Given widespread worries about low standards in U.S. schools, it would seem politically perilous for the legislature to inoculate themselves from lawsuits by creating low standards; no one wants to suggest that their state's students are entitled to only a mediocre education.[164]

The adequacy paradigm has a number of theoretical advantages over the equity paradigm. It can avoid the "equality of what?" dispute. Providing resources sufficient to help poor children reach the educational level mandated under the state standards will undoubtedly require greater spending on their behalf, but the litigants need not be stuck in the legal swamp of defining equality. Moreover, adopting state competency standards in lieu of sending the case back to the legislature for its determination of equity ends the basis for the legislative bargaining which favors wealthy school districts. A clear measure of achievement already defined by the legislature or department of education requires the legislature to create a system to meet the existing constitutional standard, but does not permit the creation of an ad hoc constitutional standard to meet the existing financing system. This result also puts courts in their more comfortable role of enforcing an educational norm created by the political majority rather than creating from the bench a norm that overrides the public choices reflected in the legislative process. Moreover, in some circumstances, adequacy standards can permit the court to order relief for poor districts without having to articulate a specific standard of educational achievement. In some cases, schools are so educationally deficient that they fail any measure of adequacy.[165] Although a court decision on this basis would be limited, it would give a clear mandate to the legislature to provide some relief to poor school districts. Finally, adequacy standards can lift the burden of proving that more resources will produce more education. The adequacy claim demands an output—the constitutionally guaranteed level of education—rather than any particular level of funding.[166]

The adequacy claim can be defined broadly or narrowly, depending on the circumstances in the state. If a majority of students at a majority of schools are failing to meet the adequacy standard, the court may find that the whole system is unconstitutional, as in the 1989 Kentucky case. If instead the majority of students at only a minority of schools are failing, the court may find that only a set of schools are unconstitutional, as in the 1990 New Jersey case. Or adequacy may focus on one aspect of schooling, inadequate capital in poor districts for example, as in the 1994 Arizona case.[167]

Adequacy claims are powerful, but not perfect. They still permit children of wealthy parents to maintain an educational advantage using public resources;[168] they risk, if the standard is defined too low, providing little benefit to poor children; and they may well, as Peter Enrich argues, surrender the moral high ground of equality for all.[169] But the advantages of adequacy claims in making a theoretical case for change and offering an effective remedy suggest they may hold more promise for equalizing the distribution of education than do equality claims.

The Remedy: Structural Shifts
in Delivering Education

The most common remedy requested under an adequacy claim is more funding for inadequate school districts. While a close cousin of the equity remedy, the adequacy remedy requires bringing all districts up to an acceptable educational level, rather than eliminating differences caused by unequal property wealth. This focus has at least two political advantages. First, the notion that every student should have an adequate education is more appealing to the public, and thus to judges and legislators, not only because it seems "just" in a democratic society, but also because it conjures up none of the fears of widespread "dumbing down" or leveling that equity claims can bring.[170] Second, although as a practical matter the wealthy will likely have to bear some of the cost of raising the level of education in poor districts, it does not require them to do so by diminishing the resources currently enjoyed by wealthy districts. Under adequacy claims, districts remain free to exploit their local property wealth in pursuit of educational excellence.

While adequacy claims sidestep some of the political pitfalls of equity claims, there remain important limitations—the limitations that arise from trying to solve the inadequacy of education by agitating for more money. States that have made efforts to raise their schools to a meaningful level of adequacy have found that it carries an enormous price tag.[171] Good intentions to support educational adequacy can erode as other demands compete for limited tax resources, and the relatively well-to-do reach a limit in their willingness to pay for the education of other people's children. That limit comes when the public discovers that their additional taxes cannot make schools adequate in especially poor districts—even when that money is targeted at compensatory educational programs to aid disadvantaged students. Thus, while the usual adequacy remedy should face less political resistance than equality remedies, plaintiffs still face formidable financial barriers to bringing students at very poor schools to a meaningful level of educational achievement.

More significant than the possible financial implications of adequacy claims, however, are the more radical remedies that can accompany them—remedies that go beyond redistributing resources to altering the basic legal structure for distributing education. These remedies that restructure education have arisen because of the political barriers that block efforts to redress inequities solely by redistributing dollars. Among these barriers are the fact that states are reluctant to undertake a large-scale redistribution from other revenue needs or from rich districts to fund poor districts; that states who eliminate local property tax as the primary source of revenue can experience reduced educational spending overall; and the fact that a prohibitive amount of money—under the current educational structure—is required to bring a chronically poor student body up to the level (in education or in spending) of a typical suburban district.

Seeking a path of less resistance, litigants and scholars have developed three models for fundamentally restructuring how school services are delivered that avoid many of the barriers that beset other reform efforts. Each model could serve as part of a court-ordered remedy in an adequacy lawsuit, or as part of the plan adopted by the legislature in response to a court order. The three options are not equally effective. The first, the choice model, has some advantages over existing financing efforts but may exacerbate the inequalities and inadequacies of the current educational delivery system. The next two, class integration and whole state reform, both have the potential to improve the situation of under-educated schoolchildren, but are useful in different contexts. Class integration is preferred for states where the schools on average provide a good education to students, but particular high-poverty school districts do not.[172] Whole state reform is appropriate where the entire state system is generally providing an inadequate education.

THE CHOICE MODEL

One approach to reform that enjoys rising popularity in certain scholarly and political circles has been tagged with the appealing label of "school choice." School choice first rose to public prominence in the 1970s as a method for avoiding public school desegregation orders in the south, although it had its advocates much earlier. It enjoyed a renaissance in the 1980s and 1990s under both the Reagan and Bush presidencies and continues to enjoy substantial political and scholarly support. In its most ambitious scheme—providing public funds in the form of a voucher that a child could use to attend any school that will accept him or her—school choice fundamentally alters the educational delivery structure.[173]

School choice could play a role in a school finance litigation, either as a court-ordered remedy or as the solution adopted by the legislature. Plaintiffs in *Jenkins v. Leininger* and *Arviso v. Dawson,* for example, urged vouchers as the court-ordered remedy.[174] Because the state failed to provide an adequate education in the public schools the plaintiffs attended, they sought a remedy that would pay their way to any private or public school that was providing an adequate education. On a broader scale, proponents of school choice have argued that replacing the current district system with a system of school choice would unleash market mechanisms to guarantee an adequate education for all. Under the current system, it costs significantly more (in most cases prohibitively more) for students to attend a school other than their assigned public school; as a result, public schools can attract students even if they do not provide the type and quality of education that families want. With vouchers, parents and students would enjoy alternatives they cannot now afford; if a school failed to provide an adequate education, students could take their voucher and go elsewhere. This would ensure an adequate education for all in two ways: the child who moves gets a better education by attending the new school, and his departure sends a warning that the old school will not be able to remain in business if it does not improve its performance.[175]

School choice suffers the disadvantages of statewide funding schemes discussed above: voters who do not have school-age children would have a reduced incentive to support state funding, funding would have to compete with other statewide priorities, and voters would have less control over the legislature than the local school board. Nonetheless, school choice has several advantages over the typical financing scheme and manages to avoid many of the pitfalls of past school finance remedies. Under a statewide voucher system, local property wealth would cease to be a factor in a student's educational opportunities; and the disadvantages of statewide financing are partially offset by the fact that parents would again have a strong incentive to support greater spending on education. Any increase in funding for schools under the voucher plan goes directly to the student's aid to be spent at the school. Parents gain the value of the increase for their children but share the cost with other taxpayers. Vouchers would also provide an immediate improvement in education to many schoolchildren who could change schools without having to wait for their neighborhood schools to change. Depending on how the voucher amount was calculated, the plan might also duck the wrath of resistant suburban school districts. If the voucher was set at what suburban schools spend per pupil, so that the schools lost no revenue, the districts and parents would have less reason to resist vouchers than they would an equalizing scheme that reduced their spending. They also have little to fear from competition. The plan would lock in suburban advantage by denying the urban and rural schools the extra dollars it would take to lure away higher-achieving students from suburban schools—giving powerful suburban interests fewer reasons to resist the plan.

Despite these advantages, however, school choice is a poor remedy for an adequacy claim in school finance litigation. Unless the remedy is carefully crafted, the distributive change would tend toward more class and race stratification, aggravating the distributional inequities of the current system. Moreover, it seems to work directly against the attainment of an adequate education for the most disadvantaged.

The irony of the school choice model is that it requires two components that are not in adequate supply: committed and interested parents, and empty desks in high quality public or private schools. The voucher plan depends on disgruntled parents removing their children from inadequate schools and placing them in better schools. This is supposed to have two beneficial results: the children who move get a better education in the different school, and the children who remain get a better education because competition rouses the teachers and administrators to improved performance. For either of those beneficial results to occur for disadvantaged children, the parents must be willing to take an active and knowledgeable role in their child's education. For a child to transfer to a better school, the parents must investigate all available options for their child. Then they must pursue whatever process is necessary to have the child enrolled and transported daily to the new school. For the loss of students to improve in the old school, there must be some risk that students will leave in sufficient numbers to close the school. If there is not a legitimate threat of widespread defection, the school will have no more incentive to change than it does now. To create a legitimate threat requires that a substantial number of parents in bad schools have the time, energy, and education to place their children in different schools. Unfortunately, there is a great deal of evidence since at least the Coleman report in 1966 that one factor that puts poor children at an educational disadvantage is that their parents lack the time, motivation, or education to get involved in their children's education.[176] It is difficult to see how these children will benefit by a shift that makes their education even more dependent on their parents' efforts.[177]

In fact, vouchers seem less likely than the current system to improve the ineffective schools. One way to produce change is the market mechanism proposed by voucher proponents—enough people abandon the system to prod reform. Another method is working for reform within the current structure. Parents of some poor children do, of course, take a very active interest in their children's education. If they have not already been able to move their child into special programs or schools in their school system, their only current option is to work to improve the school their child attends. This effort inures to the benefit of the other children whose parents are free-riding on the interested parents' efforts. With a voucher program, these interested parents can trade "voice for exit."[178] That is, they will be able to move their children to schools that require less work for the parents and a better education for the child, removing an important voice for reform from the departed school. The children left behind now attend a school that has a diminished supply of what experts agree is a crucial element of success—concerned parents willing to agitate for change. They may also have lost the most successful students, the role models that many think are crucial to achievement. Thus, whatever disadvantage children suffer because their parents are not involved is exacerbated by the removal of children whose parents are involved. Unable to exit themselves, they now are left with no one to champion their cause within the school system either.

There is more to this view than theory. For the past decade or so, urban school systems in the United States have been conducting an unplanned experiment in school choice. Most major city school districts in the nation have some type of districtwide "magnet schools" in an effort to promote racial integration. Many poor parents go to great lengths to enroll their children in these extraordinary educational programs. These magnet schools also entice white, middle-class children to remain in the system and further integration.[179] But the fact that the best students with the most energetic parents exit neighborhood schools for magnet schools does not improve the lot of those left behind.[180] Neighborhood schools in urban areas left filled with poor children are not—by almost any measure—providing a better education than they were prior to the magnet programs.

Those proposing school choice as a remedy for inadequate schools claim that it provides the biggest benefit to the children who are most disadvantaged;[181] they dismiss the contrary evidence by arguing that existing experiments, including magnet programs, do not improve the remaining schools because the programs limit school transfers. As a result, most students do not have a feasible exit option, and there is little incentive for schools to change their ways. Clearly, current examples of school choice affect a small group of children. The problem for any realistic voucher program, however, is exactly the same: the supply of alternative placements is modest. Existing private and successful public schools are not sitting empty waiting for thousands of students from poor schools to flood in. As economic theory indicates, if a substantial number of customers have no realistic alternative, the market will not force improvements.[182] The private school system in the United States is not constituted to absorb any meaningful number of public schoolchildren. There are currently only 24,690 private schools with a total enrollment of 4,673,878, as compared to 84,538 public schools with 41,217,000 students.[183] If parochial schools are excluded from the voucher program—probably still a constitutional necessity[184]—the number of eligible private schools dwindles to 4,483 schools, currently serving 649,414 children.[185] Even if the voucher system unleashed a flood of investment in nonsectarian private education—doubling the number of schools, for example—it could still serve only 3 percent of the current public school population. But even that meager goal may be far-fetched. Doubling the private school enrollment would take time and substantial amounts of capital (most of it from investors who expect a financial, not an educational return). But as private school failures suggest, it is difficult and financially risky to create a school from scratch. Add to that the risk that the legislature (up for election every two to four years) might change its mind about vouchers in general, or the level of funding, or the requirements for receiving voucher students, and the investment becomes even less attractive. In that climate, it is questionable whether a voucher program could expand the private school market to the point where a meaningful number of public schoolchildren could attend.[186]

Of course, existing private schools could expand their space to admit more students, but their financial or educational incentive to do so is unclear. The prime benefit most private schools sell is the promise of an intimate atmosphere where each child is known, with small classes, hands-on learning, opportunities for parental involvement, and exceptionally dedicated teachers.[187] All that is put at risk by a dramatic increase in student population.

Without recourse to private schools, students attending bad public schools could use their vouchers to attend better public schools. But this avenue also is blocked by inadequate supply. Many states already permit their school districts to accept students from other places, and good public schools already turn away students who wish to pay and attend.[188] These districts have no reason under the current system or the proposed voucher system to expand their programs in order to absorb a significant number of poor children from bad public schools. Even if these students would pay their own way, it is unclear what benefit a school could hope for in admitting more children. To the contrary, current educational theory suggests that smaller schools with fewer students are necessary to ensure a quality education.

The limited supply of high quality public and private schools prevent vouchers from being the quick and easy fix championed by advocates. To have a chance of success, voucher proponents would have to lure major financial investments to build and expand schools on the promise of profit to the private sector, and a promise to the public sector that a greater number of new choices in the future could improve education, even though a limited number of new choices in the past has not.

Importantly, however, even if all these predictions are wrong, school choice, unless well targeted, is still the wrong remedy for an adequacy claim. The incentive structure of the voucher system encourages class and racial stratification, furthering rather than remedying the harm alleged in the school finance litigation.

The most common voucher systems proposed are those that give students a choice of which school to attend, give schools a choice of which students to admit, and allow schools to charge more than the value of the voucher. But this structure preserves the system of incentives that have led to the current inequalities—offering every reason to believe that this system will aggravate educational inequalities and further weaken educational opportunities available to the poorest children.

The current structure—typified by good suburban and private schools surrounded by inferior and inadequate urban and rural schools—is, ironically, a problem caused by choice. Students and their families are permitted to choose their schooling by enrolling in a private school or moving to another district. As the current system indicates, most American parents prefer to send their children to schools occupied by others of roughly at least the same class and race, and they express that preference through their choice of residence or their choice of a private school.[189] The result of these choices has been a vastly unequal educational delivery system, providing an inadequate education to the most disadvantaged.

But the stratification of race and income that results from these choices is tempered by certain constraints on school choice that tend to keep middle-class students in lesser schools, or lower-income students in better schools. For example, there is a strong incentive for parents to choose public schools—even if a private school provides the type and quality of education they prefer—because public schools are heavily subsidized. More significantly, under the current system, the choice of schools is a function of the choice of housing. Even wealthy districts usually have some housing that is cheaper—townhouses, scattered apartments, dilapidated housing, perhaps even a poor section of town—that allow poorer families to take advantage of the tax dollars of their wealthy neighbors, effectively getting more education than they can afford. Or, parents' desire to be in the best school district may be tempered by a need for proximity to work, or attraction to a particular house, or the nonschool amenities of a particular neighborhood. In other words, when the school decision is tied to the housing decision, people sometimes give up their school of choice, again with the result that a wealthier student may attend a school with less well-to-do classmates.

Vouchers, however, by eliminating both the subsidy for public education and the link between school choice and housing choice, thereby also eliminate two barriers to class and race segregation. Private schooling becomes an option for more parents because public schooling is no longer subsidized. And because the housing decisions are decoupled from the school decisions, families are free to choose the best school they are willing to pay for without sacrificing housing amenity. Conversely, families will no longer be able to use a cheap housing option to slip into a school district that provides an education costing beyond the state average. These changes would lead to the very system that voucher advocates propose—a free market for expressing consumer preferences—but the educational impact of that system would not lead to the educational quality (or equality) they have advertised.

In a market, wealthier households demand more of a commodity. When the supply consumed by any household is limited (a person can eat only so much meat and a child cannot attend unlimited schools), that greater demand is reflected in the higher quality commodity the wealthier family purchases.[190] If a meat lover has fifty dollars to spend on a meal, he does not order seven hamburgers, he orders one filet mignon. If vouchers succeed in transforming the education system into a private market, we should expect the same result as with any other commodity—wealthier people buy a higher quality product than poor people. Wealthy parents will be able pay a premium above the voucher amount to enroll students in the most expensive school.[191] Middle-class parents who do not have sufficient income or desire to pay for the top echelon school but who are still willing and able to pay more than the voucher amount will send their children to a middle-tier school. The students whose parents cannot or will not pay for a superior education will be amassed in the poorest, least well funded schools.[192]

Some have suggested that this tendency to stratify students by race and class could be corrected by prohibiting schools from charging more than the value of the voucher. However, even if the court or legislature prohibited schools from charging more than a set amount, stratification by family income would still occur. By giving students the freedom and resources to choose their schools, vouchers would quicken the competition among schools to recruit the best students, enticing candidates with evidence of impressive educational performance—test scores, graduation rates, college admissions, successful careers, and so on. Studies agree that students are more likely to do well on all these measures when they come from well-to-do and well-educated families. As a result, the single best way for a school to attain exceptional results no matter what program they are offering is to begin by admitting students from wealthy families. As long as school administrators have the option of enrolling students from wealthy families, they would be foolish (assuming their aim is a high-achieving student body) to choose students with no money and poorly educated parents. Schools marketing themselves as high-achieving will undercut their own efforts by accepting students whose paper background suggests a harder road to success.

In a functioning market, some schools would seek the "difficult youth" niche, taking children whose socioeconomic backgrounds do not suggest a future of high test scores. But that is precisely the stratification that creates the problem to begin with. The market system undiluted by the need to use housing as a proxy would be even more efficient at creating separate products for different socioeconomic backgrounds. And if—as the evidence suggests—socioeconomic background is a strong indicator of academic success, then poor children, clustered together in schools unable to recruit wealthier children, will continue to fall behind. This would aggravate current inequalities and inadequacies because it would replicate—in fact worsen—the current concentration of poor students in certain schools.

The primary beneficiaries of widespread school choice plans, then, appear to be well-to-do parents who currently send their children to private schools. Under voucher plans, they are at least partially reimbursed for their private school tuition. Other beneficiaries include children of middle-income or poor families who are attractive candidates for private or elite public schools but who could not under the old school finance regime afford private school tuition or the cost of moving to a better school district. Middle-income parents of children currently attending good public schools should be unaffected, unless the disconnect from local taxes leads to an overall drop in education spending. In that case, they will be worse off under a voucher system. The clear losers will be the students who remain in the urban neighborhood school now shorn of the tax dollars of the wealthy and middle class, and the commitment to education of the poor but dedicated parents. These students, however, are the ones school finance litigation is intended to benefit.

The school choice program most likely to provide an adequate education in failing schools is one in which the court or legislature limits the eligibility to poor, failing students, prohibits schools from setting tuition higher than the vouchers, and provides transportation. This was the program originally created in the Milwaukee schools. Such a program should help some students, those who leave the failing schools for the private schools.[193] But there is no evidence that the students whose parents do not choose to participate in the program have an improved education because other parents pulled their children. Parents who are most engaged in their children's education are the ones who will take advantage of the opportunity presented by vouchers.[194] Parents of poor and failing children are statistically less likely to take an active and informed role in their child's education, and their children consequently are much more likely to be left behind in schools abandoned by students with active, involved parents. Thus, a choice plan limited to poor children may improve the educational achievement of the children who participate in the program, but holds out little hope for improving the education of those left behind.

As a method of solving the inadequacies of education that plague the poor and lower middle class, then, this remedy appears to aggravate the symptoms that led plaintiffs to bring the lawsuit to begin with. Giving each child a coupon worth the price of a minimally adequate education is an administratively easy and immediate way to alter the economic opportunities for some students in the poor districts, but it is a misguided remedy for achieving anything close to a meaningfully adequate education for all.

THE CLASS INTEGRATION MODEL

The second alternative is less prominent, but holds far greater promise for fundamentally altering the distribution of education in a direction that could provide every child an adequate education. Despite a great deal of rhetoric about the general failure of the public school system, the problem of inadequate schooling is more often not a statewide, but a local, overwhelmingly urban problem.[195] Severe poverty is highly geographically concentrated in the major urban areas.[196] New York City schools, for example, enroll 70 percent of all the students in New York State who live in concentrated poverty.[197] By drawing school district or school attendance boundaries around these poverty areas, states with large urban areas have created economically and racially isolated schools—"lonely island[s] of poverty in the midst of a vast ocean of material prosperity."[198] It is these high-poverty urban schools that are failing their students, despite increased funding and compensatory programs.[199]

Past school finance remedies have focused on gaining more funding to meet the greater needs of the students in these districts. Commentators urge greater funding in combination with accelerated educational programs designed to bring disadvantaged elementary students up to grade level. Unfortunately, after decades of lobbying and litigating for every dollar they could find in increased funding and special programs, advocates on behalf of these high-poverty districts acknowledge that students still receive an inadequate education.[200]

The class integration model suggests a completely different approach. The remedy requires not some level of funding or an educational program but the elimination of high-poverty school districts—those with enrollment of over 50 percent poor students. This remedy for the inadequate education delivered in urban school districts was requested recently by the plaintiffs in the Hartford case, *Sheff v. O'Neill.* The Connecticut Supreme Court found for plaintiffs instead on a theory of illegal racial segregation, but the plaintiffs' inadequacy theory and class integration remedy have resonated with school finance litigants and should reappear in other state cases.[201]

The class integration remedy is derived from the education research done on the results of desegregation, and from studies done to determine what factors correlate with high academic achievement. It has been known for a long time that family background is highly correlated with academic performance. Students from poor, uneducated families do worse in school than students from better off, educated families. The now familiar corollary is that income and education of parents of *fellow* students is also highly correlated with performance. In other words, poor students who attend middle-class or wealthy schools do much better in a wide assortment of measures than do poor students congregated in predominantly poor schools. Conversely, children from families above the poverty level do worse when attending high-poverty schools. Repeated and convincing social science research documents that class integration has numerous salutary educational effects for underachieving poor students, from higher test scores, to graduation rates, to college attendance, to success in the job and housing markets.[202]

One of the most thorough attempts to explain this phenomenon comes from work in economic theory. James Liebman, relying on the argument made by Albert O. Hirschman in his famous work *Exit, Voice, and Loyalty: Responses to Decline in Firms, Organizations, and States,* has argued that the advantage of middle-class and wealthy suburban and private schools can be attributed to abundant supply of "education connoisseurs," parents who actively participate in the school to make sure it is providing an adequate education for their children. Connoisseurs are the consumers most likely to complain when quality diminishes. These parents have avoided the urban public school system but do not have a convenient alternative to the suburban or private school their children now attend; there is no better school readily available. Unable to exit, these parents complain about any perceived quality decline and tell the school how to improve the education product. High-poverty schools lack a sufficient number of these education connoisseur parents, and, as a result, poor schools have no one to agitate for quality. "Quality declines are least likely to be arrested when connoisseurs can afford to exit but the remaining customers cannot."[203] When poor children attend the school with students whose parents are education connoisseurs, they too benefit from the better schooling demanded by these parents.

Others attribute the benefits to role models. Children who live and learn in areas of concentrated poverty encounter few, if any, academically successful role models. When these poor children are instead taught in the presence of a sufficient core of successful, middle-class students, they are immersed in values that encourage them to better performance.[204]

The poor results of high-poverty schools might also flow simply from the greater funding diverted to the special needs students who are always more heavily concentrated in these schools. When poor students are collected in one school, the number of children with special needs can be overwhelming, leaving little of even generous funding left over for purely academic programs. No state has yet been willing to fund poor urban schools at a level that would (after discounting costs for special needs) finance a straightforward education curriculum at the same level enjoyed by the average suburban school. When the poor students are dispersed among many schools, special needs do not squeeze out the needs of average students.

Whatever the reason, the results suggest a possible explanation for the achievement gains noted from large-scale racial desegregation, the most complete form of socioeconomic desegregation yet tried.[205] More important for the purposes of this inquiry, the achievement gains from class integration suggest a new approach for school finance cases seeking to improve the distribution of educational opportunity to a minority of failing high-poverty districts within a generally satisfactory state school system. By shifting the remedy from redistributing educational resources in the form of dollars to redistributing educational resources in the form of classmates, school finance litigation could force the fundamental structural reformation necessary to expand educational opportunity for the most disadvantaged.

The remedy of class integration would require redrawing district lines and school attendance patterns to prevent the number of low-income children in any one school from reaching 50 percent. To meet this goal, some children from high-poverty districts would be reassigned to wealthier neighboring districts, and some children would be reassigned from high-poverty schools within districts. Realistically, the remedy will likely also require some "magnet" type programs in the formerly high-poverty districts to attract children from surrounding districts into those schools. If the educators are correct, this measure would do more to improve academic achievement of currently failing students than any feasible funding increase or compensatory program.

There is no question in school finance litigation that it is hard to gain an order from the courts—or laws from the legislature—that results in real change, unless the remedies are carefully crafted with an eye to political realities. The best way for lawyers to see that successful litigation does not end in failed legislation is to build a case and recommend a remedy that reflects political reality and meets the needs of the plaintiffs while respecting—as far as possible—the perceived rights of the majority. Thus, merely defining a remedy that would work as an educational matter is insufficient; it must work as a political matter, too.

Obviously, redrawing local district lines and school assignment plans to attain greater socioeconomic integration is politically volatile. Any change in educational financing that favors poor, often minority, children will face opposition in the legislature, and white Americans have at times shown a determined resistance to having their children attend school with nonwhite children. That said, there are a number of reasons to believe that this remedy is more politically feasible than either earlier desegregation efforts or past efforts to increase school funding. In other words, this remedy is more accommodating to the interests of the politically powerful than the usual remedies for adequacy or equality that depend on spending lots of money on poor children in urban districts or capping the spending of rich districts, and thus has at least as good a chance of political implementation.

First, the class integration remedy might succeed where racial desegregation failed because it should excite less resistance from the suburban school districts. The purpose of this remedy is not to achieve numerical integration but to alleviate the overwhelming concentration of poor students in one school district. Depending on the geography, students may be dispersed through many different school districts and schools relatively easily, without dominating the demographics of any one. There is no evidence that the presence of some moderate percentage of low-income children has an adverse impact on the education of wealthier children. The state could also further limit opposition by providing a financial subsidy, or a "sweetener," to the suburban districts for each high-poverty student added to their district.

In addition, the inevitable disruption caused by shifting some of the student population can be packaged as a benefit. In the past, after court desegregation orders, school districts characteristically shook up their programs, adding cur-ricular reform, revitalized teaching staffs, enhanced parental involvement, and a revived administrative bureaucracy.[206] Similarly, the change in attendance patterns required by the class integration remedy will require the school to change, and the result may well be enhanced education for the students in the suburban school district. This too could encourage suburban parents to soften their resistance.

The class integration remedy also preserves the local financing and local control options of the current system, thus eliminating one of the major sources of political opposition. School districts continue to keep their local property taxes and the unequal funding that comes with that. This will also ensure that taxpayers remain committed to the public schools. The crucial link between property values, taxes, and quality of local schools will be preserved for most families. The suburban school districts will have some shift in students, but they retain all the tools that ensure excellence in public school education—the abundant supply of concerned and dedicated parents, control over the gover-nance of the local school, and the ability to increase funding through higher local property taxes.

Political resistance can also be reduced by enticing a sufficient number of suburban students to attend the formerly high-poverty school district volun-tarily. This could be done through magnet programs and upgrades of the facilities and programs of the formerly high-poverty schools.

A further political advantage of this approach lies in a delicious irony: the extra funding required in this remedy (an inevitable feature under any litigation remedy) goes directly to the benefit of the relatively wealthy child. It is spent on suburban districts to placate them for taking poor children, and on the magnet programs and facilities upgrades to entice suburban children into formerly high-poverty schools. Well-to-do parents and school districts should be less resistant to tax dollars spent on their own children and districts.

In addition, the overall cost of this remedy should be less than providing adequate funding to poor districts. Concentrating all the poor children in the same school districts is inefficient. The cost of a high-poverty school district is greater than the cost of each poor child added together. Teachers must be paid more to teach in those districts; large numbers of student absences and discipline problems are disruptive; class size must be significantly lower to allow teaching in the face of overwhelming student personal needs; the benefit from interaction with successful students is lost; districts must absorb the cost of constant turnover in faculty as teachers burn out and leave the profession or move to better schools; and so on. The sheer magnitude and intensity of the negative conditions and interminable problems that poor children bring to school create their own cost.[207] This extra expense of concentrated poverty can be eliminated when poor children are integrated by class. Poor children will still have special needs, but the overall cost is lower when the children are dispersed.

There may be an additional cost of transportation, but there is little reason to believe this will be substantial. The remedy is only appropriate within school districts that separate schools by class, or in the setting of urban high-poverty school districts surrounded by wealthier suburbs, an area compact enough for suburban families to commute into the city for work. Buses would need to go no farther than a reasonable commute.[208] Moreover, there is no reason the new district has to be a giant district that covers an entire metropolitan area. In some situations, lines could be redrawn to create districts no larger than currently exist.

In addition, the class integration remedy avoids one of the downfalls of desegregation—confining the desegregation order to an area so small that people find it more convenient to move rather than comply. Desegregation was most successful when it was imposed on a large geographical area, limiting the possibility that families could move to avoid integration. The more disruptive a move would be, the more likely desegregation would work.[209] If the cost of moving was high enough that families would be willing to give the schools a try for a few years, busing could succeed in integrating the schools. Polls show that a large majority of families whose children were bused to achieve desegregation had a "very satisfactory" experience.[210]

The primary impetus for "white flight" after desegregation litigation was the Supreme Court's restriction on remedy to the offending district, allowing easy escape from many court orders. This legal barrier does not exist in a class integration remedy to school finance litigation. Remedies in school finance cases have always focused on reforming the state education delivery system. This emphasis allows the class integration remedy to encompass a broad enough geographical region to encourage compliance.

THE WHOLE STATE REFORM MODEL

Adequacy claims, unlike equity claims, can also offer an avenue for improving the distribution of educational opportunities in states where the whole system fails to educate well. While most of the country faces an isolated public school problem, some poor predominantly rural states have a more comprehensive education problem. Their schools are underfunded not compared to other schools in the state, but compared to schools in the rest of the nation. The cause of the inadequate resources has little to do with local financing (in fact, most poor states derive a lesser share of school funding from local government); the cause is that the states spend relatively little on primary and secondary education, and they have well below average achievement scores to show for it.[211]

In Kentucky, for example, the court found that 80 percent of the districts were classified as poor in terms of taxable wealth, and the other 20 percent were below the national average. Not a single school district was financed at the national average. Thirty percent of the districts were "functionally bankrupt." Kentucky ranked near the bottom nationally in curricula offered, student-teacher ratios, teacher pay, provisions of basic educational materials, physical school facilities, per student annual expenditures, and achievement test scores. Thirty-five percent of the adult population had not graduated from high school, and the state ranked near the bottom in functional literacy.[212]

The adequacy paradigm is far better suited for these states than an equity claim. Although wholly inadequate school systems also contain significant inequities, their primary educational problem is a failure to provide an adequate education to the average student. Thus, students in these states have relatively little to gain from a state constitutional equity claim that would guarantee that the state "offer plaintiffs equal educational opportunity but still offer them virtually no opportunity."[213] The 1993 suit in Tennessee may well be an example. The plaintiffs in that state—rural districts with no commercial or industrial property—brought an equalization suit under the equal protection clause of the state constitution.[214] Tennessee was forty-sixth in the nation in average per-pupil expenditures in 1993, and only five states had lower average math scores, only eight had lower average reading scores.[215] While scores and expenditures are not the whole story, they suggest that a lawsuit intending to bring all schools in Tennessee up to these averages will leave the state's children without an adequate education.

The primary problem in these low spending states is not an inappropriate distribution of educational resources among schools, but an inadequate allocation of budgetary resources to schools, period. The need here is to guarantee new resources for education—a need that an equity suit does not target and cannot ensure. The adequacy claim, in contrast, directly argues that education is a state constitutional priority and must be funded before other state needs. As a result, the remedy in these states must serve to redistribute from noneducational sources, not between educational sources. Because these states are usually underfunding all state services, the redistribution will inevitably have to come from private spending through higher taxes. Successful school finance litigation based on the theory that the entire state system is failing to provide children with an adequate education can give the impetus to the political process to make the hard decision to increase taxes.

Much of the promise of adequacy claims derives from the constructive interaction between legislatures and courts that adequacy mandates can stimulate. In a number of states the court action was part of a broader political effort to transform the educational system, and the lawsuit provided cover to the political branches in pursuing education reform.[216] The Kentucky court, for example, provided the impetus for reform by breaking the legislative and executive logjam that had arisen over the cost of the proposed reforms. It did so by making clear that new revenue for schools was inevitable, and that given the other state funding mandates, the only feasible option was additional taxes.[217]

More important, in these states the adequacy paradigm provides a basis to alter education delivery more fundamentally by focusing not just on financial issues but on an overall reform of public education. Increasing revenue in these states is essential to improving the school system, but as past experience indicates, funding alone is likely insufficient to bring all students to a level of adequate educational attainment. Nor, of course, is the political commitment to large-scale funding likely to be renewed on an annual basis, if it is perceived as rewarding poor performance. The adequacy claim, by focusing on the lack of education received by students rather than inequities in funding, requires a remedy that spells out the content of an adequate education, and the steps needed to deliver it. In the remedy phase of an adequacy claim, the court can specifically require educational goals, provide the political cover to fund those goals, and require the legislature to turn to those who have expertise in education to develop the programs that will improve education.

The Kentucky case, *Rose v. Council for Better Education, Inc.*, again provides a model. In the mid-1980s Kentucky was a low spending state, spending less per pupil than any state in the south except Mississippi.[218] In *Rose* the court focused on the fact that the entire school system was failing to educate students.[219] But as with most other school finance litigation, it ordered no remedy—instead leaving to the Kentucky General Assembly the task of creating a constitutional system. The Kentucky legislature responded by raising taxes (spending over one billion additional dollars),[220] and, as a result, raising per-pupil spending to thirty-ninth in the nation by the 1991–92 school year, while guaranteeing that every student would have a set level of funding.[221] But funding was only one piece of the educational reform. After hearings that included educational policy experts, the legislature also responded with a full set of performance-oriented policies based on recent advances in education theory. The Kentucky Education Reform Act of 1990 reshaped the curriculum, governance, and financing of Kentucky schools, including mandating rewards and sanctions tied to school performance, imposing expert help on unsuccessful schools, permitting removal of the superintendent and local school board members for failing school districts, establishing a new primary school program, school-based decision making, preschool programs for at-risk children, and developing family resource and youth services centers in poor areas. To counter the widespread perception of fraud and waste in the public schools, the act also prohibited nepotism and other abusive political practices.[222] While the reforms are still recent, student test scores have already risen.[223]

In other, smaller-scale efforts, educators have developed similar reforms and techniques that have produced improvements in educational attainment. These school reforms, if implemented as part of a school finance remedy, can ensure that the extra funding needed in these poor states increases achievement, not just average per-pupil spending.[224]

A remedy of revamping the entire school system in order to ensure a particular level of educational achievement is an entirely different direction for school finance litigation, and requires attorneys to increase their reliance on educators and educational theory. While an equity theory and remedy of equal finance requires nothing unusual of a civil rights lawyer, defining the content of an adequate education and suggesting the fundamental reforms in education required to get there are not the common coin of the legal profession. In situations of statewide school failure, however, incorporating and relying on educators' expertise is necessary to achieve a politically palatable and educationally sound remedy.

CONCLUSION

School finance reform litigation under a state constitution adequacy theory cannot single-handedly transform the distribution of education. As a state-based theory, it cannot cure the national inequities in education. Whatever the success of the lawsuits, per-pupil spending, even when adjusted for cost of living, will be twice as high in New York as it is in Mississippi. As a state theory it also cannot offset the spending imbalances created by underfunded federal programs such as the Individuals with Disabilities Education Act and federal bilingual education requirements. Moreover, any court-based strategy cannot by itself end the inequities; to be effective it must be coupled with a campaign to persuade politicians and the public that the proposed remedy will meet the court requirements, achieve the desired results, and require no more resources than necessary. If the plaintiffs fail in this persuasive challenge, the political and educational establishment will find ways within the letter of the law to sabotage the spirit of the law.

While it remains to be seen whether adequacy arguments, and the associated structural remedies of class integration and whole state reform, can fare better than equity claims and funding infusions in bringing about change, there are reasons to take heart. If adequacy claimants focus attention on educational quality (rather than funding equality) and turn to educators (rather than lawyers and judges) for the models and methods to promote quality, they will have taken two important, if experimental, steps beyond the pattern of past efforts to end the rationing of educational opportunity.

NOTES

1. See Deborah A. Verstegen, *The New Wave of School Finance Litigation,* Phi Delta Kappan 243, 246 (November 1994).
2. *Brigham v. State of Vermont,* 692 A.2d 384, 389 (1997).
3. *School Spending Suits in New York Area,* New York Times, October 9, 1991, at B9.
4. See Bureau of the Census, U.S. Department of Commerce, Statistical Abstract of the United States: 1995 at 168, tbl. 257 (115th ed.) (hereinafter Statistical Abstract 1995).
5. See Statistical Abstract 1995, supra note 4, at 176, tbl. 273.
6. See Statistical Abstract 1995, supra note 4, at 174, tbl. 268.
7. See Josh Greenberg, *U.S. Students Ranked No. 2 in Literacy Report: They Trail Only the Finnish, the Education Department Finds,* Los Angeles Times, June 18, 1996, at A12.

8. As of 1991 thirty-one states had tested the constitutionality of their public school finance systems, some more than once. Of those states, ten (Arkansas, California, Connecticut, Kentucky, Montana, New Jersey, Texas, Washington, West Virginia, and Wyoming) have found their state finance schemes unconstitutional, some also more than once. See Molly McUsic, *The Use of Education Clauses in School Finance Reform Litigation,* 28 Harv. J. on Legis. 307, 307 and n. 1 (1991).

Since 1991, seven more states have found their school financing systems unconstitutional, see *Alabama Coalition for Equity v. Hunt* (Ala. Circ. Ct. 1993) (published as Appendix to *Opinion of the Justices,* 624 So.2d 107, 110 [Ala. 1993]); *Roosevelt Elementary School District No. 66 v. Bishop,* 877 P.2d 806 (Ariz. 1994); *McDuffy v. Secretary of Executive Office of Education,* 615 N.E.2d 516 (Mass. 1993); *Claremont School District v. Governor,* 635 A.2d 1375 (N.H. 1993) (declaratory judgment of constitutional duty); *DeRolph v. State of Ohio,* 677 N.E. 2d 773 (Ohio 1997); *Tennessee Small School Systems v. McWherter,* 851 S.W.2d 139 (Tenn. 1993); *Brigham v. State of Vermont,* 692 A.2d 384 (Vt. 1997).

Eight have upheld their state schemes. See *Idaho Schools for Equal Educational Opportunity v. Evans,* 850 P.2d 724 (Idaho 1993) (remanded adequacy claim); *Committee for Educational Rights v. Edgar,* 672 N.E.2d 1178 (Ill. 1996); *Skeen v. State,* 505 N.W. 2d 299 (Minn. 1993); *Gould v. Orr,* 506 N.W.2d 349 (Neb. 1993); *Reform Educational Financing Inequities Today (REFIT) v. Cuomo,* 199 A.2d 488 (N.Y. 1993); *Bismarck Public School District No. 1 v. North Dakota,* 511 N.W.2d 247 (N.D. 1994) (upheld constitutionality of school system although majority of justices found constitutional violation under provision requiring four-fifths vote); *Coalition for Equitable School Funding v. State,* 811 P.2d 116 (Or. 1991); *Scott v. Commonwealth,* 443 S.E.2d 138 (Va. 1994).

North Carolina found a constitutional right to a minimum standard of quality in education and remanded for a trial court determination whether that standard was met. *Leandro v. Ingram,* 346 N.C. 336, 488 S.E.2d. 249 (1997).

9. See Allan R. Odden, *School Finance and Education Reform: An Overview,* in Rethinking School Finance: An Agenda for the 1990s, 1, 6 (Allan R. Odden, ed., 1992); Bradley W. Joondeph, *The Good, the Bad, and the Ugly: An Empirical Analysis of Litigation-Prompted School Finance Reform,* 35 Santa Clara Law Rev. 764, 808–09 (1994) (and studies cited therein).

10. Determining an exact count of legal proceedings in all fifty states is probably impossible. For various estimates see Policy Information Center, The State of Inequality, 16–22 (Educational Testing Service 1991); Keith Henderson, *In Many States, Lawsuits Contest the Fairness of School Funding,* Christian Science Monitor, March 23, 1993, at 1 (noting that cases have been filed in forty-one states); Douglas S. Reed, *The People v. the Court: School Finance Reform and the New Jersey Supreme Court,* 4 Cornell J. of Law and Public Policy 137, 141 and n. 13 (1994) (litigation in process in 22 states).

11. See National Center for Education Statistics, U.S. Dept. of Education, Digest of Education Statistics 1994 at 37, tbl. 33 (30th ed.) [hereinafter Digest of Statistics 1994].

12. Digest of Statistics 1994, supra note 11, at 370, tbl. 349.

13. See Digest of Statistics 1994, supra note 11 at 358. Title I was renamed Chapter 1 in the 1981 reauthorization.

14. See Nathan Glazer, *Education and Training Programs and Poverty* in Fighting Poverty: What Works and What Doesn't, 152, 158–59 (Sheldon H. Danzinger and Daniel H. Weinberg, eds., 1986).

15. See U.S. Dept of Educ., National Assessment of the Chapter 1 Program: The Interim Report, 144 (June 1992) [hereinafter Chapter 1 Interim Report].

16. See U.S. Dept of Educ., Reinventing Chapter 1: The Current Chapter 1 Program and New Directions, Final Report to the National Assessment of the Chapter 1 Program, 43–44 (February 1993) [hereinafter Chapter 1 Final Report].

17. Congress has adopted amendments to Chapter 1. See Improving America's Schools Act of 1994, Pub. L. No. 103-382. For discussions of the new legislation see essays in National Issues in Education: Elementary and Secondary Education Act 55-89 (John F. Jennings, ed., 1995). President Clinton sought to target the funds by narrowing the number of school districts served; opposition in Congress prevented full realization of this goal. See Marshall S. Smith et al., *The Improving America's Schools Act: A New Partnership* in id. at 3, 12.

18. See Christopher P. Lu, *Note: Liberator or Captor: Defining the Role of the Federal Government in School Finance Reform,* 78 Harv. J. of Legislation 543, 563 (1991). For a state-by-state comparison see Policy Information Center, supra note 10, at 4–6.

19. Expenditures per pupil in 1989–90 in Massachusetts were $6,172 and in Mississippi $3,119. Policy Information Center, supra note 10, at 28. Gross domestic state product (one measure of the financial well-being of the state) in 1991 was $156 billion in Massachusetts and $41 billion in Mississippi. Statistical Abstract 1995, supra note 4, at 454, tbl. 703.

20. The percent of the population that are dropouts, defined by the Census Bureau as persons 16 to 19 years old "who is not in regular school and who has not completed the 12th grade or received a general equivalency degree" varies from over 15% of all students in Nevada to less than 5% in North Dakota. The percent of the population over 25 that are not high school graduates, a more accurate measure of educational attainment, varies from a high of 35.7% in Mississippi to a low of 13.4% in Alaska. The percent of the population who achieve a bachelor's degree varies from 18% in Colorado to 7.5% in West Virginia. See Statistical Abstract 1995, supra note 4, at 159, tbl. 242.

21. See Digest of Statistics 1994, supra note 11, at 131, tbl. 132, and 123, tbl. 120.

22. 20 U.S.C. §§1400–1491 (1994).

23. 20 U.S.C. §1400 (c) (1994).

24. See 34 C.F.R. §§300.551(a); 300.551(b)(1); 300.554 (1995).

25. See 20 U.S.C. §§1414(a)(1)(c)(iii); 1414(a)(5)(b)(1)(a); 1415(b)(1)(a); 1415(b)(1)(C); 1415(b)(1)(E).

26. See 20 U.S.C. §§1415(b)(2); 1415(c); 1415(e)(2); 1415(e)(4)(B–G) (1994).

27. See Rehabilitation Act of 1973, §504 (codified as amended at 29 U.S.C. §794 (a) (1994)). Federal regulations promulgated by the Department of Education implementing Section 504 in many instances explicitly mirror IDEA and regulations promulgated under it. Compare, e.g., 34 C.F.R. §104.33 with 34 C.F.R. §300.8, both of which define a free appropriate public education. For a discussion of the overlap and differences between IDEA and the Rehabilitation Act, see Thomas F. Guernsey and Kathy Klare, Special Education Law 8–14, 27–59, 81–85 (1993).

28. See Guernsey and Klare, supra note 27, at 3.

29. See 20 U.S.C. §1411(a); Steven R. Aleman, Congressional Research Service, Individuals with Disabilities Education Act: Reauthorization Overview 2 (November 17, 1994).

30. See Aleman, supra note 29, at 4; Stephen Chaikind et al. *What Do We Know About the Costs of Special Education? A Selected Review,* 26 J. Special Educ. 344, 345 (1993).

31. The average per-pupil current expenditure includes the higher per-pupil cost for special education, compensatory education, bilingual education, and other special programs. In surveys, the cost of the average pupil in regular education is lower. For example, in 1985–86 the average per-pupil cost for only regular education was $2,780, compared to the average per-pupil expenditure of $3,479. See Chaikind, supra note 30, at 363.

32. Chaikind, supra note 30, at 352.

33. Estimates are that average student costs for special education are 2.3 times average per-pupil expenditures. See Chaikind, supra note 30, at 345. Council for Exceptional Children, Statistical Profile of Special Education in the United States 3 (1994) (hereinafter Statistical Profile). Measuring the costs of special education is remarkably imprecise, for reasons described in U.S. Department of Education, Office of Special Education Programs, 17th Annual Report to Congress, 121–22 (1995) (hereinafter OSEP Report); Chaikind et al., supra note 30, at 347, but all estimates are that it is significantly more expensive than the cost of educating a nonhandicapped child. For other estimates, see OSEP Report supra at 125; Chaikind et al., supra note 30, at 350–52, 360–66.

34. See Statistical Profile, supra note 33, at 3.

35. See OSEP Report, supra note 33, at xxiv.

36. See Statistical Profile, supra note 33, at 1.

37. The number of special education students varies significantly between states. See Digest of Statistics 1994, supra note 11, at 66, tbl. 54. For example, 13% of New York City students—twice the national average—are special education students; see Lynda Richardson, *Special Education Loses Money, But Not Students,* New York Times, October 19, 1995, at A1, or from another angle, 51% of the state's students with severe disabilities attend the New York City public schools. See Michael A. Rebell, *Fiscal Equity in Education: Deconstructing the Reigning Myths and Facing Reality,* 21 N.Y. U. Rev. L. and Soc. Change 691 (1994–95). It is not obvious why special education students are concentrated in particular regions. One could easily assume that disabilities would be spread uniformly throughout a school-age population, but they are not. In late 1996 the University of Virginia with a grant from the Department of Education began a nationwide effort to examine why minorities are overrepresented in special education classes. See *Focusing on Minorities in Special Education,* New York Times, October 16, 1996, at A14. Whatever the reason, however, statistics indicate that the requirement for special education does not affect states or local school districts evenly.

38. In general, funds are allocated to states based on the number of disabled children ages 3–21 served. See 20 U.S.C. §1411 (a)(1)(a); Aleman, supra note 29, at 1.

39. See Christine M. Casey and Pattie Wade Dozier, *Cutting Costs in Special Ed.,* American School Board J. 27, 27 (1994). Appropriations for the state and local grant program in 1994 were $413 per child. States and intermediate educational units are permitted to set

aside some of the grant for their own use. If the entire $413 is included, rather than the $300 the local districts received, the federal funding is 3% of the total average special education cost per pupil.

40. See 42 U.S.C. §2000d (1994) (Title VI); 20 U.S.C. §§1701 et seq. (1994) (EEOA).

41. 20 U.S.C. §1706.

42. United States General Accounting Office, Report to the Chairman, Committee on Labor and Human Resources, U.S. Senate, Limited English Proficiency—A Growing and Costly Educational Challenge Facing Many School Districts, 3 (January 28, 1994) (hereinafter GAO Report—LEP). Funding figures are also available in the National Center for Education Statistics, U.S. Department of Education, Digest of Education Statistics 1995 at 380 (1995).

43. See Office of Bilingual Education and Minority Language Affairs, U.S. Department of Education, The Condition of Bilingual Education: A Report to Congress and the President, 20 (1992); GAO Report—LEP, supra note 42, at 1.

44. See GAO Report—LEP, supra note 42, at 2.

45. See *Los Angeles to Reward Speed by Bilingual Students,* New York Times, June 19, 1996, at B8 (hereinafter *Bilingual Students*).

46. Id. (New York). Statistics for 1994–95 school year from North Carolina Department of Public Instruction, Jane S. Cowan, English as a second language consultant, and Kay Long, fiscal research assistant (on file with author).

47. Insufficient funds from the federal government cannot be used as justification for refusing to serve a disabled child. See Guernsey and Klare, supra note 27, at 31–32. However, school districts are allowed to take costs into consideration when considering a range of appropriate placements. See id. at 32–33.

48. See Chaikind, supra note 30, at 344.

49. See Richard J. Murnane, *Education and the Well-Being of the Next Generation,* in Confronting Poverty: Prescriptions for Change, 289, 297 (Sheldon H. Danziger et al., eds., 1994).

50. See Charles F. Manski, *Systemic Educational Reform and Social Mobility: The School Choice Controversy* in Confronting Poverty, supra note 49, at 308, 311.

51. See School Management Information Data, Public School Districts State of Arizona (Arizona State University, College of Education, 1990); Annual Report of the Arizona Superintendent of Public Instruction, Fiscal Year 1989–90 at 160, 240 (Arizona Department of Education).

52. *Gould v. Orr,* 506 N.2d. 239, 351 (Neb. 1993).

53. It may actually increase disparities. If property taxes also fund heavy demands for police and highway services, for example, the cap may reduce school spending unevenly. This appears to be the case in Massachusetts, where communities severely constrained by Proposition 2½ (Massachusetts' property tax limitation measure) spend significantly less on schools than less constrained districts. See Katharine L. Bradbury, *School District Spending and State Aid: Why Disparities Persist?* New England Economic Review 50, 53 (Jan.–Feb. 1994).

54. The argument that common zoning laws and covenants restricting multifamily housing,

lot size, minimum square footage, setbacks, height restrictions, and so on prevent poor families from moving into suburban neighborhoods is common in land use literature. For a sampling, see, e.g., Michael H. Schill, *The Federal Role in Reducing Regulatory Barriers to Affordable Housing in the Suburbs,* 8 J. Law and Politics 703 (1992); Jesse Dukeminier and James Krier, Property 1122–40 (3d ed., 1993).

55. See sources in note 261.

56. See General Accounting Office, School Finance—Trends in U.S. Education Spending, Report to Congressional Requesters (September 15, 1995) (hereinafter GAO—Trends).

57. See Peter Enrich, *Leaving Equality Behind: New Directions in School Finance Reform,* 48 Vand. L. Rev. 101, 126 (1995). Some states, however, continued dispersing aid in the form of "flat grants," under which each school district received an equal dollar amount, or some proportionate grant, under which each district received a fixed amount per student. See William E. Thro, *To Render Them Safe: The Analysis of State Constitutional Provisions in Public School Finance Reform Litigation,* 75 Va. L. Rev. 1639, 1647 and n. 33 (1989).

58. Massachusetts and Rhode Island are fairly typical examples. In Massachusetts the poorest one-fifth of communities received almost $1,600 more state aid dollars per pupil than the richest one-fifth, and in Rhode Island state aid reduced the difference in spending of the richest and poorest quintile from 25% to 14%. See Bradbury, supra note 53, at 56, 59.

59. For a state-by-state comparison of education spending differences in high and low spending districts see Policy Information Center, supra note 10, at 7–8. As numerous plaintiffs have shown, students attending schools in underfunded school districts do worse on achievement tests, dropout rates, and other measures of educational attainment. See, e.g., *Alabama Coalition for Equity, Inc. v. Hunt* (Ala. Circ. Ct. 1993) (published as Appendix to opinion of the Justices, 624 So. 2d. 107 (Ala. 1993)); *Rose v. Council for Better Education,* 790 S.W.2d 186, 197 (1989).

60. See James S. Liebman, *Voice, Not Choice,* 101 Yale. L.J. 259, 301 (1991).

61. Average tuition paid by students in nonsectarian secondary schools in 1990–91 school year was $8,061, in Catholic schools was $3,007, and in other religious schools was $4,070. See Digest of Statistics 1994, supra note 11, at 72, tbl. 61. For a very rough comparison, if the average household with children has at least two children (Statistical Abstract 1995, supra note 4, at 63, tbl. 74) and a 1993 median pre-tax income of $36,200 (id. at 476, tbl. 735), it is easy to see how difficult it would be to pay both taxes and school tuition. As a matter of fact, U.S. Department of Education statistics indicate that only 2.5% of high school seniors from low-income families attend private schools, including Catholic schools. See National Center for Education Statistics, Statistical Analysis Report tbl. 1.3 (June 1995) (hereinafter Statistical Analysis).

62. See Digest of Statistics 1994, supra note 11, at 113, tbl. 106, 118, tbl. 112, 127, tbl. 125. There is a great deal of evidence that this difference is explained completely by socioeconomic factors.

63. See, e.g., *Milliken v. Bradley,* 418 U.S. 717 (1974); *Swann v. Charlotte-Mecklenburg Bd. of Educ.,* 402 U.S. 1 (1971); *Green v. County School Bd.,* 391 U.S. 430 (1968).

64. *Green,* 391 U.S., at 441–42.

65. See *Milliken v. Bradley (I)*, 418 U.S. 717, 724–28 (1974).

66. See *Keyes v. School Dist. No. 1*, 413 U.S. 189, 213–14 (1973).

67. See Glazer, supra note 14, at 165.

68. See, e.g., Nancy St. John, School Desegregation Outcomes for Children (1975); Robert L. Crain and Rita E. Mahard, *Desegregation and Black Achievement: A Review of the Research*, 42 Law and Contemp. Prob. 17 (Summer 1978).

69. See Digest of Statistics 1994, supra note 11, at 121, tbl. 118 (NAEP math scores by race); id. at 113, tbl. 106 (NAEP reading scores by race and region). It cannot be proved that the higher scores were a direct result of integration, but that explanation is as compelling as any other. See Christopher Jencks, *Comment*, in Fighting Poverty, supra note 14, at 173, 176.

70. See, e.g., Jencks, supra note 69, at 176; David W. Grissmer et al., Explaining Trends in NAEP Achievement Scores, 25–29 (April 1996); Robert L. Crain and Rita E. Mahard, *Minority Achievement: Policy Implications of Research*, in Effective School Desegregation: Equity, Quality, and Feasibility 55, 57–67 (Willis D. Hawley, ed., 1981); Jomills Henry Braddock II et al., *A Long-Term View of School Desegregation: Some Recent Studies of Graduates as Adults*, Phi Delta Kappan 259, 260 (Dec. 1984); Jomills Henry Braddock II and James M. McPartland, *Social-Psychological Processes That Perpetuate Racial Segregation: The Relationship Between School and Employment Desegregation*, 19 J. Black Studies 267, 267–72 (1989); William L. Taylor, *The Urban Crisis: The Kerner Commission Report Revisited*, 71 N.C. L. Rev. 1693, 1697–1704 (1993).

71. 418 U.S. 717, 744–47 (1974).

72. See J. Harvie Wilkinson III, From Brown to Bakke: The Supreme Court and School Integration: 1954–1978, at 221–23 (1979). See also Richard Briffault, *Our Localism Part II: Localism and Legal Theory*, 90 Colum L. Rev. 346, 420–22 (1990) (demonstrating that the poor and minorities have few options for residential entry).

73. See Gary Orfield, *Separate Societies: Have the Kerner Warnings Come True?* in Quiet Riots, Race and Poverty in the United States, 100, 116–17 (Fred R. Harris and Roger W. Wilkins, eds., 1988); James S. Liebman, *Desegregating Politics: "All Out" School Desegregation Explained*, 90 Colum. L. Rev. 1463, 1465, 1470 (1990); Gary Orfield, *Plessy Parallels*, in Dismantling Desegregation: The Quiet Reversal of Brown v. Board of Education, 23, 29–30 (Gary Orfield and Susan E. Eaton, eds., 1996) (hereinafter *Plessy Parallels*). Limiting the remedy to the school district was less significant a barrier in the south because much of the south had large, countywide, or metropolitanwide school districts, while many northern and western metropolitan areas had dozens of smaller school districts all within a single metropolitan area. See Gary Orfield, *The Growth of Segregation*, in Dismantling Desegregation, supra at 53, 57–61 (hereinafter *Growth of Segregation*).

74. See *Bradley v. Milliken*, 402 F. Supp. 1096, 1138–39, 1140–42 (E.D. Mich. 1975), aff'd 540 F.2d 229 (6th Cir. 1976), aff'd sub nom. *Milliken v. Bradley*, 433 U.S. 267 (1977).

75. See Susan E. Eaton et al., *Still Separate Still Unequal*, in Dismantling Desegregation, supra note 73, at 143.

76. See *Missouri v. Jenkins*, 495 U.S. 33, 37–41 (1990).

77. See *Plessy Parallels*, supra note 73, at 30.

78. For a discussion of the difficulty in proving intent in desegregation litigation see Gary Orfield, *Turning Back to Segregation,* in Dismantling Desegregation, supra note 73, at 1, 19.

79. See *Missouri v. Jenkins,* 115 S.Ct. 2038 (1995); *Freeman v. Pitts,* 503 U.S. 467 (1992); *Bd. of Educ. of Oklahoma City v. Dowell,* 498 U.S. 237 (1991). For a description of the impact of these cases on school district desegregation see Gary Orfield, *Turning Back to Segregation,* supra note 78.

80. See *Missouri v. Jenkins,* 115 S.Ct. 2038, 2049–56 (1995).

81. Enrich makes this point in his piece, and describes in detail the development of the equality theories of school finance litigation; see Enrich, supra note 57, at 115–28.

82. Augustus F. Hawkins, *Equity in Education,* 28 Harv. J. on Legis. 565, 567 (1991).

83. 411 U.S. 1 (1973). For a good description and collection of the early school finance lawsuits under a federal equal protection theory, see John E. Coons et al., Private Wealth and Public Education, 287–393 (1970).

84. See, e.g., Julius Chambers, *Adequate Education for All: A Right, an Achievable Goal,* 22 Harv. Civ. Rts.-Civ. Lib. L. Rev. 55, 68–72 (1987); James S. Liebman, *Implementing Brown in the Nineties: Political Reconstruction, Liberal Recollection, and Litigatively Enforced Legislative Reform,* 76 Va. L. Rev. 349, 405–35 (1990).

85. See Enrich, supra note 57, at 101–2.

86. Prior to 1989 only New Jersey and Washington state courts invalidated their school finance schemes on the basis of their education clauses alone. See *Robinson v. Cahill,* 303 A.2d 273, cert. denied, 414 U.S. 976 (1973); *Seattle School Dist. No. 1 v. State,* 585 P.2d 71 (1978).

87. See McUsic, supra note 8, at 312–13.

88. See, e.g., *San Antonio Ind. School District v. Rodriguez,* 411 U.S. 1, 49–50 (1973); *Milliken v. Bradley,* 418 U.S. 717, 741 (1974); *McDanial v. Thomas,* 285 S.E.2d 156, 167 (1981); *Kukor v. Grover,* 436 N.W.2d 568, 582 n.13 (1989).

89. See *Tennessee Small School Systems v. McWherter,* 851 S.W.2d 139 (Tenn. 1993); *Dupree v. Alma School District No. 30,* 651 S.W.2d 90 (1983). In an unusual case that appeared to invalidate the Alabama school system on every conceivable basis—education clause, equal protection clause, due process clause, and state statutes on disability rights—the court appeared to apply both a strict scrutiny standard, after finding education was a fundamental right, and a rational basis standard. See *Alabama Coalition for Equity v. Hunt* (Ala. Circ. Ct. 1993) (published as Appendix to opinion of the Justices, 624 So.2d 107 [Ala. 1993]).

90. See *Serrano v. Priest,* 557 P.2d 929, 957–58 (Cal. 1976); *Horton v. Meskill,* 376 A.2d 359, 374 (Conn. 1977): *Pauley v. Kelly,* 255 S.E.2d 859, 878 (W.V. 1979); *Washakie County School Dist. No. 1 v. Herschler,* 606 P.2d 310, 333–34 (Wyo. 1980).

91. See McUsic, supra note 8, at 313–14.

92. This is one of the basic critiques of the *Lochner* era jurisprudence, named for the case *Lochner v. New York,* 198 U.S. 45 (1905). For a brief summary see Geoffrey R. Stone, et al., Constitutional Law, 798–99 (2d ed., 1991).

93. States who found their school finance systems unconstitutional based on equal protection claims are *Arkansas: Dupree v. Alma School Dist. No. 30,* 651 S.W.2d 90, 93 (Ark.

1983); *California: Serrano v. Priest,* 557 P.2d 929, 957–58 (Cal. 1976); *Connecticut: Horton v. Meskill,* 376 A.2d 359, 374 (Conn. 1977); *Tennessee: Tennessee Small School Systems v. McWherter,* 851 S.W.2d 139 (Tenn. 1993); *West Virginia: Pauley v. Kelly,* 255 S.E.2d 859, 878 (W.V. 1979); *Wyoming: Washakie County School Dist. No. 1 v. Herschler,* 606 P.2d 310, 333–34 (Wyo. 1980). Cases finding the inequities of the system unconstitutional under the education clause include *Arizona: Roosevelt Elementary School District No. 66 v. Bishop,* 877 P.2d 806 (1994); *Kentucky: Rose v. Council for Better Educ.,* 790 S.W.2d 186, 189, 205–06 (Ky. 1989); *Montana: Helena Elementary School Dist. No. 1 v. State,* 769 P.2d 684, 685, 689 (Mont. 1989), modified, 784 P.2d 412 (1990); *New Jersey: Robinson v. Cahill,* 303 A.2d 273 (1973); *Texas: Edgewood Indep. School Dist. v. Kirby,* 777 S.W.2d 391, 398 (Tex. 1989); *Washington: Seattle School Dist. No. 1 v. State,* 585 P.2d 71 (1978). The Alabama and Vermont school systems were invalidated on both bases. See *Alabama Coalition for Equity v. Hunt* (Ala. Circ. Ct. 1993) (published as Appendix to opinion of the Justices, 624 So.2d 107 (Ala. 1993)); *Brigham v. State of Vermont,* 692 A.2d 384 (1997).

94. For a description and categorization of the language in each of the state's constitutions see McUsic, supra note 8, at 319–26, 333–39.

95. Examples of such arguments appear in *Roosevelt Elementary School District No. 66 v. Bishop,* 877 P.2d 806 (1994); *Rose v. Council for Better Educ.* 790 S.W.2d 186 (Ky. 1989); *Helena Elementary School Dist. No. 1 v. State,* 769 P.2d 684 (1989), modified, 784 P.2d 412 (1990); *Edgewood Indep. School Dist. v. Kirby,* 777 S.W.2d 391 (Tex. 1989); *Robinson v. Cahill,* 303 A.2d 273, 283–87 (1973).

96. See, e.g., *McDuffy v. Secretary of Executive Office of Education,* 615 N.E.2d 516 518 (1993) (describing legislative reforms during litigation); *Seattle School Dist. No. 1 v. State,* 585 P.2d 71, 95 n. 14, 101 and nn. 17–19 (1979) (describing legislative reforms during litigation).

97. A third measure, taxpayer equality—equal capacity to raise funds for education—was the focus of the earliest cases, a likely choice since the most obvious disparity was that property-rich districts could more easily generate tax revenue than property-poor districts. The principle—that the quality of a student's education operate independent of wealth other than the state's overall wealth, but not independent of the voters' willingness to tax—is generally credited to the work of Coons, Clune and Sugarman in Coons et al., supra note 83, at 2. This notion gradually receded in the cases. The remedy, however, permitting districts to raise the same amount of money with the same tax rate, is still quite common.

98. This is one example of the problem throughout law of treating differences between persons. The "dilemma of difference" arises whenever society tries to decide between establishing separate schemes for those it perceives as different and treating all individuals uniformly regardless of perceived differences. For the leading discussion of this problem generally in the legal system, see Martha Minow, Making All the Difference: Inclusion, Exclusion, and American Law (1990) and, specifically with education, Martha Minow, *Learning to Live with the Dilemma of Difference: Bilingual and Special Education,* 48 Law and Contemp. Problems 157 (1985).

99. See Richardson, supra note 37, at A1.

100. See Casey and Dozier, supra note 39, at 27 (percentage calculated from numbers provided).

101. See Rebell, supra note 37.

102. See Ronald F. Ferguson, *Paying for Public Education: New Evidence on How and Why Money Matters,* 28 Harv. J. on Legis. 465, 489 (1991).

103. See Gary Orfield, *Unexpected Costs and Uncertain Gains of Dismantling Desegregation* in Dismantling Desegregation, supra note 73, at 83.

104. See Betsy Levin, *Current Trends in School Finance Reform Litigation: A Commentary,* 1977 Duke L. J. 1099, 1109; Orfield, supra note 103, at 79.

105. Arthur Wise refers to this as the "competitive definition" of equal educational opportunity. See Arthur E. Wise, Rich Schools Poor Schools: The Promise of Equal Educational Opportunity, 153–55 (1967). For an example see *Abbott v. Burke,* 575 A.2d 359, 398 (N.J. 1990).

106. See, e.g., *Burruss v. Wilkerson,* 310 F. Supp. 572, 574 (W.D. Va. 1969), aff'd mem., 397 U.S. 44 (1970); *McInnis v. Shapiro,* 293 F. Supp. 327, 335–36 (N.D. Ill. 1968), aff'd sub nom *McInnis v. Ogilvie,* 394 U.S. 322 (1969).

107. In *Serrano v. Priest,* 577 P.2d 929 (1976), the trial court required that the state spend equally within $100 per pupil. Id., at 940 n. 21. The state supreme court rejected this measure "because of differing educational needs." Id., at 939.

108. See *Rodriguez,* 411 U.S. 1, 42 (1973); *McInnis,* 293 F. Supp. at 335–36; *Thompson v. Engelking,* 537 P.2d 635, 640–41 (Idaho 1975); *Lujan v. Colorado State Bd. of Educ.,* 649 P.2d 1005, 1018 (Colo. 1982); *Danson v. Casey,* 399 A.2d 360, 366–67 (Pa. 1979).

109. See, e.g., James S. Coleman et al. *Equality of Educational Opportunity,* U.S. Department of Health, Education, and Welfare, 290–302 (1966) (hereinafter Coleman Report); Statistical Analysis, supra note 61, at 56, tbl. 4.1a, 4.2a, 4.2b, 4.2c; John E. Chubb and Terry M. Moe, Politics, Markets, and America's Schools, 101, 105–11 (1990); Grissmer et al., supra note 70, at 13–16; Liebman, supra note 60, at 293; Murnane, supra note 49, at 290; Sara S. McLanahan, *Family Structure and the Reproduction of Poverty,* 90 American J. of Sociology 873 (1985); Lisbeth B. Schorr, Within Our Reach: Breaking the Cycle of Disadvantage (1988); William Julius Wilson, The Truly Disadvantaged: The Inner City, the Underclass, and Public Policy, 57–58 (1987); Christopher Jencks et al., Inequality: A Reassessment of the Effect of Family and Schooling in America, 158–59 (1972); Gershon M. Ratner, *A New Legal Duty for Urban Public Schools: Effective Education in Basic Skills,* 63 Tex. L. Rev. 777, 792 n.44; Mary B. W. Tabor, *Comprehensive Study Finds Parents and Peers Are Most Crucial Influences on Students,* New York Times, August 7, 1996, at A12. 1996 data from the National Center for Education Statistics, which measured reading comprehension among students from thirty-two nations, found again that students whose parents were active in their school scored significantly better than the international average, regardless of other factors. See Greenberg, supra note 7, at A12. It also found that poor students do not read as well as wealthier students and that white students do better on average than African-American children. See id.

110. See, e.g., Eric A. Hanushek, *When School Finance "Reform" May Not Be Good Policy,* 298 Harv. J. on Legis. 423 (1991) (discussing studies indicating no systematic relationship between school expenditures and student performance).

111. See William H. Clune, *New Answers to Hard Questions Posed by Rodriguez: Ending the Separation of School Finance and Education Policy by Bridging the Gap Between Wrong and Remedy,* 24 Conn. L. Rev. 721, 726 and n. 16 (1992); Richard J. Murnane and Frank Levy, *Education and Training,* in Setting Domestic Priorities: What Can Government Do? 185, 207 (Henry J. Aaron and Charles L. Schultze, eds., 1992); Marshall S. Smith, *Equality of Educational Opportunity: The Basic Findings Reconsidered,* in On Equality of Educational Opportunity 230, 315 (Frederick Mosteller and Daniel P. Moynihan, eds., 1972).

112. Examples of courts relying on experts' disagreements to find that plaintiffs have failed to prove the link between money invested and education received include: *Rodriguez,* 411 U.S. at 42–43 and n. 86, 46–47 n. 101; *Thompson v. Engelking,* 537 P.2d 635, 641–42 (Idaho 1975); *Lujan v. Colorado State Bd. of Educ.,* 649 P.2d 1005, 1018 (Colo. 1982). Even in cases where the plaintiffs won, the alleged weakness of the link between dollar input and quality of education limited the remedy ordered. See, e.g., *Horton v. Meskill,* 376 A.2d 359, 375 (Conn. 1977); *Carrollton-Farmers v. Edgewood Indep. Sch. Dist.,* 826 S.W.2d 489, 531 (Tex. 1992).

113. *Roosevelt Elementary School District v. Bishop,* No. Cv 91–1308, Statement of Facts in Support of Plaintiff's Motion for Summary Judgment (April 1992), at 2.

114. The role of public schools in creating higher property values is developed in Karl Case and Christopher Mayer, *Housing Price Dynamics Within a Metropolitan Area,* NBER Working Paper no. 5182 (July 1995).

115. See Reed, supra note 10, at 169–182 (polling data on which voters opposed or supported equalization financing measures in New Jersey and why); Clune, supra note 111, at 741 (suggesting political resistance to increased funding for poor schools flows from the "undeserved privileged status" of urban districts); Rebell, supra note 37 (describing the widespread perception of waste in urban districts that leads to political resistance to spend more). It is common for defendants to argue that the plaintiff districts have not made their best efforts to raise additional local funds. See, e.g., *Tennessee Small School Systems v. McWherter,* 851 S.W.2d 139, 142 (Tenn. 1993).

116. For discussions of the political impossibility of redistributing tax dollars from rich districts, see Clune, supra note 111, at 731, 739; James S. Coleman, *Foreword,* in Private Wealth, supra note 83, at xiii; Enrich, supra note 57, at 156–59.

117. This is known as the "fiscal neutrality" position. See John E. Coons, *Introduction: "Fiscal Neutrality" After* Rodriguez, 38 Law and Contemp. Probs. 299 (1974). It is described in Levin, supra note 104, at 1113. Advocacy of the approach is presented in Coons et al., supra note 83, at 201–42.

118. An example is Minnesota, see *Skeen v. State,* 505 N.W.2d 299, 304–05 (Minn. 1993).

119. See, e.g., *Tennessee Small School Systems v. McWherter,* 851 S.W.2d 139, 141 (Tenn. 1993) (describing the financing formula in Tennessee).

120. See, e.g., Act of June 7, 1990, 1990 Tex. Gen. Laws 1 (codified in various sections of Tex. Educ. Code Ann. §§16.001-403 (West 1991)); Kentucky Education Reform Act of 1990, ch. 476, 1990 Ky. Acts 1208 (codified as amended in scattered sections of Ky. Rev. Stat. Ann. §§156.005–446.260 (Baldwin 1995). For further description of these mixtures see McUsic, supra note 8, at 319 n.47.

121. See, e.g., GAO Report—LEP, supra note 42, at 3; Odden and Picus, supra note 9, at

188–92; Bradbury, supra note 53, at 59–63; Joondeph, supra note 9, at 774 (empirical study of five states showing they all narrowed spending gaps between poor and affluent school districts after successful litigation).

122. See John Kolbe, *School Finance DeBugged, For Now,* Arizona Republic, July 21, 1996, at H3 (describing first- and second-round legislative response).

123. For descriptions of court-ordered reform that failed to change the schools, see Note, *Unfulfilled Promises: School Finance Remedies and State Courts,* 104 Harv. L. Rev. 1072, 1075–78 (1994); Liebman, supra note 84, at 392–93.

124. See Levin, supra note 104, at 1113 (with power equalizing "the level of expenditures for a child's education is still dependent upon where he lives—the difference being that disparities in expenditures are related to the preference of local voters rather than district wealth."). See, e.g., *Seattle School Dist. No. 1 v. State,* 585 P.2d 71, 77–78 (1978) (relatively property-rich community whose school funding was low because of the voters' refusal to support school taxes); Glenna B. Musante, *Harnett Schools' Budget Reduced,* News and Observer, August 15, 1996, at 1B, 5B (system in rural North Carolina will do without $800,000 in state aid for low-wealth counties because county commissioners "believe their mandate from the voters is to hold the line" and refuse to raise level of local contribution to state requirement).

   In fact, many property-poor districts that obtained power equalization relief used this power not to increase funding of public schools but to lower property tax assessments or purchase other local goods. See, e.g., Bradbury, supra note 53, at 55 (for every additional dollar of state aid per pupil in Massachusetts, school operating spending rises by only 23 to 42 cents, as the rest goes toward nonschool local spending or property tax reductions); George P. Richardson and Robert E. Lamitie, *Improving Connecticut School Aid: A Case Study with Model-Based Policy Analysis,* 15 J. Educ. Fin. 169, 170–71 (1988) (following Connecticut Supreme Court decision in *Horton v. Meskill,* 376 A.2d 359 [Conn. 1997], much of the increased state aid went toward tax relief). This tendency is obviously not universal. Many districts populated by poor families tax themselves at an extraordinary level to pay for their schools, and without power equalizing find themselves still able to raise less than their wealthy neighbors. See, e.g., Charles S. Benson, *Definitions of Equity in School Finance in Texas, New Jersey and Kentucky,* 28 Harv. J. on Legis. 401, 407 (1991). These districts clearly benefit from the power equalizing approach.

125. This is the basic justification for progressive taxes: the diminishing marginal utility of income, with the assumption that marginal utility curves are the same across income groups. See Abba Lerner, The Economics of Control: Principles of Welfare Economics, 24–32 (1944).

126. See *San Antonio Indep. School District v. Rodriguez,* 411 U.S., 1, 56–58 (1973); See Roberto Suro, *Equality Plan on School Financing Is Upsetting Rich and Poor in Texas,* New York Times, October 9, 1991, at B9 (Houston and Dallas, which have many special needs children, were categorized as rich districts under Texas equalization plan); Peter H. Ehrenberg and Peter T. Grossi, Jr., *Note, A Statistical Analysis of the School Finance Decision: On Winning Battles and Losing Wars,* 81 Yale L. J. 1303, 1305–10, 1327 (1972) (describing evidence that poorer families do not necessarily live in poorer districts). *See*

also Kathy J. Hayes et al., *Equality and Fiscal Equity in School Finance Reform,* 12 Economics of Education Review 171, 176 (1993) (study finding that changing the finance system in Texas so that districts receive substantially equal revenues for substantially equal property tax rates would not make the distribution of educational expenditures noticeably more equal); Neil D. Theobald and Faith Hann, *Ample Provision for Whom? The Evolution of State Control Over School Finance in Washington,* 17 J. Educ. Fin. 7, 23–24 (1991) (finding that fiscal equity reform following litigation in Washington led to a smaller share of financial resources for students living in poverty).

127. See Bradbury, supra note 53, at 56. For the numbers on state revenue and taxes see Statistical Abstract 1995, supra note 4, at 308, tbl. 488. See generally Gary Natriello, et al., Schooling Disadvantaged Children: Racing Against Catastrophe, 193 (1990): "[T]he sheer volume of resources [necessary to educate the disadvantaged] greatly exceeds this society's historical commitment to education in general, and educating the disadvantaged in particular."

128. See Digest of Statistics 1994, supra note 11, at 429, tbls. 399–400.

129. See Alison Morantz, *Money and Choice in Kansas City,* in Dismantling Desegregation, supra note 73 at 241, 393 n. 41; *Abbott v. Burke,* 575 A.2d 359, 366 (N.J. 1990); *Sheff v. O'Neill,* 678 A.2d 1267, 1273 (Conn. 1996).

130. See sources in note 199 describing the failure of past efforts to improve learning in high-poverty school districts. For a sample of specific examples see Feldman et al., Still Separate, Still Unequal: The Limits of Milliken II's Educational Compensation Remedies (Harvard Project on School Desegregation April 1994). Other examples of high spending without apparent increase in achievement are presented in *Abbott v. Burke,* 575 A.2d 359, 366 (N.J. 1990) (New Jersey); Morantz, supra note 129 at 256–60 (Kansas City); Report on San Francisco School Desegregation Plan to Judge William Orrick United States District Court (July 1992) (hereinafter Report on San Francisco).

131. See *Sheff v. O'Neill,* 678 A.2d 1267, 1273, 1296–97 n.2, 1334 (Conn. 1996) (Borden, J., dissenting); id., at 1294 (Berdon, J., concurring).

132. Although total real expenditures in public elementary and secondary schools have increased since 1980, education's share of state's budgets decreased between 1987 and 1994, while Medicaid and corrections increased their shares. See GAO—Trends, supra note 56.

133. See, e.g., Benson, supra note 124, at 409 (describing Texas); *Rose,* 790 S.W.2d 186 (Ky. 1989) (describing Kentucky); Reed, supra note 10, at 188 (describing New Jersey); Bradbury, supra note 53 (describing Massachusetts).

134. See Alan Hickrod et al., *The Effect of Constitutional Litigation on Education Finance,* 18 J. Educ. Fin. 180, 189 (1992).

135. 557 P.2d 929 (1976).

136. See Joseph T. Henke, *Financing Public Schools in California: The Aftermath of Serrano v. Priest and Proposition 13,* 21 U.S.F. L. Rev. 1, 22–23 (1986).

137. See Benson, supra note 124, at 405 n.20; Henke, supra note 136, at 23.

138. On March 15, 1994, Michigan voters approved a plan that replaced the state's property tax based financing system with a plan that relies on state distribution of funds and on an increase in statewide nonproperty taxes. *See Recent Legislation, Education Law—*

School Funding—Michigan Moves Toward Statewide Collection and Distribution of Education Funds, 108 Harv. L. Rev. 1411, 1411 n.3 (1995) (hereinafter *Recent Legislation*). The legislature forced reform by abolishing local property taxes. See id. The plan increases the state portion of expenses from 35% to 79%. See id. at 1411–12 and nn. 2, 3, 8.

139. The state-run distribution plan does not allocate identical amounts to each student, but it immediately increases funding by $700 more per pupil for the poorest school districts and creates a statutory framework for reducing spending disparities by providing that any state increase in funding will be twice as great for the poorest districts as the richest. See Recent Legislation, supra note 138, at 1412, 1415.

140. See Digest of Statistics 1994, supra note 11, at 116, tbl. 110, 165, tbl. 166.

141. See William Fischel, *Exploring the Kozinski Paradox: Why Is More Efficient Regulation a Taking?* 67 Chi.-Kent. L. Rev. 865, 893 (1991).

142. This demographic process is described in Note, *Reassessing Rent Control: Its Economic Impact in a Gentrifying Housing Market,* 101 Harv L. Rev. 1835 (1988).

143. See Vincent G. Munley, *Has the Median Voter Found a Ballot Box That He Can Control?* 22 Economic Inquiry 323 (1984) (finding that in school districts the actual level of public service does not differ from the median voter's preferred level).

144. See Karl Case and James Grant, *Property Tax Incidence in Multijurisdictional Neoclassical Model,* 19 Public Finance Quarterly 379 (1991).

145. See Daniel A. Farber and Philip P. Frickey, Law and Public Choice: A Critical Introduction, 22–23 (1991).

146. Of course at least initially this will benefit the public schools, as the parents will still pay taxes but their children will no longer attend.

147. Compare Digest of Statistics 1994, supra note 11, at 153, tbl. 158 (per-pupil spending) with id. at 164, tbl. 166 (education budget by state).

148. See Joondeph, supra note 9, at 810–11 (finding that increases in current expenditures per average daily attendance in Arkansas, California, Washington, and Wyoming all trailed the national average in the years between the court decision and the 1991–92 school year, and that with the exception of Connecticut, educational funding generally increased the least in those states that reduced interdistrict disparities the most); and Patrician F. First and Louis F. Miron, *The Social Construction of Adequacy,* 20 J. of Law and Education 421, 428 (1991): "Research has shown undesirable consequences of improving measures of equity (i.e. fairness in distribution resources) without, at the same time, improving adequacy of those resources. The result is an undesirable 'leveling-down' of the acceptable minimum of educational offerings." There has also been some limited empirical work relating litigation lawsuits themselves (rather than reductions in disparities) to increased funding. These studies for the most part failed to find increased educational spending following state court equity finance decisions. See Michael Heise, *State Constitutional Litigation, Educational Finance and Legal Impact: An Empirical Analysis,* 63 U. Cinc. L. Rev. 1735, 1762–65 (1995). An exception is the study by Hickrod, which found that whether or not the plaintiffs won the suit, educational funding rates in states that experienced constitutional challenges to their school finance systems increased more than those in states that did not experience such litigation. See Hickrod, supra note 134, at 181–89. The Hickrod study is limited in a number of ways

that he describes himself, see id. at 206–08. The most important limitation is that he does not separate out other important variables that could explain variation in the growth in educational spending levels, such as student enrollment changes, economic growth in the state, overall growth in state spending, and the prior level of state educational spending. See Heise, supra, at 1752 (describing other limitations in the Hickrod study).

149. Sales taxes and particularly excise taxes on cigarettes and liquor and lottery revenues are the most regressive taxes. See Joseph A. Pechman, Who Paid the Taxes, 1966–85 (1985); Donald Phares, Who Pays State and Local Taxes, 90–91 (1980). State income tax rates vary. Most state income taxes are relatively flat (for example, Michigan has a flat income tax rate), which suggests that their incidence is proportional. However, many deductions such as homeowners' interest and charity that poor people cannot take increase regressivity. Flat exemptions that represent a greater portion of a poor person's income tend toward progressivity. Property taxes are more progressive than these replacement funding sources. See Henry J. Aaron, Who Pays the Property Tax? (1975).

150. The Michigan plan, for example, increases per-pupil funding from the state on the basis of the property wealth of the school district rather than the needs of the districts. See Recent Legislation, supra note 138, at 1412.

151. Plaintiffs won, based at least in part on an adequacy claim in Alabama, Arizona, Idaho, Kentucky, Massachusetts, New Hampshire, New Jersey, and Texas. The exceptions are Tennessee and Montana. For citations and descriptions of these cases see Enrich, supra note 57 at 185–193.

152. There were two exceptions. In *Seattle School Dist. No. 1 v. State*, 585 P.2d 71, 94–97 (Wash. 1978), and *Pauley v. Kelley*, 255 S.E.2d 859, 877–78 (W.Va. 1979), state courts overturned their state finance schemes partly in response to an adequacy claim.

153. *San Antonio Indep. School District v. Rodriguez*, 411 U.S. 1, 37 (1972).

154. See, e.g., *Shofstall v. Hollins*, 515 P.2d 590, 592–93 (Ar. 1973), *Olsen v. State*, 554 P.2d 139, 147–49 (Or. 1976).

155. See, e.g., *Rose v. Council for Better Educ.* 790 S.W. 2d 186 (Ky. 1989); *Abbott v. Burke*, 575 A.2d 359, 368–72 (N.J. 1990).

156. *Abbott*, 575 A.2d. at 397.

157. *Rose*, 790 S.W.2d at 212.

158. *Pauley*, 355 S.E.2d. at 877.

159. *McDuffy*, 615 N.E.2d at 544.

160. See Digest of Statistics 1994, supra note 11, at 145–49, tbl. 154 (listing state requirements for high school graduation); id., at 150, tbl. 155 (listing states using minimum competency testing in November 1992). Only Oklahoma did not have a state or local competency test. Id. See also Liebman, supra note 84, at 370–73 (describing state and federal efforts to adopt minimum educational standards); *President Clinton Underscores His Commitment to Education While America Goes Back to School,* The White House At Work, Press Release, September 8, 1997 (urging the adoption of national standards and testing).

161. See McUsic, supra note 8, at 330. Defining the constitutional duty by state legislature-enacted adequacy standards creates the possibility that following a court decision the

legislature simply may revoke the laws. James Liebman explains why this possibility should not prevent plaintiffs from pursuing adequacy claims based on legislatively defined requirements. See Liebman, supra note 84, at 388–89.

162. For a description of the importance of developing rigorous content-based standards, the model of such standards in Europe, and the failed attempt by the Department of Education, see Paul Gagnon, *What Should Children Learn?* Atlantic Monthly 65 (December 1995).

163. See *Idaho Sch. for Equal Educ. Opportunity v. Evans,* 850 P.2d at 728. See also *Roosevelt Elementary,* 877 P.2d 806, 819 (1994) (Feldman, C.J., specially concurring).

164. See Enrich, supra note 57, at 177.

165. See *Abbott,* 575 A.2d at 394–95.

166. For a more complete discussion of these and other advantages of adequacy claims, see McUsic, supra note 8, at 326–33; Enrich, supra note 57, at 104–15.

167. See *Rose,* 790 S.W.2d at 215 (Kentucky); *Abbott,* 575 A.2d at 403 (New Jersey); *Roosevelt Elementary School District No. 66 v. Bishop,* 877 P.2d 806 (1994) (Arizona).

168. Commentators have suggested that permitting wealthy districts to fund public education at a higher level poses no disadvantage to poorer school districts. See, e.g., Clune, supra note 111, at 739, 751. This conclusion is mistaken in a world of limited resources. So long as the supply of superior teachers, places in elite colleges, scholarships, and ideal jobs is finite, children in high-spending districts will have an advantage during their public schooling and afterward.

169. See Enrich, supra note 57, at 181.

170. See id., at 159, 168–69.

171. For example, Mass Gen. L. Ann., ch. 70, sec. 12 (authorizing additional $1.1 billion on state funding for poor local districts); Reed, supra note 10, at 153–65 (describing the cost of the response in New Jersey to successful school finance litigation); Jim Yardley, *More Money for Alabama Schools? Unlikely in Election Year,* Atlanta Journal-Constitution, Jan. 11, 1994, at A3 (describing $2 billion price tag for school improvement in Alabama).

172. "High-poverty" districts is a term of art, although seemingly not a universally accepted one. For federal purposes "high poverty" are districts with over 75% of their students from families with incomes below the poverty line. See Chapter 1 Final Report, supra note 16, at 36. Others define it as having over 41% of students in poverty. See William H. Clune, *Accelerated Education as a Remedy for High Poverty Schools,* 28 U. Mich. J. L. Ref. 655, 659 n. 18 (1995). Still others define it as more than 50% poor students. See Gary Orfield, The Growth of Segregation in American Schools: Changing Patterns of Separation and Poverty Since 1968, 21 (Harvard Project on School Desegregation, Dec. 1993).

173. This is the type of choice defined in *America* 2000, the proposal urged by the Bush administration. See Manski, supra note 50, at 310.

174. See *Jenkins,* 659 N.E.2d 1366, 1376 (Ill. App. 1995); *Arviso,* No. B 077772, slip op. (Cal. Ct. App. 2d App. Dist, 3d Div) described in Greg D. Andres, *Private School Voucher Remedies in Education Cases,* 62 U. Chic. L. Rev. 795 (1995). Commentators urging vouchers as at least a partial remedy in school finance litigation include Andres, supra; Justin J. Sayfie, *Education Emancipation for Inner City Students: A New Legal Paradigm*

for Achieving Equality of Educational Opportunity, 48 Univ. of Miami L. Rev. 913, 936–47 (1994); Clune, supra note 172, at 676–77. For a discussion of the appropriateness of vouchers as a remedy in school finance cases see Jim Hilton, *Note: Local Autonomy, Educational Equity, and Choice: A Criticism of a Proposal to Reform America's Educational System,* 72 Boston Univ. L. Rev. 973 (1992).

175. For literature favoring school choice see, e.g., John E. Coons and Stephen D. Sugarman, Education by Choice: The Case for Family Control (1978); John E. Chubb and Terry M. Moe, *Choice Is a Panacea,* Brookings Review, 4–12 (Summer 1990); America 2000, Sourcebook, U.S. Department of Education 1991; Peter W. Cookson, School Choice: The Struggle for the Soul of American Education (1994). The best articulation of the basic intellectual argument for choice remains Milton Friedman, The Role of Government in Education in Economics and the Public Interest (Robert Solo, ed., 1955). Advocates of school choice, at times, also seem to be making the claim that private schools just do a better job of educating, so shifting the system from public to private schools will alone improve education. See, e.g., Chubb and Moe, supra. Others have argued that the data does not support this interpretation. See, e.g., Murnane, supra note 49, at 299; Glen G. Cain and Arthur Goldberger, *Public and Private Schools Revisited,* 56 Sociology of Education 208 (1983).

176. See sources in note 109.

177. See Sarah Mosle, *What We Think About When We Talk About Education,* New Republic, 27, 32, June 17, 1996, at 31; Henry M. Levin, *The Economics of Educational Choice,* 10 Economics of Education Review 137 (1991); Amy Stuart Wells, *African-American Students' View of School Choice,* in Who Chooses? Who Loses? 25, 30–31, 32–35 (Bruce Fuller et al., eds., 1996) (interviews indicating that students who remained in neighborhood schools had little guidance from parents). Those who favor vouchers claim that poor parents are just as capable as middle-class parents of picking schools for their children, and suggest it is derogatory and paternalistic to claim otherwise. But those criticisms are beside the point. Whatever middle-class parents do, if it is true that a child's poor education is due in part to his or her family background—to parents who are poor, unmotivated, and uneducated themselves—then it is difficult to see how these same parents will suddenly exhibit the interest and knowledge in their children's education as predicted by voucher advocates. Moreover, surveys indicate that socioeconomic status makes a dramatic difference in the percentage of parents who contact the school about a child's academic program or academic performance, help the child with homework, belong to a parent-teacher organization, or attend parent-teacher organization meetings. See Digest of Statistics 1994, supra note 11, at 31, tbl. 25. This correlation is further suggested in a National Center for Education Statistics study that reconfirmed both that students whose parents were active in their school scored significantly better on reading comprehension tests, and that poor students did not score as well as wealthier students. See Greenberg, supra note 7, at A12. More specifically, there is substantial evidence that poor families do not make use of choice options. See Liebman, supra note 60, at 291, and sources cited therein.

178. The concept of parents using "voice" to change their situation comes from Albert O. Hirschman in his famous work, *Exit, Voice, and Loyalty: Responses to Decline in Firms,*

Organizations and States (1970). James Liebman applies Hirschman's work in clear detail to the question of school choice. See Liebman, supra note 60.

179. See Christine H. Rossell, The Carrot or the Stick for School Desegregation Policy, 41–145 (1990); Carol Ascher, *Using Magnet Schools for Desegregation*, in Magnet Schools: Recent Developments and Perspectives 3 (Nolan Estes, ed., 1990) (hereinafter Magnet Schools); Todd Silberman, *The Magnetism of Enloe: High School Excels with Innovative Teachers, Bright Kids and Lots of Support*, Raleigh News and Observer, October 15, 1996, at 1A, 7A.

180. See, e.g., Frank Esposito, *The New Improved Scoring Machine: A Recent Study*, in Concepts and Issues in School Choice, 261 (Margaret D. Tannenbaum, ed., 1995); Ascher, supra note 179, at 14–16; Valerie Martinez et al., *Public School Choice in San Antonio*, in Who Chooses? supra note 177, at 50–67; Rossell, supra note 179, at 120–21 (evidence that students in magnet schools perform better); *Sheff v. O'Neill*, 678 A.2d 1267 (Conn. 1996) (despite magnet program and voluntary transfer, students in remaining public school performing poorly); Morantz, supra note 129, at 24–25 (students in magnet programs in Kansas City did better than students in nonmagnets); Report on San Francisco, supra note 130 (suburban transfer program and magnet program in San Francisco has not raised achievement of students not participating).

181. See, e.g., Coons and Sugarman, supra note 175 at 26; John E. Chubb and Eric A. Hanushek, *Reforming Educational Reform*, in Setting National Priorities: Policy for the Nineties, 213, 239–40 (Henry J. Aaron, ed., 1990).

182. See Hirschman, supra note 178, at 26–29, 44–54.

183. See Digest of Statistics 1994, supra note 11, at 70, tbl. 59 (students and number of private schools 1990–91 school year); and at 14, tbl. 5 (number of public schools); and at 12, tbl. 3 (number of students in public schools).

184. After the Supreme Court decisions in *Mueller v. Allen*, 463 U.S. 388 (1983), and *Witters v. Washington Dept of Services for the Blind*, 474 U.S. 481 (1986), and the recent application of those cases in *Zobrest v. Catalina Foothills School District*, 509 U.S. 1 (1993), *Rosenberger v. Rectors and Visitors of the University of Virginia*, 115 S.Ct. 2510 (1995) and *Agostini v. Felton*, 117 S.Ct. 1997 (1997), many commentators and government officials assumed that voucher programs could include sectarian schools. See, e.g., *Notes, David Futterman, School Choice and the Religion Clauses: The Law and Politics of Public Aid to Private Parochial Schools*, 81 Geo. L. J. 711 (1993); Cynthia Bright, *The Establishment Clause and School Vouchers: Private Choice and Proposition 174*, 31 Calif. Western L. Rev. 193, 193, 207–20 (1995). They may be right, but I am less sure. For the reasons given in Steven K. Green, *The Legal Argument Against Private School Choice*, 62 Univ. of Cinc. L. Rev. 37 (1993), and Liebman, supra note 60 at 280–83, I think that proponents of vouchers may be reading those cases too optimistically.

185. See Digest of Statistics 1994, supra note 11, at 70, tbl. 59.

186. The Milwaukee program provides some indication of this. Milwaukee limited its voucher program to those who applied, who went to public schools, and who had incomes below a poverty threshold, and the private schools participating had to be nonsectarian. Not everyone who wished to participate could do so because there were too few spots. This occurred because many private schools were uninterested in such

children, many who were interested limited the percentages of such children admitted (for "diversity" reasons), some were financially unstable and went out of business, and the supply was not that great to begin with. See 1994 Report of John Witte to Milwaukee Public School Board. The government plan for increasing supply was to include religious schools. If constitutionally permissible, this would increase potential placements, and given that the number of students requesting vouchers has stabilized, this supply increase might be sufficient to place every child. However, proponents are also interested in increasing demand by expanding the class of students who can use the vouchers. Sectarian school placements are not unlimited, either—some will not want students, or will want only a limited number, or will not be financially stable. There is no indication that if every student could use a voucher there would be any place for them to go.

For some idea of cost, compare the start-up costs of magnet schools in Rossell, supra note 179, at 137–144.

187. See Mosle, supra note 177, at 34.

188. See Karen Diegmueller, *Districts Go On Offensive to Ferret Out Students Illegitimately Attending Schools,* Education Week, June 3, 1992, at 5; Manski, supra note 50, at 310–11 (describing a list of the range of choices offered to the public school parent).

189. See Charles Tiebout, *A Pure Theory of Local Expenditures,* 64 J. Pol. Econ. 416 (1956) (families choose to live in residential communities based upon their impressions of school quality in those communities). Polls show that most white families prefer neighborhoods and schools with a clear white majority. See Benjamin I. Page and Robert Y. Shapiro, The Rational Public: Fifty Years of Trends in Americans' Policy Preferences, 74 (1992).

190. See Karl Case and Ray C. Fair, Principles of Microeconomics, 82 (3d ed., 1994).

191. In 1990–91, the average tuition in a nonsectarian private elementary school was $3,846, and in a secondary school, $8,061. See Digest of Statistics 1994, supra note 11, at 72, tbl. 61. As a rough source of comparison, vouchers offered by Milwaukee in 1992 were $2,500, and President Bush's plan would have given $1,000 per student. See Green, supra note 184, at 40 and n. 11.

192. See Liebman, supra note 60, at 284–87; Richard F. Elmore and Bruce Fuller, *Empirical Research on Educational Choice,* in Who Chooses? supra note 177, at 187, 189–93.

193. Even this is not clear. In one study, Witte found that reading and math achievement scores of students taking advantage of the voucher were not consistently better than low-income students who stayed in the public schools. He also found no statistically significant differences in test scores between students who applied for the program but were not selected and voucher children. See John F. Witte, *Who Benefits from the Milwaukee Choice Program,* in Who Chooses? supra note 177, at 118. A different study by Paul Peterson and Jay Greene apparently did find improvements in voucher student scores compared to students who applied but did not attend. See *Insight,* New Tribune, August 18, 1996, at G4. Wisconsin's Legislative Audit Bureau found that the number of students was too small to draw meaningful conclusions about performance. See Kathy Walt, *Milwaukee Offers Learning Window on Voucher Plan,* Houston Chronicle, April 30, 1995, at 1.

194. In the Milwaukee program, not unexpectedly, the students who sought a move came from families with above average education and dedication (as measured by active involvement in the child's education), as well as smaller-than-average family size. See Witte Report, supra note 186. The same result was found by Wells, supra note 177.

195. By numerous measures, many children in public schools continue to receive a good education. Recent tests on reading comprehension show American students performing better than every industrialized country but Finland. Greenberg, supra note 7, at A12. Average reading, mathematics, and science proficiency, as measured by the National Assessment of Educational Progress, was higher for every age group tested in 1992 than in the comparison period from the 1970s. See Digest of Statistics 1994, supra note 11, at 113, tbl. 106; 121, tbl. 118; 127, tbl. 125. Average writing performance rose from 1984 for all grades tested except eleventh graders, which dropped 2 points on a 500-point scale. Id., at 118, tbl. 112. Moreover, there has been a narrowing of the gap in test scores between African American and white children. See Murnane, supra note 49, at 302. See also Grissmer et al., supra note 70, at 29 (analyses of NAEP scores "certainly do not support the more negative perceptions of declining student achievement, deteriorating families and schools, and failed educational and social programs"). Test scores are obviously not a perfect measure of educational achievement, and by some other measures American schools do less well. See Sayfie, supra note 174, at 918. But, by one important measure, there seems to be little evidence of the widespread attack on the public schools. Overall, satisfaction of parents with the public schools their children attend has remained relatively constant over the past twenty years. See Digest of Statistics 1994, supra note 11, at 30, tbl. 22. See also Peter Appelbome, *With Education in Rare Political Spotlight, Mainstream Clinton Message Seems to Sell,* New York Times, October 16, 1996, at A14 (recent poll showing 64% of the public think that public schools were good or very good). If there has been a precipitous decline in educational quality of public schools, the majority of people whose children are receiving the education are unaware of it.

196. See William Julius Wilson, *Public Policy Research and the Truly Disadvantaged,* in The Urban Underclass, 460, 461 (Christopher Jencks and Paul E. Peterson, eds., 1991). Using children who are on AFDC for more than five years as a measure of poverty, poverty is highly concentrated in cities. See Daniel Patrick Moynihan, Congressional Record, December 12, 1995 reprinted in *Congress Builds a Coffin,* New York Review of Books, January 11, 1996, at 35.

Using another measure, comparing within states, city, and suburban per-capita income, see Michael A. Stegman, *National Urban Policy Revisited,* 71 N.C. L. Rev. 1737, 1742 n. 27 (1993).

197. See Rebell, supra note 37 (statistics from plaintiffs in New York school finance litigation).

198. Martin Luther King, *I Have a Dream,* in Lend Me Your Ears: Great Speeches in History, 495 (William Safire, ed., 1992).

199. Statistics indicate that for every age tested in 1992 in reading proficiency, writing performance, geography, literature, and science, students from disadvantaged urban communities did less well than students from all other communities, including ex-

tremely rural. See Digest of Statistics 1994, supra note 11, at 113, tbl. 106; 118, tbl. 112; 120, tbl. 115; 127, tbl. 125. *See also Growth of Segregation,* supra note 73 at 1 64–67 (statistics on achievement inequalities in poor urban school districts); *College Completion Among Students from High Schools Located in Large Metropolitan Areas,* American J. of Education 562 (August 1990); Commission on Chapter 1, Making Schools Work for Children in Poverty: A New Framework Pt. II, at 1–2 (Dec. 1992) ("the most urgent needs for education improvement . . . is in schools with high concentrations of children from low-income families"); Stegman, supra note 196, at 1747 (describing the poor achievement levels of urban minority students compared to white children from more advantaged communities).

For commentary on the topic, see Gene I. Maeroff, *Withered Hopes, Stillborn Dreams: The Dismal Panorama of Urban Schools,* 69 Phi Delta Kappan 633 (1988); Heidi Marie Rock and Edward W. Hill, *Policy Prescriptions for Inner-City Public Schooling,* in The Metropolis in Black and White: Place, Power and Polarization 306 (George C. Galster and Edward W. Hill, eds., 1992); Gary Orfield and Franklin Monfort, Racial Change and Desegregation in Large School Districts: Trends Through the 1986–87 School Year, 1–2 (1988).

200. See, e.g., plaintiffs position in *Sheff v. O'Neill,* 678 A.2d 1267 (Conn. 1996); *Abbott v. Burke,* 575 A.2d 359 (N.J. 1990).

201. John C. Boger has provided a thorough explanation and endorsement of this remedy in school finance litigation (calling it a school social composition remedy) based on a detailed case study of the situation in Hartford, Connecticut. See Boger, School Finance Reform in Hartford, unpublished manuscript (February 1995). He is, to my knowledge, the first commentator to have recognized the broader potential of the plaintiffs' theory in *Sheff v. O'Neill* to enhance the successful outcomes in school finance litigation. The early response to the case suggests that the class integration remedy may be the wave of the future. See George Judson, *Civil Rights Lawyers Hope to Use Hartford Schools Case as a Model,* New York Times, August 15, 1996, at B1, B7.

202. See Chapter 1 Final Report, supra note 16, at 14–38; Coleman Report, supra note 109, at 22, 302–10; Christopher S. Jencks, *The Coleman Report and the Conventional Wisdom,* in On Equality of Educational Opportunity, supra note 111, at 69, 71; Statistical Analysis, supra note 61, at 58 and tbls. 3.2, 4.1a, 4.2a, 4.2b, 4.2c (relation between socioeconomic composition of school and achievement); Karl R. White, *The Relation Between Socioeconomic Status and Academic Achievement,* 91 Psych. Bull. 461, 463–64 (1982); Mary M. Kennedy et al., Office of Educ. Res. and Improvement, U.S. Department of Education, Poverty, Achievement and the Distribution of Compensatory Education Services, D18–D60, II-5-6 (1986); Liebman, supra note 60, at 293; Liebman, supra note 73, at 1486, and notes 675–91; Susan E. Mayer and Christopher S. Jencks, *Growing Up in Poor Neighborhoods: How Much Does It Matter?* 243 Science 1441, 1442–43 and nn. 15–16 (1989); Allan Odden, The Changing Contours of School Finance 16–17 (1991); Taylor, supra note 70, at 1702–03; Susan E. Mayer, *How Much Does a High School's Racial and Socioeconomic Mix Affect Graduation and Teenage Fertility Rates?* in The Urban Underclass, supra note 196, at 321, 325–32; Judith Anderson et al., U.S.

Department of Education, Office of Educ. Res. and Improvement, Poverty and Achievement: Reexamining the Relationship Between School Poverty and Student Achievement 2–5, 19 (1992).

There have also been a few "natural experiments" where for different reasons urban students were sent to suburban schools. The results here, too, support the conclusion that economic integration benefits poor children. See generally James E. Rosenbaum et al., *Can the Kerner Commission's Housing Strategy Improve Employment, Education, and Social Integration for Low-income Blacks?* 71 N.C. L. Rev. 1519 (1993) (describing the higher educational attainment of black poor urban children moved to middle class white suburbs as part of a settlement of the Gautreaux housing lawsuit in Chicago); Robert Crain, Finding Niches: Desegregated Students Fifteen Years Later (1992). Robert Crain and John Strauss, School Desegregation and Black Occupational Attainment: Results From a Long-Term Experiment (1985) (reporting on the results of Project Concern, which bused Hartford city students to suburbs beginning in 1966); Report on San Francisco, supra note 130 (data demonstrating large gains for low-income minority students by transfer to middle-class suburban schools).

Professor Hanushek, citing three 1970s studies, including one of his own, argues that the impact of peers is "ambiguous." See Hanushek, supra note 92, at 441. The contrary evidence from the Coleman report to the present seems overwhelming.

203. Liebman, supra note 60, at 295.

204. See Wilson, supra note 109, at 56–57, 103, 143–44. See also *Sheff v. O'Neill,* 678 A.2d 1267, 1289–90 (segregation keeps children from absorbing values and skills of "our social order."); Richard J. Murnane, *Evidence, Analysis, and Unanswered Questions,* 51 Harv. Educ. Rev. 483, 486 (1981) ("[O]ne of the most effective ways to improve children's cognitive skills is to put them in an environment with other children who want to acquire cognitive skills and whose families support such learning").

205. See Crain and Mahard, supra note 70, at 73–75; Liebman, supra note 73, at 1624–26 and n. 675; Orfield, supra notes 73 and 79.

206. See Liebman, supra note 73, at 1621.

207. Wilson describes more broadly the concentration effects of overwhelming poverty that create much more extensive and intractable problems than if the poor were dispersed. See Wilson, supra note 109, at 20–62; Wilson, supra note 196, at 462.

208. Boger offers the example of the Hartford school district—a high-poverty, failing school district surrounded by 22 suburban jurisdictions. Together they comprise a total area of 568 square miles. Both the square miles and the total number of students render Hartford almost exactly the same size as Charlotte-Mecklenburg, one of the most successfully desegregated school systems in the nation. See Boger, supra note 201, at 236. See also Growth of Segregation, supra note 83, at 60–61, 63–64 (describing the highly fragmented school districts in single metropolitan areas).

209. See Liebman, supra note 73, at 1622–23 and nn. 669–74; Orfield, supra note 172 (showing that most successful integration occurred in large school districts).

210. See Page and Shapiro, supra note 189, at 73; Liebman, supra note 73, at 1621–22 and nn. 667–68.

211. This has been true since at least the Coleman Report of 1966, which found large resource

differences between schools in the south and in other regions. See Coleman Report, supra note 109, at 12, 66–212. The correlation is rough. The fifteen states with lowest per-pupil spending are Mississippi, Louisiana, Idaho, Utah, North Carolina, Tennessee, South Dakota, South Carolina, Oklahoma, North Dakota, New Mexico, Alabama, Arizona, Arkansas, and Georgia. See Digest of Statistics 1994, supra note 11, at 165 tbl. 166. Of these states, Mississippi, Louisiana, North Carolina, Tennessee, South Carolina, Alabama, Arizona, Arkansas, and Georgia are also in the bottom fifteen of average reading proficiency scores for fourth graders. See id., at 116 tbl. 110. Of the low spending states Mississippi, Louisiana, North Carolina, Tennessee, South Carolina, New Mexico, Alabama, Arkansas, and Georgia are also in the bottom fifteen states of average math proficiency. See id., at 123 tbl. 120. California, which has the sixteenth lowest per-pupil spending of all the states, has the second lowest average reading scores and eleventh lowest math. See id. at 116, tbl. 110, and 123, tbl. 120.

212. See *Rose v. Council for Better Education,* 790 S.W.2d 186 (Ky. 1989); see also Bert Combs, *Creative Constitutional Law: The Kentucky School Reform Law,* 28 Harv. J. on Legis. 367, 367–68 (1991) (describing deficiencies of Kentucky school system); Ronald G. Dove, Jr., *Acorns in a Mountain Pool: The Role of Litigation, Law, and Lawyers in Kentucky Education Reform,* 17 J. Educ. Fin. 83 (1991).

213. *Alabama Coalition for Equity v. Hunt,* 624 S.2d 107, 151 (Ala. 1993).

214. See *Tennessee Small School Systems v. McWherter,* 851 S.W.2d 139 (Ten. 1993). For a discussion of parties and interests in the case see *Current Developments in the Law: A Survey of Cases Affecting Public Education,* 4 Pub. Int. L. J. 204, 204–12 (1994).

215. See Statistical Abstract 1995, supra note 4, at 168, tbl. 257 (per-pupil spending); Digest of Statistics 1994, supra note 11, at 116, tbl. 110; 123, tbl. 120.

216. Enrich, supra note 57, at 175–77; Rebell, supra note 37.

217. See Combs, supra note 212; Dove, supra note 212.

218. See Digest of Statistics 1994, supra note 11, at 165, tbl. 166 (1985–86 school year). Southern states include Alabama, Arkansas, Florida, Georgia, Louisiana, Mississippi, North Carolina, Oklahoma, South Carolina, Tennessee, Virginia, and Texas.

219. 790 S.W.2d 186 (Ky. 1989). See also Benson, supra note 124, at 417–20 (describing the *Rose* decision and the educational reforms that resulted from the decision).

220. See Kern Alexander, *The Common School Ideal and the Limits of Legislative Authority: The Kentucky Case,* 28 Harv. J. on Legis. 341, 343 (1991).

221. See Digest of Statistics 1994, supra note 11, at 165, tbl. 166.

222. See Benson, supra note 124, at 417–20; Clune, supra note 111, at 748.

223. See Lynn Olson, *Dramatic Rise in Ky. Test Scores Linked to Reform,* Education Week, October 5, 1994, at 13, 15.

224. Educators in the past two decades have developed many programs that promise to improve educational achievement. See, e.g., Effective Programs for Students at Risk (Robert Slavin et al., 1989); Theodore R. Sizer, Horace's School: Redesigning the American High School (1992); Henry M. Levin, Center for Policy Research in Education for At-Risk Students, Toward Accelerated Schools (1988); Stewart C. Purkey and Marshall Smith, *Effective Schools: A Review,* 83 Elementary School J. 427 (1983).

Chapter 4 Cultural, Educational, and Legal Perspectives on Immigration: Implications for School Reform

Marcelo Suárez-Orozco, Peter D. Roos, and Carola Suárez-Orozco

Nationwide, "first- and second-generation immigrant children are the most rapidly growing segment of the U.S. child population" (Landale and Oropesa 1995, 1). This influx of linguistic and ethnic minority children has significantly affected the country's public school system. Not surprisingly, schools have been largely unprepared to service these new students. Historically, schools have floundered in the servicing of non-mainstream minority and poor children and they have been even less able to provide adequate education to linguistic minority children.

Concurrently with this swift demographic shift, a nationwide preoccupation with school reform has occurred. A number of restructuring and school reform attempts have been made in school districts across the country. Unfortunately, a mounting body of evidence demonstrates that most federal, state, and local school improvement efforts have not improved the daily school experiences of immigrant and linguistic minority school children. In fact, some reform attempts have operated against the best interest of these students. If for no other reason than the sheer numbers of such students, education reform efforts that do not address the unique needs of immigrant children will be abysmal failures.

THE "NEW" IMMIGRATION

The United States and other post-industrial nations are in the midst of a major demographic transformation largely (though not exclusively)[1] related to changes in immigration patterns over the last three decades (Edmonston and Passel 1994; Portes and Rumbaut 1996; Simon 1995). The United States has undergone other waves of immigration where even larger percentages of the overall population were foreign born. However, 80 percent of today's "new immigrants" tend to be non-European in origin, emigrating from the "developing" world of Asia, Latin America, and the Caribbean (Edmonston and Passel 1994).

While these "new immigrants" experience an American context distinct from that of previous waves of immigrants to the United States, they also share many characteristics with them. Like the previous waves of immigrants, the current wave is predominantly poor and of modest education. While some have argued that the new immigrants are less inclined to settle permanently in this country, this is highly debatable; it is clear that whatever the original intention, those who have children who grow up in this country are unlikely to resettle in the country of origin.

Current immigrants are entering a country which is economically, socially, and culturally unlike the country which absorbed—however ambivalently— previous waves of immigrants. Earlier immigrants arrived on the eve of the great industrial expansion in which foreign-born workers and consumers played a key role (Higham 1955). Today, the kinds of jobs typically available to many new immigrants do not hold the same kind of promise for upward mobility (Portes 1996) available to previous immigrant groups. At the same time, the mood of the country reflects a rather bleak view of the future. As a result, these racially distinct immigrants are a visible scapegoat for much of what ails the nation; the resulting popular "immigrant bashing" has dramatically and negatively effected the receptivity of schools to immigrant children.

Demographic realities indicate that the children of these immigrants will clearly be key players in the reshaping of the American democracy, economy, and cultural pluralism. As will be discussed later in this chapter, given that the modern American economy is so much less accommodating to those with few educational skills, it becomes all the more urgent to educate the children of immigrants adequately. To complicate matters, U.S. schools are challenged to respond to children who bring to the classroom unprecedented diversity in cultural background and languages. For example:

- In California, students of limited English proficiency (LEP) jumped from fewer than 500,000 in 1985 to more than 1.2 million a decade later (Rumbaut 1995). LEP students now make up approximately 20 percent of the California school population.
- In New York, the population of foreign-born residents continues to grow at a net increase of 460,000 people between 1990 and 1995, even as the overall population of the state has declined (Pérez-Peña 1996, 27). New York City schools "have averaged an influx of 20,000 students a year, largely through immigration" (ibid).
- According to Florida Department of Education records, from 1992 to 1995, in South Florida, Dade, Broward, and Palm Beach counties, school districts experienced a growth rate for their LEP student populations of 10.4 percent, 30.47 percent, and 16.69, respectively.

SECONDARY MIGRATION

Although new immigrants are highly concentrated in a handful of states (California, New York, Florida, Texas, Illinois, New Jersey), secondary migration is bringing foreign-born children into public schools in urban, rural, and suburban communities virtually everywhere.

Immigrants who entered the United States early in the twentieth century tended to settle first in northern manufacturing centers. In contrast, almost 40 percent of immigrants counted in the 1980 U.S. census resided in just two metropolitan areas—Los Angeles and New York City. Another 20 percent were found in San Francisco, Chicago, Miami, and Dallas/Ft. Worth (First and Carrera 1988). In 1991, the ten most popular states of intended residence for legal immigrants were California, New York, Florida, Texas, New Jersey, Illinois, Massachusetts, Virginia, Pennsylvania, and Maryland (National Conference of State Legislators 1994).

A prominent characteristic of the current immigration wave is secondary migration. While immigrant families are likely to settle first in large urban centers, substantial numbers move on, motivated by a desire for family unification, improved economic prospects, and community. This, together with the fact that today's immigrants tend to be young and have large families, means that the children of immigrants are increasingly found in schools in suburbs, small towns, and rural areas, as well as the large gateway cities (National Conference of State Legislators 1994). For example:

- In Rogers, Springdale, and other small communities in northwest Arkansas, large numbers of Mexican, Mexican-American, and southeast Asian families recruited by food corporations to work in chicken-processing factories are settling in previously Ozarkan or white communities. The number of children from these families—children of color who often do not speak English—in local public schools have doubled in recent years.
- In Garden City, Kentucky, Vietnamese, Cambodian, and other Asian workers have joined first- and second-generation immigrant families from Mexico to work in local meat-packing operations. Their children also bring new challenges to schools not used to coping with a variety of languages and cultural perspectives.
- In North Dakota, refugee resettlement agencies have placed significant numbers of families from Bosnia, Afghanistan, Vietnam, and other Asian countries. Children from all these groups attend local schools which previously had little experience with cultural and language diversity.
- In Des Moines, Iowa, two-thirds of all surviving Tai Dam (members of a Laotian ethnic minority) live, work, and study.
- In Minneapolis and St. Paul, large Hmong communities must adapt to both social and meteorological climates typical of the U.S. heartland.

THE EDUCATIONAL CHALLENGE

The challenge of educating culturally and linguistically diverse student populations lies in the future for many U.S. public school districts. Although immigration tends to be highly concentrated in a handful of states, foreign-born people are found in all areas of the nation and in diverse school systems. The presence of immigrant students and linguistic minority children in U.S. schools is a reality that must be dealt with effectively. The future well-being of this nation is inexorably linked to the adequate functioning of these immigrant children. This reality will not go away, regardless of upsurges in nativism, shifts in border policies, and handwringing.

The changing faces of these communities, many of which have never had substantial numbers of residents whose culture is not that of mainstream America and who speak languages other than English, have produced and are likely to continue to produce community tensions both in neighborhoods and in schools. Constructive resolution of these tensions is most likely to occur if individuals and organizations work together, across differences in culture and language, to achieve common goals (First and Carrera 1988; National Conference of State Legislators 1994).

Growth rates such as those described earlier point to an inevitable coming crisis in U.S. public education as largely top-down reforms—devised by planners who are largely unfamiliar with the experiences and languages of these children—continue to reorganize and restructure schools for the coming century with little input from the families and communities of the children who will attend them. These demographic facts lead to several conclusions. First, reform that is not comprehensive will not succeed. Second, to the extent that institutional failure of our schools must be addressed through broad-based reform, immigrants will rise and fall with the success of that movement irrespective of specific reforms aimed at unique immigrant needs. The converse is also true. If reform is not sensitive to those unique needs or fails to be "individualized" to address barriers not confronted by others, immigrant students will not benefit from school reform. While we will focus our attention on these latter barriers, we will briefly address some of the broader reforms and how they must be sensitive to the needs of immigrant students and their families.

How might educational reform be shaped to accomplish these ambitions and goals? It is clear that, as in the past, lawyers, community advocates, parents, educators, and researchers will have to collaborate. Addressing the problems and barriers facing immigrant students—a disadvantaged and politically powerless minority—will require a range of approaches involving the skills of teachers, researchers, community leaders, and lawyers.

The language needs of these pupils were barely recognized before lawyers for the Center for Law and Education wrote the first Bilingual Education Act in Massachusetts, and San Francisco Legal Services lawyers, with the aid of a broad cross-section of supporters, secured a Supreme Court victory in *Lau v. Nichols*. Equitable financing for schools grew out of the collaboratory effort of educators such as Jose Cardenas in Texas and civil rights organizations. The right of undocumented pupils to basic access required the efforts of researchers and lawyers in the early 1980s when *Plyler v. Doe* was decided, and continues today in the fight over California's Proposition 187. Whether proceeding through litigation or other forms of advocacy, this collaboration must continue.

We have addressed the demographic and historical record that cries out for a major intervention on behalf of immigrant students as reform initiatives are debated. In our subsequent discussion, we will view the issues raised in this chapter through two lenses. We will first explore sociocultural and educational issues in the schooling of immigrant and linguistic minority children, including: (a) the strengths that immigrant families bring to this country before many sink into a morass of hopelessness that too often characterizes many second- and third-generation families; (b) structural barriers to academic success for immigrant and linguistic minority children; and (c) the school reform movement and its impact on immigrant and linguistic minority children. We will then discuss the following issues from a legal perspective: (a) historical discrimination and the crucial question of whether undocumented children should continue to be educated in American public schools—a question that cannot be segregated from the broader question of whether we are prepared to address the needs of all immigrant students in a positive manner; (b) how and why the issue of language must be part of any discussion of reform; (c) the barriers of inequitable distribution of resources; and (d) how current proposals for general education reforms must be adjusted to recognize the realities facing immigrant families.

In our final section, we discuss some of the practical issues that must be addressed if collaborative efforts are to be successful in making educational reform succeed for immigrant students.

SOCIOCULTURAL AND EDUCATIONAL ISSUES IN THE SCHOOLING OF IMMIGRANT AND LINGUISTIC MINORITY CHILDREN

Immigrant Children in Jeopardy: Hope in the Face of Barriers

The debate over immigration is as old as the American nation. Every significant cycle of new arrivals generated pro-immigration lobbies and anti-immigrant nativism. Immigration, many point out, is an enduring feature of American history.

Today, the United States has a foreign-born population of nearly 20 million people. During the decade of the 1990s the United States has been admitting, on average, nearly 1 million immigrants per annum. Although this is a significant figure, it has been noted that the proportion of immigrants in the U.S. population, today on the order of 8.5 percent, is less than in prior historical epochs. In addition to legal immigrants, an estimated 200,000 to 400,000 immigrants enter the country annually without documentation.

In 1990, there were nearly 5 million Asian and 8.5 million Latin American and Caribbean immigrants in the United States. Nearly 80 percent of the "new immigrants" come from Asia, Latin America, and the Caribbean and are therefore "of color." Some critics of immigration seem preoccupied with the cultural implications of continued large-scale immigration from third-world countries. Much of the current xenophobic outcry focuses on an unparalleled anxiety about the implications of such diversity on American culture (Brimelow 1995). Can and will today's Mexicans, Filipinos, and Dominicans be tomorrow's Americans?

The new immigrants are indeed a diverse demographic and sociocultural population. They "include at once the most educated [those from India and Taiwan] and the least educated [those from Mexico and El Salvador] ethnic groups in the United States today" (Rumbaut 1995, 17). The new immigrants come from many countries and varied socioeconomic, educational, and professional backgrounds.

Individuals of Mexican origin are by far the largest group of new immigrants; there are "more immigrants from Mexico in the United States in 1990 than from all of Europe combined" (Rumbaut 1995, 20). The 1990 census data indicate that there were 4.3 million Mexican immigrants legally residing in the United States. While there is a long history of Mexican immigration to the United States, the Central American wars of the 1970s and 1980s initiated an unparalleled wave of emigration from that part of the world, bringing close to a million Central American refugees and immigrants to the United States by 1990. In terms of socioeconomic status and school attainment, children of Central American origin tend to be closer to their Mexican peers than to their Asian peers.

In general, the new immigrants from Latin America and the Caribbean tend to be less educated and poorer than Asian immigrants, with the exception of refugees from Indochina (see Landale and Oropesa 1995; Rumbaut 1995). Though often lumped together as the "model minority," Asian students represent a heterogeneous population involving highly diverse linguistic, religious, and socioeconomic groups. Among Asian immigrant communities which send large numbers of students to U.S. schools are Vietnamese, Cambodian, Filipino, Laotian, Hmong, Chinese, and Tai Dam. The largest group of Asian immigrants to the United States is from the Philippines (close to 1 million, according to 1990 figures). Filipinos tend to have very low rates of poverty (5.9%) and a relatively high rate of labor force participation (76.3% compared to 39.7% among immigrants from the former Soviet Union). In 1990, there were slightly over a half-million Chinese, and about the same numbers of

Vietnamese and Korean immigrants in the United States. Korean immigrants have a distinctly high rate of self-employment (18%). Immigrants from India (some 450,000, according to 1990 figures) have the highest percentage of college graduates of any group in the United States (64.9% compared to 3.5% among Mexican immigrants). The U.S. Asian immigrant population, then, is exceptionally diverse and complex, a fact which is seldom recognized by public schools.

Although there are significant differences by country of origin, there are nevertheless some important similarities in the condition of the majority of immigrant children in the United States. Immigrant children, for example, "have higher rates of poverty than the general population" (Landale and Oropesa 1995, 6). The highest poverty rates are found among immigrant children from Latin America: "About half of first-generation Puerto Rican children are living in poverty, compared to about forty percent of both Mexican and Dominican children. Similarly, about forty percent of first-generation Vietnamese children are poor, a figure much higher than that for first-generation children in the other Asian subgroups" (Landale and Oropesa 1995, 6).

Refugee children bring to the immigration process the added dimension of post-traumatic stress responses owing to their experiences prior to taking refuge. The residue of these histories is carried into their new homeland, adding to the complexity of adaptation. Children coming from Central America and Indochina are particularly likely either to have been exposed to such traumas or to have parents who have undergone such levels of trauma. These experiences may lead parents to be psychologically unavailable to their children, which in turn affects the children's psychological development.

The data, in short, suggest that immigrant children come from a variety of ethnic, linguistic, religious, and socioeconomic backgrounds. In terms of their adaptation to American schooling, the children of better educated Asian immigrants tend to do quite well—often surpassing their U.S. peers in terms of grades, performance in standardized tests, and aspirations for postsecondary education. On the other hand, the children of poorer and less educated immigrants from Latin America and the Caribbean as well those of Indochinese refugees (perhaps not surprisingly) tend not to do as well academically.

What is surprising is that the longer immigrant students are in the United States the less well they tend to do in schools, a finding revealed by a number of studies (Portes and Rumbaut 1996; Kao and Tienda 1995; Rumbaut 1995; Steinberg 1996; Suárez-Orozco and Suárez-Orozco 1995). Kao and Tienda, for example, in an analysis of the first panel of the National Education Longitudinal Study of a nationally representative sample of 24,599 students from 1,052 randomly selected schools, found that, "Overall, both first and second generation youth, that is the children of immigrants, earned higher grades and math scores and expressed higher educational aspirations than children of native born parents. This generalization held even after the effects of race, ethnicity, and parental socioeconomic status were held constant" (1995, 9).

Although there are significant differences by country of origin in the school performance of immigrant children, new data suggest that length of residence in the United States seems associated with declining school achievement and aspirations for all groups. In his survey of 5,200 children of immigrants enrolled in schools in San Diego and in South Florida, Rumbaut found a "negative association of length of residence in the United States with both GPA and aspirations. Time in the United States is, as expected, strongly predictive of improved English reading skills; but despite that seeming advantage, the longer residence in the United States and second-generation status (that is, being born in the United States) are connected to declining academic achievement and aspirations, net of other factors" (Rumbaut 1995, 47–48).

If the majority of the immigrant children in U.S. schools were from middle-class English-speaking families, there probably would not be a chapter in this book on "immigrant children." While such children might confront some initial difficulties in American schools, their story would be one for an occasional Ph.D. thesis; their presence in our schools would not present major and unique issues for school reform. What is it about typical new immigrant children that distinguishes them from middle-class "mainstream" English-speaking children? First, in most cases they are not white. Second, they tend to be poor. Third, their families are not English-speaking. Fourth, their parents, who must guide their education, have very little education themselves, and often have no knowledge of how the American school system works. Fifth, the cultural values and the characteristics of the parents, and by extension the children, are often at odds with the values and characteristics of the school institution and those who carry out its mission. Finally, these children often find themselves in schools that are already the most overburdened and least equipped to deal with the needs of their students.

Balanced against these mountains that must be scaled is an opportunity that often does not exist within families that have suffered generations of oppression and poverty in the United States. Recent immigrant families and their children bring hope. They bring the belief that hard work can improve their economic and social condition. This belief provides a grand opportunity, research has demonstrated. However, unless there are major inroads into overcoming the barriers to education, hope too often turns to failure and cynicism. If education reform is to successfully break the cycle of failure for many immigrant children, it must understand the barriers to success and harness the energy of optimism that new immigrants bring with them.

In subsequent sections we will discuss the specific factors listed above and how they compel different responses to school reform. We begin, however, with a brief discussion of the research on the psychosocial framework of the recent immigrant family and how that can translate into school success. We do so to counter the sense of despair that so many seem to have about the likely prospect of breaking the cycle of failure that has burdened the children of many immigrants of color.

It has been long recognized that the immigrant generation often arrives in a new land as pioneers with dreams of making a better life for themselves as well as for their children. The objectives of first generation are relatively clear: get a job, earn money, learn a new language, if possible offer an education to the children, and in general improve their lot in life. Family reunification is another powerful motive driving many new arrivals. Some new immigrants, perhaps more than the current anti-immigration lobby may realize, often wish eventually to return home to settle there once financial considerations allow it.

The obvious difficulties that most migrants face include language inadequacies, a general unfamiliarity with the customs and expectations of the new country (what anthropologists refer to as "cultural discontinuities"), limited economic opportunities, poor housing conditions, discrimination, xenophobia, and what psychologists term the "stresses of acculturation" (Rogler, Cortes, and Malgady 1991, 585–97; for other studies of the stresses of immigration, see Arevalo 1987; Padilla and Durán 1995; Rodriguez 1989; Rogler, Malgady, and Rodriguez 1989; Salgado de Snyder 1990; Sluzki 1979).

Despite these obstacles, in many cases immigrants experience their lot as being better than it was in their country of origin (Gibson 1988). Because of a perception of relative material improvement, many migrants may fail to internalize the anti-immigrant negative attitudes of the host country toward them, maintaining their country of origin as a point of reference (Roosens 1989, 132–34). In addition, recent immigrants commonly view and experience their current lot not in terms of the ideals and expectations of the majority society but rather in terms of the ideals and expectations of the "old culture" (De Vos 1973).

This is part of an interesting orientation that has been termed "the immigrant's dual frame of reference" (Suárez-Orozco and Suárez-Orozco 1995). The Suárez-Orozcos have noted that immigrants are constantly comparing and contrasting their current lot in the host society against their experiences, opportunities, and expectations in the country of origin. During the earliest phases of immigration, the new arrivals may come to idealize the new country as a land of unlimited opportunities, concentrating on the negative aspects of life in the land left behind. The second generation, in contrast, cannot compare their own current experiences to previous experiences of relative deprivation. Instead, their standard of assessment may be the host cultures' affluent ideal (often represented in television and film) where they are likely to find themselves lacking. From the second generation's perspective, their lot in life has decidedly not improved.

Rogler, Cortes, and Malgady's (1991) exploration of the psychosocial consequences of an important generational discontinuity in a sample of Mexico-born parents and their California-born children relates to this immigrant dual frame of reference. They write, "The selectivity of the migration stream from Mexico to California tends to create a psychologically robust first-generation immigrant population who feels less deprived because migration has increased their standard of living; in contrast, the Mexican Americans born in the United States feel more deprivation because of their much higher but unrealized aspirations" (1991, 589).

The consequences of this parental optimism on the educational aspirations and achievement of first-generation immigrant children from a variety of counties of origin has long been recognized (Kao and Tienda 1995; Rumbaut 1995; Suárez-Orozco and Suárez-Orozco 1995; Gibson and Ogbu 1991) and is often translated into positive classroom behaviors (at least in the initial phases of immigration). Teachers interviewed about their experiences with immigrant students often indicated that they relished the positive attitude toward schooling and learning among new immigrant students (Suárez-Orozco and Suárez-Orozco 1995). These same teachers were puzzled to see that the longer the immigrants attended U.S. schools, the more ambivalent they became toward school and school authorities. As a perplexed teacher said, "The more Americanized they become, the worse their attitude is in school."

Researchers have suggested that sociocultural (including sociolinguistic) and socioeconomic factors, as well as overcrowded and poorly staffed schools, seem to lead many acculturated immigrant students eventually to develop ambivalent attitudes toward school and the value of education. In addition, we argue, ongoing discrimination and disparagement specially targeted to "unwanted" new immigrants is particularly destructive. Last, when learning and success in an institution of the dominant culture—that is, the school—come to be experienced as an act of ethnic betrayal, signifying a wish to "be white" learning may become a problem to some ethnic and immigrant minority students (Fordham and Ogbu 1986). As a consequence, a high drop-out rate continues to be a severe problem in some communities of minority immigrant children (see Gibson and Ogbu 1991; Suárez-Orozco and Suárez-Orozco 1995).

Barriers to Academic Success

As the largest immigration wave of the century carried growing numbers of foreign-born students into U.S. public schools in the late 1970s, educators in the public sector struggled to meet the academic and social needs of these students. They found themselves with few research findings to guide them, other than an inconclusive array of bilingual (dual language) education studies. During the early 1980s, the school reform movement had largely focused on "excellence" and paid little attention to equity issues for either U.S. or foreign-born students. Few researchers were interested in examining the many challenges that immigrant students were posing for public schools, except for the general consensus among immigrant parents and educators that these students should learn English. However, by the mid-1980s the barriers to academic success that immigrant children—and their parents—were encountering in public schools had captured the attention of advocates. In 1989 two advocacy organizations—the Boston-based National Coalition of Advocates for Students (NCAS), and one of its member organizations, California Tomorrow, released reports of studies that had examined the responses of public schools to swift demographic changes caused, in part, by immigration. A third study was released by the Rand Corporation in 1993.[2]

Today a growing body of immigrant education literature chronicles, on the one hand, the continued struggles of the schools to meet the difficult challenges posed by diverse student populations and, on the other hand, the continued struggles of students to achieve academic success while being educated by schools that are often unfamiliar with their needs and poorly equipped to meet them. According to Joan First, the executive director of the National Coalition of Advocates for Children, the following specific issues have been identified (personal communication 1996):

• Access to public education. Although, according to the *Plyler v. Doe* decision, all immigrant students who reside in the United States have a legal right to attend public schools regardless of legal immigration status, for many immigrant students and their families, school enrollment remains a fearful process. While most school districts have policies which are in compliance with the *Plyler v. Doe* decision, perceived and actual racism on the part of some school administrators, teachers, and school clerical staff may put undocumented students and their families at risk for deportation. Growing anti-immigrant sentiment during the 1990s (culminating in Proposition 187 in California, as well as a number of federal and state proposals intended to deprive undocumented students of their right to a free public education in the United States) has intensified such fears. As a result, an unknown number of immigrant families have avoided enrolling their children in schools.

- Access to comprehensible instruction. Although all limited English proficient students who attend U.S. public schools have a legal right to comprehensible instruction, many do not have access to a curriculum. Schools often fail to present curriculum in a language that the immigrant student understands and do not provide assistance from teachers or aides who speak the child's language. English as a Second Language (ESL) techniques are underutilized, as are other strategies to help the child understand what is being taught. Failure of schools to provide language appropriate instruction ranges from total absence of language acquisition supports for non-English speaking children, to provision of extremely poor quality language education services (exacerbated by severe shortages of bilingual teachers in many places), to placing students in regular curriculum classrooms before they are prepared to use English in the academic setting. These problems often result in damaging outcomes for students, including inappropriate referral for special education placement (particularly when ESL supports are prematurely removed), retention in grade (which is highly correlated to later drop-out rates), placement in low programmatic tracks, boredom during incomprehensible instruction resulting in disruptive behavior, and dropping out (First and Carrera 1988). (Ed.'s note: In California, these problems may become more severe, as voters approved a referendum in 1998 drastically limiting the use of bilingual education in public schools.)

- Language, culture, and handicapping conditions. The referral of immigrant students for special education evaluations and subsequent placements may be disproportionately high for some groups (such as Haitian students, who share with African American students a high risk of being placed in classes for the educable mentally retarded) and disproportionally low for others (e.g., Latino and Asian immigrant students are underserved groups in many school districts). The nexus between language, culture, and handicapping condition is a confusing one. While many immigrant students have special needs, and many are placed in special education, it is frequently unclear whether these children are appropriately placed (First and Carrera 1988). Some language minority children, including immigrant students, who do not succeed in the regular classroom have major learning disorders which make the regular classroom an inappropriate placement for them; however, many do not receive the special education services they need because their schools do not have bilingual special education programs. Other immigrant students are inappropriately placed in special education classes because school personnel are not equipped to adequately identify the causes for the child's failure to learn in a regular program; these causes may have to do with lack of English proficiency, cultural differences, lack of prior schooling, mobility, frequent absences from school, or placement in a classroom setting which is inappropriate to the child's learning style or otherwise does not accommodate the child's individual differences (First and Carrera 1988; Garcia and Ortiz 1988).

• Access to all of the school's programs and services. Immigrant or other limited English proficient students are often excluded from many school programs, support services, and extracurricular activities that are accessible to English-speaking students (such as internship programs, school to work transition programs, counseling services, college guidance, and so forth).

• Documentation of previous educational experience. When presenting their children for school enrollment, immigrant parents may be asked to produce documents as proof of their child's previous schooling. Producing school records, proof of a child's age, and other documents may be problematic to immigrant families, especially those who are refugees. Even when documentation can be presented, school personnel are often reluctant to believe information about the child's previous school experiences provided to them by the student and/or the family. School employees at times bring their own prejudices (and ignorance) to the enrollment interactions with students and families, resulting in low placements for students. To further complicate this issue, when such records are available, they are seldom in English. When many urban school districts have seventy-five or more languages spoken by members of their student populations, translation of students' birth, health, and academic records presents an almost impossible challenge.

APPROPRIATE GRADE PLACEMENTS FOR UNSCHOOLED IMMIGRANT STUDENTS

Immigrant children are placed in grades in the United States almost universally on the basis of age rather than the amount of schooling they have received. This practice means that a fifteen-year-old immigrant student who has completed only two or three years of schooling in his or her homeland will be placed in high school. Few teachers are prepared to teach such students; there tends to be a shortage of ESL and other educational materials which combine the student's current level of academic functioning with content which is age appropriate.

POOR RELATIONS BETWEEN THE SCHOOL AND IMMIGRANT PARENT

The low expectations many schools hold for immigrant and other limited English proficient students are frequently extended to their parents. This, together with profound barriers of language, culture, and class, impedes the ability of parents of foreign-born students to be full participants in the life of their child's school and limits their ability to effectively advocate for high quality educational services for their children.

Parents of immigrant students are often burdened by the economic need to hold more than one job, may live in unsafe neighborhoods where it is dangerous to be in the streets in the evening when many meetings are held, may lack child care, or in the case of women, the approval of their spouse to participate in community events. Some immigrant parents are fearful of contact with government agencies. Others have culturally ascribed reverence for teachers and schools and would never dream of challenging them in any way.

Many public schools lack understanding of such issues and are quick to declare parents uncaring when they do not respond to typically very limited outreach efforts, most often made in a language the parent does not understand. When public schools collaborate with ethnic constituency community-based organizations, participation of immigrant parents often increases, though such efforts remain rare. While a few immigrant parents participate in activities at their local school, very few sit on local school councils where they could be influential in making decisions about the school, its curriculum, and the deployment of its resources.

ETHNIC AND RACIAL DISCONTINUITIES

Ethnic and racial tensions and misunderstandings are manifested in a number of ways in schools.

Ethnic Tensions Immigrant students at elementary and secondary levels report high levels of racial tension and harassment in their daily school experience both from students of the "mainstream" dominant culture and from students from other minority groups. Many report longing for more opportunities to discuss these experience in comfortable, supportive settings (Kiang 1996). As one student noted, "There is hardly anything about race relation, anything about what it means to be a person of color in this country—in school. The discussion is just not happening. We do not have a place to talk about it, a place to come together and confront and share. People just walk past each other in the hallway; they sit in the same classroom, but they do not talk to one another."

Stereotypes School personnel often have preconceived notions about immigrants from different backgrounds. For example, Haitian students suffer the same expectations of other black students. Often, they are placed in low expectation tracks and ability groups. Asian students, on the other hand, tend to be held to high expectations, even if they come from low socioeconomic backgrounds. Teacher expectations are well known to have a significant impact on academic performance (Brophy and Everston 1978; Dusek and Joseph 1983; Good, Cooper, and Blakely 1980).

Guidance counselors, too, may (wittingly or unwittingly) undercut the likelihood of success for these students. This process may begin with the counselor's involvement in the child's enrollment in school and subsequent assessment and placement. Counselors also play powerful roles in determining whether students are placed in college-bound or vocational tracks. Here, again, low expectations all too frequently prevail.

Predominantly "Mainstream" Teachers The majority of U.S. public school teachers, administrators, and staff are white. Although the current immigration wave is nearing the end of its second decade, teacher training programs have been slow to address this gap. Teacher recruitment from immigrant minority groups has not occurred at the needed level, nor have teachers been provided with effective and adequate cross-cultural training about ethnic group differences as well as appropriate classroom interventions. For teachers that were trained and credentialed prior to the immigration wave that began in the 1980s, continuing education training has been even less available and effective. Without such training, teachers will be inadequately prepared to meet the needs of ethnically and linguistically diverse classrooms.

Lack of Role Models Kiang and others (1996) report that Asian immigrant students commonly describe their school experience as being one characterized by isolation and a sense of "being on my own." These students often do not feel supported by or connected to adults in the school. Like other minority children, bicultural and bilingual students have few (if any) role models in school. This compromises immigrant students' levels of social comfort within the school and may affect their ability to achieve optimal academic success.

It could be predicted that school reform efforts which fail to consider these specific barriers to academic success faced by the current wave of immigrant and linguistic minority students would not be effective. Let us now examine the school reform movement and how it has affected immigrant children.

School Reform

A decade and a half into the current school reform movement, it is reasonable to ask which schools, which children, which families, and which communities have benefited from a seemingly endless flurry of school improvement activities at every level—federal, state, district, and school site. Arguments can be made that resource inequities have resulted in middle-class children benefiting much more than poor, urban schoolchildren (Kozol 1991). Research evidence indicates that school reform efforts have not significantly changed the daily school experience of children who are poor, members of racial, ethnic and language minorities, recent immigrants, or agricultural migrants (Institute for Educational Transformation 1992).[3]

In fact, some reforms may have actually worsened the plight of these youngsters. Educational researcher Patricia Gándara (1994) notes that some reforms are "fraught with danger" for students who have limited English proficiency (LEP). Gándara particularly notes the potential negative consequences for LEP students of increased high school graduation requirements, choice programs, and reforms which have intensive testing as their centerpiece.

INCREASED GRADUATION REQUIREMENTS

The centerpiece of the first wave of educational reforms—increased high school graduation requirements—may have a far-reaching impact on LEP students. There is a relatively common belief that LEP students will catch up to rising educational standards as soon as they acquire English proficiency. Yet the data suggest otherwise. A recent study of programs for secondary LEP students demonstrated that those students who entered secondary schools without sufficient English to attend mainstream classes were at great risk of being tracked into courses which often did not yield credit for university admittance and would not even count toward high school graduation (Minicucci and Olsen 1992).

SCHOOL CHOICE

Given the evidence on choice programs which have been implemented to date, there is little reason to believe that large numbers of excellent private schools would spring up to serve the needs of LEP students whose parents are unable to supplement the basic government education allowance. Even where "choice" is limited to the public schools, LEP students can be seriously disadvantaged. Dispersion of students from a single language group to schools outside the neighborhood, whether for desegregation or development of magnet and choice schools, can deplete the critical mass of students required to mount an effective language program. On the other hand, LEP students are not likely to meet the criteria for admission to a district's selective magnet programs, which may offer better opportunities for educational advancement of students with limited English skills. Unless its implications are thought through very carefully, "school choice" could prove to be among the most devastating proposed reform initiatives for LEP students.

ASSESSMENT

With the advent of the current reform movement in the 1980s, frequent use of standardized tests has generated problems for LEP students. Decisions about students' future can be significantly influenced by their performance on such tests. Some states are requiring that all students pass an examination before being allowed to graduate from high school. Increasingly, districts are being pressured to compare their performance to that of other districts through the use of standardized tests. In some settings, pressure to do well on these assessments has reshaped teaching practice and curriculum, with class time being used to "teach to the test."

These assessment measures have largely been developed and normed on "mainstream" students. Critics have pointed out that many of these tests are not "culture free" and are in fact "culture bound." Questions are framed around issues and content that are not as familiar to minority children as they are to students brought up in the dominant culture. These issues are compounded for students whose first language is not English. In response, some districts have excluded LEP students from the testing pool (in part because it is recognized that LEP students' scores might pull down the overall districts performance scores), while other districts provide such accommodations as extended time to complete tests, bilingual dictionaries, and test administration by a teacher who speaks the students' native language. Even when the test administration is modified for a specific group, the results provide an inadequate, and probably inaccurate, profile of LEP students' skills and potential (Gándara 1994).

Immigrant students and limited English proficiency students should be left out of this accountability system altogether. If not, it is likely that LEP students will be assessed via measures that are poorly suited to assess their skills and knowledge adequately.

INCLUSION

Although not specifically mentioned by Gándara, the inclusion movement is another form of school reform that may not serve the best interests of immigrant students. As parents and special education advocates have successfully pressed for least restrictive environments for children with special needs, many school districts are developing schools or classrooms of inclusion. While inclusive instructional models are based on research for children with special needs, we currently have no data on inclusion programs designed for immigrant and other limited English proficient students who do not otherwise qualify for special education services.

Inclusionary attempts should be pursued cautiously and not be viewed as a one-time exercise. Inclusion demands an ongoing effort to make the "included" student as dynamically a part of the class as any student. Inclusion should not lead to oblivion. A student should not be included and then neglected, but rather included, integrated, and supported. Teachers working with these students will often need specialized training and support in order to adequately service their learning disabled students. Inclusion is not synonymous with "immersion," an anachronistic instructional practice that, with its unfortunate "sink or swim" connotation, leaves students unaided as they struggle in an inhospitable educational sea.

Olsen (1995) presents conclusions based upon a study of seventy-three restructuring California schools which serve diverse student populations. She notes that "school restructuring is an energetic, hopeful movement that is resulting in an increased focus by educators upon teaching and learning" (305). She notes that (1) whether restructuring will meet the needs of diverse student populations will largely depend upon the degree to which teachers develop understanding and knowledge "about how issues of race, language and culture figure in the lives and schooling of their students"; (2) "the promise of the restructuring movement to make schools better for all diverse students is dependent upon building broadly inclusive processes. However, often missing from the table are the voices of those people most connected to the communities of students"; and (3) the involvement of parents and care givers, while often a goal of restructuring schools, remains one of the most problematic aspects of reform efforts.

Another California study, *Voices from the Inside* (Institute for Educational Transformation 1992), conducted by the Claremont Graduate School, focuses upon the relational aspects of schooling and concludes that top-down reforms do not address those issues that students, teachers, and other members of school communities identify as most crucial to the motivation and academic success of students in diverse schools. Gándara (1994) provides information about the characteristics of largely local school reforms which have effectively improved the educational experiences of children from racial, ethnic, and language minority communities. Such schools have:

Comprehensive programs which are designed to support both the language
    acquisition and academic needs of limited English proficient children.
Strong parent and community involvement emphases.
High expectations for LEP students, as well as high academic standards.
Leadership of a strong principal capable of unifying faculty in support of a
    common and positive vision of schooling.

Gándara concludes that, "while many of the features of these schools are the same as those found in effective schools for non-LEP students, the schools have adapted these aspects of their program to meet the specific challenges of a non-English-speaking community" (1994, 62). "Hence, while the school may hold high standards for its students, it also makes allowances for students to meet those standards in more than one language, and while the faculty and principal may have a shared vision for its students, it also makes allowances for students to meet those standards in more than one language, and while the faculty and principal may have a shared vision for the school, that vision is also shaped by the particular concerns of the community in which the school resides" (Gándara 1994, 60).

Given the rapidly changing demographics in the United States, school reforms that fail to improve the educational and life opportunities of foreign-born students and other children whose first language is not English cannot meet the social and economic needs of the nation. If for no other reason than sheer numbers of such students, education reform that does not address the unique needs of immigrant pupils will be an abysmal failure.

LEGAL ISSUES IN THE SCHOOLING
OF IMMIGRANT AND LINGUISTIC
MINORITY CHILDREN

We turn now to a brief review of the legal perspective on discrimination along with current anti-immigrant fervor and the resulting attempts at exclusionary legislations. Taken altogether, this leads us to counsel increased protection and advocacy on behalf of immigrant students.

Historical Discrimination and Its Current
Anti-Immigrant Manifestations

The Supreme Court in *Keyes v. School District No. 1* (1973), observed:

> There is . . . much evidence that in the Southwest Hispanos and Negros have a great many things in common. . . . Hispanos suffer from the same educational inequities as Negros and American Indians. In fact, the District Court itself recognized that "one of the things which the Hispano has in common with the Negro is economic and cultural deprivation and discrimination." [313 F. Supp. at 69] This is agreement that, though of different origins, Negros and Hispanos in Denver suffers identical discrimination in treatment when compared with the treatment afforded Anglo students. (413 U.S. 189, 197–198 [1973])

The discrimination that the court recognized in *Keyes* had long been reflected in court decisions striking down practices that treated unfairly those of Mexican ancestry. A similar line of cases reflects the long-standing discrimination against those of Asian ancestry. While this documentation through court decisions has primarily centered in the west and southwest, there is ample evidence that national origin discrimination has not been limited to areas west of the Mississippi.

On the day the Supreme Court decided *Brown v. Board of Education*, it struck down the exclusion of Mexican Americans from Texas juries (*Hernandez v. Texas* 1954). Indeed, prior to *Brown*, persons of Mexican ancestry had successfully gone to courts in California, Arizona, and Texas to strike down school segregation (*Gonzalez v. Sheely,* 1951; *Mendez v. Westminister School District* 64, 1946; 9th Circuit Court, 1947; *Delgado v. Bastrop*, 1948). A number of subsequent cases found de jure segregation of Mexican American students (see, e.g., *Soria v. Oxnard Unified School District*, 1971; *United States v. Texas* (San Felipe Del Rio), 1971; 5th Circuit Court, 1972; *Cisneros v. Corpus Christi I.S.D.*, 1970; 5th Circuit, 1972). Tracking and misclassification issues have been addressed by the courts (see, e.g., *Covarrubias v. San Diego Unified School District*, 1972; *Guadalupe Organization, Inc. v. Tempe Elem. School District*, 1972; *Diana v.*

State Board of Education, 1971).[4] The quest for appropriate language program-ming has required court intervention (*Lau v. Nichols*, 1974; *Aspira v. New York Board of Education*, 1975; *Keyes v. School District No. 1, Colorado*, 1983). And the state of Texas unsuccessfully sought to exclude undocumented children from its schools in the late 1970s (*Plyler v. Doe*, 1982).

Discrimination against persons of Asian ancestry is reflected in cases ranging from *Yick Wo v. Hopkins* (1886) to *Korematsu v. United States* (1944). Indeed, it was not until 1948 that the California constitution was cleansed of a provision that mandated the segregation of Asian children in the schools of that state. *Lau v. Nichols*, the Supreme Court decision compelling schools to provide respon-sive language programming for national origin minority students, was brought by Chinese origin pupils in San Francisco (*Lau v. Nichols* 1974).

In short, there is a long and ignoble history of discrimination against immi-grant students in the United States. While this history may not compel a conclusion that every barrier must be attacked only through the courts, it suggests that heightened concern must be reflected in legislation and regula-tion, that such concern will not come about of its own accord, and that concentrated advocacy, and in many instances litigation, will be needed. This need for heightened vigilance is drawn more sharply given the current anti-immigration mood.

Public discourse on immigration has taken a decidedly post-utopian tone. Gone are the romantic narratives of poor immigrant peasants pulling them-selves up by their bootstraps to become proud and loyal Americans. The dominant image in the public debate is that of unstoppable waves of "aliens" set on (ab)using U.S. social services, refusing to "assimilate," and adding to the crime and social pathologies of the American urban landscape. Several polls suggest that many Americans believe that "immigration is now harmful" (Mills 1994, 18).

Sensing a growing anti-immigration sentiment in the population, President Clinton made clear that he would not let Republicans politically monopolize the immigration issue. The President said in his State of the Union address in 1995,

All Americans are rightly disturbed by the large numbers of illegal aliens entering our country. The jobs they hold might otherwise be held by citizens or legal immigrants; the public services they use impose burdens on our taxpayers. That's why our administration has moved aggressively to secure our borders more by hiring a record number of new border guards, by deporting twice as many criminal aliens as ever before, by cracking down on illegal hiring, by barring welfare benefits to illegal aliens. (Clinton 1995, 8)

The debate over immigration surely relates to a more general discontent in American culture. There is a sense that the structures of the welfare state have failed to solve our most pressing domestic problems (including poverty, inequality, and injustice) and are now increasingly ineffectual in light of powerful transnational impulses. There is anger over the irrelevance of a political class that is seen as arrogant, self-involved, and "out of touch." There is anger over economic decline and insecurity, diminishing expectations, and the "disappearance" of jobs. There is anger over crime and a justice system that is seen as "broken." There is anger over schools where teachers can't teach or even maintain discipline. Racial anger and divisive miscommunication seems to multiply geometrically. This general crisis of legitimacy and sense of anomie has injected urgency into the immigration debate, which seems to pose the unsettling existential question "If we can't deal with ourselves, how are we to deal with these new arrivals?"

A key ingredient in the debate over new immigrants has been the issue of schooling and more broadly the sociocultural adaptation of the children of immigrants. Indeed, an unsettling charge made by those opposing immigration is that new immigrants are not "assimilating" to the institutions of the majority society in the way previous waves of European immigrants are said to have assimilated. The image of clannish new arrivals stubbornly clinging to their counterproductive values, world-views, and languages is, of course, not new (see Suárez-Orozco and Suárez-Orozco 1995). But what we are witnessing today is the strategic deployment of this image to announce the imminent "balkanization" of the nation and eventual tearing of the American fabric. The moral of this story is unequivocal: If we don't cut back immigration, and push those already here to "assimilate," get off public support, give up their own languages, and learn English, we'll have our own version of Yugoslavia, American style.

The debate over English as the official language of the United States is structured around the cultural anxieties generated by the new immigrants. When presidential candidate Bob Dole announced on September 4, 1995, that English must be the official language of the United States, he specifically attacked bilingual education and argued that schools should conduct classes only in English. The Republican senator also proclaimed that immigrants seeking to become American citizens must learn English before being naturalized.

In short, mainstream American insecurity about the degree of social diversity it can tolerate will surely make the effort to secure schools which address the unique needs of immigrant students doubly hard and will cause a redoubling of effort. The starkest manifestation of this backlash is the effort to exclude a significant portion of the immigrant school-age population.

Legal Efforts to Exclude Undocumented Students from Public Education

The 1982 Texas ruling *Plyler v. Doe* provides both a factual and conceptual framework for understanding legal efforts to exclude undocumented students from American schools. In the majority opinion, which struck down a Texas statute denying school enrollment to undocumented immigrant children, the Supreme Court noted, "These children can neither affect their parents' conduct nor their own undocumented status" (*Plyler v. Doe*, 1982, 220). In the majority opinion, the Supreme Court noted,

> persuasive arguments support the view that a State may withhold its beneficence from whose very presence within the United States is the product of their own unlawful conduct. These arguments do not apply with the same force to classifications imposing disabilities on the minor children of such illegal immigrants. At the least, those who elect to enter our territory by stealth and in violation of our law should be prepared to bear the consequences, including, but not limited to, deportation. But the children of those illegal entrants are not comparably situated. . . . Even if the State found it expedient to control the conduct of adults by acting against their children, legislation directing the onus of a parent's misconduct against his children does not comport with fundamental conceptions of justice. (*Plyler v. Doe*, 1982, 219–20)

In the Texas case, the Supreme Court noted that even if public education is not a "right" granted to individuals by the Constitution, it is neither "merely some governmental 'benefit' indistinguishable from other forms of social welfare" (*Plyler v. Doe*, 1982, 221). Rather, "public education has a pivotal role in maintaining the fabric of our society and in sustaining our political and cultural heritage; the deprivation of education takes an inestimable toll on the social, economic, intellectual, and psychological well-being of the individual, and poses an obstacle to individual achievement" (203). The Court also noted that excluding undocumented children from school is not likely to make families return to their country of origin. Furthermore, given that—owing to amnesty and other legal factors—the "illegal alien of today may well be the legal alien of tomorrow" (207), denying access to public education to undocumented immigrant children "already disadvantaged as a result of poverty, lack of English-speaking ability, and undeniable racial prejudices, will become permanently locked into the lowest socio-economic class" (207).

The Supreme Court also commented that the spirit and the letter of the Texas statute raise "the specter of a permanent caste of undocumented resident aliens, encouraged by some to remain here as a source of cheap labor, but nevertheless denied the benefits that our society makes available to citizens and lawful residents. The existence of such an underclass presents most difficult problems for a Nation that prides itself on adherence to principles of equality under the law" (219).

Many subtle and even duplicitous efforts to exclude undocumented students have cropped up around the nation. It is a common practice to require a Social Security card as a prerequisite for school admission. Under pressure from advocates, and with *Plyler* as a tool, state superintendents in California, Texas, and Florida have issued advisories concerning this practice. Even more insidious is the "toughening" of district residency standards. The Court in *Plyler* anticipated such an evasion, expressly stating that school districts could not use residency as a false proxy for undocumented status. While school districts can assure themselves that a student is a bona fide resident of the district, standards that are unequally applied to aliens or which require an impossible standard of proof of residency for those who generally do not own homes, often share apartments, and frequently are forced to leave children with relatives or friends while on the migrant labor circuit would be viewed critically by courts in states with compulsory attendance laws built upon the recognition of the crucial importance that all school-age children should be in school.

In an unsubtle and direct exclusionary attempt, California voters on November 8, 1994, overwhelmingly approved Proposition 187, known as the "Save our State" initiative, claiming

> The People [of California] have suffered and are suffering economic hardship caused by the presence of illegal aliens in this state.
>
> That they have suffered and are suffering personal injury and damage caused by the criminal conduct of illegal aliens in this state.
>
> That they have a right to the protection of their government from any person or persons entering this country unlawfully.
>
> Therefore, the people of California declare their intention to provide for cooperation between their agencies of state and local government with the federal government, and to establish a system of required notification by and between such agencies to prevent illegal aliens in the United States from receiving benefits or public services in the State of California (Proposition 187, 1994, 91).

One of the principal objectives of Proposition 187 was to exclude an estimated 300,000 undocumented immigrant children from public elementary and secondary schools. The proposition's incendiary language, and the unsettling debate around it (for example see Lydia Chavez 1994; Rodriguez 1994; Sherwood 1994), is an index of the anxieties produced by immigration today.

Proposition 187 is currently facing several legal challenges. The provisions denying education to undocumented children are being challenged in both state and federal court (*Lulac et al. v. Wilson* 1994; *Pedro A. v. Dawson,* Case nos. 965085 and 965089, Superior Court of the City of San Francisco, 1994). The state claim primarily rests on the equal protection clause found in the state constitution. In California, education has been deemed to be "fundamental," thus requiring the state to justify its exclusion as necessary to uphold a compelling state interest[5] and narrowly tailored to that end. This is a burden that states rarely meet; it is especially unlikely that California can meet this standard in light of the U.S. Supreme Court's determination in 1982 that a similar statute enacted in Texas failed to meet a less rigorous standard of review. If the California courts agree with the undocumented students, that will end the case, as it is permissible for state courts to construe their state constitution in such a manner and thus preempt federal court review.

The federal challenge, which goes beyond education, is based on the federal equal protection clause; it is also argued that California's efforts conflict with certain specific federal laws as well as interfere with the federal government's exclusive power to regulate immigration. Many issues considered in the Supreme Court's *Plyler v. Doe* opinion are pertinent to central aspects of Proposition 187. Indeed, preliminary injunctions against its implementation in both the state and federal courts refer to the *Plyler* case.

While attention to immigrant exclusion has centered on California's Proposition 187, it would be a mistake to think that it is only a California phenomenon or that school districts are not engaged in other, less direct methods of accomplishing the same result. Proposition 187-type initiatives and bills have been under consideration in Florida, Arizona, and Colorado. Similar legislation was rejected in New York in the spring of 1995, but will likely resurface.

What would be the likely consequences of Proposition 187 and other exclusionary legislation if implemented? They may have devastating fiscal effects. State legislative analysts have suggested that while there would be some program savings by denying certain benefits and services to immigrants and their children, these savings would by far be outweighed by verification costs and potential losses of federal funds.[6]

The costs identified by the legislative analyst are likely just the tip of the iceberg. If, as most evidence would suggest, undocumented families remain in the United States, the consequences of education denied, both in economic and social terms, will be staggering. The denial of education will result in heightened criminal activity by those who have been marginalized and have idle time on their hands as children and no means of support as adults; many will ultimately rely upon the welfare system rather than contribute to the society as taxpayers and job creators; poorly educated immigrants will be totally removed from the social and political discourse which is so central to a participatory democracy; indeed, perceiving California society as one that arbitrarily created barriers to fulfillment of their potential, it is likely that they will be committed to undermining democracy's foundations rather than supporting them; and finally, the consequences will not stop with the excluded immigrant students. One can predict negative effects upon the younger citizen siblings of undocumented children, citizen peers, and ultimately their offspring, who will likely grow up in poverty because they do not have an educated parent.

Given the extraordinary efforts, resources, and losses that go into migrating to another country, it is doubtful that an appreciable number of undocumented immigrants settled in the United States will return home as a result of such exclusionary legislation. Furthermore, since a significant portion of immigrant families have both legal and undocumented members—a United States-born child is "legal," while the mother may be undocumented—"mass deportation would inevitably mean splitting of hundreds of thousands of families" (McDonnell 1994, 1). In addition, the current economic malaise in Mexico, an important source of undocumented immigration, makes it very unlikely that families from that country will return en masse. Last, there is no evidence to suggest that exclusionary legislations will act as a deterrent to likely emigrants (Cornelius 1995).

Exclusionary legislation is likely to turn every immigrant (legal and undocumented), every student with an accent, every "foreign-looking" student, into a suspect. This may engender suspicion, mistrust, and even more blatant racism in schools and elsewhere. Reports suggest that Latinos and other "foreign" individuals are now seen by some as "guilty until proven innocent." A few days after Proposition 187 was approved, a Latino cook in Los Angeles was "threatened with citizen's arrest by an Anglo customer unless he produced a green card" (Wood 1994, 2). In Palm Springs, a pharmacist refused to fill a "prescription of a regular customer because he could not produce on-the-spot evidence of citizenship" (2). In the words of immigrant attorney Lucas Guttentag, "The reign of terror has begun against lawful and unlawful immigrants alike. The racial climate is under siege" (quoted in Wood 1994, 2).

Exclusionary laws are likely to engender a much wider circle of fear—from the ever-dreaded INS or "migra," to teachers, school personnel, doctors, and nurses. It will surely reactivate—and accentuate—"persecutorial anxieties" and issues of marginality and shame, particularly among vulnerable undocumented immigrant children (Suárez-Orozco and Suárez-Orozco 1995).

There is also the troubling issue of turning teachers, school personnel, health practitioners, and administrators into de facto agents of the Immigration and Naturalization Service. If new responsibilities to report "suspected" undocumented immigrants to the immigration authorities are fully implemented, it is not clear whether these professionals would comply. If noncompliance becomes a serious issue, there could be substantial costs associated with prosecuting and punishing professionals who refuse to obey the law.

Demolishing Educational Barriers

Once school districts assume responsibility for educating immigrant children, the issue of how best to serve them must be considered. Below, we outline some key legal themes:

LINGUISTICALLY RESPONSIVE EDUCATION

Prior to 1974 there was no legal mandate for school districts to respond to the linguistic barriers that usually confront immigrant children. While there were a few disjointed and disparate efforts to address these needs, most school districts took the position that language was the child's problem, not the school's. "Sink or swim" was the common approach.

In 1974, the U.S. Supreme Court in *Lau v. Nichols* ruled that school districts had to take affirmative steps to address the linguistic needs of immigrant children. The opinion stresses that the plaintiffs did not demand a particular remedy, but merely an appropriate one. Congress later reinforced this standard, which had been based on an interpretation of the 1964 Civil Rights Act, by passing the Equal Educational Opportunities Act of 1974. This later act imposes a responsibility on school districts to take "appropriate" steps to address the linguistic needs of these children, and on states to set minimal standards and to monitor their enforcement. States can go beyond these general standards, and several have specifically mandated bilingual programs.

The mandate for "appropriate" programming found in the federal law obviously leaves a lot of room for interpretation, and that has been supplied by the federal courts. Two cases deserve special mention. In the 1981 case *Casteneda v. Pickard*, a federal appeals court established a conceptual framework for evaluating a challenge to a school district's practice. The *Casteneda* court ruled that a school district would be evaluated to determine (a) whether it had developed a pedagogically sound approach to addressing the needs of limited English proficient (LEP) children; (b) whether it had properly implemented the approach it had chosen; (c) whether it had in place an assessment program to determine if the children were succeeding; and (d) whether it was making appropriate adjustments when assessment determined that there was such a need. The *Casteneda* standard has been adopted by every court that has been confronted with the issue; indeed, the federal government in carrying out its obligation to enforce the 1964 Civil Rights Act, has, like the courts, construed that act as incorporating the *Casteneda* framework.

The second case of significance is a federal district court case, *Keyes v. School District No. 1, Denver* (1973). This latter case, which grew out of a landmark desegregation effort but eventually dealt with a language claim brought by Latino and Asian students, applies the *Casteneda* standards to a real-life factual setting. A number of fairly common practices were found by the court to violate the law. First, the court determined that subjective determinations of limited English proficiency by teachers and parents tend to overstate the English language abilities of children, and thus resulted in denial of service to students in need. Second, the court determined that the use of aides to provide ESL was a denial of equal educational opportunity. The court further found that a practice of exclusively using subjective evaluations to determine the language skills of bilingual teachers failed to meet the second priority of *Casteneda*— effective implementation of the chosen bilingual strategy. In the same vein, the court found problems with the district's recruitment and assignment practices. Materials and curricula were found deficient. Finally, the court found that an assessment program was deficient under the requirements of *Casteneda* if it failed to show that limited English proficient students were making reasonable progress in learning basic subjects and in narrowing the English language gap. The *Keyes* ruling led the parties back to the table to develop a remedial plan. After six months, a far-reaching plan was developed which addressed each of the above-stated findings and dealt with other issues.

The crucial issues today in providing educational equity for limited English proficient students were foreshadowed by the *Keyes* and *Casteneda* cases. The *Keyes* case necessarily had to consider how to reconcile the twin goals of language-appropriate instruction and integration. As with earlier cases in Boston and in Wilmington, Delaware (*Morgan v. McDonough* 1975; *Evans v. Buchanan* 1976), this was much less a problem than most commentaries suggest—at least if there is some willingness to accommodate two worthy goals. In Boston and Wilmington, students in need of bilingual programs were assigned as minority students to schools in sufficient numbers to assure an administratively viable program, but not one that segregated the schools. In Denver, notwithstanding desegregation, there were schools that had large numbers of LEP children. Classrooms have been generally integrated, though this has tended to spread too thinly the scarce bilingual teacher commodity. There is dispute over whether classroom integration (as opposed to school integration) serves the educational interests of LEP and non-LEP children.

Candor also requires a recognition that many Latino immigrant parents and others concerned with educational achievement wonder whether transportation to distant locales does more harm than good. It is argued that crucial parental involvement is substantially reduced and the non-Latino school personnel are often found to be less sympathetic to the language and other cultural needs of immigrant pupils. There are thus important policy questions surrounding integration and bilingual education, but the problems relate to policy and not inherent legal conflict.

The notion that virtually all children in need receive a bilingual program is belied by the facts. State Department statistics in California suggest that 26 percent of its limited English proficient children receive no special language assistance. Over half of the programs reviewed by the state in 1994 did not comply with basic requirements—and California is one of the more advanced states in this regard.

Even when children are in a program, there may be major implementation problems that are, in their own way, reminiscent of desegregation battles. Desegregation has a bad name in some minority communities because a hostile power structure at best reluctantly accepted it, rather than working hard to make it succeed. Language programs often result in students receiving inadequate materials, being exempted from assessment (and thus relieving the school of accountability), and being shunted into a narrow set of courses that do not lead to graduation or college admission. These problems, which are not inherent, result from inept, passive-aggressive, or outright hostile administration. Lawyers and advocates clearly must be sensitive to these and other difficulties.

A problem that has become more acute in a time of "English only" sentiment and grudging and limited acceptance of bilingual programs, is that of premature reclassification. Increasingly there are calls for strict time limits on participation in programs for limited English proficient students. Funding is typically restricted to two or three years in the belief, based on little more than legislators' gut feelings, that this should be sufficient time to learn English. Yet research suggests that, depending on the age of the child and the child's proficiency in his or her first language, the academic English skills needed for full classroom participation may take up to six years to acquire. Researchers differentiate the skills needed to merely function in the street from those required for full classroom participation. Clearly, equal educational opportunity, as measured by the Equal Educational Opportunities Act and Title VI, provide an entitlement until a child can compete in an English-only classroom. Reasonable standards must be met to measure this. An unreported order in *United States v. Texas* struck down an arbitrary two-year rule; more recently (1992), a consent decree in Florida made clear that a student's entitlement transcends the six years of funding provided in that state.

All these problems can be addressed by lawyers, but only with active and intelligent support from educators and researchers. The *Keyes* findings and other court rulings have been the product of such collaboration. The determination that evaluation of language skills can be quite subjective—and students and teachers often overstate those skills—required linguists to inform the court about the complexity of language, and educators to enlighten the court about pressures within school systems to undermine LEP programming. Issues concerning materials have required experts to testify about their availability, the differentials between those available to English-speaking and LEP students, and the educational consequences of such differences. The huge problem of LEP programs becoming watered-down tracks leading nowhere will similarly require collaboration to inform courts that LEP students are as capable as other students, that programs exist to counter such tendencies, and that the consequences of failing to deal with the problem will be devastating. Sadly, one thing we have learned is that without aggressive advocacy on those fronts, most jurisdictions take the path of least resistance and let an unsatisfactory status quo continue. It must be remembered that before that court spoke in *Lau* there was little activity to address the needs of LEP students. The needs did not change overnight—the mandate did.

A related issue that expressly deals with immigrant children should be mentioned. "Newcomer" schools are increasingly popular, built on the model of a school developed in San Francisco in the 1980s. These schools generally focus on secondary age students who have recently arrived from another country. Their conceptual premise is that to place a student, who often has limited education, no English language skills, and no orientation in American culture, into an inner-city secondary school is unlikely to result in a successful experience. The schools usually promise a faculty that is highly trained in English as a second language acquisition, some bilingual instruction, and a culturally sensitive milieu. Typically, the schools have been relatively small and have housed students from a number of countries.

While there has been no litigation challenging these newcomer schools, the Office for Civil Rights (OCR) of the U.S. Department of Education has set guidelines in an opinion concerning the propriety of such a school in Sacramento, California.[7] That opinion concludes that a newcomer school does not violate the 1964 Civil Rights Act if assignment to the school is voluntary, if it is limited to true newcomers, and if enrollment is of limited duration. An unstated but necessary condition is that it deliver a high-quality program that is genuinely shaped to the unique educational, social, and psychological needs of immigrant students.

Some argue that the promises of newcomer centers should be a matter of law and policy applying to all immigrant students, and that there should be no need for segregation. There is also concern that these schools could skim off scarce resources from other limited English proficient students. The counterargument is that a short-term, protected, transitional milieu is needed for these pupils. It does seem likely that, as a matter of law, if the conditions set by OCR are met, courts will permit their existence.

EDUCATIONAL RESOURCES

Many argue that minority pupils, particularly immigrant pupils, receive their fair share of basic educational resources; indeed in some majority communities many believe that huge resources are poured into bilingual and other supplemental programs that give an unfair advantage to immigrant students.

The perception, on the whole, is inaccurate. "Compensatory education" programs, including bilingual education, are relatively small when viewed in terms of the total costs of basic education. Not infrequently, the key components of the basic education program are not allocated equitably. Is it any wonder that we so often find that the immigrant student, full of potential, often ends up in the desperate shape of children from second- and third-generation immigrant backgrounds? Surely these pupils need more, not less than, their better advantaged, more affluent peers.

Because "the federal government has chosen to treat the funding of immigrant education as a state and local responsibility" (Cornelius 1995, 4), immigrant-related programs—including bilingual education, ESL, remedial education, and psychological services to immigrant children—are in many areas inadequately funded and staffed. The school experiences of immigrant students vary from state to state (California, for example, spends about $118 per LEP pupil, New York spends about $361, and Florida temporarily spent about $1,581 to train teachers to comply with the aforementioned consent decree).

Most are familiar with the two decades of litigation to equalize resources across district boundaries. That litigation, necessitated by undue reliance upon local property taxes, was forced into state courts by the failure of the U.S. Supreme Court to find that per-pupil disparities between districts rose to a constitutional violation under the federal constitution. (See chapter 2 for a complete discussion of school finance reform.) Very often the poorest districts have been those with the highest number of immigrant students. For example, in Texas the poorest districts, with the greatest needs, were found along the Mexican border and in the Rio Grande Valley. In California there were generally similar findings. Most states with large numbers of immigrants have gone through this litigation; it has appreciably enhanced resources in poor communities, though it has rarely achieved total equity between rich and poor. Courts and legislators have been loath to cut too deeply in affluent communities.

There is a new opening on the equalization front that should have special meaning for immigrant pupils: intra-district disparities. This litigation is obviously possible only where there are ethnic and/or wealth disparities within a district; it also is most promising in state courts, rather than federal courts. Litigation concluded against the Los Angeles Unified School District serves as a beacon (*Rodriguez v. Los Angeles Unified School District,* 1992).

A successful school requires a number of factors, among them experienced and properly trained teachers and an adequate facility. Cornelius has also noted, "The shortage of bilingual teachers is national in scope, but its effects are felt most acutely in California. During the last ten years, the number of bilingual teachers employed by the state increased by only 30 percent, while the population of LEP students grew by 150 percent" (1995, 5). It is not surprising, then, that "many California schools fall considerably short of compliance" with the state's bilingual education policies (5). In Los Angeles, like many other school systems, teachers and facilities have been allocated differentially to poor, minority, and immigrant children, on the one hand, and white, more affluent children, on the other. Pretrial discovery in *Rodriguez* uncovered that while approximately 15 percent of the pupils in minority schools were taught by teachers with incomplete credentials, the corresponding figure for students in disproportionately white schools was 6 percent. Twenty percent of the teachers at black elementary schools, 16 percent at Latino schools, and 12 percent at white schools were in their first year of teaching. These figures generally held at all levels of schooling.

The figures for overcrowded and oversized schools were even more stark—especially where Latino students predominated. At Latino elementary schools in 1992–93 there were 254 square feet per pupil, while the corresponding figure for white schools was 555. Thirty-four percent of the Latino elementary schools exceeded district size goals, while none of the white schools did. Again, these disparities were found at all levels of schooling.

A consequence of placing undertrained teachers in oversized schools is that the district pays considerably less per pupil. An independent study reported differentials of $500 per pupil between several predominantly white administrative areas and two predominantly Latino areas. Similar findings have been made in New York and Chicago.

These factors' importance to and effect on educational outcomes were developed by lawyers working with researchers and educators. For example, while the evidence predictably reflected average teacher experience differentials between minority and white schools, the lawyers were advised to focus on beginning teachers. While it might be argued that an average experience differential of, for example, several years, might not have an educational impact, few would argue that first- and second-year teachers usually lack seasoning to be fully effective teachers.

Similarly, the lawyers drew upon a burgeoning body of research about the negative consequences of large schools, especially for immigrant and minority adolescents. All of this helped the plaintiffs to sculpt a consent decree to equalize dollar resources between schools, force underspending schools to focus resources on beginning and undertrained teachers, and move the district toward both somewhat smaller schools and configurations within schools that minimize the impact of large size. Such decrees may help remedy an important disparity between the less affluent and needy immigrant students and the better-off white pupils.

There are variations on the problems caused by overcrowded and oversized schools. Each of these disproportionately strike immigrant students because the primary areas of growth are in immigrant neighborhoods. Lawsuits have challenged "waiting lists" for students where the student is not given an immediate placement in a school (*Navarette v. Long Beach Unified School District*). Even a short time lost from school can, for many of these children, hurt their educational prospects. Cross-town assignments of immigrant children without transportation have been uncovered in such geographically separate communities as Richmond, California, and Lawrence, Massachusetts. For poor parents, getting a child across town may be daunting. The assignment out of the community also destroys any realistic hope of securing parental involvement in the child's education—a factor in educational achievement that is universally recognized.

A new legal initiative to increase resources for inner-city immigrant children deserves mention, although it is still on the drawing board. A number of states either have constitutional mandates that schools provide an "adequate" education for pupils or have spelled out in outcome-based school reform legislation a specific definition of adequacy. In both cases a definition of minimal adequacy should encompass the ability of today's children to generally participate in the economic, social, and political life of the twenty-first century. Though participation may well imply different standards for different levels of participation, it cannot be denied that reading and mathematical proficiency at a high school level, as well as familiarity with the complexities of the political system, must be included.

Unfortunately, schools with high percentages of poor, immigrant, and racial or ethnic minority pupils often graduate high percentages of pupils who have not acquired these skills. With adequate resources, these schools can substantially improve upon their documented failures. Clearly, collaboration between educators and researchers will be necessary to help define skills that are needed, to overcome the common bias that the fault lies with the children, not the schools, and to suggest remedies that can point schools in the right direction.

During the past decade there has been a shift in school finance litigation from an effort to secure equality of inputs between rich and poor school districts to an effort to secure "adequate" educational resources. The long-standing case in New Jersey (*Abbott v. Burke* 1990) has recently resulted in rulings requiring not mere equality, but expanded resources in poor districts to meet the additional needs of low-income students in these districts. Litigation is contemplated in Florida and elsewhere that would extend this principle to schools with high percentages of low-income pupils. The rationale for such an extension is that resources ought to be focused on the most needy and that the school site is the most visible locus for change.

General Reform Initiatives That Are Sensitive to Immigrant Students' Needs

As stated at the outset, there are two interrelated goals in considering educational reform and the immigrant student. One realm is to assure that affirmative initiative be included and address the unique barriers immigrant students confront in the school. The preceding sections have discussed some major issues in this realm. The second area for consideration is how general reform affects immigrant students and how those initiatives ought to be shaped to maximize benefits for these students. In this section we highlight and suggest ways to resolve immigrant issues in the context of broader reform initiatives.

DEREGULATION AND DEVALUATION OF AUTHORITY

Much of the rhetoric, if not reality, of the school reform effort is based on the notion that laws, regulations, and heavy-handed administrative control have stifled teacher initiative. According to this widely held creed, if schools could operate like small businesses, with school site personnel and parents acting like business partners with a stake in the outcome, we would see a dramatic improvement in school performance. This belief often is coupled with testing initiatives that would assure accountability, which we discuss in the following section.

Several observations are in order. First, most laws and regulations which protect immigrant students were developed because most school systems failed to do so on their own. Experience does not, for example, suggest that the removal of laws and their enforcement in the area of bilingual education would result in improved language preparation for immigrant pupils. Especially at a time of anti-immigrant fervor with its attendant desire to "Americanize" these students as rapidly as possible, one can expect that many schools will revert to the "sink or swim" methods discredited in *Lau v. Nichols*. This expectation is heightened when one considers that there remains a significant gap between the ethnicity of the teaching force (largely white) and the growing immigrant student population (largely of color).

Second, the rhetoric of deregulation assumes that parents will become meaningful partners with the school in their children's education. Our experience suggests that tremendous effort, backed by financial resources, is needed to make this even a modest reality in immigrant communities. Many immigrant parents without the financial resources, educational and linguistic skills, and culturally attuned to passivity when confronted with the "expertise" of school personnel, will not likely become meaningful active partners in school reform. The problem is exacerbated by the disdain that middle-class school personnel often show toward immigrant parents.

There are models of immigrant parent participation which can serve to mitigate these problems and secure meaningful involvement in the school (Torres-Guzman 1994). Experience, however, tells us that they will rarely be implemented without an outside push. In the absence of their adoption, the school-parent partnership model is merely an empty hope.

TESTING FOR ACCOUNTABILITY

A second major focus of most school reform schemes is accountability. Conceptually the idea is to punish or reward schools based on student success or failure. Frequently this concept is viewed as the trade-off schools must accept in exchange for deregulation.

While in our view there are serious questions about accountability in practice, we would draw attention to two unique immigrant issues: measures that fail to account for culture and language, and curricular validity. High-stakes tests that confound success or failure with something other than knowledge are educationally and legally questionable. For example, in *Larry P. v. Riles* (1979; 9th Circuit Court, 1984), the court struck down the use of IQ tests for African American students with respect to placement into classes for the retarded. The court found that the test outcomes reflected cultural factors as much as ability. The same would be found if accountability were based upon tests given to children in a language that they did not fully understand. Several consent decrees have been negotiated on behalf of immigrant students on this very ground (see note 5).

While the response to this problem would seem to suggest merely that students be assessed in their own language, the solution is not quite so simple. First, there is a huge linguistic diversity in our student population that defies the creation of instruments in all languages. Equally important is the fact that most students are on a continuum of language development; there is often no "correct" language in which to assess the child. There are efforts under way to resolve these problems, but an accountability scheme without intelligent resolution will be legally and educationally suspect.

The second problem concerns curricular validity. All too often, immigrant students are in programs in which they don't have meaningful access to the curriculum. This may occur because they are placed in an English-only classroom in which they fail to follow the instruction. It may also occur when a bilingual or ESL program dumbs-down the curriculum as, unfortunately, often occurs. There is at least one powerful legal precedent, *Debra P. v. Turlington* (1979), in which high-stakes assessment of a student on matter that was not presented to him or her was ruled unlawful.

TEACHER EDUCATION

Much of the reform movement hinges on upgrading the skills of the teaching profession. In most states virtually every teacher will spend time working with immigrant students. While not every teacher needs to be a fully proficient bilingual teacher, teacher education reform will surely fail this population unless it includes efforts to improve the cultural knowledge and foreign language proficiency of the teaching force. Second, the gap between the supply of bilingual and ESL subject matter teachers and the demand of linguistically needy students is staggering. Without major efforts to narrow the gap, these students will fail to receive comprehensible instruction or acquire the English language skills needed to succeed in school and beyond.

HOW LAWYERS, EDUCATORS, AND RESEARCHERS MIGHT BETTER ADVANCE EDUCATIONAL REFORM FOR IMMIGRANT STUDENTS

By definition, the political process works more consistently and more assuredly for those with power. Power in a political sense comes from electoral clout, prestige, and wealth. Immigrant students generally lack all these. Those most directly affected by success or failure—the students and parents—rarely can vote and almost never can vote with sufficient numbers or unity to make a significant difference. Poverty being their condition, exercising power through political action committees or similar manifestations of wealth is not realistic.

What this means is that other sources of strength must be utilized. Each of these presents possibilities, but they are limited. On occasion the sheer intelligence of an idea can be reflected in law—at least when it does not appear to step on too many toes. It is not by accident that Massachusetts (with few immigrant students) in 1972 was able to pass the first bilingual education law in the country while Texas waited for a court order in 1980 before passing such a law. Thus, while limited by certain powerful realities, good ideas can be transformed into law by the coordinated effort of researchers, lawyers, and community leaders. Advocacy organizations familiar with legal processes can and should look for these opportunities. A research base coupled with the commonsense support of educators can make a difference.

Intelligent collaborative intervention can influence the regulatory process. In many agencies there are at least some individuals in leadership positions who are sympathetic to the condition of immigrant students. While ultimately these agencies often succumb to promoting the agendas of those with power, there is the possibility of modest change and/or greater change with the support of the agency leadership. An example of this process—and its limits—is the effort to secure a bilingual education regulation from the U.S. Department of Education in the late 1970s and early 1980s. After a well-coordinated campaign that included all the major national origin advocacy groups (which coordinated the effort) and educators and researchers from throughout the country, the department proposed a regulation that would have made bilingual education the law of the land. Clearly Congress was not going to go along with this. The downside—which will not soon be forgotten by the participants of that effort and their heirs—was a massive political counterattack which not only doomed the regulation but arguably created a national backlash against specific programs for immigrant students. A major lesson is that while the administrative audience might be more receptive to immigrant concerns, the goal must avoid arousing powerful passion among those with power or must be supported by others with power.

Joint projects are most likely to succeed. A recent experience in Florida provides an example. For years, minority educators in Florida had worked to secure state laws and regulations to improve the educational opportunities of immigrant students in general, and limited English proficient students in particular. At the request of a number of these pupils, a legal organization worked with a range of groups that had previously gone their individual ways. It became apparent that there were a number of cross-cutting issues—not always having to do with language. These groups, which included those with major African American, Haitian, Mexican American, and Puerto Rican membership, joined to file suit. Because of the breadth of the organization plaintiffs, and because of the strength of the legal claim, the state immediately sought to negotiate a remedy. A consent decree, which was far beyond the dreams or reach of those who had advocated for years, was the culmination of the effort. More will be said about implementation.

As with every effort described here, educators and researchers worked with lawyers to determine the contents of the decree. Yet no one is "pure" in this process. Some educators and community-based researchers stand to lose from any change in the system. While there is no formula for addressing their interests, there must be an effort to mitigate their concerns or only the narrowest legal or political victory can be assured.

Once legal victory is accomplished, the tough part begins—implementation. If at all possible, remedies for legal wrongs should be negotiated not imposed. School boards, administrators, and teachers are more likely to implement a legal mandate effectively when they have been part of the process of developing the mandate. A court-ordered finding of violation in Denver led to a negotiated remedial decree that the district leadership presented to the public as its own; it was implemented more fully and more quickly as a result. Even when this occurs, and definitely when not, lawyers and advocacy groups will need to overcome educator resistance to change. The test is to hold the line on the mandated change while giving school personnel time to adapt to the change, and to create systems where they are rewarded by successful implementation. It is interesting that passage of Proposition 187 in California was met by almost universal condemnation in Texas, which had come to see implementation of the *Plyler* requirements as the status quo. This was far different than the attitude in the late 1970s.

One in six children in the United States today is the child of immigrants. The sheer magnitude of this demographic reality alone should make the appropriate education of these children a pressing national concern. Educators, researchers, and legal advocates play crucial roles in ameliorating the educational experience of this growing population of immigrant children.

School reform efforts must be carefully conceived, coordinated, and implemented. It is crucial that organizations charged with the responsibility of supporting immigrant educational reform have the resources to reinforce one another's efforts. The degree of change in issues and individuals as well as the localized nature of educational reform requires a high degree of flexibility. A sense of shared mission and resources is the key to successful coordination on behalf of these children.

NOTES

The authors would like to thank Joan First of the National Coalition for Advocates for Students, who was the primary contributor to the section on Barriers to Academic Success. She also provided helpful critiques of the entire chapter.

1. While the presence of foreign-born students accounts for some of this change, their absence would not end it. Forces which change the face of America are also deeply rooted in young and fertile populations of established U.S. residents.

2. The National Coalition for Advocates for Students (NCAS) study entitled *New Voices: Immigrant Students in U.S. Public Schools* (First and Carrera 1988) was national in scope; the California Tomorrow study, *Crossing the Schoolhouse Border* (Olsen and Chen 1988), explored the impact of immigrant students on California schools and the schools' response to the needs of immigrant students in that state. A third study, *Newcomers in American Schools: Meeting the Educational Needs of Immigrant Youth* (McDonnell and Hill 1993), was released by the Rand Corporation. The NCAS and California Tomorrow studies focused on immigrant education issues, examining how schools might change if they are to better serve this growing and diverse group of students well. These studies used similar methodologies, which included large numbers of interviews of first-language interviews with immigrant parents and students, as well as public hearings that generated firsthand testimony from immigrant students, their parents, and advocates and concerned educators. These studies cast a wide net in their attempts to identify many factors other than comprehensible instruction which contribute to the school success or failure of immigrant students. In addition to identifying many service delivery systems which fail to meet the needs of foreign-born students, NCAS and California Tomorrow identified low teacher expectations for foreign-born children and parents and hostility and harassment of immigrant students by U.S.-born students and adults in public schools, as well as by some immigrant students from other lands of origin, as major barriers to student academic success. While the studies by NCAS, California Tomorrow, and the Rand Corporation have many findings in common, they also differ sharply with regard to certain other findings, perhaps in part because the Rand study appeared to rely upon analysis of existing data and policies, interviews with professional educators, and school observations as primary sources of information. At any rate, the Rand report did not mention low teacher expectations for newly arrived children of color, or intergroup conflict in the schools.

3. The degree to which the voices of parents and students of color, U.S. and foreign-born, have been excluded from the school reform movement of the 1980s and 1990s—and the degree to which this undercuts the success of local school reform efforts—are chronicled in several school reform reports (Institute for Educational Transformation 1992; First and Carrera 1988; Olsen 1995). Mainstream school reformers' reluctance to embrace the most critical issues to the school success of tomorrow's diverse students that two of the three documents were produced by education advocacy organizations, rather than by teacher-training institutions or mainstream school reform networks.

4. Each case resulted in court-approved consent decrees.

5. Though Proposition 187 is framed in terms of its presumed fiscal savings to the state, its implementation may prove to be costly. "The state and local governments (primarily counties) would realize savings from denying certain benefits and services to persons who can not document their citizenship or legal immigration status. These savings could be in the range of $200 million annually, based on the current estimated use of these benefits and services by illegal immigrants. . . . The state, local governments, and schools would

incur significant costs to verify citizenship or immigration status of students, parents, persons seeking health care or social services, and persons who are arrested. Ongoing annual costs could be in the tens of millions of dollars, with first-year costs considerably higher (potentially in excess of $100 million). The measure places at risk up to $15 billion annually in federal funding for education, health and welfare programs due to conflicts with federal requirements" (Proposition 187 1994: 52).

6. Supra note 5.

7. Available from Multicultural Training and Advocacy, Inc., 785 Market Street, Suite 420, San Francisco, Calif. 94103.

REFERENCES

Abbott v. Burke, 575 A.2d 359 (1990), 643 A.2d 575 (1994).

Alvarez, R., Jr. 1987. *Familia: Migration and Adaptation in Baja and Alta California,* 1800–1975. Berkeley: University of California Press.

Arevalo, L. 1987. "Psychological Distress and Its Relationship to Acculturation Among Mexican-Americans." Ph.D. diss., California School of Professional Psychology.

Aspira v. New York Board of Education, 394 F. Supp. 1161, S.D. New York (1975).

Brimelow, P. 1995. *Alien Nation: Common Sense About America's Immigration Disaster.* New York: Random House.

Brophy, J., and C. Everston. 1978. "Context Variables in Teaching." *Educational Psychologist* 12: 310–16.

Bureau of the Census. 1996. *Population Projections of the United States by Age, Sex, Race, and Hispanic Origin: 1995 to 2050.* Washington, D.C.: Government Printing Office.

Casteneda v. Pickard, 648 F.2d 989, 5th District Circuit (1981).

Chavez, L. 1994. "Immigration Politics." *Arguing Immigration.* N. Milla. New York: Simon and Schuster.

Cisneros v. Corpus Christi I.S.D., 324 F. Supp. 599 (S.D.Tex. 1970) aff'd in part, modified in part 467 F.2d 142, 5th Cir., Cert. Den. 413 U.S. 920 (1972).

Clinton, Bill. 1995. State of the Union Address. *New York Times* (January 25): A17, col. 1.

Cornelius, W. 1995. "Their Bags Are Packed in Tlacuitapa." *Los Angeles Times,* February 20.

Covarrubias v. San Diego Unified School District, C70-394 S, San Diego, CA (filed August 21, 1972).

Debra P. v. Turlington, 474 F. Supp 244, M.D. Florida (1979), 644 F.2d 397, 11th Circuit Court (1981), Reh. Den. 654 F.2d 1079 (1981).

Delgado v. Bastrop, C388, W.D. Texas (June 15, 1948).

De Vos, G. 1973. *Socialization for Achievement: Essays on the Cultural Psychology of the Japanese.* Berkeley: University of California Press.

Diana v. State Board of Education, C-70 37 REP, N.D. California (filed June 18, 1971).

Dusek, J., and S. Joseph. 1983. "The Bases of Teacher Expectancies: A Meta-Analysis." *Journal of Educational Psychology* 75: 327–46.

Edmonston, B. and J. Passel, eds. 1994. *Immigration and Ethnicity: The Integration of America's Newest Arrivals.* Washington, D.C.: Urban Institute.

Educational Testing Service.

Evans v. Buchanan, 416 F. Supp. 328. 359–60 (D. Delaware). Appeals dismissed for want of juris 97 S.Ct. 475 (1976).

First, J., and J. W. Carrera. 1988. *New Voices: Immigrant Students in U.S. Public Schools.* Boston: NCAS.

Fordham, S., and J. U. Ogbu. 1986. "Black Students' School Success: Coping with the Burden of 'Acting White.'" *Urban Review* 18 (3): 176–206.

Fudge v. Contra Costa Unified School District, C94–03756, Superior Court, County of Contra Costa, California.

Gándara, P. 1994. "The Impact of the Education Reform Movement on Limited Proficient Students." *Language and Learning: Educating Linguistically Diverse Students.* Edited by B. McLeod. Albany: State University of New York Press.

Garcia, S. B., and A. A. Ortiz. 1988. "Preventing Inappropriate Referrals of Language Minority Students to Special Education." *NCBE New Focus* 5: 1–12.

Gibson, M. A. 1988. *Accommodation Without Assimilation: Sikh Immigrants in an American High School.* Ithaca and London: Cornell University Press.

Gibson, M., and J. U. Ogbu. 1991. *Minority Status and Schooling: A Comparative Study of Immigrant and Involuntary Minorities.* New York: Garland Publishing.

Gonzalez v. Sheely, 96 F. Supp. 1004 D. Ariz. (1951).

Good, T., H. Cooper, and S. Blakely. 1980. "Classroom Interaction as a Function of Teacher Expectations, Student Sex and Time of Year." *Journal of Educational Psychology* 72: 378–85.

Guadalupe Organization, Inc. v. Tempe Elem. School District, C71-435 PHX, D. Ariz. (filed January 25, 1972).

Hernandez v. Texas, 347 U.S. 475 (1954).

Higham, J. 1955. *Strangers in the Land: Patterns of American Nativism.* New Brunswick, N.J.: Rutgers University Press.

Institute for Educational Transformation. 1992. *Voices from the Inside: A Report on Schooling from Inside the Classroom.* Claremont, Calif.: Institute for Educational Transformation at the Claremont Graduate School.

Kao, G., and M. Tienda. 1995. "Optimism and Achievement: The Educational Performance of Immigrant Youth." *Social Science Quarterly* 76 (1): 1–19.

Keyes v. School District No. 1, 413 U.S. 189, 195–98 (1973).

Keyes v. School District No. 1, Colorado, 576 F. Supp. 1503 (1983).

Kiang, P. 1996. "The Asian Family School Partnership Project." Paper presented at the National Networking Conference, National Coalition of Advocates for Students. Boston.

Korematsu v. United States, 323 U.S. 214 (1944).

Kozol, J. 1991. *Savage Inequalities: Children in America's Schools.* New York: Crown.

Landale, N. S., and R. S. Oropesa. 1995. "Immigrant Children and the Children of Immigrants: Inter- and Intra-Ethnic Group Differences in the United States." Population Research Group (PRG) Research Paper 95-2. East Lansing: Institute for Public Policy and Social Research, Michigan State University.

Larry P. v. Riles, 495 F. Supp. 926, N.D. California (1979), Aff'd in part, Rev'd in part 793 F.2d 969, 9th Circuit Court (1986).

Lau v. Nichols, 414 U.S. 563 (1974).

Lulac et al. v. Wilson, CV 94–7569 M.R.P, C.D. California (filed November 9, 1994) (federal case).

McDonnell, L. M., and P. Hill. 1993. *Newcomers in American Schools: Meeting the Educational Needs of Immigrant Youth.* Santa Monica, Calif.: RAND.

McDonnell, P. 1994. Complex family ties tangle simple premise of Prop. 187. *Los Angeles Times,* November 29, B6.

Meier, M., and F. Rivera. 1993. *Mexican Americans/American Mexicans: From Conquistadors to Chicanos.* New York: Farrar, Straus and Giroux.

Mendez v. Westminister School District, 64 F. Supp. 544, S.D., Calif. (1946).

Mills, N., ed. 1994. *Arguing Immigration.* New York: Touchstone/Simon and Schuster.

Minicucci, C., and L. Olsen. 1992. *Programs for Secondary Limited English Proficient Students: A California Study.* Washington, D.C.: National Clearinghouse for Bilingual Education.

Morgan v. Kerrigan, 401 F. Supp. 216, 241–42, D. Mass. (1975), Aff'd 530 F.2d 401, 1st Cir. (1976), cert. den. sub nom *Morgan v. McDonough* 96 S.Ct. 2648.

National Conference of State Legislatures. 1994. *America's Newcomers: An Immigrant Policy Handbook.* Washington, D.C.: National Conference of State Legislatures.

Navarette v. Long Beach Unified School District, BC135201, Superior Court of Los Angeles, Central Division (1995).

Olsen, L. 1995. *The Unfinished Journey: Restructuring Schools in a Diverse Society.* San Francisco: California Tomorrow.

Olsen, L., and M. T. Chen. 1988. *Crossing the Schoolhouse Border: Immigrant Students and the California Public Schools.* San Francisco: California Tomorrow.

Padilla, A., and D. Durán. 1995. "The Psychological Dimensions in Understanding Immigrant Students." *California's Immigrant Children: Theory, Research, and Implications for Educational Policy.* Edited by R. Rumbaut and W. Cornelius. La Jolla, Calif.: Center for U.S.-Mexican Studies, University of California, San Diego, 131–60.

Pedro A. v. Dawson Consolidated Cases nos. 965085 and 965089 Superior Court of the City of San Francisco (filed Nov. 4, 1994).

Pérez-Peña, R. 1996. "New York's Foreign Population Increases." *New York Times* (March 9): 27–28.

Plyler v. Doe, 457 U.S. 202 (1982).

Portes, A. 1996. "Children of Immigrants: Segmented Assimilation and Its Determinants." *The Economic Sociology of Immigration: Essays on Networks, Ethnicity, and Entrepreneurship.* New York: Russell Sage Foundation.

Portes, A., and R. Rumbaut. 1996. *Immigrant America.* Berkeley: University of California Press.

Quiroz, J. T. 1995. "Together in Our Differences: How Newcomers and Established Residents Are Rebuilding American Communities." Washington D.C.: National Immigration Forum.

Rodriguez, L. 1994. "View of Reaction to Proposition 187." *Houston Chronicle,* December 3, p. 33.

Rodriguez, R. E. 1989. "Psychological Distress Among Mexican American Women as a Reaction to the New Immigration Law." Chicago: Loyola University.

Rodriguez v. Los Angeles Unified School District, C611358, Superior Court for the County of Los Angeles (decree filed August 25, 1992).

Rogler, L., D. Cortes, and R. Malgady. 1991. "Acculturation and Mental Health Status Among Hispanics." *American Psychologist* 46 (6): 585–97.

Rogler, L. H., R. G. Malgady, et al. 1989. *Hispanics and Mental Health: A Framework for Research*. Malabar, Fla.: Robert Krieger.

Roosens, E. 1989. *Creating Ethnicity: The Process of Ethnogenesis*. Newbury Park, Calif.: Sage Publications.

Rumbaut, R. G. 1995. "The New Californians: Comparative Research Findings on the Educational Progress of Immigrant Children." *California's Immigrant Children: Theory, Research, and Implications for Educational Policy*. Edited by R. Rumbaut and W. Cornelius. La Jolla, Calif.: Center for U.S.-Mexican Studies, University of California, San Diego.

Rumbaut, R., and W. Cornelius, eds. 1995. *California's Immigrant Children: Theory, Research, and Implications for Educational Policy*. La Jolla, Calif.: Center for U.S.-Mexican Studies, University of California, San Diego.

Salgado de Snyder, V. 1990. "Gender and Ethnic Difference in Psychosocial Stress and Generalized Distress Among Hispanics." *Sex Roles* 22 (7–8): 11–153.

Sherwood, B. 1994. "California Leads the Way, Alas." *New York Times,* November 22, sec. 4, p. 11.

Simon, J. 1995. *Immigration: The Demographic and Economic Facts*. Washington, D.C.: Cato Institute and the National Immigration Forum.

Sluzki, C. 1979. "Migration and Family Conflict." *Family Process* 18 (4): 379–90.

Soria v. Oxnard Unified School District, 386 F. Supp. 539, C.D. California (1971).

State of California. 1994. *Proposition 187. Illegal Aliens. Ineligibility for Public Services. Verification and Reporting. Initiative Status*. Sacramento: State of California.

Steinberg, L. 1996. *Beyond the Classroom: Why School Reform Has Failed and What Parents Need to Do*. New York: Simon and Schuster.

Suárez-Orozco, C., and M. Suárez-Orozco. 1995. *Transformations: Immigration, Family Life, and Achievement Motivation Among Latino Adolescents*. Stanford: Stanford University Press.

Torres-Guzman, M. 1994. "Recasting Frames: Latino Parent Involvement." *In the Interest of Language: Contexts for Learning and Using Language*. Edited by C. Faltis and M. McGroarty.

United States v. Texas, San Felipe Del Rio, 342, F. Supp. 24 (E.D. Texas 1971), aff'd 466 F.2d 518 (5th Cir. 1972).

Westminster School District v. Mendez, 161 F.2d 774 (9th Cir. 1947).

Wood, D. 1994. "California's Prop. 187 Puts Illegal Immigrants on the Edge." *Christian Science Monitor,* November 22.

Yick Wo v. Hopkins, 118 *U.S.* 356 *(1886).*

Chapter 5 Special Education:

From Legalism to

Collaboration

Thomas Hehir and Sue Gamm

"I deal more with lawyers than I do with teachers!" said an exasperated special education director in an affluent community, describing how a large portion of his time was taken up with managing due process hearings. Another director of special education in a large urban system where parents simply did not have access to attorneys nevertheless spent a good part of his time resolving a class-action suit brought on behalf of all the children in the district. Indeed, the legal system has had a greater effect on special education than on any other area of schooling.

The positive effects of "legalization" in special education—that is, the use of lawsuits and regulatory enforcement to guarantee that school districts provide educational services to disabled children— have been beyond dispute. There is no class of children for whom schooling has improved more in the past twenty years. As a direct result of the passage and enforcement of the Education for All Handicapped Children Act of 1975 and subsequent legislation, hundreds of thousands of children who in the past were routinely excluded from school, shut away in prisonlike institutions, or isolated in depressing, dead-end programs are now learning, developing, and thriving in ways that most educators and policymakers would have thought impossible just one generation ago.

Since the mid-1980s, however, some critics have decried legalization, in part because of the enormous cost of providing an appropriate education to children with disabilities. Special education alone now accounts for about one-fourth of all public school expenditures in the United States. Kirp and Neal express a view shared by many other commentators and practitioners:

> Studies of the implementation history speak less of the promise of legalization and more of its pathology: compliance with the letter rather than the spirit of the law; preparation of standard form IEPs [individual educational plans]; resentment that handicapped children have gained a priority that does or may gain them more than their fair share of the education dollar; and defensive strategies, such as tape recording meetings, to protect the interest of the school district and teachers.[1]

Benveniste asserts that due process hearings in special education promote legalistic patterns of response that discourage mainstreaming of disabled students and move staff away from a focus on their educational needs.[2] In a monograph prepared for the largest professional group in special education, the Council for Exceptional Children, Sacken condemned the use of due process by "dissident parents" who threaten a district's resources and its "sense of competence and self esteem." He concluded that mandatory due process should be "eliminated."[3]

Critics also have pointed out that the due process protections of the law have had little impact on the problem of overrepresentation of minorities in special classes. The evidence shows that such overrepresentation, and the resulting questionable segregation of African American, Latino, and other minority students, persists, particularly in the category of mild mental retardation.

Though many criticisms of legalization may be valid, they do not tell the whole story. Though legal intervention can have unintended consequences, the view that we should abandon use of the law to secure the rights of disabled students is simplistic and unrealistic. The legal mechanisms that emerged in the past few decades to protect children with disabilities were essential for bringing about a desperately needed national reform, and they have by and large produced successful outcomes for students. Without the impartial hearing process and appeal system, there would be less incentive for school districts to implement procedural safeguards. Reflecting the strong support the law enjoys among parents and educators, Congress passed and President Clinton signed the Individuals with Disabilities Education Act (IDEA) amendments of 1997, continuing legalization as the dominant policy mode in special education.

Though it is important to recognize that the legal strategies used to implement IDEA have been successful, they have not achieved acceptable educational outcomes for many students served under the act. Children with disabilities drop out of school at double the rate of their nondisabled peers, and many who do graduate have difficulty finding jobs. This is especially true for urban and minority youth.

In order to make the promise of IDEA a reality for all its intended beneficiaries, the direction of legal reform efforts must change; they must be driven by new research on the best practices, must reach down to the local school level, and must promote optimal learning for all children.

This will happen only if educators and lawyers learn to work together more effectively. The legalistic model does, in fact, have serious limitations. Due process, by its nature, leads schools and parents to view each other as adversaries. Schools, parents, and lawyers must learn to collaborate, not just litigate. Moreover, the dynamic interaction of school systems with the legal processes established by special-education law often results in an exaggerated focus on process instead of on the needs of individual children. Educators need to recognize these limitations and take lead responsibility to develop new models for serving disabled children well. Finally, everyone involved must try to keep pace with our constantly evolving knowledge of disabilities generally and our growing understanding of how children learn.

Given the likelihood of a continued reliance on legalism, it is critical that both educators and lawyers who work in this area develop a greater understanding of and appreciation for the ways that the legal and educational systems interact in special education. With this as our purpose, we will begin with a summary of the evidence showing how much progress has been made in the educational status of people with disabilities since the passage of IDEA. This will be followed by a brief historical discussion of the legal principles underlying disabled students' right to receive public education in the "least restrictive environment." The next section will illuminate the legal dynamic and its relation to special education through the influence of due process hearings and court decisions. The final section will address current challenges facing educators and policymakers in special education. The chapter will conclude with a discussion of ways that lawyers and educators can better work together to promote educational opportunities for students with disabilities.

TWENTY YEARS OF PROGRESS

At a time when many question the efficacy of the federal government's activities, it is critically important to recognize that IDEA has resulted in demonstrable improvement in the lives of people with disabilities and their families. Research strongly supports this conclusion.

Recent studies document several positive trends in the educational status of disabled students. The number of institutionalized children with developmental disabilities is a fraction of what it was when the law was passed, going from over 90,000 children around 1970 to approximately 3,500 in 1995—at a time when the number of significantly disabled children has increased because of medical advances that keep more children alive longer.[4] Between the 1987–88 and 1992–93 school years, the number of disabled students educated in regular classrooms for more than 80 percent of the school day increased from 1.3 million to more than 2.4 million. The number of students with mental retardation in separate public schools has decreased by 38 percent from 1993 to 1997.[5] Progress in improving the lives of students with disabilities is not due solely to IDEA, but the requirement that school systems provide appropriate education in the least restrictive environment has been part of the support system children and families need.

An important sign of progress is the increased participation of disabled students in postsecondary education. The percentage of college freshmen reporting disabilities increased from 2.6 to 8.8 between 1978 and 1991. A recent study by Louis Harris and Associates found that "though the employment and income picture for the adult disability population is disturbing, trends in employment for young adults appear significantly better than for their older counterparts and may be showing the impact that access to education is having for the younger disabled population."[6]

People with disabilities are much more visible in all aspects of American life. In contrast to President Franklin Roosevelt, who hid his disability from public view, politicians like former Senator Bob Dole now run for high office acknowledging their disabilities. President Clinton has over one hundred disabled people working in his administration. An actor with Down Syndrome, Chris Burke, starred on a major network television show, and former Miss America Heather Whitestone is deaf.

IDEA has provided funds to local school districts and states to support innovation and program development as well as ongoing program support. The act also provides discretionary funds to support research, technology

development, teacher and parent training, and technical assistance to providers. The resulting innovations have been significant. The technology that
allows for the close captioning of movies and television was developed through
IDEA. It is unlikely that captioning would have been developed without
government support.

Machines that read print for the blind and devices that enable people with
communication disorders to speak were created with similar support. Cooperative learning, a popular technique whereby children assist one another in
learning, was developed by a researcher funded under IDEA. New methods for
teaching students with dyslexia are being evaluated systematically and dissemi-
nated widely with IDEA funds. Research and demonstration projects showing
how youth with significant disabilities can move into competitive employment
have been funded in almost all fifty states. Much of this research in special
education has also helped educators and parents to serve nondisabled students
better.

Not everyone supports the continuation of a national framework to address
the education of students with disabilities, however. A United States senator, in
a 1993 public television debate on the federal role in education, argued for
eliminating the Department of Education. He used IDEA as an example of a
law that overextends the reach of the federal government. The decision whether
to fund programs for disabled students should be left to local discretion, he
said.

The education of students with disabilities was a local option for the first two
hundred years of U.S. history. Throughout that time, large numbers of disabled
students were excluded from school, and few went on to independent living
and employment as adults. We do not need to relive that history—only to
remember it.

THE RIGHT TO GO TO SCHOOL

In 1975, Congress first considered what would become the Education of All
Handicapped Children Act against a long history of exclusion and segregation
of disabled children. Decades of legal activism and political advocacy by parents, and a growing body of court decisions, paved the way for the establishment of a federal right to education based on the constitutional principles of
equal protection and procedural due process, guaranteed in the Bill of Rights
and the Fourteenth Amendment. A brief history of this legal battle will help to
explain the foundations of legalism in special education and its influence on the
culture and practice of the field.

By the turn of the twentieth century, Darwin's *Origin of Species* prompted many to believe that society needed protection from the menace of hereditary "defects." The resulting eugenics movement sought to institutionalize and sterilize mentally retarded and other disabled people to prevent them from having children and passing on what was viewed as inferior genetic stock. Justice Holmes, speaking for the U.S. Supreme Court in *Buck v. Bell,* reflected the mood of the country when he wrote, "The principle that sustains compulsory vaccination is broad enough to cover the cutting of the Fallopian tubes. . . . Three generations of imbeciles are enough."[7]

Society's longstanding segregation of persons with disabilities logically transferred to schools. It was not unusual for compulsory attendance laws to exempt those with disabilities.[8] In 1883 the Massachusetts Supreme Court upheld the right of the city of Cambridge to remove a child from school "because he was too weak-minded to derive profit from instruction."[9]

Bud Beattie's case in 1919 had a similar result.[10] Beattie was born with cerebral palsy; although his speech was affected, his memory and intellect were not. He learned to read and write at an early age, and he attended school in a regular class. A representative of the state department of public instruction observed Beattie's presence one day when he was in fifth grade, and she suggested that he be placed in a special day school for the instruction of the deaf. The school board concurred, claiming that "his physical condition and ailment produces a depressing and nauseating effect upon the teachers and school children."

Beattie's parents filed suit. Although a jury reinstated Beattie, the Wisconsin Supreme Court found on appeal that his exclusion was justified because of his effect on others: "The right of a child of school age to attend the public schools of this state cannot be insisted upon when its presence therein is harmful to the best interests of the school. This, like other individual rights, must be subordinated to the general welfare." The one dissenting judge found "no evidence that as a fact this boy's presence did have any harmful influence on other children."

This line of judicial reasoning continued into the 1930s with the case of Beldene Goldman, who was excluded from the Cleveland Heights, Ohio, special school because her I.Q. was below 50. As in the Beattie case, a lower court supported the child's argument and the Court of Appeals reversed, stating: "As a matter of common sense it is apparent that a moron of very low type, or an idiot or imbecile who is incapable of absorbing knowledge or making progress in the schools, ought to be excluded."[11]

The Supreme Court's 1954 ruling in *Brown v. Board of Education* foreshadowed a fundamental change in judicial attitudes toward children with disabilities. Anticipating the application of the Court's ruling on racial segregation to the disabled, John Davis, counsel for the state of South Carolina, argued: "May it please the Court, I think if appellants' construction of the Fourteenth Amendment should prevail here, there is no doubt in my mind that it would catch the Indian within its grasp just as much as the Negro. Should it prevail, I am unable to see why a state would have any further right to segregate its pupils on the ground of sex or on the ground of age or on the ground of mental capacity."[12]

This argument initially had little impact on exclusionary practices in most states. Ohio, for example, continued to exclude students with significant cognitive disabilities from public schools. This action was legitimized on the state level with the creation, in 1967, of county boards of mental retardation that would have the responsibility of educating students "ineligible" for enrollment in a public school.[13] The Ohio law was further supported in 1969 when the state attorney general ruled that local boards of education must provide schooling for all children unless they were "unable to profit substantially from an education."[14]

That same year, however, Utah became the first state to produce a judicial opinion reflecting the Supreme Court's thinking in *Brown. Wolf v. Legislature of the State of Utah* was filed on behalf of two children with I.Q.s in the range described as "trainable." The children were excluded from school; their parents paid for their education at day care centers. Paraphrasing the Supreme Court, Judge Wilkens ordered the children to public school:

> Today it is doubtful that any child may reasonably be expected to succeed in life if he is denied the right and opportunity of an education. . . . Segregation, even though perhaps well intentioned, under the apparent sanction of law and state authority, has a tendency to retard the educational, emotional and mental development of the children. The setting aside of these children in a special class affects the plaintiff parents in that . . . they have been told that their children are not the same as other children of the state of Utah.[15]

The *Wolf* decision paved the way for *Pennsylvania Association for Retarded Children (PARC) v. Pennsylvania* in 1971. Under state law, children certified as "uneducable and untrainable" could be excluded from the public schools and were exempt from compulsory attendance laws. Following one day of testimony, the defendants in *PARC* agreed to negotiate a settlement, to be embodied in a consent decree.[16] The court later confirmed the wisdom of this outcome; the defendants' willingness to settle, it stated, "reflects an intelligent response to overwhelming evidence against their position."[17]

At the time of the *PARC* victory, laws mandating education for all children and youth with disabilities existed in only seven states; another twenty-six states had laws covering certain categories of disability.[18] The *PARC* consent decree, reinforced by similar settlements in Washington, D.C.,[19] and Orleans Parish, Louisiana,[20] firmly established not only the right of individuals with disabilities to receive an education but also the legal concept of least restrictive environment (LRE): "among the alternative programs of education and training required by statute to be available, placement in a regular public school class is preferable to placement in a special public school class and placement in a special public school class is preferable to placement in any other type of program of education and training."[21] The LRE principle is founded on the concept that when government restricts an individual's liberty in order to accomplish a legitimate state purpose, it is constitutionally required to use the least drastic means to accomplish that purpose.

The floodgates opened. Forty-six cases had been filed in twenty-eight states by 1975.[22] Many states enacted mandatory education laws for children with disabilities, but a federal law establishing the right to go to school was clearly needed. Such a law could require the revision of state statutes according to constitutional principles and provide federal financial assistance to support improved educational options.

Congress's first significant action to protect the rights of disabled children was the passage of Section 504 of the Rehabilitation Act of 1973. Arguing in favor of extending Title VI of the Civil Rights Act of 1964 to include persons with disabilities, Senator Hubert Humphrey of Minnesota said in 1972 that "we do not even have adequate statistical information on the great number of physically handicapped children who have the mental ability to attend school but are denied that right. The variety of explanations for this denial include problems of transportation and architectural barriers. But the injustice of exclusion remains."[23]

Humphrey's effort failed, but the pertinent language remained virtually intact as a separate section of the proposed Rehabilitation Act of 1972. The bill was eventually signed into law by President Nixon on September 25, 1973. Section 504 established in law the right of disabled students to be protected against discrimination in public education: "No otherwise qualified individual with a disability in the United States, . . . shall, solely by reason of his disability, be excluded from participation in, or be denied the benefits of, or be subjected to discrimination under any program or activity receiving Federal financial assistance."

The regulation implementing Section 504 relied heavily on the consent decrees in *PARC* and *Mills:* "A recipient shall place a person with a disability in the regular educational environment operated by the recipient unless it is demonstrated by the recipient that the education of the person in the regular environment with the use of supplementary aids and services cannot be achieved satisfactorily."[24] But Section 504 provided no extra funding for school districts. To address this problem, language similar to Section 504 was incorporated in the Mathias Amendment of 1974, which provided limited financial assistance to states to serve children with disabilities.[25] This reflected strong Congressional sentiment that, as Senator Harrison Williams put it, "these funds protect the rights of handicapped children to be educated together with their peers, and not be educated in a separate educational system."[26]

During the 1975 Congressional hearings on the Education of All Handicapped Children Act, the presumption that integration was its purpose became clear. Congressman George Miller spoke for placing the burden of proof on those advocating removal of the child: "I believe the burden of proof . . . ought to rest with that administrator or teacher who seeks for one reason or another to remove a child from a normal classroom, to segregate him or her from nonhandicapped children, to place him in a program of special education."[27]

Congressman C. D. Daniel argued that "the opportunity to share learning experiences with handicapped children will broaden the personal growth of classmates who are not handicapped. Lessons of patience, understanding, and the ability to provide peer encouragement are just as valuable as traditional educational lessons to the future citizens of this nation."

The House passed the bill by a vote of 404 to 7 on November 18, 1975. The Senate approved it 87 to 7 the next day. Senator Robert Stafford summed up the importance of the vote: "today Congress makes a very important statement of principle about how we intend our handicapped children to be treated in the educational process. Unfortunately we cannot by that or any other statement change the attitudes of those who would equate 'handicap' with 'inferior.' Attitudes and prejudices cannot be legislated away. They will only be changed by the good will of men."[28] President Ford signed Public Law 94–142 on November 28, the culmination of years of legal and political advocacy.

THE LEGAL DYNAMIC

Understanding how the legal system relates to special education is critical for educators, parents, advocates, and lawyers who work in this field. This interaction takes place at two levels: the individual level, through due process hearings; and the system level, through litigation and the resulting court decisions that have continued to promote the integration of students with disabilities. The combination of these two kinds of interaction creates a legal dynamic that, on balance, has served students with disabilities well, despite frequent criticisms of the type mentioned earlier. Greater understanding of how it works will, however, help educators and lawyers to serve children better.

The Impact of Due Process

Hehir's research on how due process hearings influence the programmatic decisions of special education directors sheds light on the complex relationship between the law and special education practice.[29] Though he found some evidence that due process can have unintended negative consequences, Hehir concluded that in general it has supported the goals of IDEA. Specifically, he found that, looking carefully at the way due process hearings affect the management of special education programs, the desire to avoid hearings improves both compliance with the law and the programmatic options available to disabled students.

Though relatively few parents of disabled students go through with a due process hearing, the impact of the few hearings that occur and the many more negotiated settlements between districts and parents that are designed to avoid hearings is profound. One hearing can influence the programs of many students. One adverse decision can lead to greater attention to legal compliance throughout a district, state, or region.

Some earlier researchers have called for a serious reconsideration of the procedural protections of special education law, or even their elimination, arguing that due process has not achieved the objective of providing an accessible dispute resolution mechanism between parents and districts or furthered the "least restrictive environment" requirement. Due process is correctly described in the literature as more heavily utilized by affluent, white parents, often seeking out-of-district private school placements.[30]

Hassel concluded that "excessive" legal intervention was an impediment to P.L. 94-142 implementation.[31] Sacken asserted that "dissident parents threaten not only the school district's resources and its professional sense of competence and self-esteem, but also threaten to publicly humiliate the district and its personnel."[32]

Hehir argues that most of these arguments miss the point by ignoring the influence of these hearings on the education of the individual student and other students and neglecting the impact of the formal and informal negotiated settlements that take place in special education directors' offices daily. The threat of a hearing is an essential element in the relationship between districts and parents because it raises the stakes in disputes over placement. As a result, negotiated agreements are common, and they are significantly different in both tone and impact than due process hearings.

This earlier research also misses the fact that due process has promoted integration of students with disabilities. It is true that very few disputes over integration proceed to hearings. But a closer look at the actual practice of special education directors reveals that many parents use due process to gain more integration for their children. Integration disputes rarely lead to hearings because directors usually negotiate agreements with the parents. They do this because, unlike private school placements, integrated placements are usually no more costly—and are sometimes less expensive—than segregated placements. Furthermore, special education directors know that the law favors the least restrictive environment and therefore anticipate losing if the dispute proceeds to a hearing.

Much of the earlier research, which looked only at the impact of due process hearings that took place (not at the impact of hearings that did not take place), missed these critical effects. Even at the hearings that did take place, the researchers ignored positive programmatic effects, focusing solely on cost, the adversarial nature of due process, and school "self-esteem." In the case of parents seeking integrated placements, Hehir found that procedural protections worked largely as the law intended. By taking a narrow view of due process, some researchers missed the systematic impact that the threat of hearings has had on the system as a whole. Due process hearings are one end of a continuum of dispute resolution options in special education that also includes conversation, negotiation, joint problem solving, and mediation.

Special education directors in Hehir's sample agreed that due process was a major part of their work and that their ability to deal with hearings, or the threat thereof, was a significant indicator of their effectiveness. Naturally, directors are frustrated when they lose cases that they think they should have won. They must deal with the displeasure of superintendents and school boards when they present attorneys' bills, and they complain about unreasonable parents who, in their view, abuse the system. But with few exceptions, these directors opposed the elimination of due process in special education. They simply did not trust their districts to address the needs of disabled students without this safeguard. They have learned to live quite well with procedural protections and indicated that at times they used the threat of hearings to access necessary resources for disabled children.

"If I were to say, philosophically, I think we need this vocational transition program, I'd never get it," said one urban special education director. "But if I say to my superintendent, 'We're going to get our ass beat in a hearing again unless we beef up that program,' all of a sudden the funds are available."[33]

Commentators like Kirp, Sacken, and Hassel have tried to draw a distinction between legalism and professionalism in special education practice. Benveniste views legalism as excessive attention to procedures and rules, whereas professionalism is attention to students' needs. Those who place due process on the legalism side of that line have an overly simplistic view. It is clear that districts that ignore procedural requirements—such as conducting evaluations on time, developing appropriate IEPs, and reviewing and reevaluating students according to the law—are at a serious disadvantage in a due process hearing. Losing at such a hearing spurs the district to clean up its procedural act.

If complying with the laws on special education is a worthy goal, then hearings are serving an important role. Federal monitoring has shown that, after twenty years of implementation, most districts have made major strides.

Once procedural compliance has been achieved, most hearings revolve around issues of quality: Will these services provide this student with an appropriate education as required by the law? Research shows that losing a due process hearing often prompts districts to improve services to avoid future defeats.[34] Thus legalism can promote professionalism—not undermine it—by creating incentives for school systems to address issues of quality.

The Influence of the Courts

The courts have generally supported the integration of students with disabilities with their nondisabled peers. They continue to find in favor of inclusion of children with more significant disabilities.

The first federal case to address the education of a student with a disability was *Hairston v. Drosick*,[35] filed in 1976 under Section 504. The school district had agreed to educate a child with spina bifida in a regular classroom only if the mother attended to her child's personal needs in school. Otherwise, the district argued, the child should be educated at home or in a special school that had the resources to attend to the child. The court was unpersuaded by the district's arguments of administrative burdens and costs: "A major goal of the education process is the socialization process that takes place in the regular classroom, with the resulting capability to interact in a social way with one's peers. It is therefore imperative that every child receive an education with his or her peers insofar as it is at all possible."[36] The court concluded that a child could not be removed from the regular classroom unless there were "compelling educational justification" and "every effort [has been made] to include such children . . . even at great expense to the school system."[37] Eight years later, the U.S. Supreme Court reaffirmed these principles in *Tatro v. State of Texas*[38] and other cases involving health issues and "related services" that IDEA requires.

Remarkably, until the 1989 case of *Daniel R. R.*[39] (see below) the courts were not asked to rule on the appropriateness of including students with disabilities in regular classes with supplementary aids and services, except for cases that involved the health needs of students with "normal intelligence." Previous cases involving children with mental retardation focused on their relocation from special schools to special classes with some integration in regular schools. Not one case focused on those supplementary aids and services that might be appropriate to support these children's education in regular classrooms.

For example, *Campbell v. Talladega County Board of Education and Board of Education of the State of Alabama* concerned an eighteen-year-old named Joseph with a severe cognitive disability who had a mental age of approximately two and a half.[40] He was almost entirely nonverbal and had significant delays in motor skills. Joseph's behavior was difficult: inappropriate touching, pulling hair, throwing food to the ground. His parents had initiated several due process hearings and state administrative reviews to challenge a series of transportation problems, school exclusions, inappropriate programs, and isolation from his nondisabled peers. Two levels of state due process decisions had supported the school district's placement of Joseph in a separate school.

Basing its decision on expert testimony, the court ruled that, in spite of Joseph's disabilities, "he is capable of learning" and that "students far more severely retarded had been taught skills significantly above his present levels."[41] Finding that Joseph's educational program should be geared toward "the goal of eventually integrating him into society to the greatest extent possible," the court ruled that this goal was subverted by Joseph's placement in a separate school with minimal contact with nondisabled young people. It ordered, first, the revision of Joseph's IEP to focus on acquiring functional skills in daily living activities, vocational activities, recreation, and social and community adjustment; second, in-service training for Joseph's teacher and the county special education coordinator; third, significantly increased contact between Joseph and nondisabled students, to be achieved either by placing his class in the regular public school, by placing classes for the nondisabled in Joseph's special school, or by "bearing the heavy burden of producing a plan which will satisfy the court that [Joseph's] interaction with nondisabled students will be substantially equal to that he would enjoy if his class were located in the main school building"; and, finally, compensatory education for two years past Joseph's 21st birthday.

Another case, *Pehowski v. Blatnik*,[42] addressed the widespread practice of placing children in separate schools based on the student's diagnostic label. The court ruled that "the Defendant's policy of automatically assigning all students designated by Defendants to be trainable mentally retarded to the segregated schools in the system violates Section 504 of the Rehabilitation Act, and violates the concept of mainstreaming as embodied in the Education for All Handicapped Children Act."[43]

In 1983 the Sixth Circuit Court of Appeals was the first to apply an operational analysis of the least restrictive environment standard to the question of determining whether a student required the separate day school placement recommended by the district or the regular school (special class with integrated services) requested by the parent. In *Roncker v. Walter*,[44] the court vacated a district court judgment that school officials did not abuse their discretion in recommending a separate day school with no integration opportunities for a student with severe cognitive disabilities. The court summarized its understanding of the law and previous rulings:

> [IDEA] does not require mainstreaming in every case but its requirement that mainstreaming be provided to the *maximum* extent appropriate indicates a very strong congressional preference. . . . In some cases, a placement which may be considered better for academic reasons may not be appropriate because of the failure to provide for mainstreaming. The perception that a segregated institution is academically superior for a [child with a disability] may reflect no more than a basic disagreement with the mainstreaming concept. Such a disagreement is not, of course, any basis for not following the Act's mandate.[45]

Based on its understanding, the court articulated what has come to be called the "portability" standard: "In a case where the segregated facility is considered superior, the court should determine whether the services which make that placement superior could be feasible provided in a non-segregated setting. If they can, the placement in the segregated school would be inappropriate under the Act."[46]

Regular Education Placement

The first case to focus on an inclusive educational program for a student with disabilities was *Daniel R. R. v. State Board of Education.*[47] Daniel was a six-year-old with Down syndrome. His developmental age was between two and three years, and his communication skills were not quite those of a two-year-old.

The Fifth Circuit began its analysis in Daniel's case with the guidance of the U.S. Supreme Court in *Board of Education v. Rowley.*[48] In that case, the Supreme Court held that a "free appropriate public education" under IDEA consists of educational instruction specifically designed to meet the unique needs of the handicapped child, supported by such services as are necessary to permit the child "to benefit" from the instruction. The IDEA specifically "requires participating States to educate handicapped children with nonhandicapped children whenever possible."[49] In its decision, however, the Supreme Court did not address how the courts should evaluate the least restrictive environment requirement of IDEA.[50]

The *Daniel R. R.* court broke ranks with the *Roncker* analysis, believing that it necessitates too intrusive an inquiry into the educational policy choices that Congress deliberately left to state and local officials. Instead, the court believed that the "language of [IDEA] itself provides a workable test for determining whether a state has complied with the Act's mainstreaming requirement."[51] Finding that IDEA established "a strong preference for mainstreaming" which rises to the level of a rebuttable presumption,[52] the court established the following two-prong test:

1. Can education in the regular classroom, with the use of supplementary aids and services, be achieved satisfactorily for the child?
   A. Have there been reasonable efforts to accommodate the child (with supplementary aids and services) in a regular classroom?
   B. Will the child receive educational benefits in a regular classroom (with supplementary aids and services) that are comparable to the benefits the child will receive in a special education classroom?
   C. What are the possible negative effects the child's inclusion may have on the education of the other children in the regular classroom?
2. If removal from a regular education classroom is necessary, is the child participating with nondisabled peers in academic, nonacademic and extracurricular activities to the maximum extent appropriate?[53]

Although the court in *Daniel R. R.* did not support the parents' claim that the school district improperly removed the child from the regular educational environment, it laid the foundation that was used by future courts to do so for other children. In addition, this case was the first to put school districts on notice that courts would not tolerate "mere token gestures" to accommodate the needs of students with disabilities in general education classes through the use of supplementary aids and services.[54]

Neither the IDEA's statute, nor its regulation, nor case law prior to 1992 provided specific examples of "supplementary aids and services" other than a "resource room" (learning center that provides services for a short period of time during the day) or "itinerant instruction" (special education teacher who may provide services to children in different schools for a short period of time each day or week).[55] The first court decision to do so was in *Oberti v. Board of Education.*[56]

Given the legislative and judicial void in giving meaning to the kinds of supplementary aids and services that a school district might have to consider for a child, the court in *Oberti* freely referred to expert witnesses who suggested such measures as:

- partial modification of the curriculum to accommodate the child's different level of ability;
- modification of the child's program so that he would perform a similar activity or exercise to that performed by the whole class, but at a level appropriate to his ability;
- parallel instruction (i.e., having the child work separately within the classroom on an activity beneficial to him while the rest of the class worked on an activity that would not benefit the child);
- special education training for the regular teacher;
- behavior modification programs;
- removal of the child from the classroom to receive some special instruction or services in a resource room, completely apart from the class.[57]

Relying on what it had learned from Rafael's educational experts, the *Oberti* court found that the school district had made only negligible efforts to include Rafael in a regular classroom. Rafael had been placed in a developmental kindergarten class "without a curriculum plan, without a behavior management plan, and without providing adequate special education support staff to the teacher."[58] In addition, the court found that, although the school district had "access to information and expertise about specific methods and services to enable children with disabilities like Rafael to be included in a regular class-room, . . . the district did not provide such supplementary aides and services for Rafael."[59]

Following *Oberti*, the Eleventh Circuit Court of Appeals in *Sacramento City Unified School District Board of Education v. Rachel Holland* found that all of Rachel's IEP goals could be implemented in a regular class setting with some modification to the curriculum and with the assistance of a part-time aide.[60] Since Rachel had been unilaterally placed by her parents in a school having only general education classes, they were able to produce persuasive testimony from her teacher as well as experts regarding the reasonable progress she had made in that environment.

In these pivotal decisions, the courts compared the benefits to the child of being in a regular classroom with those of being in a special education class-room. The courts in *Oberti* and *Holland* relied on expert testimony, paying special attention to their contention that disabled children are much more likely to develop critical social and communicative skills through interaction with nondisabled peers than in a segregated environment. The judges acknowl-edged that such children like Rafael and Rachel might absorb only a minimal amount of the regular education program, but held that they would still benefit enormously from the language models that nondisabled peers would provide.[61]

In *Oberti*, the court found that Rafael would benefit academically and socially from inclusion in a regular classroom. In addition, it commented that nondisabled children would benefit from having Rafael in their class. The court discounted the district's expert testimony that a regular teacher would not be able to communicate with Rafael and that the curriculum would have to be modified beyond recognition to accommodate him. Instead, the court was persuaded by the parents' experts, who pointed to various "commonly applied methods" that could be used by the teacher, with appropriate training.[62]

In *Holland*, the parents argued that Rachel needed social, behavioral, and communicative skills that she would not acquire if she were excluded from the regular class. While the school district argued that Rachel needed to focus on functional skills that she would not acquire in the regular classroom, such as handling money, doing laundry, and using public transportation, these skills were not included in her IEP.[63]

The Problem of Disruptive Behavior

That some students with disabilities engage in disruptive behavior is the single most important argument against a regular classroom placement. While the courts have been extremely sympathetic to schools on this issue, they have nevertheless strictly scrutinized behavior-based arguments. School officials have been required to describe not only the behavior of the student but the steps taken by the district to address the problem and accommodate the student in the regular classroom.

In *Oberti,* for example, the court stated that the student's disruptive behavior was relevant only to the extent that reasonable steps (in the form of supplementary aids and services) would not effectively reduce the disruption.[64] In this case, Rafael had a history of serious behavioral problems in developmental kindergarten, including repeated toilet accidents, temper tantrums, hiding under furniture, and touching, hitting, and spitting on other children. On several occasions, Rafael hit the teacher and the teacher's aide. But the court accepted the parents' expert testimony that with adequate supplementary aids and services he would no longer cause significant disruption.

The court found that Rafael's prior behavior problems were exacerbated by the inadequate level of services that had been provided to him. Although his teacher had mode some attempts to modify the curriculum for Rafael, his IEP provided no plan for addressing his behavior problems, for special education consultation for the kindergarten teacher, or for communication between the regular teacher and the special education teacher. The court found that Rafael would not have had such severe behavior problems if these additional services had been provided.[65]

In *Holland,* the court found that, with a part-time aide, Rachel did not pose a significant burden.[66] And in *Greer,* the court found that the student became less disruptive and made some progress in regular education without taking up an inordinate amount of the teacher's time.[67]

As in *Daniel R. R.,* where the court found that the child's disruptive behavior mitigated against placement in a regular education classroom, cases decided after *Holland* and *Oberti* relied on the child's difficult behavior to justify separate special education placement. In *Clyde K. v. Puyallup School District,* [68] the student violently attacked two students, assaulted staff members, and disrupted the regular education class with profanity and sexually explicit remarks. In supporting a separate school placement for the child, the court found that a personal aide was not likely to make a meaningful difference for the child in a regular class and noted that the district had offered supplementary services and accommodations through special training for staff, resource classes in academic subjects, and the assistance of behavioral specialists.

Location of Services

In the 1990s, two circuit courts examined the right of a child to be educated in the child's "home" or "neighborhood school." Following the precedent established in the 1989 Fourth Circuit case of *Barnett v. Fairfax County School Board,*[69] the Tenth and Fifth Circuits have established that, under the LRE provisions, a child should attend the neighborhood school unless the child's individualized education program requires arrangements that do not exist at that school.

In *Murray v. Montrose County School District,*[70] parents challenged the school district's decision to move their son from his neighborhood school to a school with a program for children with severe disabilities. Tyler, who was twelve years old at the time of the court decision, has multiple disabilities including cerebral palsy, significant mental and physical impairments, and speech difficulties.

In December 1990, when Tyler was in the second grade at his neighborhood school, the school district decided to transfer him to another school. Reviewing this decision, the court found that Tyler's parents never challenged his IEP "insofar as it determined how much time Tyler should spend in a regular classroom, as compared with special education or resource classrooms." Given this circumstance, the court held that it did not need to consider the district's provision of supplementary aids and services.[71] Consequently, the court determined that the only relevant issue was whether Tyler's IEP should be delivered in his neighborhood or in another school. In this regard, the court found that although the IDEA "clearly commands schools to include or mainstream disabled children as much as possible, it says nothing about where, within a school district, that inclusion shall take place. . . . [T]he LRE mandate does not include a presumption of neighborhood schooling, and a school district accordingly is not obligated to explore supplementary aids and services before removing a child from a neighborhood school. It is only so obligated before removing a child from a regular classroom with nondisabled children."[72]

The *Murray* court commented that *Oberti,* which found a presumption in favor of placing the child in the neighborhood school, conditioned that placement on the grounds of feasibility: if that placement is not feasible, the child should be placed as close to home as possible.[73]

With this rationale, the *Murray* court indicated that it did not need to select a standard of review, such as one followed by the courts in *Roncker, Daniel R. R.,*

Oberti, or *Holland.* Instead, the court simply concluded that the school district did not violate the law when it rejected the neighborhood school for Tyler. The only factual rationale used by the court was evidence that the selected school's "severe needs program was more appropriate" and "more physically accessible" than that of the neighborhood school.[74]

The Fifth Circuit reached the same result the following year in *Flour Bluff Independent School District v. Katherine M.*[75] In that case, the court held that the "neighborhood school is only one of many factors to be considered in determining placement and there is no presumption in favor of neighborhood school."[76] With this decision, the court found that the school district properly placed Katie, a third-grader with a hearing impairment, at a regional day school attached to an elementary school in another district, rather than her home school. As in *Murray,* the issue before the court was the *location* of services, not the type or amount.

In reaching its decision, the *Flour Bluff* court found that the hearing officer (who ruled for the neighborhood school placement) improperly concluded that the "close to home" provision of IDEA's regulatory language should be "accorded significant weight": "[The] district court [presumed incorrectly] that [Katie's] neighborhood school was the proper placement even though [she] required other arrangements which were not then in existence at *Flour Bluff.* Nor did the district court apparently afford any weight to the testimony of *Flour Bluff* officials concerning the scarcity of educational resources upon which the district had grounded its policy decision to send disabled students who required certain services to the regional day school."[77]

As outlined in *Murray,* Katie had been receiving services in her neighborhood school at the time of the appellate court's decision. Thus, the court advised that the "IEP for the forthcoming year should consider the fact that Katie is currently attending the neighborhood school, which may now have the support services she requires."[78]

The Fifth (*Flour Bluff*) and Tenth (*Murray*) Circuits were reluctant to review the educational decisions of the school districts as aggressively as the Third (*Oberti*) and Ninth (*Holland*). Although the courts framed their decisions in the context of location, as opposed to program, they were unwilling to require the school districts to adjust their service delivery systems to educate the students in the neighborhood school. By contrast, the courts in *Oberti* and *Holland* asserted that school districts have an affirmative duty to adjust their programs and provide reasonable supplementary aids and services. It could appear that school districts have more discretion when location, rather than program, is at issue. In reality, it is difficult to analyze these cases consistently. As a result, more litigation is likely to follow as parents and school districts strive to understand the operational boundaries of the law.

Considerations of Cost

While several court decisions give lip service to the issue of cost, few have denied services because of it. The *Holland* court articulated two questions for considering cost: First, will the need for curricular modifications monopolize the school's budget? And second, will the cost of educating a child with a disability in a regular classroom be so great that it would significantly reduce the quality of education for other children in the district?[79]

Although the issue of cost has rarely been used as a deciding factor in determining the appropriateness of an educational program for a child with a disability, the Fourth Circuit in *Barnett* referred to the programmatic as well as financial costs involved in replicating an integrated educational program for a seventeen-year-old student with severe multiple disabilities at her home school. Similarly, in *Flour Bluff,* the Fifth Circuit cited educational and financial reasons behind the state's provision of regional day schools throughout the state to serve students with hearing impairments.

Given the large number of court decisions that require school districts to fund expensive programs for students with disabilities, including costly residential placements, financial concerns have not substantially influenced the judiciary. This is not surprising, since courts address the needs of the individual child before the bench. No decision has considered the financial impact with regard to similarly situated children. While many children with the same needs may significantly affect a district's budget, it is rare that the needs of one child would have such an impact.

Much evidence indicates that the increased attention of both the courts and federal Department of Education to the integration and inclusion of children with disabilities has had a notable impact on the field. The number of students in integrated settings has grown greatly. During the 1987–1988 school year approximately 30 percent of school-age students with disabilities received services in general education classrooms. By the 1993–1994 school year, that figure had jumped to 44 percent. During the same period, the number of students educated outside regular school buildings dropped from 7.2 percent to 5.1 percent.[80]

Class Actions and State Educational Agency Responsibility

Twenty-three years after the passage of the Education of All Handicapped Children Act, a court for the first time held a state educational agency liable under IDEA for failing to ensure that children with disabilities were educated in the least restrictive environment. In 1992, *Corey H. et al. v. City of Chicago, et al.*[81] was filed in federal court on behalf of all current and future children with disabilities in the Chicago public schools against the school district and the Illinois State Board of Education (ISBE). In a decision reached six years later, on February 19, 1998, the court found: "Children with disabilities in the Chicago public schools have been and continue to be segregated into separate and unequal educational environments, contrary to established federal law. Although the local school district has recognized its deficiencies and agreed to a remedial plan, the State educational agency has continued to deny its responsibilities. . . . That denial squarely conflicts with the clear Congressional intent to make the State ultimately responsible for compliance with the long-standing federal mandate that children with disabilities be educated in the least restrictive environment."[82]

Although the Chicago Board of Education reached a settlement of its case and was not a party to the trial, the court's decision nevertheless cited the school district's historical practice of placing children in educational settings according to their category of disability, a practice which did not begin to change until 1992. The court relied on expert testimony that found insufficient educational justification to support the extent to which children with disabilities continued to be educated in separate settings, outside of the general education classroom. With this factual foundation, the court considered the contributory liability of the ISBE and found the agency in violation of IDEA because it "has failed and continues to fail to ensure that: (1) placement decisions are based on the child's individual needs as determined by his or her IEP; (2) LRE violations are identified and corrected; (3) teachers and administrators are fully informed about their responsibilities for implementing the LRE mandate and are provided with the technical assistance and training necessary to implement the mandate; (4) teacher certification standards comply with the LRE mandate; and (5) state funding formulas that reimburse local agencies for educating children in the least restrictive environments are consistent with the LRE mandate."[83] In reaching its conclusions, the court determined that the ISBE "in certain respects impeded [Chicago's] compliance by what appears to be a disregard of its duties."[84]

As the first judicial decision involving a finding of liability by a state educational agency for systemic violation of IDEA's least restrictive environment, a road map exists for future litigation. Defendants with fact patterns comparable to Chicago and the ISBE would be wise to take heed of the court's clear language, which praised the school district because it "has recognized its past failures and has embarked on a program to correct them" and admonished the ISBE for failing to do so: "Unfortunately, and inexplicably, the ISBE continues to deny the undeniable and defend the undefendable. . . . An objective observer—including this court—can conclude only that the ISBE has engaged in this exercise more to delay the inevitable result than to change or avoid it."[85]

THE CHALLENGES AHEAD

Though the educational trends for disabled students in general have been largely positive, much remains to be done before the promise of IDEA becomes a reality. The National Longitudinal Transition Study of Special Education Students (NLTS), which followed a sample of students who were in high school in the mid-1980s for five years after graduation, offers a revealing picture of the status of disabled students. The study documents both positive and disturbing trends.

Of particular concern is the fact that disabled students are twice as likely to drop out of school as their nondisabled peers. Those who drop out are more likely to be unemployed or in jail. The study documented a much higher rate of maternity among high-school-age disabled girls. These negative outcomes were most heavily represented in the "severely emotionally disturbed" category: 48 percent of these students dropped out of school. Within two years of dropping out, 37 percent of this group had been arrested; within five years, 58 percent had been arrested.[86] It would be reasonable to expect that emotionally disturbed young people would have somewhat higher rates of dropping out, unemployment, and incarceration than their nondisabled peers. But the differential rates observed by researchers are unacceptable, given what we know about the positive outcomes that can be achieved when disabled students get the services they need.

Another important study conducted by Larson provides a disturbing picture of how urban youth identified as disabled fare in the system. Using a mixed qualitative and quantitative design, Larson showed how students with disabilities—particularly those with behavior problems—are frequently moved from program to program. With little continuity in their educational plan, and the resulting inability to accrue academic credits, these students become prime candidates for dropping out of school. Larson found that students at times were moved with good intentions, and with adherence to procedural compliance well documented. Nevertheless, between grades 7 and 9, Larson reports, one-third of learning disabled and seriously emotionally disturbed students had three or more changes in educational setting; this far exceeds the rate for nondisabled students.

There is still more disturbing news from research. Nationally, about half of all disabled students are not part of any publicly reported accountability system in education—including the National Assessment of Educational Progress.[87] Indeed, Allington's research suggests that students may be referred to special education as a way to avoid accountability for low-achieving students in high-stakes assessment programs.

Among the complex issues related to including students with disabilities in state and local assessment and testing programs is the desirability of using standardized tests to measure the efficacy of schooling. In standardized assessment practices, half the students will fall below the mean. But does that approach answer the broader question of whether students have learned what the curriculum purports to teach?

Another set of issues arises when states or districts move toward innovative "portfolio" assessments designed to address the problems of standardized tests. Are such measures reliable and valid predictors of future academic performance or merely episodic samplings of a student's work? Do such measures reflect the biases of the assessor more than the actual quality of student work?

What degree or type of accommodation should be made for students with disabilities taking standardized tests, and how can these accommodations be kept from compromising the integrity of the measuring instruments? These are not trivial concerns, considering that such assessments are often high-stakes events for both the student and the professionals involved.

Though the issue is complex, the inclusion of students with disabilities in assessment systems is fundamentally an access issue. If assessments are an essential element of the accountability system in education, by which important decisions about instruction are made, excluding students with disabilities from those assessments raises fundamental civil rights concerns.

The Overrepresentation Dilemma

When Public Law 94-142, was passed in 1975, it was believed that the law's procedural protections would reduce the disproportionately large number of racial minority children educated in separate special education settings. In 1997, this has yet to occur. As a result, the perception of special education and its implications have created suspicion and opposition among parents of students who could benefit greatly from the law's provisions.

One congressman recently expressed frustration with the complaints about special education that he regularly hears in his district from minority parents, who wanted their children out of these programs, not in them. As a strong supporter of disability rights in Congress, he was beginning to question how his support for IDEA squared with his constituents' views of special education.

New research is giving us a more accurate view of the problematic relation between minority children and special education. In his 1974 essay, Kirp accurately described how minority students were being placed in separate special education classes in disproportionately large numbers and that such placement was of dubious benefit to them. He described these placements as a form of "exclusion" that carried with it social stigma and lower expectations. Relying on the pioneering work of Erving Goffman on the harmful effects of stigma, Kirp argued that special-class placement resulted in the loss of post school opportunity:

> The effects of school-imposed stigmas do not cease when the child leaves school, for schools are society's most active labelers. Slow-track assignment makes college entrance nearly impossible and may discourage employers from offering jobs; assignment to a special education program forecloses vocational options. While many children labeled retarded by the school do come to lead normal lives, the stigma persists. For the children who cannot escape their past—as by moving from the South to the North to seek employment, leaving all school records except a diploma behind them—the retarded label may stick for life.[88]

Kirp suggested that special class placement raised constitutional issues of equal protection and due process. His concerns were embraced by the designers of Public Law 94-142. Significant due process protections were built into the law, along with requirements that the placement of children in special education had to be regularly reviewed and reevaluated. Further, the law implicitly recognized that the provision of special services should not automatically mean the removal of students from the mainstream. Nevertheless, twenty years after the passage of the law there continues to be evidence of significant overrepresentation of African American, Latino, and Native American children in separate special education settings.

Some degree of differential rates is to be expected because of the well-documented links between poverty, race and disability. An extensive 1995 study in Rhode Island showed how factors related to the development of disabilities are far more prevalent among the poor.[89] For instance, pregnant women in the core cities were far more likely to have received inadequate prenatal care: 20.9 percent of them, compared with 9.4 percent for the rest of the state. Children in Providence tested positive for exposure to lead at a rate 22 percent higher than other children. The rate of low birth weight in Providence was 8.3 percent; it was 5.1 percent for the rest of the state. Lack of prenatal care, low birth weight, and exposure to lead are all strongly correlated to disability and far more likely among the poor.

Given the high rate of poverty in the African American, Latino, Native American, and other populations, we can expect a higher rate of disabilities in those groups. It is useful to note, for example, that there is significant overrepresentation of African Americans in populations of what are known as "nonjudgmental" disabilities—such as blindness and deafness. Blacks make up approximately 15 percent of the school-age population, but more that 20 percent of blind, visually impaired, and deaf people. No one argues that schools are placing hearing children in programs for the deaf—so what accounts for this overrepresentation? These numbers simply reflect the link between poverty and disability. Even taking this into account, however, the data are disturbing: close to 40 percent of the children identified as mildly mentally retarded are black.[90]

Both Section 504 and IDEA include regulatory language designed to limit the impact of race in the evaluation and classification process. They require assessments to be

- selected and administered so as not to be racially or culturally discriminatory;
- tailored to assess specific areas of educational need and not merely those that provide a general intelligence quotient;
- provided and administered in the child's native language or other mode of communication unless it is clearly not feasible to do so;
- validated for the specific purpose for which they are used; and
- administered by trained personnel in conformity with the instructions provided by their producer.[91]

Lawsuits and government monitoring efforts have usually been triggered by numerical findings of overrepresentation and have relied on "input" remedies such as changing referral and assessment procedures of the district.

There are a variety of promising nonlegalistic strategies and approaches that schools can use to address the problem of overrepresentation at the critical point of referral.

First, the general practice of including as many students with disabilities as possible in regular classes will naturally tend over time to reduce the number of inappropriate referrals by regular classroom teachers. If those teachers know that a referral for special education services will not necessarily result in a child's removal from the regular class, they will be less likely to seek classification as a way of getting rid of kids they would rather not teach.

Second, school administrators should look critically at the differential rates of referral in individual schools and by individual teachers. Sometimes the problem of overrepresentation can be traced to the practices of just a few teachers in the school. Once identified, these teachers can be helped to find better ways of serving their students with disabilities.

Third, schools can implement a variety of interventions to help students who may have disabilities before a formal referral is made. Schools that maximize individual attention to students and focus on small-group and cooperative learning techniques are better able to do this, and are less likely to make unnecessary special education referrals.

Finally, educators and parents should be wary of relying too heavily on testing procedures that are keyed to IQ or other suspect measures.

While these "input" remedies have been important, they have not promoted significant reform in how students of color fare in the special education system. A critical question remains: What happens to students once they are identified as having a disability? Do they receive services that truly benefit them? State-reported data and the NLTS show that disabled students in cities are almost three times more likely to be segregated in separate schools and far more likely to be kept out of challenging academic programs than their suburban counterparts. Almost 11 percent of urban youth with disabilities go to special schools, compared with about 3 percent of suburban youth. Adding the figures for those in special schools with those served in regular schools but not in regular classes, the NLTS found that over 26 percent of disabled students were segregated, compared with 13 percent of suburban youngsters. The same study found that only 38 percent of urban students had the option of integration into some or all regular academic classes, compared with 59 percent of disabled suburban students. Urban parents need alternatives, such as those available to their suburban counterparts, that offer real benefits for their children.

Those who seek to improve special education in large urban systems must go beyond a simple numerical analysis of evaluation and referral practices and move to a more sophisticated kind of "benefit" analysis. The goal should be not simply to reduce the numbers of students identified as needing special education, but to ensure that all who need appropriate services receive them. All who are designated as eligible for services under IDEA should receive valuable benefits.

For most students with disabilities, special education should be seen not as places but as services—including a challenging, appropriate curriculum. The problem of overrepresentation, therefore, must be viewed through a wider lens, which takes in not just the determination of eligibility but also the results of that identification. Indeed, this kind of benefit analysis would well serve every child covered by IDEA.

The Foundations of a Benefit Analysis

Because of recent research and innovative programs in serving students with disabilities, our understanding of what works and what doesn't work is growing. Kathy Larson, for example, has done important work with urban minority youth, who have experienced the poorest outcomes of all disabled students. Though her research paints a pessimistic picture of the current situation of many of these youngsters, Larson has designed an intervention strategy that is very promising. Studying young people whose education had been interrupted, she found that 67 percent of her intervention group returned to and remained in school, compared with 45 percent of a comparison group.

Larson's interventions included

- remediation of the student's "deficient social and task-related problem-solving skills";
- intensive attendance monitoring;
- recognition and bonding activities;
- frequent teacher feedback to the parent and student; and
- teaching parents about management skills and promoting their participation in school activities.

Larson singled out the importance of having an adult in the school who saw his or her role as being an advocate for the student—one person who cared deeply for the child and took responsibility for keeping him or her in school. She also emphasized the negative impact of frequent program changes.

The NLTS also identified characteristics of programs associated with improved outcomes. Students who were integrated in school generally had better outcomes than those who had been segregated. This varied by disability group, however, with physically disabled students showing the greatest difference between those who had been segregated and those who had been integrated. Controlling for race, IQ, socioeconomic status, and sex, the NLTS revealed that integrated students with physical disabilities had a 50 percent higher likelihood of being employed after leaving school than those who were segregated. The NLTS also showed that certain interventions, including counseling, tutoring, and access to vocational education, were related to staying in school and to postschool success, even after controlling for the factors above.

Other studies point to the importance of early intervention. Too often educators ignore the early signs of school failure and take no action until much later when the problem has become intolerable. Children who do not learn to read in the primary grades, for example, fall into a pattern of failure and are more likely to be referred for special education in the intermediate grades. By this time, unfortunately, the child has fallen far behind his or her peers in almost every academic area. Early reading problems call for immediate intervention, which has been shown to reduce inappropriate referrals to special education and to ensure that students get a positive start in school. We also know that intervening early with children exhibiting serious behavior problems in the early grades can prevent the development of graver school adjustment problems later.

The following six general principles emerge strongly from twenty years of research on implementing IDEA.

1. Appropriate integration, as a rule, leads to more positive outcomes than segregation for most children with disabilities.
2. Early intervention to arrest reading and behavior problems in the primary grades is effective in preventing later deficits and inappropriate special education referrals.
3. Access to vocational education is often a critical variable related to the success of disabled students.
4. Modifications in traditional teaching techniques are important to the success of many disabled students.
5. The counseling and support of a caring adult advocate in the school system is often a critical variable for disabled high school students.
6. Ensuring students' success in one setting by providing appropriate support and modifications is apt to be more effective than moving students frequently from setting to setting.

These principles are not all-inclusive, but they provide a basis for conducting a benefit analysis. Educators and lawyers seeking systemic reform can look at the programs in their school districts and assess the degree to which they conform to good practice. Are students routinely segregated? Do students who are integrated receive support and appropriately modified curricula within the regular classroom? Are students who are experiencing difficulty frequently moved from school to school? Do students in large secondary schools have a support person available who knows them well enough to be an effective advocate for their interests?

Input-oriented approaches, which focus on such measures as the number of students being assessed and placed in special education programs and the number of staff hired, may work to compel school systems to establish the evaluation and service delivery systems contemplated by the law. But these approaches alone are not likely to bring about fundamental reform in the way children are educated. Indeed, some systems with heavily input-oriented approaches, focusing on whole-system remedies rather than school-by-school improvement, may have inadvertently promoted segregation of students with disabilities. Boston and New York City are examples. A 1994 New York University study found that 60 percent of these cities' special education populations were in restrictive settings—three times the national average.

Input-oriented approaches to enforcement therefore usually foster centralized rather that school-based accountability. The system feels pressure mainly to get students evaluated and placed. Concentrating on these elements of compliance is not wrong, but it is equally important to look at what happens to students after placement. Moreover, focusing on the central office takes the school principal—an important actor—out of the loop.

Centralized approaches are based on the questionable assumption that school systems are "machine bureaucracies."[92] In fact, these systems are more likely to operate as "loosely coupled" organizations.[93] The shortcomings of interventions like those in *Allen* and *Jose P.* are related to a failure to understand this organizational nature of schools. Central office bureaucracies tend to establish special programs for disabled students. Some school administrators get themselves off the hook by pleading that they are unable to serve students with disabilities and that the central office must place them elsewhere. These centralized bureaucratic approaches often impede implementation of services in the least restrictive environment.

Under a benefit analysis applied to special education reform, each school would build its capacity to educate those children who would naturally attend that school, so that relatively few students require services elsewhere.

A COLLABORATIVE MODEL
OF EDUCATION REFORM

School principals are at the heart of the process of finding solutions to the emerging challenges of special education reform. The legalistic model, with its emphasis on input measures, was successful in addressing the pervasive problems of exclusion and segregation of children with disabilities. But now a second generation of problems has emerged. Chief among these issues, argues Jay Heubert of Columbia, are the fragmentation and balkanization of educational programs and instructional staff. In many schools and districts, he points out, there are separate staffs and administrators for general education, special education, vocational education, bilingual education, and Title I programs. Too often, these programs exist in isolation, with little communication among staff members. If students with disabilities are to be educated effectively in their local schools, integrated appropriately in regular classrooms with nondisabled peers, the staffs of these fragmented programs will have to collaborate with each other in new and innovative ways.[94]

School and district administrators are the only people in the system with the authority to require the various players in the organization to work with and support each other in finding the best interventions for individual students. Unfortunately, this collaboration rarely happens. More often than not, school principals and district administrators have little background in or knowledge of special education and see it as just one more in a long list of administrative headaches. As a result, they leave it to the "experts"—the program directors who lack the authority, time, and often the incentive to overcome fragmentation.

Related to the problem of fragmentation, Heubert adds, is the widespread incapacity of general education personnel to address the needs of disabled students. Inadequate pre-service and in-service training, scheduling conflicts, and lack of administrative support all contribute to the problem. Moreover, the American system of education has long operated on the unstated but powerful premise that the best teachers should be rewarded by getting to teach the ablest students. This presumption has several negative effects. It leads teachers to see the inclusion of students with disabilities in their classes as a kind of punishment, and it prevents them from experiencing the enormous rewards that can come from working with the disabled. Thus they remain predisposed to let someone else take the responsibility for these children.

The solution, again, lies with the active intervention and advocacy of school administrators. Only they can establish the institutional expectation of inclusiveness and sense of mission that are necessary if these longstanding beliefs and practices are to change. But not all administrators are currently prepared to do this.

Where administrators have taken on the challenge of creating a collaborative team structure to serve students with disabilities, the results have been dramatic. At the O'Hearn School in Boston, educators have developed an inclusive approach in which students with disabilities learn in regular classes. The principal, Bill Henderson, was permitted to use the funds the district would have spent to educate students with disabilities in separate settings, as well as the school's Title I money, to provide two teachers in each classroom. In effect, all O'Hearn students have individualized programs.

A magnet school, O'Hearn now has parents seeking to enroll many more children than there are places. Students with significant disabilities can be found in virtually every classroom. At the same time, test scores have gone up and teachers compete for jobs in the school. At a meeting with the author (Hehir) in 1994 one mother told how her nondisabled daughter had "tested for" the district's gifted program and was offered admission. After visiting the gifted program in another school, however, she reported that the children there were all doing the same thing, and the work they were doing was below the level her daughter had already achieved at O'Hearn. "My daughter has had an individualized program ever since she started at the O'Hearn," she said, "one that has recognized her potential and challenged her. Why should I place her in the gifted program?"

This nondisabled child is learning at a high level in the same classroom that serves a child with significant cognitive disabilities. But this classroom is not staffed by a lone teacher attempting to address such diverse needs. At schools like O'Hearn, special education and Title I resources are used not as "pull-outs" but as vehicles for the fundamental rethinking of classroom instruction.

In our vision for school reform, students with disabilities must be a natural part of the education system, and special education must be the modifications, aids, and services needed to ensure their success. As such, special education transcends a place and becomes the supports children need to be successful in school.

This vision holds enormous potential benefit for all students, not just those with disabilities. Indeed, many programs and interventions originally developed for disabled children have proved to be superior tools for promoting learning in all children. With its history of individualization and innovation, special education at its best has much to offer American education as we seek to create schools where all children can do their best.

The IDEA Amendments of 1997

The fundamental structure of existing special education laws is unlikely to change, as there is broad recognition that the rights of children and families must be protected through procedural safeguards. Indeed, the IDEA 97 amendments signed by President Clinton in June 1997 reaffirm the basic rights-based structure of IDEA while requiring increased accountability for educational results. Under current law, students with disabilities must be included in state and district assessments of educational progress. School districts and states will be held publicly accountable for the educational outcomes of students with disabilities, just as they are for the performance of nondisabled students. The majority of students with disabilities are capable of full participation in state-wide assessments. Alternative assessments should be developed for those few students with significant cognitive disabilities for whom the regular assessments are not appropriate, and results duly reported to the public. This reform is important because large numbers of students are currently excluded from this important accountability measure. As schools assess students with disabilities and report the results, they will be more likely to provide these students access to the general curriculum.

Although IEPs have served a central role in implementing IDEA, their potential contribution has not been fully realized. Research on IEPs has found that they often have limited relevance to the general classroom and that they have increasingly become the sole curriculum offered to many students, often addressing only a narrow range of content with few linkages to the general curriculum.[95] Used solely for process accountability, IEPs have lacked connection to system goals or to the general curriculum. Given the individualized nature of the IEP, it has not allowed teachers to compare the progress of disabled students with their nondisabled peers.[96]

In the IDEA Amendments of 1997, the primary focus of the IEP is to enable students with disabilities to participate in the general curriculum and to promote changes in regular classrooms that would make this possible. Children with disabilities should be learning in school what other children are learning, and the IEP should lay out the plan for achieving that objective. Though the IEP must also address those needs that cannot be part of the general curriculum, such as a blind child's need to learn Braille or a cognitively disabled student's need to learn community skills, such as crossing streets, its primary thrust should be a plan for accessing the curriculum and identifying services and accommodations needed to make that access possible. The IEP must also articulate measurable annual goals related to the attainment of curricular outcomes. Parents must be more regularly informed of their child's progress in meeting these goals. Special education evaluations must go beyond the mere determination of disability; they should include additional relevant information on how the student's disability affects his or her access to the general curriculum.

In addition to the reinforced IEP, states must establish performance goals for their special education programs. To the greatest extent possible, these goals should be consistent with those developed under other federal programs. Further, states are required to have a state improvement plan that at minimum addresses the performance of students with disabilities on assessments, dropout rates, and school completion rates. The establishment of state performance standards is a significant departure from the current process orientation of state plans.

To provide better support to students in the least restricted environment, state finance systems must be "placement neutral"—that is, they should not encourage any particular type of placement. Many states' current funding systems favor segregated settings by giving districts higher levels of reimbursement for such placements. Some districts have even lost state aid by moving toward more inclusive practices.

Finally, states must monitor their local districts in regards to overplacement of minority students.

CONCLUSION

After twenty years of implementation of IDEA, public education has at last become a reality for all our children. We have done this within a "legalized" mode of policy implementation that has generally served the interests of students with disabilities and their families well. Much remains to be done, however.

We have learned a great deal in those twenty years about how to educate disabled students. Now that we have incorporated that knowledge into the structure of IDEA, it needs to be incorporated into the everyday workings of schools and special education practices. The power of the procedural protections embodied in IDEA and enforced through due process hearing, the courts, and the federal government has demonstrated that our education system can be fundamentally changed within just one generation. Continued progress will depend on changing the process orientation of current enforcement efforts to one that incorporates a benefit analysis and an emphasis on collaboration. Those involved in IDEA enforcement efforts must engage regular education administrators and teachers, particularly principals, in meaningful ways. New remedies must be found for a new generation of more complex implementation problems.

These changes will require that lawyers and others involved in enforcement efforts work much more closely with educators. New remedies will have to be based on best practice in special education, which lawyers are generally not competent to judge. Educators and lawyers alike will need to understand the ways their interactions can promote or inhibit educational reform; they must resolve to use the power of law to promote true reform.

If these positive changes take place, the future holds great promise for reforms that will benefit all children. The practices that promote better results for students with disabilities will help other students as well, by establishing the principles that each child is unique, individual, and infinitely valuable; and that every child deserves an education that is suited to his or her needs and abilities.

NOTES

1. D. Kirp and D. Neal, "The Allure of Legalism Reconsidered: The Case of Special Education," in D. Kirp and D. Jensen, *School Days, Rule Days* (1986).

2. G. Benveniste, "Implementation and Intervention Strategies: The Case of 94-142," in D. Kirp and D. Jensen, *School Days, Rule Days*.

3. D. Sacken, *Reflections on an Adversarial Process: The Confessions of a Special Education Hearing Officer*, Monograph distributed by the Council of Administrators of Special Education (1988).

4. C. Lakin, et al., "Longitudinal Change and Interstate Variability in the Size of Residential Facilities for Persons with Mental Retardation," 28 *Mental Retardation* 6 (1990).

5. U.S. Department of Education, *Twelfth and Nineteenth Annual Reports to Congress on the Implementation of the Individuals with Disabilities Education Act* (1990, 1996).

6. American Council on Education, Health Resource Center, *College Freshmen with Disabilities: A Statistical Profile* (1992).

7. 274 U.S. 200 at 207 (1926).

8. See D. L. Miller and M. A. Miller, "The Handicapped Child's Civil Right as It Relates to the 'Least Restrictive Environment' and Appropriate Mainstreaming," 54 *Indiana Law Journal* 1 at 10 (1987); F. J. Weintraub, A. R. Abeson, and D. L. Braddock, *State Law and Education of Handicapped Children: Issues and Recommendations* 11 (1972).

9. *Watson v. City of Cambridge*, 157 Mass. 561, 32 N.E. 864 (1893).

10. *Beattie v. Board of Education,* 172 N.W. 153 (1919).

11. *Board of Education of Cleveland Heights v. State ex rel. Goldman,* 47 Ohio Appendix 417, 191 N.E. 914 at 914, 915 (1934).

12. T. Gilhool and E. Stutman, *Integration of Severely Handicapped Students: Toward Criteria for Implementing and Enforcing the Integration Imperative of P.L. 94-142 and Section 504,* at 5 (1980) (citing Friedman [ed.], Argument 51, 1969).

13. Ohio Rev. Code Ann. §5127.01.

14. Opinion of Attorney General of the State of Ohio, 69-040 (1969).

15. No. 182 646 (3d Jud. Dist. Utah, Jan. 8, 1969), as cited in R. Burgdorf, "The Doctrine of the Least Restrictive Alternative," in R. Burgdorf (ed.), *The Legal Rights of Handicapped Persons: Cases, Materials, and Text,* 1980, n. 80 at 71–72.

16. An agreement between the parties approved by the court, violations of which constitute contempt of court.

17. 343 F. Supp. 279, 291 (E.D. Pa. 1972).

18. R. Roach, "The Least Restrictive Environment Section of the Education for All Handicapped Children Act of 1975: A Legislative History and an Analysis," 13 *Gonzaga Law Review* 717, n. 48 at 740 (1978); See H.R. Rep. No. 332, 94th Cong., 1st Sess. 10 (1975).

19. *Mills v. Board of Education of the District of Columbia,* 348 F. Supp. 866 (D.D.C. 1972).

20. *Labanks v. Spears,* 60 F.R.D. 135 (1973).

21. 334 F. Supp. at 1260.

22. H.R. Rep. No. 332, 94th Cong., 1st Sess. 3 (1974).

23. 161 *Cong. Rec.* 525 (1972).

24. 34 C.F.R. 104.33(a).

25. §611–621, 88 Stat. 579–85 (1975).

26. 120 *Cong. Rec.* 15,271 (1974).

27. 121 *Cong. Rec.* H7764 (1975).

28. 121 *Cong. Rec.* §20429 (1975).

29. Hehir's study investigated whether special education directors in Massachusetts develop programs to protect themselves from adversarial proceedings. It included a review of documents related to hearing decisions over a five-year period and intensive interviews with twenty-eight randomly selected special education directors. Hehir, "The Impact of Due Process on the Programmatic Decisions of Special Education Directors" (Ph.D. diss., Harvard Graduate School of Education, 1990).

30. M. Kirst and K. Bertken, "Due Process Hearings in Special Education: Some Early Findings in California," in *Special Education Policies,* J. Chambers and W. Hartman, eds. (1983); M. Budoff, A. Orenstein, and M. Kervick, *Due Process in Special Education: On Going to a Hearing* (1982); N. Wolf, "Due Process and the Least Restrictive Environment: An Analysis of Special Education Due Process Hearings in California," 43 *Dissertation Abstracts International* 3877A (Ph.D. diss., University of California, 1983).

31. C. Hassell, "A Study of the Consequences of Excessive Legal Intervention on the Local Implementation of PL 94-142," 42 *Dissertation Abstracts International* 3105A (Ph.D. diss., University of California, Berkeley, 1981).

32. Sacken, *Reflections on an Adversarial Process,* 7.

33. Hehir, "The Impact of Due Process on the Programmatic Decisions of Special Education Directors," 78.

34. Hehir, "The Impact of Due Process of the Programmatic Decisions of Special Education Directors."

35. 423 F. Supp. 180 (S.D. W.Va. 1976).

36. Id. at 183.

37. Id. at 184.

38. 468 U.S. 883 (1984).

39. 874 F.2d 1036 (5th Cir. 1989).

40. No. 79-M-277 (N.D. Ala. March 31, 1981).

41. Id., slip op. at 4.

42. No. 78-9939-W(H) (N.D. W.Va. April 11, 1980).

43. Id., slip op. at 11.

44. 700 F.2d 1058 (6th Cir. 1983); cert. denied, 464 U.S. 864 (1983).

45. Id. at 1063. The Act's mainstreaming requirement applies to non-academic activities such as lunch, gym, recess, and transportation to and from school.

46. Id.

47. 874 F.2d 1036 (5th Cir. 1989).

48. 488 U.S. 176 (1982).

49. *Daniel R. R.,* 874 F.2d at 1044; *Rowley,* 488 U.S. at 188–89, 202.

50. *Daniel R. R.,* 874 F.2d at 1046; *Murray v. Montrose County School Dist.,* 51 F.3d 921, 926 (10th Cir. 1995); cert. denied. 116 S.Ct. 278 (1995). Since neither the IDEA statute nor regulation define "mainstreaming," "inclusion," or "regular education placement," the courts have provided a variety of meanings to these terms: "Mainstreaming means educating a handicapped child with non-handicapped peers." *Briggs v. Board of Educ.,* 882 F.2d 688, 691 (2d Cir. 1989). "Full-inclusion" means that "the handicapped child is a full member of a regular education class. . . . Under full-inclusion, the child need not be in the classroom 100% of the time. . . . The child may be removed from that class to receive supplementary services such as physical or speech therapy when these services cannot be provided in the classroom. Under full-inclusion, the child's primary placement is in the regular education class, and the child has no additional assignment to any special class for handicapped children." *Board of Education v. Holland,* 786 F. Supp. 874, 878 (E.D. Calif. 1992). "Education in the regular classroom" means "placement in a regular class for a significant portion of the school day." Such children are likely to receive "some special education and related services outside of the regular classroom, such as speech and language therapy or use of a resource room." *Oberti v. Board of Educ.,* 995 F.2d 1204, 1215 (3rd Cir. 1993).

51. *Daniel R. R.,* 874 F.2d at 1046.

52. Id. at 1044–1045.

53. Id. at 1048–1050.

54. Id. at 1048; See also *Greer v. Rome City School District,* 950 F.2d 688, 696 (11th Cir. 1991).

55. 34 C.F.R. 551(b) (2).

56. 995 F.2d 1204 (3rd Cir. 1993).

57. Id. at 1211, 1216.

58. Id. at 1220.

59. Id. at 1221.

60. 14 F.3d 1398 (9th Cir. 1994); cert. denied. 114 S.Ct. 2679 (1994).

61. *Oberti,* 995 F.2d at 1216–1217, 1221–1222; *Holland,* 14 F.3d at 1401, 1404.

62. 995 F.2d at 1216–1217.

63. 786 F. Supp. 874, 881 (E.D. Calif. 1992).

64. 995 F.2d at 1217; See *Greer,* 950 F.2d at 697.

65. 995 F.2d at 1223.

66. 286 F. Supp. at 883.

67. 1950 F.2d at 698.

68. 35 F.3d 1396 (9th Cir. 1994).

69. 927 F.2d 146 (4th Cir. 1991); cert. denied., 502 U.S. 859 (1991).

70. 51 F.3d 921 (10th Cir. 1995); cert. denied., 116 S.Ct. 278 (1995).

71. 51 F.3d at 930.

72. Id. at 928–930.

73. 995 F.2d 1204, 1224. See *Barnett,* 927 F.2d 146, 153. Section 300.552 does not impose an absolute obligation to place a child in the neighborhood school, but requires the school district to take into account geographical proximity of placement.

74. 995 F.2d at 924, 926, 927; *Urban by Urban v. Jefferson County School District R-1,* 89 F.3d 720 (10th Cir. 1996). (Separate program with job-site training was appropriate for Tyler, a nineteen-year-old student with multiple disabilities.) Ironically, by the time the *Murray* appellate court issued its decision, Tyler had been in his home school for five years and was in the seventh grade. Pursuant to the "stay put" provision of the IDEA, Tyler's placement in his neighborhood school was maintained during the pendency of the court hearings. Because his current IEP established that Tyler should be placed in his neighborhood school, the court's decision had no effect on his placement. The court, nevertheless, ruled that it would decide the case because the issue could come up again. 995 F.2d at 931.

75. 91 F.3d 689 (1996).

76. Id. at 693.

77. Id. at 695; See *Barnett,* 927 F.2d at 152. "Whether a particular service or method can feasibly be provided in a specific special education setting is an administrative determination that state and local school officials are far better qualified and situated than we are to make."

78. Id. at 695.

79. 786 F. Supp. at 880; See *Greer,* 950 F.2d at 697; *Greer,* 700 F.2d at 1063.

80. U.S. Department of Education, *Twelfth and Nineteenth Annual Reports to Congress on the Implementation of the Individuals with Disabilities Education Act.*

81. Civil Action No. 92 C 3409 (E.D. Ill.).

82. *Corey H. et al. v. City of Chicago et al.,* F. Supp., 1998 U.S. Dist. LEXIS 2485, Slip Opinion at 2 (E.D. Ill. February 18, 1998).

83. Id. at 12–15.

84. Id. at 4.

85. Id. at 5.

86. M. Wagner, J. Blackorby, R. Cameto, K. Hebbeler, and C. Newman, *The Transition Experiences of Young People with Disabilities* (1993).

87. The inclusion rate of disabled students in public accountability systems varies widely from state to state, with Kentucky including more than 98 percent while other states include fewer than 50 percent. The NAEP has begun to remedy its heretofore systematic exclusion of the disabled.

88. D. Kirp, "Student Classification, Public Policy and the Courts," reprinted in T. Hehir and T. Latus, eds., *Special Education at the Century's End: Evolution of Theory and Practice Since 1970* (Cambridge, Mass.: Harvard Educational Review, 1992), 15.

89. *Rhode Island Kids Count Fact Book* (1995).

90. Hume, "A Longitudinal Study of Children Screened and Served by Early Childhood Special Education Programs," 13 *Journal of Early Intervention* (Spring 1989).

91. 34 C.F.R. §300.532; 34 C.F.R. 104.33.35.

92. T. Skertic, "An Organizational Analysis of Special Education Reform," 8 *Counterpoint* (1987).

93. K. Weick, "Educational Organizations as Loosely Coupled Systems," 21 *Administrative Science Quarterly* 1 (1976).

94. Conversation with Jay Heubert, Harvard Graduate School of Education, October 1996.

95. G. M. Giangreco et al., "Dressing Your IEPs for the General Education Climate: Analysis of IEP Goals and Objectives for Students with Multiple Disabilities," 15 *Remedial and Special Education* 5 (September 1994).

96. M. Brauen, F. O'Reilly, and M. Moore, *Issues and Options in Outcomes-Based Accountability for Students with Disabilities* (1994).

Chapter 6 Service Integration and Beyond: Implications for Lawyers and Their Training

Martin Gerry

For almost three decades, educators, policymakers, and lawyers have attempted to create comprehensive infrastructures of supports and services in order to advance the healthy development and learning of various groups of American children.[1] Using one or more "service integration" approaches, they have sought to coordinate a variety of categorical grant programs and to effectively integrate these services with those provided by the public schools. This strategy has not yielded a universal infrastructure of child and family supports and services and appears unlikely to do so in the foreseeable future. The time has come to consider seriously more fundamental system reform strategies.

This chapter explores the roles of lawyers in assisting both traditional service integration efforts and in crafting more sweeping system reform efforts and the professional training which they need to play them successfully. As an understanding of the context and rationale for both approaches is necessary, much of this chapter is devoted to an exploration of the contextual matters (e.g., differing origins, evolution, cultures, and financing mechanisms) which surround universal public education, the current array of categorical grant programs for children and their families, and the range of service integration approaches which have been or are being tried. The first section examines the underlying problem—the absence of an accessible and comprehensive infrastructure of community-based supports and services which could optimize ongoing child development, learning, and health. The second section reviews service integration strategies and alternative approaches for creating such an infrastructure and posits principles which might guide more fundamental system reform. In the final section, the varied roles of lawyers and educators in supporting both service integration and more fundamental system reforms are discussed and the implications of these roles for professional training are briefly explored.

CHILD GOALS, SERVICE STRUCTURES, AND OUTCOMES

This section profiles the current structures through which both public education and other services and supports for children are provided, reviews the shortfall between child wellness goals and actual outcomes, and identifies and discusses factors within the current structures that appear to have most impeded progress towards these goals.

Current Program Structures

As the twentieth century began, the primary role of government in supporting the development and wellness of children was to fund and operate systems of public elementary and secondary education. It was generally assumed that children lived in intact families that would provide for their own economic and social well-being and otherwise raise their children successfully (Olasky 1992). It was generally understood that families confronted by problems that overwhelmed their internal resources could call upon informal community support structures to help them through periods of crisis until family self-sufficiency could be restored (McKnight 1995).

UNIVERSAL PUBLIC EDUCATION

From its origins early in the nineteenth century, public education has been seen as a basic responsibility, and even as a prerogative of local government. Until the past two decades, states have played a minimalist role in the administration of public schools.

Due largely to major shifts in what the nation wanted from its schools, this century has witnessed several successive waves of "school reform." From about

1900 to 1930, American society considered the assimilation of the children of immigrants a central responsibility of the public schools. During this period, the wellness of large numbers of children in immigrant families in the crowded ghettos of many American cities was threatened by a range of serious and persistent health, family, and environmental problems related to severe and chronic poverty. Social reformers, such as Jacob Riis and Robert Hunter, called for school-based health and social services to prevent or remedy the ill health, hunger, and neglect of immigrant children attending the nation's urban schools. Most of these early school-based programs were based on a *deficit* model that assumed not only that immigrants knew little about proper health care, dental care, or nutrition, but also that they did not know how to raise children. Virtually all were undertaken by urban school systems working in collaboration with both professional (e.g., doctors) and nonprofessional (e.g., women's organizations) voluntary groups (Tyack 1992).

The impetus for most school-based services came from forces outside the schools who saw the schools as an attractive locus for health and social service reform. During the 1920s, physicians and dentists took the lead in introducing health and dental services in the schools. Nonprofessional voluntary groups were most often responsible for the development of numerous school-based social services, including the provision of free or inexpensive breakfasts and lunches, the operation of vacation schools, and the creation and supervision of playgrounds and other recreational facilities for the out-of-school hours. New forms of school-linked social work and counseling were also pioneered; "visiting teachers" often served as advocates for immigrant families seeking to adjust to a new land (Tyack 1992). By 1928, the evolution of school-based health and social services had come far enough for one prominent sociologist to recommend that all agencies working with neglected children and those with behavioral problems be coordinated under the aegis of the school (Eliot 1928). The principal social policy assumption driving this era of school-based services was that the expanded needs of poor children could be met by investing public money (chiefly local) into the general support for the public schools (Tyack 1992).

For the next quarter of a century, from about 1930 to 1955, increasing school attendance was the focal point of the era of "progressive education," a period of school reform in which many school reformers believed that academic learning was useful for some but not necessary for all. During these years, mastery of the curriculum was less significant than simply participating in school life (Graham 1993). The school-based health and social services of this era were chiefly those that enjoyed external support from influential constituencies (such as doctors and women's groups) and those that did not challenge the central core of classroom instruction or require teachers to behave differently. In practice, some of these service programs had to be altered to better mesh with school operations (Tyack 1992).[2]

The twentieth century's third wave of school reform (1955–1983) focused on expanded and improved "access," primarily for groups of children who had been previously denied equal educational opportunity (e.g., poor children, children of color, girls, and children with disabilities). In support of access-oriented school reform, for the first time, large federal categorical programs were created to focus on public education. Of these, the largest were the compensatory education program created by Title I of the Elementary and Secondary Education Act of 1965 (ESEA) and the program of special education and related services mandated by the Education for All Handicapped Children Act of 1975 (P.L. 94-142). By 1983, the United States had achieved much broader access to its educational institutions than had existed in the past (Graham 1993).

The publication of *A Nation at Risk* in 1983 launched the current school reform effort, one focused on attaining high levels of academic achievement for all children (National Commission on Excellence in Education 1983). Unlike earlier reform efforts, its central focus on educational accountability raised expectations for both children and schools and propelled a dramatic expansion of state regulation of virtually every aspect of public education (e.g., teacher qualifications, teacher-pupil ratios, and standards for grade progression and graduation).

Implementation of various provisions of the Personal Responsibility and Work Opportunity Reconciliation Act of 1996 (commonly referred to as "welfare reform") has already begun to have a significant impact on public schools and the school reform efforts under way within them. As required by the new law, in the fall of 1997, nearly half a million out-of-school, unwed teenage mothers enrolled in public secondary schools or other programs to complete their high school education.[3] This mandated enrollment has already generated serious pressures on secondary vocational education programs and public school-based school-to-work initiatives (Ambach 1996).

Several provisions of the 1996 welfare reform legislation may also have a significant adverse effect on the health and development of large numbers of both preschool and school-age children. Federal support to poor families has been reduced (as discussed in greater detail below), and implementation of the new law is also likely to increase the percentage of preschool and school-age children who have no health insurance. Decreased "school readiness" (both at school entry and thereafter) for large numbers of children of all ages in the families adversely affected by these changes is likely. A corollary demand for compensatory education and special education services for affected children is predictable, as are pressures to divert significant amounts of public education resources to offset reductions in the availability of food and nutrition services, afterschool child care, and health insurance (Ambach 1996).[4]

A serious shortage of affordable child care (particularly for working poor families) is an inevitable consequence of implementation of the new law, and public secondary schools can anticipate a substantial demand for full-day, school-based child care for the preschool children (particularly those under the age of two) of teen parents required by the welfare reform to attend school (Urban Institute 1996).[5]

Over the next five years, several million adults will be required by the new welfare reform legislation to participate in "work activities."[6] More than half of the adults who have been on the welfare caseload for more than two years have not completed high school, and a substantial number have educational skills below the eighth-grade level (Meyers, Lukemeyer, and Smeeding 1997). The initial work activity for most of these adult mothers is likely to be enrollment in either a secondary school or an adult basic education (or GED) program. During the 1995–96 school year, the total enrollment of adults in these programs was only about 2.3 million; fewer than 20 percent of these adults were receiving public assistance (U.S. Department of Education 1996). To accommodate the enrollment of adults now on the Temporary Assistance to Needy Families (TANF) caseload, the capacity of adult basic education programs must more than double.

NONEDUCATIONAL CATEGORICAL GRANT PROGRAMS

Prior to the passage of the Social Security Act in 1935, the federal government played a minor role in supporting the wellness of children.[7] With the exception of providing public education, state government was generally limited to protecting child health through quarantine and immunization and ensuring the welfare of children who were orphaned, neglected, or delinquent (Gardner 1994; Olasky 1992).

The New Deal and the Shift of Basic Social Policy Assumptions The creation in 1935 of the Aid to Families with Dependent Children (AFDC) program (under the Social Security Act of that year) signaled the emergence of a new and different social policy approach to meeting the needs of poor children. It embedded the notion of a targeted social welfare obligation into a social insurance construct (Olasky 1992). In place of the indirect approach of strategic investment in school capacity that had characterized the era of assimilation, the new strategy sought to meet the needs of what was perceived to be a deserving subset of children and families by focusing public funds directly on their categorical (e.g., health, social service) needs. Over the next thirty years, the notion of targeted social welfare obligations slowly overtook and eventually replaced school investment as the primary strategy for responding to the needs of poor children and their families.

The Great Society and the Proliferation of Categorical Programs From 1960 to 1970, Congress more than tripled the number of federal categorical grant programs related to children and families (Tyack 1992) as government (both state and federal) sought to intervene directly to solve a broad range of problems (e.g., educational disadvantage and inadequate health care and nutrition) experienced by various categories of children and families (Gerry 1993). Structurally, these new categorical programs fell into three major groups: uncapped entitlements; capped formulas (e.g., Title I of ESEA) and "block grants"; and discretionary grants. In an uncapped entitlement program (such as Medicaid), states and localities draw down federal funds as needed to meet the actual costs of providing covered services to eligible individuals. In most of these programs, new federal funds must be matched with funds from a nonfederal (usually state or local) source.

In a formula or block grant program (such as Title I of ESEA or the Maternal and Child Health Block Grant), a grant is made to each state on the basis of a formula related to the number of potential categorical beneficiaries within the state. States have varying flexibility in distributing these grant funds within the state (usually greater under block grants than formula grants). Like formula and block grants, discretionary grants (e.g., Head Start) operate within a fixed or "capped" budget, but unlike formula and block grants, discretionary grant awards are competitive and no state or community is guaranteed annual funding.

This proliferation of new federal categorical programs reflected the perception of federal policymakers that the federal government had the technical and administrative capacity, the financial resources, and the will to solve the major social and economic problems facing low-income children and their families. Through the enactment of new federal categorical grant programs, state and local governments (which had the traditional responsibility for service delivery) were enlisted as agents of the federal government (Reischauer 1986).

Several factors contributed to this rapid growth of categorical programs. First, triangular relationships existed (and continue to exist) at the federal and state levels among professional organizations, legislators and their staffs, and executive branch specialists. Working together, these coalitions helped to expand the number of federal categorical grant programs by arguing that a combination of special expertise and dedicated or targeted funding was needed to ensure that vulnerable populations of children received needed services (Gardner 1994). Indeed, the creation of new categorical grant programs represented an excellent political opportunity for legislators to take credit for meeting the needs of various groups of children and families, even if new programs were funded only at token levels.

Second, the resistance of several states and hundreds of localities to the equal educational opportunity guarantees of new federal civil rights laws[8] argued strongly in favor both of a federal program base and of strict eligibility and fund use requirements which would prevent state and local governments from subverting basic program purposes. Children at the center of these converging movements were the same: the children of poverty, of color, and with disabilities.

Third, the expansion of categorical programs that targeted children and families was also fueled by a desire to circumvent states and raise the quality of services by creating new national standards. For example, states seeking to participate in the Medicaid programs and localities interested in operating a Head Start program were required to establish (or raise existing) licensing and credentialing standards in order to receive the new federal funds (Gardner 1994).

Finally, the expansion of categorical programs also created new fields of employment for a large labor force of service workers (particularly women entering the labor market) who, in turn, became economically dependent upon the expanded funding of categorical programs (McKnight 1995).

The Reagan Revolution and the Omnibus Reconciliation Act of 1981   On the heels of the extraordinary expansion of federal entitlement and discretionary grant programs during the late 1960s and early 1970s, pressure mounted to create block grants which would bring order and simplicity to the proliferation of categorical programs which were increasingly being perceived as inherently inefficient and ineffective (Pressman and Wildavsky 1984).

The first major block grant legislation, the Omnibus Reconciliation Act of 1981 (OBRA), was passed early in the Reagan Administration in order to transfer important program decisions and administrative authority from the federal government to states. OBRA created nine new or revised block grants which consolidated fifty-seven separate programs. The funds consolidated represented about 10 percent of total federal grant funds to state and local governments and the block grants, in turn, represented a 12 percent reduction in the total funding level of the consolidated categorical grant programs. Unlike earlier block grants, OBRA was used openly as a device for reducing overall federal spending (Hayes 1995). States were given broad discretion to decide which programs and services to provide, as long as they were related to the categorical goals of the overall grant (e.g., health prevention, maternal and child health).

Following the passage of OBRA in 1981, most states did not radically alter their programs, management systems, and service delivery structures, and most found a way to offset the federal funding reductions which accompanied it.[9] In programs employing income eligibility standards, states generally tightened their focus, excluding large numbers of children living in near-poor or working poor families. Under the education block grants, states redefined "need" in a manner which shifted funds away from big city schools with high concentrations of minority children (Hayes 1995).

For several reasons, the momentum for block grants which had seemed irresistible in the early 1980s was virtually spent by the end of the decade. Block grants, by their nature, lack a clear expression of purpose and, thus, clear political constituencies. Because block grants were accompanied by significant funding cuts and congressional inaction in the face of rising service costs, it was difficult to attribute tangible results or successful outcomes to them. Over time, the state flexibility intended by OBRA was diminished substantially by congressional actions to create categorical set-asides and expenditure ceilings (e.g., the Maternal and Child Health Block Grant). Finally, because of their inattention to problems of equity and fairness, vocal constituencies successfully attacked them for short-changing vulnerable populations of children and families (Hayes 1995).

Ironically, the OBRA block grants did little to stem the growth of federal categorical programs. As finally enacted, the 1995 budget included more than 550 federal grant programs. These programs covered a broad range of categorical areas outside of elementary and secondary education, maternal and child health, food and nutrition, early care and education, and family support services.[10] In seventy-seven categorical programs that targeted children and families, annual federal appropriations in fiscal year 1995 were in excess of $100 million (Bureau of the Census 1997).

Welfare Reform and the Balanced Budget Act of 1997 After almost four years of wrangling, vetoes, and apparent stalemate, sweeping welfare reform legislation (the Personal Responsibility and Work Opportunity Reconciliation Act of 1996) was enacted with major implications for the three largest child-family focused income support and substitution programs: AFDC, Supplemental Security Income (SSI), and food stamps. These programs form the core of what President Reagan labeled the "safety net" for children and their families.

Almost one in four American families (60 percent of families with incomes below 130 percent of the poverty level) receives assistance from at least one of these programs. Their combined effect has been to reduce poverty substantially, especially for families with children (Urban Institute 1996). The new welfare reform legislation as modified and expanded by the Balanced Budget Act of 1997 reduces federal government spending on these core programs by over $10 billion annually as compared to current law.[11] Over the next five years, more than two million children (23 percent of the current caseload) will lose AFDC support, over two million children (15 percent of the current caseload) will lose food stamp eligibility,[12] and approximately 200,000 disabled children (22 percent of the current caseload) will no longer receive SSI income support.

Several provisions of the new law combine to reduce incomes of families in the lowest income groups and to significantly increase the number below the poverty line. Over one million children in low-income families are moving into poverty as a result of these cuts, an increase of about 12 percent (Urban Institute 1996). More than 20 percent of American families with children will see their incomes fall by about $1,300 per year, on average. Over 80 percent of these families are "working poor," with incomes below 150 percent of the poverty line (Urban Institute 1996).[13]

The welfare reform legislation merges several child care grant programs into the existing Child Care and Development Block Grant and eliminates guarantees of child care assistance for welfare recipients participating in work or training. This block grant is a primary source of child care funding for working poor families, and the number of working poor families is significantly larger than the number of families receiving welfare. Under the new law, states must use at least 70 percent of the mandatory funds to provide child care assistance to welfare recipients in work programs and attempting to leave welfare and to those at risk of going on welfare. Although the annual funding for this unified program is more than the total funding of the constituent programs, these changes will dramatically reduce the access of working poor families to affordable child care while not meeting the needs of welfare families—even if all states meet their welfare-to-work targets. OMB estimates that annually almost 2.5 million children, most in working poor families, will lose child care subsidies (Urban Institute 1996).

The welfare reform legislation also cuts close to $3 billion over six years from child nutrition programs, with much of the reduction coming from cuts in nutrition aid to family day care providers that do not operate within a low-income geographic area or are not operated by a low-income provider. Once again, the primary adverse impact will be on children in working poor families (Urban Institute 1996).

Although comprehensive Medicaid reform was not included in the welfare reform legislation, several important changes were made with respect to categorical eligibility. Children in most families that become ineligible for income support under the new block grant for reasons other than gainful employment continue to be eligible for Medicaid.[14] However, children in families that discontinue participation in the new block grant program because of gainful employment will be eligible for Medicaid only for one transitional year. Because most of the jobs obtained by former welfare recipients are likely to be without employer-based health insurance benefits, these provisions will significantly increase the number of uninsured children and adults in working poor families (Robert Wood Johnson Foundation 1996).

The consolidation of categorical programs (e.g., child care) and the elimination of open-ended entitlements (e.g., AFDC and related child care) accomplished by the new welfare reform provisions makes it much easier for states to both integrate their public assistance programs[15] and devolve greater program authority to the local level (Watson and Gold 1997). While New York was the only state which considered a major shift in state-local responsibilities for AFDC prior to the federal welfare reform legislation, Watson and Gold believe that this legislation will likely be a catalyst for further state-local devolution. They predict that the thirteen states with the most decentralized systems (those with county-administered AFDC and child welfare programs) are the most likely to shift responsibilities further from the state to the counties. History would suggest that governors and state legislatures, faced with serious consequences of the $10 billion per year in funding cuts, are just as likely as Congress to set their own "categorical" restrictions on the use of block grant funds when they reach the local level.

Does the Current "System" Need To Be Fixed?

Over the past two decades, America has established ambitious goals to improve the learning and health of all of its children. The National Education Goals and the Healthy People 2000 goals established at the beginning of the 1990s provide excellent measures of the overall effectiveness of the current array of categorical programs and institutional arrangements in ensuring the healthy development of all American children and particularly of those most at risk. An analysis of progress to date in meeting these child wellness goals strongly suggests that, despite recognition of the need both to interconnect federal and state categorical grant programs effectively and to link them in an integrated fashion to public education, most American communities do not have a comprehensive infrastructure of children's services and supports.

A NATION AT RISK AND THE NATIONAL EDUCATION GOALS

In 1983, the authors of *A Nation at Risk* established high levels of academic achievements by *all* students as the goal of the current era of school reform (National Commission on Excellence in Education 1983). Eleven years later, Congress formally adopted a set of eight national education goals for the year 2000 (Goals 2000: Educate America Act 1994). From a vantage point over fifteen years after publication of the Commission's report, have we made serious progress toward ensuring high levels of academic achievement for all children? The general consensus has ranged from "no" to a hesitant "maybe" (Holton and Goroff 1995; Asayesh 1993).

Progress reports issues by the U.S. Department of Education in 1993 and 1996 conclude that the nation has fallen behind its own expectations and behind the progress of our global competitors. The 1993 report concludes that almost half of American babies start life behind and never have the support to catch up. Most American children enrolled in public elementary and secondary school cannot read and do mathematics at levels that are necessary for success in today's world (U.S. Department of Education 1993). The only measure where child outcomes are approaching the goals set by the National Education Goals is high school graduation.[16]

While the 1996 progress report reveals a significant increase in the average mathematics performance of nine- and thirteen-year-olds (i.e., the equivalent of at least one grade level); it concludes that these gains in mathematics performance, while significant, are not sufficient. The results in reading performance (which remained relatively unchanged) are extremely disturbing, and the gap in performance between white and minority students unacceptably large (U.S. Department of Education 1996).

Graham (1993) observes that this era of school reform may not prove as successful as its predecessors in meeting public expectations,[17] and several prominent school reformers have argued that this generation of school reform requires a broader focus than just school restructuring (Asayesh 1993). Pointing out that American schools are not well equipped or adapted to serve the many needs of American children, Graham argues that the current school reform effort must be nested in a larger "social reform," which recognizes that children "require and deserve support from a varied fleet, not just from a battleship." Such a reform would focus not only on schools but on the broader needs of children (Holton and Goroff 1995). Echoing these thoughts, active school reformers have noted that the direction of systems change must be more toward the community as a whole than toward the school alone. Ted Sizer has observed that until the non-schooling problems of children are addressed effectively at the community level, few schools will have the time needed for school reform to succeed (Asayesh 1993).

HEALTHY PEOPLE 2000 AND CHILD HEALTH AND DEVELOPMENT

Early in the current decade, over one hundred child wellness objectives for infants, children, and youth were established as part of the *Healthy People* 2000 report developed under the leadership of the Public Health Service (Public Health Service 1991). Many of these objectives focused on improved maternal and child health and nutrition status, immunization rates, and child cognitive and emotional development. Others sought reductions in the incidence of child abuse, high-risk behaviors, and violence among adolescents and in persistent environmental health problems (e.g., lead poisoning). One objective anticipated increasing to at least 95 percent the proportion of children who have a stable source of ongoing primary care (Public Health Service 1991). Revisions to these objectives made by the Public Health Service in 1995 added new special population sub-objectives and updated the original objectives in light of new science, information, and data (Public Health Service 1995b). The adverse consequences for large groups of American children (particularly the almost 25 percent of American children living in poverty) of the failure to create comprehensive infrastructures of supports and services are clear and well documented. They include impaired health as a result of poor prenatal care, malnutrition, and high rates of preventable disease, accidental injury, abuse and neglect, and high-risk social behaviors (Public Health Service 1995a; Children's Defense Fund 1992; National Commission on Children 1991; National Center for Children in Poverty 1990).[18] In fact, during the 1980s, American children lost ground in every major area of child development and health as compared to children in the rest of the world,[19] and large numbers of American youth fail to achieve acceptable levels of physical, mental, and social well-being (Children's Defense Fund 1992).

The learning of most of these children is particularly at risk because of the causal relationship between child health and development problems and disrupted school attendance, impaired ability to concentrate and lack of readiness to learn, and the erosion of both self-confidence and self-respect (National Commission on Children 1991).[20]

What's Wrong with the Present Structures?

As we have seen, large and increasing numbers of American children, particularly those living in poverty and others with multiple problems, are unable to obtain the supports they need to optimize their wellness and learning, for several reasons.

CONFLICTING POLICIES AND UNDERLYING ASSUMPTIONS

From the foregoing discussion, it should be apparent that the social policy assumptions underlying American public education are very different from those which drive the hundreds of other child services grant programs which have been created by government over the past three decades. Figure 6.1 compares some of these assumptions.

Policy Assumptions About Clientele In contrast to the primary assumption which underlies public education (i.e., that all children need, deserve, and must receive public education services), the structures of most categorical grant programs that serve children reflect an underlying policy assumption that only some children should have access to publicly funded services and supports. This assumption appears based on two discrete propositions: children and families only need access to external services and supports if the child or family is "deficient" in some respect; and some of these children do not deserve to

Public Education	Other Child Services
All children need, deserve, and must participate in a free program of school-based learning	Only some children need and deserve publicly funded services and supports
The need for teaching (instruction) is a normal and essential part of learning	Child service needs are not a normal part of development and stem from internal or family deficiencies
An infrastructure of neighborhood-based schools is a basic obligation of state and local government	Government has no duty to ensure that a primary care infrastructure (e.g., health or child care) exists within the community
Educators create a climate for child learning, provide a variety of tools for children to use, and motivate children to learn	Professionals providing compartmentalized services to meet (fix) the deficiency-based needs of children and families
Parents and community members need to actively support school-based teaching and learning	Parents and community members need to help identify child needs and provide child access for professionals

Figure 6.1. A Comparison of Underlying Social Policy Assumptions

receive such external services and supports at public expense (McKnight 1995; Gerry and Paulsen 1995).

The Myth of Child-Family Self-Sufficiency. Despite its popularity, the first of these propositions, the myth of child-family self-sufficiency, conflicts directly with what we know about healthy child development as well as with one of the basic policy assumptions underlying universal public education: the public school classroom provides a unique social environment in which educators stimulate and engage with children in an interactive teaching-learning process (Dewey 1937).[21]

In reality, almost all children have ongoing developmental, health, and learning needs which can be met only through some interaction between children (and their families) and the social and institutional environments within their communities. No two children are exactly alike, and each child is constantly changing through a variety of interactions with other adults and children in the child's and family's social, economic, and physical environment. For example, access to good quality child care and health care, parental employment, and the presence or absence of racism or sexism can have profound impacts on child development. A child's learning is directly affected by a variety of people within the overall community outside of the child's nuclear family and school, such as playmates, adult neighbors, soccer coaches, ministers, and police officers (Gerry, Fawcett, and Richter 1996).

Within most American communities, an informal network of "primary services" *external* to the family has for generations provided a natural source of support for child development and learning. Mothers day-out programs, library-based story hours, park- and recreation-based sports programs and nature walks, and neighborhood-based toddler play and cooperative child care groups are ready examples of primary services focused on young children (Wynn, Merry, and Berg 1995). In most communities, an informal network of community-based primary services also exists for children and adolescents (e.g., youth orchestras and sports teams, special religious activities for youth, and volunteer service). These "services" contribute significantly to building important social, civic, and cognitive skills (Pittman and Cahill 1992).

Finally, all children and families need help, both routinely and on an emergency basis, from a variety of professionals outside of public education. For example, all children need preventive health care (e.g., immunization and routine health screening), and, from time to time, outpatient health and dental care. Some require ongoing health maintenance (e.g., prescription drugs for asthma). A rapidly growing number of families with young children need early care and educational services and, for a variety of reasons, family supports (including nourishing food or emergency shelter).[22] In fact, what most differentiates children and families within the present structure is not the nature or extent of their need for "external" services and supports but the degree of access which they enjoy to the human, financial, and technical resources which must be brought to bear if those needs are to be met successfully (Gerry and Paulsen 1995).

The myth of undeserving children. The second proposition underlying the restricted access assumption is that some of the children who need services and supports do not "deserve" to receive them at public expense. (Gerry and Paulsen 1995). This myth is in direct conflict not only with the approach taken by American public education but also with the approach to child and family services used by virtually all Western European countries.[23]

While one can make a rational argument that publicly supported services and supports should not be provided to adults who are judged to have behaved badly (e.g., unwed pregnancy, drug abuse), it is difficult to understand why the infant or three-year-old child of such an adult who needs medical care or food should suffer the consequences. Indeed a social policy that punishes a child (by denying access to needed services) because of prior acts of a parent is both irrational and immoral (Rawls 1971). In practice, the attempt to separate needy children into those who are deserving of assistance and those who are not inevitably produces extraordinary equity problems with large numbers of children and families with severe service needs being found ineligible. The irrationality of this approach is perhaps best evidenced by the fact that the largest group of children who are most often sorted out (i.e., found to be undeserving) are those living in two-parent working-class families,[24] many of whom have lower income levels than single-parent families who receive public assistance (Bureau of the Census 1997).

Policy Assumption About Access and Infrastructure In America, the concept of universal public education has traditionally assumed that state and local governments will establish and maintain an infrastructure of neighborhood-based public elementary and secondary schools readily accessible to all children.[25] In contrast, the design of most other children's service programs implicitly assumes that government has no duty to ensure that a primary care infrastructure exists within every neighborhood or community or that children have meaningful access to and the ability to pay for such services.

In practice, there simply is no infrastructure of available and affordable health care or child care services for "categorically eligible" children (let alone all children) in most American communities. The absence of a local infrastructure for child health care is directly manifested in the location and geographic inaccessibility of health care clinics and hospitals and in the distribution and availability of different types of health care providers (e.g., pediatricians, physical therapists, and substance abuse counselors) (Politzer et al. 1991). It poses serious problems for meeting the needs of children and families in both rural and urban areas.

For children and pregnant women, health insurance coverage is not tantamount to health service access. Indeed, of the 14 million children who are covered by Medicaid, each year over half fail to receive a Medicaid-reimbursed preventive or primary health care service (Gerry 1993). Disincentives to effective health access are also created by the design of health care environments, including the hours and days of service, availability of child care, and the location of facilities (Halfon, Inkelas, and Wood 1995).

There are also serious gaps in the infrastructure of early care and education services in most American communities. Indeed, only about 40 percent of all children entering kindergarten in the United States have had some type of formal early education. Regardless of increased need, participation of young children living in high-poverty areas in some form of early childhood education is as low as 25 percent (GAO 1993). In fact, only 39.5 percent of all children under the age of one year, 43.4 percent of children of all one-year-olds, 51.4 percent of all two-year-olds, 60 percent of all three-year-olds, and 89 percent of all four-year-olds received early care and education services of any kind. In sum, only 57.5 percent of all American children below the age of five now receive early care and education services of any kind (Regenstein, Silow-Carroll, and Meyer 1995; Bureau of the Census 1992b).[26]

Policy Assumptions About the Role of Professionals Within the context of universal public education, Dewey (1937) believed that the central "professional" role of the educator is to create within the classroom a "purified medium" in which the child can "act" (i.e., learn). This learning is, in turn, a "shared activity" between teacher and student, one in which "the teacher is a learner, and the learner is without knowing it, a teacher." Indeed, to Dewey the "art of instruction" is to simultaneously motivate and empower every child to learn;[27] within such a vision the need for "teaching" is a healthy and normal part of child development.

For a century (from its origins during the era of assimilation to its codification in 1994 as the first national education goal), "school readiness" has been recognized by universal public education to be an important prerequisite to learning (Tyack 1992). Underlying the concern for readiness is a realization both that teaching necessarily involves engaging and empowering the whole child and that learning necessarily involves balancing the diverse influences of the various social environments (e.g., family, street, church) in which the child functions (Dewey 1937). Thus, the provision of instruction to a child who is chronically ill, exhausted, or physically abused by a parent is unlikely to lead to learning (Gerry 1993).

In contrast to Dewey's vision of the empowering professional, most federal categorical grant programs targeted at children appear to have started from a therapeutic vision of society which assumes first, that the primary factors impairing child wellness are *internal* to the child and family, and second, that professionals and the services they provide are crucial to ensure ongoing wellness. "Problems" that are heavily determined by external social and economic realities (e.g., chronic poverty) have been recast as pathological and endemic to the child or family (McKnight 1995).

From this vantage point, families cannot know whether they have a need or what the remedy is, cannot understand the process that purports to meet the need, and cannot even know whether the need has been met. Here, the child is seen to be "as a set of manageable parts" and the professional is a "service mechanic" whose job is to provide a compartmentalized service in order to solve a specific child wellness problem (McKnight 1995).

Child wellness is the product of both personal and environmental factors (Gerry, Fawcett, and Richter 1996). The notion that the primary factors contributing to impaired child wellness are *internal* to the child and family neglects the crucial role played by the child's social, economic, and physical environment. As is discussed at length earlier, in America today, the link between poverty and impaired child wellness is overwhelming. For example, the link between poverty and lead poisoning is so strong that one major research center declared: "as family income decreases, blood lead concentration increases" (National Commission on Children 1991).

Nevertheless, some have argued that the external social, economic, and political environment is simply a stage upon which more deeply rooted pathologies of children and families are played out. They see the rapid increase in unwed parenthood and the operation of the welfare state as responsible for creating families in which the work ethic and the values of the traditional family are devalued. The resulting absence of the love and discipline which could be provided by a father, they argue, has led to a generation of "emotionally impoverished" children and to poor child wellness outcomes (Olasky 1992; Murray 1984).

These critics seem oblivious to the fact that, for the past three decades, the number of children living in single-parent families as a result of divorce has greatly exceeded the number of children in never-married single parent families (Bureau of the Census 1997). If the absence of paternal love and discipline is a key to child wellness problems, then why haven't the outcomes for children in working-, middle-, and upper-middle-class families been similarly affected? The National Commission on Children (1991) rejected such an interpretation by making clear the link between the external social, economic, and physical environment of the child and family and the pattern of adverse outcomes.

In practice, the therapeutic vision has worked at cross-purposes with what should be a central social policy objective—strengthening the ability and increasing the opportunities for a family to solve all or most of its own problems without fostering the need for ongoing service intervention.

The therapeutic vision has also incorporated an assumption that each service provided competently by the appropriate mechanic to each part of the child (education, health, nutrition) will make an incremental contribution to the child's overall development, learning, and/or wellness (Gerry 1993). The difference between this service mechanic model of most large categorical programs and "whole-child" assumption underlying public education can be illustrated by an analogy to construction and quality control. The service mechanic adopts an approach akin to the quality control needed for house-building. In most cases, a board left out here or there may weaken but not defeat the overall structure. In contrast, the whole-child paradigm leads to the type of quality control needed for boat-building where the omission of virtually any plank will completely undermine the overall structure. In reality, the literature is replete with numerous examples of unsuccessful single-strategy approaches.

Policy Assumptions About the Roles of Parents and Communities The social policy assumptions underlying the current structure of public education envision an active involvement of parents and other community members in support of the teaching and learning that are crucial to its success. Indeed, one of the national education goals calls for the formation of partnerships that will increase parental involvement and participation in promoting the social, emotional, and academic growth of children (Goals 2000: Educate America Act 1994). Within this construct, the learning of children is viewed as an ongoing joint enterprise between educational professionals and families.

In contrast, most federal categorical grant programs assume a very different role for parents and community members. Here, the prevailing myth of professional services asserts that child needs can be met only be the right combination of external professional services. In this context, parents and community members are expected to help identify child needs and to provide child access for professionals but not to become actively involved in responding to the needs of their children. Because the situation is defined as the service professional *produces* and the child and/or family *consumes,* answers to child and family needs other than professional services—such as family empowerment, peer support, and changes within the overall political, social and economic environment—are effectively ruled out. In many instances, the active involvement of families may even be regarded as problematic (McKnight 1995).

While the increasing inclusion of a "case management" component in service integration strategies represents an expansion of the focus to families, by its very nature, case management accomplishes this expansion by creating a new professional or quasi-professional mediator/overseer between the family and other service professionals and agencies (Kagan and Neville 1993).

As is also discussed earlier, child development in inexorably tied to the community, and child learning is a local product. The behaviors that affect child development and learning occur among a variety of people within the overall community. Thus, the engagement of diverse groups within the community in an array of contexts and settings is required to solve many important child wellness problems such as high-risk behaviors among adolescents[28] (Gerry, Fawcett and Richter 1996). The culture of most large federal categorical grant programs has, however, compelled professionals to translate child needs into "deficiencies" to justify ongoing program eligibility. Although unintended, this "translation" process has worked to isolate children, families, and professionals from the community context. As a result, friends and neighbors have often been discouraged from attempting to help the family solve its own problem because the family is presented as "sick" rather than simply in need of help.[29] One important outcome of this process of pathologizing child needs has been the collective erosion of both the inclination and capacity of communities to assist children and families directly.

OTHER FACTORS IMPAIRING PROGRAM EFFECTIVENESS

In addition to the conflicts in policies and underlying assumptions discussed above, the inability of states and communities to establish and maintain effective infrastructures of child wellness supports can be attributed to at least four other factors.

First, although the breadth of the numerous federal categorical programs targeted on children and families appears impressive, most are overly rigid. Categorical service definitions severely restrict the use of funds to promote child wellness through proactive prevention strategies. For example, despite the fact that parental literacy is generally acknowledged to be an excellent predictor of child health status, few categorical grant programs would permit funds to be used to provide short-term child care so that single parents could learn to read.

Second, in practice, the current financing structures punish rather than reward program success. Because the bias of most educational and noneducational grant programs is to provide financial support for services to those least well served by the current system, often the only feasible way to increase program support is to demonstrate the ineffectiveness of current services and supports. For example, if the measures of child well-being increase, the potential for continued funding may be jeopardized. It makes no sense for programs to reward those communities who serve at-risk children poorly while penalizing those communities who serve the same type of children well. Indeed, the principal measure of "success" for providers has become input (has the budget level grown?) rather than output (how many needs were met or problems solved?) (Gerry 1993).

Third, many of the most important categorical child and family social and human service programs suffer from a crisis-orientation. Eligibility is often triggered only when a child's problem or family dysfunction has progressed to the point that family stability is threatened. Funds are available only in response to a clearly diagnosed problem—usually a problem that has gone unattended for some time (Farrow and Joe 1992). These restrictions make it virtually impossible to finance a child development and wellness system whose core values are heavily oriented toward prevention and early intervention.

Finally, management responsibility for categorical grant programs is widely dispersed at the state and local government levels (Gerry 1993; National Commission on Children 1991). As a result, most children and families encounter an inaccessible, highly uncoordinated array of narrowly focused services and benefits that target different and often conflicting goals, use inconsistent eligibility criteria and conflicting rules, and are administered by different agencies and staffed by overspecialized professionals. Within this disjointed, fragmented, and incomplete nonsystem, no service professional or agency is accountable to a particular child and family for the effective provision of all services that the child needs (Gerry 1993; National Commission on Children 1991).

CREATING A COMPREHENSIVE CHILD SERVICE INFRASTRUCTURE

This section reviews service integration strategies and alternative approaches for building and maintaining an accessible and comprehensive infrastructure of children's services and supports.

Service Integration Strategies

This section discusses the origins, evolution, and diversity of service integration strategies, offers an inclusive working definition, analyzes the potential of service integration strategies, and concludes by outlining a set of principles which might guide a more fundamental system reform.

ORIGINS AND EVOLUTION

The demand for service integration arose from the proliferation of categorical programs and the persistent failure of large numbers of children and families to gain access to needed services. Service integration emerged as both a strategy and a process which could be used to offset some of the worst features of the disjointed array of categorical programs.

As is discussed earlier, the great expansion of federal categorical grant programs occurred during the late 1960s and 1970s. In 1971, Secretary of Health, Education and Welfare Elliot Richardson, concerned about the proliferation of these programs and the inability of the federal government to manage centrally what were in reality local initiatives, launched a major effort to integrate "allied" services. Research and demonstration projects were funded, technical assistance was provided to states and localities, and new "allied services" legislation was prepared and submitted to Congress which would have greatly aided service integration efforts at all governmental levels (Kagan and Neville 1993). During this period, Congress also imposed specific coordinated planning and accountability requirements at state and local levels.[30]

In the early 1980s, interest in comprehensive service integration efforts waned as states tried to respond to the opportunities and challenges posed by the OBRA block grant strategy. However, by the mid-1980s, service integration activities at the federal and state levels were revived with the original service coordination emphasis.

GOALS AND DEFINITIONS

As Kagan and Neville (1993) suggest, a review of the literature reveals that over the past twenty-five years the primary goals of service integration have remained unclear. Alternative goal formulations have included: improvements in the service system; improved outcomes for families and children; and better and more efficient use of limited resources. Some have argued that improvements in the service system and in child outcomes are interdependent (Kagan, et al. 1995). Others have disagreed (Martin et al. 1983). Bruner (1989, 1996) and Gerry and Paulsen (1995) have attempted to merge these themes by arguing that the primary goal of service integration is not improved caretaking but helping families gain or regain control over their lives.

Partly as a result of this confusion over goals, no clear and agreed-upon definition of service integration has emerged over the past three decades (Kagan and Neville 1993). Some have suggested outcome-oriented definitions. To Rein

(1970), service integration is the set of strategies needed to solve pervasive service system problems (e.g., duplication of effort across agencies, the absence of any overall accountability for child outcomes). In contrast, Gans and Horton (1975) defined service integration from a client impact outcome perspective: linking service providers to allow treatment of a child's needs in a more coordinated and comprehensive manner. Levy and Shephardson (1992) have defined service integration in terms of its ability to prevent the foreseeable problems of a child or family, remediate identified problems, and strengthen family self-sufficiency.[31]

Others have suggested a variety of process-oriented definitions. The HEW Task Force envisioned a process for planning the coordinated delivery of a comprehensive range of services (with resources allocated rationally) at the local level (U.S. Department of Health, Education, and Welfare 1972). Agranoff and Pattakos (1979) defined service integration as essentially a process of administrative streamlining in which the mechanics of service delivery would be smoothed out without altering basic policy or the front-line behavior of service professionals. Kagan and Neville (1993) approached the definition of service integration descriptively by defining it as a blend of administrative strategies (i.e., client-centered, program-centered, policy-centered, and organization-centered) to integrate service. Kagan and others (1995) later proposed a definition of service integration that combines these descriptive elements with both child outcome and system-reform goals. To date, only a few definitions of service integration have included a link between service integration and the need to expand neighborhood social capital, community economic resources, and family employment (Bruner 1996; Annie E. Casey Foundation 1995; Gerry and Paulsen 1995).

For purposes of discussing the entire range of roles which lawyers and educators play and may come to play in designing and implementing service integration strategies, I suggest the following working definition.

> Services integration is a set of strategies by which a community seeks to ensure the immediate and uninterruped access of all children and families to those children's service and family supports needed by the family to optimize the cognitive, social, emotional, and physical development of each of its children, and to ensure the healthy functioning, stability, social and economic integration, and economic self-sufficiency both of the family and of the neighborhood of which it is a part.

CURRENT SERVICE INTEGRATION INITIATIVES

Today, hundreds of service integration initiatives are being operated by state and local governments and nonprofit agencies. Important state-level service integration focused on linking education and noneducational services include California's Healthy Start program, Indiana's Step Ahead initiative, Florida's Supplemental School Health Program, Kentucky's Family Resource and Youth Services Center, Missouri's Caring Communities initiative, New Jersey's School-Based Youth Services Program, and Oregon's local Commissions on Children and Families.

Major multistate service integration initiatives include the Danforth Foundation's State Policymaking Program, the Ensuring Student Success Through Collaboration project of the Council of Chief State School Officers, the Robert Wood Johnson Foundation's Making the Grade program and the Carnegie Corporation's Early Start program. Important community-level service integration initiatives focused on children include the Annie E. Casey Foundation's New Futures initiative, the Kellogg Foundation's Youth Initiatives Program, The Robert Wood Johnson Foundation's America's Promise initiative, New York City's Beacon Schools, the Children's Aid Society's Community Schools, Philadelphia's Youth Access Centers, and San Diego's New Beginnings. Among these hundreds of "service integration" initiatives, there are both similarities and significant differences.

Which Children and What Perspective? The population of children to be served varies among current service integration initiatives. While most statewide initiatives target economically disadvantaged or "at-risk" children and families,[32] local efforts are focused on both universal and categorical service populations. However, virtually all local initiatives targeting all children serve geographic areas with high concentrations of categorically eligible children (Levy and Shephardson 1992; Bhaerman 1994).

While virtually all current service integration initiatives are child centered (National Commission on Children 1991; Kagan and Neville 1993), they diverge markedly on the extent to which they are also family centered. Those focused on younger children are for the most part family centered (Farrow and Joe 1992); those service integration initiatives focused on older youth often are not.

What Services Are Being Integrated? The services integrated by current initiatives vary widely, depending on the age of the children involved, the comprehensiveness of the program's vision, the locus of activity and the availability of resources (Levy and Shephardson 1992).[33] The child/family services which form the grist for most service integration initiatives include: education; health services (both preventive and primary); food and nutrition services; mental health services; early care and education services; child welfare services (e.g., adoption and foster care); and family support services (e.g., family counseling and family preservation services, adult education, and job training). For youth, these services would be expanded to include: substance abuse prevention and treatment; pregnancy prevention; delinquency prevention; and school-to-work transition (Gerry and Paulsen 1995; Kadel 1992).

Where Do Service Integration Activities Take Place? Among current service integration initiatives focused on children, three approaches have been used to connect public schools to programs providing noneducational child and family services. In the school-based approach, "full service schools" merge concepts of school reform with the integration of support services and prevention programs. They serve as the hub for a wide range of psychological, health, social, recreational, and treatment services directed not only at educational remediation but also at changing a whole array of negative behaviors (Dryfoos 1994). Important components of emerging full service school models include school-based health centers, family resource and youth service centers, and settlement house-in-the-school programs.[34]

While similarly school-focused, a school-linked services approach provides services to children and their families through a collaboration among schools, health care providers, and social service agencies. Schools are among the central participants in planning and governing the collaborative effort, and services are provided (or coordinated by personnel located) at or near the school. The school-linked approach often requires agencies that typically provide health and social services off the school site to move some of their staff and/or services to the school (Larson et al. 1992).[35]

Despite the relative popularity of school-based and school-linked approaches, some experts have expressed concern about selecting the school or any other single community institution as the locus for all or most service integration activity. For example, Chaskin and Richman (1992) argue that an exclusive focus on any one institutional locus could cause services to conform primarily to the requirements, priorities, and world view of that institution. While schools are the most extensive institutional provider of children's services, a significant number of community residents (particularly those who were former students) may view the school as a hostile environment in which they both failed and often suffered humiliation (Levy and Shephardson 1992). In most communities, the attitudes of families toward nearby schools run the gamut. In some neighborhoods, elementary schools have become true community institutions, trusted centers of community activity. In these instances, the school would be an ideal locus for child and family support. In other neighborhoods, schools are more like fortress outposts in openly hostile country. In these locations, where no trust exists between families and schools, any other community site would be a better locus for child and family support. Chaskin and Richman (1992) observe: "The nature of community life is too diverse and the array of services and opportunities required for children is far too broad for the school, or any single institution, to plan or provide. To constrain points of access to a school-based system would be to lose the richness and diversity required in such an array of services" (112).

Community-based service integration initiatives may be sponsored by community-based organizations separate from the public service delivery system or by programs that maintain strong links to a local government agency or program (Chaskin and Richman 1992). Because of the tension surrounding the provision of health care services to adolescents, service integration efforts focused on elementary school-age children are more likely to be school-linked or school-based, and those focused on youth are more likely to be community based (Gerry and Paulsen 1995).[36]

How Are Services Linked or Coordinated? Across current service integration sites, a wide range of strategies is used in an effort to improve the coordination of services to children and families. Interagency service coordination involves integrating the work of different agencies and professionals. It necessarily entails negotiating new roles and implementing more collaborative decision-making among previously autonomous public and private agencies, providers, and funders.

Possible service coordination objectives range from the isolated, programmatic structure that characterizes the status quo to collocation, integration, and at the other end of the spectrum, a total unification of all programs into a fully integrated child service system. Initiatives have combined managerial, operational, organizational, and physical linkage strategies to pursue different service coordination objectives (U.S. Department of Health, Education, and Welfare 1972).

Managerial linkages include planning, programming, budgeting, evaluation, and training. Operational linkages include common outreach, intake, diagnosis, referral, information gathering, tracking, and record keeping. Organizational linkages include common governance and decision-making procedures. Physical linkages include collocation and shared transportation and communications. Governance arrangements and locus of service integration activities play a major role in determining both service coordination objectives and the proper mix of these service linkage strategies.

IMPROVED SERVICE INTEGRATION OR FUNDAMENTAL SYSTEM REFORM?

After nearly thirty years of experience with service integration strategies, serious questions exist about whether service integration approaches are the proper vehicle to create an accessible and comprehensive infrastructure of child wellness services and supports. This subsection analyzes both the empirical and the theoretical evidence regarding the potential of service integration strategies to create the desired infrastructure, and concludes that, while efforts to improve the effectiveness of service integration must continue, serious consideration should be given to a more fundamental system reform. The principles that should drive such a reform are then outlined.

The Empirical Evidence In assessing the potential of service integration strategies to significantly improve child wellness and learning, one would expect to find empirical evidence of effectiveness after active experimentation involving a broad range of service integration strategies at hundreds of sites over nearly thirty years. Remarkably, a careful review of the literature yields no such evidence. In fact, relatively few methodologically sound evaluations of complex service integration initiatives have been conducted, and the results of these have been inconclusive or mixed.

Bill Morrill and I (Morrill and Gerry 1990), after reviewing the evaluation literature then available on service integration, noted that a relatively limited description of these initiatives existed and even less had been done to analyze and evaluate results. We concluded that both the effectiveness and efficiency of service coordination and integration remain to be systematically tested.

In a more recent review of the evaluation literature on school-linked service integration initiatives, Gomby and Larson (1992) concluded that the existing school-linked service evaluation literature varies greatly in quality. They pointed out that many studies were plagued with one or more serious methodological problems (e.g., overly small sample sizes, poor measurement instruments) and that few studies followed children for a number of years to see if program effects are maintained over time. After reviewing sixteen multifocus and multiagency school-linked service integration initiatives in progress, Gomby and Larson observed that "evaluation of these efforts is in a preliminary stage. . . . Some programs have not undertaken any formal evaluation at all. . . . Given the scope and complexity of these initiatives, it is not surprising that methodologically rigorous evaluations have not yet been conducted" (80).

Where the evaluations have been conducted, the results have not always been positive. For example, Kirby, Waszak, and Ziegler (1991) in a comprehensive study of school-based health clinics reported no appreciable effects on a range of important child wellness outcomes. Kisker, Brown, and Hill (1994), in a preliminary evaluation report of the School-Based Adolescent Health Program funded by the Robert Wood Johnson Foundation, expressed frustration with the methodological problems inherent in school-based outcome evaluation and reported no evidence of reductions in high risk adolescent behavior owing to the presence of school-based clinics. Writing about early childhood service integration initiatives in four states, Kagan and others (1995) concluded that crucial steps in evaluating service integration initiatives, such as outcome specification and assessment, have yet to be fully implemented. Dryfoos, Brindis, and Kaplan (1996), in an analysis of the research to date on school-based health care, report findings are fragmented and have many methodological shortcomings. They conclude that, in the aggregate, this research provides encouraging but not overwhelming evidence of success.

There is little significant empirical evidence to support an assertion that the implementation of service integration strategies has materially affected child wellness outcomes. This is, or course, not proof that they have been ineffective. Indeed, I believe that they have undoubtedly improved child wellness. What I am much less sure of is that service integration strategies can serve as the primary vehicle for creating an infrastructure of supports and services which enables all or most American families to ensure the ongoing wellness of their children.

From Conversing to Teaming From its inception, the cooperation and collaboration of service professionals and providers has been viewed as a crucial element of service integration (Gans and Horton 1975). Gerry and Paulsen (1995) suggest that these approaches can be arrayed along a continuum (see fig. 6.2).

Conversing represents the initial effort by service professionals administering different programs focused on the same child and family to consider the parallel efforts of other service professionals.

Communication occurs when formerly isolated service professionals talk with each other about the scheduling and sequencing of different services and to

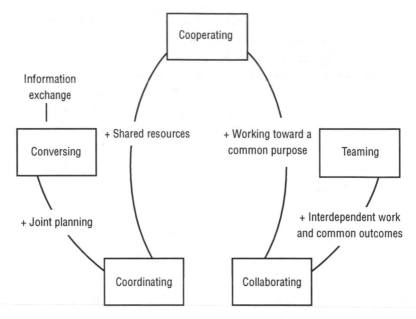

Figure 6.2. A Continuum of Relationships Among Professionals and with Families

some extent about the needs of the child and family. Here, the key question concerns: How can we stay out of each other's way?

Cooperation is reached when simple communication gives way to integrated service planning and coordinated service delivery. Now, the key question can become: How can we help each other?

Traditional collaboration is reached when professionals, across a broad range of programs and disciplines, work together to achieve their respective program goals. At this stage, the key question becomes: How can we work together to achieve our individual goals?

Teaming, the final point on the continuum, occurs when the traditional program goals of agencies give way to a common set of child outcome goals and work becomes interdependent. The key teaming question is: How can we best pool our professional talents and abilities to accomplish our common goals?

The distinction between the last two points in the continuum, traditional collaboration and teaming, is a critical one. In practice, the central focus of most traditional collaboration approaches is to gain help in better accomplishing one's separate programmatic objectives for a child (McKnight 1995; Hagedom 1995). Indeed, a central flaw of such a strategy is that the participating service professionals do not assume a joint responsibility for the achievement of all child-specific wellness outcomes (e.g., school achievement, and healthy physical development). As a result, the success or failure of each of the cooperating or collaborating agencies is not based on any collective accountability for the wellness of the child (Gerry 1993).[37]

This approach to collaboration for the most part squanders the opportunity for service professionals from different disciplines to assist each other. Despite the elaborate graduate education, credentialing, and licensing systems which have grown in lock-step with the expansion of categorical programs, child and family service professionals (including teachers) are engaged in only three basic types of interactions with children: informing, nurturing, and protecting. Irrespective of graduate degrees or licenses, human chemistry is neither an exact nor a predictable science. Some professionals are simply more effective doing certain tasks with certain families.[38]

Unlike traditional collaboration approaches, teaming strategies can take advantage of this positive chemistry by assigning different roles to different professionals with different children and families based on their collective judgment as to who is most likely to possess the combination of skills and temperament needed to be most effective with a particular child and family (Gerry 1993).[39]

Experience has demonstrated that if a collaboration is not working with children and families, it will inevitably be perceived as doing something *to* children and families (Annie E. Casey Foundation 1995). Nevertheless, implementers of traditional collaborative approaches have not viewed family members as part of the overall collaboration, although they often "consult" parents or assign case managers to represent their interests. A new generation of service integration initiatives, particularly those linked to family resource centers, have actively involved families in both priority-setting and day-to-day decision-making.[40] Finally, traditional collaborations exclude both important service professionals and community volunteers from the overall collaborative activity.

With respect to professionals, this exclusionary process is perhaps best understood by seeing service professionals as located at various different developmental stations of a train line on which the child and parent are riding. For example, at the first station—prenatal care—a health counselor provides information and ongoing support to the expectant mother. At a second station—infant care—a neonatologist, visiting nurse, and parent-teacher work with the child and family. Finally, at a third station—early childhood education—a Head Start teacher works with the child and parents for two years. In this example, over the first five years of life, three groups of service professionals have become familiar with the child and family. Some have important insights into the child's development, parental attitudes, and the home environment. A few have built up trust with the child and parents. As the child gets older, these professionals are left behind as the child and parents get on the train to go to the next developmental "station."

Most collaborative efforts to integrate services for a school-age child fail to include these service professionals because none is currently providing services to either the child or the family.[41] As a result, valuable information and valued relationships developed at the preschool are left out of collaboration.

In a similar vein, most collaborative efforts to integrate services for both preschool and school-age children fail to include the staff and volunteers of neighborhood-based organizations who provide primary services (mothers' day-out programs, recreation, and cooperative child care) to young children (Wynn, Merry, and Berg 1995) or youth services (e.g., service learning and mentoring) to adolescents (Pittman and Cahill 1992). For families uncomfortable with public employees, these community resources could contribute valuable information to the overall service integration process.

WHAT ELSE HAVE WE LEARNED?

Experience with a broad range of service integration initiatives over twenty-five years has yielded two additional insights into how they might be made more effective or how an alternative approach to system reform might be designed.

Empowering Families As is discussed earlier, most categorical program structures currently impair the ability and decrease the opportunities for families to respond effectively to the needs of their own children and solve all or most of their own problems without ongoing service intervention. The impact of this disempowerment process on families can be measured using four basic questions, comparing the answers of a typical empowered family ("normal" family) with those of a disempowered family. The four basic questions are (1) Who determines whether and what children's services are needed? (2) Who sets service priorities and specific service goals? (3) Who determines when, where, and by whom services will be provided? and (4) Who determines whether services are provided effectively, i.e., who must be satisfied? (Gerry, Fawcett, and Richter 1996)[42]

"Normal" families determine their own service needs, sometimes with outside advice when they solicit it. By contrast, program agencies and service providers, often influenced heavily by criteria for categorical eligibility and budget constraints rather than by child or family need, usually determine whether disempowered families need services, and if they do, what services are needed by them. Normal families set their own service priorities and use their purchasing power to reach agreement with service providers on service goals.

For disempowered families, service professionals usually determine service priorities and goals, with limited input from family members. Normal families often specify or negotiate desired service locations and schedules with prospective service providers. Disempowered families, however, are usually presented with limited service locations and fixed schedules by service professionals with a take-it-or-leave-it philosophy. Normal families determine service effectiveness and hold providers directly accountable through their checkbooks. In contrast, service professionals (or the agencies that retain them) working with disempowered families usually determine service effectiveness with little consultation with the affected families (Gerry, Fawcett, and Richter 1996).[43] In short, because the disempowered family is viewed as deficient, the important and evaluated outcome of the service is the service professional's own assessment of his or her efficacy. McKnight (1995) observes that it is becoming more and more evident that service systems are creating sensitive but frustrated professionals, unable to understand why their love, care, and service do not reform society, much less help individuals to function. In the professionals' view, any fundamental reform should help these servicers while allowing families to perceive and deal with their own problems.

Empowering Neighborhoods and Communities The behaviors that affect child wellness occur among a variety of people within the overall community.[44] Poor child outcomes (physical, social, psychological, economic and educational) are geographically concentrated in seriously distressed neighborhoods where substantial disinvestment has occurred (Jencks and Peterson 1991; Haveman and Wolfe 1994; Bruner 1996). Eliminating this neighborhood distress therefore must become an important objective of service integration initiatives. In practice, comparatively few initiatives have actually involved neighborhoods and communities in advancing the wellness of all children who live within them. As Bruner (1996) remarks: "While the emphasis on collaboration to address child and family needs has moved from an end vision of 'service collaboration' and 'service integration' to a broader one of 'community collaboration' and 'community building,' only the first tentative steps have been taken to make this a reality" (16).

New Strategies for Accountability As a result of several inherent problems, few service integration initiatives are truly accountable for the ongoing wellness of the children who are their clients (Levy and Shephardson 1992). Indeed, most service integration strategies effectively preclude the use of an outcomes-based accountability strategy. For example, if the focus of accountability for a service integration initiative is to be child wellness, then the design of an accountability mechanism should begin with the realization that major child wellness outcomes are significantly affected by both personal and environmental factors outside the immediate control of schools and noneducational service providers.[45] The restricted membership (i.e., current service professionals) of most service integration efforts makes it impossible to bring all the necessary parties to the accountability "table."[46]

In looking toward more fundamental reforms, Philadelphia School Superintendent David Hornbeck has defined accountability in a way that provides an excellent starting point: "Outcomes based accountability includes a system of rewards and penalties that impact teams of responsible staff directly" (Gardner 1994).

Future Directions and Guiding Principles for System Reform

The adverse impacts of unmet child wellness needs on the overall development and learning of American children are direct, severe, and worsening. While service integration strategies have been used as the primary vehicle for creating an accessible and comprehensive infrastructure of child wellness supports, the current combination of categorical grant programs and service integration innovation is unlikely to accomplish that task in the foreseeable future.

The time has come to consider seriously an alternative approach, one that would create a child wellness infrastructure capable of both responding to the comprehensive needs of individual children and addressing the cross-cutting social and environmental factors within their community that affect their physical, intellectual, emotional, and social wellness. Our experience with categorical programs and service integration has yielded seven important insights which should guide a more fundamental system reform.

First, communities, not schools, should assume the overall responsibility for the ongoing wellness and learning of all of the children who live within them. Within this context, schools should be seen as learning organizations.

Second, every American child should have ready access to a comprehensive and equitable system of care and support which is designed to optimize her or his healthy development and learning and which is based in a wellness-oriented community.

Third, families and other community residents should invest, tailor, negotiate, control, and answer for the outcomes of the new service and support infrastructures for children and their families.

Fourth, the reformed system should invest its resources in a manner that enhances the capacity and well-being of the families, neighborhoods, and community it serves.

Fifth, children and their families should have the freedom to choose among individual care and service providers.

Sixth, mechanisms must be fashioned to ensure overall equity and fairness in the treatment of all community members.

Seventh, the funding and financing of such a system should be unitary, sufficient, equitable, and stable and should reward rather than punish success.

AN ALTERNATIVE APPROACH

With my colleagues Steven Fawcett and Kim Richter, I (1996) offered at least a partial vision of the type of fundamental system reform suggested by the guiding principles outlined above. Alexis de Tocqueville (1991) in his monumental treatise on American democracy describes empowered American communities—communities in which groups of citizens define a social problem, decide how to solve it, and become key actors in implementing the solution they devise. At the core of the system reform which we suggest is this exact but demanding blend of community proactivity, leadership, and contribution.

Specifically, I envision the creation of a new network of community-based child wellness systems. Within this new network, decision-making and control of noneducational child wellness resources would be transferred to community partnerships that are owned, controlled, and shared by families, adolescents, and others most directly affected and by the various social, economic, and service systems (e.g., schools, clubs, businesses) that influence the community environment.

These community partnerships would serve as catalysts for system change and would be responsible for the creation of a child wellness oriented community and accountable for the wellness of all children who live within it. To carry out this responsibility, they would have the power to define child wellness needs and problems within the community, design a local child wellness system to meet such needs and respond effectively to such problems, and exercise control over the human, material, and economic resources essential to the successful operation of such a system (McKnight 1995).

Each community system would ensure universal access to an infrastructure of integrated child development and wellness services and supports for individual children and their families, and a process for actively addressing cross-cutting health and wellness issues. The configuration of community systems would vary, based both on assessments by the community partnership of child wellness outcomes, needs, capabilities, and assets[47] and on an identification of existing channels of child wellness influence within the community.[48]

Community partnerships would also develop and coordinate the implementation of locally acceptable methods for addressing cross-cutting child development and wellness issues, such as the prevention of accidental injuries and adolescent pregnancy.[49]

Children needing individual care would be able to choose among service providers, and health care would be provided on a fee-for-service basis under a capped annual child wellness budget.[50] Service costs and payment mechanisms would be negotiated periodically at the local level, and community partnerships would enjoy broad discretion in structuring the financing of child wellness capacities. For example, the community partnership might choose to employ child wellness care professionals directly, enter into contractual arrangements with public or private providers, rely on informal support structures, or issue vouchers to children and families to support the purchase of child wellness services from a competitive market.

In support of new community-based child wellness systems, state agencies could play two important roles. States could help build community capacity to support the day-to-day operations of the system and create structures to prevent recurrence of the types of abuses in the provision of individual child and family care under what is sometimes referred to as the old "county" health and welfare system.[51]

The ongoing operations of such a network of child wellness systems would be financed through dedicated trust funds. The annual revenue for these trust funds would be obtained through a combination of reprogramming existing resources and a new uncapped payroll tax.[52] Close on the heels of the recent welfare reform legislation, which removed more than $10 billion annually from the child wellness safety net, it may seem strange to some observers to suggest the creation of a new payroll tax (along with the reprogramming of existing funds) as a mechanism for financing the proposed system reform. But for several reasons, I think it the right path to pursue.

For more than thirty years, public support for payroll-tax-based financing of the Social Security retirement and Medicare programs has been consistently strong.[53] At the same time that the categorical safety net was being partially dismantled by the enactment of welfare reform legislation, legislators supporting changes in the Social Security and Medicare safety nets scrambled for their political lives.

As is discussed earlier, welfare reform is also likely to drive states to experiment with greater devolution of responsibilities for children's services to local communities (Watson and Gold 1997). The proposed system reform would create a universal rather than a categorical infrastructure of services to ensure child wellness and would devolve responsibility for the detailed design and operation of the system to these communities. The next step in building support for such a fundamental system reform would be the design and implementation of an aggressive social marketing strategy (Andreasen 1995).[54]

It is against a backdrop of both this expanded notion of community child wellness systems and more traditional service integration approaches that we turn to a consideration of the lawyer's role.

THE ROLE AND TRAINING OF LAWYERS

This section explores the varied roles of lawyers in supporting both service integration and more fundamental system reform approaches and discusses the implications of these roles for their professional training. Before proceeding, however, it may be helpful to consider two important questions: why should this work be done by lawyers rather than social scientists or management experts, and what are the risks inherent in such a work allocation decision?

Lawyers and the Work to Be Done

Three key roles must be played skillfully if service integration initiatives (or bolder system reform) are to be well crafted and implemented successfully. These roles are those of interagency translator, broker, and problem solver. Most lawyers are not, themselves, products of the discipline-specific training and credentialing structures and categorical program-driven service systems that have led to many underlying problems. As a result and because they should be more sensitive to the complex legal rights and responsibilities which surround children's services, lawyers are on balance better candidates for these roles than their likely competitors (i.e., service professionals, program administrators, or management experts). However, in order to play these roles successfully, lawyers must not be caught in a series of intellectual traps embedded within their own profession.

First, there is little question that the implementation of well-designed service integration strategies or more fundamental system reform would advance important civil rights objectives (reducing or eliminating serious disparities in educational performance or health outcomes). However, at the core, service integration is not primarily about ensuring equity by simply eliminating outcome disparities that exist among subgroups. Rather, at its best, service integration represents a clear and egalitarian answer to what Glendon (1991) calls the bottom-line question of every democracy: How well do the institutions of government and civil society serve the needs of those who cannot help themselves? By seeking to optimize the development and learning of *all* children, service integration is an important expression of a moral and social commitment by public and private agencies, families, and communities.

Second, American legal and political discourse about children and government programs regularly fails to consider the social environment of which children and families are a part. This environment is characterized by crisscrossing networks of associations and relationships that constitute the "fine grain of society," what Glendon (1991) eloquently describes as:"the mediating institutions that stand as buffers between individuals and the state, the diverse groups that share with families the task of nurturing, educating and inspiring the next generation" (134).

Because lawyers are more familiar with and disposed toward more formal institutions of society, in designing and implementing service integration initiatives they must take into full account the informal social institutions (e.g., neighborhood organizations, churches, clubs, and other communities of interest) that directly affect child development and learning (Gerry, Fawcett, and Richter 1996; McKnight 1995; Glendon 1991).

Third, usually during their first year of law school, most law students enrolled in torts classes are dismayed to learn that, in most instances, under the common law there is no "duty to rescue" a child in peril. After expressing reactions that range from outrage to chagrin, they are presented with (and often overcome by) a series of technical, and probably wrongheaded, rationales that attempt to distinguish legal duties from moral imperatives. One of the lawyer's greatest strengths in helping to fashion service integration initiatives is the ability to rise above the eccentricities of specific organizational cultures and avoid the blinders imposed by overspecialized disciplines. The need to rise above the absence of a duty-to-rescue rule may be the lawyer's greatest initial challenge.

The Lawyer and Service Integration
Strategies

Because of its origins in the explosion of categorical programs targeted on children and families in the two decades that followed the Great Society era, service integration has always been a fertile field for lawyers and other legal institutions. Because much service integration activity has been school based or school linked, educators seeking to improve the overall development and wellness of their students have also often found themselves in the midst of one of several highly legalistic processes associated with service integration initiatives. If lawyers are to make constructive contributions to the design and implementation of successful service integration initiatives, they must do so in two interrelated ways.

First, lawyers must stop designing and maintaining categorical program structures that both create the need for service integration and impede its successful implementation. Second, they must work closely with educators, families, community members, and other service professionals to design, implement, and support successful, ongoing, and equitable service integration initiatives.

STOP CONTRIBUTING TO THE PROBLEM

The fragmented array of categorical programs has been and continues to be designed by lawyers who act as the eligibility gatekeepers and the fund-use police of present program structures. They devise statutes, regulations, standards, and procedures that perpetuate and institutionalize many features of categorical programs that both impair the ability of children and families to benefit from a particular program and create the greatest obstacles to the overall improvement of child wellness.

Lawyers involved in the development of law and regulation in the legislative and executive branches of federal and state government can help increase the likelihood of improved child development, learning, and wellness for large numbers of American children by:

1. revising laws and regulations to create consistent program goals, philosophies, and incentives within educational grant programs and across all categorical programs targeted on children and families;

2. changing the structure of categorical programs (e.g., Head Start, Medicaid) to permit children living in families with incomes above the current eligibility threshold to participate in such programs upon payment by the family of a sliding-scale cost contribution;

3. eliminating or reducing current restrictions on the use of categorical grant funds in return for strengthened outcome accountability standards and a system of related rewards and penalties;

4. redesigning confidentiality and privacy provisions that significantly impair integrated service planning, delivery, and evaluation;[55]

5. overhauling categorical licensing and credentialing systems that create program-based sinecures and restrict the operation of informal support networks; and

6. amending existing laws and regulations to incorporate service expansion within the structures of existing categorical grant programs rather than through the creation of new programs.

In addition to these policy and regulatory reform activities, lawyers administering laws and regulations at the federal, state, and local levels can help develop and implement consolidated state plans and local application strategies and innovative waiver approaches which can dramatically improve the operating efficiency and outcome effectiveness of service integration initiatives.[56]

DESIGNING AND IMPLEMENTING SERVICE INTEGRATION INITIATIVES

Lawyers must work closely with educators, families, community leaders, other service professionals to design, implement, and support the successful, ongoing operation of school-based and school-linked service integration efforts. Much of this work involves identifying and dismantling the legal and programmatic barriers to coordination and integration of child and family services (described in detail earlier) which continue to be erected within the current array of federal and state categorical grant programs.

In addition to barrier removal, lawyers must work with educators, parents, and a variety of other child and family professionals to design, manage, and evaluate a wide range of service integration initiatives. To this end, lawyers should be seriously involved on an ongoing basis in the design of governance arrangements, blueprints for interagency service coordination, new mechanisms for ensuring accountability, the crafting of flexible financing strategies, and the adjudication of disputes between collaborating agencies.[57]

Governance Arrangements Governance refers to the permanent consolidation of leadership and decision-making that is needed within local communities to improve the delivery of services to children and families. In practice, it is the mechanism by which public agencies, acting in concert, can integrate the efforts of service providers (Center for the Study of Social Policy 1991). In some community-based initiatives, governance also incorporates strategies to promote and facilitate citizen participation in planning and decision-making (Chaskin and Garg 1995).

The governance structures of multiagency service integration initiatives vary greatly, based on the initiative's goals and objectives and the politics of agency relationships and government entities within the community (Gardner 1992). For the lawyer, the development of governance arrangements throws into contrast, perhaps most vividly, the extraordinary differences among the child- and family-serving organizations within a comprehensive service integration partnership.

The two most important and controversial variables associated with such governance structures have proven to be the nature and legitimacy of "community" representation and participation within the governance structure and the relation between governance and government within the affected community (Chaskin and Garg 1995; Center for the Study of Social Policy 1991).

Questions of legitimacy have been raised about both resident self-selection and processes that call for participation by members of neighborhood organizations that appear to some to have become informal agents of local government. Selecting individuals to act as neighborhood representatives who also represent their own institutional interests and perspectives frequently poses the appearance of conflict of interest. The issues of legitimacy focus on notions of fair or adequate representation and necessarily involve the question of for whom individual family or neighborhood representatives are presumed to speak and with what authority.

Experience demonstrates that the manner of structuring this type of community participation may be crucial to the overall success of the initiative because the perceived legitimacy of this participation[58] can make a substantial difference in whether the initiative is seen as truly connected to and in the best interests of the community—whether it has credibility (Chaskin and Garg 1995).

Arriving at the proper linkage of government and governance within a service integration initiative raises issues primarily of organization. Most com-

munity-level initiatives have used one of the following structures: (1) an institution parallel to local government which offers an alternative mechanism for
providing services and supports now provided by government; (2) a separate
but complementary institution to local government; or (3) direct incorporation
into local government, usually through the creation of a formal subunit of
government (Chaskin and Garg 1995). The selection of any of these alternatives
poses difficult questions for the lawyer.

The use of an institution parallel to local government which offers an alternative mechanism for providing services and supports now provided by government has been urged as a central strategy in the needed reinvention of government. Proposals for this type of linkage have ranged from outright privatization
of governmental functions by assigning them those functions to a single nongovernmental agency, to so-called managed care approaches, to voucher arrangements that would enable families to select among competing institutions
(Osborne and Gaebler 1992).

Finally, because the direct incorporation of a multiagency governance structure into local government has often occurred through the creation of either a
new subunit of local government or a new type of local governmental unit,
lawyers are frequently confronted with complex questions of state law related to
the formation of new governmental units. For example, state laws and even
state constitutions often expressly designate the unit of local government (e.g.,
city, county, or school district) which is empowered to carry out a public
function (e.g., manage a public health clinic).

Complex legal questions often arise where an intent exists to delegate some
or all of these roles and functions to a new subunit of local government without
the express approval of the state legislature or the voters. A decision to create a
separate but complementary institution to local government raises an equally
complex set of issues and questions, including:

1. Is the institution to be created public, quasi-public or nonpublic? State law
   varies greatly on the extent to which responsibilities of public agencies can be
   transferred or delegated to each of these types of institutions.
2. Will the separate but parallel institution enjoy sovereign immunity? Will it
   be constrained by merit system personnel requirements? Will it be required
   to hold all meetings in public?
3. How will laws governing confidentiality and privacy apply to it?

Blueprints for Interagency Service Coordination Interagency service coordination involves integrating the work of different agencies and professionals,

particularly those involved in the direct provision of child and family services. The common understandings of these agencies and professionals as to how they will work together are captured in interagency service coordination agreements. In practice, these agreements vary significantly, based primarily on the politics of agency relationships and government entities within the community (Gardner 1992). Unfortunately, such agreements have been used frequently as a substitute for real collaboration rather than as a tool to achieve it.

The majority of child-serving organizations operate in a highly unstable environment. Strong incentives exist to participate in mechanisms that can reduce uncertainty in those external factors critical to the life and work of the organization. Against this background, interagency agreements often represent an important mechanism for managing environmental uncertainty, particularly if they include provisions addressed to present and future interorganizational exchanges of scarce, important, and transferable resources, for example, money, clients, services, and information (Center for the Study of Social Policy 1991).

Some of the most important factors affecting the viability and usefulness of interagency service coordination agreements have proven to be the range of programs and agencies which need to be coordinated;[59] the nature of the envisioned interdependence among them; the degree to which conflicts and other differences in organizational cultures can be resolved; and incentives for each of the organizations to coordinate with others.[60]

The role of lawyers in the framing of interagency service coordination has involved translating and brokering among agencies and disciplines. It requires a working knowledge of the issues of organizational and interorganizational structure and organizational behavior which lie just beneath the surface of service coordination (Meyers 1993).[61]

One important challenge for the lawyer attempting to reach a common understanding on service coordination is to be sure that the appropriate players are at the table. A fatal flaw of many unsuccessful service integration efforts has been a serious misfit between the global outcome goals being pursued for children and families and the limited membership of the strategic partnerships formed to pursue them. If successful service integration requires reliance on a boat-building paradigm (as discussed earlier), the lawyer's task is to ensure that no organizational plank is omitted.[62]

The nature and extent of interdependence among the participating agencies substantially affect the allocation of legal, programmatic, and financial responsibility for the provision and outcomes of the children's services and family supports. Moreover, the nature of agency interdependence should be a decisive factor in resolving fundamental competition over resources or power within the collaboration.

Lawyers exploring potential interagency linkages (i.e., managerial, operational, organizational, and physical) often have little understanding of the organizational cultures they are trying to link. Major differences in cultural assumptions and values exist among child- and family-serving organizations. The lawyer's clients are usually familiar with only one of the involved cultures. As a result, and usually by default, lawyers must attempt to become translators of both professional and organizational assumptions and ultimately of underlying organizational values.

Among the public institutions likely to participate in interorganizational service coordination, only the school systems are dedicated to providing services to all school-age children within the community. For educators, basic service eligibility is a question of birth date. However, eligibility is a preoccupation of virtually all other child-serving organizations which must, on a continuing basis, determine which children and families are "entitled" to services and which are not. This gate-keeping orientation brings with it a set of very different organizational characteristics (Meyers 1993).

In the context of public education, the services provided to most children are seen as normative and developmentally appropriate. Many health care provider organizations are involved simultaneously in providing normative, prevention-oriented services (e.g., immunization, vision screening) on a universal basis; and disease- or injury-triggered services to specific children on both case-by-case and categorical bases. This disparity often creates a type of intraorganizational schizophrenia which mirrors the problems faced in interagency arrangements.

Another source of underlying conflict in organizational culture derives from the crisis orientation of many child and family service programs. As is discussed earlier, eligibility for many of these services requires proof that a child or family problem has progressed to a dangerous point (Farrow and Joe 1992). Services that respond to the crisis are often quite different from those needed to address the multifaceted problems of which the crisis is only a symptom. Agencies and programs focused on prevention or early intervention (e.g., Head Start, parenting education) and those focused on normative development (e.g., public schools) approach the question of service access and design quite differently.

The lawyer's role in first explaining and then resolving the conflict in underlying organizational cultures within the overall array of categorical grant programs for children and their families is frequently crucial to the overall success of the service integration effort. To play this role successfully, lawyers must be vigilant to prevent jargon (legal and programmatic) from destroying efforts at meaningful collaboration and negotiation.

Accountability Mechanisms Today, the watchword of almost every service integration initiative at both the state and community levels is accountability. As a result, lawyers are increasingly being asked to help craft mechanisms that will ensure that coordinated programs and agencies are accountable to both families and the community at large for both short-term and long-term child and family outcomes. The design of a service integration accountability mechanism is a particularly daunting task.

For the lawyer, the success of the design effort is likely to depend on three key matters: (1) the degree of agreement among families and those agencies and professionals to be held accountable; (2) the role of the lead or "integrating" agency; and (3) the motivation of professionals and families to work together. An important first step in designing an accountability mechanism, therefore, is to define *accountability*. In different contexts, it has been defined as: measurement; measurement together with an explanation of the reason for outcomes; or measurement, an explanation of the reason for the outcome, and a duty to correct a measured shortfall in outcomes or expectations (Gerry and Paulsen 1995). The selection of the appropriate definition is linked to the earlier question of the membership of the service coordination partnership. For example, assuming the most expanded notion of accountability, an active role for families and neighborhoods in the overall collaboration will likely be essential because important child outcomes are significantly affected by factors outside the immediate control of child-serving organizations.

In most service integration initiatives, one or more of the participating agencies plays an overall management and coordination role (U.S. Department of Health, Education, and Welfare 1972; Kagan and Neville 1993). For the lawyer seeking to design an accountability mechanism, an understanding of the nature of this coordination role is crucial to allocating legal, programmatic, and financial accountability. In practice, these basic types of coordination have emerged: voluntary coordination, where an agency provides direct services and oversees the provision of services by other agencies to ensure comprehensiveness; mediating coordination, where an agency develops linkages among autonomous service providers and provides no direct services itself; and directing coordination, where an agency can mandate linkages among subordinate agencies (Gans and Horton 1975).

In developing an accountability mechanism, lawyers must also pay careful attention to the internal structures, control arrangements, reward systems, and socialization techniques of the participating organizations. An understanding of these factors is crucial to the development of mechanisms that will influence effectively the attitudes and behaviors of both mid-level managers and front-line professionals (Meyers 1993). Research shows, for example, that public school administrators choose to cooperate with other child-serving organizations when doing so can satisfy demands to improve their performance on particular problems. In the absence of new demands, the same administrators may resist the extra work of service coordination, no matter how great the agreement about its inherent value (Weiss 1987).

Financing and Funding Strategies Financing strategies represent a key element of most comprehensive service integration initiatives. As Farrow and Joe (1992) point out, current methods of financing affect program priorities, shape the incentives that drive service systems, and ultimately influence how useful services are to families. They reinforce an initiative's underlying policy and programmatic direction and contribute significantly to organizational incentives for service coordination (Center for the Study of Social Policy 1991).

The lawyer seeking to design flexible financing strategies to support comprehensive service integration needs to be familiar with: the diverse financing structures that provide funding for children's services and family supports; the service integration barriers created by these structures; and a range of flexible funding alternatives. As Farrow and Joe (1992) point out:

"Pulling together the needed funding sources is neither simple nor a short-term venture. It requires detailed and extensive knowledge of how money is now spent and of the rules that govern the spending. It requires creativity in combining previously separate funding sources to achieve a new collaborative goal" (67). These financing structures and some of the barriers created by them are discussed above.

Lawyers developing financing strategies must be able to identify refinancing opportunities that involve a wide variety of federal, state, and local funding sources, including approaches designed to make better use of existing resources such as staff reassignment and budget reallocation. Even after interagency financing strategies have been implemented, lawyers must also participate sufficiently in the budgetary and allocation decisions of the coordinating service agencies to ensure that budget decisions are consistent with interagency service coordination agreements (Center for the Study of Social Policy 1991).

Lawyers working to develop flexible funding strategies need a working knowledge of two flexible funding approaches: the decategorization of funding streams, through waivers, pooling arrangements, and blended funding approaches; and the increased leveraging of federal entitlement funds. Both strategies have proven successful in expanding the overall financial resources available to support service integration initiatives (Center for the Study of Social Policy 1991).[63]

Decategorization removes categorical restrictions on the use of federal and state grants funds so that services and supports can be better tailored to meet the individual needs of all children and families. Decategorization approaches seem particularly suited to financing a comprehensive infrastructure of children's services and a logical consequence of the increasing devolution of responsibilities from state to local government. As the Center for the Study of Social Policy (1991) points out, state governments seeking to encourage local communities to develop comprehensive school-linked service strategies can do so by providing greater flexibility in available funding streams.

Waivers are tools for creating pooled and blended funding arrangements by decategorizing significant amounts of federal grant funds provided under the Social Security Act (e.g., Medicaid, child welfare). Upon application by states, federal agencies can remove categorical restrictions in order to expand eligibility of needy children and families and allow flexibility in the use of grant funds. In many instances, because the administrative overhead of these programs is inflated by categorical restrictiveness, the granting of such a waiver results in more services for children and families without an increase in overall program cost.[64]

In a pooled funding strategy, two or more funding sources are used to support the same service or to support it consistent with categorical restrictions applicable to each. Funding may be integrated for the family, but the funding sources must remain separate at the administrative level.[65] In a blended funding financing strategy, all categorical restrictions are waived so that funds from different categorical funding sources may be integrated both for families and for the purposes of day-to-day administration (Gerry and Paulsen 1995).[66]

Financing strategies that maximize the leveraging[67] of federal entitlement funds can make substantially more federal dollars available to support comprehensive service integration efforts without increasing overall service expenditures. The level of federal-state entitlement funding received by local communities is based on three factors: the number of people within the community who meet the categorical eligibility criteria of the program; the capped or uncapped nature of the program and related matching requirements, if any; and the amount of nonfederal money that is available to the state or locality for matching.

While the first factor in this equation would appear to be a given, a few communities have shown great creativity in discovering previously unknown characteristics of residents that have allowed these residents to become categorically eligible for income support benefits with a lower state/local fiscal contribution (e.g., AFDC-TANF to SSI). In such situations, the likelihood of state collaboration is greatly enhanced.

NEEDED SKILLS AND ABILITIES

The work expected of lawyers in connection with the design, implementation, and ongoing operation of service integration initiatives requires an expertise in ever-broadening areas of law and regulation (including categorical program structures and operations), demography and ethnography, child development and learning, family dynamics and wellness, community building and supports, labor economics, social psychology, and organizational theory. This information must be distilled and brought to bear in connection with a variety of service integration initiatives.

Lawyers involved in service integration need a much greater range and depth of information about a wide variety of legal areas and topics rarely addressed by law schools. First, lawyers working with service integration need a much better than average grasp of the law in several specific areas: universal public functions (e.g., public education, public and environmental health and safety, parks and recreation); federal and state programs, categorical and universal, which provide benefits, services, and supports to children and families (e.g., public education, health, and mental health); civil rights and liberties (e.g., non-discrimination, confidentiality and privacy); state and local police powers (e.g., law enforcement and juvenile detention, parental rights and child abuse and neglect, foster care and guardianship, and child support); the creation of special purpose government and quasi-public agencies; and the operation of public and private finance systems.

Second, they need an awareness of widely differing features (e.g., training, working protocols, and operating realities) of the professional cultures of the different organizations and professions (e.g., teaching, nursing, social work, law enforcement) to cooperate. Most lawyers have had scant preparation for learning the maze of program, administrative, and service arrangements and related organizational cultures. They must become familiar with the various program and administrative jargons (and underlying assumptions) which now defeat service coordination, professional collaboration, and meaningful attempts at family or community participation or empowerment.

Third, lawyers need to become aware of the social psychology (e.g., expectations, fears, motives, hopes, anxieties, and jealousies) that affect the attitudes and behaviors of the front-line professionals who are the prospective spouses of the service integration marriage. One of the cardinal errors of service integration initiatives for two decades has been to confuse the marriage brokers (i.e., the agency heads) with the actual bride and groom.

Fourth, lawyers need to understand better the day-to-day reality of the children, families, and neighborhoods which form both the purpose and the context of all service integration work. If service integration is, itself, to be a universal strategy, then that understanding must begin with (but extend beyond) the situation of those children who are most disadvantaged, those families that are most dysfunctional, and those neighborhoods that are least vibrant. For example, often children within working poor families are least well served by the present categorical system. One great danger for many lawyers involved in service integration is to ignore the services and supports which are available to the most advantaged children and families. Social justice demands that the opportunities, services, and supports available to the most advantaged child be a principal benchmark in measuring the effectiveness of the opportunities, services, and supports available to the least advantaged (Rawls 1971).[68]

In addition to the expansion of knowledge, lawyers must also acquire the skills needed to be effective translators and brokers of systems change. Lawyers must learn to observe and listen more in the fashion of social anthropologists and psychologists and less in the style of adversaries or Socratic debaters. The case method of the common law will be of little use in the support of service integration initiatives. Instead, the skills of mediation, conflict resolution, and negotiation are of the utmost importance.

The system of professional preparation and training must respond to these important information and skill needs through a program of interdisciplinary courses and seminars that focus on service integration in the context of systems change and that provide a range of opportunities for learning by doing.

The Lawyer's Role in More Fundamental
System Reform

If lawyers are to participate in designing, implementing, and supporting the ongoing operation of new community infrastructures of children's service, they need to play a combination of old (i.e., those identified in connection with service integration) and new roles. Again, they will have to work closely with families, communities, educators, and other service professionals and will need to continue to be involved in the development of state and federal laws and regulations.

Rather than trying to make various categorical grant structures more compatible, lawyers involved in more fundamental system reform efforts will need to focus increasingly on system design at the state or national level and on supporting decision-making and ensuring equity at the community level. In lieu of identifying and dismantling the legal and programmatic barriers, they will need to focus on developing new roles as counselors and advisers to community partnerships. These partnerships will need substantial assistance in establishing common goals and setting priorities. Lawyers working in support of broader system reform will be increasingly expected to help community partnerships carry out new roles, for example, as a direct payer for individual care and as an investor of community wellness resources, which pose complex legal issues and require the creation and maintenance of ongoing relationships with a host of outside organizations that depend on regular and reliable fulfillment of responsibilities.

The only interagency service coordination agreements needed by these new systems will involve the structuring of their relation with the local public schools. Nevertheless, lawyers will need to work with community partnerships to overcome differences in organizational and disciplinary cultures that will continue to exist and pose problems within the systems. In this regard, lawyers will need to continue to be particularly vigilant to prevent jargon (legal and programmatic) from undermining a system's successful operation.

While lawyers and educators must work together (in collaboration with parents and a broad range of other child and family professionals) to design, implement, and manage these new systems, the development of governance arrangements that ensure legitimacy, informed and free choice by families, and overall outcome accountability will be much more at center stage (Gerry, Fawcett, and Richter 1996).

Lawyers working to design, implement, and support the ongoing operation of new community-based child wellness systems will need extensive preparation in understanding community structures, formal and informal, that both influence child wellness and form the social, economic, and political context for the new community systems.

Because these new community partnerships will have a moral and programmatic "duty to rescue," lawyers will need to reject traditional notions of absoluteness and focus on the essential interplay between rights and responsibilities (Glendon 1993). Thus, it is even more important that their professional preparation and training emphasize practicum experience and provide a range of opportunities for learning by doing.

NOTES

1. In this chapter the healthy development and learning of children are also referred to as child "wellness."
2. For example, "visiting teachers" who had been advocates for improving the general social conditions of children and families when transformed into school social workers became part of the school attendance machinery. David Tyak (1992) calls this phenomenon "goal displacement."
3. This number includes all mothers below the age of twenty who have not received a high school diploma (or equivalent) with the youngest dependent children over the age of twelve weeks.
4. The increased demand for preventive and primary health care arises from the loss of Medicaid eligibility for children currently in those TANF families when the custodial parent leaves the program to be employed in a job that does not provide access to dependent health insurance. After a year of eligibility for "transitional" Medicaid, most of these children are likely to become uninsured. Although Congress established a new federal categorical grant program in the Balanced Budget Act of 1997 to help states provide health insurance for uninsured children, that program is unlikely to provide assistance to more than 40 percent of uninsured children.
5. The new welfare reform legislation repeals the prior child care entitlement for children of AFDC recipients participating in education and job training.
6. This requirement applies to adults who have received income support assistance for twenty-four months. States must achieve at least 50% work participation rate by fiscal year 2002.
7. Federal categorical grant programs had their origins in the agricultural extension legislation of 1887. Between 1914 and 1921, Federal categorical grants targeted at maternal and child health and vocational education were enacted (Gardner 1994).
8. Discrimination against children by public schools and other public and private agencies receiving federal financial assistance was prohibited on the basis of race and ethnicity (Title VI of the Civil Rights Act of 1964), gender (Title IX of the Education Amendments of 1972), and physical and mental disability (Section 504 of the Rehabilitation Act of 1973).

9. During this period, states took steps to offset important cuts by the federal government in other categorical aid programs such as Medicaid (Nathan and Doolittle 1984). This was made easier by the fact that virtually all federal entitlement programs with matching requirements (with the exception of AFDC and Medicaid) had been capped by 1980.

10. The current federal contribution toward the total costs of public elementary and secondary is less than 7%.

In fiscal year 1995, total government expenditures for maternal and child health services were approximately $52 billion (or 21% of all expenditures). During that year, federal expenditures were approximately $30.5 billion, with three program areas—Medicaid ($13.5 billion), public health programs ($14.5 billion), and Title V maternal and child health programs ($2.2 billion)—making up over 95 percent of the total. State and local government expenditures were approximately $20 billion (Bureau of the Census 1997).

Federal financincing for most child food and nutrition services and supports is currently provided through several categorical structures operated by public and private agencies. In fiscal year 1995, public expenditures for food and nutrition services for pregnant women and children exceeded $26 billion. Of this, approximately $22.5 billion (86%) was from federal sources and $3.8 billion (14%) was from state or local sources. Federal funding was primarily through food stamps ($11.4 billion), school nutrition programs ($6 billion), and the Special Supplemental Program for Women, Infants, and Children (WIC) ($3.6 billion) (Bureau of the Census 1997).

The principal sources of financing for early care and education services are nonpublic (e.g., family resources or funds made available by business organizations). In fiscal year 1996, more than $52 billion was spent on child care and early childhood services. Of this, about 40% was paid by government directly or through tax credits; the balance (60%) came from out-of-pocket expenditures by individuals and employers. Government expenditures for child care and early childhood services ($21 billion) were split between federal (56%) and state and local (44%) sources, with three program areas—the Child Care and Development Block Grant ($3 billion), AFDC-linked child care ($1.3 billion), and early childhood services, including Head Start, ($3.8 billion)—and federal tax benefits ($3.5 billion) accounting for over 95% of federal expenditures (Bureau of the Census 1997).

In fiscal year 1995, total annual public expenditures, for family support services exceeded $27 billion. Approximately $8.5 billion, or 27% or these expenditures, was from federal sources, with the largest program expenditures occurring through the Family Preservation and Support Program ($1 billion), the Child and Family Services programs ($4.5 billion), the Social Services Block Grant ($2 billion), the Community Mental Health Services Block Grant ($131 million), and the Prevention and Treatment of Substance Abuse Block Grant ($610 million) (Bureau of the Census 1997).

11. Specifically, AFDC program spending is reduced by $5.3 billion, with the prospect that nearly one million families will lose all AFDC assistance. Even after allowing legal alien children currently to stay on the caseloads by the Balanced Budget Act of 1997, spending on the SSI program will decrease by nearly $3 billion and food stamp spending will be reduced by nearly $5 billion. The 1996 legislation also cuts another billion dollars of annual federal funding for child care nutrition programs and the Social Services Block

Grant by almost half a billion dollars. In contrast, the Balanced Budget Act of 1997 creates new child health insurance ($4 billion annually) and welfare-to-work grant programs ($1.5 billion).

12. By capping the food stamp deduction for shelter costs, the 1996 welfare reform legislation reduces food stamp help for millions of poor families with children that pay more than half of their income for housing. Adjustments to the Thrifty Food Plan, a low-cost food budget which is used to calculate the amount of food stamps a family receives, also reduce the level of aid provided to millions more. Overall, families with children are bearing about 70% of these cuts (Urban Institute 1996).

13. The new welfare reform legislation will reduce the incomes of families who do not rely on cash welfare payments by almost $1,000 annually. As a result of the new legislation, the "poverty gap"—the difference between poor families' incomes and the poverty threshold—will increase by around $6 billion for all families, a 12% increase relative to current policies (Urban Institute 1996).

14. Children in families who have qualified for AFDC under old guidelines (including those used to determine income and resources) but who become ineligible because of new TANF provisions (such as the five-year time limit or lower eligibility guidelines) will still qualify for Medicaid.

15. Thirty-one states provide ongoing cash or in-kind assistance (often labeled "general assistance") to children and/or families with children who are ineligible for federally funded income support programs. Eligibility criteria, program elements, and benefits (both level and duration) vary widely by state (Uccello, McCallum, and Gallagher 1997).

16. While the current rate of 88% is within striking distance of the goal, the high school completion rates for poor and minority students are dramatically lower, with rates in many urban areas below 50% (Department of Education 1996).

17. Graham suggests three reasons for this shortfall. First, while American schools have been historically very successful in educating healthy, well-motivated children of stable, supportive families, the fraction of such children currently enrolled in the public schools is diminishing. Second, high levels of academic achievement have never been widely expected of students in this country. Third, while circumstances for children have become more difficult and expectations for schools have dramatically expanded, we have not improved the educational effectiveness of schools (Graham 1993).

18. Despite the Surgeon General's 1979 goal of immunizing 90% of all American two-year-olds against common childhood diseases, by 1990 only about 70% percent (in many inner cities only 50%) of these young children had been immunized against measles, mumps, and rubella. On a community level, over 12 million children, most in low-income families, are at risk of lead poisoning (National Commission on Children 1991).

19. For example, the United States lags behind nineteen other countries in the proportion of children who survive their first year (National Commission on Children 1991).

20. Preventable health problems that reduce a child's capacity to learn include prenatal alcohol, tobacco, and drug exposure, malnutrition, child abuse and neglect, and lead poisoning (National Commission on Children 1991).

21. Dewey notes a marked difference between the education that every child gets from life within the family and the deliberate education that takes place in schools. The former he

sees as natural and important but incidental (i.e., not the express reason of the association). In contrast, formal education represents the work of intentional agencies (schools) using explicit material to develop a child's ability to think and to master the skills needed to share effectively in a wide range of adult activities. This type of education, Dewey asserts, gives children experiences that would not be accessible to them if they were left to pick up their training in informal association with others.

22. When discussed in the context of more economically advantaged families, this help is almost never described as "services." For example, all children need immunization and periodic health screening. For those with private insurance, these services are usually described as well-baby care; for those on Medicaid this is usually described as an Early Periodic Screening, Diagnosis and Treatment "service."

23. Structures within these countries ensure access of all children and families to a broad array of children's services, with gradually increased family cost participation. Thus, "poverty" is treated as a relative and highly variable condition that affects financial contribution rather than participation (Gerry and Paulsen 1995).

24. Inexplicably, the most severe impact of recent welfare reform legislation will almost certainly be on children in working poor families, the same group of children who are most likely to be without insurance coverage (Gerry, Fawcett and Richter 1996).

25. Prior to passage of civil rights laws of the 1960s and 1970s, the neighborhood school access of both children in certain racial and ethnic minority groups and children with physical and mental disabilities was not routinely assumed or provided for by all states.

26. For purposes of these estimates, children enrolled in organized child care facilities or receiving early care from a nonrelative are regarded as receiving early care and education services. Children receiving care from relatives are not included. These participation rates are much lower than those of most Western European countries. For example, the preschool participation rate in Italy exceeds 95% for three- and four-year-olds (General Accounting Office 1993).

27. Dewey believed that "the educator's part in the enterprise of education is to furnish the environment which stimulates responses and directs the learner's course" (212). Another important role of the educator identified by Dewey is to structure subject matter (i.e., curricula) in a progressive order so that experience and "luminous familiar spots" (184) of prior learning assist children in solving "new problems large enough to challenge thought" (Dewey 1916).

28. More than 14% of eighteen-nineteen-year-olds do not graduate from high school, and nearly one in five teenagers looking for work cannot find a job. Although these factors represent serious threats to the well-being of more than a million American adolescents, the professionalized needs assumption, of course, offers no response or solution (Gerry, Fawcett, and Richter 1996).

29. By translating a child or family need (e.g., help for a young mother dealing with stresses posed by a colicky baby) into pathological terms (e.g., parenting education to help prevent child abuse or neglect), the likelihood that members of the community will come forward to help the family solve the problem (e.g., offer to babysit) is dramatically decreased. Is there any reason to believe that providing a parenting education service to the parents of a colicky child twice a week is likely to be more effective than babysitting

provided informally by friends and neighbors? (Gerry, Fawcett & Richter 1996; McKnight 1995).

30. Congress included explicit requirements for the coordinated planning and delivery of services for preschool children (Head Start) and for school-age children with disabilities (IDEA). Similar requirements were later made part of the Part H program, the Vocational Rehabilitation Program, the Social Services Block Grant, the Job Training and Partnership Act, and in 1995 in the Family Preservation and Support Program.

31. Most statewide and comprehensive community-based initiatives are pursuing the two interdependent goals cited by Kagan and Neville (1993), together with some of the thematic objectives noted by Levy and Shephardson (1992). For example, Ensuring Student Success Through Collaboration, a project of the Council of Chief State School Officers, is simultaneously focused on system change (collaboration), strengthening families, and improving outcomes for children. Similarly, the New Futures initiative of the Annie E. Casey Foundation has sought to transform educational, social, and health outcomes through major changes in the underlying service systems and institutions (Annie E. Casey Foundation 1995).

32. New Jersey's School-Based Youth Services Program is a notable exception.

33. Significant problems also exist within schools with respect to the coordination and integration with general class instruction of categorical educational services (special education, bilingual education, and compensatory education). These programs feature deficit-based eligibility criteria, highly compartmentalized service structures, and process-based accountability. Specifically, the "pull-out" model associated with many categorical programs makes it difficult for classroom teachers to reserve sufficient time for uninterrupted instruction for all of their students and insufficient coordination of pull-out instruction with general class instruction has been shown to impede student learning. Past practices and historical traditions in how resources are used pose much larger barriers to the integration of categorical education services than statutory or regulatory requirements (Carlson and O'Reilly 1996).

34. New Jersey's School-Based Youth Services Program, Florida's Supplemental School Health Program, and California's Healthy Start program as well as similar programs in Connecticut and Colorado, provide good statewide examples. The Robert Wood Johnson Foundation's School-Based Adolescent Health and Making the Grade programs provide support to a network of good community-based examples. California's Healthy Start program and Extended Service Schools initiative of the DeWitt Wallace–Reader's Digest Fund represent good examples of family resource and youth service centers. New York City's Beacon Schools, the Children's Aid Society's Community Schools, and San Diego's New Beginnings initiative provide good examples of settlement house in the school.

35. Kentucky's Family Resource and Youth Services Centers, Missouri's Caring Communities initiative, the Casey Foundation's New Futures initiative, Kellogg's Youth Initiatives Program, and Philadelphia's Youth Access Centers are excellent examples.

36. Indiana's Step Ahead initiative, Oregon's local Commissions on Children and Families, Carnegie's Early Start program, Casey's New Futures initiative, Kellogg's Youth Initiatives Program, Robert Wood Johnson's America's Promise initiative, Indianapolis's

Building Better Neighborhoods project, and Chicago's Children, Youth, and Family Initiative represent important examples of this approach.

37. The notion of collective or joint accountability for child wellness outcomes has, however, begun to be a feature of some service integration initiatives. Oregon's local Commissions on Children and Families, Iowa's Child Welfare Decategorization Initiative, the Carnegie's Early Start program, and Casey's New Futures initiative are examples of service integration initiatives focused on collective accountability.

38. While the focus of this "informing" may vary (e.g., from academic instruction to personal hygiene to greater self-realization), the talents needed to be a successful teacher, pediatrician, social worker, parent, or psychologist are remarkably similar (Gerry 1993).

39. Osborne and Gaebler (1992) describe this approach in terms as "decentralized government," where neighborhood- or site-based professionals and administrators make key decisions now made by centralized bureaucracies.

40. Indiana's Step Ahead initiative, Kentucky's Family Resource Centers, Missouri's Caring Communities initiative, Chicago's Children, Youth and Family Initiative, New York City's Beacon Schools and Community Schools, and San Diego's New Beginnings are examples of this newer generation of family-friendly service integration initiatives.

41. In many Western European countries (e.g., Italy, Denmark), multiyear involvement of service professionals with the same child and family is the rule rather than the exception. For example, in Italy, early childhood professionals work with elementary school teachers for two years before and after a child enters elementary school. For one or two years prior to elementary school enrollment, teachers from the elementary school participate in monthly preschool staffings related to the child and with the child's parents.

42. As used in this discussion, *empowerment* refers to the process of extending the influence of families and communities over the conditions and outcomes that matter to them, including the health and wellness of their children (Gerry, Fawcett, and Richter 1996).

43. A few federal categorical programs have attempted to involve families actively in service planning and delivery. For example, in the Title I program, parent advisory committees were first required to assist school districts in determining learning priorities and strategies. Most of these efforts have sought collective rather than individual involvement of parents, and problems of legitimacy have been raised frequently with respect to the selection of "representative" parents. Under the IDEA, however, all parents are expected to participate actively in the development of individualized educational programs for their children and in decisions made about the children's educational placement. While these provisions stem from the civil rights background of the statute rather than from a desire for family empowerment per se, the involvement which they seek is individual and child-specific. The principal problems with this approach have been the failure of large numbers of low-income parents of children with disabilities to participate and the concomitant failure of school districts to create a receptive climate for such participation. The most effective family empowerment component of a federal categorical program has been pioneered by the Head Start program. The primary reasons for this success have been the active involvement of Head Start families in virtually all aspects of program planning and operations and the hiring and training of large numbers of family members as program staff.

44. As used in this chapter, *community* means the social place used by family, friends, neighbors, neighborhood associations, clubs, civic groups, local businesses, churches and synagogues, local government, local unions, and local media (McKnight 1995).

45. As discussed earlier in this section, major methodological problems in evaluating the outcomes of complex service integration initiatives have been reported by numerous researchers.

46. For example, if curbing adolescent smoking were to be seen as an important child wellness objective, then public officials who regulate the sale of tobacco products and local merchants who sell cigarettes should be part of the collaboration.

47. The development of a conceptual design for a community-based system of children's services and supports might begin with twelve core capacities: (1) disease prevention; (2) safety and accident prevention; (3) prevention and reduction of high-risk behavior among adolescents; (4) health and developmental screening at all ages; (5) primary care, including outpatient and home-based health and dental care, mental health care, prenatal care, sick-child care, and early intervention services; (6) health maintenance; (7) early care and education; (8) hospital or inpatient care, including substance abuse treatment and rehabilitation; (9) food and nutrition counseling; (10) emergency shelter; (11) family support; and (12) environmental health and wellness. The term *capacity* (rather than *service* or *program*) is used because communities may wish to organize their response to different types of child needs in other than a traditional "services" model (Gerry, Fawcett, and Richter 1996; McKnight 1995).

48. These channels might include community leaders and advisers, media, and both formal and informal organizations. Some of these channels (e.g., businesses, churches, and public schools) may provide services that are not core system capacities and may yet be crucial to the operation of the overall community system (Gerry, Fawcett, and Richter 1996).

49. For example, in a wellness-oriented community, the use of safety devices, such as protective helmets and seat belts, would be actively promoted by parents and neighbors, and merchants would not sell alcohol and tobacco to minors. Streets, parks, and homes would be safe and violence-free and teenagers would be able to find jobs (Gerry, Fawcett, and Richter 1996).

50. The cap would operate with respect to the entire program budget and a reserve fund of approximately 5 percent would be created to expand funding to respond to emergency circumstances.

51. For example, states might wish to create a state ombudsman system to oversee the operation and decision-making of community partnerships from the standpoint of individual child and family decision-making and overall equity and fairness.

52. The payroll tax option is familiar, highly efficient, and very easy to administer. It requires no significant additional tax collection overhead to businesses and creates no new government bureaucracies. It is automatically adjusted for inflation and has proven to be the least unpopular of all major taxation strategies. In addition, it avoids the generational/political problem of taxing unearned as well as earned income. (Gerry, Fawcett, and Richter 1996).

53. No politically feasible alternatives to such a financing approach are readily apparent.

Surely, continuing to fight an uphill battle against the "block and cut" grant requires at least as much optimism.

54. Social marketing is a process that creates a receptive and ultimately supportive climate for a proposed change, particularly where the envisioned change may (1) require a substantial period of time to accomplish, (2) involve highly sensitive issues which may give rise to culture conflicts, (3) be subject to public scrutiny, and (4) involve the active support of multiple publics or audiences (Andreasen 1995).

55. Space does not permit an extended discussion of the range and complexity of the legal issues associated with the needed redesign of current confidentiality and privacy provisions. Failure to carefully consider these issues has proven fatal to many serious efforts to integrate service planning, delivery, and accountability.

56. For example, two consolidated state plans approved by the Clinton Administration, Indiana's Step Ahead program and West Virginia's School Health Initiative, represent crucial components of major statewide service integration initiatives in both states.

57. Within the context of service integration initiatives, lawyers should also be directly involved in the investigation and resolution of complaints by families.

58. Family and neighborhood members of local governance structures have been selected through approaches ranging from statistical sampling to direct election. In some situations, local political leaders, lead agencies, or community foundations have selected neighborhood participants. In other situations, representatives of designated neighborhood organizations have assumed ex-officio membership (Chaskin and Garg 1995).

59. These child- and family-serving organizations generally include public or publicly funded elementary and secondary school districts (and schools), health and nutrition agencies, community mental health agencies, center-based child care providers, early childhood education programs, and social service and child welfare agencies.

60. The potential added costs of service coordination can act as a significant organizational disincentive unless at least a small amount of special funding is dedicated to supporting core staff (Center for the Study of Social Policy 1991).

61. Understanding these issues, in turn, requires at least some familiarity with bureaucratic-administrative contingency theories, which examine control structures and the management of work within organizations; resource dependence theories, which analyze the dynamics of interdependent organizational networks; and bureaucratic bargaining theories, which examine power and control relationships within complex organizations (Meyers 1993).

62. Examples of fatal omissions include transportation needs, neighborhood safety factors, and a community infrastructure of needed child care services.

63. Indiana, Iowa, Maryland, Missouri, and Vermont all take such approaches to finance major service integration initiatives successfully.

64. For example, when over 90% of the families in a neighborhood are Medicaid eligible, the administrative cost of sorting out the eligible from the ineligible may well exceed the cost of simply declaring everyone eligible (Gerry and Paulsen 1995).

65. Maryland uses a "pooled funding" arrangement to finance an integrated program for out-of-state residential placements. In Iowa, several counties currently pool child welfare funding.

66. Wisconsin and California currently use "blended funding" strategies to decategorize funding going to the county level. Indiana and West Virginia blend categorical grant funds at the local level.

67. "Leveraging" is a process by which state and local funds are used to obtain federal funds which would not otherwise be available. New federal funds are allocated as a function (usually 1:1) of the amount of state and local funds which are staked. The amount of new federal funds which can be leveraged is determined by a combination of the leveraging ratio and the amount of new state and local funds that can be brought to the leverage.

68. Rawls (1971) argues that a just social policy is properly developed by a policymaker who fully understands the dimensions of the overall situation but does not know anything about her or his personal characteristics. A rational person in such a position, he concludes, would develop a set of social policies which would be seen as "fair" by the least favored individuals in society. Thus, in deciding what outcomes of social policy are fair, the worst outcomes for the least advantaged members of society would be set at what are perceived as "normal" outcomes for the more favored members of society.

REFERENCES

Agranoff, R. A., and Pattakos, A. (1979). *Dimensions of human services integrations: Service delivery, program linkages, policy management, organizational structure.* Human Services Monograph Servies. Dekalb, Ill.: Center for Governmental Studies, Northern Illinois University.

Aid to Families with Dependent Children; Social Security Act, as amended, Title IV, Part A, 42 U.S.C. 601–617 (1950).

Ambach, G. (1996, October). The Personal Responsibility and Work Opportunity Reconciliation Act of 1996 (P.L. 104–193) and implications for public education. *Memorandum to chief state school officers.* Washington, D.C.: Council of Chief State School Officers.

Andreasen, A. (1995). *Marketing social change: Changing behavior to promote health.* San Francisco: Jossey-Bass.

Annie E. Casey Foundation. (1995, August). *The path of most resistance.* Baltimore: Author.

Asayesh, G. (1993). Ten years after "A Nation at Risk." *School Administrator, 50,* no. 4, pp. 8–14.

Balanced Budget Act of 1997 (not yet codified).

Bhaerman, R. (1994). *Integrating education, health and social services in rural communites: Service integration through the rural prism.* Philadelphia: Research for Better Schools.

Bruner, C. (1989). "State innovations in children and family services collaboration and financing." In C. L. Romig (ed.), *Family policy recommendations for state action,* pp. 163–172. Washington, D.C.: National Conference of State Legislators.

———. (1996). *Realizing a vision for children, families and neighborhoods: An alternative to other modest proposals.* Des Moines, Iowa: National Center for Service Integration.

Bureau of the Census, U.S. Department of Commerce. (1992a). *Who's minding the kids? Child care arrangements: Fall 1988.* Current Population Reports, ser. (30), 70. Washington, D.C.: U.S. Government Printing Office.

———. (1992b). *Federal expenditures by state for fiscal year* 1991. FES/91. Washington, D.C.: U.S. Government Printing Office.

———. (1993). *Government finances:* 1990–91 *(Preliminary report).* GF/91-59. Washington, D.C.: U.S. Government Printing Office.

———. (1997). *Statistical abstract of the United States,* 1996. Washington, D.C.: U.S. Government Printing Office.

Carlson, E., and O'Reilly, F. (1996, January). Integrating Title I and special education. *Remedial and Special Education,* 17, no.1, pp. 21–29.

Center for the Study of Social Policy. (1991, September). *Building a community agenda: Developing local governance entities.* Washington, D.C.: Author.

Chaskin, R., and Garg, S. (1995). *The issues of governance in neighborhood-based initiatives.* Chicago: University of Chicago, Chapin Hall.

Chaskin, R., and Richman, H. (1992, Spring). Concerns about school-linked services: Institution-based versus community-based models. *The Future of Children,* 2, no. 1, pp. 107–117.

Child and Adult Care Food Program, National School Lunch Act, Sections 9, 11, 14, 16, and 17; as amended, 42 U.S.C. 1758, 1759a, 1762a, 1765, and 1766.

Child Care Development Block Grant Act of 1990, Omnibus Budget Reconciliation Act of 1990, Section 5082, Public Law 101-508, as amended.

Children's Defense Fund. (1992). *The state of America's children.* Washington, D.C.: Author.

De Tocqueville, A. (1991). *Democracy in America.* Trans. G. Lawrence, ed. J. P. Mayer. Garden City, N.Y.: Doubleday Anchor.

Dewey, J. (1937). *Democracy and education.* New York: Macmillan.

Dryfoos, J. (1994). *Full service schools: A revolution in health and social services for children.* San Francisco: Jossey-Bass.

Dryfoos, J., Brindis, C., and Kaplan, D. (1996, June). Research and evaluation in school based health care. In *Adolescent medicine: State of the art reviews.* Philadelphia: Hanley & Belfus. vol. 7, no. 2., pp. 207–220.

Education for All Handicapped Children Act of 1975 (P.L. 94-143), now codified as the Individuals with Disabilities Education Act, Part B, Sections 611–617, and 620, as amended; 20 U.S.C. 1411–1417 and 1420.

Eliot, T. (1928, September). Should courts do case work. *The Survey,* 60, pp. 601–603.

Farrow, F., and Joe, T. (1992, Spring). Financing school-linked, integrated services. *The Future of Children,* 2, no. 1., pp. 56–67.

Food Stamp Act of 1977, as amended, Public Law 95–113, 91 Stat. 958, 7 U.S.C. 2011 et seq.

Gans, S., and Horton, G. (1975). *Integration of human services: The state and municipal levels.* New York: Praeger.

Gardner, S. (1992, Spring). Key issues in developing school-linked, integrated services. *The Future of Children,* 2, no. 1, p. 85.

———. (1994, December). *Reform options for the intergovernmental funding system: Decategorization policy issues.* Washington, D.C.: Finance Project.

———. (1995, September). Babies, bathwater and muddy waters. In *Dollars and sense.* Washington, D.C.: Finance Project and the Institute for Educational Leadership.

General Accounting Office. (1993, July). *Poor pre-school-aged children: Numbers increase but most not in pre-school.* GAO/HRD-93-111BR. Washington, D.C.: Author.

Gerry, M. (1993). *A joint enterprise with America's families to ensure student success.* Washington, D.C.: Council of Chief State School Officers.

Gerry, M., Fawcett, S., and Richter, K. (1996, July). Community health and wellness systems for all of our children. In *Providing universal health insurance coverage to children: Four perspectives.* Princeton, N.J.: Robert Wood Johnson Foundation.

Gerry, M., and Paulsen, R. (1995). *Building community-based networks of children's services and family supports.* New York: Aspen Institute.

Glendon, M. A. (1991). *Rights Talk.* (New York: Free Press).

Goals 2000: Educate America Act, Title III, Public Law 103-227. (1994).

Gomby, D., and Larson, C. (1992, Spring). Evaluation of school-linked services. *The Future of Children,* 2, no. 1, p. 68.

Graham, P. A. (1993, February). What has America expected of its schools over the past century? *American Journal of Education,* 101, no. 2, pp. 83–98.

Hagedom, J. M. (1995). *Forsaking our children: Bureaucracy and reform in the child welfare system.* Chicago: Lakeview Press.

Halfon, N., Inkelas, M., and Wood, D. (1995). Non-financial barriers to care for children and youth. In *Annual Review of Public Health, Volume 16.* Palo Alto, Calif.: Annual Reviews of Public Health.

Haveman, R., and Wolfe, B. (1994). *Succeeding generations: On the effect of investments in children.* New York: Russell Sage Foundation.

Hayes, C. (1995, April). *Rethinking block grants: Toward improved intergovernmental financing for education and other children's services.* Washington, D.C.: Finance Project.

Head Start Act: Omnibus Budget Reconciliation Act of 1981, as amended; 42 U.S.C. 9801 et seq.

Holton, G., and Goroff, D. (1995, Fall). Where is American education going? Report on a convocation. *Daedalus,* 124, no. 4, pp. 1–42.

Jencks, C., and Peterson, P. (eds.). (1991). *The urban underclass.* Washington, D.C.: Brookings Institution.

Kadel, S. (1992). *Interagency collaboration: Improving the delivery of services to children and families.* Greensboro, N.C.: Southeast Regional Vision for Education.

Kagan, S., and Neville, P. (1993). *Integrating services for children and families: Understanding the past to shape the future.* New Haven: Yale University Press.

Kagan, S., Goffin, S., Golub, S., and Pritchard, E. (1995). *Toward systemic reform: Service integration for young children and their families.* Falls Church, Va.: National Center for Service Integration.

Kirby, D., Waszak, C., and Ziegler, J. (1991, October). *An assessment of six school-based clinics: Services, impact and potential.* Houston: Center for Population Options.

Kisker, E., Brown, R., and Hill, J. (1994). *Health caring: Outcomes of the Robert Wood Johnson Foundation's school-based adolescent health care program.* Princeton, N.J.: Mathematica Policy Research.

Larson, C., Gomby, D., Shiono, P., Lewit, E., and Behrman, R. (1992, Spring). Analysis. *The Future of Children,* 2, no. 1, pp. 6–18.

Levy, J., and Shephardson, W. (1992, Spring). A look at current school-linked service efforts. *The Future of Children*, 2, no. 1. pp. 44–55.

Martin, P. Y., Chackerian, R., Imershein, A., and Frumkin, M. (1983). The concept of integrated services reconsidered. *Social Science Quarterly*, 64, no. 4, pp. 747–763.

Maternal and Child Health Services Block Grant to the States: Social Security Act, Title V, Section 501(a)(1), 42 U.S.C. 701, as amended. 1981.

McKnight, J. (1995). *The careless society: Community and its counterfeits*. New York: Basic Books.

Medical Assistance Program (Medicaid): Social Security Act, Title XIX, as amended; 42 U.S.C. 1396, et seq.

Meyers, M. (1993). Organizational factors in the integration of services for children. *Social Service Review*, 67, no. 4. pp. 547–575.

Meyers, M., Lukemeyer, A., and Smeeding, T. M. (1997). *Work, welfare and the burden of disability*. Income Security Policy Series, Paper no. 12. Maxwell School, Syracuse University.

Morrill, W., and Gerry, M. (1990, February). *Integrating the delivery of services to school-aged children at risk*. Washington, D.C.: U.S. Department of Education.

Murray, C. (1984). *Losing ground: American social policy, 1950–1980*. New York: Basic Books.

Nathan R., and Doolittle, F. (1984, June). *Effects of the Reagan domestic program on states and localities*. Princeton, N.J.: Princeton University, Urban and Regional Research Center.

National Center for Children in Poverty. (1990). *Five million children*. New York: Author.

National Commission on Children. (1991). *Beyond rhetoric: A new agenda for children and families, final report*. Washington, D.C.: U.S. Government Printing Office.

National Commission on Excellence in Education. (1983). *A nation at risk: The imperative for educational reform*. Washington, D.C.: U.S. Department of Education.

National Educational Goals Panel. (1993, September). *The national education goals report: Building a nation of learners*. Washington, D.C.: Author.

National School Lunch Program: National School Lunch Act, as amended, 42 U.S.C. 1751–1769. 1946.

Olasky, M. (1992). *The tradegy of American compassion*. Washington, D.C.: Regnery.

Omnibus Reconciliation Act of 1981, Public Law 97-35.

Osborne, D., and Gaebler, T. (1992). *Reinventing government: How the entrepreneurial spirit is transforming the public sector*. Reading, Mass.: Addison-Wesley.

Personal Responsibility and Work Opportunity Reconciliation Act of 1996, as amended, Public Law 104-193, 110 Stat. 2150.

Pittman, K., and Cahill, M. (1992, July). *Pushing the boundaries of education: The implications of a youth development approach to education policies, structures and collaborations*. Washington, D.C.: Council of Chief State School Officers.

Politzer, R., Harris, D., Gaston, M., and Mullan, F. (1991, July). Primary care physician supply and the medically underserved: A status report and recommendations. *Journal of the American Medical Association*, 266, no. 1, p. 104.

Pressman, J., and Wildavsky, A. (1984). *Implementation*. Berkeley and Los Angeles: University of California Press.

Public Health Service, U.S. Department of Health, Education and Welfare. (1991). *Healthy*

People 2000: *National Health Promotion and Disease Prevention Objectives.* Washington, D.C.: U.S. Government Printing Office.

Public Health Service, U.S. Department of Health and Human Services. (1995a). *Healthy People 2000 Midcourse Review.* Washington, D.C.: U.S. Government Printing Office.

————. (1995b). *Healthy People* 2000: *Proposed Revisions.* Washington, D.C.: U.S. Government Printing Office.

Rawls, J. (1971). *A theory of justice.* Cambridge: Harvard University Press.

Regenstein, M., Silow-Carroll, S., and Meyer, J. (1995, June). *Early childhood education: Models for expanding access.* Washington, D.C.: Economic and Social Research Institute.

Rein, M. (1970). *Social policy: Issues of choices and change.* New York: Random House.

Reischauer, R. (1986). Fiscal federalism in the 1980s: Dismantling or rationalizing the great society. In M. Kaplan and P. Cuciti (eds.), *The Great Society and its legacy.* Durham, N.C.: Duke University Press.

Robert Wood Johnson Foundation. (1996, July). *Providing universal health insurance coverage to children: Four perspectives.* Princeton, N.J.: Author.

School Breakfast Program: Child Nutrition Act of 1966, as amended, 42 U.S.C. 1773, 1779, 1779.

Social Security Act of 1935, as amended, 42 U.S.C. 301 et seq.

Social Services Block Grant: Social Security Act, Title XX, as amended; 42 U.S.C. 1397 et seq.

Supplemental Security Income: Title VI of the Social Security Act of 1935, as amended; 42 U.S.C. 1381–1383d.

Temporary Assistance to Needy Families Program: Title IV, Part A of the Social Security Act of 1935, as amended by the Personal Responsibility and Work Opportunity Reconciliation Act of 1996, Public Law 104-193, 110 Stat. 2150.

Title I of the Elementary and Secondary Education Act of 1965, Part A, as amended; 20 U.S.C. 6301 et seq.

Tyack, D. (1992, Spring). Health and social services in public schools: Historical perspectives. *The Future of Children,* 2, no. 1, pp. 19–31.

Uccello, C., McCallum, H., and Gallagher, L. (1997). *State general assistance programs, 1996: Introduction and summary.* Washington, D.C.: Urban Institute.

Urban Institute. (1996, July). *Potential effects of congressional welfare reform legislation on family incomes.* Washington, D.C.: Author.

————. (1996, Fall). *Goals* 2000: *A progress report.* Washington, D.C.: Author.

U.S. Department of Health, Education, and Welfare. (1972). *Report of the task force on administrative and organizational constraints to services integration.* Washington, D.C.: Author.

Watson, K., and Gold, S. (1997). *The other side of devolution: Shifting relationships between state and local governments.* Washington, D.C.: Urban Institute.

Weiss, J. (1987). Pathways to cooperation among public agencies. *Journal of Policy Analysis and Management,* 7, no. 1, pp. 94–117.

Wynn, J., Merry, S., and Berg, P. (1995). *Children, families, and communities: Early lessons from a new approach to social services.* Washington, D.C.: Institute for Educational Leadership.

Chapter 7 School Reform and Enforceable Rights to Quality Education

Paul Weckstein

I. UNITING DESIRE, KNOWLEDGE, AND AUTHORITY

A. The Puzzle

Normally, we expect that when desire, know-how, and authority converge, things get done. So imagine that the great majority of families in the United States strongly wanted something from their local governments, that there was broad agreement that those families should have it, that there was substantial knowledge about how to provide it, and, finally, that local governments were not merely authorized but actually required to provide it. You would probably assume that this area of public policy would be largely resolved—until told that "it" in this case is high-quality public education.

This essay is driven by six basic premises:

Families in the United States tend to feel strongly about the importance of high-quality education—and are supported in that belief by the statements of public officials and business leaders.

Leading reform movements of the last decade embody professional knowledge about at least some key elements of high-quality education and what it takes to provide it.[1]

State and federal laws mandate and support many of those key elements.[2]

Millions of children in the United States do not, by any measure, currently receive a high-quality education.[3]

The denial of a good education cuts across student demography and, at the same time, disproportionately hits those who have been the special concern of education law—the poor, racial minorities, students with limited English proficiency, and students with disabilities.[4]

For most children, no one is doing anything sufficient to remedy that denial.[5]

In other words, if we continue our current course, millions of students will be deprived of a high-quality education, despite the widespread desire for it, the know-how to achieve it, and the mandate to provide it.

These premises do not seem to add up. If the will, the expertise, and the legal mandates all exist, we would expect to see those who want quality education working with those who know how to provide it and those who can see that the laws supporting it are carried out. One would expect to see this collaboration at the front end—in designing and implementing new programs and reforms to achieve high outcomes for all. Failing that, one would expect collaboration at the back end—in quick and vigorous legal challenges to inadequate programs. (With millions of children denied a critical public good to which they are legally entitled, the number of lawsuits alleging denial of an adequate education is actually troubling—for its paucity.)

B. The Isolation of Desire, Knowledge, and Authority

We live in an era when waves of feeling that most social problems are intractable, beyond the reach of concerted efforts to solve them, are clashing against, and perhaps eroding, the longer-standing bedrock of American can-do optimism.[6] It is tempting to retreat to cynicism or nihilism: to assert that families don't in the end really care much about their kids' education, or that little we know about teaching actually works, or that the mere fact that a law explicitly calls for something to happen doesn't mean anything and never will. In other words, despite appearances to the contrary, we don't really have the desire, knowledge, or authority. Or, even if desire, knowledge, and authority do converge here, we still shouldn't expect action, because, for ineffable reasons, things just don't work that way. It is a sign of our times that these assertions don't strike us as bizarre.

So this essay is dedicated to the alternative proposition—that families (and others) do care about education, that we have substantial knowledge about what it takes (in a nonmechanistic way) to provide it, that the authority and obligation to do so exist—and that when desire, knowledge, and authority do converge, things should happen. Reflection on that proposition, together with the fact that we are nevertheless not on a path that will secure high-quality education for all children in a timely way, suggests that desire, knowledge, and authority, even though all focused on the same basic core, actually are not converging because they remain isolated from each other.

The effort to draw them together is the basis for the collaboration between law and education called for here. Parents who want a good education for their children, and particularly the parents of children in schools most in need of reform, remain isolated from educators with important knowledge about what it takes to provide it, and from the very few lawyers who understand the relevant legal levers. (Much the same can be said about many teachers and other building-level staff who do not want to accept their students' current levels of achievement as the best they can hope for.)

Thus, we must focus resources on community education: educators and lawyers together need to translate and help parents and school staff understand these legal and educational structures. Then, of course, they will need more than information—they will need help (including legal representation for parents where necessary) in making use of it, including help in confronting the political and economic inequalities which largely produced the isolation in the first place. The basic, accessible questions below, used here to frame the legal and education structure of standards-based reform, should aid in this effort.

C. Framework for Standards-Based School Reform

This inquiry into collaboration focuses on standards-based reform—the effort first to define what students should know and be able to do and then to develop and implement strategies for enabling students to meet those standards.[7] Standards-driven reform has been the basis for much recent federal and state education legislation. It also provides a framework for analyzing and revitalizing older legal doctrines in both federal and state law.[8]

That framework is summarized in the chart below, to help understand the terms of standards-based school reform and connect them to potential legal standards:

Questions	School Reform Terms
1. What do we want all students to know and be able to do?	Content and performance standards
2. What do we have to do to get there?	Program plan/
a. Curriculum	Opportunity-to-learn standards/
b. Instructional methods	Delivery standards/
c. School/class structure	Program implementation
d. Staff development	
e. Individual help	
f. Other	
[Resources for above]	
3. How do we know when (and to what extent) we get there?	Assessment
4. What happens if we don't get there?	Improvement/Enforcement
5. Who's "we"?	Governance/Participation/Partnership

Figure 7.1. Five Questions of School Reform

This basic structure characterizes most state-level school reform initiatives, although one or more major pieces may be missing from the effort in any one state. Since 1994, it also characterizes the explicit structure of federal elementary and secondary education law. In that year, Congress enacted Goals 2000: Educate America Act, a national framework for reform, based on national education goals espoused by President Bush and the nation's governors (including Bill Clinton) in 1990,[9] and rewrote other federal laws to incorporate the elements of this reform structure to achieve those goals.

This framework itself unites desire, knowledge, and authority—with the expectation that their union will produce effective action. It starts with defining desired outcomes—the knowledge and skills that all students should have (content and performance standards).[10] Then it focuses on how to achieve what we want by organizing the elements of school—curriculum, instruction, school and classroom structure, staffing and staff development, governance, specialized services for particular students, financial resources, outside assistance—to enable all students to reach those outcomes. (This is done through developing and implementing a program plan—and is sometimes captured in "opportunity-to-learn" or "delivery" standards.)[11]

Next, the framework asks if we are getting there, through assessments designed to identify the degree to which students have attained the desired knowledge and skills (not just how they are doing relative to each other). Then, it requires the use of that information to identify and change schools that are not making enough progress to reach the goals. Finally, the framework raises the sometimes unasked question of "Who's we?"—in terms of who is involved, through what structures, in deciding and implementing the goals, the plan, and the follow-up.

The notion behind this framework—that high-quality education for all students depends upon a school community adopting a set of high standards for what it wants all its students to achieve (and is committed to the belief that its students can reach those goals), focusing its practices on those goals, assessing itself in relation to those goals, and making changes in areas needing improvement—seems obvious. We're more likely to end up where we want to go if we clearly identify the destination, focus our efforts on getting there, and check in regularly to make sure we're staying on course.

D. Empirical Support

That common-sense notion is now supported as well by research, showing that students, including disadvantaged students, can perform at high levels when their education is organized around that framework.[12]

OVERALL (STANDARDS, PLANNING, IMPLEMENTATION)

For example, in analyzing five years of data from more than 1,500 schools, the Center on Organization and Restructuring of Schools (CORS)[13] found that schools could dramatically boost overall performance and decrease disparities in student outcomes by engaging students in what the researchers call "authentic student achievement." This is a concrete vision of what students should be able to do in learning to use their minds well—grounded in a picture of authentic adult achievement—in which students "construct" knowledge, through disciplined inquiry, to produce discourse and performance that has meaning beyond school. "Constructing knowledge" involves manipulating information and ideas by analyzing, synthesizing, and interpreting in ways that produce new meanings or understandings. "Disciplined inquiry" goes beyond mere application to elaborate definitions: make connections to other concepts within the discipline and to other disciplines; use theories, concepts, and principles from the discipline to explain concrete events; and demonstrate understanding through elaborated written communication. The third characteristic involves studying problems that have significance beyond school and demand communication with audiences beyond school. Students in schools with this kind of authentic pedagogy learn much more.[14]

Schools which produce these kinds of gains ask themselves, and answer as a community, questions like those in the chart above, in relation to authentic student achievement. CORS found that *successful* restructuring depends upon creating clarity and consensus about central goals for student learning, specific enough to sustain coherent focus and yet flexible enough to encourage further development of mission through debate, discussion, and experimentation within the framework—a process of continuous reflection.[15] Thus, CORS concluded that "restructuring" (for example, keeping students in the same homeroom throughout high school, multidisciplinary learning teams, mixed ability classes, smaller subunits or schools-within-a-school, parents volunteering, etc.), while correlated with authentic pedagogy, is not enough by itself— the school must have the organizational capacity to figure out *how* to use the new structure to promote authentic pedagogy.

CORS found that such organizational capacity—to form an effective collective enterprise focused on clarity and consensus about, and sense of collective responsibility for attaining, central learning goals for all students—is enhanced when the school is created as a schoolwide teacher professional community (STPC). This focuses the staff on the learning goals and on authentic pedagogy, and it also creates student expectations that they will work hard to master challenging material, they will succeed, and they will get help and support.[16] Staff development that enhances the skills to carry out the schools' learning mission and interdependent work structure with enough time for teachers to communicate and collaborate[17] were found to be among the conditions that support high STPC.[18] Human resources and leadership (teaching staff and principal) were also aligned with the authentic pedagogy.

In a similar vein, Valerie Lee, Julia Smith, and Robert Croninger analyzed data from more than 11,000 students in 280 high schools and concluded that overall achievement improved, and the achievement gap between high and low socioeconomic groups was reduced, in schools that are organized "organically" rather than bureaucratically: with a common academic curriculum that clearly focuses on high-level learning for all; communication of expectations of high academic standards; authentic models of instruction (as discussed above); teachers' sense of collective responsibility for student learning; and a related set of restructuring practices used toward those ends—such as interdisciplinary teaching teams, elimination of ability grouping in math and science, cooperative learning, common teacher planning time, flexible class time, and schools-within-a-school.[19]

RESOURCES

In summarizing "what has been learned since 1988," Congress has found, "Equitable and sufficient resources, particularly as such resources relate to the quality of the teaching force, have an integral relationship to high student achievement."[20] From the vantage point of the research above, resources matter, in the following sense. Schools starting with a low base of human and social resources have a harder time making good use of school reform principles that can result in higher achievement—high standards, staff development, parent involvement, school-level autonomy.[21] These schools require more extensive and complex forms of outside support to take advantage of these principles, but rarely get the right mix.

Similarly, Richard Murnane and Frank Levy found dramatic improvements in student achievement when high-poverty elementary schools used extra funding to reduce class-size, *if* part of a larger program of intensively revising curriculum and instruction around high achievement goals for all students and engaging teachers, parents, and students in consensually pursuing those goals—in contrast to the more prevalent practice of reducing class size without changing classroom practice.[22]

ASSESSMENT

Much of the standards-based school reform literature emphasizes reforming assessment practices to ensure that they are aligned with new, more challenging standards of student achievement—in terms of (a) higher content; (b) performance-based assessment tasks (including elaborated answers, projects, and portfolios), instead of solely relying on multiple-choice questions; and (c) reporting results in terms of criterion-based statements of proficiency in the desired skills and knowledge, instead of norm-referenced statements of percentile score comparisons among students.[23] This is intended both to produce more useful information for purposes of program improvement and to prevent low-level, norm-referenced tests from continuing to drive curriculum and instruction. The CORS research very much supports that reform, but because engaging students in learning tasks where they are asked to demonstrate what they know is at the heart of classroom teaching and learning, CORS classifies "authentic assessment" as an element of teachers' authentic pedagogy, rather than viewing assessment simply as an external evaluation occurring *after* instruction has been provided.[24]

GOVERNANCE/PARTICIPATION

In terms of the final question in the reform framework—who's "we" in all this?—the research above, emphasizing the school as the unit of analysis, a professional school community taking collective responsibility for student achievement, the nature of high-level authentic teaching and learning, and so on, points to the need for governance structures in which the entire school community, including teachers and students, actively assumes responsibility, *provided* that this authority is focused on the goals of high achievement.[25] The need to embrace common learning goals and to embed assessment in curriculum and instruction, as noted above, demands a robust role for the school community in establishing standards and assessments, which must be reconciled with needs for external accountability and for overcoming the vast inequality in expectations between schools serving predominantly disadvantaged and advantaged populations.[26]

There is also a substantial body of evidence that student achievement is promoted by practices that encourage parent involvement in schools, and that this involvement is most effective when it engages parents in a full range of roles—as advocates for their children and decision-makers, as well as teachers of their children at home and supporters of school activities.[27] Further, parent involvement in a broad range of school affairs has been identified as a condition that actually supports creation of a schoolwide professional teacher community on behalf of authentic student learning—contrary to any assumptions that strong parent involvement undermines teachers' professional role.[28] Moreover, parents were found to be among the most active and influential outside forces for supporting positive reform.[29]

A study of local site councils in Chicago found a strong correlation between the degree of democratic decision-making and the degree to which the school is engaged in the kind of academic reform that promotes learning to high standards.[30] Strongly democratic schools, with joint decision-making based on a school-parent consensus about mission, had the best impact when compared with either adversarial or consolidated principal power models. On the other hand, it was found that parent involvement born out of conflict can ultimately lead to a stronger school, even though conflict usually tends to undermine it.

E. Legal Support

The standards-based framework as a vehicle for obtaining high quality education also has considerable legal support.

STUDENTS' RIGHTS

Many laws protect a child's right to be in a school that does a good job of helping him or her to meet high standards for what all students should know and be able to do.[31] For example:

- In schools receiving federal Title I funds, children have a right to a high-quality education that will enable them to master those high standards. In particular, students must get an "accelerated" and "enriched" curriculum, not a slower, watered down one. Teachers must be "highly qualified," use "effective" instructional strategies, and get intensive training on a regular basis about how to provide this kind of enrichment. They must also recognize when individual students are having difficulty mastering any of the standards and intervene with timely, effective extra help. Schools must make enough progress in achievement results each year for every child to reach proficient and advanced levels of proficiency.
- Children with disabilities have the right to a program designed to help them meet the same high standards expected for all children. The written individualized education plan (IEP) should spell out how the child's special needs will be addressed so that they do not pose a barrier to reaching those standards. An IEP that sets lower goals and does not focus on these standards is usually illegal. Nor is it generally legal to assign a student with disabilities to a low-track regular program that does not teach to these standards. These rights are protected by the federal Individuals with Disabilities Education Act (IDEA) and Section 504 of the Rehabilitation Act of 1973.
- Children should not be placed in low-track classes disproportionately composed of students of one race if those classes have lower academic content and do not fully address the challenging subject matter identified in standards for all students. Children are protected against such placement by Title VI of the federal 1964 Civil Rights Act.
- Children from a different language background with limited ability to write, read, or speak English have the right to a program effectively designed to overcome these language barriers so that they can meet the standards expected for all children. These rights are protected by Title VI and by the federal Equal Educational Opportunities Act of 1974.
- In schools that get federal aid for vocational or school-to-work programs,

students have a right to a program that integrates high-level academic and vocational skills and that prepares them for a four-year college as well as for work. The program must provide strong understanding and experience in "all aspects of the industry" students are studying—such as planning, finance, management, principles of technology, and labor issues—not just the skills to do a single job that may not be there when they graduate. Students with special needs—because of low income, low achievement, a disability, or limited English-language skills, or because they are trying to enter a field that is not traditional for their sex—have a right to the extra help necessary to succeed in the program. These rights are protected by the Carl D. Perkins Vocational and Applied Technology Education Act and the School-to-Work Opportunities Act.

• In many states, students are guaranteed rights to high-quality education which allows them to reach high standards—under the state constitution, state school-reform laws, and the plans states and school districts adopt to get federal Goals 2000 (and Title I) funds.

PARENTS' RIGHTS

Parents also have rights they can use to make sure that their children get a high-quality education.[32] For example:

• In Title I schools, parents have the right to develop the program plan jointly with the school. Exactly how that happens should be spelled out in a parent involvement policy, developed jointly with and agreed upon by the parents, including a parent-school "compact" that specifies what both the school and the parents will do to make sure the child's education meets the standards. Parents also are entitled to good training and information about the program, their rights, and how their own child is doing in meeting the standards.

• Parents of children with disabilities must be fully involved in the evaluation of the child and in designing and approving the child's IEP. If a school does not agree to provide the education the parent believes the law calls for, the parent can recover the lawyer's fees and other costs involved in winning a hearing or court case.

• Under the First Amendment, parents concerned about the quality of their children's school have the right (as do students) to speak out, pass out literature, form an organization with others, peacefully demonstrate, and petition for change. Various federal laws and state procedures also spell out ways to file complaints.

• Under the federal Family Educational Rights and Privacy Act, parents have the right to see the information the school system and its staff keeps about their child. In most states, under public records laws, parents and others can also see the information that is not specific to an individual, such as program evaluations, aggregate achievement data, etc.

F. Legal and Educational Process: The Nature of Collaboration

Professionals often feel that those outside their field have a simplistic view of their discipline. Part of working together across fields is getting past the stage of feeling—and being—misunderstood, oversimplified, stereotyped, or reified.

Thus, educators need to understand that the law is not necessarily "top down." It often does reshape authority, but not necessarily in the direction of moving it to higher levels. It can help give those on the ground (including parents, students, and teachers), and among them those who are least enfranchised, the power to better control the events that affect them. And power in turn affects attitudes—the very things we typically say cannot be legislated. People perceived to have power are treated, and treat themselves, differently.

Lawyers, for their part, need to understand how schools change, in light of the volitional nature of both teaching and learning. They need to recognize, on the one hand, that educational research generally cannot support an argument that a particular educational approach or curriculum can be mechanically adopted or imposed in a way that will make big differences.[33] On the other hand, they need to see that they cannot assume that if they simply legislate the outcomes, along with sanctions for failing to meet them, then educational institutions can be left to themselves to figure out how to produce those outcomes.[34]

Thus, the argument that federal law can and should provide one important basis for actualizing the right of all children to a good education must be placed in context. It is *not* an argument for a command-and-control approach to change, in which the federal government (or, for that matter, the state) runs the schools.

First, federal law in this context is not principally about outside enforcement. The main way that legal advocates and educators need to collaborate on implementation of the law is to work together, with parents, to ensure that people at the school and community level understand the quality-oriented aspects of this body of law and how it can be used as a tool for the school community to create programs that, in complying with these provisions, provide a good education.

Second, where this is not enough, this community education and support role should give the knowledge and tools to correct problems to those at the ground level—particularly parents, whose desire for their own children's well-being is generally less constrained by bureaucratic considerations. In other words, where enforcement becomes necessary, we are primarily talking about bottom-up enforcement—whether the parents successfully convince the school to change voluntarily, file a lawsuit, or file a complaint with state or federal agencies.

Finally, even though federal agency monitoring and enforcement will not be the primary vehicle for implementation of federal law, there *is* a need to change the expectation about monitoring and enforcement of education law relative to other federal laws. But even in that arena, a focus on enforcement should not and need not translate into federal control of the classroom. Part of the reason that most schools and families are unaware of the important quality provisions summarized in the list above is that there is so little expectation at the federal level of responsibility for implementation and enforcement, or for ensuring that parents, teachers, and others have enough information to work on implementation themselves.

Indeed, the problem is difficult to document (except through personal experience) because it is so endemic.[35]

- The Department of Education maintains virtually no data by which it could gauge, and inform the rest of us about, the implementation of key provisions summarized above.
- Funded research studies of implementation, even when looking at the impact of federal programs, rarely analyze the extent to which the programmatic provisions were understood and implemented as intended. Thus, one recommendation from this essay is that educators and lawyers work together to frame implementation research in ways that better reflect key quality-oriented provisions of the law.
- Congressional oversight and reauthorization hearings look at evaluation data on program participation and impact, anecdotes that relate to the program's usefulness, and experts' recommendations for change, but Congress almost never inquires into the degree to which the provisions it wrote actually were implemented. Thus implementation and enforcement are defined as a non-issue.[36]

In addition to frustrating the realization of students' rights to high-quality education, this impedes improving the federal role and creating more sensitive and sensible federal legislation. Congress continually rewrites the law without knowing whether the problems it seeks to address have persisted because the strategies it adopted last time don't work or because they were never adequately tried.

Legal principles and the structure of standards-based school reform mutually support each other in focusing on the creation and strengthening of a school community capable of taking responsibility for high-level student learning. As the research on authentic learning confirms, that requires teacher and student engagement in volitional, autonomous activity; it cannot be programmed.[37] The provisions of federal law with which we are concerned here support, rather than substitute for or negate, that kind of learning community, the kind of school-level planning necessary to create it, the development of a staff with the skills and orientation needed to make it work, and the rights of students to seek redress when they are denied access to it. The federal government must speak for those provisions in a more effective way.

G. Education and Accountability

As we look at schools' responsibility and accountability for providing a high-quality education, it is worth comparing education with other fields where accountability comes largely in the form of a duty to meet standards of accepted practice, along with potential liability for failure to utilize those standards when that failure results in harm to individuals. The point here is not primarily to pave the way for damage actions for educational malpractice. The most immediate legal relevance of educators' accountability for standards of practice is its potential impact on enforcement of other education laws. Nevertheless, because of emerging new standards for teaching practice, along with higher expectations for education, I will, in section III.A.2.b ("Potential Emergence of Malpractice Standards") briefly revisit the concept of educational malpractice, which was largely dismissed twenty years ago.

Teaching is often, though not universally, regarded as a profession.[38] Like other professions it involves the real-world application of specialized knowledge and skills, usually acquired in part through advanced academic training, including a credentialing process. While opinions differ on the extent to which teaching is a science, an art, or a craft, the same can be said of other professions such as medicine or law.[39] Perhaps more important, like other professions, good teaching is very much about the exercise of discretion—professional judgment, creative initiative, and perceptive responsiveness to the particular learning context (including what the students bring to it), rather than rote implementation of precise instructions—as any of us will recall when we think about those teachers who managed to help us learn something.

Yet teaching has remained quite distinct from other professions in terms of individual, professional accountability for the exercise of discretion in the actual teaching process (as distinct from accountability for custodial functions). In medicine, for example, keeping up with all the relevant research in one's field, applying that research in the treatment of all one's patients, and being held responsible for any deviation from best practice that results in harm to one's patients are accepted as basic to the professional role. Indeed, any deviation is clearly regarded as such and, when it comes to light, frequently becomes the subject of legal proceedings. In education, the parallel notion—that each teacher is responsible for reading all the relevant research journals, applying their findings each day in class, and being held responsible for any student's educational deficiency that is caused by the failure to apply that research or use best practice—has been quite foreign.[40]

Another important contrast is in responsibility for operating within government regulation. When the Food and Drug Administration issues a rule regarding the use of a particular medication, we all count on the fact that the norm among doctors will be both virtually immediate awareness of the new rule and a high degree of compliance. Again, as with best practice based on research, instances in which these regulations are not followed are regarded as deviations, calling for remedial action, with official watchdog agencies in place and active. In education, the norm is quite the opposite. Few teachers (or even building administrators) are familiar with the specific substantive provisions of many of the largest federal programs that supposedly regulate their schools.[41] When those provisions[42] are ignored, no alarm bells sound,[43] and it is not regarded as a deviation from the norm—because it is not.[44] Noncompliance is the norm.[45]

Thus, in regard to both discretionary and regulatory responsibility, there has not been the same sense of accountability as in the medical profession.

Since the mid-1990s, the traditional reluctance to hold educators accountable for the outcomes of their work has begun to weaken. Heightened concern about school failure is fueling this movement. Although overall levels of educational performance have not been declining, the consequences of continued poor performance are increasingly viewed as unacceptable.[46]

Greater educator accountability may also be stimulated by a more sophisticated and widely held consensus within education circles noted above about the kinds of school-based reforms that promote student achievement, along with a growing public consensus, at least at the level of public policy, that all children can learn and virtually all children can meet relatively rigorous academic standards.[47]

At the same time, a variety of countervailing forces threaten the recognition of enforceable rights to high-quality education—such as the failure to set aside adequate resources (particularly as state and local budgets are squeezed by the need to fill in for federal cutbacks in noneducation funding); lack of federal agency resources and political will to monitor and enforce state and local compliance with existing key quality mandates; the current Congressional attacks on the notion of federally established rights (whether called "entitlements" or "unfunded mandates") and proposals to replace more specific mandates with block grants giving governors considerable discretion; attacks on standards-based reform by some parents and conservative groups who view it as imposition of "secular humanist" values; some ambivalence by school-based reformers who fear that state-generated standards could interfere with school autonomy; and informed resistance and/or lack of capacity to implement reform on the part of some administrators and teachers.[48]

H. The Risks

This chapter focuses mainly on the opportunities that standards-based reform provides for advancing the rights of all children to a good education—for challenging and changing the structure of programs that do not effectively teach students the high-level skills and knowledge all are expected to learn, for challenging the denial of resources sufficient to provide such programs, and ultimately for challenging these students' eventual employers, whose jobs and workplace organization fail to utilize and adequately compensate those skills and knowledge. But there are also risks—that "standards" will become a substitute for, rather than a stimulus for, the structural changes and the resources necessary for real opportunity to learn, and will only validate, rather than help eliminate, vast inequalities in educational outcomes and economic opportunity.

I. STANDARDS WITHOUT RESOURCES

It is, of course, much easier to declare a new set of standards for students than to create a system that will actually enable all students to achieve them.[49] Similarly, in a tight job market, it is far easier to raise standards for hiring and promotion than to restructure the workplace to create enough jobs that actually use and pay well for the skills specified in those standards. While setting

standards poses some methodological problems and can engender controversy,[50] these latter tasks require marshaling political and economic where-
withal in the face of persistent political and economic inequality in both
educational resources and the employment sector.

2. VALIDATION OF INEQUALITY

The risks are not simply in students failing to attain the standards. There is also
the risk of adding insult to injury. Having identified certain skills and knowledge as essential for success, a society that denies some students the education
needed to master those skills will then, when it tries to assess those skills and
knowledge, be measuring its own inequality. Instead of remedying the inequality, however, using individual test results to label students as lacking essential
skills and knowledge provides a ready-made justification for inequality. As
performance on new forms of standards-based assessments becomes an accepted criterion for promotion, graduation, college admission, and so on, this
inequality will then be reinforced—with early denial of benefits becoming the
rationale for later denials.

Moreover, the harm is heightened to the extent that there is any looseness
between the assessments and their ability to predict later success with absolute
certainty. For example, during the period before Florida's competency test
could be used as a criterion for high school graduation, a study found that many
high school graduates who had failed the test were succeeding in college.[51]
Further, if one controls for educational attainment (years of school completed),
the association between cognitive test performance and socioeconomic success
is quite weak, suggesting that imposing a new set of educational credentials may
inadvertently cut off opportunities for people who would otherwise succeed.[52]

Unequal access to high-quality education is not a misfortune randomly
visited on students, but is much more common for poor and minority families.[53] Thus, any inequalities that are validated through a system of standards-
based assessment will further reinforce race and class inequalities. Any optimism over the prospects for the current reform movement, and its ability to
evade these negative consequences, must reckon with our history, in which
cognitive assessment has indeed been used to rationalize inequality and reinforce class and race stereotyping.[54]

3. SCAPEGOATING FOR LACK OF GOOD JOBS

The potential use of standards-based assessments for employment decisions
also heightens the danger of new barriers for low-income students and others.

The notion that we have rapidly moved to a knowledge-based economy, in which cognitive skills are rewarded with high-paying jobs, easily leads to the conclusion that our economic woes, both collective and individual, are attributable to a lack of skills. Introducing new standards-based assessments—with claims that they measure the skills necessary for success—into this climate will strengthen that conclusion.

There is evidence, however, that our economy often is simply not producing enough good jobs and that, matched against the actual pattern of low-wage, low-skill jobs, there is often no major skill shortage.[55] This is not to say that higher educational levels do not confer a competitive advantage on individuals in obtaining the too few jobs. But increasing the skills of workers (the supply side of the labor market) will not by itself address the scarcity of good jobs (the demand side). In fact, increases in the numbers of workers at any specific skill level, by increasing supply relative to demand, usually depress wages. This is consistent with the erosion in real wages.[56] In this context, the growing numbers of economic losers become the scapegoats for what is in fact a structural economic problem: too few good jobs.

That students will actually receive the benefits of standards-based reform is by no means a foregone conclusion, and the risks are equally real. The point is not to predict the outcome of this effort, but to shape it. Educators and lawyers need to work together, particularly in concert with parents and communities, to help realize the benefits and prevent the harms.

II. LAWS SUPPORTING SCHOOL REFORM

The tremendous flux in education legislation at both state and federal levels should not obscure the fact that there is now an extensive body of law that supports the school reform elements discussed above. The federal and state laws are interwoven. In particular, provisions found under state statutory law play a critical role in making federal legal standards concrete.

Following are brief sketches of some of the more important bodies of law— just enough to identify their overall structure and, at the most general level, their relationship to school reform principles.[57]

A. State Statutes

State legal requirements that address various elements of standards-based reform are not new. State legislatures and departments of education have long issued requirements for what should be taught, student-teacher ratios, teacher qualifications, and so on, which can be fit within the framework of standards, opportunity to learn, assessment, and improvement.

In recent years, new state laws have been designed explicitly as standards-based reforms, and thus tend to have more of the elements discussed above in the section on frameworks of reform.[58] This trend got a push from the meeting of the governors and President Bush in 1990 that resulted in the National Education Goals[59] and, even more, from federal education legislation in 1994, discussed below. The influences are varied, however, including state finance equity litigation,[60] discussed in the next section.

In some states, legislation sets out standards and other reform elements in some detail, while elsewhere broad legislation leaves details to state education agency policy. In either case, the ultimate result is typically a package of (1) content and performance standards for what all students should know and be able to do; (2) at least some elements of local planning to help schools enable students to reach the standard;[61] (3) new assessments of whether the standards have been met; (4) a set of consequences for failing to meet them; and (5) allocation or reallocation of some resources toward these changes.

Whether these education standards are directly enforceable as a matter of state statutory law depends on both the specific mandates and the background of state law on private causes of action. Regardless of their direct enforceability, these emerging state education standards can greatly invigorate the role of both state constitutional law and federal statutory law, as discussed below. State pronouncements about what schools should provide—the "opportunity to learn" portion—may help fill in the meaning of state constitutional and federal statutory requirements. Even more, the state's articulation of what all students should know and be able to do can reverberate throughout these other laws.

B. State Constitutions

Students' rights to high-quality education can be grounded on the education clauses that appear in almost all state constitutions, often in terms of a duty to provide a thorough and efficient system of education in the state. These clauses help explain the continued liveliness of claims that financial inequalities among school districts are unconstitutional, long after the window for asserting such claims under federal constitutional law all but closed.[62] Such education clauses have also been invoked, in a manner that supports a state constitutional right to education, in cases challenging the charging of fees to parents and students for essential educational services.[63]

These education clauses, together with school finance case law and emerging state education standards, can have a vital role in establishing and defining a substantive state constitutional right to education that goes beyond the issues of school finance and fees. In some of the litigation, the focus has been on a direct substantive right to education under the education clause itself.[64] At other times, the presence of the education clause has been used to establish a standard of strict scrutiny of inequalities under the state's equal protection clause, in contrast to the U.S. Supreme Court's more restrained review under the federal equal protection clause, based on the absence of explicit reference to education in the U.S. Constitution.[65]

Some of these cases establish education as a fundamental state right, and then move straight to a determination that the gross levels of school finance inequality cannot survive the high standards for judging state interference with fundamental rights, whether directly under the education clause or the equal protection clause.[66] Other cases, however, provide important additional guidance in defining education standards by inquiring into what level of education is required by the state constitution.[67]

For example, the court in *Pauley* found it necessary to identify the elements of the state constitutional mandate for a "thorough and efficient" system of education, in order to determine whether the state's system of finance deprived students in low-wealth districts of such education. It therefore appointed masters (experts) to help it first define, in elaborate detail, standards for curriculum, instruction, and facilities and then analyze the extent to which the low-wealth districts failed to meet those standards.[68]

The job for which the court in *Pauley* sought masters' help—defining the contours of a constitutional right to education—can now in many states be assigned in part to emerging education standards.[69] The fact that students in certain schools, or certain tracks within the school, are not receiving an education that effectively addresses the standards that the state itself has set for all students is relevant to whether the mandate for a thorough and efficient system of education has been met, or whether the qualitative differences in education meet the high standards of scrutiny under the state equal protection clause.

As elsewhere, the relation between state constitution and state statute is two-way. While standards-related state education laws can help establish the nature and contours of the constitutional right, Kentucky is a good example of how successful state constitutional litigation can also spawn additional state legislative standards.[70]

C. Federal Statutes

By 1994, all federal elementary and secondary education law began to be organized around standards-based reform. As of spring 1998, we have been through three years in which the life expectancy of many of the federal statutes discussed below has been in question. Republican proposals would have replaced some of the laws with block grants containing fewer requirements, or in some cases would simply have repealed pieces of the laws. Most of this new structure survived the 104th Congress; the 105th has appeared somewhat less anxious to wipe the slate clean, although some such proposals remain alive.

In any event, the impact of these statutes is not necessarily limited to the life of their authorization—both because they interplay with ongoing state reform efforts and because it can take a long time before state and local education agencies move off prior legislation to orient themselves around a new program—in part the result of weak federal dissemination and enforcement. While this often impedes reform, in this context it may mean that school administrators who first begin to understand and get comfortable with the structure of the 1994 reforms may be slow to shift to a new paradigm.

I. GOALS 2000

The Goals 2000: Educate America Act[71] was enacted on March 31, 1994, with the overall purpose to "provide a framework for meeting the National Education Goals established by Title I of this Act."[72] While the National Education Goals include school readiness, high school graduation rates, school safety and discipline, teacher professional development, parent involvement, and adult literacy and competency, the operational focus of the Act is largely on developing academic standards for student achievement and programs designed to reach them. The Act's purpose puts it squarely behind standards-based reform in much the terms described section I.C above. Because it serves mainly as a stimulus to state efforts that have now begun, Goals 2000 may have an impact beyond its statutory life.

As originally enacted, the Act's Title II provided a national process for assisting and certifying voluntary efforts to develop content, performance, and opportunity to learn standards by states, discipline groups, and others. Much of this structure was repealed in 1996—the one significant casualty for standards-based legislation in the 104th Congress.[73] Title V, the National Skills Standards Board, does remain fully in place, designed to assist and certify development of occupational skill standards for various industries by education-business-labor partnerships (see section II.C.3.d).

The bulk of Goals 2000 funding is for Title III, providing for a system of state and local grants to stimulate and support standards-based reform.[74] States apply to develop and, once approved, implement a state improvement plan. The state's plan must contain strategies for meeting the National Educational Goals by improving teaching and learning and students' mastery of basic and advanced skills in core content areas. It must include content and performance standards for all students, along with state assessments of all students, curricula, instructional materials, teacher training, monitoring and accountability, and various other measures—all aligned with and designed to enable all students to meet the standards.

While Goals 2000 funds may be used for a wide variety of state activities, the bulk of the funds (90 percent after the first year) must be passed through as subgrants to local educational agencies (LEAs),[75] which apply (on a competitive basis) for one-year planning grants, and subsequently for grants to implement their local school improvement plans. The local plan requirements, structured like the state plan, must: "address districtwide education improvements directed at enabling all students to meet the State content standards," reflect the state improvement plan priorities, and "include a strategy for—(i) *ensuring that all students have a fair opportunity to learn;* (ii) improving teaching and learning, (iii) improving governance and management; (iv) generating, maintaining, and strengthening parent and community involvement; and (v) expanding improvements throughout the local educational agency."[76]

In turn, the bulk of LEA funds (85 percent after the first year) must be used for development and implementation of individual school improvement plans, with at least 50 percent going to schools with special needs, such as high percentages of low-income or low-achieving students.[77] The LEA must monitor, in close consultation with parents and others, the implementation and effectiveness of the plan and report progress to the state, which decides whether to recommend revisions. States make separate competitive, peer-reviewed subgrants to LEAs or consortia of LEAs, in cooperation with higher education institutions or nonprofit organizations, for improving preservice teacher education and providing inservice professional development necessary to prepare all students to meet state standards.[78]

Despite the absence of enforceable provisions for explicit state "opportunity-to-learn" (OTL) standards,[79] students can seek remedies for failure to implement the other state and local requirements of the act above that bear upon the quality of their education. First (as discussed in section I.C), the elements of a program plan or improvement plan that determine whether students will have good opportunities to learn can and do go well beyond formally designated OTL standards. The repeal of the OTL section did not diminish the enforce-ability of the parts of Goals 2000 state or local improvement plans that relate to curriculum, pedagogy, resources, teaching staff, and so on, and indeed local plans must include a strategy for ensuring that all students have a fair oppor-tunity to learn. In fact, except where noted, states and local educational agen-cies are legally obligated by the General Education Provisions Act to operate their programs in accordance with the plans and applications they have submit-ted for receipt of federal funds.[80]

Second, regardless of its direct enforceability, Goals 2000 can play an impor-tant role in establishing the parameters of enforcement under other laws. The plans submitted under Goals 2000 are often reflected in state law and regula-tion—either because they were already developed independently before receipt of Goals 2000 funds or because Goals 2000 has pushed the state to enact laws and regulations in order to obtain the funds.[81]

Further, as noted in section II.B above, official state standards and pronounce-ments concerning what all students should learn and what schools should provide in order to make sure students can learn it—whether found in Goals 2000 submissions or not—are likely to be relevant in giving more specific meaning to the state's constitutional duty to provide a thorough and efficient education.

Finally, as will be discussed below, the mandates of other federal programs, civil rights laws, and even federal constitutional obligations can gain particular meaning from the standards, program plans, assessments, and improvement steps developed under Goals 2000, just as from those reform structures devel-oped entirely under state law.

2. TITLE I OF THE ELEMENTARY AND SECONDARY EDUCATION ACT

Low-achieving students who are not effectively taught the high-level knowl-edge and skills expected of all children may claim a violation of Title I.[82] Title I has been the centerpiece of the Elementary and Secondary Education Act since ESEA's enactment in 1965, and it remains the largest federal education pro-gram, totaling $7.69 billion in fiscal 1997. Funds go to school districts based on numbers of low-income children, and then are used in each district's higher poverty schools to improve the academic achievement of students, especially the lowest achieving students, regardless of income. While traditionally focused more on the early grades, Title I funds go to many high schools, and the number is growing because of a new allocation rule in the law.

As amended in 1994, Title I now imposes duties on states, school districts, and schools, composed largely of the standards-based reform elements discussed in section I.C. above—including high state content and performance standards;[83] programming that addresses school readiness, curriculum, instructional methods, program structure, staff qualifications and training, and individual assistance; performance assessment; and improvement and enforcement activities—which together constitute, for participating students, a right to a high-quality educational program.

The contrast between the actual operation of Chapter 1 and the emerging consensus on the shape of school reform (as described in sections I.C and I.D above) largely provoked the 1994 revision. Amendments in 1988, designed to ensure that Chapter 1 students mastered the skills all students were expected to learn, had not been clear enough and strong enough to overcome a twenty-year pattern of low expectations and fragmented programs focusing on remedial drill and minimal gains on norm-referenced tests of basic skills.[84] The stated purpose of the 1994 revision—"to enable schools to provide opportunities for children served to acquire the knowledge and skills contained in the challenging content standards and to meet the challenging state performance standards for all children"—is to be accomplished by a set of activities that are explicitly organized around those elements of school reform.[85]

Consistent with emerging reform principles, the new law focuses much more attention than previously at the school level. It articulates two school-level options—targeted assistance schools and schoolwide programs. Targeted assistance schools continue to follow rules to ensure that funds are used only for extra services for those students who are most educationally disadvantaged.[86] Schoolwide programs, an option that schools with particularly high poverty rates may choose, are permitted to use Title I funds for overall school improvement.[87]

While both options were available before 1994, the new law makes significant changes. For both models, there are much more detailed, comprehensive program requirements, covering many of the noted school reform elements and linked with the standards. The programmatic changes respond to past concerns that, on the one hand, targeted programs were fragmented and marginal and did not deal with the overall education program of the disadvantaged children, and, on the other hand, schoolwide program funds became unfocused general aid, with neither one resulting in reform of the core academic program.

In place of remediation, both types of programs now require "accelerated," "enriched," and "high-quality" curricula, "effective instructional strategies," "highly qualified instructional staff," and "high-quality" staff development—all aimed at enabling all students to achieve proficiency.[88] Moreover, targeted assistance schools must now take on responsibility for the overall program of those low-achieving students being served—not just for the extra federal dollars used to assist those students. Schoolwide programs, for their part, must ensure that individual student difficulties in mastering any of the standards are identified and addressed with effective additional assistance in a timely manner[89] and, like targeted assistance schools, must show enough gains in performance of low-income and limited-English-proficient students as well as of all students being served—so that "schoolwide" includes, rather than substitutes for, an effective system for meeting individual need. Thus, the difference between the two program models should not be overdrawn, since in most ways they are now more like each other and less like their predecessors.

States must develop new, valid, multiple methods for annually assessing all students to determine the extent of mastery of the performance standards. Schools and school districts that do not make enough annual progress to result in all participating students reaching proficient and advanced levels of performance[90] must develop and implement improvement steps and ultimately are subject to sanctions. States must also have transitional systems for assessing performance of complex skills and challenging subject matter and for ensuring that participating students are taught the same knowledge and skills as all other children during the period before standards and assessments are fully developed.

Critical implementation documents for these Title I reforms include schools' program plans, incorporating the elements above and jointly developed with the parents;[91] school-parent compacts spelling out what the school will do to enable the student to meet the standards, how the parent will support student learning, and how teachers and parents will communicate; district plans addressing staff development and technical assistance, also developed with parents; school- and district-level parent involvement policies, which are jointly developed with and agreed upon with the parents, spelling out, among other things, the specific methods for jointly developing the school and district program plans; state plans addressing content and performance standards, assessment, adequate progress, local improvement and enforcement, and how the state will help each district and school develop the capacity to carry out the local planning and implementation requirements; and improvement plans for schools and districts not making adequate yearly progress.[92]

Particularly in schoolwide programs, whose numbers are increasing substantially under the new law, the promise of whole-school restructuring hangs in the balance. Title I must not become general aid to do more of the same, filling holes caused by state and local budget constraints (common practice among schoolwide programs under the prior law), and "schoolwide" reform cannot become a banner for ignoring individual students' needs in relation to high standards. For targeted assistance schools, the challenge will be actualizing those parts of the law that link extra Title I services to reform of the regular program for low-achieving students.

Parents and student advocates can intervene in several ways in programs that are not working.[93] First, there are the substantial, detailed rights above to participate in designing, implementing, and evaluating the programs at the state, district, and school level. Second, there is the process above for addressing the needs of an individual child having difficulty becoming proficient in particular areas. Third, there are the opportunities above for getting involved in and overseeing the improvement process and interventions for schools and districts that are not making adequate progress. Fourth, each state must have a system for addressing complaints of noncompliance and failure to implement these and other provisions; complaints may also be filed with the U.S. Department of Education.[94] Fifth, parents and students may seek to enforce the Act in court, at least in regard to district- and school-level obligations.[95]

The relationship between Title I and state standards is dynamic. Like Goals 2000, Title I prods states to set standards and develop new assessment tools, as a quid pro quo for continued Title I funding. Title I also provides a set of strong requirements to design and implement high-quality programs to ensure that all students, and disadvantaged students in particular, are able to reach those standards.[96]

3. VOCATIONALLY ORIENTED PROGRAMS AND OVERALL HIGH SCHOOL REFORM

Quality standards have been incorporated into federal vocational education law, and again, state standards can play a vital role. It is not merely that standards-based reform can now be used to overcome problems associated with vocational education, but rather that innovative federal principles for vocationally oriented programs can play a leading part in overall school reform, creating higher quality, more vital whole-school programs for all students.

a. Carl D. Perkins Vocational and Applied Technology Education Act This law rewrote the provisions governing approximately one billion dollars in federal vocational education aid; it also indirectly affects several times that amount in state and local funding for vocational programs receiving federal aid. Key requirements for vocational education now focus on whether programs:[97]

1. integrate academic and vocational education and provide strong student development and use of basic and advanced problem-solving and *academic skills* (including math, reading, writing, science, and social studies) in the vocational setting, so that vocational programs do not form a separate, academically inferior track;

2. provide students with strong experience in and understanding of *all aspects of the industry* they are preparing to enter, including planning, finance, management, technical and production skills, principles of technology, labor, community issues, and health, safety, and environment—instead of trying to predict exactly what jobs future workers will have and exactly what skills will be required for those jobs, and then providing only narrow training for that particular definition; and

3. provide access and the supplemental services needed for success to students who are members of *special populations,* including those who are economically disadvantaged, academically disadvantaged, limited-English-proficient, disabled, single parents and displaced homemakers, or seeking to enter fields not traditional for their sex.[98]

These three sets of requirements, for example, are the constants in state planning, which must target the funds at state and local levels to the needs identified by a state assessment of these elements.[99] They are also the constant elements in annual local program evaluations, based upon state performance standards, which trigger a program improvement process similar to that in Title I.[100] All programs assisted with basic grant funds must be of sufficient size, scope, and quality to give reasonable promise of meeting the vocational education needs of the students involved.[101] Further, recipients are required to review programs annually, with full and informed participation of special populations, to identify and adopt strategies to overcome barriers resulting in lower rates of special populations' access to or success in such programs.[102] There also must be effective, state-developed procedures by which students, parents, teachers, and area residents can participate in state and local program decisions and make expedited appeals.[103]

The law opens up possibilities for low-income students and communities, including ways to meet the mandates through involving youth in community development projects, where they assess their community and then plan, start, and run enterprises to address unmet community needs.[104] Major inadequacies in understanding and implementing the new provisions have been identified.[105] In seeking remedies, advocates should examine the interplay between state academic standards and federal mandates concerning academic skills for vocational students. Students should be receiving effective academic instruction that meets the state education standards applicable to all.

b. School-to-Work Opportunities Act of 1994 This law provides federal funds to underwrite initial costs of planning and establishing statewide school-to-work systems that will be maintained with other resources (including Perkins funds).[106] These systems must integrate school-based and work-based learning, academic and vocational education, and secondary and postsecondary education.

The required components complement those in Perkins and, like Perkins, can both contribute to and gain strength from academic reform requirements and initiatives. States can receive initial development grants and, after an adequate plan is developed, implementation grants. Local partnerships—consisting of public secondary and postsecondary institutions or agencies, educators, employers, labor, and students (and, optionally, community-based organizations, parent organizations, and others)—can receive grants through the states which receive implementation grants, or directly from the federal government, either in states that are not beyond the first year of a state implementation grant or for partnerships in high-poverty areas in any state.[107]

The program for each student must include and connect a school-based component and a work-based component and offer the opportunity to complete a career major, including attainment of a skill certificate.[108] The same themes sounded in Perkins—strong academic skills, broadening vocational skills to focus on all aspects of an industry, and ensuring equity—are found throughout the School-to-Work requirements:

- Academic and vocational learning must be integrated. The program must meet the same *academic standards* established by states for all students, including any under Goals 2000. It must also meet the requirements necessary to prepare them for postsecondary education, including four-year college programs, without additional academic preparation.[109]
- Students must, to the extent practicable, gain strong understanding of and experience in *all aspects of an industry.* This is part of the basic program requirements, the definition of a career major, and the requirements for both school-based and work-based components.[110]

- The program must provide "all students" with *equal access* to the full range of its components, including recruitment, enrollment, and placement activities.[111] Career counseling must devote attention to surmounting gender, race, ethnicity, disability, language, or socioeconomic impediments to career options and encouraging careers in nontraditional employment.[112]

The state plan must describe how the state will ensure effective, meaningful opportunities for all students to participate in programs that meet these requirements.[113] It must also describe how the state has and will continue to enlist the active participation of students, parents, and community organizations, as well as employers, labor organizations, education agencies, teachers, and other members of the public.[114] Local partnerships must also develop compacts—a process by which the responsibilities and expectations of students, parents, employers, and schools are clearly established and agreed upon when the student enters a career major program.[115]

Performance measures—to be developed by the Secretaries of Education and Labor in collaboration with the states for assessing state and local programs—also must address the three areas above (academic standards, all aspects of the industry, and equitable participation). They must measure progress in development and implementation of state plans that meet the requirements; participation rates, including information on students and dropouts, by gender, race, ethnicity, socioeconomic background, limited English proficiency, disability, and "academically talented" status; and outcomes for students and dropouts, broken out in the same way, including academic learning gains, attainment of strong experience in and understanding of all aspects of the industry the students are preparing to enter, school continuation, graduation, and later placement outcomes.[116]

c. High School Reform Themes in Perkins and School-to-Work The focus on academic-vocational integration and on learning all aspects of an industry in these two laws is designed to address long-standing problems associated with vocational education. Traditionally designed to link school with work for students viewed as not academically inclined, the industrial model of vocational education hinged on employers' identifying the specific technical and production skills needed for future jobs and the schools' identifying students to be taught those skills. While equity problems were sometimes raised in terms of race, class, gender, and disability discrimination in admission to higher-status training programs, the larger equity issues—whether the very existence of a vocational program created an inferior, inequitable track for certain students—

remained mostly a matter of individual concern. Parents and students harboring that concern voted with their feet and enrolled in the college-prep track.

Two related developments created an atmosphere more hospitable to challenging the traditional industrial model of vocational education. First, increasing academic requirements began squeezing the room in students' schedules for vocational courses. Second, critics began to question vocational education on its own terms—trading off higher-level academics for access to good jobs. Research showed limited if any employment or wage benefit to high school vocational enrollment for most groups of students in most occupational areas, not only in comparison to college-prep track enrollment but even when compared with the widely condemned "general" track.[117] Further, accelerated economic, technological, and personal change made it harder to forecast the precise number of stable jobs, the precise skills needed for those jobs, or the long-term career goals of youth.[118]

These reforms reflect a belief that vocational students must achieve the same high academic standards as others. But they also reflect a recognition that the benefits are not one-sided—that there are pedagogical benefits from infusing stronger academic content with teaching methods borrowed from vocational education and from using the world of work as a context for learning activities and reflection. Indeed, many of the most favored elements of current academic reform share a great deal with traditional vocational pedagogy—such as hands-on work and active exploration in cooperative learning teams, project-based learning, teacher as guide rather than lecturer, performance-based demonstration of student competency, and long-block scheduling.[119]

The melding of academic and vocational reforms is also stimulating efforts to restructure schools into smaller subschools, houses, or academies—each with a different multidisciplinary theme (such as arts, communication, transportation, or health) but of equal academic quality and depth.[120] Thus, integrated implementation of the federally mandated vocational reforms can play a vital role in making academic reform real and creating more engaging schools that enable all students to meet high standards.

The focus on all aspects of an industry is, in turn, central to making this academic-vocational integration real and is a central element of program quality in its own right. Academic-vocational integration runs the risk of both appearing and being watered-down or "dumbed-down" applied academics unless the vocational side is conceptualized much more broadly than the skills needed to perform a narrowly defined job. When, in contrast, the task is to explore all the issues confronting an industry—planning, management, finances, labor issues, principles of technology, community issues, and health, safety, and environmental issues—there is a much richer platform for integrating high-level academics, bringing to bear literature and language arts, mathematics and science, history and other social sciences. At the same time, the all-aspects-of-the-industry approach allows students to focus on a particular industry (as opposed to a single occupation) and engage in practical activity, while not being limited to a particular set of job skills when labor markets, job requirements, or career goals change. It directly overcomes the distinction between planners and workers, ensuring that students get, and get involved in, the "big picture" of the whole industry. In this sense, it is a direct challenge to the most fundamental basis for tracking in school and work.

Finally, while preparing students for high-performance, high-skill workplaces with decentralized decision-making, it also prepares them to deal with the local economy in low-income communities with not enough good jobs;[121] the enumerated elements of all aspects of the industry are the skills needed for community development, job creation, and entrepreneurship. Indeed, some of the best models for teaching all aspects of the industry engage students and teachers in assessing their communities and planning and running enterprises that meet significant community needs.[122]

As in other areas of federal education law, the lack of serious federal implementation, oversight, and enforcement means that a visitor could easily show up at a Perkins- or School-to-Work-funded program and find that key required elements, including academic-vocational integration, all aspects of the industry, or adequate attention to the needs of various populations, are not fully implemented or even fully understood.[123] Nevertheless, the shift away from narrow skill training embodied in these reforms has gained momentum at the state and local levels in many places. In particular, the School-to-Work Opportunities Act's strategy of phasing in planning and implementation grants has been fairly successful in garnering attention at state and local levels. Thus, even if either Act were repealed,[124] there would be some hope that their thrust will have already been institutionalized in at least some states and localities.

d. National Skill Standards Act of 1994 This law, which was incorporated as Title V of Goals 2000,[125] establishes a National Skill Standards Board to stimulate development and adoption of "a voluntary national system" of workforce skill standards and assessment.[126] The National Board is to identify broad clusters of occupations; facilitate the establishment of business-labor partnerships to develop skill standards and assessment and certification systems for each such cluster; recommend that the Secretary of Labor award grants to those partnerships; develop (after extensive public consultation) objective criteria for endorsing skill standards, assessments, and certification systems for those clusters; endorse those systems; and conduct related research, clearinghouse, dissemination, and coordination functions, including encouraging the development and adoption of curricula and materials for attaining the skill standards that provide for structured work experiences and related study programs leading to progressive levels of certification and postsecondary education.

To be endorsed, the skill standards must take into account international standards and the requirements of high-performance work organizations; meet or exceed the highest standards used in the United States; allow for regular updating; promote portability of credentials and worker mobility within and among occupational clusters and industries; and be nondiscriminatory. Endorsed systems of assessment and certification must take into account relevant international methods, use a variety of evaluation techniques (including, where appropriate, oral and written evaluations, portfolio assessments, and performance tests), and include methods for establishing that the system is not discriminatory. Endorsed systems for promoting use of these standards and systems must include dissemination of information about relevant civil rights laws regarding their use.

The use of these skill standards, assessments, and individual certifications in both the school setting and the workplace raise a number of questions. On the school side, it is not clear how skill standards that are designed to certify workers as being able to perform the work in a particular occupational cluster will affect high school curriculum, including the required focus on all aspects of an industry and the effort to move away from narrow skill training.[127] Indeed, for many, this high school reform effort is about using work and industry as a context for learning but not necessarily assuming that the goal is to prepare students to emerge from high school trained with the technical skills for a specific job or even a cluster of jobs. An occupational cluster can be quite different from an industry or industry sector and holds the potential for reinforcing rather than overcoming school tracking based on career paths of unequal power and status.

For example, a high school academy built around the health industry need not and should not segregate students and curriculum into groupings such as aides, nurses, and doctors, but "occupational clusters" might well do so. The skill standards partnerships funded by the Departments of Labor and Education vary in specificity of focus (with one developing standards for industrial launderers and another developing separate standards for hotel bellpersons, cashiers, servers, and other hospitality and tourism positions).

And then there is the practical question of whether, if both new academic standards and workplace skill standards are as rigorous as they are supposed to be, students' schedules will really allow for successful mastery of both in high school. In these regards, while the School-to-Work Opportunities Act requires that programs lead to certification by the completion of the program, the program typically includes postsecondary education, and many aspects of a particular set of skills standards may be most appropriate for the postsecondary portion.

In the workplace, the questions hinge largely on the distinction between using the standards, assessments, and certifications for training workers or evaluating a workplace on the one hand or using them to make hiring or promotion decisions on the other. As discussed in section III.B.2 below, employment discrimination laws bar hiring and promotion criteria that have disparate impact on the basis of race, national origin, sex, religion, or disability unless they have been validated as necessary for job performance. If the leaders of an industry develop skill standards at the high level called for by the act, extreme vigilance will be needed to prevent employers in an industry whose workplaces do not yet in fact require that level of skill from using certification as a hiring or promotion criteria, thereby producing discrimination.

4. SPECIAL EDUCATION

Among the most developed areas of education law, both in statute and case law, are those governing the "special education" of students with disabilities—both their rights to a free, appropriate public education in the least restrictive environment under the Individuals with Disabilities Education Act, first enacted in 1975,[128] and the parallel and complementary rights to nondiscriminatory education Section 504 of the Rehabilitation Act of 1973.[129] From a standards-reform perspective, however, these laws can be cast in terms of requirements to assist students with disabilities to master the core curriculum expected for all students.[130]

Much programming for students with disabilities is based on assumptions, usually unstated and unproven, that they cannot master the full range of skills expected for others.[131] For example, individualized education plans (IEPs), supposedly developed by staff and parents based on a thorough assessment of individual needs, are often not plans for how the school will help the students overcome any barriers to their mastery of the skills taught in the mainstream curriculum but instead are built on a set of lower expectations. Similarly, when students with disabilities are "mainstreamed" into "regular" classes, those classes are often (as with Title I students) low-track groupings not aimed at teaching the full range of academic skills expected for others. These two practices directly conflict with the requirements of both laws concerning non-discrimination, least restrictive environment, and appropriate education—except in those cases where it can be clearly demonstrated through the objective, professional evaluation process that the student is so severely disabled that, even with appropriate assistance, he or she is unable to master those skills and that curriculum.[132]

Here again, independent state and local education standards for what students should know and be able to do are highly relevant. When students with disabilities (with the narrow exception above) are not in programs that are effectively aimed at mastery of those standards or their special education services are not designed to meet their special needs in relation to that mastery, then their effective exclusion from the benefits of the mainstream curriculum constitutes discrimination on the basis of their disability,[133] a denial of their right to "appropriate" education,[134] and a failure to provide their education in the least restrictive environment. IDEA and Section 504 should be seen to bar educational practices that provide disabled students with less effective opportunities to meet those standards.[135]

In 1997, IDEA was amended,[136] with an explicit focus on standards-based reform and success in the general curriculum, drawing on findings concerning low expectations for children with disabilities and the need for maintaining high academic standards and providing maximum opportunities to achieve them for these students, addressing their needs in carrying out education reform, and ensuring that staff serving them have the skills and knowledge to do so.[137] States must have: goals for the performance of children with disabilities that "are consistent, to the maximum extent appropriate, with other goals and standards for children established by the State;"[138] and biannually report on their performance indicators for assessing progress toward those goals, including performance on assessments, drop-out rates, and graduation rates.[139]

The state must demonstrate that children with disabilities are included in general state- and district-wide assessment programs, with appropriate accommodations, where necessary. The state or LEA, as appropriate, must develop guidelines for participation in alternative assessments by those children who cannot participate in state- and district-wide assessments, with such alternative assessments to be in use by July 1, 2000. Reports to the public on student assessment must include the numbers of children with disabilities participating in regular and alternative assessments and their performance.[140] (It is important to distinguish alternative assessments which assess the same standards through a different vehicle, because a student's disability prevents him or her from demonstrating their level of mastery of the same knowledge and skills through the regular assessment, from alternative assessments which fail to measure performance on the same standards. The latter, except for the most limited of exceptions discussed in this section, generally conflict with the overarching legal requirements of IDEA and Section 504.)

The student's IEP must include a statement of how the disability affects the child's involvement or progress in the general curriculum; measurable annual goals, including benchmarks or short-term objectives, related to meeting the needs resulting from the disability to enable the child's involvement and progress in that curriculum, and how progress toward those goals will be measured and reported to the parents (including information on the extent to which the progress is sufficient to reach the goals by the end of the year); and the special education, related services, and supplemental aids and services to be provided for purposes of that involvement and progress. Regarding state- or district-wide assessments of achievement, the IEP must include any individual modifications needed in administering the assessments and, if the IEP team determines that the child will not participate in all or part of such an assessment, a statement of why the assessment is not appropriate and how the child will be assessed.[141] The LEA representative on the team developing the IEP must be knowledgeable about the general curriculum, as well as qualified to provide, or supervise, specially designed instruction to meet the unique needs of children with disabilities. One of the team members must be qualified to interpret the instructional implications of evaluation results.[142]

Recognizing changing demographics and increasing proportions of minority populations, and the issues raised for students and staffing,[143] the amendments require, when the various data that the state must report to the federal government reveal significant racial disproportions in identification of children with disabilities or placement in particular educational settings, state review and, if appropriate, revision of the policies, procedures, and practices used to ensure compliance with IDEA.[144]

A new set of state improvement grants are established to identify and address those critical aspects of early intervention, general education, and special education programs that must be improved to enable children with disabilities to meet the state's performance goals. The state's improvement plan, which must be integrated to the maximum extent possible with state plans under ESEA (including Title I) and the Rehabilitation Act of 1973, and must be revised based on assessment of progress toward the state's performance goals, describes how the state will: change state policies and procedures to address systemic barriers to improving these children's results; hold LEAs and schools account- able for these children's educational progress; provide technical assistance to LEAs and schools to improve such results; and address the identified needs for inservice and preservice preparation to ensure that all personnel (including those in general education) working with such children have the skills and knowledge to meet their needs. At least 75 percent of the grant must be used for ensuring such sufficient personnel or for working with other states on common certification criteria (or at least 50 percent if the state demonstrates it already has such personnel).[145]

The specific references in the IDEA amendments to performance goals, assessments, and the general curriculum do not displace, but instead must be read in tandem with, the overarching legal standards in IDEA and Section 504.[146] While the amendments clearly call for inclusion in these activities to the maximum extent appropriate, the overarching legal standards—on non-dis- crimination, free appropriate public education (FAPE), and least restrictive environment (LRE), for example—provide meaning to "maximum extent appropriate." Reliance on "whatever the IEP says" for guidance on the appro- priateness of including a child, with individual assistance to the extent needed, in the regular curriculum or in the regular assessment, will only replicate the history of lower expectations discussed above and noted by Congress,[147] unless and until IEP teams rigorously apply those overarching standards. In the vast majority of cases, any setting of lower goals, exclusion from any portion of the regular curriculum or regular assessment,[148] or any placement in a lower "regular" program track that does not teach to the standards expected for all— instead of providing the assistance and accommodation needed for the child to meet those goals and fully participate—constitutes discrimination on the basis of disability and denial of FAPE in the least restrictive environment. Again, the exception is only in the narrowest of circumstances, where a student with the most severe cognitive disabilities is clearly proven through objective, profes- sional evaluation to be unable, even with full assistance and accommodation, to fully reach those goals or fully participate or to show any level of mastery on an assessment, in which case the exclusion and provision of alternative goals, curricula, or assessment must still be carefully tailored to be the least restrictive departure from the mainstream.

Other, standards-oriented federal laws also make explicit provision for students with disabilities. Title I requires, for example, that, in assessing the performance of all students, reasonable adaptations and accommodations for students with diverse learning needs, necessary to measure their achievement relative to the state standards, be made;[149] that results be disaggregated, including by students with disabilities;[150] that district and school services for these students be coordinated with Title I;[151] and that they be eligible for Title I services on the same basis as other children.[152] Under the Perkins Act, students with disabilities constitute a "special population," guaranteed equal access, nondiscrimination, individualized determination, provision of the supplemental services needed for successful participation, and annual local evaluation (with representatives of the population) to identify and take steps to remove barriers resulting in unequal rates of participation or success (see section II.C.3.a). Both Goals 2000 and the School-to-Work Opportunities Act focus heavily on inclusion of "all children" and specifically include children with disabilities in the definition of that term.

5. CIVIL RIGHTS LAWS

The Civil Rights Acts protect students against discrimination by recipients of federal aid on the basis of race and national origin, sex, or disability.[153] Central to these acts is protection against assumptions, differences in treatment, or practices with disparate impact, when those assumptions, treatment differences, or practices have not been sufficiently justified.[154] This provides an important lens for looking at differences in educational outcomes among groups of students. The two examples below highlight this analysis.

a. Tracking and Similar Practices The common practice of creating tracks for students within the regular program, based upon purported differences in student ability, illustrates the connection between these civil rights laws and the increased focus on higher student achievement standards. These tracks can take the form of separate classes within a school (e.g., college-prep, vocational, and general tracks within a high school), separate but relatively permanent groupings within a single classroom (e.g., the "hawks" and the "sparrows"), or separate schools (e.g., magnet or exam schools). In some cases, the tracks may not be acknowledged by, or even self-evident to, the school staff but are nevertheless quite apparent to the students and observable by researchers.[155] In the low tracks, students typically receive a watered-down curriculum taught at a slower rate, in which teachers' expectations for students are often more focused on good behavior than on academic mastery or intellectual inquiry.[156] As a result, these students fall further and further behind their peers.

Where racial minorities are overrepresented in the low tracks, the relevant legal inquiry under Title VI focuses on the relation between the nature of the education in those tracks and the student selection methods. *If* the program in the low tracks were enriched and accelerated, so that students selected were effectively helped to catch up and achieve academic mastery, the relevant inquiry would be largely limited to whether the students selected are those who can benefit from this arrangement—those who need extra help in reaching the standards set for all.[157] In contrast, when the low tracks do not teach the same skills and knowledge taught to other students, then the practice can be justified as nondiscriminatory only if the school could clearly demonstrate that the selection mechanisms identify just those students who are simply, and permanently, incapable of mastering or benefitting from the curriculum made available to others. Otherwise, the system consigns certain students to a lesser curriculum on the basis of race and without adequate justification. The grades, teacher recommendations, tests, and other methods typically used to select students for low tracks cannot meet that criterion—again except for students with the most severe mental disabilities.[158]

Thus, educators—whether in the courtroom or in the preventive context of designing a program that is equitable and effective—must look carefully at both the educational programs to which students are assigned and the mechanisms used to assign them, to see whether the match is legally sufficient. First, in terms of the programs to which students are assigned: Are the programs (their curriculum, pedagogy, staffing, etc.) designed to enable the students with the identified characteristics to meet the standards, taking into account the need for accelerated progress for those who start out further behind? The application of Title I, Goals 2000, and state standards to this inquiry could help reduce the risk—present in the pre-standards tracking cases—of a battle of the experts in which the court simply shrugs and defers to whatever the school system asserts in the face of a difference of opinion the court feels incapable of resolving. The question moves beyond a relatively vague inquiry into whether the program is good or "appropriate" to whether it effectively incorporates instruction in the particular standards that have been identified as applicable to all students, including the elements of instruction identified in the school-level provisions of

Title I (and any state requirements)—areas in which disagreements of experts should narrow, at least in regard to low-track programs obviously not aimed at the same standards other students are expected to attain, or not as rich and intensive, in relation to those standards, as the programs in which minorities are underrepresented.

The second area of inquiry for educators involves analyzing what the selection mechanisms are capable of, and validated for, measuring—*in relation to* what the programs are actually providing.[159] It is a grave injustice to consign any student to a program which, by its very nature, ensures that she or he will not master the skills and knowledge in the standards for "all students" in the absence of clear proof that the student is incapable, with extra assistance, of learning those things. When that mistake is made systematically in ways that disproportionately impact students on the basis of race, the injustice is compounded. Thus, this is an area where the ability of educational experts to recognize the distinction between assessing a student's current achievement and making judgments about that student's permanent and fixed capacity to learn is especially important.

b. Language Programs for Students with Limited English Proficiency Students are entitled to affirmative steps designed to overcome the barriers to learning caused by limited English proficiency, under both Title VI of the 1964 Civil Rights Act[160] and the Equal Educational Opportunities Act of 1974.[161] A three-part quality-oriented test has emerged for evaluating the sufficiency of language programs for LEP students under these two statutes.[162] First, the program must be based on an educational approach that is supported by research. Second, steps must be taken to implement that approach effectively. Third, after a legitimate trial period, the program must either be shown to work or be modified toward that end.

The independent emergence of new state and local education standards should strengthen and add precision to this legal standard.[163] Programs for LEP students can be assessed in terms of whether they are designed to teach, have the resources to teach, and over time are in fact successful in actually teaching those skills and knowledge.

The Bilingual Education Act (BEA)[164] was rewritten in 1994 to help LEP children and youth meet the same rigorous academic standards expected of all, including the State content and performance standards required under Title I.[165] Unlike Title VI and EEOA, which apply to all recipients of federal funds, the BEA reaches only as far as its funding—at least 75 percent of which must be used for bilingual programs which make instructional use of both English and the student's native language, enabling LEP students to achieve English proficiency and academic mastery of subject matter content and higher order skills.

Federal laws oriented to standards-based reform also make specific provision for the education of students with limited English proficiency. Title I—which actually serves a much larger number of LEP students than the BEA—requires, for example, adequate yearly progress for LEP students sufficient for all to reach proficient and advanced levels, along with inclusion of all LEP students in performance assessments, which must, to the extent practicable, be in the language and form that will most reliably measure their achievement.[166] Under the Perkins Act, LEP students constitute a "special population," with the same guarantees for access and services discussed for students with disabilities, above.[167] Both Goals 2000 and the School-to-Work Opportunities Act focus heavily on inclusion of "all children" and specifically include children with limited English proficiency in the definition of that term.

D. Federal Constitutional Standards

The claims above, relying on state law and federal statutory law, may render federal constitutional argument unnecessary. Nevertheless, claims under the equal protection clause and due process clause of the Fourteenth Amendment can be made using a similar analysis. Despite the optimism that lies behind both the federal education agenda that passed between 1990 and 1994 and the raft of state reform packages, we may be entering a period in which reliance on the Constitution becomes more important again—in light of (a) possible judicial, legislative, and administrative weakening of the ability to enforce federal law that is not based on civil rights, and (b) the potential for state budgetary problems to weaken state mandates.[168]

I. EQUAL PROTECTION

The presence of new standards for student achievement as well as clearer standards or duties for educators in enabling achievement could add considerable vigor to equal protection claims.[169]

First, unjustified assumptions about selected student groups' ability to learn, which emerge when the content of their educational programs is compared with academic standards for all students, may satisfy the requirement of showing discriminatory intent in order to establish a suspect classification meriting strict scrutiny under the equal protection clause[170] (in contrast to the effects standard under federal civil rights laws[171] and some state equal protection clauses). Discriminatory intent requirements would also be satisfied by show-ing that students' current placement in inferior programs with weaker curricula is in part the result of *prior* intentional discrimination, such as the students' prior attendance in an intentionally segregated system.[172]

Second, the Court in *San Antonio Independent School District v. Rodriguez* left open the possibility of showing that provision to some students, and denial to others, of the skills and knowledge needed for exercising other constitutional rights of citizenship, such as voting, regardless of intent, could burden funda-mental rights and trigger heightened equal protection scrutiny.[173] The public statements accompanying adoption of higher academic standards are at least an indication of new social and governmental consensus about the skills and knowledge needed for effective exercise of fundamental rights.[174]

Third, placement of students in programs that, by their very nature and content, cannot result in mastery of state-articulated education goals, without a rational basis for determining that these students are incapable of achieving those goals, may constitute an equal protection claim even under restrained, rational relationship review.[175]

2. DUE PROCESS

Involuntary placement of students by the state in a program not designed to provide the skills that the state has articulated as the purpose of compulsory education could be viewed as a deprivation of liberty without due process of law, analogous to *Successful School Restructuring* right-to-treatment cases.[176] Here again, success would appear to depend on a clear contrast between state achievement standards and the content of the program.

In addition, after the state or school district has identified the standards all students are expected to meet, students can claim liberty and property interests in an educational program that teaches those things—interests students cannot then be deprived of without due process.[177] Placement in a program that does not teach to those standards, in the absence of proof that the students are not capable of mastering the very things that the state has said all children can and should master, would seem to fail the test of fundamental fairness that is part of substantive due process.[178]

Probably the most important federal constitutional claim, however, rests on a different due process analysis. It is fundamentally unfair to condition educa-tional decisions with high stakes for students on demonstrating mastery of educational content that the students have not had an adequate opportunity to learn. Thus, the court in *Debra P. v. Turlington* held that Florida could not require passage of a minimum competency test for high school graduation until a sufficient period had passed for students to prepare to meet the new standards and for schools to align their curricula and instruction with those standards, so that it was a fair test of what was actually taught.[179] While the remedial focus in *Debra P.* was on overturning diploma denials, remedies could also focus directly on ensuring that students received an education adequate to master the standards.

This last approach, while very powerful, has one condition. It works only where the education system seeks to impose high stakes (such as diploma denial or nonpromotion) on the student for failing to meet the standards. The other statutory and constitutional claims described above are in this sense more intrinsic—the right to education that they posit can be asserted regardless of whether the state imposes additional punishment for failure to obtain it.

III. THE NATURE OF LEGAL AND EDUCATIONAL ACCOUNTABILITY

Each of the reform elements in this section—the development of standards, the design of a plan to reach the standards, the implementation of that plan, assessment of its results, and follow-up action—presents enormous opportunities for proactive collaboration among lawyers, educators, and parents. Focusing on the nature of students' rights to a high-quality education from the vantage point of enforcement—and the nature of the potential legal claims when students are denied a good education—is also critical, however, for several reasons.

First, in at least some places, it is only after such claims have been asserted and get some publicity that these rights will be fully secured. Second, in light of the analysis that began this chapter—of the need to unite legal authority and educational expertise with parents' desires for their children's education—a crucial engine for reform is community education of parents and school staff about children's rights, in terms concrete enough for them to understand when those rights are denied. Third, as we will see, the nature of these legal claims reveals something important about standards-based reform and helps us avoid oversimplifying the reform process.

A. Nature of Claims

Few would argue for a pure individual outcomes model for legal claims arising under these various laws, in which failure to "produce" a student who meets performance standards is in itself a violation of a legal duty to the student.[180] Commonly articulated as a basis for explaining current state and federal reforms, however, is the notion that we stop regulating processes and inputs; instead, we should hold schools "accountable for results." While perhaps not a legal guarantee of proficiency to each student, this perspective does trigger enforcement activity based on student assessment results and, in the case of Title I, specifically on whether there is yearly progress adequate to achieve the goal of all students reaching proficient and advanced levels of performance (see section II.C.2).

To say that outcomes are now being regulated *instead of* process and inputs, however, is a vast oversimplification of Title I and similar efforts. Even if all goes as planned, outcome-based sanctions tied to high performance standards for failing schools will not have to be imposed for roughly ten years—the time needed to develop content and performance standards, develop and validate new assessments, generate multiple years of comparable data for assessing progress toward the standards, planning for improvements where progress is not adequate, assessing the results of those improvements, and only then moving toward sanctions.

Imagine, then, a state that has adopted an ambitious definition of adequate yearly progress. If the teeth of Title I consisted only of outcome-based enforcement, then a parent who complained that his child was not learning might be told, "Don't worry. In ten years, we're going to take action against the school if it isn't decreasing by 5 percent the proportion of students in fourth grade who are not proficient."[181] To a parent whose child may not be in the fourth grade now, most certainly won't be in ten years, and, in any event, even in ten years might not be among the extra 5 percent who are becoming proficient, such an answer won't do. The point is not that this timeline or standard for adequate yearly progress is too lax. Rather, it reveals a problem with relying solely on an outcome-based enforcement system.

There are other difficulties. Overreliance on outcome-based enforcement is likely to produce distortions and incentives for counterproductive tactics. If all students are to achieve proficiency, those who are further behind must make more rapid progress (part of the notion of "accelerated curriculum" in Title I), so schools with higher proportions of such students will have to show greater gains in order to make adequate yearly progress. The notion of equal gains or average gains for those who are further behind (underlying the NCE concept of the former Chapter 1) is no longer acceptable under Title I. If this accelerated responsibility is viewed primarily as a sanction, then high-poverty schools will feel they are being punished for serving a more disadvantaged student body. The existing dangers of distortion (such as watering down the standards, "teaching to the test," excluding low-achieving students from the assessment results, encouraging students to drop out, and so on) are likely to increase. Thus, it is important to focus attention primarily on planning and implementing good programs up front and cooperative steps for improvement where results are not adequate, triggering additional resources and assistance, with outcome-based enforcement measures reserved for breakdowns. Meeting the minimum level of adequate yearly improvement needed to avoid outside intervention should be the by-product of implementing a good plan for all students to meet the standards, not the educational goal of the school in itself.

Another problem arises from focusing on "results" without also focusing on the kinds of program components needed to produce good results. This is likely to lead to a lack of knowledge, capacity, and focus in program design; a tendency to sit on one's hands, allowing ineffective programs to continue to run as they have always run, for the several years it will take to produce consistent, reliable data under new assessment systems;[182] and even once a program has been identified as ineffective, a lack of focus in the improvement process—that is, inability to identify the program elements leading to the poor results.[183]

In fact, Title I (and most of the other laws discussed in section II above) is far more than a promise to impose rewards and sanctions for student performance. It has a structured set of requirements for developing programs designed to produce the desired levels of performance.

I. AN INTEGRATED, OUTCOME-ORIENTED, HYBRID MODEL

In general, the legal claims discussed in section II primarily focus neither on specific instructional practices nor on a specific educational outcome. Rather, their main focus is most often on required process, but it is an *outcome*-oriented process (and an input-sensitive one).

For example, under Title I, it is not a violation per se to fail to produce the requisite level of student achievement. It *is* a violation to fail to take the requisite steps designed to reach that level, such as identifying standards for all children, aligning an accelerated curriculum and effective instructional strategies with those standards, devoting resources of sufficient size, scope, and quality—including a highly qualified instructional staff, staff development, and tailored help for students having difficulty—toward that end, and evaluating the program on that basis. It is also a violation to fail to take the required improvement actions when the evaluation shows that the requisite amount of progress has not been made (see section II.C.2).

The distinctions here, however, should not be overdrawn. Ultimately, under Title I, states will impose sanctions on schools and districts that fail to make adequate progress.[184] Before that step, Title I also requires that failing schools and LEAs develop or revise plans "in ways that have the greatest likelihood of improving the performance of participating children in meeting the State's student performance standards,"[185] thereby bringing the focus closer to particular, research-established practices. At an even more specific level, certain practices may eventually become incorporated into legal standards. For example, the professional standards issued by the National Council of Teachers of Mathematics have gained widespread support.[186] Aside from their potential for achieving a professional status similar to the accepted standards of good medical practice (see section III.A.2), such teaching standards may be directly incorporated into future formal state education standards.

The framework that emerges under the various bodies of law discussed in section II parallels the framework for school reform in section I.C. It links achievement goals for all students to responsibilities for designing a program to reach those goals (or scrutiny of programs not designed to achieve them), marshaling adequate resources for carrying out that design, evaluating progress toward the goals, and intervening in programs that are not reaching them, along with (in some cases) efforts to give parents and others new ways to help shape these steps. It generally does not mandate specific curricula or instructional techniques,[187] but it does provide a framework for applying important research[188] and for choosing and implementing curriculum and instruction appropriate to achieving the required goals.

At the broadest level, the mandates of law thus capture the essence of the educational process—deciding on goals, thinking through what those goals mean and how to get there, implementing the agreed-upon plan, critically examining whether the results are what was intended, and then revising one's actions in light of the results. The law thus asks schools to act like institutions of *education* in addressing their own problems.

a. Failure to Set Outcome Standards Properly Failure to develop and adopt a uniform and sufficiently high set of content and performance standards would run afoul of many state statutory requirements, state constitutional guarantees, the mandates of key federal programs (starting with Goals 2000 and Title I), and, arguably, the equal protection clause. With virtually all states undertaking this effort, legal claims are more likely to focus on (a) failure to meet statutory or court-ordered deadlines for adoption; (b) failure to go through the mandated processes for development, including failure to include those with expertise in the needs of various populations; or (c) setting standards that are too low,[189] are too vague,[190] or allow the continuation of unequal expectations for different localities or groups of students.[191] These problems are linked: if standards for all students are set low or defined very loosely, they are likely to be a cover of false uniformity hiding great inequalities. Vague standards will prompt widely varying and unequal local interpretations, while low standards will prompt some districts, but not others, to supplement them.[192]

Failures in setting standards properly may also arise at the level of the individual program or individual student—such as when a program for specific groups of children (e.g., LEP or homeless students) or the individualized plan for a student with disabilities sets goals without proper connection to the outcomes adopted for all students (see sections II.C.4 and II.C.5).

b. Inadequate Program Design to Reach the Standards Program design is where federal and state statutes, and the mandates that emerge from constitutional and civil rights case law, are often most descriptive. Failures subject to legal challenge can emerge in any of three broad forms.

First, when a program's design is described in vague generalities, or when a required program description is little more than a statement that a plan will later be developed (e.g., a declaration that certain parties will meet to figure it out), then no one can determine whether that design meets the requirements of the law. While there may be no single right form for an adequate description of a program component, and there may be disagreements about how specific a plan needs to be, it ought to say concretely what will be done, when, how, and by whom. State and local program plans often fail this basic test.[193]

Second, the adequacy of program design components, once sufficiently described, may be challenged under the various legal principles in section II. These plans might previously have received rather restrained scrutiny—as to whether they had the support of any reasonable theory supported by at least some experts.[194] More recent developments, however, should now sharpen the scrutiny: the presence of clear content and performance standards, so that the question is not whether the program will provide some educational benefit to students but whether it is at least reasonably tailored to enabling all students to achieve proficiency on those standards (again, a critical question for looking at low tracks); the requirements for specific program components found in federal and state statutory law;[195] and greater research-based consensus about at least some elements of school reform. Research also indicates that neglecting to align programs with the achievement goals is often the norm in schools.[196]

Third, the adequacy of participation of key stakeholders in the program design is subject to challenge under the various planning requirements of state and federal law.[197]

c. Failure to Implement the Program Design Assuming an adequate plan (or absent specific planning requirements), implementation problems may be subject to a variety of challenges. This is particularly important in light of recent findings that good strategies for educating disadvantaged students are successful only when rigorously implemented.[198]

First, poor implementation may be challenged as a violation of the direct implementation requirements of the laws themselves—in other words, regardless of what may or may not be in a plan, the school, district, or state is not in fact taking the steps required by the law.[199]

Second, failure to follow an approved plan may be the basis for a challenge.[200] This avenue can become important in short-circuiting some legal disputes about whether a particular approach is necessary to meet a statute's requirements. The primary forum for such disputes should not be the courts but the initial planning process set out in the law, in which state or local stakeholders hammer out the design. Having decided on a path, however, they are then responsible for following it—and that responsibility is enforceable in the courts if necessary.

Third, under some mandates, adequate implementation may include application of research and adoption of "best practices."[201] The law may require, for example, that a program be of sufficient size, scope, and quality to achieve program goals.[202] Such a requirement can be interpreted in light of available information about the program's success to date[203] and research findings from elsewhere. Similarly, adequacy of implementation means more than finding the standards "covered" somewhere in the curriculum but demands attention to quality, depth, and approach[204] sufficient to permit mastery—in the classroom, not merely on paper.

Fourth, the question of whether the resources devoted to the program are adequate—taking into account variations in need—is open to legal analysis under state constitutional law (see section II.B and chapter 3), as well as provisions in statutory law, again such as "size, scope, and quality" requirements. This means money.[205]

It also means a staff that is well prepared to teach the program effectively. A massive reorientation to a much higher, more challenging set of standards, through radically different curriculum and instructional methods, will not work unless teachers unaccustomed to teaching in that way are given substantial assistance and training regarding both new subject matter and new ways to teach, including the ability to meet the needs of diverse populations and to relate to the community and families which the school serves; and that in turn requires a much more active and sustained approach to staff development, integrated into the fabric of the school day, than the limited, fragmented, passive approach teachers often experience.[206] In addition to the general legal standards in section II for judging the adequacy of staff resources, some of the reform mandates now make quite specific reference to the quality and intensity of required staff development efforts.[207]

d. Failures in Assessment Inadequate assessment of progress and student achievement in relation to the standards is subject to challenge, for example, under Goals 2000, Title I, Perkins and School-to-Work, IDEA (for individual students with disabilities), the EEOA (for programs serving LEP students), and state law. Further, where the assessments have a significant impact on students and that impact is disproportionate in terms of race, national origin, gender, or disability, there is an obligation to demonstrate that the assessments are valid and reliable for the purposes (and with the populations) for which they are being used, and that those purposes are legitimate.

Inadequacies subject to challenge may show up in the assessment design— for example, not developing valid and reliable measures of extent of student mastery of the skills and knowledge in the standards; not developing and adopting valid criteria for establishing a particular cut-off score for "proficiency;" not validating the assessment for the various populations for which it will be used; or relying on a single measure where multiple measures are required. An obvious case is continued use of norm-referenced tests that have not been validated for determining criterion-referenced proficiency on new, higher standards. Inadequacies may also show up in implementation—such as failures in accommodation or adaptation to ensure the assessments' accuracy as applied to particular students with disabilities or limited English proficiency; purposeful or unintentional exclusion of certain students from the assessment process;[208] irregularities that make the requisite comparisons (for example, between years) impossible; or failure to meet requirements for disseminating results, along with information and assistance in understanding them, to parents, teachers, and others.[209]

While less apparent to the public than the state and district systems of uniform student assessment, the ongoing tasks that students are asked to perform in classrooms—whether on teacher-constructed exams, papers, or projects—form another level of student assessment critical to the success or failure of school reform. Indeed, these ongoing assessment tasks, by defining students' classroom work, are a central part of curriculum and instruction (see section I.D). Aside from efforts to apply legal standards to these assessments,[210] they form a central body of evidence, for parents and others, as to whether required reforms are being successfully implemented. Reviewing student assignments, assessment tasks, and work is among the best ways to tell whether students are being asked to focus on the knowledge and skills found in challenging standards, and how well they are doing.

e. Failure to Take Required Steps When Outcomes Are Unsatisfactory Failure to make appropriate use of assessment results to improve programs and services has been common.[211] However, requirements to do so—through improvement plans, extra assistance from the state or other outside sources, or, ultimately, coercive action to change the schools or the personnel—are now well articulated in state reform statutes, federal program law (including Title I[212] and Perkins[213]), and case law.[214] Both the adequacy of the improvement steps and the process through which they were developed may be subject to challenge.

Properly defining the point at which inadequate performance triggers required improvement is also key. Under Title I, states must define it in terms of enough yearly progress for all students actually to reach proficient and advanced levels of achievement.[215] This stands in stark contrast to the minimal standard to which states and localities had long been accustomed—*any* improvement in yearly scores on standardized tests, under which many students would never approach proficiency on challenging standards. This contrast from past practice, along with the political pressures against identifying "too many" schools for program improvement, suggests potential implementation failures which may need to be challenged.

f. Failure in Other Forms of Monitoring and Enforcement As noted at the beginning of this section (on the nature of claims) and throughout this essay, there is a tendency to assume that, in an outcome-oriented system, there is only monitoring and enforcement of outcomes. As also discussed, this is a serious misreading.[216] For the reasons noted above, accountability *in the present* for planning and implementing programs that conform to basic quality-oriented requirements and ensure that students have real opportunities to achieve those outcomes is critical to success *for the future*—such as the setting of standards, the development of core programs, the development of staff capacity, the devotion of adequate resources, the establishment of effective parent participation mechanisms, etc.

In legal terms, the new responsibilities for monitoring student outcomes supplements, rather than replaces, state[217] and federal[218] responsibilities for monitoring and, where necessary, enforcing the basic programmatic requirements of the law. As discussed in sections I.F and I.G, gaps in this monitoring and enforcement are widespread, to say the least, and need to be highlighted and challenged. This is particularly important since those who stand to gain or lose most from the success or failure of standards-based reform—children and their parents, especially those who are disadvantaged—are also disadvantaged in their power to make these reforms happen on their own.

2. THE ROLE OF PROFESSIONAL TEACHING STANDARDS

a. Current Status Efforts to develop discipline-based standards for teachers and other education professionals are also changing the landscape in which claims to high-quality education may be asserted.[219] Numerous state statutes, many of long standing, establish minimum levels of teacher proficiency.[220] Some statutes also establish professional teacher standards commissions.[221]

Standards may come from subject-matter professional groups. The National Council of Teachers of Mathematics has created, in addition to curriculum and evaluation standards, a widely respected, and increasingly widely used, set of professional standards for teaching mathematics. In addition, a set of related national initiatives are being linked to cover accreditation standards for institutions preparing teachers, licensing standards for new and early-career teachers, and board certification standards for experienced teachers.

The National Board for Professional Teaching Standards (NBPTS) was established, in the wake of three highly publicized 1986 reports,[222] "to establish high and rigorous standards for what accomplished teachers should know and be able to do, to develop and operate a national voluntary system to assess and certify teachers who meet these standards, and to advance related education reforms for the purpose of improving student learning in American schools."[223] Committees of classroom teachers, teacher educators, and subject experts are creating standards in more than thirty fields (such as early childhood/generalist or adolescence and young adulthood/science), subject to final approval by the board. Performance-based assessments are the basis for teachers applying for national board certification. NBPTS describes its standards as symbols of teaching excellence for experienced teachers, in contrast to entry-level standards set by state licensing systems.[224] The standards are based on five core propositions—that accomplished teachers:

1. are committed to students and their learning (and understand how students develop and learn and act on the belief that all can learn);
2. know the subjects they teach, and how to teach those subjects to students (and are adept at creating multiple paths to the subjects, teaching students how to pose and solve their own problems, and developing their students' critical and analytical capacities);
3. are responsible for managing and monitoring student learning (creating, enriching, maintaining, and altering instructional settings to capture and sustain students' interest, make the most effective use of time, and allow the school's goals for students to be met; being as aware of ineffectual or damaging practice as they are devoted to elegant practice; and assessing, and clearly explaining to parents, individual and classroom-wide progress through multiple measures);
4. think systematically about their practice and learn from experience (serving as models of the virtues and intellectual capacities they seek to nurture, such as reasoning, creatively taking multiple perspectives, and adopting an experimental and problem-solving orientation—using knowledge of human development, subject matter and instruction, and their understanding of their students, grounded in findings, theories, and ideas from the literature and in their own experience); and
5. are members of learning communities (working collaboratively with other professionals and parents on making the whole school more effective and tapping school and community resources for the benefit of their teaching and their students).[225]

The Interstate New Teacher Assessment and Support Consortium, involving more than thirty states, has developed ten core standards—with knowledge, dispositions, and performances for each—similar to NBPTS, but for beginning teacher licensing and development.[226] INTASC also developed standards for beginning mathematics teachers in 1995. INTASC standards are the basis for initial license tests and for performance assessments during the first two years of supervised teaching to be used for granting a continuing license.

The Interstate School Leaders Licensure Consortium has similarly adopted six standards—along with knowledge, disposition, and performance indicators—for licensing school administrators.[227]

The National Council for Accreditation of Teacher Education (NCATE) has developed quality standards for accrediting postsecondary teacher preparation schools, departments, and colleges.[228] Many states are moving to ensure that new teachers graduate from NCATE-accredited programs in order to be certified.

The National Commission on Teaching and America's Future is pushing for greater state and local use of such professional standards so that by the year 2006, "we will provide every student in America with what should be his educational birthright: access to competent, caring, qualified teaching in schools organized for success."[229] Among its recommendations are that professional standards boards be established in every state; teachers and principals be licensed, hired, and retained based on their ability to meet professional standards of practice and incompetent teachers be removed; NBPTS standards be the benchmark for accomplished teaching; all teacher education programs be organized around standards for students and teachers and either meet professional accreditation standards or be closed; and other steps be taken to improve recruitment, staff development, teacher incentives, and school organization.

The existence of these standards for teachers, administrators, and programs, alongside structures for student-outcome-based reform, raises two possibilities for legal advocacy. First, they may resurrect the question of a viable tort action of "educational malpractice," analogous to malpractice claims against doctors or lawyers. Second, they have implications for the other legal claims discussed in this chapter.

b. Potential Emergence of Malpractice Standards Past efforts to sue school officials for educational malpractice were both unsuccessful and relatively rare in comparison to the numbers of students affected by poor practice.[230]

In most of these cases, one or more of the necessary components of a negligence action were found missing—a duty of care, a breach of that duty, an injury, and establishment of the breach as a proximate cause of the injury. In the end, though, that conclusion was based on public policy grounds.

Those policy grounds may now be shifting toward countenancing liability, given the emergence of professional standards, public policy pronouncements that all students can and must meet challenging standards, and a more general concern about the high cost of school failure, to both individual and society. Moreover, these changes may satisfy each of the required elements of a negligence action: the emergence of professional standards, together with obligations under standards-based education laws, may provide sufficient clarity to establish a duty and criteria for whether it is breached. The establishment of new assessments for measuring proficiency, together with public policy pronouncements about the unacceptable nature of failing to attain the proficiency standards, may provide a clearer, more consensual notion of injury. Those same pronouncements that, properly taught, children will achieve, together with research establishing the impact of good educational practice on achievement, should help establish causation.[231] Causation is, in any event, relatively obvious in those cases where the school program clearly fails to focus on the content and skills addressed in the standards.

Policy arguments about the danger of putting public fiscal resources in jeopardy also seem less convincing, particularly in instances of long-term breach of educational duties resulting in injuries to children that cannot otherwise be fully compensated.[232] The public has strong interests in assuring high-quality education, avoiding these harms, and ensuring that its resources are not wasted on failing programs and practices.

This approach is not suggested lightly, but it deserves at least exploration—considering the harms and the comparison with medicine (see section I.G), which suggests that few other approaches may be as effective in making professionals aware of and responsible for following accepted standards of practice. In any event, courts and legislatures that conclude that damages are not the best remedy for the harm can fashion other forms of relief.

c. Use of Professional Standards with Other Laws Regardless of whether independent malpractice tort actions gain recognition, the emergence of professional standards will certainly be relevant in shaping educational rights under the other state and federal laws discussed in this essay. For example, Title I requires instruction by "highly qualified" staff (see section II.C.2), on which NBPTS can be informative. The content of various of the professional standards may be helpful in clarifying the extent of student access to good teaching and qualified staff from the perspective of students' rights to a high-quality program under state constitutional law, stark disparities in that access under civil rights laws, the adequacy of interventions required for particular groups of students or for programs that are not succeeding, and so on.

3. THE IMPORTANCE OF PARTICIPATORY PROCESS AND PLANNING

The fact that what ultimately seems enforceable is often process—development and implementation of plans (along with equalization of inputs, taking into account differing needs)—highlights the need to ensure that the process is participatory. Requirements for involvement of parents, students, teachers, or community members in decision-making exist, for example, in Title I, the Perkins and School-to-Work vocational acts, IDEA, and the Bilingual Education Act.[233] The 1994 Title I provisions for parents to develop plans, policies, and compacts jointly with the school and district are particularly noteworthy (see section II.C.2). These requirements, often treated cavalierly, should be seriously implemented, improved, and extended as an important adjunct to other forms of monitoring and enforcement. Practical and political limits of substantive enforcement by higher state or federal agencies are at least a current reality. Further, an emerging, more sophisticated consensus about the desired outcomes (active, higher-order thinking and decision-making skills), the complex nature of human learning and development, and the nature of successful school change (including establishment of an active and intentional learning community of teachers and students) also poses limits on mechanical notions of enforcement.[234]

In view of these limits, those at the local level who have a stake in positive outcomes—particularly parents and students—must be empowered, with information and authority, to be at the table, deciding on the desired outcomes, seeing that the mandated processes are followed, and seeking remedies when they are not.[235] This is particularly important in communities where educators may not fully reflect the cultural diversity of their clients.

If the new Title I and other federal programs are to work, federal policy must be far better understood and embraced at the local level, changing the culture of "plans" and "planning." Planning can no longer consist of the federal programs director in the central office filling out an application for funds. It must become an informed, active process of teachers and parents grappling with what high standards means in their school, what stands in the way, and what needs to be done.

Research supports the positive impact of parent involvement in a range of roles in the school, including decision-making, on student achievement.[236] For ineffective schools that are not structured to provide high-quality instruction in their core programs, however, the question is not whether parent involvement is an effective component of an effective overall reform program, but what can parents do, working with others, to obtain an effective program for their children? In this setting, and given the limited expectations for top-down enforcement, being an effective advocate for your children (and others') is a critical role. Many wealthy parents take it for granted that they can and should play that role, and schools respond when parents intervene.[237] This type of parent activity, of course, is much harder to evaluate through normal research studies.

B. Student Accountability for Standards

I. EDUCATIONAL SANCTIONS AND REWARDS

While federal standards-based reform has focused accountability on schools, districts, and states, a growing number of states and districts are moving toward tying graduation and promotion to success on performance-based assessments connected to new standards—or, in some cases, on older standardized tests not well connected to new standards—in part because of pressure to show their seriousness about reform. As discussed in section II, such actions must pass legal muster: students must have an adequate opportunity to learn the skills and knowledge being tested (and that the assessment results accurately distinguish between students who have and have not mastered those skills and knowledge). Due process, in terms of fundamental fairness, demands this (see section II.D.2). Civil rights law also demands this whenever sanctions would have a disproportionate impact by race, national origin, gender, or disability (see section II.C.5). Yet research indicates that few districts pay attention to whether curriculum and instruction are designed and aligned to provide that opportunity.[238]

The meaning and scope of this "opportunity to learn" should be shaped by the details of the state and federal reform statutes (as well as state constitutional law) that have been evolving, and perhaps by new professional teaching standards as well. State or local failures in various statutory duties that were part of the reform packages connected to new graduation requirements should become more relevant.[239] Further, these developments in the law and in our knowledge about the elements of successful reform should mean that families will be better able to seek remedies that provide the requisite levels of education, not just protection against sanctions (e.g., the granting of diplomas despite low proficiency test scores).[240]

This last is important in countering the charge that, by challenging the use of such tests for sanctions against students who have not been taught, advocates are slowing reform. To the contrary, when "reformers" who call for "raising the bar" brand as antireform those advocates who seek to ensure that the education students actually receive conforms to new standards, it is those who want only to raise the bar whose commitment to reform should be questioned. At the expense of students, they are going after the easy symbols of raising standards but not implementing the substance of reform to meet them.

In fact, this premature use of high-stakes tests puts even those administrators who most want reform in the position of arguing in effect that further reform of assessment, curriculum, or instruction is not really necessary—since the legal defense of the practice requires a demonstration that the tests already measure accurately the desired skills and knowledge and that the curriculum and instruction already teach those skills and knowledge adequately.[241]

Thus, educators and lawyers should instead be collaborating at a much earlier stage outside the courtroom—working together to design and implement the serious reforms that ensure that assessments, curriculum, and instruction adequately reflect and enable mastery of the standards we want for all children. Vigorous application of the legal principles then becomes the ally of reformers within the system—by pushing the questions, and having rigorous, disciplined criteria for the answers, of whether our assessments are really an accurate measure of what we want students to know and be able to do, and whether our curriculum and instruction are really adequate for teaching them to all our students.

2. WORK-RELATED SANCTIONS

As new competency-based standards and assessments are phased in, there is increased possibility that employers will look to them in making hiring decisions. This could happen in at least three ways. First, if assessments are linked to high-school graduation requirements, then employer reliance on a diploma will incorporate the assessment results. Second, if not, employers may look separately to the assessment results. Third, as school-to-work partnerships become the basis for work-based learning opportunities while students are in school (see section II.C.3.b), and as those work-based placements then provide a leg up in seeking post-graduation employment, the possibility arises that the assessments will be used to determine which students get the limited number of placements.

Some education, government, and business leaders are encouraging precisely this development. Few of them are calling attention to the need for employers to comply with civil rights laws before using these assessments in hiring—despite the fact that the key civil rights case in this area was largely about the improper use of a high-school diploma requirement for jobs that were not demonstrated to require the skills represented by that diploma.[242] Indeed, civil rights advocates are likely to be viewed as hindrances to educational reform and economic productivity. In fact, the reverse is true.

The current focus on new education standards poses great opportunity and great dangers for the economic rights and fates of young people. Far too few jobs actually fit the ideal of a high-skill, high-wage economy waiting to employ the talents of a well-educated populace—as demonstrated by the continued growth of low-wage, low-skill jobs.[243] The interaction between historical inequalities and an economy that provides only limited slots for full use of that talent is also evident in the fact that the wage gap has continued to grow over the past thirty years even though educational attainment has become more equal, both among workers as a whole and between white workers and African American and Latino workers.[244]

In the face of the shortage of jobs in the American economy that fully utilize or compensate the higher skills we want our schools to teach, the two most obvious responses are inadequate. On one hand, lowering education standards to the skills demanded by most jobs available would compound the injury of wasted careers with the matching injury of minimal education. On the other hand, allowing employers to use higher educational certification standards, such as tougher graduation requirements, for hiring or promotion when jobs do not in fact demand those skills would unfairly turn away qualified people, in direct violation of Title VII of the 1964 Civil Rights Act, banning employment discrimination.[245]

A third path is needed—one that embraces high standards for education but is careful about their use for employment purposes. From this point of view, civil rights law can and must be seen as an engine of economic growth and efficiency, not an obstacle. It tells employers that the problems of the economy cannot be blamed on students and workers, or shifted to the schools, inadequate as the schools may be. It tells them that pretending to have a high-skills workplace, and screening out people on that basis, is not enough. Instead, before using these standards for employment decisions, they must actually have a high-skills workplace that actually utilizes and values the learning we want our schools to foster. Employers' demonstrating that they have such a workplace as a condition of partnership with the schools, whether for student work placements or for purposes of using educational certification requirements, is both a legal requirement and a significant stimulus for eliminating the waste of human talent that limits our society.

CONCLUSION: COLLABORATING TO SCALE

Obviously, lawyers and educators can meet in the courtroom, where research and expert testimony are needed to adjudicate claims that students have been denied their rights to high-quality education. Indeed, given the extent of denial of those rights, there are strong arguments for many more such meetings. There are, however, critical opportunities for collaboration at earlier stages that may avoid the need for litigation.

The first question about such collaboration is whether it will take the high road or the low road to reducing litigation. Educators and lawyers can work together to make standards unenforceable, using vague and obfuscatory educational language on the one side and drafting legislative and regulatory clauses that deny enforcement rights on the other. Or they can work together to articulate what students are entitled to, and to ensure that those entitlements are well understood by school professionals, parents, students, and the wider community. In this process, a key role for educators is in taking seriously the claim, embodied in the push for new standards, that all students can and must learn.

If the high road is chosen, there are several places along the way for this collaboration: (1) the standard-setting process; (2) state planning, including steps to ensure the real adequacy of state solicitation and review of local plans; (3) local planning, including integration of special population issues with program quality improvements; (4) program assessment design; and (5) monitoring and enforcement.

As the standards-based reform movement has promoted the rhetoric of "all children" achieving at high levels, we are haunted by the sense of how far we are from strategies for "going to scale" at a level sufficient to reach that result, and humbled by the limited impact of past efforts.[246] Our tendency to seek out, study, and celebrate the exceptions to the norm teaches us much about the practices and structures that support high-level learning. But it probably doesn't teach us much about going to scale, since these are most often schools that changed through an unusual amount of dedication, vision, and extraordinarily long hours on the part of a small number of individuals, in the face of resistant conditions.[247] Instead, it feeds the belief in "exceptionalism" that is antithetical to going to scale.

In a sense, this parallels traditional attitudes about student achievement: having organized our schools and our society in a way that is not supportive of many children's learning and development, we then focus on figuring out why a few stars succeed in the face of hostile conditions and developing theories of personal pathology about the rest—instead of working to change the conditions that make success so difficult.

It also teaches misleading lessons about the role of policy, since most successful individual school reformers have, in the context of a hostile environment, experienced policy as something they needed to get around in order to succeed. From within their own experience, freedom from external policy creates the possibility of change. Yet leaving schools alone is clearly not a prescription for successful reform on a scale that goes beyond those schools with the drive and know-how to implement reform; instead, it reproduces the current situation.

This chapter began with the need to overcome the isolation of desire, knowledge, and authority—for example, the isolation of parents who want quality education from the knowledge of educators who understand some of the keys to providing it and from the legal authority that requires it. From this, we can derive a parallel set of three strategies that run through this chapter and that, if united, can help take us to scale:

1. stimulating demand for change—by parents who, aided by educators and advocates, understand what to look for in schools and their rights to obtain it;
2. building school and staff capacity—by combining adequate resources with a committed focus on the kinds of pedagogy, curriculum-embedded assessment, teacher preparation and staff development, supporting structures, and so on, that the research shows stimulate high-level student learning;[248] and
3. enforcing accountability for implementing policy—not just for long-term outcomes but for implementing the pieces of the standards-based framework that are key to producing good outcomes.

While one of the three parties is in a lead role for each strategy, all strategies involve all parties. The basis for this collaboration—if we are to avoid the potential harms and fulfill the potential promise of standards-based reform—must be a recognition by all of the rights of students to quality education.

We must be confronted by the question, from the parents of children *currently in school*, "How are you going to ensure that my child gets the high-quality education to which she has a right?" And we must then approach school reform with an urgent commitment to do what it takes to answer that question affirmatively and fulfill that basic right for that child. Unless collaboration is premised on confronting that question and acting on that commitment, then neither bottom-up organic school change and staff development efforts nor top-down outcome accountability structures will respond in time to those parents who continue to send their children off to schools and classrooms that do not deliver on that promise. In the school life of a child, even a year is a long time. In but a few, educational opportunity is lost. The urgency of each one's right to a good education must be the driver as we negotiate our way through school reform.

NOTES

Portions of this chapter were adapted from a much briefer article by the author, "New Educational Standards and the Right to Quality Education," in University of Pennsylvania Law Review, *Child, Parent, and State: Law and Policy Reader,* 351–363 (Philadelphia: Temple University Press, 1994).

1. See section I.D. Stated in the negative, there is also a fair degree of agreement that certain educational practices will result in denial of a high-quality education.
2. See sections I.E and II. In large part, the connection between these laws and those reform elements is the subject of this essay. Again stated negatively, many of those key practices recognized as inconsistent with a high-quality education are barred by state or federal law.
3. For example, regarding the widely respected National Assessment of Educational Progress, 77% of 8th graders in the nation were below the proficient level on the 1996 NAEP 8th grade mathematics test, and even in the highest scoring state, Minnesota, 66% were not proficient. In reading, 72% of 4th graders in the nation were below the proficient level on the 1994 NAEP 4th grade exam, and even in the best state, Maine, 59% could not read proficiently. U.S. Department of Education, National Center for Education Statistics (NCES), *NAEP 1996 Mathematics Report Card for the Nation and the States* (1997) and *NAEP 1996 Reading Report Card for the Nation and the States* (1996). Similarly, results from the Third International Mathematics and Science Study (TIMSS), showed 12th-grade performance in the United States was among the lowest of the participating countries in mathematics and science general knowledge, physics, and advanced mathematics, even though the usually high-performing East Asian nations were not included in the comparison. NCES, *Pursuing Excellence: A Study of U.S. Twelfth-Grade Mathematics and Science Achievement in International Context* (1998). For additional background and state-by-state comparisons on NAEP and other measures of educational quality, see Editorial Projects in Education, *Quality Counts, 1997: A Report Card on the Condition of Public Education in the Fifty States* (Special Report of *Education Week,* January 1997), and *Quality Counts, 1998: The Urban Challenge: Public Education in the Fifty States* (January 1998). See also Education Trust, *Education Watch: The 1996 Education Trust State and National Data Book;* National Commission on Teaching and America's Future, *What Matters Most: Teaching for America's Future* (1996), pp. 24–50, documenting pervasive low expectations for student performance, unenforced standards for teachers, major flaws in teacher preparation,

slipshod teacher recruitment and induction, lack of professional development, and schools structured for failure instead of success.

4. See, for example, *Education Watch, supra* note 3 (documenting that poor and minority students who have less to begin with get less in school—in terms of less qualified teachers, less adequate textbooks and other resources, lower-level and watered-down curricula, and less exposure to the classes needed to progress to higher levels of education); Jeannie Oakes, *Multiplying Inequalities: The Effects of Race, Social Class, and Tracking on Opportunities* (RAND Corporation, 1990); National Coalition of Advocates for Students, *The Good Common School: Making the Vision Work for All Children* (1991). Concerning students with disabilities, see also Dorothy Kerzner Lipsky and Alan Gartner, "Inclusion, School Restructuring, and the Remaking of American Society," 66 (4) *Harvard Ed. Review* 762 (Winter 1996). For continuing inequity in access to fiscal resources, see Molly McUsic in chapter 3 of this volume, as well as *Quality Counts 1997* and *Quality Counts 1998,* supra note 2. The latter also examines urban/non-urban differences, including evidence that being in an urban school tends to have a large negative effect on achievement over and above being in a high-poverty school.

5. This is not to gainsay the real reform efforts under way in various places. It is simply to recognize the many millions of children in this large nation who are not directly or sufficiently reached by those efforts.

6. And, indeed, eroding the fundamental notion of democracy—that the government is we the people. Fully realized, this is not a naive notion, for its corollary is a keen sensitivity to disjunctures between our current government and ourselves, but accompanied by a determination to remedy them, rather than assuming they are endemic to federal government and either retreating into passive cynicism or actively seeking to all but abolish key elements of that instrument of our will.

7. Thus other strategies, such as vouchers or desegregation, are not discussed except insofar as they are sometimes linked to standards-based reform. Nor are a variety of other issues that often are viewed as related to achievement, such as school safety, human services, and preschool programs. Indeed, even excluding such topics, the remaining discussion—in connecting standards-based reform with students' rights—is so wide here that in-depth treatment of many particulars, such as assessment, staff development, and enforcement schemes, is not possible within the limits of an essay.

8. See section II, infra.

9. 20 U.S.C. §5801 et seq.

10. For examples, see the New Standards Project, *Performance Standards: English Language Arts, Mathematics, Science, and Applied Learning* (1997). NSP, a joint project of the Learning Research and Development Center and the Center for Education and the Economy, is an association of states and school districts. These standards, which build upon those developed by some discipline-based professional groups, are published in three volumes—for elementary, middle, and high school—and contain related examples of student work.

11. The terms "delivery standards" and "opportunity-to-learn standards" are currently in some political disfavor (which raises questions about the commitment to make sure

students get an education that enables them to meet the performance standards), but requirements for program plans often capture many of the same elements, although perhaps in less specific terms, and provoke much less controversy as an essential element of reform.

12. Beyond the sources discussed here, see *The Good Common School, supra* note 4; Linda Darling-Hammond, "Creating Standards of Practice and Delivery for Learner-Centered Schools," 4 *Stanford Law & Policy Review* 37 (Winter 1992–93); T. L. Good and J. E. Brophy, *Looking in Classrooms* (1994); Margaret E. Goertz, Robert E. Floden, and Jennifer O'Day, *Studies of Education Reform: Systemic Reform* (Consortium for Policy Research in Education, 1995); Policy Study Associates, *Raising the Educational Achievement of Secondary School Students: An Idea Book* (U.S. Department of Education, 1995); Lipsky and Gartner, supra note 4; Consortium for Policy Research in Education, *Public Policy and School Reform: A Research Summary* (University of Pennsylvania, 1996); Sam Stringfield et al., *Special Strategies Studies for Educating Disadvantaged Children: Findings and Policy Implications of a Longitudinal Study* (U.S. Department of Education, 1997).

13. Fred M. Newmann and Gary G. Wehlage, *Successful School Restructuring: A Report to the Public and Educators* (Wisconsin Center for Education Research, University of Wisconsin—Madison, 1995), jointly distributed by the American Federation of Teachers, the Association for Supervision and Curriculum Development, the National Association of Elementary School Principals, and the National Association of Secondary School Principals. See also Fred Newmann and Associates, *Authentic Achievement: Restructuring Schools for Intellectual Quality* (1996); issue on "Teaching for Authentic Student Performance," *Educational Leadership* (January 1997).

Given space limitations, focusing on the CORS research is useful for several related reasons: (1) It is derived from, and integrates, a very large information base. (2) It provides a coherent overall framework for linking (a) high student achievement to (b) good teaching practice to (c) school organizational conditions that support good teaching to (d) external factors which promote those conditions. As such, it can organize and clarify a good deal of other research about the impact of particular practices or conditions on student achievement. (3) It has identified practices and conditions with a much greater impact on achievement than most other research. This is largely because of the research model—instead of simply asking whether reduced class size, elimination of ability grouping, etc., improve achievement, it looks as well at the intervening variables, curriculum and pedagogy, since a variety of school changes can provide new opportunities for improved teaching but do not by themselves guarantee that the school staff are prepared to use those opportunities to engage students in high-level intellectual work. (Thus, it found that even in most highly restructured schools, the kind of authentic pedagogy which results in high achievement is still not the norm.) This helps explain the relatively weak correlations in much other research. (4) Its conclusions are useful for policymakers, parents, and advocates confronting a wide range of educational philosophies and trying to find the right middle ground between being too prescriptive of teaching practice and too laissez-faire. For example, while stressing the importance of students "constructing," rather than simply regurgitating, knowledge, it emphasizes that this construction requires building on a base of prior existing knowledge. Similarly, while stressing connections among disciplines, it also emphasizes use of the principles and methods of particular disciplines. It prescribes neither the specifics of content and performance standards nor the particular methods to teach them.

14. "For example, an average student who attended a 'high authentic instruction' school would learn about 78 percent more mathematics between grades 8 and 10 than a comparable student in a 'low authentic instruction' school." Supra note 13 at 25. Moreover, authentic pedagogy was found equally effective for students regardless of gender, socioeconomic status (SES), race, and ethnicity, and it reduced the impact of SES on achievement gain. Further, students in such schools achieved high marks not only on performance assessments designed to measure these higher-level skills but on traditional tests as well. For example, "Regardless of social background, an average student would increase from about the 30th percentile to about the 60th percentile as a result of experiencing high versus low authentic pedagogy." Id. at 22.

15. *Successful School Restructuring,* supra note 13.

16. Similarly, schools where teachers report high levels of collective responsibility for learning demonstrate 54–137% higher levels of achievement, depending on grade and subject matter. For example, students would learn more than twice as much science (116% higher) between grades 10 and 12. Student achievement is also much higher in schools which score high on other indicators of STPC, such as common curriculum (with low variation in course-taking among students) and high "academic press" (where students are pressed toward academic pursuits, expected to do homework, and place high priority on learning).

17. This teacher release time from classes is typically the biggest cost of intensive staff development.

18. See also National Foundation for the Improvement of Education, *Teachers Take Charge of Their Learning: Transforming Professional Development for Student Success* (1996).

19. V. Lee, J. Smith, and R. Croninger, "Another Look at High School Restructuring: More Evidence That It Improves Student Achievement, and More Insight into Why," *Issues in Restructuring Schools,* 9 (Fall 1995).

20. U.S.C. §6301(c)(12), revising Title I of the Elementary and Secondary Education Act in 1994.

21. *Successful School Restructuring,* supra note 13.

22. "Evidence from Fifteen Schools in Austin, Texas," in Gary Burtless, ed., *Does Money Matter?* (Brookings Institution, 1996). The successful schools, for example, adopted for all students the curriculum previously used only for "gifted and talented" students, used the curriculum to leverage change in instructional methods, mainstreamed students with disabilities in regular classes, focused professional development on implementing these changes, heavily invested in involving parents (including in governance), and improved attendance by introducing health services for students.

23. See, for example, Linda Darling-Hammond and Beverly Falk, *Assessment for Equity and Inclusion: Embracing All Our Children* (1997); Ruth Mitchell, *Testing for Learning: How New Approaches to Evaluation Can Improve America's Schools* (1992).

24. *Successful School Restructuring*, supra note 13. See also Linda Darling-Hammond, "Performance-Based Assessment and Educational Equity," 64 (1) *Harvard Educational Review* 5 (Spring 1994).

25. *Successful School Restructuring*, supra note 13; Lee, Smith, and Corninger, supra note 19.

26. See, for example, sections I.F, I.G, and III.A.3 for further discussion.

27. Anne T. Henderson and Nancy Berla, *A New Generation of Evidence: The Family Is Critical to Student Achievement* (Center for Law and Education, 1994); Chrissie Bamber, Nancy Berla, and Anne T. Henderson, *Learning from Others: Good Programs and Successful Campaigns* (Center for Law and Education, 1996); *The Good Common School*, supra note 4. As with add-on programs and other isolated interventions, we should not expect dramatic gains in achievement from schools' efforts to involve parents if they do not engage the parents in helping to improve the core educational program for students. See also Anne C. Lewis and Anne T. Henderson, *Urgent Message: Families Crucial to School Reform* (Center for Law and Education, 1997); Annenberg Institute, *Reasons for Hope, Voices for Change: A Report of the Annenberg Institute on Public Engagement for Public Education* (1998). (Information about Center for Law and Education publications and resources referred to in this chapter is available at www.cleweb.org.)

28. Gary Wehlage and Eric Osthoff, *Consensus and Conflict: Parent Participation in Twenty-Four Restructured Schools* (1996); *Successful School Restructuring*, supra note 13.

29. Id. Further, as noted in section III.A.3, when students are *not* getting a program effectively organized to promote high achievement, parents have an important, and all too often unique, role in seeking to remedy the problem—a phenomenon not typically studied.

30. Anthony Bryk et al., *A View from the Elementary Schools: The State of Reform in Chicago* (Consortium on Chicago School Research, University of Chicago, 1993). See also *Successful School Restructuring*, supra note 13. Chicago is one of the few places where parent involvement in decision-making goes deep enough in some schools to mount a comparative study with a full range of variation.

31. Some of these laws were recently written or rewritten explicitly to address standards-based reform. Others are older laws with more general legal standards that take on new meaning when applied in the context of standards-based reform. These laws are discussed more fully in section II.

32. These are process rights (in addition to going to court) that parents can use to see that the child's substantive rights to high-quality education, illustrated in the previous list, are actually implemented.

33. See section I.D, supra, on school reform research.

34. Id. See Fred M. Newmann, M. Bruce King, Mark Rigdon, "Accountability and School Performance: Implications for Restructuring Schools," 67 (1) *Harvard Educational Review* 41 (Spring 1997), finding that external accountability for results does not by itself translate into greater organizational capacity to produce those results. See also section III.A, below, on why meaningful implementation and enforcement of standards-based reform cannot be reduced to a pure shift to enforcing performance outcomes but must remain concerned with outcome-sensitive processes and resources.

35. But see note 44, infra.

36. It is not clear if this is because Congress and others assume that programs are implemented as intended, so the focus is naturally on whether they are working, or because there is little expectation of, or interest in the degree of, implementation. There appears to be at least a small element of the latter reason at work, since the issue has been pointed out to the Congressional education committees without provoking much attention.

37. See section I.D. Thus, while calling for a stronger federal role, I have also been among the most vigorous proponents (for example, during the reauthorization process for Title I) of both more emphasis on school-level, teacher-based assessment of student performance and a school community focus on shaping the standards for its children rather than focusing solely on state standards.

38. *Webster's New World Dictionary* defines "profession" as "a vocation or occupation requiring advanced training in some liberal art or science, and usually involving mental rather than manual work; as teaching, engineering, writing, etc.; especially, medicine, law, or theology (formerly called *the learned professions*);" and "professional" as "of, engaged in, or worthy of the high standards of a profession." The historical issues surrounding teacher "professionalization," however, have been more complicated and controversial—not only in terms of definition but in terms of whether professionalization is a positive or negative development. For a critical view, see, for example, David F. Larabee, *Power, Knowledge, and the Rationalization of Teaching: A Genealogy of the Movement to Professionalize Teaching*, 63 (2) Harvard Educational Review 123 (Summer 1992. For a historical perspective, see, for example, Christine E. Murray, Teaching as Profession: The Rochester Case in Historical Perspective, 63 (4) Harvard Educational Review 494 (Winter 1992). The point here is a limited one—concerning comparison with other occupations regarded as professions, in terms of the nature and extent of the duty and accountability for discretionary judgment and action in using the specialized knowledge and skills of the profession.

39. Indeed, Richard F. Elmore argues that the "massive failure of schools to harness their institutional incentive to the improvement of practice" is rooted in a deep, very limiting cultural belief "that successful teaching is an individual trait rather than a set of learned professional competencies acquired over the course of a career." "Getting to Scale with Good Educational Practice," 66 (1) Harvard Educational Review 1, 16 (Spring 1996).

40. Changing that pattern could raise resource issues. If substantially more time were added to teachers' expected work week to keep up, comparison of salaries between teachers and other professionals might be pressed. On the other hand, freeing up sufficient time during the regular work week for substantially more staff development, without increasing class size, can also cost money.

41. These are not trivial provisions. See highlighted examples, starting on page 314, of key requirements that go directly to the quality of children's education.

42. This is distinct from fiscal compliance provisions (such as those listing eligible uses of funds or requiring maintenance of effort, for example), where patterns of federal enforcement were established a quarter-century ago, compliance appears to be relatively high, and noncompliance has the very real possibility of provoking an audit exception.

43. See, for example, the National Education Goals Panel, *The 1996 National Education Goals Report: Building a Nation of Learners*, 61, in which only 41% of K-8 principals (or

their designees) reported that parent input is considered in policy decisions in three or more areas, despite federal requirements to do so—an indication of not only noncompliance but also lack of awareness that they were describing non-compliance.

44. For example: even under Chapter I, the law that was in place from 1989 to 1995 (before being replaced by a stronger Title I), of the millions of children in programs receiving the funds, none should have been in a program that was not designed to teach the basic and advanced skills expected for all children—but most were. None should have had a regular classroom placement in a low track that was also not designed to teach those high-level skills—but most did. And no child should have gone for more than a year of not making substantial progress toward those goals without a careful individual review involving the teacher and parent—but most did. Similarly, the common disproportionate representation of African American and Latino students and students with disabilities in low-track classes should always trigger a vigorous inquiry under Title VI and Section 504; it rarely does. See also note 123, infra.

45. For those who question whether this conclusion is overdrawn or just plain cynical, I suggest an empirical test: Go into the schools in your area with the list of programmatic legal rights relating to high quality education in section I.E. and see how many are known and understood, let alone implemented, by teachers or administrators, not to mention parents.

46. For example, in reframing the Elementary and Secondary Education Act in 1994, "The Congress declares it to be the policy of the United States that a high-quality education for individuals and a fair and equal opportunity to obtain that education are a societal good, are a moral imperative, and improve the life of every individual, because the quality of our lives ultimately depends on the quality of the lives of others." 20 U.S.C. §6301(a)(1).

47. Thus, in rewriting Title I of ESEA in 1994, Congress included findings titled "What Has Been Learned Since 1988," which begin with: "(1) All children can master challenging content and complex problem-solving skills. Research clearly shows that children, including low-achieving children, can succeed when expectations are high and all children are given the opportunity to learn challenging material." 20 U.S.C. §6301(c)(1).

48. See, for example, Jeannie Oakes, Amy Stuart Wells, and Associates, *Beyond the Technicalities of School Reform: Policy Lessons from Detracking Schools* (1996); Richard F. Elmore, supra note 39.

49. Thus, in New Jersey, despite the state supreme court long ago having declared the inequities in the school finance system unconstitutional, the state has recently alleged that its adoption of higher standards for students is the remedy rather than finance reform—*instead of* ensuring that the resources are provided to bring the quality of education in poor districts up enough to enable students to meet those standards. (The New Jersey Supreme Court has now firmly rejected the state's argument. *Abbott v. Burke,* C.A. No. 622-96 [5/14/97].)

50. See Newmann, King, Rigdon, supra note 34.

51. In *Debra P. v. Turlington,* discussed infra.

52. See Henry M. Levin, "An Economist's View of Educational Standards," presentation to Annual Meeting of American Educational Research Association, March 26, 1997.

53. See note 4.
54. See Stephen Jay Gould, *The Mismeasure of Man* (1981); *Larry P. v. Riles,* 495 F.Supp. 926 (N.D.Cal. 1979), aff'd, 793 F.2d 969 (9th Cir. 1986).
55. See note 243, infra, and accompanying text.
56. See Lawrence Mishel, Jared Bernstein, and John Schmitt, *The State of Working America* (Economic Policy Institute, 1996). While the notion of an overall decline in real wages has recently been called into dispute by some economists (who believe that inflation has been overstated in measuring real wages), the trend of growing income and wealth inequality (even when differences in educational attainment have narrowed) has not been seriously challenged. See note 244, infra.
57. As with the educational side of this topic, full discussion of the legal issues is not possible here—particularly for the extensive bodies of relevant constitutional and civil rights law treating such issues as desegregation, school finance, students with limited English proficiency, and students with disabilities, as well as the details of states' reform laws.
58. See, for example, the Kentucky Education Reform Act of 1990 (KERA), ch. 476, 1990 Ky. Acts 1208, widely regarded as among the most advanced and extensive. The Council of Chief State School Officers and the Education Commission of the States both issue a substantial variety of publications and updates on the status of states' standards-based reform initiatives. See also National Council on Education and Testing, *Raising Standards for American Education* (1992).
59. A second summit, with governors and corporate CEOs, occurred in March 1996, in large part to renew momentum for standards-based reform.
60. The Kentucky Education Reform Act, KERA, for example, grew out of plaintiffs' court victory in Kentucky.
61. The second category—the focus of "opportunity to learn" the new standards—is in many cases given the least attention. As discussed below, however, even then these statutes may provide a key element in establishing a right to various opportunity-to-learn elements because of the potential use of the content and performance standards in connection with other laws.
62. Compare *Edgewood Indep. Sch. Dist. v. Kirby,* 777 S.W.2d 391 (Tex. 1989), with *San Antonio Indep. Sch. Dist. v. Rodriguez,* 411 U.S. 1 (1973), reh'g denied, 411 U.S. 959 (1973). See also, for example, *Alabama Coalition for Equity v. Hunt,* (Ala. Cir. Ct. 1993), published as *Opinion of the Justices,* 624 So.2d 107 (Ala. 1993); *Roosevelt Elementary School District No. 66 v. Bishop,* 877 P.2d 806 (1994); *Dupree v. Alma School District No. 30,* 651 SW.2d 90 (Ark. 1983); *Serrano v. Priest,* 487 P.2d 1241 (Cal. 1971), 557 P.2d 929, cert. denied, 432 U.S. 907 (1977); *Horton v. Meskill,* 376 A.2d 359 (Conn. 1977); *Rose v. Council for Better Educ., Inc.,* 790 S.W.2d 186 (Ky. 1989); *McDuffy v. Secretary of Executive Office of Education,* 615 N.E.2d 516 (Mass. 1993); *Helena Elementary Sch. Dist. No 1 v. State,* 769 P.2d 684 (Mont. 1989); *Claremont School District v. Governor,* 635 A.2d 1375 (N.H. 1993); *Abbott v. Burke,* 575 A.2d 359 (N.J. 1990), 643 A.2d 575 (1994); *Tennessee Small School Systems v. McWherter,* 851 S.W.2d 139 (Tenn. 1993); *Seattle School District No. 1 v. State,* 585 P.2d (1978); *Pauley v. Kelly,* 255 S.E.2d 859 (W.Va. 1979). The school finance cases are discussed in more detail by Molly McUsic in chapter 3 of this volume.
63. See, e.g., *Hartzell v. Connell,* 679 P.2d 35 (Cal. 1984).

64. See, e.g., *Alabama, Roosevelt, Rose, McDuffy, Helena, Claremont, Edgewood, Seattle,* supra note 62.

65. See *Serrano, Horton, Pauley,* and *Washakie,* supra note 62. Fiscal inequalities have also been subject to state equal protection challenges based upon the establishment of a suspect class (*Serrano*); or the absence of a rational relationship between the finance system and the state's legitimate goals (*Dupree, Tennessee,* and *Alabama,* supra note 62); but these avenues generally are somewhat less directly relevant to this essay's focus on establishment of a right to education.

66. See, for example, *Serrano, Horton, Helena,* and *Tennessee,* supra note 62.

67. See, for example, *Alabama, Rose, McDuffy, Claremont,* and *Pauley,* supra note 62. Thus, it is common now to summarize finance litigation history as having an older phase based on "equity" or equalization claims and a newer phase of "adequacy" claims. See, for example, McUsic, chapter 3 in this volume; "Adequacy Litigation in School Finance Symposium," 28 (3). *U. Mich. J. Law Reform* (Spring 1995). As often noted in the commentary, however, both types of claims are sometimes asserted in the same litigation, and for purposes of this discussion, successful equity rulings, while typically not providing as much detail concerning the substantive nature of the state constitutional right, can also play a role in establishing students' rights to high quality education when put in the context of standards-based reform.

68. See also Martha I. Morgan, Adam S. Cohen, and Helen Hershkoff, "Establishing Education Program Inadequacy: The Alabama Example," 28 (3) *U. Mich. J. Law Reform* 599 (Spring 1995), describing various sources of evidence, including the use of older, more traditional types of input and output standards, not tied to newer content and performance standards, in defining the contours of constitutional adequacy in *Alabama Coalition for Equity,* supra note 62.

69. McUsic, supra note 67, points out that courts are likely to be much more comfortable relying on legislatively adopted standards for this purpose than having to create their own.

70. As a remedy for the constitutional violations found in *Rose,* supra note 62, the legislature passed the Kentucky Education Reform Act, supra note 58, establishing a more detailed standards-based reform framework.

71. 20 U.S.C. §5801 et seq.

72. 20 U.S.C. §5801. The goals were first set out at the meeting of the governors and President Bush in 1990 and then modified in developing Title I of the act. Each goal is accompanied by more specific objectives.

73. National-level activities in other sections of the act remain in place regarding technology, technical assistance, data gathering, research, evaluation, dissemination, and demonstrations relating to state and local improvement plans.

74. Among the findings in support of Title III, "Congress finds that—(1) all students can learn and achieve to high standards and must realize their potential if the United States is to prosper; (2) the reforms in education from 1977 through 1992 have achieved some good results, but such reform efforts often have been limited to a few schools or to a single part of the educational system; . . . (5) strategies must be developed by communities and States to support the revitalization of all local public schools by fundamentally

changing the entire system of public education through comprehensive, coherent, and coordinated improvement in order to increase student learning; . . . (15) all students are entitled to participate in a broad and challenging curriculum and to have access to resources sufficient to address other educational needs." 20 U.S.C. §5881.

75. 20 U.S.C. §5888.

76. 20 U.S.C. §5889(a)(3) (emphasis added).

77. The Secretary of Education also has a much smaller pot of funds for direct, competitive grants to urban and rural school districts with high numbers or concentrations of low-income or limited-English-proficient students to develop and implement local improvement plans, but the funds may not go to schools already receiving money under the state grants. 20 U.S.C. §5894(b)(1).

78. 20 U.S.C. §5889(b).

79. Congress repealed a section of the Act requiring opportunity-to-learn standards or strategies in the state plan, but, in any event, implementation of the standards developed under that section would have been voluntary.

80. See note 200, infra.

81. See section II.A, supra, on enforceability of state law.

82. 20 U.S.C. §§6301 et seq. Between 1981 and 1994, the program was called Chapter 1.

83. The state must use any such standards for all students it already has adopted or is developing, under Goals 2000 or otherwise, or if it has not already done so, must develop them at least for mathematics and reading or language arts for the 1997–98 school year. 20 U.S.C. §6311(b)(1)(B) and (C) and (6).

84. This weakness was recently confirmed by a long-term study of the limited impact of Chapter 1 prior to the 1994 revision. Abt Associates, *Prospects: Impact of Participation in Chapter 1 on Student Outcomes* (U.S. Department of Education, 1997). Where particular schools showed major gains, however, they implemented the reforms called for by the act and supported by the research cited in section I.D. Indeed, a separate study of schools during 1990–93 identified ten strategies that work for disadvantaged students and found that Chapter 1 funds were clearly the primary engine for reform, where reform did happen. Sam Stringfield et al., supra note 12.

85. 20 U.S.C. §6301(d).

86. This may, however, include staff development costs for improving the ability of all teachers to meet the needs of these children.

87. In order to encourage greater use of that option, the low-income threshold for becoming a schoolwide program, which had been 75% of the student body, was reduced to 50% starting with the 1996–97 school year.

88. 20 U.S.C. §6314(b)(1), 6315(c)(1), 6320(a)(1).

89. 20 U.S.C. §6314(b)(1)(H). There are also to be teacher-parent conferences for any student who has not met such standards, focusing on what the school will do, what the parent can do, and any additional assistance available in the school or community to help meet the standards.

90. 20 U.S.C. §6311(b)(2)(B)(I). The Department of Education has noted that this definition must be sufficiently rigorous to achieve that goal during a student's school career. *Guidance on Standards, Assessments, and Accountability,* p. 57, 61 (1997).

91. Written school plans are explicitly mentioned only for schoolwide programs, but planning is clearly required for targeted assistance schools as well. See 20 U.S.C. §6315(c)–(e). Moreover, the requirements for written parent involvement plans and school-parent learning compacts do apply to targeted assistance schools.

92. 20 U.S.C. §6319 and §§6311(b), 6312, 6314(b), 6317, and 6319(c)(3).

93. See Margot Rogers, *Planning for Title I Programs: Guidelines for Parents, Advocates, and Educators* (Center for Law and Education, 1995), for more detail on Title I content and implementation strategies.

94. On March 26, 1996, the Department of Education published proposed revisions of complaint procedures for this purpose. 61 *Fed. Regis.* 13324, under authority of 20 U.S.C. §1221e-3(a)(1).

95. See *Valdez v. Grover,* 563 F.Supp. 129 (W.D. Wis. 1983); *Nicholson v. Pittenger,* 364 F. Supp. 669 (E.D. Pa. 1973). See also note 196, infra.

96. In November, 1997, Congress also appropriated $150 million for the 1998–1999 school year for a new initiative, the Comprehensive School Reform Demonstration Program. It provides grants of at least $50,000 to schools to implement whole-school change programs using innovative strategies proven successful by research (which may draw from but is not limited to seventeen programs specifically listed by Congress), to enable all students to meet state standards, planned and implemented with meaningful parent and community involvement. Public Law 105-79, H. Conf. Rpt. 105-309. The U.S. Department of Education issued guidance for the program on March 12, 1998. At least 83% of the local competitive grants, which run through the states, will go to Title I-eligible schools, and the law and guidance emphasize the connections to Title I.

97. 20 U.S.C. §2301 et seq., funded at $1.13 billion in fiscal 1997. As of April 1, 1998, revision of the Perkins Act was under consideration in Congress. See note 52, infra.

98. See also the Office for Civil Rights Guidelines for nondiscrimination in vocational programs, note 151, infra. The guidelines (which cover nondiscrimination on the basis of race, national origin, sex, and disability status) and the Perkins special populations provisions (covering the groups identified above) are complementary and only partially overlapping.

99. See 20 U.S.C. §§2323(a)(3)(B), (b)(1)–(3); 2326(a); 2328.

100. See 20 U.S.C. §§2327 and 2325(b)(1).

101. 20 U.S.C. §2468e(b).

102. See 20 U.S.C. §2327(a)(1)(A).

103. See 20 U.S.C. §2328(d).

104. See also §2468e(c)(3). For fuller discussion of the law, program options, and advocacy strategies, see Center for Law and Education, "Vocational Education: A New Opportunity for Educational and Community Change," *Newsnotes,* 43 (December 1991, special issue on vocational education).

105. See, e.g., Center for Law and Education, *Problems in Implementing the Perkins Act: Preliminary Report Concerning State Plans* (1991).

106. 20 U.S.C. §§6101 et seq. For a fuller description, analysis, and discussion of the Act's relationship to other laws, see Lauren Jacobs, *The School-to-Work Opportunities Act of 1994: A Guide to the Law and How to Use It* (Center for Law and Education, 1995).

107. The bulk of local money comes through the states, which must through 70–90% of their state implementation grants. For fiscal 1997, total funding for the Act is $400 million.

108. Students' work-based learning components may include school-sponsored, student-run enterprises. 20 U.S.C. §6113(b). Skill certificates are discussed below in section II.C.3.d.

109. 20 U.S.C. §6112(3); House Conference Report No. 103-480, pp. 46–47, 51.

110. 20 U.S.C. §§6103(5)(D), 6111(2) and (4), 6112(4), and 6113(a)(5). "All aspects of an industry" is defined to include "planning, management, finances, technical and production skills, underlying principles of technology, labor and community issues, health and safety issues, and environmental issues, related to such industry." 20 U.S.C. §6103(1).

111. 20 U.S.C. §6111(5). "[A]ll students means both male and female students from a broad range of backgrounds and circumstances, including disadvantaged students, students with diverse racial, ethnic, or cultural backgrounds, American Indians, Alaska Natives, native Hawaiians, students with disabilities, students with limited English proficiency, migrant children, school dropouts, and academically talented students." 20 U.S.C. §6103(2). See also Conference Report, p. 50, stressing the need to design and implement the programs to serve all students.

112. 20 U.S.C. §§6103(4)(C) and 6112(1).

113. 20 U.S.C. §§6103(3) and (19) and 6143(d)(13).

114. 20 U.S.C. §6143(d)(5).

115. 20 U.S.C. §6145(b)(5).

116. 20 U.S.C. §6192(a).

117. See National Assessment of Vocational Education, *Final Report* (Office of Educational Research and Improvement OERI, U.S. Department of Education, 1989).

118. See Senate Report No. 98-57 (1984), pp. 5, 9–10.

119. See, for example, Kathleen Cushman, "What's 'Essential' About Learning in the World of Work," 14 (no. 1) *Horace* (Coalition of Essential Schools, September 1997). See also Tamara Berman and Adria Steinberg, *The VIA Book: A Best Practices Manual from the Vocational Integration with Academics Project* (Rindge School of Technical Arts, Cambridge Rindge and Latin School, 1997); "Changing the Subject: The New Urban High School," www.bpic.org.

120. See, for example, Edward Pauly, Hilary Kopp, Joshua Haimson, *Homegrown Lessons: Innovative Programs Linking Work and High School* (Manpower Demonstration Research Corporation 1994); Lee, Smith, and Croninger, supra note 19; *Raising the Educational Achievement of Secondary School Students,* supra note 12; Judith Warren Little, "What Teachers Learn in High School: Professional Development and the Redesign of Vocational Education," 27 (3) *Education and Urban Society* 274 (May 1995); National Association of Secondary School Principals, *Breaking Ranks: Changing an American Institution* (1996).

121. This is why the provision in the School-to-Work Opportunities Act allowing school-based enterprises to fulfill the work-based component program requirement is important. The numbers of high-quality employer-based work-based learning placements is, not surprisingly (particularly in light of employment opportunities in low-income communities), still very low.

122. For further discussion, including program examples, see Paul Weckstein, "Teaching Workplace Competencies and All Aspects of an Industry," in Naomi Thiers, ed., *Successful Strategies: Building a School-to-Career System,* 293–302 (American Vocational Association, 1995); Erica Nielson Andrew, ed., *As Teachers Tell It: Implementing All Aspects of the Industry* (National Center for Research in Vocational Education, 1996). See also Statement of Senator Edward M. Kennedy, 130 *Cong. Record* S.12959 (1984), explaining forerunner all-aspects-of-the-industry provisions in the 1984 Perkins Act and citing AAI as an antidote to the notion of "throwaway" workers.

123. For example, in explaining why nothing was yet being done to meet a clear requirement in the School-to-Work Opportunities Act to develop, as part of the national system of performance measures, a measure of student attainment of strong understanding of and experience in all aspects of the industry, the consultants to the School-to-Work Office at the U.S. Departments of Education and Labor noted that "few states—if any—have developed appropriate assessment instruments in this area." Karen Levesque and Elliott A. Medrich, *Designing a System of Performance Measures for School-to-Work,* p. 7 (MPR Associates, January 17, 1995). Yet, since 1990, assessing AAI is one of the very few things that *all* states have been required to do as the basis for developing and revising their state plan, and one of the few things that *all* local recipients are required to do as part of their annual evaluation for purposes of program improvement.

124. Efforts in the 1995–96 Congress to replace Perkins, School-to-Work, the Job Training Partnership Act, and a host of other youth and adult training and literacy programs with a block grant fell short. In 1997, the House instead passed a revised version of Perkins, which addresses the same principles discussed above, although in different form. While the Senate has taken no final action, it now appears likely that Perkins will remain a separate program, albeit with significant amendments, and that the School-to-Work Act will not be rewritten or eliminated.

125. 20 U.S.C. §§5931 et seq. Goals 2000 is discussed in section II.C.1, supra. Interestingly, the establishment of a National Skill Standards Board has not generated the same level of hostility as the academic skills standards board established by Goals 2000 (the National Educational Standards and Improvement Council). Apparently, an industry-based national body involved in standard setting is not as troubling as a public sector one.

126. 20 U.S.C. §5932.

127. There have been some efforts to complement specific technical skills with "general" occupational and workplace readiness skills, sometimes drawing on the Secretary's Commission on Achieving Necessary Skills, *What Work Requires of Schools: SCANS Report for America 2000* (U.S. Department of Labor, 1991). The SCANS Commission identified five competencies—(1) resources: identifies, organizes, plans, and allocates resources; (2) interpersonal: works with others; (3) information: organizes and uses information; (4) systems: understanding complex interrelationships; and (5) technology: works with a variety of technologies—supported by a foundation of basic skills, thinking skills, and personal qualities. There is some risk, however, that these skills either will remain abstract or, when they take on more specific content, will cease to remain equal and generally applied, so that, for instance, while all workers must be able

to "work with others" or "use information," these will mean radically different things in a hierarchical workplace for an executive and a lower-level worker. See also Diana C. Pullin, "Learning to Work: The Impact of Curriculum and Assessment Standards on Educational Opportunity," 64 (1) *Harvard Educational Review* 31 (Spring 1994). In contrast, the Perkins Act states: "The term 'general occupational skills' means experience in and understanding of all aspects of the industry the student is preparing to enter, including planning, management, finances, technical and production skills, underlying principles of technology, labor and community issues, and health, safety, and environmental issues." 20 U.S.C. §2471(17). As discussed in section II.C.3.c, supra, this all-aspects-of-the-industry focus allows students to gain skills that are both concrete *and* transferrable, and is specifically designed to resist the reinforcement of class hierarchy and division in the vocational program.

128. 20 U.S.C. §§1400–1487, formerly the Education of the Handicapped Act.

129. 29 U.S.C. §794. See also the discussion of civil rights in Section 63, below. For a more detailed overview of the educational rights of students with disabilities under IDEA and Section 504, see Center for Law and Education, *Educational Rights of Children with Disabilities* (1991).

130. For an in-depth analysis, see Eileen L. Ordover, Kathleen B. Boundy, and Diana C. Pullin, *Students with Disabilities and the Implementation of Standards-Based Education Reform: Legal Issues and Implications* (forthcoming).

131. See Lipsky and Gartner, supra note 4.

132. Ordover et al., supra note 125. Even then, when the student is clearly not able to fully achieve those standards, the program should be designed to allow him/her to do so to the maximum extent possible, rather than becoming totally detached from the standards once there is such a finding. (Because this notion of maximum potential is proffered here where "maximum potential" is lower than the education standards the state or district has set for all, it does not run counter to *Board of Hendrick Hudson School District v. Rowley*, 458 U.S. 176 (1982). The Supreme Court's denial of additional services there relied on the fact that the student *was* meeting, and indeed surpassing, what were then the education standards for all students. Here the claim is simply that, in the few cases where it can be shown that the standards for all are not fully applicable, the differential treatment should be the least possible. This is also a concomitant of "least restrictive environment.")

133. Cf. *Muscogee (GA) County School District*, EHLR 257:540 (OCR 6/30/84), in which the Office for Civil Rights found a section 504 violation when a separate high school program for students with cognitive impairments and learning disabilities did not teach biology, a subject required by state standards for receipt of a regular diploma.

134. IDEA's definition of "free appropriate public education" requires special education and related services that "meet the standards of the State educational agency" and "include an appropriate preschool, elementary, or secondary education in the State involved." 20 U.S.C. §1401(a)(18)(B) and (C).

135. 34 C.F.R. §104.4(b)(1) (implementing §504) prohibits the provision to students with disabilities of "an aid, benefit or service that is not as effective as that provided to others." These various IDEA and §504 protections extend to assessment as well—both in terms

of inclusion and in terms of accommodations necessary to ensure that the assessments are equally effective in measuring the relevant performance.

136. P.L. 105-17, Individuals with Disabilities Education Act Amendments of 1997.

137. See 20 U.S.C. §§1400(c)(4); 1451(a)(6); 1471(a).

138. 20 U.S.C. §1412(a)(16)(A)(ii). This should be seen as a reference to goals and standards for students with disabilities that are additional to or build on the "other goals and standards" established by the state for all students, and not as substitution for or dilution of such other goals and standards, particularly since wholesale setting of lower goals for such children would violate the provisions against nondiscrimination and requirements for individualized determination of FAPE in the least restrictive environment. See discussion of these overarching standards elsewhere in this chapter.

139. 20 U.S.C. §1412(a)(16).

140. 20 U.S.C. §1412(a)(17). See also §1413(a)(6).

141. 20 U.S.C. §1414(d)(1)(A).

142. 20 U.S.C. §1414(d)(1)(B)(iv) and (v). The variety of assessment tools and strategies must include those which gather information, including from the parent, related to enabling the child to be involved in and progress in the general curriculum. §1414(b)(2)(A).

143. 20 U.S.C. §1400(c)(7)–(10).

144. 20 U.S.C. §1418.

145. 20 U.S.C. §1451 et seq. See also 20 U.S.C. §1412(a)(16)(D). The SEA may also give LEAs authority to permit schools to operate under school-based improvement plans to improve results for all children with disabilities. The plan must be (a) designed, evaluated, and, as appropriate, implemented by a school-based standing panel, and (b) approved by both a majority of the parents on the panel and a majority of the nonparent members. The LEA assumes sole responsibility for oversight of all plan-related activities. 20 U.S.C. §1413(g). National programs of research, personnel preparation, technical assistance, support, and information dissemination are also now more explicitly focused on maximizing success in the mainstream curriculum and meeting the same standards established for all children. 20 U.S.C. §1461 et seq. The parent-governed Parent Training and Information Centers (PTICs) must now, among their other duties, assist parents of children with disabilities to "participate in school reform activities." 20 U.S.C. §1482(b)(4)(F). Local Community Parent Resource Centers, parallel to the PTICs, carry out similar activities, but focus on underserved parents of children with disabilities, including low-income parents, parents of children with limited English proficiency, and parents with disabilities.

146. See also 20 U.S.C. §1417(l), providing that nothing in IDEA shall be construed to restrict or limit rights, procedures, and remedies available under the Constitution, the Americans with Disabilities Act, the Rehabilitation Act, or other federal laws protecting the rights of children with disabilities.

147. 20 U.S.C. §1400(c)(4).

148. But note the discussion above concerning alternative methods for assessing the same knowledge and skills, as distinguished from assessments of lower standards.

149. 20 U.S.C. §6311(b)(3)(F).

150. 20 U.S.C. §6311(b)(3)(I).

151. 20 U.S.C. §6312(b)(4)(B). The IDEA amendments now provide that a school's IDEA Part B funds may be used for schoolwide programs under Title I. 20 U.S.C. §1413(a)(2)(D).
152. 20 U.S.C. §6315(b)(2)(A)(I). Title I funds may not cover services otherwise required by law for these children, but may be used to supplement or coordinate those services. 20 U.S.C. §§6315(b)(2)(A)(ii); 6314(a)(3)(B).
153. Title VI of the 1964 Civil Rights Act, 42 U.S.C. §2000d, Title IX of the Education Amendments of 1972, 20 U.S.C. §1681; and section 504 of the Rehabilitation Act of 1973, 29 U.S.C. §794, respectively.
154. The Title VI regulations that bar unjustified practices which have racially disparate impact, despite being facially neutral, were upheld in *Guardians Association v. Civil Service Commission,* 463 U.S. 582 (1983). See *Larry P. v. Riles,* 793 F.2d 969 (9th Cir. 1986) (applying the standard to use of IQ tests in California schools). More specific guidelines for applying the Title VI, Title IX, and Section 504 regulations to vocational programs, including a disparate impact analysis modeled in part on the Title VII Equal Employment Opportunities Commission guidelines, were issued by the Office for Civil Rights in 1978, 34 C.F.R. Part 100, Appendix B.
155. See Jeannie Oakes, *Keeping Track: How Schools Structure Inequality* (1985); John I. Goodlad, *A Place Called School* (1984); Oakes, supra note 4.
156. Id.
157. See *McNeal v. Tate,* 508 F.2d 1017 (5th Cir. 1975); *Georgia Conference of Branches of NAACP v. State of Georgia,* 775 F.2d 1403 (11th Cir. 1985). See also *Larry P. v. Riles,* supra note 154; *Hobson v. Hansen,* 269 F.Supp. 401 (D.D.C. 1967), aff'd, 408 F.2d 175 (D.C.Cir. 1969). Compare the "disparate impact" standard under Title VI with Constitutional equal protection claims, such as those rejected in *People Who Care v. Rockford Board of Education,* discussed at note 172, which instead require proof of racially discriminatory intent.
158. See section II.C.4 for further discussion of tracking and students with disabilities.
159. See American Educational Research Association, American Psychological Association, National Council on Measurement in Education, *Standards for Educational and Psychological Testing* (1985); National Forum for Assessment, *Principles and Indicators for Student Assessment Systems* (1996).
160. 42 U.S.C. §2000d. See *Lau v. Nichols,* 414 U.S. 563 (1974).
161. 20 U.S.C. §§1703(f), 1706.
162. The leading case in the development of this standard is *Castañeda v. Pickard,* 648 F.2d 989 (5th Cir. 1981). See also Multicultural Education, Training and Advocacy, *The Rights of Limited English Proficient Students: A Handbook for Parents and Community Advocates* (1993).
163. See, for example, California Department of Education, *Designing a Standards-Based Accountability System for Language Minority Students* (1996).
164. Title VII, Part A, of the Elementary and Secondary Education Act, 20 U.S.C. §7401 et seq., funded at $157 million in fiscal 1997.
165. 20 U.S.C. §§7402(c), 7421(2)(B).
166. 20 U.S.C. §6311(b)(2)(B)(I), (3)(F)(iii). The state must identify the languages in which

such assessments are needed but not currently available, must make every effort to develop them, and may request federal assistance on linguistically accessible assessment. 20 U.S.C. §6311(b)(5). Title I provisions for disaggregating achievement data, LEP student eligibility, coordination of services for LEP students, and nonsupplanting of services required by other laws are the same as those for students with disabilities described in the text accompanying notes 147–149, supra. See also Diane August, et al., *LEP Students and Title I: A Guidebook for Educators* (1995).

167. See text following note 153, supra.

168. See, for example, *New York Times,* May 2, 1996, page B5 ("Education Panel Adopts New Academic Standards"), citing concerns that the standards adopted in New Jersey were watered down and made too easy in order to reduce implementation costs of meeting them.

169. Under traditional equal protection analysis, government's differential treatment of people is subject to strict scrutiny, and the government must demonstrate that it is necessary to a compelling state interest, if either the basis for the difference is an intentional, suspect classification (such as race) or the difference impinges on a fundamental right (such as voting). Otherwise, the difference will be upheld unless there is no rational relationship to any legitimate government purpose, a much lower standard of scrutiny. Some more recent cases indicate either a three-level range or more of a continuum of scrutiny, depending on the interests at stake, rather than a simple high-low dichotomy. See, e.g., *Plyler v. Doe,* 457 U.S. 202 (1982), stressing the importance of education in using an intermediate standard of heightened review to strike down the exclusion of undocumented immigrant children from school.

170. See *Washington v. Davis,* 426 U.S. 229 (1976); *Personnel Administrator v. Feeney,* 442 U.S. 229 (1976). Intentional differences in educational programming explicitly based on status are likely to be most evident in the case of disability. An intermediate standard of heightened scrutiny may apply to such disability-based differences. See *City of Cleburne v. Cleburne Living Center,* 43 U.S. 432 (1985). Previously accepted "benign" justifications for differential treatment may no longer be acceptable, given the confluence of content and performance standards for all students adopted as a matter of policy, a slower and more diluted lower track with less breadth and depth in relation to those standards, and the courts' rejection of a lower standard of scrutiny for benignly motivated racial classifications. See *City of Richmond v. J. A. Croson Co.,* 488 U.S. 469 (1989); *Aderand Constructors, Inc. v. Pena,* 115 S.Ct. 2097 (1995).

171. See section II.C.5, supra.

172. See *Debra P. v. Turlington,* 474 F. Supp. 244, 254–57 (M.D.Fla. 1979), modified, 644 F.2d 397 (5th Cir. 1981) (state "functional literacy examination" requirement for high school graduation unconstitutionally perpetuated effects of prior unconstitutional denial of equal educational opportunities) (discussed further in section III.B.1, infra). See *Dayton Board of Education v. Brinkman,* 443 U.S. 526 (1979); *U.S. v. Fordice,* 112 S.Ct. 2727 (1992).

For challenges to tracking on this basis, see *McNeal v. Tate,* 508 F.2d 1017 (5th Cir. 1975); *Castaneda v. Pickard,* 648 F.2d 989 (5th Cir. 1981); *Georgia Conference of Branches of NAACP v. Georgia,* 775 F.2d 1403 (11th Cir. 1985); *Montgomery v. Starkville Municipal*

Separate School District, 665 F. Supp. 487 (N.D. Miss. 1987), aff'd, 854 F.2d 127 (5th Cir. 1988). In examining whether ability grouping perpetuated or helped to overcome the effects of prior segregation, however, these courts did not have the benefit of new standards and related policies for scrutinizing differences among the tracks. See also *People Who Care v. Rockford Board of Education,* C.A. No. 96-2410 (7th Cir. 4/15/97) (reversing a lower court order to prohibit tracking as an overbroad remedy for the alleged wrong of having misused it to produce greater segregation than would have occurred through "objective" tracking alone). Compare with the analysis of tracking under Title VI in section II.C.5.a, supra.

Courts also have frequently ordered substantive education improvements as a remedy to eliminate the vestiges of unconstitutional segregation. See David S. Tatel, "Desegregation Versus School Reform: Resolving the Conflict," 4 *Stanford Law and Policy Review* 61 (Winter 1992–93). One court has ordered standards-based reforms: *Pennsylvania Human Relations Commission v. School District of Philadelphia,* 168 Pa. Cmwlth. 542, 651 A.2d 186 (1994) (requiring the district to establish exemplary content and performance standards, processes for assessing performance in relation to those standards, and various program changes and practices to reach them).

Some desegregation remedies have focused directly on raising test scores. See *Reed v. Rhodes,* 455 F. Supp. 569 (N.D. Ohio 1978), aff'd in part and remanded in part, 607 F.2d 714 (6th Cir. 1979), cert. denied, 445 U.S. 935 (1980); *Berry v. School District of Benton Harbor,* 515 F. Supp. 344, 369 (W.D. Mich. 1981), aff'd and remanded, 698 F.2d 813 (6th Cir. 1983). It is now clear, however, that the remedy in such cases must be targeted to eliminating the incremental effect that segregation had on achievement—a difficult task to identify. See *Missouri v. Jenkins,* 115 S.Ct. 2038 (1995); *People Who Care,* supra (reversing an order to eliminate half the gap between white and nonwhite test scores within four years).

173. 411 U.S. 1, 37 (1973). See *Papasan v. Allain,* 478 U.S. 265, 286 (1986): "As *Rodriguez* and *Plyler* indicate, this Court has not yet definitively settled the questions whether a minimally adequate education is a fundamental right and whether a statute alleged to discriminatorily infringe that right should be accorded heightened equal protection review."

174. See, e.g., Goals 2000, 20 U.S.C. §5812; Title I, 20 U.S.C. §1001; *National Education Goals Report,* supra, note 43; National Council on Educational Standards and Testing, *Raising Standards for American Education: A Report to Congress, the Secretary of Education, the National Education Goals Panel, and the American People* (1992). Further, there remains the possibility—opened up by *Plyler v. Doe,* supra note 169—of getting at least heightened, if not strict, review because of the importance of education, even if not a fundamental right. But compare *Kadrmas v. Dickinson Public Schools,* 478 U.S. 450 (1988). See James S. Liebman, "Implementing Brown in the Nineties: Political Reconstruction, Liberal Recollection and Litigatively Enforced Legislative Reform," 76 *Virginia Law Review* 349, 420 (1990).

175. The burden of showing that there is *no* possible rational basis for the students' treatment and the restrained nature of the judicial review make this third approach much more difficult than claims under Title VI or other federal statutes. See, e.g., *Heller v. Doe,* 113

S.Ct. 2637 (1993); *FCC v. Beach Communication, Inc.,* 113 S.Ct. 2096 (1993); *Sandlin v. Doe,* 643 F.2d 1027 (4th Cir. 1981); *Bond v. Keck,* 616 F. Supp. 565 (E.D. Mo. 1985). Yet the rationality of codifying the skills and knowledge that the state says all students can and must master and then setting up an education program for large numbers of those students which is clearly not designed to teach those things is highly questionable. Thus, the presence of new standards and related state policy may provoke a different judicial response even under this theory. See Liebman, supra note 174. Cf. state court decisions finding no rational relationship between school finance schemes and legitimate state policy, in note 65, supra.

176. See, e.g., *Nelson v. Heyne,* 491 F.2d 352 (7th Cir. 1974), cert. denied, 417 U.S. 976 (1974); *Wyatt v. Aderholt,* 503 F.2d 1305 (5th Cir. 1974).

177. See *Goss v. Lopez,* 419 U.S. 565 (1975).

178. *Debra P. v. Turlington; St. Ann v. Palisi,* 495 F.2d 423 (5th Cir. 1974).

179. 474 F. Supp. at 266–67, 644 F.2d at 403–7. See also *Brookhart v. Illinois State Board of Education,* 697 F.2d 179 (7th Cir. 1983); *Crump v. Gilmer Independent School District,* 797 F. Supp. 552 (E.D. Tex. 1992); *Board of Education v. Ambach,* 436 N.Y.S.2d 563 (Sup.Ct. 1981).

180. But see *People Who Care,* supra note 172, overturning the portion of a desegregation remedy that ordered a reduction in half the white-minority test-score gap within four years. The appeals court said that this was a remedy beyond the defendants' control and that it was not tied to proof that half the gap was caused by illegal segregation. Neither on this point nor in its discussion of tracking does the opinion address the kind of standards-based analysis suggested below.

181. This was the standard for adequate yearly progress proposed by the Commission on Chapter 1 and considered to be quite ambitious.

182. This appears to be the pattern for nonimplementation during the first year of the revised Title I, in disregard of the fact that Title I *does* have major reform-oriented input and process requirements. See Center for Law and Education, *Consolidated State Plans: School Reform at Risk* (1996).

183. Thus, Newmann, King, and Rigdon, supra note 34, find that external accountability for results does not by itself translate into internal capacity to achieve those results. See also Darling-Hammond, supra note 12.

184. Again, however, individual students are entitled not to the outcome but to a system that takes the requisite steps—including this state action—toward that outcome.

185. 20 U.S.C. §6316(c)(2)(A)(I) and (d)(4)(A).

186. *Curriculum and Evaluation Standards for School Mathematics* (1989); *Professional Standards for Teaching Mathematics* (1991).

187. This is true at least at the federal level; state mandates are often more specific.

188. See the research discussed in section I.D above. Indeed, as discussed there, the elements researchers now find central to high achievement for all students—i.e., schools which adopt those goals and develop the organizational focus, sense of shared responsibility, and capacity to reach them—provides the empirical basis for this framework.

189. See 20 U.S.C. §6311(b)(1)(D) (Title I's criteria for high state standards). Note report of efforts in New Jersey to lower standards, note 165, supra.

190. For example, standards for English language arts, developed by the National Council of Teachers of English and the International Reading Association, have been criticized by some as too vague. See *Education Week,* March 20, 1996, p. 1. Of course, the standards developed by a disciplinary group are not subject to challenge per se, but only if adopted to fulfill legal mandates by a state or locality. Further, in examining whether the standards are specific enough, it is necessary to view them in their totality. For example, in Kentucky and other states, standards adopted by the state legislature are quite general, but the state education department has developed more specifics. Further, opinions may vary as to where to strike the balance between being to vague and being so specific that the standards become a laundry list of fragmented tasks and pieces of knowledge.

191. See standard-setting difficulties and controversies discussed in Newmann et al., supra note 34.

192. That a district or school grapples with what the standards mean and then chooses to adopt additional standards—to go deeper or get more specific in certain areas or to address topics not covered in state standards—is not the problem, and indeed should be a critical part of making the standards real. See the research discussed in text accompanying note 15, supra, concerning the importance of school-level reflection and consensus on goals. The problem is when the state standards are low or too vague so that optional local action is needed even to have standards that meet the legal criteria, and when assessments of success on local standards substitute for, rather than supplement, assessment of success on the state standards, so that a dual system of what "proficiency" means is perpetuated—particularly in comparing high- and low-poverty schools and systems.

193. See, for example, *consolidated State Plans,* supra note 182.

194. See *Castañeda,* supra note 162.

195. Such as the Title I requirements for enriched, accelerated curriculum tailored to high standards (which is typically not found in the low-track classes which disproportionately serve disadvantaged students) and a system for ensuring timely, effective identification and intervention by teachers for students having difficulty mastering particular standards. See section II.C.2, supra.

196. According to a National Center for Education Statistics report, school districts pay insufficient attention to opportunity to learn. In a survey of 142 school districts, the study found that "almost all of the districts did not investigate whether different groups of students did or did not have access to the content of the test." The districts made no attempt to infer meaning from the test scores in terms of teachers' instructional practices, access to the knowledge tested, or any other dimension. The study found that differences in student achievement are not being related to opportunities to learn, and that this is hampering teachers' ability to improve their teaching and making knowledge accessible to students. Attempts to ensure congruence between the skills taught and the skills tested are not made. Floraline I. Stevens, *Opportunity to Learn: Issues of Equity for Poor and Minority Students* (National Center for Education Statistics, 1993), 23.

197. For example, was the reform plan—as required by Title I—*jointly* developed with the

parents of the school, through a process agreed upon by the school's parents and spelled out in the parent involvement policy, with adequate training and information for those parents? 20 U.S.C. §6319(a)(2)(A) and (c)(3).

198. Sam Stringfield, et al., supra note 12.

199. The Supreme Court has ruled recently that private parties may not sue *states* to enforce federal legislation enacted *under authority of the spending clause* of the Constitution unless the state has explicitly waived its immunity under the Eleventh Amendment. *Seminole Tribe v. Florida,* 64 USLW 4167 (1996). However, three points should be noted. (a) The Court left open the ability to bring such suits for injunctive relief against individual state officials (rather than the state itself) under certain conditions. (b) This decision does not limit the ability to enforce against states those federal laws that have been enacted *under authority of the Fourteenth Amendment,* which includes at least the Civil Rights Acts and the Individuals with Disabilities in Education Act, and 42 U.S.C. §1983, which is the most common basis for enforcing other federal education legislation. (c) The decision does not limit enforcement of federal legislation against *local* government units, including school boards, which do not enjoy Eleventh Amendment immunity. Thus, clear duties set out in Title I and other federal program laws, including the requirement (described in note 200) to comply with the assurance to operate programs consistent with the plans and applications submitted by the recipient, are enforceable through Section 1983. See *Lampkin v. District of Columbia,* 27 F.3d 605 (D.C. Cir.), *cert. denied,* 115 S.Ct. 578 (1994), distinguishing *Suter v. Artist M.,* 503 U.S. 347 (1992).

200. Federal law requires assurances by states and local applicants that their programs will be carried out in accordance with all applicable statutes, regulations, *program plans, and applications.* See 20 U.S.C. §§1232d(b)(1), 1232e(b)(1), 8853(a)(1), and 8856(a)(1). See also *Lampkin,* supra. Also, as discussed in section II.C.5.b, civil rights law requires that, having chosen an approach to meeting the needs of LEP students, an education agency must take steps to implement that approach effectively.

201. See various Title I requirements for basing instructional strategies and staff development on effective approaches and on analysis of data, such as 20 U.S.C. §§6314(b)(1)(A), (B)(ii) and (iii), and (2)(b); 6315(c)(1)(B) and (D); 6320(b)(1)(A) and (h)(1)(B); Title II professional development grant requirements, such as 20 U.S.C. §§6645(b)(2), 6648(d)(1)(E), 6650(b)(2). Expert evidence is regularly brought to bear in administrative hearings and litigation on the appropriateness of special education programs for individuals with disabilities under IDEA. See section II.C.4.

202. Perkins-supported programs, for example, must be "of such size, scope, and quality as to be effective." 20 U.S.C. §2342(c)(1)(A).

203. See *Nicholson v. Pittenger,* supra note 95, and discussion in section III.A.1.e of size, scope, and quality issues in relation to failure to respond to data showing the program is not working.

204. See *Successful School Restructuring,* supra note 13 and accompanying text.

205. See text accompanying notes 20–22, supra, concerning the impact of resources on schools' capacity to effectively implement reform. Even some states whose finance systems were successfully challenged, however, continue to receive very poor grades for

equitably funding local reform. *Quality Counts,* supra note 3. See also Jonathan Kozol, *Savage Inequalities* (1991).

206. See *Successful School Restructuring,* supra note 13. The need for intensive staff development is further highlighted by research showing that teachers in restructuring schools have an easier time adopting new teaching methods—such as encouraging students to talk more—than using those methods well, in terms of both depth of subject matter content and ability to push the student dialogue to a high level (with probing questions, etc.). David K. Cohen et al., chapter 6 of Deborah Lowenberg Ball, et al., *Understanding State Efforts to Reform Teaching and Learning: The Progress of Instructional Reform in Schools for Disadvantaged Children* (Michigan State University and University of Michigan, 1994).

207. Title I, aside from its requirement of "highly qualified" instructional staff, builds on knowledge that "Intensive and sustained professional development for teachers and other school staff, focused on teaching and learning and on helping children attain high standards, is too often not provided," 20 U.S.C. §6301(c)(5); and requires devotion of sufficient resources to effectively carry out the plans for intensive, sustained professional development to enable all students to meet the standards, §§6314(a)(5) and 6315(c)(3). See also §§6312(e)(2) and (3); 6317(c)(1); 6319. Goals 2000 spells out a national goal and specific objectives for staff development, 20 U.S.C. §5812(4); requires states and localities to focus on improving teaching, including familiarizing teachers with the standards and developing their capacity to provide high-quality instruction, §§5886(c)(1) and 5889(a)(3); and awards a separate set of professional development grants, §5889(b). Requirements for professional development grants under Title II of ESEA are found at 20 U.S.C. §§6601 et seq.

208. For example, the National Center for Educational Outcomes found that most national and state assessments exclude large numbers of students with disabilities who were capable of participating. Kevin McGrew et al., *Inclusion of Students with Disabilities in National and State Data Collection Programs* (1992).

209. For other problems in developing consensus on assessment, see Newmann, King, Rigdon, supra note 34.

210. Some explicit provisions may be found in Title I, for example, 20 U.S.C. §6312(a)(1). Adequate, classroom-based assessment is also critical to meeting other requirements which cannot be met with the yearly assessments of certain grades used for school accountability, such as the Title I requirement to identify and remedy on a timely basis the difficulties that students are having with particular standards during the course of the year. Further, to the extent that these assessments, in the form of grades, are also used by schools to make high-stakes decisions about students' futures, such as placement in low tracks or non-graduation, they may be subject to the analysis discussed in sections II.C.5, II.D.2, and III.B.1.

211. See Stevens, supra note 196.

212. Title I improvement actions must be those with greatest likelihood of success; see text accompanying note 185, supra.

213. In addition to improvement plans for programs making inadequate progress, Perkins

requires, as part of the annual evaluation, steps to identify and remove barriers resulting in unequal rates of participation or success for special populations; see text accompanying note 102, supra.

214. See section II.C.5.b for civil rights case law requiring changes in programs for LEP students if, after a trial period, they are not working. Similarly, in *Nicholson v. Pittenger,* supra note 95, the court found a violation of the size, scope, and quality requirement of the old Title I—before the law contained an explicit school improvement structure—because programs were approved without change despite evaluation data showing they were ineffective.

215. See note 90 and accompanying text, supra.

216. This misreading is partially responsible, for example, for the failure to pay much attention to the critical, school-based requirements of the new Title I while we wait for state standards and assessments to be fully developed. As a result, a multibillion dollar reform program is discussed at the national level as if it were nothing but a state planning grant, while too often in the schools the programs, with notable exceptions, continue to look like the former Chapter 1 programs.

217. States and localities receiving federal funds sign an assurance that the programs will be administered in conformity with these requirements, and states are responsible for monitoring local implementation. Also, under state constitutions, it is typically the state which is ultimately responsible for ensuring that a thorough and efficient system of education is established.

218. In addition to the overall responsibilities the U.S. Department of Education has for ensuring that its programs are administered at state and local levels in conformity with the terms set out by Congress, the Perkins Act requires, for example, a federal monitoring plan, developed through a participatory process, and including monitoring the states' efforts to monitor local recipients. 20 U.S.C. §2466e.

219. These efforts also overlap with efforts to establish delivery and practice standards for educational institutions. See Darling-Hammond, supra note 12.

220. See, for example, Cal. Stat. art. 2.5, §51215; Md. Code Ann. §7-202(a).

221. See, for example, Ala. Code tit. 16, §16-23-16.1 (1995).

222. Carnegie Forum on Education and the Economy, *A Nation Prepared: Teachers for the Twenty-First Century;* The Holmes Group, *Tomorrow's Teachers;* National Governors' Association, *Time for Results: Task Force on Teaching.*

223. National Board for Professional Teaching Standards, "Backgrounder."

224. The direct reach of NBPTS standards may initially be more limited than the licensing standards discussed below, since only a small number of teachers have sought board certification to date, and even current proposals to increase the number dramatically set a goal of 105,000, or one for every school. Nevertheless, as in medicine, the potential relationship between board certification standards and the overall development of accepted standards of the profession extends beyond those who actually seek certification.

225. NBPTS, "National Board Certification: Five Principles of Successful Implementation." (The parenthetical material summarizes points made in explanatory materials for each principle.)

226. *Model Standards for Beginning Teacher Licensing and Development: A Resource for State Dialogue* (1992). INTASC is housed at the Council of Chief State School Officers.

227. *Standards for School Leaders* (Council of Chief State School Officers, adopted by Full Consortium, November 2, 1996).

228. *Standards, Procedures and Policies for the Accreditation of Professional Education Units* (1994 revision). These standards are evolving; for instance, a parent involvement standard is under consideration. 5(1) *NCATE Reporter* 1 (Winter 1997).

229. *What Matters Most: Teaching for America's Future* (1996), p. 21.

230. See *Peter W. v. San Francisco Unified School District,* 60 Cal. App. 3d 814 (1976). *Tirpak v. Los Angeles Unified School District,* 187 Cal. App. 3d 639 (Ct. App. 1986); *Donohue v. Copaigue Union Free School District,* 407 N.Y.S.2d 874 (App. Div. 2d Dep't 1978), aff'd, 418 N.Y.S.2d 375 (1979); *Hoffman v. City of New York,* 410 N.Y.S.2d 99 (App. Div. 1978), rev'd, 424 N.Y.S.2d 376 (1979); *Suriano v. Hyde Park Central School District,* 611 N.Y.S.2d 20 (App. Div. 1994); *D.S.W. v. Fairbanks North Star Borough School District,* 628 P.2d 554 (Alaska 1981); *Hunter v. Board of Education,* 439 A.2d 582 (Md. Ct. App. 1982); *Myers v. Medford Lakes Board of Education,* 489 A.2d 1240 (N.J. App. Div. 1985). But see *B. M. v. State,* 649 P.2d 425 (Mont. 1982).

231. These pronouncements presumably would not, however, bar schools and educators from claiming that the student did not make the requisite effort (a kind of contributory negligence). In contrast, the public policy agreement that all children can learn would seem to bar most defenses that the students did not achieve proficiency because they were incapable. Further, even the defense of lack of student effort would seem questionable in those instances where there was massive failure to follow good educational practice, since the presence or absence of such practice has a major impact on whether children are engaged in school. Indeed, the imposition of higher achievement standards without effective school practices for enabling students to meet them is likely to *decrease* the motivation of large numbers of students who—as generations before them—learn to see themselves as school failures.

232. The risk is presumably indirect in most cases—through liability insurance premiums—rather than through directly exposing schools or individual educators to direct payment of a major damage claim.

233. Strong parent involvement provisions also operate in Head Start. 42 U.S.C. §9837(b); 45 C.F.R. Part 1304, Subpart E (Parent Involvement Objectives and Performance Standards) and Appendix B (Head Start Policy Manual: The Parents).

234. See section I.D. See also Newmann et al., supra note 34, on the role of internal accountability.

235. See *Urgent Message,* supra note 27. The National Education Goals Panel has found a striking degree of alienation among parents. Very low percentages of parents (20% in first grade, 17% in fourth, 10% in eighth) report that they have a say in setting school policy, while 58–62% of principals report that parents participate. Few parents agree that their child is challenged at school (15–27%) or gets any additional help in school he or she needs (17–27%). Only a minority of parents at any grade level agree that they (23–39%) or their children (26–42%) are respected by teachers and principals. *Data for the National Education Goals Report* (Volume I: National Data, 1995).

236. See section I.D, notes 27–30 and accompanying text, supra. For description of the limited nature of even most of the best parent involvement efforts, see Chapter 3, "What Falls Short," in *Learning from Others,* supra note 27.

237. See James S. Liebman, "Voice, Not Choice," 101 *Yale L. J.* 259 (1991).

238. See discussion of NCES data in Stevens, supra note 196.

239. See also 20 U.S.C. §1401(a)(18)(B), providing that part of the definition of "appropriate" education for students with disabilities under IDEA is conformance with state standards for provision of that education.

240. Thus, in both these respects, these developments allow lawyers and educators working together to move beyond *Debra P.,* supra note 172, in which—while it remains the leading case holding that students must have an adequate opportunity to learn the material on such tests before being subjected to major penalties—(a) the court subsequently relied on a questionable study in eventually determining that Florida's curriculum and instruction had been modified sufficiently to provide, after four years, adequate opportunity; and (b) the plaintiffs sought only to overturn the diploma denial.

241. The internal contradictions are heightened because measures of student performance are simultaneously being used to assess schools (which is premised on the notion that low scores indicate that students have *not* yet been taught the skills and knowledge adequately) and to impose sanctions on students (which must be premised on the notion that they *have* been taught adequately).

242. *Griggs v. Duke Power Co.,* 401 U.S. 424 (1971).

243. For example, the Bureau of Labor Statistics' updates on job growth regularly show that relatively low-wage, low-skill jobs continue to dominate the list of areas producing the largest number of new jobs. BLS can simultaneously report that "Jobs requiring the most education and training will be the fastest growing and highest paying," *and* that "Jobs requiring the least education and training will provide the most openings, but offer the lowest pay" (*Tomorrow's Jobs: Overview*), because doubling an area with 5,000 jobs will produce far fewer jobs than even a 1% gain in an area with 5 million jobs. Thus, the ten occupations for which BLS predicts the largest growth are, in order: cashiers, janitors/cleaners, retail salespersons, waiters/waitresses, registered nurses, general managers/top executives, systems analysts, home health aides, guards, and nursing aides/orderlies/attendants (*Employment Outlook:* 1994–2005). In addition to dominating the list of largest number of new jobs, low-wage/low-skill occupations also produce the most replacement openings. See also Commission on the Skills of the American Workforce, National Center on Education and the Economy, *America's Choice: High Skills or Low Wages!* (1990); Lawrence R. Mishel and Ruy A. Teixeira, *The Myth of the Coming Labor Shortage: Jobs, Skills, and Incomes of America's Workforce 2000* (1991); David Howell, "The Skills Myth," 18 *The American Prospect,* 81–90 (Summer 1994); Edward N. Wolff, *Technology and the Demand for Skills* (Jerome Levy Economics Institute, Working Paper No. 153, December 1995).

244. Martin Carnoy and Richard Rothstein, "Are Black Diplomas Worth Less?" 30 *The American Prospect,* 42-45 (January–February 1997); Elaine Reardon, "Black/White Wage Inequality in the 1980's," 4 *Jobs and Capital,* Feature Article No. 4 (Summer 1995);

Jared Bernstein, *Examining the Puzzle: The Gap Between Black Educational and Labor Market Progress* (Economic Policy Institute, February 1995); Frank Levy and Richard Murnane, "U.S. Earnings Levels and Earnings Inequality: A Review of Recent Trends and Proposed Explanations," *Journal of Economic Literature,* September 1992. As Barry Bluestone explains, greater equality in schooling does not necessarily produce more equal earnings, in part because smaller and smaller differences in education count for more and more in obtaining the limited number of good jobs. *The Polarization of American Society: Victims, Suspects, and Mysteries to Unravel* (1995). See also note 52 and accompanying text, infra.

245. 42 U.S.C. §2000e. See *Griggs,* supra note 242; Civil Rights Act of 1991, P.L. No. 102-166, codifying the *Griggs* line of cases and overturning the contrasting decision in *Wards Cove Packing Co. v. Atonio,* 490 U.S. 642 (1989).

246. See Elmore, supra note 39.

247. One can argue that meaningful change *always* comes about, at least in part, through extraordinary efforts on the part of a dedicated few. But the point is that, for people who want to dedicate their energies to helping take reform to scale, their strategy should not be getting all schools to replicate the histories of these lead schools.

248. Elmore, supra note 39, at 19, addresses this piece of the scale question and suggests that one key for staff development of sufficient scale and depth is *external* normative structures for good practice, such as the professional teaching standards and credentialing systems discussed in section III.A.2, because "it institutionalizes the idea that professionals are responsible for looking outward at challenging conceptions of good practice, in addition to looking inward at their values and competencies." At the same time, he stresses the importance of teachers working on their practice in small, personalized groupings, rather than anonymous, bureaucratic structures, and of having one or more explicit models for organically increasing the numbers involved in strong staff development.

Afterword: Reform Law and Schools

Martha Minow

We are in the midst of a wave of school reform, a reprieve actually from the disillusionment and frustration generated by the last wave.

The last wave started, many observe, when the launch of the Soviet Sputnik satellite stimulated fears that American education was failing to prepare Americans for global competition. Public will sponsored federal dollars and experimental curricula in public schools. This coincided with more vigorous enforcement of the desegregation mandate. In addition, young men seeking to avoid the draft or exercising conscientious objection became teachers, usually for a short time, but long enough to excite classrooms with new energy and ideas. And then a movement to integrate children with special needs in mainstream classrooms and to provide needed services animated litigation and legislation. Advocates for immigrant children successfully argued for bilingual instruction. Lawyers associated with civil rights and equality coalitions filed suits to equalize per-pupil expenditures. The experiment called Head Start offered an expansive model for preschool education and also for connecting schools, medical and social services, and disadvantaged families throughout public education.

But reaction and retrenchment followed. Courts set limits on school desegregation remedies. Special education bureaucracies and even due process hearings began to seem the problem rather than the solution in many districts. The
federal courts and some state courts rebuffed school finance litigation. Bilingual
education created a battleground over the best way to teach English and,
indeed, over the very purposes of education. Public schools scrambled to
reclaim their "core missions" of instruction rather than participate in the fights
over dwindling resources for schools-based services. Legal commentators decried excessive judicial involvement in institutional reforms. And depending on
your viewpoint, beleaguered teachers' unions built understandable defenses
against relentless criticism or stood in the way of effective reforms.

Yet rather than waiting another twenty or thirty years—or the passage of a
generation burned by failure—school reforms promptly started up again with
support in diverse quarters. Some reformers simply never stopped, shifting to
state courts when federal courts made obstacles, or building bridges between
teachers' unions and universities. Martin Gerry traces the recent and current
reform wave to the publication of *A Nation at Risk* in 1983. The report, like
Sputnik in 1957, directed the attention of opinion leaders, legislators, and
business people to the challenge of higher expectations for all American children and schools. In addition, James Comer, Theodore Sizer, and Robert
Slavin, among others, demonstrated that individual schools could be much
better, and perhaps fleets of schools as well. Yet, as the chapters in this volume
demonstrate, the current generation of school reforms owes much to lawyers,
and the lawyers involved are beginning to learn to collaborate with educators in
ways that could make change endure.

The new movement is under construction. This volume sketches its hopeful
themes, and important warnings. Thus, as Molly McUsic documents, lawyers
who seek to develop state constitutional rights to "adequate" education must
work with educators to give form and content to that notion. The law of special
education could steer away from attacks for diverting too many dollars from
mainstream classes and also away from parental fears, and especially minority
parents' fears, about segregation by implementing inclusionary practices. Look
at how children are educated, and build the capacity of each school, and each
classroom, to educate all students; this is the strategy that could win legally,
politically, fiscally, and ethically. If lawyers and educators collaborate in the new
technologies of reform—standard setting, program assessment, and monitoring—reforms could connect desire, know-how, and authority, Paul Weckstein
advises. Indeed, as Jay Heubert describes, educators can play greater roles in

litigation and lawyers should spend more time mediating, building solutions to problems, and convening teams to collaborate on school reform with greater successful results than when the two kinds of professionals stay in conventional roles.

Some authors give important cautions. Absent thoughtful responses to the needs of a new influx of immigrant children, current reforms could make their situations, attitudes, and futures worse. Without the presence of representatives for Latino children, for example, school desegregation remedies terminate programs they need and deserve. Moreover, warn Marcelo Suárez-Orozco, Peter Roos, and Carola Suárez-Orozco, immigrant children's length of stay in the United States seems associated with a worsening of their attitudes toward schooling. Like the proverbial canary in the mine shaft, immigrant children whose school aspirations and achievement decline with successive years in American schools may simply be demonstrating to everyone else the suffocation that results in too many current educational settings. Reinventing systems, not just individual schools, is crucial for real and long-term improvement. This is a lesson Martin Gerry pulls from the piecemeal efforts to integrate services with schools.

Perhaps most sobering is Gary Orfield's observation that "today's activist conservative judges and educators are pushing harder and faster for [racial] resegregation than their predecessors ever did for integration." This resegregation by activist judges could actually be accelerated by some versions of school choice, performance standards, heightened graduation requirements, and the undermining of programs for Latinos and economically disadvantaged children. The very mentality that looks for quick fixes and simple mantras in school reform matches the tendency Orfield discovers in a number of resegregation cases "toward speedy and superficial consideration of the very complex and critical decisions." Yet equally disturbing is Martin Gerry's assessment that "the largest group of children in need of [services] who are most frequently excluded (i.e., found to be *undeserving*) are children living in two-parent working-class families, many of which have lower income levels than single parent families which receive public assistance benefits." Equality may be restored, sadly, simply because the recent welfare reforms will strip benefits from children in single parent families as well.

What shards of the old paradigm, framed by rights and remedies, enforced by courts, can and should be salvaged in this new time, marked by talk of higher expectations for students and teachers, incentives, investment, and outcome measures? Thomas Hehir and Sue Gamm quote an urban special education director who said, "If I were to say, philosophically, I think we need this vocational transition program, I'd never get it, but if I say to my superintendent, 'We're going to get our ass beat up in a hearing again unless we beef up that program,' all of a sudden the funds are available." One current challenge involves preserving that ability to ensure needs are met because law so demands while attending to the collaborative processes necessary to improve day-to-day instruction and supports in actual classrooms. These processes require political give-and-take, restructuring school days to permit common planning and learning time for teachers, along with management and incentive techniques to change entire systems. Rights talk, in contrast, amplifies the claims of precisely the students who risk neglect in those processes, students who are immigrants, who have special needs, who are poor, and whose own parents cannot or do not provide vigorous advocacy.

To be frank, schools probably will never get it right once and for all. It seems improbable that even ideal schools today would not need reforms again, if not tomorrow then in a few years. But it is possible, I believe, to gather the ingredients for continual school reform, developed as much within school systems as without. For that, the entire public needs educators' help in really understanding what it takes for learning to happen and lawyers' assistance in devising and revising structures to translate dreams into enforceable realities. The enterprise represented by this book both reflects and summons this kind of sustained coalition work by teachers and lawyers to integrate the starkness of rights and the texture of day-to-day education. Parents and business people, politicians and students also need to be part of this effort. Without the integration of rights and educational insights, this will be just another short-lived and failed cycle of reform.

Contributors

Sue Gamm, J.D., is Chief Specialized Services Officer in the Chicago Public Schools, with responsibility for special education, pupil support services, gifted and talented programs, and alternative schools. She is also a member of the Illinois State Advisory Council on Special Education and has served as director of the elementary and secondary education division of the regional Office for Civil Rights, U.S. Department of Education. Her publications include *Serving Children With Disabilities: A Procedural Manual* (1992).

Martin Gerry, J.D., directs the Center for the Study of Family, Neighborhood, and Community Policy at the University of Kansas, where he heads the National Technical Assistance Center on Welfare Reform. He has also served as Assistant Secretary for Planning and Development in the U.S. Department of Health and Human Services and as director of the Office for Civil Rights in the U.S. Department of Health, Education, and Welfare. He is the author of numerous articles, including "Service Integration and Beyond" (1998).

Thomas Hehir, Ed.D., is director of the Office of Special Education Programs in the U.S. Department of Education. He has also directed special education in the Chicago and Boston school districts. His publications include "Special Education: Successes and Challenges" (1994) and *Special*

Education at the Century's End: Evolution of Theory and Practice Since 1970 (coeditor, 1992).

Jay P. Heubert, J.D., Ed.D., is an associate professor of education at Teachers College and an adjunct professor of law at Columbia Law School. He has also served as chief counsel to the Pennsylvania Department of Education and as trial attorney in the Civil Rights Division of the U.S. Department of Justice. His publications include "Schools Without Rules? Charter Schools, Federal Disability Law, and the Paradoxes of Deregulation" (1997) and "The More We Get Together: Improving Collaboration Between Educators and Their Lawyers" (1997).

Harold Howe II, M.A., served as U.S. Commissioner of Education during the Johnson Administration; as vice president for education at the Ford Foundation; as chair of the Educational Testing Service; and as the Francis Keppel Senior Lecturer on Education at the Harvard Graduate School of Education. He is the author of numerous articles and *Thinking About Our Kids* (1993).

Molly S. McUsic, J.D., professor of law at the University of North Carolina at Chapel Hill, currently serves as counselor to the Secretary of the Interior. McUsic served as law clerk to the Hon. Harry A. Blackmun of the U.S. Supreme Court; her publications include "The Use of Education Clauses in School Finance Reform Legislation" (1991).

Martha Minow, J.D., Ed.M., is a professor of law at Harvard Law School, a lecturer in education at the Harvard Graduate School of Education, and a co-executive director of Children's Studies at Harvard. She served as law clerk to the Hon. Thurgood Marshall of the U.S. Supreme Court. Her numerous publications include *Not Only for Myself: Identity, Politics and Law* (1997) and *Making All the Difference: Inclusion, Exclusion and American Law* (1990).

Gary Orfield, Ph.D., is a professor of education and social policy at Harvard University and co-director of the Harvard Project on Civil Rights. Among his recent books, both coauthored, are *Dismantling Desegregation: The Quiet Reversal of Brown v. Board of Education* (1996) and *The Closing Door: Conservative Policy and Black Opportunity* (1991).

Peter D. Roos, J.D., is co-director of Multicultural Education, Training and Advocacy, Inc., in San Francisco. He has served as lead attorney in a number of civil rights cases concerned with the education of immigrant children. He successfully argued *Plyler v. Doe* (1982), in which the U.S. Supreme Court ruled that children of undocumented immigrants have a constitutional right to a free public education.

Carola Suárez-Orozco, Ph.D., is a lecturer in human development and psychology at the Harvard Graduate School of Education and co-director of the Harvard Immigration Projects. She coauthored *Transformations: Immigration, Family Life, and Achievement Motivation Among Latino Adolescents* (1995).

Marcelo Suárez-Orozco, Ph.D., is a professor in human development and psychology at the Harvard Graduate School of Education and co-director of the Harvard Immigration Projects. His most recent books are *Transformations: Immigration, Family Life, and Achievement Motivation Among Latino Adolescents* (co-author, 1995) and *Crossings: Mexican Immigration in Interdisciplinary Perspective* (editor).

Paul Weckstein, J.D., Ed.M., is co-director of the Center for Law and Education. He has played an important role in shaping past and current reforms of Title I, the Perkins Act, and the School to Work Opportunities Act and has initiated national projects to help implement those reforms. He is the author of "New Education Standards and the Right to Quality Education" (1993).

Index

Accountability: and student achievement, 28, 196–97, 313, 358; and law-driven school reforms, 196–97, 247; and children with disabilities, 228, 237, 243n87, 350; and service integration, 273, 276, 287–88, 298n37; and categorical grant programs, 282; and assessments, 310, 352–53, 359; and standards-based reforms, 318- 20, 346–64, 368n34; and legal claims, 346–59; and outcome measures, 347–50, 353; integrated model for, 348–54; and program design, 350–52; and monitoring, 353–54, 386n217; and teacher standards, 354–57; and participatory process, 358–59; and student accountability for standards, 359–62; and collaboration, 362–64

Advocates' collaboration: and law-driven school reform, 8, 17, 33–34, 200n3; and immigrant children, 164, 171, 198;

and limited English proficiency children, 190; and special education, 214

Affirmative action: debate over, 2, 4; and politics, 26; and outcome measures, 30; and immigrant children, 32; and Reagan Administration, 45, 85n36; civil rights remedies for, 49; and conservative activists, 50; and reverse discrimination, 77

African Americans. *See* Black students; Blacks

Agranoff, R. A., 266

Aid to Families with Dependent Children (AFDC), 27, 248–49, 249n9, 252, 253, 294n10, 294n11, 295n14

Alabama, 144n89

Alaska, 94, 114, 139n20

Allen v. McDonough, José P. v. Ambach, 234

Allington, Richard, 228

Arizona, 98, 107–8, 110, 118, 180, 185

Arkansas, 150n148, 163

Armor, David, 64

Arviso v. Dawson, 120–21

Asia, 161, 165–67, 175–76

Asian Americans, 10, 11, 29, 74, 180, 181, 188

Assessments: and immigrant children, 32, 177–78, 352; and children with disabilities, 228, 338–41, 352, 377–78n135, 378n142, 385n208; portfolio assessments, 228, 336; and accountability, 310, 352–53, 359; and standards-based reform, 310, 321; and student achievement, 312–13; authentic assessment, 313; and state law, 323, 352; and student performance, 329, 388n241; and Title I, 329, 352; and vocational education, 335–36; and Individuals with Disabilities Education Act, 339, 352; and limited English proficiency children, 344, 352, 380n166; classroom-based assessment, 353, 385n210; of teachers, 355–56, 357, 391; and employment-related sanctions, 360; and authentic pedagogy, 367n14; teacher-based assessment, 369n37. *See also* Testing

Austin, Texas, 74

Authentic pedagogy, 311, 313, 366n13, 367n14

Balanced Budget Act of 1997, 252–54, 293n4, 294–95n11

Barnett v. Fairfax County School Board, 223, 225

Beattie, Bud, 210

Benefit analysis, 231–34

Benveniste, G., 206, 216

Bilingual education: and immigrant children, viii, 22, 32, 171, 187, 192; and court orders, 7, 197–98; and service integration, 24, 297n33; and school finance reform, 106; and adequacy claims, 137; per-pupil expenditures for;

140n31; and English language instruction, 182, 391; and teachers, 188, 192, 197; and integration, 189; and educational resource distribution, 191; and intra-district disparities, 193; and law-driven school reform, 195; and participatory process, 358

Bilingual Education Act of 1968, 22, 25, 96–97, 164, 343–44

Black students: and segregation, 2, 41; student performance of, 3, 15, 49, 71, 89, 100–101, 146n109; and desegregation, 10, 41, 42, 44, 46; and educational exclusion, 10, 11; racial isolation of, 15, 17; and racial stereotypes, 16; and poverty, 65, 101, 230; and special education, 65, 96, 206, 229; population of, 73; and Latino students, 74; and compensatory education programs, 77; test scores of, 156n195, 196; and federal law compliance, 370n44

Blacks, viii, 60, 64–65, 77, 180, 361

Block grants, 249, 250–52, 294n9, 294n10, 325

Board of Education v. Dowell (1991), 50, 54, 59, 60

Board of Education v. Rowley, 219

Boger, John C., 157n201

Bohannon, Luther, 60

Boston, Massachusetts, 70, 189, 234, 236

Brindis, C., 271

Broward County, Florida, 59–60, 70

Brown, R., 271

Brown v. Board of Education of Topeka (1954): and desegregation, vii, 46, 52, 56, 57; and immigrant children, vii, 13; and school finance reform, vii, 11, 12; and discrimination, viii, 180; and law-driven school reforms, 1; and segregation, 2, 10, 28, 42, 43, 45, 100; and children with disabilities, 14, 210–11; and resegregation, 39, 40; and conservative activists, 53–54, 66; and judges, 55; and new school construction, 68

Brown II, 62, 75
Bruner, C., 265
Buck v. Bell, 210
Buffalo, New York, 55, 67–69, 70
Burke, Chris, 208
Bush Administration, 45, 49, 54–55, 120, 309, 323
Busing: as leading issue, 44, 85n48; and *Swann v. Charlotte-Mecklenburg Board of Education* (1971), 47, 63, 80; and Reagan Administration, 49, 85n36; and local control, 56, 57, 58; and desegregation, 59, 63, 86n55, 100; and parents, 61; and politics, 101; and integration, 133
Byrd, Janelle, 60

California: and undocumented children, ix, 184, 185–86; and Proposition 187, 5, 13, 32, 164, 172, 184–85, 199, 200–201n5; and English language learners, 22; and Latino students, 73, 180; and resegregation, 73–74; and Proposition 13, 111–12; and school finance reform, 111–12, 114; per-pupil expenditures of, 150n148; and immigration, 162, 170, 172; and limited English proficiency students, 162, 189, 192; and restructuring of schools, 178; and law-driven school reform, 179; and Asian Americans, 181; and immigrant children, 200n2; and service integration, 267, 297n34, 301n66
California Tomorrow, 171
Cambodian immigrants, 166
Campbell v. Talladega County Board of Education and Board of Education of the State of Alabama, 217
Cardenas, Jose, 164
Caribbean, 161, 166
Carl D. Perkins Vocational and Applied Technology Education Act: and enforceable performance mandates, 23; and outcome measures, 30, 353, 385–

86n213; and educational quality, 315; and standards-based reform, 330–35, 376n124; and children with disabilities, 341; and limited English proficiency children, 344; and assessment, 352; and participatory process, 358; and monitoring, 386n218
Carnegie Corporation, 27
Carter Administration, 73, 74
Castaneda v. Pickard (1981), 188, 189
Categorical grant programs: problems with, x–xi, 263–64; and school reform, 247; and New Deal, 248–49; and proliferation of, 249–50; and block grants, 250–52, 294n10; and welfare reform, 252–54; and children's services system, 260; and parents' role, 262; and community context, 263; management of, 264; and service integration, 265, 281, 282; and lawyers' roles, 281–82, 290, 292; and families, 298n43
Center for Law and Education, 164
Center for the Study of Social Policy, 289
Center on Organization and Restructuring of Schools (CORS), 310–13, 366–67n13
Central America, 166, 167
Chapter 1, 94, 139n17, 328, 370n44, 373n84. *See also* Title I
Charlotte, North Carolina, 70, 97
Chaskin, R., 268, 269
Chicago, Illinois, 77, 162, 193, 226, 227, 313
Child and Family Services programs, 294n10
Child care, 248, 252–53, 259, 293n5, 294n10
Child Care and Development Block Grant, 252, 294n10
Child food and nutrition services, 253, 268, 294n10, 294n11
Child wellness: and school-based services, 246–48; evaluation of, 254; and

Child wellness (*continued*)
Healthy People 2000, 255–56; and
children's services system, 260–61,
263–64; and communities, 262–63,
275–76, 277, 299n44; financing of,
263–64, 277, 278; and high-school
graduation rates, 263, 296n28; and service integration, 270–73, 276, 280,
298n37; and categorical grant programs, 281; and lawyers' roles, 281–82,
290, 291

Children with disabilities: discrimination
against, viii, 293n8, 341; and law-
driven school reforms, ix, 1, 2, 3, 9;
and student achievement, 2, 3–4; and
educational equality, 4, 6; and educational exclusion, 14–15, 16, 35n2, 390;
and litigation, 14, 32; and classroom
placement, 17, 19–20; and enforceable
performance mandates, 23; and outcome measures, 31, 232, 237; and collaboration, 34; and compulsory
education laws, 35n2; and desegregation, 67; and educational delivery, 95;
and federal education funds, 141n47;
and lawyers' roles, 205; and costs, 206;
progress of, 208–9; and segregation,
209, 210, 211, 213, 218–19, 226, 229,
231, 232–33, 234; and disruptive behavior, 221–22, 233; and accountability, 228, 237, 243n87, 350; and
assessments, 228, 338–41, 352, 377–
78n135, 378n142, 385n208; and poverty,
229, 230; and benefit analysis, 231–34;
and categorical grant programs, 250;
and Supplemental Security Income,
252; and neighborhood schools,
296n25; and educational quality, 307,
314; and vocational education, 331, 333;
and standards-based reforms, 338,
377n132, 378n138; and educational
sanctions, 359; and federal law compliance, 370n44; and equal protection
clauses, 380n170

Children's services system: program
structures, 245–54; evaluation of, 254–
56; policy assumptions of, 256–63;
problems with, 256–64; public education compared to, 257; and child wellness, 260–61, 263–64; financing of,
263–64, 277, 278–79, 282, 285, 288–
90; service integration strategies for,
264–76, 285, 300n59; system reform
directions, 276–79; and communities,
277–78, 299n47, 299n48, 299n51; and
poverty, 296n23

Chinese immigrants, 166–67, 181

Choice programs: debate over, viii, 4,
392; and desegregation, 31, 41–42, 120;
and courts, 100; and school finance reform, 120–28; and adequacy claims,
121, 122, 125, 128; and private and parochial schools, 121, 153n175; and reading proficiency, 155n193; and
immigrant children, 176, 177

Civil rights: and courts, viii, 56; and deregulation, 4; and educational equality, 16, 250, 293n8, 390; and
decentralization, 31; and lawyers' role,
32–33, 290; and desegregation, 39, 45,
47, 53, 71; and resegregation, 43, 60,
61, 66, 67, 80; and conservative activists, 44, 50; and Reagan Administration, 44–45; and Justice Department,
46; and Meese, 49, 85n36; and voting
rights, 49; and Savannah, 62; and trial
courts, 79; of Latino students, 81; and
school finance reform, 89, 102, 105;
and equal protection clause, 103, 344,
379n157; and immigrant children, 164;
and service integration, 280; and
neighborhood schools, 296n25; and
individualized educational programs,
298n43; and educational quality, 314–
15; and student achievement, 341; and
Goals 2000, 342; and Title I, 342–43;
and employment-related sanctions,
360–61

Civil Rights Act of 1964: and desegregation, 10, 42, 46; Title VI of, 18, 96, 190, 212, 293n8, 314, 342, 343, 370n44, 379n157; and Supreme Court, 44; and linguistically responsive education, 187, 188; and newcomer schools, 191; Title IX of, 293n8; and standards-based reform, 341–44; Title VII of, 361; and accountability, 384n199

Class integration model, 91, 120, 128–34, 133, 137, 157n201, 158n208

Classroom placements: and educational quality, 17–20; and immigrant children, 21, 29, 172–73, 175; and desegregation, 64, 65, 66; and resegregation, 76; and children with disabilities, 141n47, 229, 339; and discrimination, 180–81

Cleveland, Ohio, 55

Cleveland Heights, Ohio, 210

Clinton, Bill, viii, 139n17, 181, 206–7, 208, 237, 309

Clyde K. v. Puyallup School District, 222

Coleman Report, 11, 19, 122, 158–59n211

Collaboration: and school finance reform, viii, 21; and immigrant children, ix, 197–99; and service integration, xi, 25, 272–73, 274, 275; and educational equality, 2; and educational policy, 5, 6, 8, 33, 34, 35; and law-driven school reforms, 5–8, 17, 34–35, 308, 316–18; and classroom placement, 18; and limited English proficiency children, 22; and litigation, 31, 33, 34, 362; and special education, 235–38; and standards-based reform, 308–10, 362–64, 389n247; and enforceable performance mandates, 316–18, 362–64; and educational quality, 362, 393. *See also* Advocates' collaboration; Educators' collaboration; Lawyers' collaboration; Parent collaboration; Scholars' collaboration

College graduates: and minority students, 41; and educational resource distribution, 94, 139n20; and class integration model, 129; and immigrant children, 167; and Indian immigrants, 167; and children with disabilities, 208

Colorado, 73, 139n20, 185, 297n34

Columbus II, 43

Comer, James, 391

Communities: and child wellness, 262–63, 275–76, 277, 299n44; and children's services system, 277–78, 299n47, 299n48, 299n51; and service integration, 281, 282, 283–84, 300n58; and lawyers' roles, 290, 291, 292, 293; and law-driven school reform, 308; and vocational education, 331–32, 333, 335; and accountability, 358

Community Mental Health Services Block Grant, 294n10

Compensatory education programs: and black students, 77; and adequacy claims, 119; and urban areas, 129; and student achievement, 131; per-pupil expenditures for, 140n31; and immigrant children, 191; and children with disabilities, 218; as grant programs, 247; and welfare reform, 248; and service integration, 297n33

Comprehensive School Reform Demonstration Program, 374n96

Compulsory education laws, 35n2, 93, 184, 210

Confidentiality, 282, 300n55

Congress: and welfare reform, 27, 254; and civil rights, 42; and desegregation, 44, 49; and Latino students, 73; and linguistically responsive education, 187; and bilingual education, 198; and special education, 206–7, 209, 212; and children with disabilities, 213; and block grants, 251; and Goals 2000, 254; and service integration, 265, 297n30; and standards-based reform, 309, 325, 372–73n74; and educational

Congress (*continued*)
   resource distribution, 312; and implementation, 317–18, 369n36; and educational quality, 370n46; and accountability, 386n218
Connecticut, 111, 150n148, 297n34
Consent decrees, 7, 198, 211–12
Conservative activists: and courts, 40, 43, 44, 49, 51, 54, 78, 103, 392; and resegregation, 44, 54, 392; and civil rights, 50; and Latino students, 73; and standards-based reform, 320
Constitutional rights: and educational equality, 4; and school finance reform, 102–3; and standards-based reforms, 344–46. *See also* Supreme Court
Cooper v. Aaron (1958), 46
Cooperative learning, 41, 209, 231, 311–12, 334
Corey H. et al. v. City of Chicago et al., 226
Cornelius, W., 192
CORS (Center on Organization and Restructuring of Schools), 310–13, 366–67n13
Counseling and guidance programs, 64, 175, 192, 233, 333
Court orders: and bilingual education, 7, 197–98; and desegregation, 7, 40, 67, 390; and urban areas, 7; compliance with, 69; and resegregation, 76; and unitary status, 78–79, 81–82; termination of, 80; and choice model, 120–21; and school finance reform, 120; and class integration model, 131
Courts: and school finance reform, viii, 6, 15, 89, 103–4, 137, 192, 391; and resegregation, 2, 40, 41, 43, 55, 78–79; and educational policy, 5, 7, 18; and desegregation, 7, 10–11, 39, 42, 80–83, 93, 100, 391; and educational exclusion, 9; and Proposition 187, 13; and classroom placement, 19; and student performance, 29; and law-driven

school reform, 32; and conservative activists, 40, 43, 44, 49, 51, 54, 78, 103, 392; and segregation, 42–53, 78–79, 83n7; trial courts, 45, 50, 53–61, 71, 75–79; district courts, 46, 49, 51–52, 57–60, 63, 75–79, 101, 102; appellate courts, 49, 50, 60, 61, 67, 75–79, 87n75; and practicality principle, 62–69; and local control, 70; and ending remedies, 71–73; and adequacy claims, 116, 117, 118; and choice model, 126–27, 128; and whole state reform model, 135–36; and language programming, 181; and undocumented children, 184, 185; and linguistically responsive programs, 188; and special education, 209, 214, 216–19, 222, 223–25. *See also* Supreme Court, U.S.
Croninger, Robert, 311
Crotes, D., 170
Curtin, John, 67–68

Dallas, Texas, 68, 74, 162
Daniel, C. D., 213
Daniel R. R. v. State Board of Education, 217, 219–20, 222, 223
Darwin, Charles, 210
Davis, John, 211
Dawson, Warren, 58
Dayton II, 43
Debra P. v. Turlington (1979), 197, 345–46
Decentralization, 3, 4, 9, 26, 28–31, 32, 253, 298n38
Delaware, 64, 86n74, 114
Delivery standards, 309, 365–66n11
Denver, Colorado, 55, 70, 73, 189, 199
Deregulation, 3, 4, 9, 26, 28–31, 32, 195–96
Desegregation: compliance with, viii, 39, 57; and law-driven school reform, 3, 4; and court orders, 7, 40, 67, 390; and courts, 7, 10–11, 39, 42, 80–83, 93, 100, 391; and classroom placement,

17–19; and educational quality, 20–21; in South, 20, 42–47, 51, 71, 85n46, 100, 102, 143n73; and politics, 26–27; and outcome measures, 30; and choice programs, 31, 41–42, 120; and decentralization, 31; and litigation, 32; and resegregation, 39–40; and Latino students, 47, 67, 392; and conservative activists, 50; and student achievement, 50, 53, 100; and unitary status, 52, 56, 57–59, 85–86n55; as leading issue, 85n48; and school finance reform, 93, 109; and educational resource distribution, 100–102; and class integration model, 129, 130, 131, 133; problems with, 189–90; and standards-based reform, 365n7; and equal protection clause, 381n172; and accountability, 382n180

Detroit, Michigan, 100, 101

Dewey, J., 260, 295–96n21, 296n27

Dilemma of difference, 106, 145n98

Dole, Bob, 182, 208

Dominican Republic, 167

Dropout rates: and school funding inequalities, 13, 94; and English language learners, 23; and outcome measures, 29; and school finance reform, 111; and state funding, 111, 142n59; measurement of, 139n20; and immigrant children, 171, 172; and children with disabilities, 207, 227, 228, 338; and vocational education, 333. *See also* High-school graduation rates

Dryfoos, J., 271

Due process: and special education, 32, 205, 206, 207, 209, 214–16, 229, 240n29, 391; and court orders, 69; and minority children, 79, 229; and Individuals with Disabilities Education Act, 95; and limited English proficiency children, 96; and standards-based reforms, 345–46, 359

Eagleton-Biden Amendment, 73

Early childhood education, 259–60

Edenfield, Avant, 62–63

Education clause, 103, 104, 116, 323–24

Education for All Handicapped Children Act of 1975 (P.L. 94–143), 205, 209, 213, 218, 226, 247

Education Writers of America project, 86n60

Educational delivery: and whole state model, 91–92, 120, 134–37; legal structure for, 93–100; structural shifts in, 119–37; and choice model, 120–28; and class integration model, 128–34

Educational equality: and lawyers' roles, vii, 16, 102; and collaboration, 2; and law-driven school reforms, 4, 9, 16–26; and local control, 12; and judges, 16, 90; and segregation within schools, 16, 17–20, 65–66; and desegregation, 41–42, 56; and resegregation, 41, 44; and district courts, 51, 101; and federal mandates, 89; and state funding, 99; and private schools, 100; and school finance reform, 102, 103, 107, 115; and equity paradigm, 105–8; and adequacy standards, 118; and choice model, 125; and competitive definition, 146n105; and school-based services, 247; and civil rights laws, 250, 293n8; and enforceable performance standards, 321

Educational exclusion: and law-driven school reforms, 3, 9, 10–16, 35n2; of undocumented children, 183–87; and special education, 209–13, 217, 229, 235

Educational policy: and federal law, 4; and collaboration, 5, 6, 8, 33, 34, 35; and courts, 5, 7, 18; and law-driven school reforms, 20; and school finance reform, 21, 90; and enforceable performance mandates, 24; and resegregation, 40; and desegregation, 53; and legislature, 108; and whole state re-

Educational policy (*continued*)
form model, 136; and bilingual education, 189; and special education, 219; and social policy, 256–63; and standards-based reform, 320, 363; and state law, 323; and teacher standards, 357

Educational quality: and lawyers' roles, vii; and enforceable performance mandates, x, 23–24, 307, 314–15, 346; and classroom placements, 17–20; and immigrant children, 21–23; and service integration, 24–26; and poverty, 91; and state courts, 116; and equity claims, 119; and choice model, 124; and parents, 130, 156n195, 315–16, 368n29, 368n32; and urban areas, 130; and adequacy claims, 137; and whites, 155n189; and isolation of desire, knowledge and authority, 207–8; and due process hearings, 216; and families, 306–7, 308; empirical support for, 310–13, 391; and accountability, 318–20, 357; and access, 321; and state constitutions, 323; and Title I, 328; and collaboration, 362, 393; and Congress, 370n46; and federal law compliance, 370n45

Educational resource distribution: and per-pupil expenditures, 88; and student achievement, 89, 90, 312; and legal structure, 92–102; and desegregation, 100–102; and school finance reform, 102, 115–37; and poverty, 106, 312, 367n22; and class integration model, 130–31; and rural areas, 134, 158–59n211; and immigrant children, 165, 191–95; and teacher accountability, 319, 369n40; and standards-based reform, 320–21; and state law, 323; and accountability, 351–52, 357, 384–85n205

Educators: and law-driven school reforms, ix, 8, 17, 32; and service fragmentation, 25; and politics, 28, 33–34; and desegregation, 40; and resegregation, 40; and conservative activists, 44, 392; and school finance reform, 90, 109; and adequacy claims, 92, 117, 137; and educational equality, 102; and whole state reform model, 136–37; and immigrant children, 171, 197–99; and special education, 206, 214; and service integration, 266. *See also* Teachers

Educators' collaboration: and educational quality, vii, 362; and law-driven school reforms, x, 5–8, 17, 18–19, 34–35, 391–92; and service integration, x, 25, 281, 282, 292; and educational equality, 2; and school finance reform, 21; and legislation, 33; and litigation, 34; and immigrant children, 164, 194, 197–99; and limited English proficiency students, 190; and special education, 207, 235–38, 239; and standards-based reform, 308, 316, 346; and implementation, 317

EEOA (Equal Educational Opportunities Act of 1974), 22–23, 96, 187, 190, 314, 343, 352

Eisenhower Administration, 43

El Salvador, 166

Elementary and Secondary Education Act of 1965 (ESEA), viii, 94, 247, 340, 370n46. *See also* Title I

Eleventh Amendment, 384n199

Eleventh Circuit Court of Appeals, 78–79, 221

ELLs (English language learners), 22, 23, 24, 29, 31

Elmore, Richard F., 369n39

Employment discrimination laws, 337

Employment rates: and children with disabilities, 4, 207, 208, 209, 227, 229, 233; and outcome measures, 29; and child wellness, 296n28; and standards-based reforms, 321–22; and vocational education, 333; and wages, 371n56

Employment-related sanctions, 360–62

Enforceable performance mandates: and educational quality, x, 23–24, 307, 314–15, 346; and law-driven school reform, 3, 4; and parents, 23, 24, 315–16, 317; and litigation, 32; and school finance reform, 136; and standards-based reforms, 309; and collaboration, 316–18, 362–64; and educational resource distribution, 320–21; and state law, 322–23; and state constitutions, 323–24; and federal law, 325–44; and constitutional rights, 344–46. *See also* Accountability; Standards-based reforms

English as a Second Language (ESL), 172, 173, 192, 197

English as official U.S. language, 182, 391

English language arts standards, 383n190

English language learners (ELLs), 22, 23, 24, 29, 31. *See also* Limited English proficiency (LEP) children

Epps, Garrett, 53

Equal Educational Opportunities Act of 1974 (EEOA), 22–23, 96, 187, 190, 314, 343, 352

Equal protection clauses: and school finance reform, 89, 103, 372n65; and civil rights, 103, 379n157; and undocumented children, 185, 380n169; and special education, 209; and state constitutions, 324; and standards-based reforms, 344–45, 350, 380n169, 380n173, 380n174, 381–82n175; and children with disabilities, 380n170

ESEA (Elementary and Secondary Education Act of 1965), viii, 94, 247, 340, 370n46

ESL (English as a Second Language), 172, 173, 192, 197

Expert witnesses, 80–81, 221, 222, 226

Extracurricular activities, 77, 86n55, 219

Families: and service integration, 265, 266, 267, 268, 273, 274–75, 281, 282, 298n40; and neighborhood schools, 268–69; and accountability, 287; and lawyers' roles, 291, 292; and categorical grant programs, 298n43; and Head Start, 298n43; and complaints, 300n57; and educational quality, 306–7, 308. *See also* Parent collaboration; Parent involvement; Parents

Family Educational Rights and Privacy Act, 315–16

Family Preservation and Support Program, 294n10, 297n30

FAPE (free appropriate public education), 340

Farrow, F., 288

Faubus, Orval, 46

Fawcett, S., 277

Federal education funds: and school funding inequalities, 12–13, 92–93; and desegregation, 42, 46; level of, 94, 99, 294n10, 390; and Individuals with Disabilities Education Act, 95, 96; and Bilingual Education Act of 1968, 96–97; and special education, 96, 97, 212, 213; and children with disabilities, 141n47; and local educational agencies, 326

Federal law: and educational policy, 4; and educational delivery, 93, 94–97; and standards-based reforms, 308–9, 316, 323, 325–44, 350–51, 384n200; implementation of, 317–18; compliance with, 319, 325, 369n42; and special education, 337–41; and accountability, 354, 386n218; and black students, 370n44

Federal mandates: and educational equality, 89; and children with disabilities, 95, 226; and Individuals with Disabilities Education Act, 97; and educational quality, 307; and standards-based reforms, 349. *See also* Enforceable performance mandates

Fifth Circuit Court of Appeals, 43, 46, 219, 223, 224, 225

Filipino immigrants, 166
First, Joan, 171, 199
Flat grants, 109, 142n57
Florida: and desegregation, 55; and limited English proficiency students, 162, 190, 192, 198; and undocumented children, 184, 185; and school finance reform, 194; and service integration, 267, 297n34; and high-school graduation requirements, 321; and opportunity-to-learn standards, 388n240
Flour Bluff Independent School District v. Katherine M., 224, 225
Food stamps, 252, 294n10, 295n12
Ford, Gerald, 213
Foreign born students, 161, 171, 200n1
Fort Worth, Texas, 74, 162
Fourteenth Amendment, 344, 384n199
Fourth Circuit Court of Appeals, 223, 225
Free appropriate public education (FAPE), 340
Freeman v. Pitts, 50, 58, 62, 68
Fried, Charles, 50

Gamm, Sue, ix, 3, 14, 15, 18, 33, 392–93
Gándara, Patricia, 176, 178, 179
Gans, S., 266
Gender, 293n8, 331, 333, 341, 352, 359, 367n14
Gerry, Martin, xi, 5, 14, 25–26, 33, 265, 270–71, 277, 391–92
Glendon, M. A., 280
Goals 2000: Educate America Act 1994: and enforceable performance mandates, 23; and outcome measures, 30; and Congress, 254; and standards-based reform, 309, 325–27, 349, 376n125; and educational quality, 315; and vocational education, 332, 335; and children with disabilities, 341; and civil rights, 342; and limited English proficiency children, 344; and assess-

ment, 352; and staff development, 385n207
Goffman, Erving, 229
Gold, S., 253
Goldman, Beldene, 210
Gomby, D., 270
Governance, 283–84, 300n58, 313
Graham, P. A., 255, 295n17
Green v. New Kent County School Board, 30, 46, 56, 62, 68, 79, 80
Greer, 222
Guttentag, Lucas, 187

Hairston v. Drosick, 216–17
Haitian immigrants, 175
Hartford, Connecticut, 111, 129, 157n201
Hartsdale, New York, 106
Hassel, C., 214, 216
Hawaii, 97
Hawkins, Augustus F., 102
Head Start, viii, 249, 250, 294n10, 297n30, 298n43, 390
Health insurance, 247–48, 253, 259, 295n11, 296n24
Health services, 259, 267–68, 269, 271
Healthy People 2000, 254, 255–56
Hegarty, Stephen, 58
Hehir, Thomas: and lawyers' role, ix, 33; and children with disabilities, 3, 14, 15, 19, 236, 392–93; and due process hearings, 214, 215, 240n29
Henderson, Bill, 236
Hernandez v. Texas (1954), 180
Heubert, Jay, ix, 235, 391
Hickrod study, 150–51n148
High-school graduation rates: and children with disabilities, 4, 232, 233, 338; and segregation, 15, 41, 56, 66; and Individuals with Disabilities Education Act, 29; and black students, 64–65, 66, 89; and Latino students, 73, 74, 89; and class integration model, 129; in Kentucky, 134; and National Educa-

tion Goals, 254, 295n16; and child wellness, 263, 296n28. *See also* Dropout rates

High-school graduation requirements: and immigrant children, 176, 177; and teen pregnancy, 247–48; and standards-based reform, 321, 380n172; and due process, 345–46; and accountability, 359; and employment-related sanctions, 360, 361; and resegregation, 392

Hill, J., 271

Hirschman, Albert O., 129

Hispanics. *See* Latino students; Latinos

Hmong immigrants, 166

Holmes, Oliver Wendell (Justice), 210

Hornbeck, David, 276

Horton, G., 266

Housing policies: and school segregation, 11, 82, 100; and desegregation, 48, 71; and resegregation, 79; and state funding, 98; and choice model, 125–26, 127; and immigration, 169

Houston, Texas, 74

Humphrey, Hubert, 212

Hunter, Robert, 246

Idaho, 116

IEP. *See* Individualized educational program (IEP)

Illinois, 162

Illinois State Board of Education (ISBE), 226–27

Immigrant children: and *Brown v. Board of Education of Topeka*, vii, 13; and discrimination, viii, 171, 180–83; growth in population of, viii-ix, 160, 165, 199; and sociocultural issues, viii, ix, 165–79, 182; and educational exclusion, xi, 13–14, 15, 16; and linguistically responsive education, xi, 187–91; and law-driven school reforms, 1, 2, 3, 9, 160–61, 164, 165, 169, 171, 176–79, 195–97,

392; and welfare reform, 2, 14; debate over services for, 4, 6; and Proposition 187, 5; and classroom placements, 21, 29; and educational quality, 21–23; and politics, 26–27, 28; and outcome measures, 29; and assessment, 32, 177–78, 352; and litigation, 32; educational barriers, 159, 187–95; educational challenge of serving, 163–65; and educational resource distribution, 165, 191–95; and student achievement, 165, 167–68, 171–76, 200n2, 392; and poverty, 167, 246; hope of, 168–69; legal issues concerning, 180–97; and newcomer schools, 191; and intra-district disparities, 192–93; and educational sanctions, 359

Immigration: and civil rights, viii; demographic transformations in, 161–62, 165–66, 199; and secondary migration, 162–63; and sociocultural issues, 166, 168, 169–71, 182; and second generation perspective, 168, 170; anti-immigrant sentiment, 172, 181, 195; and child wellness, 246

Immigration and Naturalization Service, 187

Immunization, 248, 255, 295n18

Incarceration, 227

Inclusion, x, 20, 178–79, 216, 225, 235, 241n50

Income support assistance, 293n6

India, 166, 167

Indiana, 267, 301n66

Indianapolis, Indiana, 55

Individualized educational program (IEP): and outcome measures, 31; requirements of, 95, 206, 216, 339, 340; and courts, 217–18, 221, 226, 242n74; and neighborhood schools, 223, 224; and special education reform, 237–38; and parents, 238, 298n43, 315; and educational quality, 314; lowered expectations in, 337–38

Individuals with Disabilities Education
Act (IDEA): and classroom placement, 19; and enforceable performance mandates, 23; and outcome
measures, 29–30; and educational delivery, 95; and federal education funding, 95, 96; and per-pupil
expenditures, 95, 140n31; and Rehabilitation Act, 95, 139n27; and federal
mandates, 97; and adequacy claims,
137; amendments of 1997, 207, 237–
38, 338; and progress, 208–9; and due
process, 214; and courts, 217; and
mainstreaming, 218, 219; and supplementary services, 220; and special education challenges, 227; and
overrepresentation of minorities, 229,
339; and race, 230; and benefit analysis, 232; implementation of, 233, 238–
39; and service integration, 297n30;
and educational quality, 314; and
standards-based reforms, 338, 377n134;
and assessments, 339, 352; and participatory process, 358; and accountability, 384n199
Indochina, 166, 167
Integration: and whites, 44; and South,
56; class integration model, 91, 128–
34; and magnet schools, 123; and busing, 133; and limited English proficiency children, 189; and children
with disabilities, 213, 214, 215, 216, 225,
232–33; and resegregation, 392. See
also Desegregation
Interagency service coordination, 269–
70, 284–87, 289, 292, 300n60, 300n61
Interstate New Teacher Assessment and
Support Consortium (INTASC),
355–56
Interstate School Leaders Licensure Consortium, 356
Iowa, 163, 300n65
ISBE (Illinois State Board of Education),
226–27

Jenkins v. Leininger, 120–21
Job Training and Partnership Act,
297n30, 376n124
Joe, T., 288
Johnson Administration, 42, 45, 46
Judges: and collaboration, 5, 6, 7; and
educational equality, 16, 90, 105; role
of, 35–36n11; and resegregation, 39–
40, 44, 57, 62, 78, 392; and conservative activists, 43, 44, 49, 50; and desegregation, 45, 52–53, 56, 58–59, 69; and
Meese, 49–50; and Brown v. Board of
Education of Topeka, 55; and practicality principle, 67, 69; and educational resource distribution, 90, 108;
and equal protection clause, 103; and
adequacy claims, 119
Justice Department, U.S., 42, 43, 46,
62, 73

Kagan, S., 265, 266, 271, 297n31
Kansas City, Missouri, 70, 71
Kao, G., 167
Kaplan, D., 271
Kentucky: and school finance reform, 21,
136; and desegregation, 64, 86n74;
and adequacy standards, 118, 135; and
poverty, 134; and immigration, 163;
and accountability system, 243n87;
and service integration, 267; and
standards-based reform, 324,
372n70
Kentucky Education Reform Act of
1990, 136
Keyes v. School District No. 1 (1973): and
desegregation, 47, 48, 70, 71, 80;
and Latino students, 73, 74, 180, 188;
and linguistically responsive education, 188, 189, 190
Kiang, P., 175
Kirby, D., 271
Kirp, D., 206, 216, 229
Kisker, E., 271
Korean immigrants, 167

Korematsu v. United States (1944), 181
Kovachevich, Elizabeth, 57–58

Laotian immigrants, 166
Larry P. v. Riles (1979), 196
Larson, C., 270
Larson, Kathy, 227–28, 232
Latin America, 161, 165–66, 167
Latino students: and segregation, 2, 10, 13, 41, 73, 180; and educational exclusion, 10; and socioeconomic status, 11; racial isolation of, 15, 17; and racial stereotypes, 16; and school finance reform, 22; dropout rates of, 29; and desegregation, 47, 67, 392; and California, 73, 180; and poverty, 73, 74, 230; and resegregation, 73–75, 80; civil rights of, 81; and linguistically responsive education, 188; and intra-district disparities, 193; and special education, 206, 229; and federal law compliance, 370n44
Latinos, viii, 180, 361, 392
Lau v. Nichols (1974), 22, 164, 181, 187, 190, 195
Law-driven school reforms: and children with disabilities, ix, 1, 2, 3, 9; and immigrant children, 1, 2, 3, 9, 160–61, 164, 165, 169, 171, 176–79, 195–99; and educational equality, 4, 9, 16–26; and collaboration, 5–8, 17, 34–35, 308, 316–18; interdisciplinary perspectives on, 5, 9–31; and advocates' collaboration, 8, 17, 33–34, 200n3; and educational exclusion, 10–16; challenges of, 26–31; and lawyers' roles, 31–35; and accountability, 196–97, 247. *See also* Standards-based reforms
Lawyers' collaboration: and educational quality, vii, 362; and law-driven school reform, x, 5–8, 17, 18–19, 34–35, 391–92; and service integration, x, xi, 25, 26, 281, 282; and school finance reform, 21; and legislation, 33; and litigation, 34, 392; and whole state reform model, 136–37; and immigrant children, 164; and limited English proficiency students, 190; and special education, 207, 239; and standards-based reform, 308, 316, 346; and implementation, 317
Lawyers' roles: and educational equality, vii, 16, 102; and law-driven school reforms, vii, ix-x, 4, 5–8, 17, 31–35, 316; and politics, 28; and special education, 33, 205, 214; and resegregation, 41, 44, 72–73; and civil rights, 79; and educational resource distribution, 89, 92; and school finance reform, 115; and class integration model, 131; and limited English proficiency children, 190; and intra-district disparities, 193; and immigrant children, 197–99; and service integration, 244, 266, 279–91; and professional training, 291, 293; in fundamental system reform, 292–93
LEAs (local educational agencies), 326, 338, 339, 340, 378n145
Least restrictive environment (LRE): and Individuals with Disabilities Education Act, 208, 337; consent decrees, 212; and due process, 214, 215; and segregation, 218; and Supreme Court, 219; and neighborhood schools, 223; and class actions, 226; and litigation, 227; and standards-based reforms, 338, 340–41
Lee, Valerie, 311
LEP. *See* Limited English proficiency (LEP) children
Leveraging, 289, 301n67
Levy, Frank, 312
Levy, J., 266, 297n31
Liberals, 55, 78
Liebman, James, 129
Limited English proficiency (LEP) children: and special education, 14, 173, 178; and Equal Educational Oppor-

Limited English proficiency (LEP) children (*continued*)
tunities Act, 22; and federal education funding, 96–97, 373n77; and New York City, 106; and California, 162, 189, 192; and comprehensible instruction, 172; and high-school graduation requirements, 176; and law-driven school reforms, 176, 179; and choice model, 177; and testing, 177–78; and inclusion, 178; and undocumented children, 183–84; and courts, 188; and premature reclassification, 190; and educational quality, 307; and Title I, 329; and vocational education, 331, 333; and standards-based reforms, 343–44; and assessment, 344, 352, 380n166; and accountability, 350, 384n200; and children with disabilities, 378n145

Linguistic minority children: educational challenge of serving, 163–65; sociocultural issues of, 165–79; immigrant children as, 168, 176; and classroom placements, 173; and law-driven school reforms, 176, 179; legal issues concerning, 180–97

Linguistically responsive education, 187–91

Litigation: and lawyers' role, x, 31–32, 392; changing nature of, 4; costs of, 7–8; and children with disabilities, 14, 32; and collaboration, 31, 33, 34, 362; and school finance reform, 31, 89, 90; and special education, 32, 207, 214; and discrimination, 181; and limited English proficiency students, 192; and least restrictive environment, 227; and education clause, 324. *See also* School finance reform

Little Rock, Arkansas, 56, 78

Local Community Parent Resource Centers, 378n145

Local control: and Supreme Court, 11, 12, 51, 80, 101, 103; and Rehnquist

Court, 40; and district courts, 51; and resegregation, 55–56, 58, 69–71, 76; and practicality principle, 68; and courts, 70; and white outmigration, 71; and class integration reform model, 91; and school finance reform, 93, 103, 109, 112–13; and educational delivery, 97; and taxation, 98; and class integration model, 132; and immigrant children, 192; and special education, 209

Local educational agencies (LEAs), 326, 338, 339, 340, 378n145

Local governments: and suburban areas, 112; and public education, 245–48; and categorical grant programs, 249–50, 264; and block grants, 251; and neighborhood schools, 259; and service integration, 266, 267, 282, 284, 289, 297n34; and children's services system, 279

Lockett v. Board of Education of Muscogee County, 78–79

Long Island, New York, 88

Los Angeles, California, 73, 97, 162, 192–93

Louisiana, 212

Low-wage/low-skill jobs, 361, 388n243

LRE. *See* Least restrictive environment (LRE)

Madison, Wisconsin, 5

Magnet schools: and unitary status, 67; and resegregation, 68–69, 70, 86n55; and choice model, 123; and class integration model, 131, 132; and limited English proficiency children, 177; and children with disabilities, 236; and tracking, 341

Maine, 364n3

Mainstreaming, 218, 219, 241n50, 338

Malgady, R., 170

Mandates. *See* Enforceable performance mandates; Federal mandates

Marshall, Thurgood, 49

Maryland, 162, 300n65

Massachusetts: per-pupil expenditures of, 94, 110, 139n19; and adequacy claim, 116; and property taxes, 141n53; and state funding level, 142n58; and immigration, 162; and bilingual education, 197; and children with disabilities, 210

Maternal and Child Health Block Grant, 249, 251

Mathematics proficiency: and school funding inequalities, 13, 95; in Tennessee, 134; and vouchers, 155n193; national level of, 156n195, 364n3; and immigrant students, 194; and National Education Goals, 255

Mathias Amendment of 1974, 213

McUsic, Molly, viii, 10–12, 19, 21, 31–32, 33, 34, 391

Medicaid: as uncapped entitlement program, 249; and credentialing standards, 250; eligibility for, 253, 293n4, 295n14; and health services access, 259; and block grants, 294n9; federal spending levels, 294n10; and preventive health services, 296n22

Medicare, 279

Meese, Edwin, 49–50, 85n36

Mental health services, 268

Merrow, John, 1, 14

Mexican Americans. *See* Latino students; Latinos

Mexico, 166, 167, 170, 186

Miami, Florida, 162

Michigan, 111, 112, 149–50n138, 151n150

Miller, George, 213

Milliken I: and desegregation, 43, 48, 51, 73, 101; and local control, 69–70

Milliken II: desegregation, 20, 30, 34, 48, 50, 52, 101, 102; and state funding, 20, 81; and educational equality, 64, 72; and remedial education programs, 71; and compensatory remedies, 102

Mills v. Board of Education of the District of Columbia, 213

Milwaukee, Wisconsin, 128, 154–55n186, 156n194

Minnesota, 163, 364n3

Minorities: and integration, 44; and urban areas, 47–48, 232; and law-driven school reforms, 179, 200n3; discrimination against, 293n8

Minority children: and educational quality, viii, 307, 365n4; and law-driven school reforms, 1, 9; achievement gap with white students, 2, 15, 89, 255; segregation within schools, 6; and educational exclusion, 11, 16; and classroom placement, 17, 18, 19; and college education, 41; and desegregation, 41, 50, 52, 100; and resegregation, 41, 44, 54, 61, 72; and race neutral policies, 69; civil rights of, 79; and Milliken rulings, 102; and special education, 140n37, 206, 229; and testing, 177; and intra-district disparities, 193; and children with disabilities, 207; and categorical grant programs, 250; and block grants, 251; and high-school graduation rates, 295n16; and neighborhood schools, 296n25; and vocational education, 333; and authentic pedagogy, 367n14

Minow, Martha, 28

Mississippi, 46, 88, 94, 112, 136, 139n19, 139n20

Missouri, 267

Missouri v. Jenkins (1995), 30, 50–52, 70, 71, 72, 80, 101, 102

Morrill, W., 270

Murnane, Richard, 312

Murray v. Montrose County School District, 223, 224

Nation at Risk, A, 247, 254–55, 391

National Assessment of Educational Progress (NAEP), 3, 364n3

National Association for the Advancement of Colored People (NAACP), 57, 58, 60, 74
National Board for Professional Teaching Standards (NBPTS), 354–55, 356, 357, 386n224
National Center for Education Statistics (NCES), 364n3, 383n196
National Center for Educational Outcomes, 385n208
National Coalition of Advocates for Students (NCAS), 171, 199
National Commission on Children, 261
National Commission on Teaching and America's Future, 356
National Committee on Children, 27
National Council for Accreditation of Teacher Education (NCATE), 356
National Council of Teachers of Mathematics, 349, 354
National Education Goals, 254–55, 323, 325
National Education Longitudinal Study, 167–68
National Educational Standards and Improvement Council, 376n125
National Longitudinal Transition Study of Special Education Students (NLTS), 227, 231, 232–33
National Skill Standards Act of 1994, 325–26, 335–37
National Skills Standards Board, 325–26, 335, 376n125
Native Americans, 10, 229, 230
NBPTS (National Board for Professional Teaching Standards), 354–55, 356, 357, 386n224
NCAS (National Coalition of Advocates for Students), 171, 199
NCATE (National Council for Accreditation of Teacher Education), 356
NCES (National Center for Education Statistics), 364n3, 383n196
Neal, D., 206

Nebraska, 98
Neighborhood schools: and desegregation, 46, 52; and segregation, 53, 82, 98; and white outmigration, 71; and Eagleton-Biden Amendment, 73; and choice model, 121; and children with disabilities, 223–25, 242n73, 242n74; and public education, 259; and families, 268–69
Nevada, 55, 139n20
Neville, P., 265, 266, 297n31
New Hampshire, 116
New Jersey, 88, 118, 162, 194, 267, 297n34, 370n49, 380n168
New Standards Project (NSP), 365n10
New York, 94, 96, 162, 185, 192, 193, 253
New York City, 97, 106, 128, 140n37, 162, 234, 267, 297n34
Ninth Circuit Court of Appeal, 224
Nixon Administration, 42, 43, 45, 46, 212
NLTS (National Longitudinal Transition Study of Special Education Students), 227, 231, 232–33
North, and desegregation, 47, 51, 101, 102
North Dakota, 139n20, 163
NSP (New Standards Project), 365n10

Oakes, Jeannie, 64
Oberti v. Board of Education, 220–21, 222, 223, 224
OBRA (Omnibus Reconciliation Act of 1981), 250–52, 265
Office for Civil Rights (OCR), 191
Ohio, 211
Oklahoma City, Oklahoma, 60–61, 75
Oliphant, Miriam, 59
Olsen, L., 178
Omnibus Reconciliation Act of 1981 (OBRA), 250–52, 265
Opportunity-to-learn standards: and standards-based reform, 309; and state law, 323, 371n61; and Goals 2000, 325; implementation of, 326–27, 373n79;

and accountability, 359, 383n196, 388n240; and politics, 365–66n11

Optional attendance zones, 100

Oregon, 267

Orfield, Gary, viii, 7, 10–11, 17, 32, 392

Outcome measures: of student achievement, 4, 9; and law-driven school reform, 28–31; and children with disabilities, 31, 232, 237; and immigrant children, 194; and service integration, 265, 266, 271, 276, 277, 287; and categorical grant programs, 282; and standards-based reform, 309, 316, 365n10; and accountability, 347–50, 353

Parent collaboration: and law-driven school reforms, x, 5–8, 17, 18, 34–35; and educational equality, 2; and school finance reform, 21; and litigation, 34; and immigrant children, 164; and special education, 207; and service integration, 282, 292; and standards-based reform, 308, 346

Parent involvement: and student achievement, 107, 194, 313, 368n27; and poor children, 122–23, 128, 153n177; and private and parochial schools, 124; and reading proficiency, 146n109, 153n177; and immigrant children, 179; and deregulation, 195–96; and service integration, 262; and Title I, 329, 374n96; and vocational education, 333; and accountability, 358–59

Parent Training and Information Centers (PTICs), 378n145

Parents: and law-driven school reforms, 8, 17, 32, 195–96; and educational equality, 16; and classroom placement, 22; and enforceable performance mandates, 23, 24, 315–16, 317; and student performance, 29; and lawyers' role, 33; and politics, 33–34; and desegregation, 44; and resegregation, 58, 60, 61; and Individuals with Disabilities Education Act, 95; and limited English proficiency children, 96, 188; educational level of, 107; and school finance reform, 109, 112, 114; and adequacy standards, 118; and choice programs, 121, 122, 128, 153n177, 156n194; and suburban areas, 129–30; and educational quality, 130, 156n195, 315–16, 368n29, 368n32; and class integration model, 132; satisfaction of, 156n195; of immigrant children, 168, 170, 171, 174, 194, 195–96, 197, 200n2; and special education, 178, 206, 207, 209, 214, 220, 221, 222, 229, 231; and student achievement, 189, 194; and due process hearings, 214–15, 216, 217; and neighborhood schools, 224–25; of minority children, 229; and urban areas, 231; and individualized educational program, 238, 298n43, 315, 338; and social policy assumptions, 262–63; education services, 296–97n29; and Title I, 315, 329, 330, 358, 383–84n197; and standards-based reform, 320, 326, 363; and vocational education, 334; and federal law compliance, 370n43; and assessments, 378n142; alienation of, 387n235

Pattakos, A., 266

Pauley v. Kelly, 324

Paulsen, R., 265, 271

Payroll taxes, 278–79, 299n52

Pehowski v. Blatnik, 218

Pennsylvania, 162

Pennsylvania Association for Retarded Children (PARC) v. Pennsylvania (1971), 211–12, 213

People Who Care v. Rockford Board of Education, 75–76, 379n157

Perkins Vocational Education Act. *See* Carl D. Perkins Vocational and Applied Technology Education Act

Per-pupil expenditures: and educational resource distribution, 88, 94, 139n19, 159n211; and Individuals with Disabilities Education Act, 95, 140n31; and property taxes, 98; and school finance reform, 103, 109–12, 114, 137, 150n139, 150n148, 192; and educational equality, 106–7, 390; and whole state reform model, 134, 136

Personal Responsibility and Work Opportunity Reconciliation Act of 1996, 247, 252

Philippines, 166

Plessy v. Ferguson (1896), 28, 41, 45–46

Plyler v. Doe (1982), 13, 15, 164, 171–72, 183–84, 185, 199, 380n169

Politics: and law-driven school reform, x, 21, 26–28, 391; and standards-based reform, 3, 365n11; and educational equality, 16, 102; and school finance reform, 28, 34, 89, 90, 108–15, 137, 147n115; and outcome measures, 30; and desegregation, 31; and judges' role, 36n11; and resegregation, 40, 82–83; ideological changes in, 54–56; and busing, 101; and standards, 117, 118; and adequacy claims, 119; and choice model, 120; and class integration model, 131–32; and whole state reform model, 135–36; and out of touch political class, 182; and immigrant children, 197; and children with disabilities, 209; and categorical grant programs, 250; and block grants, 251; and service integration, 283, 285; and educational resource distribution, 321; and opportunity-to-learn standards, 365–66n11

Poor children: and educational equality, viii, 106; and remedial education, viii; and categorical grant programs, x, 250; and law-driven school reforms, 1, 3, 8, 176; and welfare reform, 2, 252; and educational exclusion, 16; and

student achievement, 105, 111, 129, 130, 146n109, 158n204; and school finance reform, 106; and adequacy claims, 116–18; and choice model, 122–28, 153n177, 154–55n186; and parent involvement, 122–23, 128, 153n177; and class integration model, 131–32, 133, 158n202; and children's services system, 256; and high-school graduation rates, 295n16

Porter, Ann, 58

Portfolio assessments, 228, 336

Posner, Richard, 76–77

Poverty: and segregation, 2, 41, 42, 98–99; and welfare reform, 2, 247, 252, 296n24; and special education, 19, 96, 130; and urban areas, 19, 21, 110, 128–29, 156n196; and National Committee on Children, 27; and black students, 65, 101, 230; and Latino students, 73, 74, 230; and student achievement, 89, 99, 105; and educational quality, 91, 307, 365n4; and Title I, 94, 327, 328, 329; and educational equality, 104; and educational resource distribution, 106, 312, 367n22; and school finance reform, 110, 111, 114–15, 148n124, 149n127; and class integration model, 120, 129, 158n207; and magnet schools, 123; and Kentucky, 134; and private schools, 142n61; and suburban neighborhoods, 142n54; definitions of, 152n172; and immigration, 161; and Filipinos, 166; and immigrant children, 168, 192, 197; and undocumented children, 183, 186; and intradistrict disparities, 193; and children with disabilities, 229, 230, 378n145; and categorical grant programs, 249–50, 252; and early childhood education, 259–60; and child wellness, 261; and working poor, 291, 296n24, 392; and children's services system, 296n23; and federal education funding, 326,

373n77; and vocational education, 331, 332

Powell, Lewis, 116

Power equalization relief, 110, 148n124

Preventable disease, 256, 295n20

Prevention and Treatment of Substance Abuse Block Grant, 294n10

Preventive health services, 258, 296n22

Preventive law, 32–33, 34

Prince George's County, Maryland, 78

Private and parochial schools: subsidized system of, 89, 93, 99–100; and children with disabilities, 95, 215; and state/federal laws, 99–100; and school finance reform, 114; and choice model, 121, 122, 123–26, 127, 128, 153n175, 155–56n186; and parents, 129–30; tuition for, 142n61; and immigrant children, 177

Progressive education, 246–47

Promotion rates, 29

Property taxes: and school finance reform, 12, 103, 104–5, 109, 111–12, 114–15, 148n124, 149–50n138, 192; and educational resource distribution, 98; and wealth, 98, 99, 103, 104, 105, 109, 111–12, 114, 115; and state funding, 99, 120; and property values, 113; and choice programs, 121; and class integration model, 132; and police and highway services, 141n53; as progressive taxes, 151n149

Proposition 13, 111–12

Proposition 187, 5, 13, 32, 164, 172, 184–85, 199, 200–201n5

PTICs (Parent Training and Information Centers), 378n145

Public education: local government's responsibility for, 245; and school reform history, 245–47; and child wellness services, 246; and welfare reform, 247; social policy of, 256–63, 286; Dewey on, 260, 295–96n21, 296n27; and parent involvement,
262; free appropriate public education, 340

Public health, 294n10

Public Health Service, 255

Puerto immigrants, 167

Quarantine, 248

Race: discrimination against, viii, 293n8, 341; and school finance reform, 11; and racial isolation, 15, 17; racial stereotypes, 16; and housing, 98; and private schools, 99; and equal protection clause, 103; and choice model, 122, 125, 126; and urban areas, 128; and whites, 155n189; and immigrant children, 168, 172, 174–75, 186; and undocumented children, 172, 184, 187; and law-driven school reforms, 176, 179; and American discontent, 182; and immigration, 186–87; and children with disabilities, 229, 339; and Individuals with Disabilities Education Act, 230; and child development, 257; and neighborhood schools, 296n25; and educational quality, 307, 314; and assessment, 321, 352; and vocational education, 333; and tracking, 342; and student achievement, 343; and educational sanctions, 359; and authentic pedadogy, 367n14

Rand Corporation, 171

Rawls, J., 301n68

Reading proficiency: in Mississippi, 112; in Tennessee, 134; and parent involvement, 146n109, 153n177; and vouchers, 155n193; national level of, 156n195, 364n3; and urban areas, 156–57n199; and immigrant children, 168, 194; and special education, 233; and National Education Goals, 255

Reagan Administration, 44–45, 49–50, 54–55, 63, 74, 120, 250–52

Refugee children, 167

Regular education: and children with disabilities, ix, 19–20, 208, 217, 219–22, 225, 241n50; and service fragmentation, 24; per-pupil expenditures for, 95, 140n31; educational resource distribution and, 97; and overrepresentation, 231

Rehabilitation Act of 1973, Section 504: and children with disabilities, 95, 212–13, 337, 338, 340, 377n133; and Individuals with Disabilities Education Act, 139n27; and segregation, 218; and race, 230; and discrimination, 293n8; and educational quality, 314; and assessments, 339; compliance with, 370n44

Rehnquist, William, 48, 49

Rehnquist Court, 40, 44, 49, 51, 79

Rein, M., 265–66

Remedial programs, viii, 99, 192, 232

Researchers. *See* Scholars; Scholars' collaboration

Resegregation: and courts, 2, 40, 41, 43, 55, 78–79; and desegregation, 39–40; and judges, 39–40, 44, 53, 57, 62, 78, 392; and educational equality, 41, 44; and conservative activists, 44, 54, 392; and trial courts, 56–61; complexities of, 67–69; and local control, 69–71; and ending remedies, 71–73, 80–83; and Latino students, 73–75, 80; and appeals courts, 75–78

Reverse discrimination, 69, 76–77, 86n55

Rhode Island, 142n58, 230

Richardson, Elliot, 265

Richman, H., 268, 269

Richter, K., 277

Riis, Jacob, 246

Robinson, Sue L., 65–67

Rockford, Illinois, 75–77

Rogler, L., 170

Roncker v. Walter, 218, 219, 223

Roos, Peter D., 8, 13, 23, 33, 34, 392

Roosevelt, Franklin D., 208

Rose v. Council for Better Education, Inc., 136

Rural areas: and choice model, 122, 125; and whole state reform model, 134; and immigration, 163; and health care access, 259; and federal education funding, 373n77

Ryskamp, Kenneth, 59

Sacken, D., 206, 214–15, 216

Sacramento, California, 191

Sacramento Unified School District Board of Education v. Rachel Holland, 221, 222, 224, 225

San Antonio Independent School District v. Rodriguez (1973), 12, 15, 22, 103, 116, 193, 345

San Diego, California, 297n34

San Francisco, California, 74, 78, 162, 191

Sarokin, Lee (Judge), 87n75

SAT scores, 13, 94–95

Savannah, Georgia, 62–63

Scalia, Antonin, 54

SCANS Commission, 376–77n127

Scholars: and law-driven school reforms, 8, 17, 18, 32; and resegregation, 40, 54; and black student achievement, 49; and educational equality, 66; and courts, 78; and class integration reform model, 91; and adequacy paradigm, 115–16; and choice programs, 120; and immigrant children, 164, 168–71, 193; and special education, 208–9, 215; and student achievement, 349, 382n188

Scholars' collaboration: and educational equality, 2; and law-driven school reforms, 5–8, 17, 18, 34–35; and school finance reform, 21; and litigation, 34; and limited English proficiency students, 190; and immigrant children, 194, 197–99

School finance reform: and *Brown v.*

Board of Education of Topeka, vii, 11, 12; and courts, viii, 6, 15, 89, 103–4, 137, 192, 391; and law-driven school reform, 2, 3; and student performance, 2, 29; debate over, 4; educational exclusion and, 11–13; and state constitutions, 12, 89, 138n8, 323; and educational quality, 21; and politics, 28, 34, 108–15; and litigation, 31, 89, 90; and desegregation, 47; and civil rights, 89, 102; and equal protection clauses, 89, 103, 372n65; and adequacy claims, 90–92, 194, 372n67; background on, 102–5; and education as basic right, 103–4, 144n89; and equity paradigm difficulties, 105–8; and student achievement, 107; and adequacy paradigm, 115–19; and educational delivery structure, 119–37; and choice model, 120–28; and class integration model, 128–34; and whole state reform model, 134–37; and immigrant children, 192, 194; and standards-based reform, 323, 370n49

School readiness, 248, 260

School reform: history of, 245–47, 390; and Nation at Risk, 254, 391; and educational quality, 307; as continual process, 393. *See also* Law-driven school reform; School finance reform; Standards-based reforms

School-based enterprises, 375n21, 375n108

School-based improvement plans, 378n145

School-to-work initiatives, 247

School-to-Work Opportunities Act: and educational quality, 315; and standards-based reforms, 332–35, 337, 376n124; and children with disabilities, 341; and limited English proficiency children, 344; and assessment, 352; and participatory process, 358; and school-based enterprises, 375n121

Schoolwide programs, 328, 329, 330

Schoolwide teacher professional community (STPC), 311

Science proficiency, 156n195, 156–57n199

Segregation: and law-driven school reforms, ix, xi, 2, 3, 9, 15; and *Brown v. Board of Education of Topeka* (1954), 2, 10, 28, 42, 43, 45, 100; and Latino students, 2, 10, 13, 41, 73, 180; and poverty, 2, 41, 42; segregation within schools, 2, 6, 9, 15, 16, 17–20, 65–66, 76, 77; and housing segregation, 11, 82, 100; and educational equality, 16, 48; educational consequences of, 41–42; and courts, 42–53, 78–79, 83n7; and trial courts, 53–56; and practicality principle, 62–69; and children with disabilities, 209, 210, 211, 213, 218–19, 226, 229, 231, 232–33, 234; and equal protection clause, 381n172

Serrano v. Priest, 111

Service integration: interagency service coordination, x–xi, 269–70, 284–87, 289, 292, 300n60, 300n61; and law-driven school reform, 3, 5, 9; and educational quality, 24–26; and immigrant children, 200n2; and lawyers' roles, 244, 266, 279–91; reform in, 244, 270–74, 276–79; and case management, 262–63; strategies for, 264–76, 281–91; goals of, 265–66; initiatives towards, 266–70, 281, 282–90, 390; and California, 267, 297n34, 301n66; and accountability, 273, 276, 287–88, 298n37; and family empowerment, 274–75; and community empowerment, 275–76; governance arrangements for, 283–84, 300n58; financing strategies for, 288–90; and special education, 297n33

SES. *See* Socioeconomic status (SES)

Sheff v. O'Neill, 129, 157n201

Shephardson, W., 266, 297n31

Sizer, Theodore, 255, 391

Slavin, Robert, 391

Smith, Julia, 311

Social justice, 291, 301n68

Social marketing, 279, 300n54

Social reform, 255

Social Security, 279

Social Security Act of 1935, 248

Social Services Block Grant, 294n10, 294–95n11, 297n30

Social workers, 250, 293n2

Socioeconomic status (SES): and educational exclusion, 11, 15; and minority students, 11; and desegregation, 19; and litigation, 31–32; and housing, 98; and choice model, 122, 125, 126–27, 153n177; and student achievement, 127, 311, 367n14; and urban areas, 128; and immigration, 166, 167, 170; and immigrant children, 174; and assessment, 321; and vocational education, 333; and authentic pedagogy, 367n14. *See also* Poor children; Poverty; Wealth; Wealthy children

South: desegregation in, 20, 42–47, 51, 71, 100, 102, 143n73; and integration, 56; and new school construction, 68, 85n46; and student achievement, 101; and choice programs, 120; and educational resource distribution, 159n211

Special education: and law-driven school reform, vii, 3, 391; debate over, 4, 390; and court orders, 7; and limited English proficiency, 14; and poverty, 19, 96, 130; and immigrant children, 21, 29, 172–73, 178; and English language learners, 23, 24; and service integration, 24, 25, 297n33; and politics, 28; and outcomes measures, 29–30; and bilingual education, 32; and lawyers' role, 33, 205; and black students, 65, 96, 206, 229; and federal mandates, 95, 97; per-pupil expenditures for, 95–96, 140n31, 140n33; distribution of, among states, 96, 140n37; and school finance reform, 106, 109; federal education funds for, 140–41n39; and minority children, 140n37, 206, 229; legalism of, 205–7, 209, 214–27, 235, 238, 240n29; costs of, 206, 225; and least restrictive environment, 208, 212; progress in, 208–9; and courts, 209, 214, 216–19, 222, 223–25; and educational exclusion, 209–13; and regular education placement, 219–21; and supplementary services, 219, 220, 222, 223, 241n50; and disruptive behavior, 221–22, 233; and service location, 223–25; and class actions, 226–27; challenges of, 227–34; and overrepresentation, 228–32, 339; and benefit analysis, 231–34; and collaboration, 235–38; reform of, 235–38; and welfare reform, 248; and federal law, 337–41

Special needs students, 93

Special Supplemental Program for Women, Infants, and Children (WIC), 249n10

SSI (Supplemental Security Income), 252, 294n11

Stafford, Robert, 213

Standards-based reforms: and politics, 3, 365n11; risks of, 30–31, 320–22; and adequacy claims, 91, 116–18; and collaboration, 308–10, 316–18, 362–64, 389n247; framework for, 308–10; and state law, 308, 322–23, 327; and Congress, 309, 325, 372–73n74; and outcome measures, 309, 365n10; empirical support for, 310–13; and student achievement, 310, 345, 362–63, 365n7, 366–67n13; legal support for, 314–16, 368n31; and accountability, 318–20, 346–64, 368n34; and high-school graduation requirements, 321, 380n172; and state constitutions, 323–24; and federal law, 325–44; and constitutional rights, 344–46, 380n168; and equal protection clauses, 344–45, 350, 380n169, 380n173, 380n174, 381–

82n175; and supplemental standards, 350, 383n192

State constitutions: and segregation, 10; and school finance reform, 12, 89, 102, 103–4, 115, 138n8, 150–51n148; role of, 35–36n11; and education clause, 103, 104; and equal protection clause, 103–4; and adequacy claim, 116, 118, 137; and whole state reform model, 136; and service integration, 284; and educational quality, 315; and standards-based reforms, 323–24, 327, 349

State funding: and Milliken II, 20, 81; geographical basis of, 89, 93, 97–98, 100; and property taxes, 99; and student achievement, 99, 142n59; supplemental appropriations, 99, 109; education compared with other services, 111, 121, 149n132; and school finance reform, 112–13, 114, 150–51n148; and choice model, 121; low levels of, 134–35; and flat grants, 142n57; and immigrant children, 192

State government: and child wellness, 248; and categorical grant programs, 249–50, 264; and block grants, 251, 294n9; and welfare reform, 252–54, 295n15; and neighborhood schools, 259; and service integration, 266–67, 278, 282, 289, 297n34, 299n51, 300n56; and accountability, 354, 386n217

State law: and law-driven school reform, 29; and educational delivery, 97–99; and service integration, 284, 292; and educational quality, 307, 315; and standards-based reforms, 308, 322–23, 327, 349, 350–51; and assessment, 323, 352; and federal law, 327; and teacher standards, 354

State legislatures: and school finance reform, viii, 108–11, 113, 192; and educational policy, 108; and adequacy standards, 116, 118, 119, 151–52n161; and standards, 117; and choice model,

120, 121, 124, 126–27, 128; and class integration model, 131; and whole state reform model, 136; and immigrant children, 185–86; and welfare reform, 253–54

State regulations, 247

STPC (schoolwide teacher professional community), 311

Student achievement: and children with disabilities, 2, 3–4; gap between white and minority students, 2, 15, 89, 255; outcome measures of, 4, 9; accountability for, 28, 196–97, 313, 358; cross-racial comparisons of, 30, 74, 77, 89, 146n109, 156n195; and segregation, 41, 56, 66; and resegregation, 44, 60–61; and desegregation, 50, 53, 100; and educational resource distribution, 89, 90, 312; and poverty, 89, 99, 105; and wealthy children, 89, 99, 153n177; and private schools, 99–100; and state funding, 99, 142n59; and poor children, 105, 111, 129, 130, 146n109, 158n204; and parent involvement, 107, 194, 313, 368n27; and adequacy claims, 118, 119, 194; and choice model, 123; and socioeconomic status, 127, 311, 367n14; and class integration model, 129, 131; and whole state reform model, 136; and testing, 156n195; and urban areas, 156–57n199, 365n4; and immigrant children, 165, 167–68, 171–76, 200n2, 392; and immigration, 165, 166, 167–68; and transportation, 189; and school reform, 247, 254–55, 295n17; and standards-based reform, 310, 345, 362–63, 365n7, 366–67n13; and assessments, 312–13; and National Education Goals, 325; and federal education funding, 326; and Title I, 327, 329, 348; and civil rights, 341; and race, 343; and equal protection claims, 344; and teachers, 367n16; and opportunity-to-learn standards, 383n196

Student performance: and school funding formulas, 2; of black students, 3,
15, 49, 71, 89, 100–101, 146n109; and
law-driven school reform, 28–30; of
immigrant children, 168; and teacher
expectations, 175; and children with
disabilities, 228, 340; and assessment,
329, 388n241; and vocational education, 333, 336; and accountability, 347;
and educational sanctions, 359–60;
national level of, 364n3; and student
effort, 387n231; and resegregation, 392.
See also Enforceable performance
mandates
Suárez-Orozco, Carola, 8, 13, 23, 33, 34,
170, 392
Suárez-Orozco, Marcelo, 8, 13, 23, 33, 34,
170, 392
Suburban areas: and desegregation, 48,
101; and school finance reform, 106,
112–13; and local governments, 112;
and choice model, 121–22, 125; and
parents, 129–30; and class integration
model, 131–32, 158n202; and poverty,
142n54; and immigration, 162; and
children with disabilities, 231
Supplemental Security Income (SSI),
252, 294n11
Supplementary services, 219, 220, 222,
223, 241n50
Supreme Court, U.S.: and undocumented children, ix, 183–84; and law-
driven school reforms, 1; and desegregation, 10–11, 20–21, 42, 45–53, 55,
83n7, 86n61; and local control, 11, 12,
51, 80, 101, 103; and school finance reform, 12, 22, 89, 103, 192; and immigrant children, 13, 181; and outcome
measures, 30; attacks on, for desegregation decisions, 41, 43; and resegregation, 43, 71–72, 75, 80; and
civil rights, 44–45, 50; and unitary
status, 52, 56, 60; directives of, 83; and
compensatory remedies, 102; and district court limitations, 102; and children with disabilities, 210, 211, 217,
219, 377n132; and equal protection
clause, 324; and accountability,
384n199
Swann v. Charlotte-Mecklenburg Board of
Education (1971), 47, 63, 80

Tai Dam immigrants, 166
Taiwan, 166
Tampa, Florida, 57–59, 70
TANF (Temporary Assistance to Needy
Families), 248, 293n4, 295n14
Tatel, D., 31
Tatro v. State of Texas, 217
Taxation: and local control, 98; and private school tuition, 99; and school finance reform, 110, 111, 113–14, 148n124;
and state income taxes, 114, 151n149;
and whole state reform model, 135;
and educational equality, 145n97; and
progressive taxes, 148n125, 151n149. See
also Property taxes
Teacher certification, 30, 226
Teacher education, 197, 326, 356, 364–
65n3
Teacher testing, 32
Teachers: and immigrant children, 170,
175, 178, 200n2; and bilingual education, 188, 192, 197; and limited English
proficiency children, 188, 199; and
intra-district disparities, 193; as whites,
195; and special education, 209, 220,
221, 235; and least restrictive environment, 226; and overrepresentation,
231; visiting teachers, 246, 293n2; and
service integration, 297n33; and staff
development, 311, 326, 329, 352, 356,
363, 367n17, 373n86, 385n206,
385n207, 389n248; and Title I, 314,
329, 373n86; accountability of, 318–20,
354–57, 369n40; and professionalism,
318–19, 369n38; standards for, 318, 349,
354–57, 359, 364n3, 389n248; and fed-

eral law compliance, 319, 369n42; and
vocational education, 333, 334; assessments of, 355–56, 357, 391; and student
achievement, 367n16; teacher-based
assessment, 369n37; and opportunity-
to-learn standards, 383n196. *See also*
Educators; Educators' collaboration
Teen pregnancy, 227, 247–48, 278
Temporary Assistance to Needy Families
(TANF), 248, 293n4, 295n14
Tennessee, 134–35
Tenth Circuit Court of Appeals, 223, 224
Testing: and educational quality, 17–20;
and enforceable performance mandates, 23; and immigrant children, 29,
32, 167, 176, 177–78; and outcome
measures, 31; and resegregation, 60–
61; and adequacy claims, 91; and private schools, 99–100; and district
courts, 102; and school finance reform,
107, 136; and class integration model,
129; in Kentucky, 134; and student
achievement, 156n195; and accountability, 196–97; and children with disabilities, 228; and overrepresentation,
231; and standards-based reform, 321.
See also Assessments
Texas: and undocumented children, ix,
181, 183–84; and school finance reform, 12, 103, 116, 149n126; and Latino
students, 73; per-pupil expenditures
of, 88, 94, 103; and immigration, 162;
and segregation, 180; and poverty, 192;
and bilingual education, 197–98; and
Proposition 187 reaction, 199
Third Circuit Court of Appeals, 224
Third International Mathematics and
Science Study (TIMSS), 364n3
Thomas, Clarence, 45, 49
Tienda, M., 167
Title I: and English language learners,
22; and enforceable performance mandates, 23; and service fragmentation,
24–25, 235; and outcome measures,
30, 353; and children with disabilities,
236, 340, 341; as categorical grant program, 247; as capped grants, 249; and
parent advisory committees, 298n43;
and educational quality, 314; and parents, 315, 329, 330, 358, 383–84n197;
and standards-based reform, 327–30;
and assessment, 329, 352; and civil
rights, 342–43; and limited English
proficiency children, 344, 380n166;
and accountability, 347–49, 382n182,
383n195, 384n199, 386n216; and
teacher standards, 357; and participatory process, 358; revisions of, 370n47.
See also Chapter 1
Title V programs, 294n10
Tocqueville, Alexis de, 277
Tracking, 341–43, 380–81n172
Transportation: and school finance reform, 109; and choice model, 128; and
class integration model, 133, 158n208;
and limited English proficiency children, 189; and immigrant children,
194; and children with disabilities,
212, 217
Truman Administration, 43
Tyak, David, 293n2

Undocumented children, ix, 164, 165,
172, 181, 183–87, 185, 380n169
Unitary status: and Supreme Court, 52,
56, 60; and *Green v. New Kent County
School Board,* 56, 68, 79; and Tampa,
57–59, 85–86n55; and practicality
principle, 62, 67–69; and local control, 70; and court orders, 78–79, 81–
82; and segregation, 80
United States v. Texas, 190
Urban areas: and court orders, 7; and
poverty, 19, 21, 110, 128–29, 156n196;
and desegregation, 20, 47–48; and minorities, 47–48, 232; and resegregation, 71; and Latino students, 73, 74;
demographics of, 112; and choice

Urban areas (*continued*)
model, 122, 123, 125, 127–28; and class integration model, 128; and student achievement, 156–57n199, 365n4; and immigration, 162; and immigrant children, 173; and law-driven school reforms, 176; and children with disabilities, 207, 227, 230, 231; and special education, 231–32; and child wellness, 246; and block grants, 251; and health care access, 259; and high-school graduation rates, 295n16; and educational quality, 365n4; and federal education funding, 373n77
Utah, 211

Vermont, 88
Vietnamese immigrants, 166, 167
Virginia, 162
Vocational education: and enforceable performance mandates, 23; and service fragmentation, 24; and collaboration, 33; and children with disabilities, 233; and teen pregnancy, 247; and educational quality, 314–15; and standards-based reform, 330–37, 376–77n127
Vocational Rehabilitation Program, 297n30
Voting rights, 49
Voting Rights Act, 44, 50
Vouchers, 120–27, 153n177, 154–55n186, 155n193, 365n7

Waldman, Ali, 59
Warren Court, 54, 55
Washington, 114, 150n148
Washington, D. C., 212
Waszak, C., 271
Watson, K., 253
Wealth: and private and parochial schools, 93; and property taxes, 98, 99, 103, 104, 105, 109, 111–12, 114, 115; and adequacy claims, 119; and housing choices, 125–26; and choice model,

126, 127; and politics, 197; and due process hearings, 214; and preventive health services, 296n22; and parent involvement, 359
Wealthy children, 89, 99, 118, 132, 152n168, 153n177, 193
Weckstein, Paul, xi, 4, 23, 24, 25, 33, 391
Welfare reform: and immigrant children, 2, 14; and poverty, 2, 27, 247, 252, 295n13; and child care, 248, 293n5; and categorical grant programs, 252–54; and children's services system, 278–79; and health care, 293n4; and federal funding levels, 294–95n11, 295n12; and working poor, 296n24, 392
Welfare-to-work grants, 253, 295n11
West, and desegregation, 101, 102
West Virginia, 139n20, 301n66
White students: achievement gap with minority students, 2, 15, 89, 255; and desegregation, 10, 50–51; and school finance reform, 11; and racial stereotypes, 16; and student achievement, 74, 100, 146n109; and intra-district disparities, 193
Whites: and integration, 44; and out-migration, 47, 68, 70–71, 102, 133; and resegregation, 56; and desegregation, 59; and sociological factors, 64–65; and reverse discrimination, 69, 76–77, 86n55; and school finance reform, 109; and class integration model, 131; and educational quality, 155n189; and race, 155n189; test scores of, 156n195; educators as, 175; and due process hearings, 214; and wage gap, 361
Whitestone, Heather, 208
Whole state reform model, 91–92, 120, 134–37
WIC (Special Supplemental Program for Women, Infants, and Children), 249n10
Wilkens, Judge, 211

Williams, Harrison, 213
Wilmington, Delaware, 63–64, 75–76, 189
Wisconsin, 210, 301n66
Wise, Arthur, x
Witte, John F., 155n193
Wolf v. Legislature of the State of Utah, 211
Women, viii, 250. *See also* Gender

Work-based components, 332, 375n108
Working poor, 291, 296n24, 392
Wyoming, 150n148

Yick Wo v. Hopkins (1886), 181

Ziegler, J., 271
Zoning laws, 98, 141–42n54